Alaska, Canada, United States

NATIVE AMERICAN DIRECTORY

Galleries
Indian Stores
Trading Posts

Events
Organizations
Media Outlets
Tribal Office & Reserves

Published by National Native American Cooperative
Fred Synder, Director

Native American Directory, Alaska, Canada, U.S.

Library of Congress Catalog No: 970.004/970025; LC E 76.2.N37
ISBN 0-9610334-3-6 (library), ISBN 0-9610334-5-2 (paperback).

Published by: National Native American Cooperative
P.O. Box 1000
San Carlos, AZ 85550-1000
U.S.A.

January 1996

ISBN 0-9610334-3-6
90000>
9 780961 033439

ISBN 0-9610334-5-2
54995>
9 780961 033453

Library Edition

SPECIAL ACKNOWLEDGEMENT TO THE FOLLOWING:

TECHNICAL ASSISTANCE

Carole J. Garcia, M.P.H., Tohono O'odham - Proofreader/Consultant
Maxine Norris, Tohono O'odham - Pow-wow format
Debbie Sakiestewa, Hopi/Navajo - Canadian Information Specialist/ Data Input
Dawn Culver - Typesetting
Wilfried Wegener - Technical Advisor

RESEARCH AND INFORMATION ASSISTANCE

Dr. Eddie Brown, Yaqui/Tohono O'odham - Bureau of Indian Affairs
Veronica Murdock, Colorado River Tribe - Bureau of Indian Affairs
Paul Ortega, Mescalero Apache - Indian Health Service
DIANA, Communication KIOSK, Ottawa, Ontario, Canada

Table of Contents

ALASKA

CANADA

⋙ CANADA (continued) ⋘

⋙ UNITED STATES ⋘

➳ UNITED STATES (continued) ➳

➳ BUYER'S GUIDE ➳

➳ TRACING YOUR INDIAN ANCESTRY ➳

Author's Forward

The computer age is upon us and a comprehensive directory written on Native Americans, Natives, Indians, and Alaska Natives exclusively is now a reality. The layers of information circulated by individual agencies such as Bureau of Indian Affairs, Bureau of the Census, Public Health Service, Indian Health Service, Native Organizations and associations, and others is over whelming, scattered and inaccurate at best. The majority of information in the Native American Directory, Alaska, Canada and U.S. was compiled from these resources. However, each tribe, print and broadcast medium, and event was contacted for verification- with less than a 20% response. Therefore, many other unique resources were used to collect the most current information used in the Directory. Still, when networking with over 2,000 tribes, organizations, associations, media, and events, there will be some shortcomings. However, the editor has used every effort to insure that the information collected is accurate and current. It can only improve with the networking of Indian people in the future.

The first edition of the Native American Directory, published in 1982, was reviewed in Booklists by the American Library Association as, "...a unique and valuable source ...." which hurtled it into almost every library in the world. Additionally, it became the "red page bible" on American Indians of today. The editor is not a publisher, writer, or resource researcher, but has merely gathered information while being on the red road pow-wow trail for over 25 years.

It was hoped that the first edition would establish or inspire an educational/cultural center to undertake a major clearinghouse with continued updated information for everyone in all areas of education, health, social and cultural needs. This did not happen, and will not be possible without tribal commitment to establish such a clearinghouse. Therefore, a revision of the Native American Directory was needed.

The Native American Directory, Alaska, Canada, United States is divided into five sections in its revision. It was impossible for uniformity in Alaska, Canada, and U.S. sections due to the many variances particular to each region. The Buyers Guide to Acquiring Native Art and Researching Your Indian Ancestry follows the tribal information.

Ancestry identification was added in the revision of both editions.

An index has been included in the revision for general areas of interest, but it would take another book to index all the statistics. We did not index these statistics.

This is the first time, to our knowledge, that using the American Indian as the common denominator, Indians of North America, Indian Hobbyist groups in the USA, and European Indian Support Groups, organizations, media and events are listed side-by-side in one directory.

This is also the first time that each tribe, pueblo, rancheria, and Indian Territory is addressed as an independent Nation - Nations within the Nation of the United States. There is much controversy over this. However, the Editor personally feels and maintains that the President's American Indian policy has not been taken seriously by all concerned; both Indian and non-Indian.

Also, many of the tribal nations have returned to the traditional name each has called themselves for centuries and most of these tribes are listed accordingly. for example, Papago have changed to Tohono O'odham. Sioux to Lakota, Dakota, Nakota and so forth.

The purpose of the <u>Native American Directory</u> is not to interpret, analyze, or judge, but to pull together all information available into one single source. We have experienced differences in statistics, ways of collecting data, tribal and cultural differences and indifference- all hurdles that we did not let stand in our way to give you, the reader, the most comprehensive Directory written on Indians of today.

We need your help to continue this flow of information. Newspaper clippings, press releases, mailing lists, photo copied stories of interest, and statistics would be appreciated. Also, add us to your mailing list.

Funds from the Directory are earmarked for the N.A^2.I.I.T.C., North American, Native American, Indian Information and Trade Center, to file, store and retrieve, and distribute information pertinent to the continued preservation of Native culture, crafts and education of First Nations people.

The Alaska, Canada and U.S. sections generally follow this sequence:
...General description, demographics and statistics of the Native People in that region.
...Tribal profiles (historic and economic) listing each tribe of that area.
...National, regional, governmental organizations.
...Print, broadcast and television media.
...Calendar of events for each region.

The Buyers Guide to Acquiring Native Arts follows and is arranged in this sequence:
...How to buy, invest in, and evaluate American Indian art.
...Where to buy Indian art.
...Who to evaluate/sell your Indian art.
Information gathered is mostly from the editor's personal experience as the Director of the National Native American Cooperative for 24 years.
Researching your Indian Ancestry is arranged in this sequence:
...Records in the federal archives.
...How do I trace my ancestry.
...Where to find more information

All listings in this directory are alphabetical by the respective states and/or provinces. All events are listed alphabetically by month and weekend of occurrence. Most sections have footnotes of credit for information in that chapter. The editor wishes to thank these people and organizations for sharing this information. The Directory could not have been completed without their help!

The three most requested suggestions from our readers and critics in the 1982 publication were some pictures/maps, ancestry identification, and an index.

Pictures and maps are very expensive in the printing business and again we tried to put out a product that everyone could afford. The paperback edition ISBN Number 09610334-5-2 has no pictures and limited maps. The library edition ISBN number 09610334-3-6 includes a wall map of Indian Land Areas, and measures 42" x 45", that was printed recently by the U.S. Geological Service, and that has an updated detailed listing of all state and federally recognized tribes in the U.S. and Alaska. It also contains more detailed information.

All correspondence should include $3.00, self-addressed (priority mail) stamped envelope if requesting a reply to:

N.A^2.I.I.T.C.
PO Box 27626
Tucson, AZ 85726

Sincerely,
Fred Synder, Editor, Director
National Native American Cooperative

Fred Synder, Director, Consultant

N.A^{2}I.I.T.C

North American Native American
Indian Information & Trade Center

This book is dedicated in loving rememberance of:

Wilfred Henry Garcia

(June 20, 1920 - November 10, 1995)

Tohono O'Odham Nation
Sells, Arizona

Fred Synder, Director, Consultant

N.A.²I.I.T.C.

North American Native American
Indian Information & Trade Center

ALASKA

ALASKA

Ahtna, Inc.
Aleut Corporation
Arctic Slope Regional Corporation
Bering Straits Native Corporation
Bristol Bay Native Corporation
Calista Corporation
Chugach Alaska Corporation
Cook Inlet Region, Inc.
Doyon, Ltd.
Koniag, Inc.
NANA Regional Corporation
Sealaska Corporation
Thirteenth Regional Corporation

ALASKA

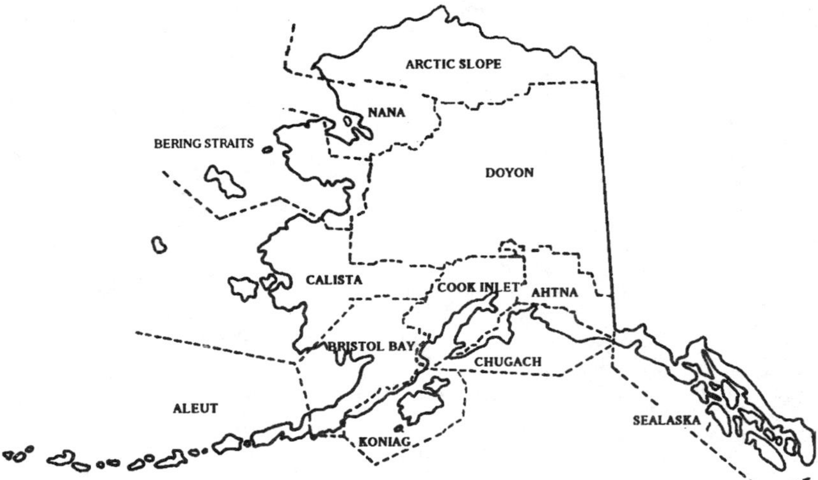

NATIVE REGIONAL CORPORATIONS

SPECIAL FEATURES OF NATIVE REGIONAL CORPORATIONS

Origins and Purposes: On December 18, 1971, the Alaska Native Claims Settlement Act (ANCSA) became law, awarding Alaska Natives $962.5 million and 44 million acres in settlement of their aboriginal claims. The law called for creation of 12 regional and more than 200 village corporations to manage the settlement land and money. The corporations were given the broad and elusive task of using the land and the money to produce economic and social benefits for Alaska Natives.

Shareholders: Persons of at least one-quarter Alaska Eskimo, Indian or Aleut blood who were alive in December 18, 1971 were to benefit from the settlement by virtue of owning the corporations. About 75,000 enrolled as shareholders of the corporations and received stock.

Restriction on Stock Sales: For the first 20 years after ANCSA was passed, shareholders were prohibited from selling their stock. This provision was to insure that the corporations stayed in Native ownership for at least that long. The original ANCSA called for stock to automatically become transferable after 1991. But in 1987 ANCSA was amended so that a majority of the shareholders would have to approve in order for stock to come on the market after 1991. Then, in late 1991, Congress made yet another change: as of now, stock sales are prohibited until 1993. That move came at the request of the Alaska Federation of Natives, which was worried about the prospect of hostile takeovers of corporations if the stock came on the market.

Shareholder Voting Rights: The original ANCSA allowed shareholders to will their shares to whomever they chose, but only Natives or descendants of Natives were to have shareholders voting rights until after 1991, when stock was to automatically come on the market. In 1987 amendments to ANCSA, Congress gave share holder the option of keeping their stock off the market after 1991- and to prohibit non-Native shareholders from voting as long as the stock remained non-transferable.

Net Resource Revenue Sharing: ANCSA requires the regional corporations to share 70 percent of net revenues (revenues minus expenses) from timber and subsurface resources among themselves and the village corporations.

Issuing New Stock: Under the original ANCSA, only Natives alive on December 8, 1971 could enroll as shareholders, and all shareholders were issued equal numbers of shares. In 1987 Congress approved amendments to allow current shareholders to approve issuing new stock to Natives born since 1971, to elders, and to any eligible Native who missed the original enrollment. This amendment provides a way for young Natives to benefit more directly from ANCSA, and for older Natives to get more benefits now. ASRC has already issued new stock to young Natives, and NANA is planning to do so.

Land Protections: The original ANCSA protected undeveloped Native lands from taxation and loss for debt just until 1991. After 1980, Corporations got the option to extend that protection by putting undeveloped land in a land bank. Then, in 1987, amendments to ANCSA made all undeveloped lands automatically safe from taxation and loss through corporate debt or bankruptcy for as long as they remained undeveloped. Developed lands can revert to undeveloped status once there is no more development activity.

Corporations have, from the beginning, had the authority to sell land if they chose.

Settlement Trusts: A provision in the 1987 amendment allows shareholders to put money and surface land (but not subsurface rights) in settlement trusts that are shielded from corporations operations. Establishing such trusts is complicated, and once assets are in they can't be taken out. Trust assets are protected even if the corporation goes bankrupt, and they can't be seized for corporate debt. Settlement trusts can invest money to create dividends for shareholders, but can not develop or sell lands.

FINANCIAL PERFORMANCE OF NATIVE REGIONAL CORPORATIONS

Twenty years ago this month, December 1991, Congress passed the Alaska Native Claim Settlement Act (ANCSA). That act ended the claim struggle but set in motion a new process: the establishment of business corporations, owned by Alaska Natives, to manage their claims settlement of nearly $1 billion and 44 million acres.

Twelve regional and more than 200 village corporations were organized soon after the act was passed, and by 1973 about 75,000 Alaska Natives had enrolled as shareholders. The corporations have since become a familiar part of the Alaska landscape, and in 1991 employed nearly 7,500 Alaskans including about 2,500 shareholders.

The ANCSA corporations were given broad but elusive task of benefiting their shareholders and future generations of Natives. But what form those benefits ought to take, and how the corporations should achieve them was not clear. The shareholders, Congress, and others expected the corporations to do everything from earning profits and creating jobs to improving conditions in the villages and protecting subsistence resources.

The Review examine one narrow measure of how well the corporations have done: it describes the financial performance of the regional corporations from their beginning in 1973 through 1990. We also report available information on shareholder employment.

The regional corporation got about half the ANCSA cash settlement, full ownership of some land, and subsurface rights to their own village and corporation land. The endowment of natural resources in each region explains a lot about the relative financial success of the corporations: some regions just have more marketable resources than others. But besides the differences attributable to random resource distribution, we can make several points about the corporations cumulative financial performance from their start through 1990.

- The regional corporations made more than $575 million, adjusted for inflation. But public policies implemented after ANCSA accounted for most of that.
- Second, a special tax law allowed them to collect real proceeds of $445 million by selling their net operating losses (NOLs) to other corporations.
- Aside from those two special sources of income , investments in stocks and other securities worked well for the corporations, producing real returns of $439 million.
- As a group they lost money on many of their business ventures, for a cumulative real loss of $352 million. However a few individual corporations did well in business ventures, and some suffered losses while providing jobs for their shareholders.

Our analysis is based largely on annual reports of the corporations themselves. This publications marks the first time such comprehensive data on the financial gains and losses of the regional corporations have been drawn together. Previous studies have looked at standard measures of financial performance like return on equality. We concentrate instead of on how the corporations achieved the results they did by examining where they got their financial wealth, how they used it, and what strategies proved most profitable for them. We look at the corporation as a group and individually, and at total and per shareholder figures.

We do not report on finances of village corporations. Also, our financial analysis does not directly include the value of Native lands. For the most part, corporations have not assigned a dollar value to ANCSA lands. We do of course include any income that ANCSA lands held by regional corporations have generated.

CONCLUSIONS

All of the regional corporations survived the first twenty years, but several just barely did. A big part of their relative financial success or failure can be traced to their different resources endowments: some corporations got more natural resources to begin with, and a few were able to win rich resource lands through negotiations and trades.

Most-not all- were held back by business losses. CIRI was the clear exception, bringing in hundreds of millions of dollars for its shareholders. A number of the other corporations lost by putting too much of their money into single big, risky business ventures.

But they certainly weren't alone in business failures. Hundreds of Alaska business went into bankruptcy during the recession of the late 1989s. Alaska, especially rural Alaska, is a hard place to do business. The regional corporations in rural areas often involved themselves in marginal ventures-partly to sustain jobs.

The tenacity and political skills of their leaders also helped the corporations. With strong backing from Alaska's congressional delegation, potential than the ones originally opened to them. And later they won the right to sell the net operating losses (NOLs) they said were the result of the federal's government's long delays in conveying ANCSA lands. In both cases, their success meant financial gains.

A few corporations-NANA being the outstanding example chose to create jobs for their shareholders even though they knew that could mean foregoing profits. What most consistently paid off for the corporations over time were investments in stocks and other securities and natural resource development. So it seems to make sense for them to concentrate on that basic logic.

But for the next 20 years and beyond, the corporation face not only questions about how to make profits for their shareholders but about the much broader issue of how best to serve the Alaska Native people. And in recent years, Natives have become increasingly split over how to benefit from and at the same time protect the asset they won after the long settlement battle.

Under the original terms of ANCSA, the ability of Native people to hold onto and benefit from their settlement was in many ways linked to the financial success of the corporation. They were given 20 years of partial protection, by prohibiting stock sales until 1991, ANCSA guaranteed that the corporations would stay in Native hands at least that long. After that, the corporations were to have become more or less like other U.S. corporation, with stock automatically becoming transferable.

Land was actually less well protected than stock in the early years of the corporations. Under the original terms of ANCSA, management could sell land but shareholders could not sell stock.

As time went on Native leaders became increasingly concerned about losing control of corporations after 1991. They persuaded Congress to enact major amendments ANCSA in 1987. Those amendments keep stock off the market unless a majority of the shareholders vote to sell. (In late 1991 Congress precluded stock sales until at least 1993, in a move designed to prevent hostile takeovers of the corporations.) They automatically protect all undeveloped Native lands from taxation or loss through corporate failure. An shareholders can vote to put surface land and money in settlement trusts to insulate them from corporate operations. The trusts can not develop lands or undertake business activities, but they can create investment funds and pay dividends to shareholders. However, once assets are in a trust, they can't be removed.

So as it stands now, Alaska Natives have more choice about keeping and using their settlement assets. But the 75,000 shareholders of the corporations are a diverse group. They share a native heritage, but differ in many ways. Some live in tiny remote villages and others live in cities. Some rely on the land and subsistence and some on the sea. A significant share live outside the regions to which they are enrolled and some don't live in Alaska at all.

Some shareholders want their corporations to concentrate less on profits and more on jobs, education and training. Others want them to be more aggressive in going after profits and distributing dividends.

And there is the issue whether to emphasize benefits for current or future generations of Natives. Originally, only Natives alive on December 8, 1971 could enroll as shareholders. The 1987 amendments gave corporations the option of issuing new stock to young Natives, elders, or to others who may have somehow missed the original enrollment. So far only Arctic Slope (ASRC) has issued new stock. NANA plans to enroll shareholders. It remains to be seen to what extent current shareholders in other corporations will be willing to share the value of their corporations with the new generation.

At the other end of the generational spectrum, many Native elders may not live to reap the financial benefits of their share in the corporations.

That's because more profits re-invested for the future means less money for the dividends today. Sealaska and ASRC have addressed the issue by establishing special trust funds to pay distributions to elders.

For most U.S. business corporations, these profound questions about who should benefit and when are not relevant because shareholders can sell their stock for cash, and those unhappy with a companies business strategy can shop around for stock in another with a management philosophy they like.

Native shareholders have had no such choice for the past 20 years: they have had to stick with their corporations receive direct financial benefits mainly in the form of dividends. Within a few years they will have the choice of selling their stock. But even if shareholders are able to sell, many who want cash still wouldn't want to give up their stake in their land by selling stock.

From the shareholders perspective, therefore, Congress may have gotten things backwards when it allowed the corporations to sell ANCSA lands and prohibited the shareholders from selling stock.

The 1987 amendments to ANCSA included provisions that allowed shareholders to approve stock sales, and provisions which allow protection of undeveloped land in permanent settlement trusts. Many of the diverse issue facing the corporations might be resolved if there were a way, short of locking it up permanently, for shareholder to insure that they don't lose their land. It remains to be seen whether they will seek such a solution, and if so whether they can succeed under current law.

Re-printed with permission from:
ALASKA REVIEW OF SOCIAL AND ECONOMIC CONDITIONS
Institute of Social and Economic Research
University of Alaska Anchorage
E. Lee Gorsuch, Director
3211 Providence Drive
Anchorage, Alaska 99508

ALASKA

KEY TO TRIBAL GRAPHS ON PAGES 10 TO 35

This graph format is divided into three sections, ie. Historical Profile on the left hand page, Economic Profile on the right hand page and down the middle of each page in the shaded area is the full name, address, state, zip, phone and fax information of each tribal nation.

HISTORICAL PROFILE

B.I.A. AGENCY:

The Bureau of Indian Affairs has divided Alaska and the United States into twelve area offices, each is responsible for several Indian tribes/nations. In Alaska there are five regional agencies for the Bureau of Indian Affairs, each is listed in the legend at the bottom of each graph.

FIRST TREATY:

Alaska native tribes did not sign treaties with the United States government. Traditional villages never signed a treaty. Villages were divided under thirteen regional corporations in 1972.

FORM OF GOVERNMENT:

Alaska native tribes and villages are divided between the I.R.A. group, which is the Indian Reorganization Act, and the T.C., which are Traditional Councils.

POPULATION 1990:

The population figures are those reported by the 1990 census and only the figures they report. A census figure is available from the Bureau of Indian Affairs, I.H.S. public health census and the tribal census office. All with great differences in the count. Some villages are used seasonally; these show no population by the U.S. Census.

ECONOMIC PROFILE

L - Lodging, Resort, Motel
F - Fishing
N - Newspaper
R/T - Radio/TV
M/C - Museum/Cultural Center

HISTORICAL PROFILE

BIA Agency *	First Treaty **	Form of Govt. ***	Pop 1990 ****	Village	Address
AN	1972	IRA	67	ATKA, NATIVE VILLAGE OF	PO BOX 47030
BE		TC	250	ATMUATLUAK, VILLAGE OF	PO BOX ATT
FA		TC	201	ATQASUK VILLAGE COUNCIL	GENERAL DELIVERY
JU		TC		AUKQUAN TRADITIONAL COUNCIL	9296 STEPHEN RICHARDS MEMORIAL DR
FA	1972	IRA	2217	BARROW, NATIVE VILLAGE OF	PO BOX 1139
FA		TC	98	BEAVER VILLAGE CCL	PO BOX 24029
AN		TC	0	BELKOFSKI, NATIVE VILLAGE OF	PO BOX 57
BE		TC	2986	BETHEL NATIVE CCL ORUTSARARMUIT NATIVE CCL	PO BOX 927
FA		TC	27	BETTLES FIELD/EVANSVILLE VILLAGE	GENERAL DELIVERY
BE		TC	0	BILL MOORE'S SLOUGH NATIVE VILLAGE	PO BOX 20037
FA		TC	38	BIRCH CREEK VILLAGE CCL	PO BOX KBC
NM		TC	183	BREVIG MISSION TRADITIONAL CCL	GENERAL DELIVERY
NM	1972	IRA	302	BUCKLAND, NATIVE VILLAGE OF	PO BOX 67
AN		TC	33	CANTWELL, NATIVE VILLAGE OF	PO BOX 94
FA		TC	33	CENTRAL CCL OF THE TLINGIT & HAIDA INDIANS	320 W WILLOUGHBY AVE, #300
FA		TC	83	CHALKYITSIK TRADITIONAL CCL	PO BOX 57
BE		TC	312	CHEFORNAK TRADITIONAL CCL	PO BOX 29

LEGEND:

AN - Anchorage
BE - Bethel
FA - Fairbanks
NM - Nome
JU - Juneau
PO - Portland

* BIA Agency - Bureau of Indian Affairs Area Offices, Abbreviations

** First Treaty - Traditional villages never signed a treaty, villages divided under 13 regional corporations in 1972.

*** I.R.A. - Indian Reorganization Act. T.C. - Traditional Council

**** Some villages are used seasonally: These show no population by US Census

ECONOMIC PROFILE

City	State	Zip	Phone Fax	L	F	N	R/T	M/C
ATKA	AK	99574	907-839-2233 907-839-2234		X			
ATMAUTLUAK	AK	99559	907-553-5610		X			
ATQASUK	AK	99723			X			
JUNEAU	AK	99801	907-465-4120					
BARROW	AK	99723	907-852-4411		X			
BEAVER	AK	99724	907-628-6126		X			
KING COVE	AK	99612	907-497-2304		X			
BETHEL	AK	99559	907-543-2608 907-543-2639		X			
BETTLES	AK	99726	907-692-5035		X			
KOTLIK	AK	99620	907-899-4712		X			
FORT YUKON	AK	99740	907-221-9133		X			
BREVIG MISSION	AK	99785	907-642-4301 907-642-4311		X			
BUCKLAND	AK	99727	907-494-2171		X			
CANTWELL	AK	99729	907-768-2151	X	X			
JUNEAU	AK	99801	907-586-1432	X	X			
CHALKYITSIK	AK	99788	907-848-8893		X			
CHEFORNAK	AK	99561	907-867-8850 907-867-8429		X			

Legend:

L - Lodging, Resort, Motel
F - Fishing
N - Newspaper
R/T - Radio/TV
M/C - Museum / Cultural Center

HISTORICAL PROFILE

BIA Agency *	First Treaty **	Form of Govt. ***	Pop 1990 ****	Village	Address
AN	1972	IRA	65	CHENEGA, NATIVE VILLAGE OF	PO BOX 8079
BE		TC	556	CHEVAK TRADITIONAL CCL	PO BOX 5514
AN		TC	9	CHICKALOON, NATIVE VILLAGE OF	PO BOX 1105
AN	1972	IRA	30	CHIGNIK LAGOON, NATIVE VILLAGE OF	GENERAL DELIVERY
AN	1972	IRA	122	CHIGNIK LAKE, NATIVE VILLAGE OF	GENERAL DELIVERY
AN		TC	85	CHIGNIK LAKE, NATIVE VILLAGE OF	PO BOX 33
JU	1972	IRA	112	CHILKAT INDIAN VLG OF KLUKWAN	PO BOX 210
JU	1972	IRA	240	CHILKOOT INDIAN ASSOC	PO BOX 490
AN		TC	37	CHISTOCHINA, NATIVE VILLAGE OF	PO BOX 241
AN		TC	23	CHITNA, NATIVE VILLAGE OF	PO BOX 31
BE		TC	87	CHUATHBALUK, VILLAGE OF	PO BOX 31
BE		TC	0	CHULOONAWICK, NATIVE VILLAGE OF	GENERAL DELIVERY
FA		TC	63	CIRCLE VILLAGE CCL	PO BOX 8
AN		TC	53	CLARK'S POINT, NATIVE VILLAGE OF	PO BOX 16
AN	1972	N/A	155	COPPER RIVER NATIVE ASSOCIATION	PO BOX 68
NM		TC	5	COUNCIL, NATIVE VILLAGE OF	PO BOX 2050
JU	1972	IRA	333	CRAIG COMMUNITY ASSOCIATION	PO BOX 828

LEGEND:

AN - Anchorage
BE - Bethel
FA - Fairbanks
NM - Nome
JU - Juneau
PO - Portland

* BIA Agency - Bureau of Indian Affairs Area Offices, Abbreviations

** First Treaty - Traditional villages never signed a treaty, villages divided under 13 regional corporations in 1972.

*** I.R.A. - Indian Reorganization Act. T.C. - Traditional Council

**** Some villages are used seasonally: These show no population by US Census

ECONOMIC PROFILE

City	State	Zip	Phone Fax	L	F	N	R/T	M/C
CHENEGA BAY	AK	99574	907-573-5132		X			
CHEVAK	AK	99563	907-858-7428 907-858-7812		X			
CHICKALOON	AK	99674	907-746-0505		X			
CHIGNIK LAGOON	AK	99565	907-840-2206		X			
CHIGNIK	AK	99563	907-749-2285		X			
CHIGNIK LAKE	AK	99548	907-845-2212		X			
KLUKWAN	AK	99827	907-767-5505 907-767-5515		X			
HAINES	AK	99827	907-766-2243 907-766-2328		X			
GAKOMA	AK	99586	907-822-3503		X			
CHITINA	AK	99566	907-563-6643		X			
CHUATHBALUK	AK	99557	907-467-4313	X	X			X
CHULOONAWICK	AK	99581	907-949-1147		X			
CIRCLE	AK	99733	907-733-5498		X			
CLARK'S POINT	AK	99569	907-236-1221		X			
COPPER CENTER	AK	99573	907-822-5541		X			
NOME	AK	99762	907-443-3443 907-443-2618		X			
CRAIG	AK	99921	907-826-3321 907-826-3980		X			

Legend:

L - Lodging, Resort, Motel
F - Fishing
N - Newspaper
R/T - Radio/TV
M/C - Museum / Cultural Center

HISTORICAL PROFILE

BIA Agency *	First Treaty **	Form of Govt. ***	Pop 1990 ****	Village	Address
BE		TC	96	CROOKED CREEK, VILLAGE OF	PO BOX 69
NM	1972	IRA	148	DEERING, NATIVE VILLAGE OF	PO BOX 36043
AN		TC	1125	DILLINGHAM VILLAGE CCL	PO BOX 216
NM	1972	IRA	167	DIOMEDE, NATIVE VILLAGE OF	PO BOX 7099
FA		TC	38	DOT LAKE VILLAGE CCL	PO BOX 2272
JU	1972	IRA	134	DOUGLAS INDIAN ASSOCIATION	PO BOX 20478
FA	1972	IRA	33	EAGLE VILLAGE CCL	PO BOX 19
BE		TC	243	EEK, NATIVE VILLAGE OF	PO BOX 87
AN		TC	86	EGEGIK VILLAGE CCL	PO BOX 189
AN		TC	48	EKLUTNA, NATIVE VILLAGE OF	36339 EKLUTNA VILLAGE ROAD
AN		TC	2	EKUK, NATIVE VILLAGE OF	GENERAL DELIVERY
AN		TC	67	EKWOK VILLAGE CCL	PO BOX 49
NM	1972	IRA	242	ELIM, NATIVE VILLAGE OF	PO BOX 39010
BE	1972	IRA	591	EMMONAK VILLAGE CCL	PO BOX 126
AN		TC	144	ENGLISH BAY CORP	PO BOX KE8
FA				EVANSVILLE VILLAGE	PO BOX 26025
AN	1972	IRA	250	EYAK, NATIVE VILLAGE OF	PO BOX 1388

LEGEND:

AN - Anchorage
BE - Bethel
FA - Fairbanks
NM - Nome
JU - Juneau
PO - Portland

* BIA Agency - Bureau of Indian Affairs Area Offices, Abbreviations

** First Treaty - Traditional villages never signed a treaty, villages divided under 13 regional corporations in 1972.

*** I.R.A. - Indian Reorganization Act.
T.C. - Traditional Council

**** Some villages are used seasonally: These show no population by US Census

ECONOMIC PROFILE

City	State	Zip	Phone Fax	L	F	N	R/T	M/C
CROOKED CREEK	AK	99575	907-432-2227		X			
DEERING	AK	99736	907-363-2148		X			
DILLINGHAM	AK	99576	907-842-2384		X			
DIOMEDE	AK	99762	907-686-3021		X			
DOT LAKE	AK	99737	907-882-2669 907-882-2112		X			
JUNEAU	AK	99802	907-586-1798		X			
EAGLE	AK	99738	907-547-2271		X			
EEK	AK	99578	907-536-5426		X			
EGEGIK	AK	99579	907-233-2231		X			
CHUGIAK	AK	99567	907-688-6020 907-688-6021		X			
EKUK	AK	99476	907-842-5937		X			
EKWOK	AK	99580	907-464-3311		X			
ELIM	AK	99739	907-890-3741 907-890-3072		X			
EMMONAK	AK	99581	907-949-1720 907-949-1926		X			
ENGLISH BAY	AK	99603	907-281-9219		X			
EVANSVILLE	AK	99726	907-692-5467					
CORDOVA	AK	99574	907-424-3622		X			

Legend:

L - Lodging, Resort, Motel
F - Fishing
N - Newspaper
R/T - Radio/TV
M/C - Museum / Cultural Center

HISTORICAL PROFILE

BIA Agency *	First Treaty **	Form of Govt. ***	Pop 1990 ****	Village	Address
AN		TC	52	FALSE PASS VILLAGE CCL	PO BOX 29/180 UNIMAK DRIVE
FA	1972	IRA	493	FORT YUKON, NATIVE VILLAGE OF	PO BOX 126
AN		TC	0	GAKONA, NATIVE VILLAGE OF	PO BOX 124
FA		TC	377	GALENA VILLAGE CCL	PO BOX 182
NM		TC	505	GAMBELL, NATIVE VILLAGE OF	PO BOX 99
BE		TC	60	GEORGETOWN, NATIVE VILLAGE OF	GENERAL DELIVERY
NM		TC	118	GOLOVIN CHINIK ESKIMO COMM, VLG OF	PO BOX 62020
BE		TC	231	GOODNEWS BAY, NATIVE VILLAGE OF	PO BOX 3
FA	1972	IRA	194	GRAYLING (HOLIKACHU) ORGANIZED VILLAGE OF	GENERAL DELIVERY
AN		TC	61	GULKANA VILLAGE CCL	PO BOX 254
BE		TC	0	HAMILTON, NATIVE VILLAGE OF	PO BOX 20130
FA		TC	40	HEALY LAKE VILLAGE CCL	PO BOX 667
FA		TC	259	HOLY CROSS VILLAGE CCL	PO BOX 203
JU	1972	IRA	534	HOONAH INDIAN ASSOCIATION	PO BOX 402
BE		TC	811	HOOPER BAY, NATIVE VILLAGE OF	PO BOX 2193
FA		TC	50	HUGHES VILLAGE CCL	PO BOX 45010
FA		IRA	188	HUSLIA VILLAGE CCL	PO BOX 10

LEGEND:

AN - Anchorage
BE - Bethel
FA - Fairbanks
NM - Nome
JU - Juneau
PO - Portland

* BIA Agency - Bureau of Indian Affairs Area Offices, Abbreviations

** First Treaty - Traditional villages never signed a treaty, villages divided under 13 regional corporations in 1972.

*** I.R.A. - Indian Reorganization Act.
T.C. - Traditional Council

**** Some villages are used seasonally: These show no population by US Census

ECONOMIC PROFILE

City	State	Zip	Phone Fax	L	F	N	R/T	M/C
FALSE PASS	AK	99583	907-548-2227 907-548-2214		X	X		
FORT YUKON	AK	99740	907-662-2581 907-662-2222		X			
GAKONA	AK	99586	907-822-3497		X			
GALENA	AK	99741	907-656-1666		X			
GAMBELL	AK	99762	907-985-5346 907-985-5520		X			
GEORGETOWN	AK	99557			X			
GOLOVIN	AK	99589	907-779-3521 907-779-3261		X			
GOODNEWS BAY	AK	99589	907-967-8929		X			
GRAYLING	AK	99590	907-453-5128		X			
GAKONA	AK	99586	907-822-3746		X			
KOTLIK	AK	99620	907-899-4313 907-899-4826		X			
DELTA JUNCION	AK	99737	907-452-7915		X			
HOLY CROSS	AK	99602	907-476-7134		X			
HOONAH	AK	99829	907-945-3220 907-945-3445		X			
HOOPER BAY	AK	99604	907-758-4915 907-758-4815		X			
HUGHES	AK	99745	907-899-2206		X			
HUSLIA	AK	99745	907-829-2256		X			

Legend:

L - Lodging, Resort, Motel
F - Fishing
N - Newspaper
R/T - Radio/TV
M/C - Museum / Cultural Center

HISTORICAL PROFILE

BIA Agency *	First Treaty **	Form of Govt. ***	Pop 1990 ****	Village	Address
JU	1972	IRA	387	HYDABURG COOPERATIVE ASSOC	PO BOX 305
AN		TC	26	IGIUGIG VILLAGE CENTER	PO BOX 4008
AN		TC	62	ILIAMNA, NATIVE VILLAGE OF	PO BOX 286
FA	1972	IRA	328	INUPIAT COMM OF ARCTIC SLOPE	PO BOX 1232
AN		TC	33	IVANOF BAY VILLAGE CCL	PO BOX K 1 B
JU	1972	IRA	514	KAKE, ORGANIZED VILLAGE OF	PO BOX 316
FA		TC	66	KAKTOVIK VLG BARTER ISLAND	PO BOX 8
NM		TC	222	KALTAG, NATIVE VILLAGE OF	PO BOX 9
AN	1972	IRA	86	KANATAK, NAT VLG OF FT ANCHORAGE AG	1675 'C' ST #110
AN	1972	IRA	65	KARLUK, NATIVE VILLAGE OF	PO BOX 22
JU	1982	IRA	29	KASAAN, NATIVE VILLAGE OF	GENERAL DELIVERY
BE		TC	405	KASILGLUK, NATIVE VILLAGE OF	PO BOX 19
AN	1972	IRA	535	KENAITZE INDIAN TRIBE	PO BOX 988
JU	1972	IRA	1404	KETCHIKAN INDIAN CORP	429 DEERMONT AVENUE
NM		TC	360	KIANA TRADITIONAL CCL	PO BOX 69
AN		TC	177	KING COVE TRADITIONAL CCL	PO BOX 18
NM	1972	IRA	311	KING ISLAND NATIVE COMMUNITY	PO BOX 992

LEGEND:

AN - Anchorage
BE - Bethel
FA - Fairbanks
NM - Nome
JU - Juneau
PO - Portland

* BIA Agency - Bureau of Indian Affairs Area Offices, Abbreviations

** First Treaty - Traditional villages never signed a treaty, villages divided under 13 regional corporations in 1972.

*** I.R.A. - Indian Reorganization Act.
T.C. - Traditional Council

**** Some villages are used seasonally: These show no population by US Census

City	State	Zip	Phone Fax	L	F	N	R/T	M/C
HYDABURG	AK	99922	907-285-3139 907-285-3944		X			
IGIUGIG	AK	99613	907-553-3211		X			
ILIAMNA	AK	99606	907-571-1246		X			
BARROW	AK	99723	907-825-6907		X			
IVANOF BAY	AK	99502	907-699-2204		X			
KAKE	AK	99830	907-785-6471 907-785-4902		X			
KAKTOVIK	AK	99501	907-640-6120		X			
KALTAG	AK	99748	907-534-2230		X			
ANCHORAGE	AK	99924	907-263-9820 907-274-3721		X			
KARLUCK	AK	99609	907-241-2218 907-241-2203		X			
KASAAN	AK	99611	907-542-2214 907-542-2215		X			
KASIGLUK	AK	99901	907-477-6927		X			
KENAI	AK	99749	907-283-3633		X			
KETCHIKAN	AK	99612	907-225-5158 907-247-0429		X			
KIANA	AK	99762	907-475-2109		X			
KING COVE	AK	99614	907-497-2648 907-497-2444		X			
NOME	AK	99750	907-442-5494 907-443-5487		X			

Legend:

L - Lodging, Resort, Motel
F - Fishing
N - Newspaper
R/T - Radio/TV
M/C - Museum / Cultural Center

HISTORICAL PROFILE

BIA Agency *	First Treaty **	Form of Govt. ***	Pop 1990 ****	Village	Address
BE		TC	458	KIPNUK, NATIVE VILLAGE OF	PO BOX 57
NM	1972	IRA	309	KIVALINA, NATIVE VILLAGE OF	PO BOX 50051
JU	1972	IRA	427	KLAWOCK COOPERATIVE ASSOCIATION	PO BOX 112
AN		TC	31	KNIK VILLAGE CCL	PO BOX 872130
NM		TC	62	KOBUK TRADITIONAL CCL	GENERAL DELIVERY
AN		TC	845	KODIAK, NATIVE VILLAGE OF	PO BOX 1974
AN		TC	137	KOKHANOK VILLAGE CCL	PO BOX 1007
JU	1972	IRA	174	KOLIGANEK VILLAGE	PO BOX 5057
BE		TC	286	KONGIGANAK TRADITION CCL	PO BOX 5069
BE		TC	447	KOTLIK, VILLAGE OF	PO BOX 20096
NM	1972	IRA	2067	KOTZEBUE, NATIVE VILLAGE OF	PO BOX 296
NM	1972	IRA	219	KOYUK, NATIVE VILLAGE OF	PO BOX 30
FA		TC	123	KOYUKUK VILLAGE CCL	PO BOX 49
BE	1972	IRA	538	KWETHLUK, ORGANIZED VILLAGE OF	PO BOX 54
BE	1972	IRA	264	KWIGILLINGOK, NATIVE VILLAGE OF	PO BOX 49
BE		TC	407	KWINHAGAK (QUINHAGEK), NATIVE VILLAGE OF	PO BOX 58
AN		TC	124	LARSEN BAY, NATIVE VILLAGE OF	PO BOX 35

LEGEND:

AN - Anchorage
BE - Bethel
FA - Fairbanks
NM - Nome
JU - Juneau
PO - Portland

* BIA Agency - Bureau of Indian Affairs Area Offices, Abbreviations

** First Treaty - Traditional villages never signed a treaty, villages divided under 13 regional corporations in 1972.

*** I.R.A. - Indian Reorganization Act.
T.C. - Traditional Council

**** Some villages are used seasonally: These show no population by US Census

ECONOMIC PROFILE

City	State	Zip	Phone Fax	L	F	N	R/T	M/C
KIPNUK	AK	99925	907-896-5515 907-896-5420		X			
KIVALINA	AK	99750	907-645-2153		X			
KLAWOCK	AK	99751	907-755-2265 907-755-8800		X			
WASILLA	AK	99687	907-376-2845		X			
KOBUK	AK	99751	907-948-2214		X			
KODIAK	AK	99615	907-486-4449	X	X			
ILIAMNA	AK	99606	907-282-2202		X			
KOLIGANEK	AK	99606	907-596-3434	X				
KONGIGANAK	AK	99559	907-557-5226 907-557-5611		X			
KOTLIK	AK	99620	907-889-4326		X			
KOTZEBUE	AK	99752	907-442-3467 907-442-2162		X			
KOYUK	AK	99753	907-984-6414 907-984-3442		X			
KOYUKUK	AK	99754	907-927-2214		X			
KWETHLUK	AK	99621	907-757-6814 907-757-6328		X			
KWIGILLINGOK	AK	99622	907-588-8114 907-588-8429		X			
QUINHAGAK	AK	99655	907-556-8449		X			
LARSEN BAY	AK	99624	907-847-2207		X	X		

Legend:

L - Lodging, Resort, Motel
F - Fishing
N - Newspaper
R/T - Radio/TV
M/C - Museum / Cultural Center

HISTORICAL PROFILE

BIA Agency *	First Treaty **	Form of Govt. ***	Pop 1990 ****	Village	Address
AN	1972	IRA	87	LEVELOCK IRA CCL	PO BOX 70
BE		TC	40	LIME VILLAGE CCL	GENERAL DELIVERY
FA	1972	IRA	0	LOUDEN VILLAGE CCL	PO BOX 182
BE		TC	286	LOWER KALSKAG, VILLAGE OF	PO BOX 27
FA		TC	14	MANLEY VILLAGE CCL	GENERAL DELIVERY
AN		TC	368	MANOKOTAK VILLAGE CCL	PO BOX 169
BE		TC	253	MARSHALL, NATIVE VILLAGE OF	PO BOX 10
NM		TC	0	MARY'S IGLOO, VILLAGE OF	PO BOX 572
BE		TC	248	MCGRATH NATIVE VILLAGE	PO BOX 134
BE	1972	IRA	176	MEKORYUK, NATIVE VILLAGE OF	PO BOX 66
AN		TC	70	MENTASTA VILLAGE AKA MENTASTA LAKE	PO BOX 6019
PO	1972	IRA	1500	METLAKATLA INDIAN COMM CCL	PO BOX 8
FA	1972	IRA	212	MINTO VILLAGE CCL	PO BOX 26
BE		TC	614	MT VILLAGE, NATIVE VILLAGE OF	PO BOX 32249
AN				NAKNEK NATIVE VILLAGE	PO BOX 106
BE		TC	3	NAPAIMUTE, NATIVE VILLAGE OF	PO BOX 96
BE	1972	IRA	300	NAPAKIAK, NATIVE VILLAGE OF	GENERAL DELIVERY

LEGEND:

AN - Anchorage
BE - Bethel
FA - Fairbanks
NM - Nome
JU - Juneau
PO - Portland

* BIA Agency - Bureau of Indian Affairs Area Offices, Abbreviations

** First Treaty - Traditional villages never signed a treaty, villages divided under 13 regional corporations in 1972.

*** I.R.A. - Indian Reorganization Act.
T.C. - Traditional Council

**** Some villages are used seasonally: These show no population by US Census

ECONOMIC PROFILE

City	State	Zip	Phone Fax	L	F	N	R/T	M/C
LEVELOCK	AK	99625	907-287-3030		X			
LIME VILLAGE	AK	99627	907-526-5126		X			
GALENA	AK	99741	907-656-1666		X			
LOWER KALSKAG	AK	99626	907-471-2307		X			
MANLEY HOT SPRINGS	AK	99756	907-672-3331		X			
MANOKOTAK	AK	99628	907-289-2067		X			
FORTUNA LEDGE	AK	99585	907-679-6215 907-679-6220		X			
TELLER	AK	99778	907-642-3731		X			
MCGRATH	AK	99627	907-524-3024		X			
MEKORYUK	AK	99630	907-827-8828 907-827-8215		X			
TOK	AK	99780	907-291-2319		X			
METLAKATLA	AK	99926	907-886-4411 907-886-7997		X			
MINTO	AK	99758	907-798-7112		X			
MT VILLAGE	AK	99632	907-591-2841 907-591-2811		X			
NAKNEK	AK	99633	907-246-4210					
ANIAK	AK	99557			X			
NAPAKIAK	AK	99634	907-589-2227		X			

Legend:

L - Lodging, Resort, Motel
F - Fishing
N - Newspaper
R/T - Radio/TV
M/C - Museum / Cultural Center

HISTORICAL PROFILE

BIA Agency *	First Treaty **	Form of Govt. ***	Pop 1990 ****	Village	Address
BE		TC	311	NAPASKIAK VILLAGE CCL	PO BOX 6109
AN			67	NELSON LAGOON, VILLAGE OF	PO BOX 13 NLG
FA		TC	188	NENANA NATIVE ASSOCIATION	PO BOX 356
AN	1972	IRA	375	NEW STUYAHOK VILLAGE	PO BOX 49
AN			151	NEWHALEN VILLAGE CCL	PO BOX 207
BE		TC	193	NEWTOK VILLAGE CCL	PO BOX NWT
BE	1972	IRA	146	NIGHTMUTE, NATIVE VILLAGE OF	GENERAL DELIVERY
FA		TC	97	NIKOLAI VILLAGE CCL	GENERAL DELIVERY
AN	1972	IRA	29	NIKOLSKI, NATIVE VILLAGE OF	GENERAL DELIVERY
AN		TC	89	NINILCHIK, NATIVE VILLAGE OF	PO BOX 39070
NM		TC	322	NOATAK, NATIVE VILLAGE OF	GENERAL DELIVERY
NM	1972	IRA	1824	NOME ESKIMO COMMUNITY	PO BOX 1090
AN		TC	159	NONDALTON VILLAGE CCL	GENERAL DELIVERY
NM	1972	IRA	498	NOORVIK NATIVE COMM	PO BOX 71
FA		TC	107	NORTHWAY VILLAGE CCL	PO BOX 516
FA		TC	328	NUIQSUT, NATIVE VILLAGE OF	GENERAL DELIVERY
FA		TC	365	NULATO VILLAGE CCL	GENERAL DELIVERY

LEGEND:

AN - Anchorage
BE - Bethel
FA - Fairbanks
NM - Nome
JU - Juneau
PO - Portland

* BIA Agency - Bureau of Indian Affairs Area Offices, Abbreviations

** First Treaty - Traditional villages never signed a treaty, villages divided under 13 regional corporations in 1972.

*** I.R.A. - Indian Reorganization Act.
T.C. - Traditional Council

**** Some villages are used seasonally: These show no population by US Census

ECONOMIC PROFILE

City	State	Zip	Phone Fax	L	F	N	R/T	M/C
NAPASKIAK	AK	99559	907-737-7626		X			
COLD BAY	AK	99571	907-989-2204 907-989-2234		X			
NENANA	AK	99760	907-832-5662		X			
NEW STUYAHOK	AK	99636	907-693-3173		X			
ILIAMNA	AK	99606	907-571-2410		X			
NEWTOK	AK	99559	907-237-2314		X			
NIGHTMUTE	AK	99690	907-647-2313					
NIKOLAI	AK	99691	907-293-2226		X			
NIKOLSKI	AK	99638	907-576-2225 907-576-2205		X			
NINILCHIK	AK	99639	907-567-3313 907-567-3308		X			
NOATAK	AK	99761	907-485-2173		X			
NOME	AK	99762	907-443-2246 907-443-3539		X			
NONDALTON	AK	99640	907-294-2254 907-294-2254		X			
NOORVIK	AK	99763	907-636-2144		X			
NORTHWAY	AK	99764	907-778-2271		X			
NUIQSUT	AK	99723	907-480-6714		X			
NULATO	AK	99765	907-898-2231		X			

Legend:

L - Lodging, Resort, Motel
F - Fishing
N - Newspaper
R/T - Radio/TV
M/C - Museum / Cultural Center

HISTORICAL PROFILE

BIA Agency *	First Treaty **	Form of Govt. ***	Pop 1990 ****	Village	Address
BE	1972	IRA	367	NUNAPITCHUK, NATIVE VILLAGE OF	PO BOX 130
BE		TC	0	OHOGAMIUT, NATIVE VILLAGE OF	GENERAL DELIVERY
AN		TC	252	OLD HARBOR, VILLAGE OF	PO BOX 62
BE		TC	52	OSCARVILLE, TRADITIONAL CCL	PO BOX 1554
AN		TC	178	OUZINKIE, VILLAGE OF	PO BOX 13
AN		TC	38	PEDRO BAY VILLAGE CCL	PO BOX 47020
AN	1972	IRA	102	PERRYVILLE, VILLAGE OF	PO BOX 101
JU	1972	IRA	373	PETERSBURG INDIAN ASSOCIATION	PO BOX 1418
BE		TC	0	PIAMUIT, NATIVE VILLAGE OF	GENERAL DELIVERY
AN		TC	45	PILOT POINT, VILLAGE OF	PO BOX 449
BE		TC	440	PILOT STATION TRADITIONAL CCL	PO BOX 5040
BE		TC	129	PITKA'S POINT, NATIVE VILLAGE OF	PO BOX 127
BE		TC	59	PLATINUM VILLAGE CCL	GENERAL DELIVERY
FA	1972	TC	113	POIN LAY, NATIVE VILLAGE OF	PO BOX 101
NM	1972	IRA	587	POINT HOPE VILLAGE CCL	PO BOX 91
AN		TC	150	PORT GRAHAM VILLAGE CCL	PO BOX 5510
AN		TC	86	PORT HEIDEN, VILLAGE COUNCIL OF	PO BOX 49007

LEGEND:

AN - Anchorage
BE - Bethel
FA - Fairbanks
NM - Nome
JU - Juneau
PO - Portland

* BIA Agency - Bureau of Indian Affairs Area Offices, Abbreviations

** First Treaty - Traditional villages never signed a treaty, villages divided under 13 regional corporations in 1972.

*** I.R.A. - Indian Reorganization Act. T.C. - Traditional Council

**** Some villages are used seasonally: These show no population by US Census

ECONOMIC PROFILE

City	State	Zip	Phone Fax	L	F	N	R/T	M/C
NUNAPITCHUK	AK	99641	907-527-5705		X			
FORTUNA LEDGE	AK	99585	907-679-6740		X			
OLD HARBOR	AK	99643	907-286-2215		X			
OSCARVILLE	AK	99559	907-737-7321		X			
OUZINKIE	AK	99644	907-680-2259		X			
PEDRO BAY	AK	99647	907-850-2225		X			
PERRYVILLE	AK	99648	907-852-2203		X			
PETERSBURG	AK	99833	907-772-3636 907-772-3637		X			
HOOPER BAY	AK	99604	907-758-4420		X			
PILOT POINT	AK	99649	907-797-2208		X	X		
PILOT STATION	AK	99650	907-549-3512		X			
PITKA'S POINT	AK	99658	907-438-2833		X			
PLATINUM	AK	99651	907-979-8126		X			
POINT LAY	AK	99759	907-833-2428		X			
POINT HOPE	AK	99766	907-368-2453		X			
PORT GRAHAM	AK	99603	907-284-2227		X			
PORT HEIDEN	AK	99549	907-837-2218		X			

Legend:

L - Lodging, Resort, Motel
F - Fishing
N - Newspaper
R/T - Radio/TV
M/C - Museum / Cultural Center

HISTORICAL PROFILE

BIA Agency *	First Treaty **	Form of Govt. ***	Pop 1990 ****	Village	Address
AN		TC	150	PORT LIONS, VILLAGE OF	PO BOX 69
AN		TC	3	PORTAGE CREEK VILLAGE CCL	GENERAL DELIVERY C/O CHOGGIUNG
AN		TC	259	QAWALANGIN TRIBAL CCL (UNALASKA)	PO BOX 334
FA		TC	64	RAMPART VILLAGE CCL	PO BOX 67029
BE		TC	27	RED DEVIL, VILLAGE OF	PO BOX 49
FA		TC	126	RUBY NATIVE CCL	PO BOX 21
BE		TC	233	RUSSIAN MISSION, NATIVE VILLAGE OF	PO BOX 9
AN		TC	104	SALMATOK, VILLAGE OF	PO BOX 2682
AN		TC	433	SAND POINT (SHUMAGIN CORP), VILLAGE OF	PO BOX 447
NM	1972	IRA	494	SAVOONGA, NATIVE VILLAGE OF	PO BOX 129
JU	1972	IRA	494	SAXMAN, ORGANIZED VILLAGE OF	RT 2, BOX 2
BE		TC	331	SCAMMON BAY, NATIVE VILLAGE OF	PO BOX 126
NM	1972	IRA	569	SELAWIK, NATIVE VILLAGE OF	PO BOX 59
BE	1972	IRA	48	SELDOVIA, NATIVE VILLAGE OF	PO DRAWER L
BE	1972	IRA	132	SHAGELUK IRA CCL	GENERAL DELIVERY
NM	1972	IRA	168	SHAKTOOLIK, NATIVE VILLAGE OF	PO BOX 100
BE		TC	101	SHELDON'S POINT, NATIVE VILLAGE OF	GENERAL DELIVERY

LEGEND:

AN - Anchorage
BE - Bethel
FA - Fairbanks
NM - Nome
JU - Juneau
PO - Portland

* BIA Agency - Bureau of Indian Affairs Area Offices, Abbreviations

** First Treaty - Traditional villages never signed a treaty, villages divided under 13 regional corporations in 1972.

*** I.R.A. - Indian Reorganization Act. T.C. - Traditional Council

**** Some villages are used seasonally: These show no population by US Census

ECONOMIC PROFILE

City	State	Zip	Phone Fax	L	F	N	R/T	M/C
PORT LIONS	AK	99550	907-454-2234 907-454-2434		X	X		
PORTAGE CREEK	AK	99576	907-842-5218		X			
UNALASKA	AK	99685	907-581-2920 907-581-3644	X	X			
RAMPART	AK	99767	907-358-3312		X			
RED DEVIL	AK	99656	907-447-9901		X			
RUBY	AK	99768	907-468-4406		X			
RUSSIAN MISSION	AK	99657	907-584-5511		X			
KENAI	AK	99611	907-283-7864	X				
SAND POINT	AK	99661	907-383-3525 907-383-5356		X	X		
SAVOONGA	AK	99769	907-984-6414 907-984-6027		X			
KETCHIKAN	AK	99901	907-225-5163 907-225-6450		X			
SCAMMON BAY	AK	99662	907-558-5113 907-558-5626		X			
SELAWIK	AK	99770	907-484-2225 907-484-2226		X			
SELDOVIA	AK	99663	907-234-7625		X			
SHAGELUK	AK	99665	907-473-8239		X			
SHAKTOOLIK	AK	99771	907-995-3701 907-995-3151		X			
SHELDON'S POINT	AK	99666	907-498-4226		X			

Legend:

L - Lodging, Resort, Motel
F - Fishing
N - Newspaper
R/T - Radio/TV
M/C - Museum / Cultural Center

HISTORICAL PROFILE

BIA Agency *	First Treaty **	Form of Govt. ***	Pop 1990 ****	Village	Address
NM	1972	IRA	431	SHISHMAREF, NATIVE VILLAGE OF	PO BOX 72110
AN		TC	0	SHOONAQ TRIBE OF KODIAK	PO BOX 1974
NM	1972	IRA	211	SHUNGNAK, NATIVE VILLAGE OF	GENERAL DELIVERY
JU	1972	IRA	1900	SITKA COMMUNITY ASSOCIATION	PO BOX 1450
JU		TC	0	SKAGUAY TRADITIONAL VILLAGE CCL	PO BOX 399
BE		TC	92	SLEETMUTE, VILLAGE OF	PO BOX 21
NM		TC	6	SOLOMON, VILLAGE OF	PO BOX 243
AN		TC	108	SOUTH NAKNEK VILLAGE CCL	PO BOX 70106
AN		TC	131	ST GEORGE ISLAND CCL	PO BOX 940
BE		TC	366	ST MARY'S VILLAGE (ALAGANCIA)	PO BOX 48
NM	1972	IRA	269	ST MICHAEL, NATIVE VILLAGE OF	PO BOX 59090
NM	1972	IRA	379	STEBBINS COMMUNITY ASSOCIATION	PO BOX 2
FA	1972	IRA	93	STEVENS NATIVE VILLAGE CCL	GENERAL DELIVERY
BE		TC	45	STONEY RIVER, VILLAGE OF	PO BOX SRV
BE		TC	17	TAKOTNA VILLAGE CCL	PO BOX TYC
FA	1972	IRA	100	TANACROSS VILLAGE CCL	PO BOX 77130
FA	1972	IRA	270	TANANA IRA NATIVE CCL	PO BOX 77093

LEGEND:

AN - Anchorage
BE - Bethel
FA - Fairbanks
NM - Nome
JU - Juneau
PO - Portland

* BIA Agency - Bureau of Indian Affairs Area Offices, Abbreviations

** First Treaty - Traditional villages never signed a treaty, villages divided under 13 regional corporations in 1972.

*** I.R.A. - Indian Reorganization Act. T.C. - Traditional Council

**** Some villages are used seasonally: These show no population by US Census

ECONOMIC PROFILE

City	State	Zip	Phone Fax	L	F	N	R/T	M/C
SHISH-MAREF	AK	99772	907-649-3821 907-649-3583		X			
KODIAK	AK	99615	907-486-4449		X			
SHUNGNAK	AK	99773	907-437-2170		X			
SITKA	AK	99835	907-747-3207 907-747-4915		X			
SKAGWAY	AK	99840	907-983-2885		X			
SLEETMUTE	AK	99668	907-449-9901					
SOLOMON	AK	99762	907-443-2844 907-443-5098		X			
SOUTH NAKNEK	AK	99670	907-246-6566		X	X		
ST GEORGE ISLAND	AK	99591	907-859-2205 907-859-2242		X			
ST MARY'S	AK	99658	907-438-2932		X			
ST MICHAEL	AK	99659	907-923-3222 907-923-3142		X			
STEBBINS VILLAGE	AK	99671	907-934-3561 907-934-3560		X			
STEVENS VILLAGE	AK	99774	907-478-9226		X			
STONEY RIVER	AK	99557	907-537-3214		X			
TAKOTNA	AK	99675	907-298-2212		X			
TANACROSS	AK	99776	907-883-4131		X			
TANANA	AK	99777	907-366-7160 907-366-7195		X			

Legend:

L - Lodging, Resort, Motel
F - Fishing
N - Newspaper
R/T - Radio/TV
M/C - Museum / Cultural Center

HISTORICAL PROFILE

BIA Agency *	First Treaty **	Form of Govt. ***	Pop 1990 ****	Village	Address
AN	1972	IRA	103	TATITLEK, VILLAGE OF	PO BOX 171
AN		TC	57	TAZLINA, VILLAGE OF	PO BOX 188
FA		TC	10	TELIDA VILLAGE CCL	PO BOX 217
FA	1972	IRA	83	TELLER VILLAGE CCL	PO BOX 520
NM		TC	131	TELLER VILLAGE CCL	PO BOX 509
FA		TC	3526	TLINGIT & HAIDA COMM CCL	320 W. WILLOUGHBY #300
AN		TC	535	TOGIAK, VILLAGE OF	PO BOX 209
BE		TC	401	TOKSOOK BAY, NATIVE VILLAGE OF	NELSON ISLAND
BE	1972	IRA	342	TULUKSAK NATIVE COMMUNITY	PO BOX 156
BE		TC	290	TUNTUTULIAK, NATIVE VILLAGE OF	PO BOX 77
BE	1972	IRA	304	TUNUNAK, NATIVE VILLAGE OF	PO BOX 77
AN		TC	61	TWIN HILLS VILLAGE TRIBAL COUNCIL	PO BOX TWA
AN	1972	IRA	142	TYONEK, NATIVE VILLAGE OF	PO BOX 82009
AN		TC	6	UGASHIK VILLAGE COUNCIL	GENERAL DELIVERY
BE		TC	0	UMKUMIUT VILLAGE CCL	GENERAL DELIVERY
NM	1972	IRA	584	UNALAKLEET IRA	PO BOX 270
AN		TC		UNGA, NATIVE VILLAGE OF	PO BOX 508

LEGEND:

AN - Anchorage
BE - Bethel
FA - Fairbanks
NM - Nome
JU - Juneau
PO - Portland

* BIA Agency - Bureau of Indian Affairs Area Offices, Abbreviations

** First Treaty - Traditional villages never signed a treaty, villages divided under 13 regional corporations in 1972.

*** I.R.A. - Indian Reorganization Act.
T.C. - Traditional Council

**** Some villages are used seasonally: These show no population by US Census

ECONOMIC PROFILE

City	State	Zip	Phone Fax	L	F	N	R/T	M/C
TATITLEK	AK	99677	907-325-2311		X			
GLENALLEN	AK	99588	907-822-5965		X			
MCGRATH	AK	99627	907-843-8115		X			
TETLIN	AK	99780	907-883-2321		X			
TELLER	AK	99778	907-642-3381 907-642-4014					
JUNEAU	AK	99801	907-586-1432	X	X			
TOGIAK	AK	99678	907-493-5920		X	X		
TOKSOOK BAY	AK	99637	907-427-7114 907-427-7714		X			
TULUKSAK	AK	99679	907-695-6828		X			
TUNTUTULIAK	AK	99680	907-256-2128		X			
TUNUNAK	AK	99681	907-652-6527 907-652-6011		X			
TWIN HILLS	AK	99576	907-525-4820		X			
TYONEK	AK	99682	907-583-2201		X	X		
KING SALMON	AK	99613			X			
NIGHTMUTE	AK	99690	907-647-6213		X			
UNALAKLEET	AK	99684	907-624-3013 907-624-3099		X			
SAND POINT	AK	99661	907-271-4088 907-271-4083		X			

Legend:

L - Lodging, Resort, Motel
F - Fishing
N - Newspaper
R/T - Radio/TV
M/C - Museum / Cultural Center

HISTORICAL PROFILE

BIA Agency *	First Treaty **	Form of Govt. ***	Pop 1990 ****	Village	Address
BE		TC	146	UPPER KALSKAG, VILLAGE OF	GENERAL DELIVERY
FA	1972	IRA	171	VENETIE VILLAGE COUNCIL	PO BOX 99
FA		TC	464	WAINWRIGHT VILLAGE TRADITIONAL CCL	PO BOX 184
NM	1972	IRA	143	WALES, NATIVE VILLAGE OF	PO BOX 549
NM	1972	IRA	158	WHITE MOUNTAIN NATIVE VILLAGE	PO BOX 84082
JU	1972	IRA	535	WRANGELL COOPERATIVE ASSOCIATION	PO BOX 868
JU		TC	341	YAKUTAT NATIVE ASSOCIATION	PO BOX 418

LEGEND:

AN - Anchorage
BE - Bethel
FA - Fairbanks
NM - Nome
JU - Juneau
PO - Portland

* BIA Agency - Bureau of Indian Affairs Area Offices, Abbreviations

** First Treaty - Traditional villages never signed a treaty, villages divided under 13 regional corporations in 1972.

*** I.R.A. - Indian Reorganization Act. T.C. - Traditional Council

**** Some villages are used seasonally: These show no population by US Census

ECONOMIC PROFILE

City	State	Zip	Phone Fax	L	F	N	R/T	M/C
KALSKAG	AK	99607	907-471-2248		X			
ARCTIC VILLAGE	AK	99781	907-849-8212		X			
WAINWRIGHT	AK	99782	907-763-2726		X			
WALES	AK	99783	907-664-3511 907-664-3641		X			
WHITE MOUNTAIN	AK	99784	907-638-3651 907-638-3421		X	X		
WRANGELL	AK	99929	907-874-3747		X			
YAKUTAT	AK	99689	907-784-3932 907-784-3595		X			

Legend:

L - Lodging, Resort, Motel
F - Fishing
N - Newspaper
R/T - Radio/TV
M/C - Museum / Cultural Center

NATIVE CLAIMS SETTLEMENT ACT REGIONAL CORPS (PROFIT)

AHTNA, INC.
PO Box 649
Glennallen, Alaska 99588
907-882-3476

ALUET CORPORATION
4000 Old Seward Hwy,
Ste 300
Anchorage, Alaska 99503
907-576-4300

ARCTIC SLOPE REGIONAL CORPORATION
PO Box 129
Barrow, Alaska 99723
907-852-8633

BERING STRAITS NATIVE CORPORATION
PO Box 1008
Nome, Alaska 99672
907-443-5252

BRISTOL BAY NATIVE CORPORATION
PO Box 3310
Dillingham, Alaska 99576
907-842-5257

CALISTA CORPORATION
601 W. 5th Ave., Suite 200
Anchorage, Alaska 99501
907-297-5516

CHUGACH ALASKA CORPORATION
300 "A" Street
Anchorage, Alaska 99503
907-563-8866

COOK INLET REGION, INC.
2525 "C" Street
Anchorage, Alaska 99509
907-275-8636

DOYON, Ltd.
Doyon Building,
201 First Ave.
Fairbanks, Alaska 99701
907-452-4755

KONIAG, INC.
4300 "B" Street, Suite 407
Anchorage, Alaska 99503
907-561-2668

NANA REGIONAL CORPORATION
PO Box 49/4706 Harding Drive
Kotsebue, Alaska 99752
907-442-3301

SEALASKA CORPORATION
One Sealaska Plaza, Suite 400
Juneau, Alaska 99801
907-586-1512

* See pages 10-35 for Village Entities categorized by region

THE THIRTEENTH
REGIONAL CORPORATION
The First Place Plaza, 12503
S.E. Mill Plain Road,
Suite 200
Vancouver, Washington 98684
206-254-0688

NATIVE ASSOCIATIONS -- PROFIT AND NON-PROFIT CORPORATIONS

NON-PROFIT

ASSOC OF VILLAGE
COUNCIL PRESIDENTS
Pouch 29 Box 219
Bethel, AK 99559
907-543-3521

BRISTOL BAY NATIVE
ASSOC
PO Box 310
Dillingham, AK 99576
907-842-5257

COOK INLET TRIBAL
COUNCIL
670 W Firewood Ln # 200
Anchorage, AK 99503
907-272-7529
907-277-9071 FAX

COPPER RIVER NATIVE
ASSOC INC
Richardson Hwy Mile 104
Drawer H
Copper Center, AK 99573
907-822-5241
907-822-5247 FAX

INUPIAT COMM OF
ARCTIC SLOPE
PO Box 934
Barrow, AK 99723

KAWERAK INC
PO Box 948
Nome, AK 99762
907-443-5231

MANIILAQ ASSOCIATION
PO Box 256
Kotzebue, AK 99742
907-442-3311

TANANA CHIEFS
CONFERENCE INC
122 1st Ave
Fairbanks, AK 99701
907-452-8251
907-451-8936 FAX

TLINGIT & HAIDA
CENTRAL COUNCIL
320 W Willoughby # 300
Juneau, AK 99801
907-586-1432
907-586-8970 FAX

PROFIT

AHTNA INC
Anchorage Office
406 W Firewood Ln # 101
Anchorage, AK 99503
907-274-7662
907-274-6614 FAX

ARCTIC SLOPE REGIONAL CORP
PO Box 129
Barrow, AK 99723
907-852-8533
907-852-5733 FAX

BERING STRAITS NATIVE CORP
PO Box 1008
Nome, AK 99762
907-443-5252

BRISTOL BAY NATIVE CORP
PO Box 100220
Anchorage, AK 99510
907-278-3602
907-276-3924 FAX

CALISTA CORP
601 W 5th Ave # 200
Anchorage, AK 99501
907-279-5516
907-272-5060 FAX

CHUGACH ALASKA CORP
3000 A Street # 400
Anchorage, AK 99503
907-563-8866
907-563-8402 FAX

COOK INLET REGION INC
PO Box 93330
Anchorage, AK 99509
907-274-8638

DOYON LIMITED
201 First Ave
Fairbanks, AK 99701
907-452-4755
907-456-6785 FAX

KONIAG INC
4300 "B" St # 407
Anchorage, AK 99503
907-561-2668
907-562-5258 FAX

NANA REGIONAL CORP
PO Box 49
Kotzebue, AK 99752
907-442-3301

SEALASKA CORPORATION
One Sealaska Plaza # 400
Juneau, AK 99801
907-586-1512

THE ALEUT CORPORATION
4000 Old Seward Hwy # 300
Anchorage, AK 99503
907-561-4300
907-563-4328 FAX

VILLAGE CORPORATIONS BY REGION

AHTNA REGION

AHTNA INC*

Chitina Native Corp

*Villages in the Region that merged into the Regional Corp., AHTNA, Inc. are: Cantwell, Christochina, Copper Center, Gakona, Gulkana, Mentasta, Tazlina.

ALEUT REGION

Akutan Corporation

Atxam Corporation

Belkofski Corporation

Chaluka Corporation

Isanotski Corporation

King Cove Corporation

Nelson Lagoon Corporation

Ounalashka Corporation

Sanak Corporation

St. George Tanaq Corp

St. George Traditional Council

Tanadgusix Corporation

Unga Corporation

Village Council

ARCTIC SLOPE REGION

Atqasuk Traditional Council

Cully Corporation

Kaktovik Inupiat Corp

Kuukpik Corporation

Nunamiut Corporation Inc

Olgoonik Corporation Inc

Tigara Corporation

Ukpeagvik Inupiat Corp

BRISTOL BAY REGION

Alaska Peninsula Corp*

Aleknagik Natives Limited

Bay View Incorporated

Becharof Corporation

Chignik Lagoon Native Corp

Chignik River Limited

Choggiung Limited**

Ekwok Natives Limited

Far West Incorporated

Igiugig Natives Limited

Iliamna Natives Limited

Kijik Corporation

Koliganek Natives Limited

Levelock Natives Ltd

Manokotak Natives Ltd

Oceanside Corporation

Paug-Vik Incorporated, Ltd

Pedro Bay Native Corp

Pilot Point Native Corp

Saguyak Incorporated

Stuyahok Limited

Togiak Natives Limited

Twin Hills Native Corp

*Villages merged to form ALASKA PENINSULA CORPORATION: Port Heinden, Ugashik, Newhalen, South Naknek, Kokhanok.

** Villages merged to form CHOGGINUNG: Dillingham, Ekuk, Portage Creek.

BERING STRAITS REGION

Brevig Mission Native Corp

COUNCIL NATIVE CORP

Elim Native Corporation

Golovin Native Corporation

Inalik Native Corporation

King Island Native Corp

Koyuk Native Corporation

Mary's Igloo Native Corp

SAVOONGA NATIVE CORP

Shaktoolik Native Corporation

Shishmaref Native Corporation

Sitnasuak Native Corp

Solomon Native Corporation

St. Michael Native Corporation

Stebbins Native Corporation

Teller Native Corporation

Unalakleet Native Corporation

Wales Native Corporation

White Mountain Native Corp

CALISTA REGION

Akiachak, Limited

Alakanuk Native Corp

Arviq Incorporated

Askinuk Corporation

Atmautlauk Limited

Azachorok Incorporated

Bethel Native Corp

Chefarnrmute Incorporated

Chevak Company Corp

Chuloonawick Corporation

Chinuruk, Incorporated*

Emmonak Native Corporation

Iqfijoug Company

Kasigluk Incorporated

Kokarmuit Corporation

Kongnikilnomuit Yuita Corp

Kotlik Yupik Corporation

Kugkaktlik Limited

Kuitsarak Inc

Kuskokwim Corporation**

Kwethluk Incorporated

Kwik Incorporated

Maserculiq Incorporated

Mekoryuk IRA Council

Napakiak Corporation

Napakiak IRA Council

Napaskiak Incorporated

Nerklikmute Native Corp

Newtok Corporation

Nima Corporation

Nunakauiak Yupik Corp

Nunapiglluraq Corporation

Oscarville Native Corporation

Paimiut Corporation

Pilot Station Native Corp

Pitka's Point Native Corp

Qanirtuug Corporation

Russian Mission Native Corp

Sea Lion Corporation

St. Mary's Native Corporation

Swan Lake Corporation

Tulkisarmute Incorporated

Tuntutuliak Land Limited

*Villages merged to form CHINURUK, INCORPORATED: Nightmute, Umkumiut. *Villages merged to form KUSKOKWIM CORPORATION: Aniak, Crooked Creek, Georgetown, Upper Kalskag, Lower Kalskag, Napaimute, Red Devil, Chuathbaluk, Sleetmute, Stong River.

CHUGACH REGION

Chenega Corporation

English Bay Corporation

Eyak Corporation

Mount Marathon Native Assoc

Port Graham Corporation

Tatitlek Corporation

Valdez Native Assoc

COOK INLET REGION

Alexander Creek Inc

Chickaloon-Moose Creek Assoc

Eklutna Incorporated

Knikatnu Incorporated

Ninilchik Native Association

Salamatoff Native Association

Seldovia Native Association

Tyonek Native Corporation

DOYON, LTD REGION

Baan-O-Yeel Kon Corp

Bean Ridge Corporation

Beaver Kwit'Chin Corp

Chalkyitsik Native Corp

Danzhit Hanlaii Corp

Deloycheet Incorporated

Dineega Corporation

Dot Lake Native Corporation

Evansville Incorporated

Gana-A'Yoo Limited

Gwitchyaazhee Corporation

Hee-Yea-Lingde Corporation

Hungwitchin Corporation

Ingalik, Inc

K'oyitl'ots'ina Ltd*

Medfra Traditional Council

Mendas Cha-Aq Native Corp

Mtnt Limited**

Northway Natives Inc

Seth-De-Ya-Ah Corporation (Mint)

Tanacross Incorporated

Tihteet'Aii Incorporated

Toghetthele Corporation

Tozitna Limited

Zho-Tse, Inc

*Villages merged to form KOYITL'OTS'INA, LIMITED: Alatna, Allakaket, Hughes, Huslia

**Villages merged to form MTNT LIMITED: MaGrath, Nikolai, Takotna, Teleida

KONIAG REGION

Afognak Native Corporation*

Akhiok, Native Village of

Akhiok-Kaguyak, Inc**

Anton Larsen Incorporated

Ayakulik Inc

Bells Flats Native Inc

Koniag Inc***

Old Harbor Native Corporation

Ouzinkie Native Corporation

Shuyak Incorporated

Uganik Natives Incorporated

Uyak Natives Incorporated

*Villages that merged to form AFOGNAK,NATIVE CORPORATION: Afognak, Port Lions

*Villages that merged to form AHKIOK-KAGUYAK, INC: Ahkiok, Kaguyak

*Villages that merged to form KONIAG, INC: Larsen Bay, Klarluk

NANA REGION

Kikiktagruk Inupiat Corp

Nana Corp*

*Villages that merged to form the NANA REGIONAL CORPORATION: Ambler, Buckland, Deering, Kiana, Kivalina, Kobuk, Noatak, Noorvik, Selawik, Shungak

SEALASKA REGION

Cape Fox Corporation

Haida Corporation

Huna Totem Corporation

Kake Tribal Corporation

Kavilco Incorporated

Klawock Heenya Corporation

Klukwan, Incorporated

Kootznoowoo Inc

Shaan-Seet Incorporated

Shee Atika Inc

Yak-Tat Kwaan Inc

B.IA. AREA OFFICES AND TRIBAL AGENCIES

Anchorage Agency
Bureau of Indian Affairs
1675 C St
Anchorage, AK 99501
907-271-4088
907-271-4083 FAX
69 TRIBAL ENTITIES*

Bethel Agency
Bureau of Indian Affairs
PO Box 347
Bethel, AK 99559
907-543-2727
907-543-3574 FAX
60 TRIBAL ENTITIES*

Fairbanks Agency
Bureau of Indian Affairs
101 12 Ave
Box 16
Fairbanks, AK 99701
907-456-0222
907-456-0225 FAX
45 TRIBAL ENTITIES*

★JUNEAU AREA OFFICE
Bureau of Indian Affairs
PO Box 25520
Juneau, AK 99802
907-586-7177
907-586-7169 FAX
20 TRIBAL ENTITIES*

Nome Agency
Bureau of Indian Affairs
PO Box 1108
Nome, AK 99762
907-443-2284
907-443-2317 FAX
33 TRIBAL ENTITIES*

Metlakatla Field Station
Bureau of Indian Affairs
PO Box 450
Metlakatla, AK 99926
907-886-3791
907-886-7738 FAX

★AREA OFFICES HEADQUARTERS

* See pages 10-35 for listings cross referenced by BIA Areas

QUICK NOTES !

**Information for this page is only available in the Library Edition.

Fred Synder, Director, Consultant

N.A.²I.I.T.C.

North American Native American Indian Information & Trade Center

QUICK NOTES !

**Information for this page is only available in the Library Edition.

QUICK NOTES !

**Information for this page is only available in the Library Edition.

Fred Synder, Director, Consultant

N.A.²I.I.T.C.

North American Native American Indian Information & Trade Center

PUBLIC LAW 93-638 TRIBAL AND TRIBAL ORGANIZATION CONTRACTORS (NON-PROFIT)

ALUETIAN/PRIBILOF ISLANDS ASSOCIATION
401 East Fireweed Lane, Suite 201
Anchorage, Alaska 99503
907-276-2700

ASSOCIATION OF VILLAGE PRESIDENTS
PO Box 219
Bethel, Alaska 99559
907-543-3521

BRISTOL BAY NATIVE ASSOCIATION
PO Box 310
Dillingham, Alaska 99576
907-842-5257

CENTRAL COUNCIL TLINGIT & HAIDA
Indian Tribes of Alaska
320 W. Willoughby Ave., Suite 300
Juneau, Alaska 99801
907-586-1432

COOK INLET TRIBAL COUNCIL
670 W. Fireweed Lane, Suite 200
Anchorage, Alaska 99503
907-272-7529

COPPER RIVER NATIVE ASSOCIATION
Drawer H
Copper River, Alaska 99573
907-882-5241

FAIRBANKS NATIVE ASSOCIATION
310-1/2 First Avenue
Fairbanks, AK 99701
907-642-1648
907-456-5151

FORT YUKON, NATIVE VILLAGE OF
PO Box 125
Fort Yukon, Alaska 99740
907-662-2587
907-662-2581

GAMBELL, NATIVE VILLAGE OF
PO Box 133
Gambell, Alaska 99742
907-985-5127

KAKE, ORGANIZED VILLAGE OF
PO Box 163
Kake, Alaska 9974
907-785-4177

KAWERAK, INC
PO Box 948
Nome, Alaska 99762
907-443-5231

KENAITZIE INDIAN TRIBE
PO Box 988
Kenai, Alaska 99611
907-283-3633

KETCHIKAN INDIAN CORPORATION
429 Deermount Avenue
Ketchikan, Alaska 99901
907-225-5158

KIANA TRADITIONAL COUNCIL
General Delivery
Kiana, AK
907-457-2014

KODIAK AREAS NATIVE ASSOCIATION
402 Center Avenue
Kodial, Alaska 99615
907-486-5725

KODIAL TRIBAL COUNCIL
PO Box 1974
Kodial, Alaska 99615
907-486-4449

KOTZEBUE IRA COUNCIL
PO Box 296
Kotzebue, Alaska 99557
907-675-4384

KUSKOKWIM NATIVE ASSOCIATION
PO Box 106
Aniak, Alaska 99557
907-675-4384

MANIILAQ ASSOCIATION
PO Box 256
Kotzebue, Alaska 99752
907-442-3311

NATIVE VILLAGE OF LARSEN BAY
PO Box 35
Larsen Bay, Alaska 99624
907-847-2207

METASTA TRADITIONAL VILLAGE COUNCIL
Drawer U
Tok, Alaska 99780
907-291-2319

NOME ESKIMO VILLAGE
PO Box 401
Nome, Alaska 99762
907-443-2246

NOORVIK IRA COUNCIL
PO Box 71
Noorvik, Alaska 99763
907-636-2144

THE NORTH PACIFIC RIM, INC
3300 "C" Street
Anchorage, Alaska 99503
907-562-4155

ORUTSARARMUIT NATIVE
COUNCIL
PO Box 927
Bethel, Alaska 99559
907-543-2608

SELAWIK NATIVE
VILLAGE
PO Box 59
Selawik, Alaska 99770
907-484-2225

SITKA COMMUNITY
ASSOCIATION
PO Box 1450
Sitka, Alaska 99835
907-747-3207

TANANA CHIEFS
CONFERENCE, INC
122 First Avenue
Fairbanks, Alaska 99701
907-452-8251

TANANA IRA COUNCIL
Tanana, Alaska 99777
907-366-7160

UNITED CROW BAND,
INCORPORATED
PO Box 131
Tok, Alaska 99780
907-833-5137

YAKUTAT NATIVE
ASSOCIATION
PO Box 418
Yukutat, Alaska 99689
907-784-3238

ALASKA NATIONAL NATIVE ORGANIZATIONS

A F N
ALASKA FEDERATION OF NATIVES
1577 C St # 100
Anchorage, AK 99501
907-276-7989
907-276-7989 FAX

...advocate for Alaskan Eskimos, Indians, and Aleuts before Congress...
FOUNDED 1966

ALASKA NATIVE COALITION
PO Box 200908
Anchorage, AK 99520
907-258-6917

...to protect Native ancestral lands, strengthen tribal governments, and protect the subsistence way of life...

ALASKA NATIVE EDUCATION COUNCIL
PO Box 200923
Anchorage, AK 99520
907-272-3399

ASSOCIATION OF ALASKA NATIVE CONTRACTORS
700 W 58th Unit F
Anchorage, AK 99518
907-562-1866
907-272-5060 FAX

I A N A
INSTITUTE OF ALASKA NATIVE ARTS
455 Third Ave # 117
PO Box 70769
Fairbanks, AK 99707
907-456-7491
907-451-7268 FAX

...continuation of Alaska Native traditions, crafts, food, art...

I B C
INDIGENOUS BROADCAST CENTER
ALASKA PUBLIC RADIO NETWORK
810 E Ninth Ave
Anchorage, AK 99501
907-263-7409
907-263-7497 FAX

...national training center...for native participation in the media...

I C C
INUIT CIRCUMPOLAR CONFERENCE c/o A F N
1577 C St # 100
Anchorage, AK 99501
907-258-6917

...committed to upholding rights of indigenous peoples across the Arctic rim...
FOUNDED 1966

KLUKWAN HERITAGE FOUNDATION
PO Box 972
Haines, AK 99827

N A R F
NATIVE AMERICAN RIGHTS FUND
310 K St # 708
Anchorage, AK 99501
907-276-0680

...see Colorado listing...

N N N
NATIONAL NATIVE NEWS
ALASKA PUBLIC RADIO NETWORK
810 E Ninth Ave
Anchorage, AK 99501
907-263-7409
907-263-7497 FAX

...programing over public radio stations...

ORRE DRUMRITE WALKING HERITAGE
PO Box 221689
Anchorage, AK 99522-1689
907-243-2421

...unite all tribes to pray our street Indians back to responsible lives...

ALASKA STATEWIDE NATIVE ORGANIZATIONS

AHTNA INC
PO Box 649
Glenallen, AK 99588
907-822-3476
907-822-3495 FAX

AHTNA INC
Anchorage Office
406 W Fireweed Ln # 101
Anchorage, AK 99503
907-274-7662
907-274-6614 FAX

ALASKA ESKIMO WHALING COMMISSION
PO Box 570
Barrow, AK 99723
907-852-2392

ALASKA FEDERATION OF NATIVES INC
1577 "C" St # 100
Anchorage, AK 99501
907-276-7989
907-276-7989 FAX

ALASKA HEALTH PROJECT
1818 W Northern Lights #103
Anchorage, AK 99517
907-276-2864
907-279-3089 FAX

ALASKA LEGAL SERVICE CORP
1016 W 6th Ave # 200
Anchorage, AK 99501
907-276-6282
907-279-7417 FAX

ALASKA NATIVE COALITION
PO Box 104024
Anchorage, AK 99510
907-276-0680
907-243-8203

ALASKA NATIVE HEALTH BOARD
1354 Rudakof Cir # 206
Anchorage, AK 99508
907-337-0028
907-333-2001 FAX

THE ALASKA SEA OTTER COMMISSION
PO Box 83177
Fairbanks, AK 99708
907-479-4362
907-479-4931 FAX

ALASKA VILLAGE ELECTRIC COOPERATIVE INC
4831 Eagle
Anchorage, AK 99503
907-561-1818
907-561-2388 FAX

THE ALEUT CORPORATION
4000 Old Seward Hwy # 300
Anchorage, AK 99503
907-561-4300
907-563-4328 FAX

ALEUTIAN/PRIBIL OF ISLANDS ASSOC
401 E Fireweed Ln # 201
Anchorage, AK 99503
907-276-2700

ARCTIC SLOPE REGIONAL CORP
PO Box 129
Barrow, AK 99723
907-852-8533
907-852-5733 FAX

ASSOC FOR STRANDED RURAL ALASKANS IN ANCHORAGE
101 E 9th Ave # 10B
Anchorage, AK 99501
907-277-7043

ASSOC OF VILLAGE COUNCIL PRESIDENTS
Pouch 29 Box 219
Bethel, AK 99559
907-543-3521

BRISTOL BAY AREA HEALTH CORP
PO Box 130
Dillingham, AK 99576
907-842-0520

BRISTOL BAY NATIVE ASSOC
PO Box 310
Dillingham, AK 99576
907-842-5257

BRISTOL BAY NATIVE CORP
PO Box 10220
Anchorage, AK 99510
907-278-3602
907-276-3924 FAX

CALISTA CORP
601 W 5th Ave # 200
Anchorage, AK 99501
907-279-5516
907-272-5060 FAX

CENTRAL COUNCIL OF TLINGIT & HAIDA TRIBES
3320 W Willoughby Ave #300
Juneau, AK 99801
907-586-1432
907-586-8970 FAX

CHUGACH ALASKA CORP
3000 A Street # 400
Anchorage, AK 99503
907-563-8866
907-563-8402 FAX

COMMUNITY ENTERPRISE DEVELOPMENT CORP OF ALASKA
1577 C St Plaza # 304
Anchorage, AK 99501
907-274-5400

COOK INLET TRIBAL COUNCIL
670 W Firewood Ln # 200
Anchorage, AK 99503
907-272-7529
907-277-9071 FAX

COOPERATIVE EXTENSION SERVICE, UNIVERSITY OF AK FAIRBANKS
2221 E Northern Lights # 118
Anchorage, AK 99508
907-279-5582
907-277-5242 FAX

COPPER RIVER NATIVE ASSOC
Drawer H
Copper Center, AK 99573
907-822-5241
907-822-5247 FAX

COPPER RIVER NATIVE ASSOC
1689 "C" St # 211
Anchorage, AK 99501
907-272-2762
907-274-2329 FAX

DOYON LIMITED
201 First Ave
Fairbanks, AK 99701
907-452-4755
907-456-6785 FAX

ESKIMO WALRUS COMMISSION
PO Box 948
Nome, AK 99762
907-443-5682
907-443-3708 FAX

INDIGENOUS SURVIVAL INTERNTL
PO Box 200908
Anchorage, AK 99520
907-279-2511
907-279-6343 FAX

INUIT CIRCUMPOLAR CONFERENCE
1577 "C" St # 100
Anchorage, AK 99501
907-258-6917
907-276-4330 FAX

KAWERAK INC
PO Box 948
Nome, AK 99762
907-443-5231

KODIAK AREA NATIVE ASSOC
402 Center Ave
Kodiak, AK 99615
907-486-5725

KONIAG INC
4300 "B" St # 407
Anchorage, AK 99503
907-561-2668
907-562-5258 FAX

KUSKOKWIM NATIVE ASSOCIATION
PO Box 127
Aniak, AK 99557
907-675-4384

MANIILAQ ASSOCIATION
PO Box 256
Kotzebue, AK 99742
907-442-3311

NANA REGIONAL CORPORATION INC
PO Box 49
Kotzebue, AK 99752
907-442-3301

NORTH PACIFIC RIM
3300 "C" St
Anchorage, AK 99503
907-562-4155
907-563-2891 FAX

NORTH SLOPE BOROUGH DEPT OF HEALTH AND SOCIAL SERVICES
PO Box 69
Barrow, AK 99723
907-852-3999
907-852-0268 FAX

NORTON SOUND HEALTH CORP
PO Box 966
Nome, AK 99762
907-443-3311

RURAL ALASKA HONORS INSTITUTE
Univ of Alaska
507 Gruening Bldg
Fairbanks, AK 99775
907-474-6886
907-474-5624 FAX

RURAL ALASKA RESOURCES ASSOC
PO Box 200908
Anchorage, AK 99520
907-279-2511
907-279-6343 FAX

SEALASKA CORPORATION
One Sealaska Plaza # 400
Juneau, AK 99801
907-586-1512

SOUTHCENTRAL FOUNDATION
670 W Fireweed Ln # 236
Anchorage, AK 99503
907-265-4900
907-265-5925 FAX

SOUTHEAST AK REGIONAL HEALTH CORP
3245 Hospital Dr
Juneau, AK 99801
907-463-4000

TANANA CHIEFS CONFERENCE INC
122 1st Ave
Fairbanks, AK 99701
907-452-8251
907-451-8936 FAX

UNIVERSITY OF ALASKA -
FAIRBANKS
Rural Student Services
303 Tanana Dr 5th Flr
Gruening
Fairbanks, AK 99775
907-474-7871

YUKON-KUSKOKWIM
HEALTH CORP
PO Box 528
Bethel, AK 99559
907-543-3321
907-543-5277 FAX

URBAN INDIAN HEALTH CENTERS

ALASKA NATIVE HEALTH CENTER
255 Gambell
Anchorage, AK 99501
907-279-6661

ALASKA NATIVE HEALTH CENTER
3289 Tongass Ave
Ketchikan, AK 99901
907-225-4156

ALASKA AREA INDIAN HEALTH SERVICE
250 Gambell
Anchorage, AK 99501
907-257-1393

BARROW PHS ALASKA NATIVE HOSPITAL
Barrow, AK 99723
907-852-4611

CHIEF ANDREW ISAAC HEALTH CENTER
11638 Cowles
Fairbanks, AK 99701
907-451-6682

CHIEF ANDREW ISAAC HEALTH CENTER
PO Box 107
Tanana, AK 99701
907-366-7222

MANIILAQ MEDICAL CENTER
MANIILAQ ASSOCIATION
PO Box 43
Kodiak, AK 99615

NORTON SOUND OPERATING UNIT
Po Box 966
Nome, AK 99762
907-443-3139

SEARHC JUNEAU MEDICAL CENTER
3245 Hospital Dr
Juneau, AK 99801
907-463-4000

SEARHC MT EDGECUMBE HOSPITAL
222 Tongass Dr
Sitka, AK 99801
907-966-2411

YUKON-KUSKOKWIM DELTA SERVICE UNIT
Pouch 3000
Bethel, AK 99559
907-543-3711

NATIVE HEAD START PROGRAMS

PROJECT HEAD START ADMIN
CHILDREN, YOUTH AND FAMILIES DEPT.
HEALTH & HUMAN SERVICES
330 C STREET SW ROOM 2231 (ZIP 20201)
PO BOX 1182
WASHINGTON, DC 20013
202-205-8437
202-401-5916 FAX

Association of Village Council Presidents Head Start
PO Box 219
Bethel, AK 99559
907-543-3157
907-543-5590 FAX

Central Council of Tlingit-Haida Head Start
320 W Willoughby Ste 300
Juneau, AK 99801
907-586-1432
907-586-8970 FAX

Chugachmiut Head Start
4201 Tudor Centre Dr Ste 210
Anchorage, AK 99508
907-562-4155
907-563-2891 FAX

Fairbanks Native Association Head Start
201 First Ave Ste 200
Fairbanks, AK 99701
907-456-4989
907-456-5311 FAX

Kawerak, Inc. Head Start
PO Box 948
Nome, AK 99762
907-443-5294
907-443-5570

Metlakatla Indian Community Head Start
PO Box 8
Metlakatla, AK 99926
907-886-5151/5313
907-886-7997 FAX

Southcentral Foundation Head Start
670 W Fireweed Ln Ste 105
Anchorage, AK 99503
907-265-4983
907-265-5925 FAX

Tanana Chiefs Conference, Inc. Head Start
122 First Ave Ste 600
Fairbanks, AK 99701
907-452-8251 Ext. 3172
907-459-3851 FAX

MUSEUMS AND CULTURAL CENTERS (NATIVE OWNED AND OPERATED)

ALUTIIQ CULTURE CENTER, KANA
402 Center Ave
Kodiak, AK 99615
907-486-1992

CHICKALOON NUK DIN ITNU TRIBAL MUSEUM
Box 5
Sutton, AK 99674
907-745-0707

CULTURAL HERITAGE MUSEUM COMMITTEE
Ganmbell Street
Lawrence Island, AK

DINJII ZHUU ENJIT MUSEUM
PO Box 42
Fort Yukon, AK 99740

DUNCAN COTTAGE MUSEUM
PO Box 282
Annette Island Reserve
Matlakatla, AK 99926

INUPIAK MUSEUM
PO Box 429
Barrow, AK 99723

KENAITZE INTERPRETIVE SITE IN THE CHUGACH NATIONAL FOREST
c/o Kenaitze Indian Tribe IRA
PO Box 988
Kenai, AK 99611
907-283-3633

KUZHGIE CULTURAL CENTER
PO Box 401
Nome, AK 99762

NANA MUSEUM OF THE ARCTIC
PO Box 49
Kotzebue, AK 99752
907-442-3301

SEALASKA HERITAGE FOUNDATION
1 Sealaska Plaza Ste 201
Juneau, AK 99801
907-463-4844

SIMON PANEAK MEMORIAL MUSEUM
PO Box 21085
Anaktuvuk Pass, AK 99721
907-661-3413

SOUTHEAST ALASKA INDIAN CULTURAL CENTER
106 Metlakatla St
Sitka, AK 99835
907-747-8061

TATITLEK MUSEUM AND CULTURAL CENTER
General Delivery
Tatitlek, AK 99677

TOK NATIVE ASSOCIATION
PO Box 372
Tok, AK 99780
907-883-4761
907-883-4761 FAX

TRIBAL HOUSE OF THE BEAR
Foot of Shakes St
Box 868
Wrangell, AK 99929
907-874-3505

WRANGELL MUSEUM
PO Box 1050
Wrangell, AK 99929
907-874-2345

YUP'IIT PICIRYARAIT CULTURAL CENTER AND MUSEUM
PO Box 219
Bethel, AK 99559
907-543-3521

NON NATIVE OWNED MUSEUMS

DILLINGHAM HERITAGE MUSEUM
Pouch 202
Dillingham, AK 99576
907-842-5601

SHELDON JACKSON MUSEUM
104 College Dr
Sitka, AK 99835
907-747-8981

KETCHIKAN INDIAN MUSEUM
PO Box 5454
Ketchikan, AK 99901
907-228-5600

KOTZEBUE MUSEUM INC
PO Box 46
Kotzebue, AK 99752
907-442-3401

UNIVERSITY OF ALASKA MUSEUM
907 Yukon Dr
College, AK 99708
907-474-7505

YUTARVIK REGIONAL MUSEUM
PO Box 388
Bethel, AK 99559
907-543-2098

CRAFT GUILDS - COOPERATIVES

MUSK OX PRODUCERS
COOPERATIVE
604 H St
Anchorage, AK 99501
907-272-9225

NATIONAL NATIVE
AMERICAN COOPERATIVE
PO Box 27626
Tucson, AZ 85726
520-622-4900

ST LAWRENCE ISLAND
ORIGINAL IVORY
COOPERATIVE
PO Box 189
Gambell, AK 99742
907-985-5112

TAHETA ARTS AND
CULTURAL GROUP
605 A St
Anchorage, AK 99501
907-272-5829

PERFORMING NATIVE DANCE GROUPS

AHTNA DANCERS
C/O Jackie Ewan
Copper River Native Assoc
Drawer H
Copper Center, AK 99573

ALAKANUK DANCERS
C/O John James
General Delivery
Alakanuk, AK 99554

ARCTIC VILLAGE DANCERS
C/O Sarah James
General Delivery
Arctic Village, AK 99723

ATHABASCAN DANCERS
C/O Mike Demientieff
4101 Wilson St
Anchorage, AK 99503

ATHABASCAN FIDDLERS
C/O Bill Stevens
PO Box 84325
Fairbanks, AK 99707

BARROW DANCERS
C/O Martha Aiken
PO Box 494
Barrow, AK 99723

BETHEL TRADITIONAL DANCERS
C/O Nick & Elena Charles
Box 36
Bethel, AK 99559

CHEVAK DANCERS
C/O John Pingayak
PO Box 5518
Chevak, AK 99563

CHITNA DANCERS
C/O Maggie Eskilida
PO Box 31
Chitna, AK 99566

CHOMILLKSCHTOON
C/O Larry Matfay
PO Box 2
Old Harbor, AK 99643

EAGLE RAVEN DANCERS
C/O Agnes Bellinbger
711 W 11th St
Juneau, AK 99801

EMMONAK DANCERS
C/O Jasper Joseph
General Delivery
Emmonak, AK 99581

FORT YUKON DANCERS
C/O John Alexander
PO Box 21
Fort Yukon, AK 99740

GAJAA HEEN TLINGIT DANCERS
C/O Isabella Brady
JOM Indian Ed Program
PO Box 6210
Sitka, AK 99835

MT FAIRWEATHER DANCERS
Hoonah Indian Assoc
PO Box 144
Hoonah, AK 99829

MT JUNEAU TLINGIT DANCERS
C/O Rosa Miller
2225 Arctic Blvd # 212
Anchorage, AK 99503

MT VILLAGE ESKIMO DANCERS
C/O Alponsus Chiklak
PO Box 32074
Mt Village, AK 99632

NAA KAHIDI THEATER
C/O Tim Wilson
Sealaska Heritage Foundation
One Sealaska Plaza
Juneau, AK 99801

NENANA ATHABASCAN DANCERS
C/O Mitch Dementieff
201 First Ave
Fairbanks, AK 99701

NORTHWAY ATHABASCAN DANCERS
C/O Becky Gallen
PO Box 483
Northway, AK 99764

NORTHERN LIGHTS DANCERS
C/O Rachel Craig
PO Box 801
Kotzebue, AK 99752

NUNAMUIT DANCERS
C/O Raymond Paneak
PO Box 21084
Anaktuvuk Pass, AK 99701

NUNAMTA (OF OUR LAND) YUPI
C/O Chuna Macintyre
917 Dorine Ave
Rohnert Park, CA 94928

PILOT STATION DANCERS
General Delivery
Pilot Station, AK 99650

POINT HOPE DANCERS
C/O Charlie Kinneaveauk
General Delivery
Point Hope, AK 99766

SAVOONGA COMEDY PLAYERS
C/O Cathy Noonegwook
PO Box 28
Savoonga, AK 99769

SHAGELUK DANCERS
C/O Earl Dutchman
Shageluk, AK 99665

SHOONAQ' TRIBAL DANCERS
C/O Connie Chya
Kodiak, AK 99615

STEBBINS DANCERS
C/O Jean Ferris
General Delivery
Stebbins, AK 99671

GAMBELL DANCERS
C/O Jerry Tungiyan
PO Box 57
Gambell, AK 99742

GEISAN DANCERS
C/O Matilda Lewis
PO Box 183
Haines, AK 99827

GIT LAX LIKSHTAA DANCERS
C/O Barbara Fawcett
PO Box 44
Metlakatla, AK 99926

GREATLAND TRADITIONAL DANCERS
C/O Walter Kalerak
670 W Fireweed Ln Ste 201
Anchorage, AK 99503

JUNEAU DANCERS
C/O Ozzie Sheley
320 W Willoughby Ste 300
Juneau, AK 99801

KAKE DANCERS
General Delivery
Kake, AK 99803

KASIGLUK AKUL HIGH SCHOOL DANCERS
General Delivery
Kasigluk, AK 99609

KING ISLAND DANCERS
C/O Paul Tiulana
4400 E Fourth Ave
Anchorage, AK 99508

KING ISLAND DANCERS
C/O Michael Saciamana
PO Box 992
Nome, AK 99762

KODIAK DANCERS
Kodiak Native Assoc
C/O Rick Knecht
PO Box 172
Kodiak, AK 99724

KOTLIK DANCERS
General Delivery
Kotlik, AK 99620

KWITCHEN DANCERS
C/O Elsie Pitka
Beaver, AK 99724

MEAD RIVER DANCERS
General Delivery
Atgasuk, AK 99791

MENTASTA LAKE DANCERS
C/O Ruth Hicks
Mile 81.5 Tok Cutoff
Mentasta Lake, AK 99780

METLAKATLA DANCERS
C/O Richard Booth
PO Box 474
Metlakatla, AK 99926

MINTO DANCERS
C/O Geraldine Charlie
Minto Senior Service
PO Box 43
Minto, AK 99758

ST LAWRENCE / NOME DANCERS
C/O Nick Wongittilin
PO Box 568
Nome, AK 99762

ST MARY'S DANCERS
C/O Peter M Andrews
or Larry Mike
PO Box 171
St Mary's, AK 99658

TAHETA DANCERS
C/O Jim Richards
606 A St
Anchorage, AK 99501

TANACROSS ATHABASCAN DANCERS
C/O Debby Thomas
General Delivery
Tanacross, AK 99776

TIKIQAQ TRADITIONAL DANCERS
C/O Lillian Lane
General Delivery
Point Hope, AK 99766

TLINGIT-HAIDA DANCERS
C/O Bea Halkett
8040 Cranberry St
Anchorage, AK 99502

TOKSOOK BAY ESKIMO DANCERS
C/O James Charlie Sr
Toksook Bay Traditional Council
General Delivery

Toksook Bay, AK 99637

TYONEK DANCERS
C/O Emil McCord Sr President
Native Village of Tyonek
Tyonek, AK 99682

WAINWRIGHT DANCERS
C/O Rossman Peetok
PO Box 43
Wainwright, AK 99782

information provided by: Walter Kalerak, Anchorage, AK

NATIVE AMERICAN PRINT MEDIA							
PUBLICATION	**INDIVIDUAL**	**TRIBE**	**ORGANIZATION**	**INDEPENDENT**	**OFF RESERVATION**	**MAJOR**	**FREQUENCY**
ALASKA							
AFN NEWSLETTER 1577 C STREET #100 ANCHORAGE, AK 99501 907-274-3611 907-276-2989 FAX			X				M
COASTAL CROSSINGS KETCHIKAN MUSEUMS TOTEM HERITAGE CENTER 629 DOCK STREET KETCHIKAN, AK 99901 907-228-5600 907-228-5602 FAX			X		X		M
HAN ZAADLITL GE PO BOX 309 NANANA, AK 99760			X				M
JOURNAL OF ALASKA NATIVE ARTS INSTITUTE OF ALASKA NATIVE ARTS PO BOX 70769 FAIRBANKS, AK 99707 907-456-7491 907-451-7268 FAX			X		X		Q

KEY

B - BI-MONTHLY
U - BI-WEEKLY
Q - QUARTERLY
Y - YEARLY
W - WEEKLY
M - MONTHLY
D - DAILY
I - IRREGULAR

NATIVE AMERICAN PRINT MEDIA							
PUBLICATION	INDIVIDUAL	TRIBE	ORGANIZATION	INDEPENDENT	OFF RESERVATION	MAJOR	FREQUENCY
MANILLAQ ASSOCIATION PO BOX 256 KOTZEBUE, AK 99742			X				Q
NEWSLETTER INDIGENOUS BROADCAST CENTER 810 EAST 9TH AVENUE ANCHORAGE, AK 99501 907-263-7409 907-263-7497 FAX			X		X		Q
NEWSLETTER SEALASKA HERITAGE FOUNDATION ONE SEALASKA PLAZA #201 JUNEAU, AK 99801 907-463-7491			X				M
THE TCC COUNCIL 122 FIRST AVENUE FAIRBANKS, AK 99701 907-452-8251 907-459-3851 FAX			X				M
TUNDRA TIMES PO BOX 92247 ANCHORAGE, AK 99509-2247 907-274-2512 800-764-2512 907-277-7217 FAX			X		X		U

NATIVE AMERICAN RADIO STATIONS						
STATION	AIR TIME	N.N.N.	A.I.H.	TRIBAL	INDEPENDENT	OTHER
BWANDAK PUBLIC BROADCASTING PO BOX 126 FORT YUKON, AK 99740 907-662-2587 907-662-2222					X	
NATIONAL NATIVE NEWS SERVICE 810 E 9TH AVE ANCHORAGE, AK 99501 907-277-2776 907-263-7450		X			X	
KBBI-AM 890 PO BOX 1085 HOMER, AK 99603	1:00 PM				X	
KBRW-AM 680 INUIT PO BOX 109 BARROW, AK 99723 907-852-6811	8:30 AM 11:30AM 5:50 PM				X	
KCAW-FM 104.7 NATIONAL NATIVE NEWS PO BOX 1766 SITKA, AK 99835	8:30 PM	X			X	

KEY:
N.N.N. - NATIONAL NATIVE NEWS
A.I.H. - AMERICAN INDIAN HOUR
TRIBAL - TRIBALLY OWNED
INDEPDENDENT - MAJOR STATION
OTHER - EDUCATIONAL STATION

NATIVE AMERICAN RADIO STATIONS						
STATION	AIR TIME	N.N.N.	A.I.H.	TRIBAL	INDEPENDENT	OTHER
KCHU-AM 770 VALDEZ, AK 99686	12:25 PM 4:45 PM				X	
KCUK-FM 88.1 KASHUNANIUT SCHOOL DIST CHEVAK, AK 99563 907-858-7014 907-858-7114					X	
KCZP-FM 91.9 KENAI, AK 99611	6:30 PM				X	
KDLG-AM 670 PO BOX 670 DILLINGHAM, AK 99576 907-842-5281 907-842-5645	4:45 PM				X	
KFSK-FM 100.9 NATIONAL NATIVE NEWS PO BOX 149 PETERSBURG, AK 99833	4:24 PM	X				
KHNS-FM 102.3 NATIONAL NATIVE NEWS PO BOX O HAINES, AK 99827	8:30 AM	X				
KIAL-AM 1450 UNALASKA, AK 99685	5:40 PM				X	
KIYU-AM 910 GALENA, AK 99741	12:20 PM				X	

NATIVE AMERICAN RADIO STATIONS						
STATION	AIR TIME	N.N.N.	A.I.H.	TRIBAL	INDEPENDENT	OTHER
KMXT-FM 100.1 NATIONAL NATIVE NEWS PO BOX 484 KODIAK, AK 99615	10:00 AM 4:00 PM	X				
KNOM-AM 780 NATIONAL NATIVE NEWS PO BOX 988 NOME, AK 99615	11:30 AM	X				
KNSA PO BOX 178 UNALAKLEET, AK 99684 907-624-3101					X	
KOTZ-AM 720 PO BOX 78 KOTZEBUE, AK 99752 907-442-3435	11:00 AM				X	
KRBD-FM 105.9 NATIONAL NATIVE NEWS 716 TOTEM WAY KETCHIKAN, AK 99901	1:10 PM	X				
KSDP-AM 840 SAND POINT, AK 99661	5:40 PM				X	
KSKA-FM 91.1 NATIONAL NATIVE NEWS APU PROVIDENCE DR ANCHORAGE, AK 99503	5:55 PM	X				
KSKO-AM 870 MCGRATH, AK 99627	12:20 PM				X	

NATIVE AMERICAN RADIO STATIONS							
STATION	AIR TIME	N.N.N.	A.I.H.	TRIBAL	INDEPENDENT	OTHER
KSRD-FM 88.1 SEWARD, AK 99664	6:30 PM				X	
KSTK-FM 101.7 NATIONAL NATIVE NEWS PO BOX 282 WRANGELL, AK 99929	12:35 PM	X				
KTOO-FM 104.3 224 4TH JUNEAU, AK 99801	8:15 AM				X	
KUAC-FM 104.7 UNIVERSITY OF ALASKA FAIRBANKS, AK 99701	12:40 PM				X	X
KUHB-FM 91.9 PRIBILOFF SCHOOL DISTRICT ST PAUL, AK 99660 907-546-2254	5:40 PM				X	X
KYUK-AM PO BOX 468 BETHEL, AK 99559	12:30 PM				X	

ALASKA NATIVE GIFT SHOPS

ALASKA LEGACY ART GALLERY
311 Mill Street, Suite 202
Ketchikan, AK 99901
907-225-1234 or 907-225-6676
Catalogue ✓ No Yes
✓ Retail ✓ Wholesale

ALASKA NATIVE ARTS AND CRAFTS ASSOC INC (ANAC)
425 D Street
Anchorage, AK 99501
907-274-2932
Catalogue ✓ No Yes
Retail Wholesale

AMOS WALLACE
PO Box 478
Juneau, AK 99802
907-586-9000
Catalogue ✓ No Yes
Retail Wholesale

CHILKAT VALLEY ARTS
PO Box 145
Haines, AK 99827
907-766-2990 or 907-766-2216
Catalogue ✓ No Yes
✓ Retail Wholesale

ESKIMO BOW DRILL GALLERY
PO Box 812
Cooper Landing, AK 99572
907-595-1221
Catalogue ✓ No Yes
✓ Retail Wholesale

MARLINDA DOLLS
PO Box 611
Wrangell, AK 99929
907-874-3854
Catalogue ✓ No Yes
Retail ✓ Wholesale

NANA MUSEUM OF THE ARCTIC CRAFT SHOP
PO Box 49
Kotzebue, AK 99752
907-442-3304 or 907-442-3747
Catalogue ✓ No Yes
Retail Wholesale

ST LAWRENCE ISLAND ORIGINAL IVORY COOPERATIVE LTD
PO Box 111
Gambell, AK 99642
907-985-5826
Catalogue ✓ No Yes
Retail Wholesale

SAVOONGA NATIVE STORE
PO Box 100
Savoonga, AK 99769
Catalogue ✓ No Yes
Retail Wholesale

TAHETA ARTS AND CULTURAL GROUP
605 "A" Street
Anchorage, AK 99501
907-272-5829
Catalogue ✓ No Yes
✓ Retail ✓ Wholesale

QUICK NOTES !

**Information for this page is only available in the Library Edition.

Fred Synder, Director, Consultant

N.A.²I.I.T.C

North American Native American Indian Information & Trade Center

ALASKA

EVENTS

The Chamber of Commerce of each city or the sponsoring tribe or organization should be contacted to verify all events.

January
Early Jan Thru Mar

Alaska Dog Mushers Races
Each Weekend, Fairbanks, AK

2nd Weekend

All Alaska Juried Art Exhibition
Anchorage Fine Arts Museum
Fairbanks, AK
907-264-4326

February
2nd Weekend

Fur Rendezvous
Alaska's largest winter celebration with World Champion Sled Dog Races,
c/o Greater Anchorage, Inc.
327 Eagle St.
Anchorage, AK 99501-2628
907-277-8615

3rd Weekend

Festival of Alaska Native Arts
James Ruppert
508 Gruening
Univ. of Alaska
Fairbanks, AK 99775-0140
907-474-7181

2nd, 3rd, 4th Weekends

Festival of the North
Cultural event encompassing music, visual arts, Native arts and culture, and myriad workshops.
907-225-2211

March
1st Weekend

Annual Beaver Round-up Festival
Dillingham Beaver Round-up Assoc.
PO Box 267
Dillingham, AK 99576
907-842-2209

March	
2nd full Week	**Iditarod Native Arts Show/Sale** Visitors Center PO Box 240 Nome, AK 99762 907-443-5535
3rd Weekend	**Potlach Celebration of Spring** Fairbanks Native Assoc. 310 ½ First Ave. Fairbanks, AK 99701 907-452-1648
2nd to 3rd Week	**Fairbanks Winter Carnival** Week-long festivities. 907-452-1105 or 907-452-6279
4th Weekend	**Camai Festival** Linda Curda, Chat Program Kuskokwim Campus Yukon Community College PO Box 368 Bethel, AK 99559 907-543-4540
July	
1st Weekend	**AHTNA Native Arts and Crafts Show** Copper Center, AK 907-822-5241
3rd Weekend	**World Eskimo Indian Olympics** Euphrasia Dayton World Eskimo/Indian Olympics Committee PO Box 2433 Fairbanks, AK 99707 907-452-6646
August	
1st Weekend	**Founders Day, Metlakatla Birthday** Metlaktla, AK

August **2nd Weekend**	**Tanana Valley Fair** Tanana Valley Fairgrounds Fairbanks, AK
September **1st Full Week**	**Alaska State Fair** Palmer, AK 907-745-4827
October **Varies**	**Alaska Federation of Native's Annual Convention**
November **2nd Week**	**Annual Athabascan Fiddling Festival** I.A.N.A. Fairbanks, AK 907-456-7491

CANADA

CANADA

Algonkian
Assiniboine
Blackfoot
Blood
Cree
Delaware
Dene
Huron
Iroquois
Maliseet
Micmac
Mohawk
Ojibway
Seneca
Shuswap
Sioux
Tlingit
Tsimshean

CANADA

KEY TO FIRST NATION GRAPHS ON PAGES 3 TO 84

This graph format is divided into three sections ie, Historical Profile on the left hand page, Economic Base on the right hand page and full name, address, providence, postal code, phone and fax information down the middle of each page with each first nation shaded.

HISTORICAL PROFILE

TREATY:

This reflects the first signing of a treaty for that first nation. Some first nations have circumstances that include several treaty signings, some no treaty signing. The Canadian Government was under England's rule when most of the original treaties were signed and the current Canadian Government has had difficulty interpreting with each first nation re-negotiating with each respective province.

LANGUAGE:

Most all tribes in Canada are bilingual; we have listed their mother language if it is still spoken among the people.

TRIBAL CLASS:

Most tribes of Canada were categorized by tribal groups ie Algonkian, Athapaskan, Siouan, Salish, etc.

POPULATION:

These statistics were provided by the D.I.A.N.A. - Department of Indian and Northern Affairs, Ottawa, Canada.

ACREAGE:

These statistics were provided by the D.I.A.N.A. - Department of Indian and Northern Affairs, Ottawa, Canada. As each province uses different measurements we left all numbers in acreage, put **h** if reported in hectares, and others are measured in square kilometers **sq.k.**

ECONOMIC BASE

L = LODGING, MOTEL, RESORT, RV PARK

Lodging available on each reserve is marked with an X. We could not differentiate if there were motels, resorts or R.V. parks.

E. B. = ECONOMIC BASE

Denotes the main economic base that the members of each first nation is involved ie A - agriculture, F - fish / aquaculture, M - minerals, R - ranching, T - timber. In some cases what the tribe's main source of income and its members source of income varies greatly.

N = NEWSPAPER

This denotes that each tribe has a tribal newspaper with an emphasis on its unique culture, tribal meetings, current events death/births and common information important to its members. It must be emphasized that the tribal media is usually the first to be cut in tribal economic hard times; therefore often these publications have been around on an irregular basis for several years often operating for several months cut for a month or two and then reinstated.

M = MUSEUM / CULTURAL CENTER

This denotes that each first nation has a museum or cultural center with an emphasis on it's unique culture, crafts, oral history and artifacts from that area. These facilities can range from a department within the first nation office to a multi million dollar complex including museum, theater, library, R.V. camping, restaurant, meeting rooms, rodeo and fairgrounds.

HISTORICAL PROFILE

ALBERTA

Treaty	Language	Tribal Class	Pop	Acreage*	Nation
1876	CREE	ALGONKIAN	997	17,990	ALEXANDER FIRST NATION
1876	DAKOTA	SIOUAN	944	15,259	ALEXIS FIRST NATION
1871	CREE	ALGONKIAN	3,017	120,154	BEARSPAW FIRST NATION (STONEY)
					BEAVER FIRST NATION BAND
1876	CREE	ALGONKIAN	505	15,185	BEAVER LAKE FIRST NATION
1889	CREE	ALGONKIAN	3,715	52,292	BIGSTONE CREE FIRST NATION
1871	BLACKFOOT	ALGONKIAN	7,273	354,490	BLOOD FIRST NATION
1889	BEAVER	ATHAPASKAN	543	17,483	BOYER RIVER FIRST NATION
1871	DAKOTA	SIOUAN	3,017	120,154	CHINIKI FIRST NATION (STONEY)
1876	CHIPEWYAN	ATHAPASKAN	1,595	46,193	COLD LAKE FIRST NATION
1889	CREE	ALGONKIAN	1,583	12,628.9	CREE FIRST NATION
1889	SLAVE	ATHAPASKAN	1,858	74,224	DENE THA'TRIBE FIRST NATION
1889	CREE	ALGONKIAN	1,395	15,688	DRIFTPILE FIRST NATION
1889	CREE	ALGONKIAN	106	5,995	DUNCAN'S FIRST NATION
1876	CREE	ALGONKIAN	1,246	12,960	ENOCH FIRST NATION
1876	CREE	ALGONKIAN	2,191	30,191	ERMINESKIN FIRST NATION
1889	CHIPEWYAN CREE	ATHAPASKAN ALGONKIAN	496	52,398.7	FORT CHIPEWYAN FIRST NATION

* Note: Some Provinces use hectares, denoted by h. All others are in acres.

ALBERTA

Address		Phone Fax	L [1]	EB [2]	N [3]	M [4]
PO BOX 510, MORINVILLE, AB	CANADA T0G 1P0	403-939-5887 403-939-6166	X			
PO BOX 7, GLENEVIS, AB	CANADA T0E 0X0	403-967-2225 403-967-5484				
PO BOX 40, MORLEY, AB	CANADA T0L 1N0	403-881-3770 403-881-2187	X			
PO BOX 270, HIGH LEVEL, AB	CANADA T0H 1Z0	403-927-3697 403-927-3496				
PO BOX 960, LAC LA BICHE, AB	CANADA T0A 2C0	403-623-4549 403-623-4523	X			
GENERAL DELIVERY, DESMARAIS, AB	CANADA T0G 0T0	403-891-3836 403-891-3942		T		
PO BOX 60, STANDOFF, AB	CANADA T0L 1Y0	403-737-3753 403-737-2336		RM		
PO BOX 270, HIGH LEVEL, AB	CANADA T0H 1Z0	403-927-3697 403-927-3496		FA		
PO BOX 40, MORLEY, AB	CANADA T0L 1N0	403-881-3770 403-881-2187	X			
PO BOX 1769, GRAND CENTRE, AB	CANADA T0A 1T0	403-594-7183 403-594-3577		T		
PO BOX 90, FORT CHIPEWYAN, AB	CANADA T0P 1B0	403-697-3740 403-697-3826				
PO BOX 120, CHATEH, AB	CANADA T0H 0S0	403-321-3842 403-321-3886		A		
GENERAL DELIVERY, DRIFTPILE, AB	CANADA T0G 0V0	403-355-3868 403-355-3650		A		
PO BOX 148, BROWNVALE, AB	CANADA T0H 0L0	403-597-3777 403-597-3920		AM		
BOX 2 SITE 2 RR 1, WINTERBURN, AB	CANADA T0E 2N0	403-470-4505 403-470-3057		A		
PO BOX 219, HOBBEMA, AB	CANADA T0C 1N0	403-585-3741 403-585-2550				
PO BOX 90, FT CHIPEWYAN, AB	CANADA T0P 1B0	403-697-3740 403-697-3500		F		

Legend

1. Lodging - Resort, Motel, RV Park
2. Economic Base - Farming, Fishing, Ranching Operations
3. Tribal Newspaper
4. Museum/Cultural Center

A - Agriculture
F - Fish, Aquaculture
M - Mineral
R - Ranching
RV - Recreational Vehicle
T - Timber
TC - Tribal Contract

HISTORICAL PROFILE

Treaty	Language	Tribal Class	Pop	Acreage*	Nation
ALBERTA					
1889			379	13,465	FORT MCKAY FIRST NATION
1876	CREE	ALGONKIAN	1,283	45,567	FROG LAKE FIRST NATION
1871	DAKOTA	SIOUAN	3,017	120,154	GOODSTONEY FIRST NATION (WESLEY GROUP)
1889	CREE	ALGONKIAN	182	1,069	GROUARD FIRST NATION
1876	CHIPEWYAN CREE	ATHAPASKAN ALGONKIAN	181	11,100	HEART LAKE FIRST NATION
1889	BEAVER	ATHAPASKAN	407	7,658	HORSE LAKE FIRST NATION
1889	CHIPEWYAN CREE	ATHAPASKAN ALGONKIAN	429	4,034	JANVIER FIRST NATION
1876	CREE	ALGONKIAN	1,186	20,261	KEHEWIN FIRST NATION (LONG LAKE CREE)
1889	CREE	ALGONKIAN	2,228	60,471	LITTLE RED RIVER FIRST NATION
1991	CREE	ALGONKIAN			LOON RIVER CREE FIRST NATION
1876	CREE	ALGONKIAN	1,080	13,122	LOUIS BULL FIRST NATION
1889	CREE	ALGONKIAN	240		LUBICON LAKE FIRST NATION
1876	CREE	ALGONKIAN	559	11,730	MONTANA FIRST NATION
1876	OJIBWAY	ALGONKIAN	525	34,280.2	O'CHIESE FIRST NATION
1876	CREE DAKOTA	ALGONKIAN SIOUAN	1,171	18,112	PAUL FIRST NATION
1871	BLACKFOOT	ALGONKIAN	2,519	112,656	PEIGAN FIRST NATION
1876	CREE	ALGONKIAN		11,205	SADDLE LAKE #128 FIRST NATION GOODFISH LAKE GROUP

* Note: Some Provinces use hectares, denoted by h. All others are in acres.

Address		Phone Fax	L [1]	EB [2]	N [3]	M [4]

ALBERTA

Address		Phone / Fax	L	EB	N	M
PO BOX 5360, FT MCMURRAY, AB	CANADA T9H 3G4	403-828-4220 403-828-4393				
GENERAL DELIVERY, FROG LAKE, AB	CANADA T0A 1M0	403-943-3737 403-943-3966		R		
PO BOX 40, MORLEY, AB	CANADA T0L 1N0	403-881-3770 403-881-2187				
GENERAL DELIVERY, GROUARD, AB	CANADA T0G 1C0	403-751-3800 403-751-3664				
PO BOX 447, LAC LA BICHE, AB	CANADA T0A 2C0	403-623-2130 403-623-3505		M		
PO BOX 303, HYTHE, AB	CANADA T0H 2C0	403-356-2248 403-356-3666		RA		
GENERAL DELIVERY, CHARD, AB	CANADA T0P 1G0	403-559-2259 403-791-0946				
PO BOX 6218, BONNYVILLE, AB	CANADA T0A 0L0	403-826-3333 403-826-2355		TA		
PO BOX 1165, HIGH LEVEL, AB	CANADA T0A 1Z0	403-759-3912 403-759-3780		TA		
BOX 189, RED EARTH, AB	CANADA T0G TX0	403-649-3600 403-649-3873				
PO BOX 130, HOBBEMA, AB	CANADA T0C 1N0	403-423-2064 403-585-3978				
PO BOX 6731, PEACE RIVER, AB	CANADA T8S 1S5	403-639-3945 403-629-3939				
PO BOX 70, HOBBEMA, AB	CANADA T0C 1N0	403-585-3744 403-585-3264		RA		
PO BOX 1570, ROCKY MTN HOUSE, AB	CANADA T0M 1T0	403-989-3943 403-989-3795		T		
PO BOX 89, DUFFIELD, AB	CANADA T0E 0N0	403-892-2691 403-892-3402				
PO BOX 70, BROCKET, AB	CANADA T0K 0H0	403-965-3940 403-965-3931		RA		
GENERAL DELIVERY, GOODFISH LAKE, AB	CANADA T0A 1R0	403-636-3622 403-636-3755	X	A		

Legend

1. Lodging - Resort, Motel, RV Park
2. Economic Base - Farming, Fishing, Ranching Operations
3. Tribal Newspaper
4. Museum/Cultural Center

A - Agriculture
F - Fish, Aquaculture
M - Mineral
R - Ranching
RV - Recreational Vehicle
T - Timber
TC - Tribal Contract

HISTORICAL PROFILE

Treaty	Language	Tribal Class	Pop	Acreage*	Nation
			ALBERTA		
1876	CREE	ALGONKIAN	5,926	63,704	SADDLE LAKE FIRST NATION (MAIN GROUP)
1876	CREE	ALGONKIAN	4,183	38,569	SAMSON CREE FIRST NATION
1871	SARCEE	ATHAPASKAN	1,048	67,399	SARCEE FIRST NATION (TSUU T'INA NATION)
1889	SARCEE	ATHAPASKAN	243	5,296	SAWRIDGE FIRST NATION
1871	BLACKFOOT	ALGONKIAN	4,008	175,406	SIKSIKA NATION
1889	CREE	ALGONKIAN	1,462	38,317.9	STURGEON LAKE FIRST NATION
1889	CREE	ALGONKIAN	1,475	14,794	SUCKER CREEK FIRST NATION
1876	CREE	ALGONKIAN	601	12,894	SUNCHILD CREE FIRST NATION
1889	CREE	ALGONKIAN	651	10,672	SWAN RIVER FIRST NATION
1889	CREE	ALGONKIAN	619	9,206	TALLCREE FIRST NATION
1876	CREE	ALGONKIAN	1,255	11,974	WHITEFISH LAKE FIRST NATION (GOODFISH) #459
1889			596		WOODLAND CREE BAND #474 FIRST NATION

* Note: Some Provinces use hectares, denoted by h. All others are in acres.

Address		Phone Fax	L[1]	EB[2]	N[3]	M[4]
ALBERTA						
PO BOX 100, SADDLE LAKE, AB	CANADA T0A 3T0	403-726-3829 403-726-3788		A		
PO BOX 159, HOBBEMA, AB	CANADA T0C 1N0	403-421-4926 403-585-2226		TAR	X	
3700 ANDERSON RD SW BOX 69, CALGARY, AB	CANADA T2W 3C4	403-281-4455 403-251-5871				X
PO BOX 326, SLAVE LAKE, AB	CANADA T0G 2A0	403-849-4311 403-849-3446	X	M		
PO BOX 249, GLEICHEN, AB	CANADA T0J 1N0	403-264-7250 403-734-5110	X	RA		
PO BOX 757, VALLEYVIEW, AB	CANADA T0H 3N0	403-524-3307 403-524-2711	X			
PO BOX 65, ENILDA, AB	CANADA T0G 0W0	403-523-4426 403-523-3111		RA		
PO BOX 747, ROCKY MTN HOUSE, AB	CANADA T0M 1T0	403-989-3740 403-989-2533		T		
PO BOX 270, KINUSO, AB	CANADA T0G 1K0	403-775-3536 403-927-4375	X	TFA		
BOX 100, FORT VERMILLION, AB	CANADA T0H 1N0	403-927-3727 403-927-4375				
GENERAL DELIVERY, ATIKAMEG, AB	CANADA T0G 0C0	403-767-3914 403-767-3814		TM		
GENERAL DELIVERY, CADOTTE LAKE, AB	CANADA T0H 0N0	403-629-3803 403-629-3898				

Legend

1. Lodging - Resort, Motel, RV Park
2. Economic Base - Farming, Fishing, Ranching Operations
3. Tribal Newspaper
4. Museum/Cultural Center

A - Agriculture
F - Fish, Aquaculture
M - Mineral
R - Ranching
RV - Recreational Vehicle
T - Timber
TC - Tribal Contract

HISTORICAL PROFILE

Treaty	Language	Tribal Class	Pop	Acreage*	Nation
					BRITISH COLUMBIA
		SALISHAN	572	2,885.2 h	ADAMS LAKE FIRST NATION
			1,269	595 h	AHOUSAHT FIRST NATION
			20	21.4 h	AITCHELITZ FIRST NATION
			120	1,142.3 h	ALEXANDRIA FIRST NATION
			486	3,993.3 h	ALEXIS CREEK FIRST NATION
			518	3,960.3 h	ALKALI FIRST NATION
			1,005	5,656.2 h	ANAHAM FIRST NATION
			189	804 h	ANDERSON LAKE FIRST NATION
1894		SALISHAN	121	2,018 h	ASHCROFT FIRST NATION
			169	296 h	BEECHER BAY FIRST NATION
			1,030	2,203.9 h	BELLA COOLA FIRST NATION
1889			208		BLUEBERRY RIVER FIRST NATION
			531	1,331.9 h	BONAPARTE FIRST NATION
1878	NTLAKYAPUMUK	SALISHAN	187	2,122 h	BOOTHROYD FIRST NATION
1878	NTLAKYAPUMUK	SALISHAN	180	608.8 h	BOSTON BAR FIRST NATION
1881			262	3,840.5 h	BRIDGE RIVER FIRST NATION
1983			130	619.7 h	BROMAN LAKE FIRST NATION

* Note: Some Provinces use hectares, denoted by h. All others are in acres.

Address		Phone Fax	L[1]	EB[2]	N[3]	M[4]
BRITISH COLUMBIA						
PO BOX 588, CHASE, BC	CANADA V0E 1M0	604-679-8841 604-679-8813	X	T	X	X
GENERAL DELIVERY, AHOUSAHT, BC	CANADA V0R 1A0	604-670-9563 604-670-9589	X	F		
8150 AITKEN RD, RR 1, SARDIS, BC	CANADA V2R 1A9	604-792-2404			X	
BOX 4 RR #2, QUESNEL, BC	CANADA V2J 3H6	604-993-4324 604-398-5798		TA		
PO BOX 69, CHILANKO FORKS, BC	CANADA V0L 1H0	604-481-3335 604-481-1197				
PO BOX 4479, WILLIAMS LAKE, BC	CANADA V2G 2V5	604-440-5611 604-440-5721		TAR		
GENERAL DELIVERY, ALEXIS CREEK, BC	CANADA V0L 1A0	604-394-4212 604-394-4275		RA		
PO BOX 88, D'ARCY, BC	CANADA V0N 1L0	604-452-3221 OR 604-452-3295	X	T	X	
PO BOX 440, ASHCROFT, BC	CANADA V0K 1A0	604-453-9154 604-453-9156	X		X	
BOX 2 RR #1, SOOKE, BC	CANADA V0S 1N0	604-478-3535 604-478-3585				
PO BOX 65, BELLA COOLA, BC	CANADA V0T 1C0	604-799-5613 604-799-5426		TF		
PO BOX 3009, BUCK, BC	CANADA V0C 2R0	604-630-2584 604-830-2589				
PO BOX 669, CACHE CREEK, BC	CANADA V0K 1H0	604-457-9624 604-457-9550		TR	X	
PO BOX 295, BOSTON BAR, BC	CANADA V0K 1C0	604-867-9211 604-867-9747			X	
SS NO 1, BOSTON BAR, BC	CANADA V0K 1C0	604-867-9349	X		X	
PO BOX 190, LILLOOET, BC	CANADA V0K 1V0	604-256-7423 604-256-7999		TF		
PO BOX 760, BURNS LAKE, BC	CANADA V0J 1E0	604-698-7330 604-698-7480	X	T		

Legend

1. Lodging - Resort, Motel, RV Park
2. Economic Base - Farming, Fishing, Ranching Operations
3. Tribal Newspaper
4. Museum/Cultural Center

A - Agriculture
F - Fish, Aquaculture
M - Mineral
R - Ranching
RV - Recreational Vehicle
T - Timber
TC - Tribal Contract

HISTORICAL PROFILE

BRITISH COLUMBIA

Treaty	Language	Tribal Class	Pop	Acreage*	Nation
			68	164 h	BURNS LAKE FIRST NATION
			249	108.3 h	BURRARD FIRST NATION
1888			438		CAMPBELL RIVER FIRST NATION
			426	2,059.3 h	CANIM LAKE FIRST NATION
			448	5,582.5 h	CANOE CREEK FIRST NATION
			679	1,648 h	CAPE MUDGE FIRST NATION
1881			132	687 h	CAYOOSE CREEK FIRST NATION
			248	614 h	CHAWATHIL FIRST NATION
			283	502 h	CHEAM FIRST NATION
			650	906.8 h	CHEHALIS FIRST NATION COMPT. 66
			737	1,202 h	CHEMAINUS FIRST NATION
			185	1,403 h	CHESLATTA CARRIER FIRST NATION
					CLAYOQUOT FIRST NATION
1878	NTLAKYAPUMUK	SALISHAN	482	2,498.9 h	COLDWATER FIRST NATION
1884		KOOTENAYAN	188	3,401.5 h	COLUMBIA LAKE FIRST NATION
			205	694 h	COMOX FIRST NATION
1878	NTLAKYAPUMUK	SALISHAN	236	4,058.2 h	COOK'S FERRY FIRST NATION

* Note: Some Provinces use hectares, denoted by h. All others are in acres.

BRITISH COLUMBIA

Address		Phone Fax	L[1]	EB[2]	N[3]	M[4]
PO BAG 9000, BURNS LAKE, BC	CANADA V0J 1E0	604-692-7097 604-692-7097		T		
3082 GHUMLYE DR, NORTH VANCOUVER, BC	CANADA V7H 1B3	604-929-3454 604-929-4714			X	
1400 WEIWAIKUM RD, CAMPBELL RIVER, BC	CANADA V9W 5W8	604-286-6949 604-287-8838		TFM	X	
PO BOX 1030, 100 MILE HOUSE, BC	CANADA V0K 2E0	604-397-2227 604-397-2769		TA	X	
GENERAL DELIVERY, DOG CREEK, BC	CANADA V0L 1J0	604-440-5645 604-440-5679		A	X	
PO BOX 220, QUATHIASKI COVE, BC	CANADA V0P 1N0	604-285-3316 604-285-2400	X	TFM	X	
PO BOX 484, LILLOOET, BC	CANADA V0K 1V0	604-256-4136 604-256-4030	X	TR	X	
PO BOX 1659, HOPE, BC	CANADA V0X 1L0	604-869-9994 604-869-7614	X	F		
379-10704 #9 HWY, ROSEDALE, BC	CANADA V0X 1X0	604-794-7924 604-794-7456		TFA		
RR #1 CHEHALIS RD, AGASSIZ, BC	CANADA V0M 1A0	604-796-2116 604-796-3946		TF	X	
RR #1, LADYSMITH, BC	CANADA V0R 2E0	604-245-7155 604-245-3012	X		X	
PO BOX 909, BURNS LAKE, BC	CANADA V0J 1E0	604-694-3334 604-694-3632		T		
PO BOX 18, TOFINO, BC	CANADA V0R 2Z0	604-725-3233				
PO BAG 4600, MERRITT, BC	CANADA V0K 2B0	604-378-6174 604-378-5351		TRA	X	
PO BOX 130, WINDERMERE, BC	CANADA V0B 2L0	604-342-6301 604-342-9693	X		X	
3320 COMOX RD, COURTENAY, BC	CANADA V9N 3P8	604-339-7122 604-339-7053		TF		
PO BOX 1000, SPENCES BRIDGE, BC	CANADA V0K 2L0	604-458-2224 604-458-2312		RA	X	

Legend

1. Lodging - Resort, Motel, RV Park
2. Economic Base - Farming, Fishing, Ranching Operations
3. Tribal Newspaper
4. Museum/Cultural Center

A - Agriculture
F - Fish, Aquaculture
M - Mineral
R - Ranching
RV - Recreational Vehicle
T - Timber
TC - Tribal Contract

HISTORICAL PROFILE

BRITISH COLUMBIA

Treaty	Language	Tribal Class	Pop	Acreage*	Nation
			51	88.9 h	COQUITLAM FIRST NATION
			2,511	2,493 h	COWICHAN FIRST NATION
			11	40 h	COWICHAN LAKE FIRST NATION
		KASKA TAHLTAN	128		DEASE RIVER FIRST NATION
			357	727 h	DITIDAHT FIRST NATION
1889			178		DOIG RIVER FIRST NATION
			161	432.3 h	DOUGLAS FIRST NATION
					EHATTESAHT FIRST NATION
			123	18 h	ESQUIMALT FIRST NATION
			178		FORT GEORGE FIRST NATION
					FORT NELSON FIRST NATION
			266		FORT WARE FIRST NATION
			665	1,572.2 h	FOUNTAIN FIRST NATION
			270	966.3 h	FRASER LAKE FIRST NATION
			1,286		GITANMAAX FIRST NATION
					GITANYOW FIRST NATIONN (KITWANCOOL)
	TSIMSHEAN	NISAGA'A	1,346	1,999.7 h	GITLAKDAMIX FIRST NATION

* Note: Some Provinces use hectares, denoted by h. All others are in acres.

Address		Phone Fax	L[1]	EB[2]	N[3]	M[4]

BRITISH COLUMBIA

Address		Phone Fax	L	EB	N	M
65 COLONY FARM RD, PORT COQUITLAM, BC	CANADA V3C 3V4	604-941-4995			X	
PO BOX 880, DUNCAN, BC	CANADA V9L 3Y2	604-748-3196 604-748-1233		FA	X	
PO BOX 1376, LAKE COWICHAN, BC	CANADA V0R 2G0	604-745-3548			X	
GOOD HOPE LAKE BAG 3500, CASSIAR, BC	CANADA V0C 1E0	604-239-3000 604-239-3003	X	M		
PO BOX 340, PORT ALBERNI, BC	CANADA V9Y 7M8	OPERATOR N-692932		TF		
PO BOX 55, ROSE PRAIRIE, BC	CANADA V0C 2H0	604-827-3776 604-827-3778		RA		
PO BOX 339, HARRISON HOT SPG, BC	CANADA V0M 1K0	604-820-3082 604-820-3083				
BOX 716, CAMPBELL RIVER, BC	CANADA V9W 6J3	604-287-4353 604-287-2330				
1000 THOMAS RD, VICTORIA, BC	CANADA V9A 7K7	604-381-7861 604-384-9309		T		
RR 1 SITE 27 COMP 60, PRINCE GEORGE, BC	CANADA V2N 2H8	604-963-8451 604-963-8324		A		
RR #1 293 ALASKA HWY, FORT NELSON, BC	CANADA V0C 1R0	604-774-7688 604-774-7260				
1257 4TH AVE # 3, PRINCE GEORGE, BC	CANADA V2L 3J5	604-563-4161 604-563-2668		T	X	
PO BOX 1330, LILLOOET, BC	CANADA V0K 1V0	604-256-4227 604-256-7505		TR	X	
PO BOX 36, FORT FRASER, BC	CANADA V0J 1N0	604-690-7211 604-690-7316		TA		
PO BOX 440, HAZELTON, BC	CANADA V0J 1Y0	604-842-5297 604-842-6364	X	T	X	
PO BOX 340, KITWANGA, BC	CANADA V0J 2A0	604-849-5222				
PO BOX 233, NEW AIYANSH, BC	CANADA V0J 1A0	604-633-2215 604-633-2514	X		X	

Legend

1. Lodging - Resort, Motel, RV Park
2. Economic Base - Farming, Fishing, Ranching Operations
3. Tribal Newspaper
4. Museum/Cultural Center

A - Agriculture
F - Fish, Aquaculture
M - Mineral
R - Ranching
RV - Recreational Vehicle
T - Timber
TC - Tribal Contract

HISTORICAL PROFILE

Treaty	Language	Tribal Class	Pop	Acreage*	Nation
BRITISH COLUMBIA					
			626		GITSEGUKLA FIRST NATION
			818		GITWANGAK FIRST NATION
	TSIMSHEAN	NISHGA'A	273		GITWINKSIHLKW FIRST NATION (CANYON CITY)
					GLEN VOWELL FIRST NATION
			440	1,857 h	GWA'SALA-'NAKWAXDA 'XW FIRST NATION
			440		HAGWILGET FIRST NATION
			163	165 h	HALALT FIRST NATION
1889			173		HALFWAY RIVER FIRST NATION
			588	520.3 h	HARTLEY BAY FIRST NATION
			1,720	1,369 h	HEILTSUK FIRST NATION
			488	235 h	HESQUIAHT FIRST NATION
1881	SHUSWAP	SALISHAN	35	1,506.3 h	HIGH BAR FIRST NATION C/O FRASER CANYON INDIAN ADMIN
			275	623.8 h	HOMALCO FIRST NATION
	SEKANI		248		INGENIKA FIRST NATION
	TAHLTAN	ATHAPASKAN	234	270.5 h	ISKUT FIRST NATION
1871		SALISHAN	720	13,249 h	KAMLOOPS FIRST NATION
1881	SHUSWAP	SALISHAN	127	228.8 h	KANAKA BAR FIRST NATION

* Note: Some Provinces use hectares, denoted by h. All others are in acres.

Address		Phone Fax	L[1]	EB[2]	N[3]	M[4]

BRITISH COLUMBIA

Address		Phone / Fax	L	EB	N	M
36 CASCADE AVE RR #1, SOUTH HAZELTON, BC	CANADA V0J 2R0	604-849-5595 604-849-5252		T	X	
BOX 400, KITWANGA, BC	CANADA V0J 2A0	604-849-5591 604-849-5746		TF	X	
PO BOX 1, GITWINKSIHLKW, BC	CANADA V0J 3T0	604-633-2294 604-633-2539		TF	X	
PO BOX 157, HAZELTON, BC	CANADA V0J 1Y0	604-842-5241 604-842-5601				
BOX 998, PORT HARDY, BC	CANADA V0N 2P0	604-949-8343 604-949-7402		TFM	X	
PO BOX 460, NEW HAZELTON, BC	CANADA V0J 2J0	604-842-6258 604-842-6924			X	
RR #1, CHEMAINUS, BC	CANADA V0R 1K0	604-246-4736 604-246-2330		T	X	
PO BOX 59, WONOWON, BC	CANADA V0C 2N0	604-787-4452 604-785-2021		A		
GENERAL DELIVERY, HARTLEY BAY, BC	CANADA V0V 1A0	604-841-2500 604-851-2581		F		
PO BOX 880, WAGLISLA, BC	CANADA V0T 1Z0	604-957-2381 604-957-2544	X	F		
PO BOX 2000, TOFINO, BC	CANADA V0R 2Z0	CH466-98077 604-724-8570		F		
BOX 99, CLINTON, BC	CANADA V0K 1K0	604-455-2279 604-455-2772		R	X	
PO BOX 789, CAMPBELL RIVER, BC	CANADA V9W 6Y4	604-287-4922 604-287-9590		TF		
101-1551 OGILVIE, PRINCE GEORGE, BC	CANADA V2N 1W7	604-562-8882 604-562-8899		T	X	
GENERAL DELIVERY, ISKUT, BC	CANADA V0J 1K0	604-234-3331 604-234-3200			X	
315 YELLOWHEAD HWY, KAMLOOPS, BC	CANADA V2H 1H1	604-828-9700 604-372-8833	X	TRAM	X	
PO BOX 210, LYTTON, BC	CANADA V0K 1Z0	604-455-2279 604-455-2772		A	X	

Legend

1. Lodging - Resort, Motel, RV Park
2. Economic Base - Farming, Fishing, Ranching Operations
3. Tribal Newspaper
4. Museum/Cultural Center

A - Agriculture
F - Fish, Aquaculture
M - Mineral
R - Ranching
RV - Recreational Vehicle
T - Timber
TC - Tribal Contract

HISTORICAL PROFILE

Treaty	Language	Tribal Class	Pop	Acreage*	Nation
BRITISH COLUMBIA					
			303	340 h	KATZIE FIRST NATION
			1,347		KINCOLITH FIRST NATION
			970		KISPIOX FIRST NATION
		KWAGUITLH	1,200	665.4 h	KITAMAAT FIRST NATION
			393	598.2 h	KITASOO FIRST NATION
			1,167	1885.2 h	KITKATLA FIRST NATION
					KITSEGUKLA FIRST NATION
	TSMISHEAN	TSMISHEAN	243	1,103.4 h	KITSELAS FIRST NATION
	TSMISHEAN	TSMISHEAN	410	558.7 h	KITSUMKALUM FIRST NATION HOUSE OF SIM-OI-GHETS
			481		KITWANCOOL FIRST NATION
			179	1,357.6 h	KLAHOOSE FIRST NATION
			136	1,652.7 h	KLUSKUS FIRST NATION
			23	505 h	KWA-WA-AINEUK FIRST NATION
			427	725 h	KWAKIUTL FIRST NATION
1979			29	62.78 h	KWAW-KWAW-A-PILT FIRST NATION
			15	169 h	KWIAKAH FIRST NATION
			232	443 h	KWICKSUTAINEUK-AH-KWAW-AH-MISH FIRST NATION

* Note: Some Provinces use hectares, denoted by h. All others are in acres.

Address		Phone Fax	L[1]	EB[2]	N[3]	M[4]

BRITISH COLUMBIA

10946 KATZIE RD, PITT MEADOWS, BC	CANADA V3Y 1Z3	604-465-8961 604-465-5949		F		
PO BOX 325, KINCOLITH, BC	CANADA V0J 1B0	604-326-4212 604-326-4208		TF	X	
PO BOX 25 RR 1, KISPIOX, BC	CANADA V0J 1Y0	604-842-5248 604-842-5604		F	X	
HAISLA PO BOX 1101, KITAMAAT, BC	CANADA V0T 2B0	604-639-9361 604-632-2840		F	X	
GENERAL DELIVERY, KLEMTU, BC	CANADA V0T 1L0	604-839-1255 604-839-1256		TF		
GENERAL DELIVERY, KITKATLA, BC	CANADA V0V 1C0	604-628-9305 604-628-9266			X	
36 CASCADE AVE RR 1, SOUTH HAZELTON, BC	CANADA V0J 2R0	604-849-5543				
4562 QUEENSWAY, TERRACE, BC	CANADA V8G 3X6	604-635-5084 604-635-5335		F	X	
PO BOX 544, TERRACE, BC	CANADA V8G 4B5	604-635-6177 604-635-4622	X	F	X	
PO BOX 340, KITWANGA, BC	CANADA V0J 2A0	604-849-5222 604-849-5445		TF	X	
PO BOX 9, SQUIRREL COVE, BC	CANADA V0P 1T0	604-935-6650 604-935-6997		TF		
395 KINCHANT #A, QUESNEL, BC	CANADA V2J 2R5	604-992-8186 604-992-3929		T		
PO BOX 344, PORT MCNEILL, BC	CANADA V0N 2R0	604-949-8732		T	X	
PO BOX 1440, PORT HARDY, BC	CANADA V0N 2P0	604-949-6012 604-949-9066		AFM	X	
PO BOX 412, CHILLIWACK, BC	CANADA V2P 6H7	604-858-0662 604-858-7692			X	
1440 ISLAND HWY, CAMPBELL RIVER, BC	CANADA V9W 2E3	604-286-1295			X	
GENERAL DELIVERY, SIMOON SOUND, BC	CANADA V0P 1S0	604-974-8099 604-974-8100		T	3	

Legend

1. Lodging - Resort, Motel, RV Park
2. Economic Base - Farming, Fishing, Ranching Operations
3. Tribal Newspaper
4. Museum/Cultural Center

A - Agriculture
F - Fish, Aquaculture
M - Mineral
R - Ranching
RV - Recreational Vehicle
T - Timber
TC - Tribal Contract

HISTORICAL PROFILE

BRITISH COLUMBIA

Treaty	Language	Tribal Class	Pop	Acreage*	Nation
			336	382 h	KYUQUOT FIRST NATION
			232	489.7 h	LAKAHAHMEN FIRST NATION
	TSMISHEAN	NISGA'A	1,091	1,835.9 h	LAKALZAP FIRST NATION
			1,413		LAKE BABINE FIRST NATION
					LAKE COWICHAN INDIAN BAND % 1ST NATION SOUTH ISL TBL CCL
			105	556.7 h	LANGLEY FIRST NATION
					LAX-KW-ALAAMS FIRST NATION
					LHEIT LIT'EN FIRST NATION
1881			231	700.6 h	LILLOOET FIRST NATION
			245	3,135.2 h	LITTLE SHUSWAP FIRST NATION
					LOWER KOOTENAY INDIAN BAND
1878	NTLAKYAPUMUK	SALISHAN	664		LOWER NICOLA FIRST NATION
1876		SALISHAN	304	15,726.4 h	LOWER SIMILKAMEEN FIRST NATION
			158		LYACKSON FIRST NATION
1881	NTLAKYAPUMUK	SALISHAN	1,359	5,908.7 h	LYTTON FIRST NATION
			203	237 h	MALAHAT FIRST NATION
			264	580 h	MAMALELEQALA-QWE-QWA-SOT-ENOX FIRST NATION

* Note: Some Provinces use hectares, denoted by h. All others are in acres.

BRITISH COLUMBIA

Address		Phone Fax	L [1]	EB [2]	N [3]	M [4]
GENERAL DELIVERY, KYUQUOT, BC	CANADA V0P 1J0	604-332-5259 604-332-5210		TF		
41290 LOUGHEED HWY, DEROCHE, BC	CANADA V0M 1G0	604-826-7976 604-826-0362		T	X	
GENERAL DELIVERY, GREENVILL, BC	CANADA V0J 1X0	604-621-3212 604-621-3320		TF	X	
PO BOX 879, BURNS LAKE, BC	CANADA V0J 1E0	604-692-7555 604-692-7559		TFM		
PO BOX 62, MILL BAY, BC	CANADA V0R 2P0	604-743-3228				
PO BOX 117, FORT LANGLEY, BC	CANADA V0X 1J0	604-888-2488 604-888-2442		FA		
206 SHASHAAK ST, PORT SIMPSON, BC	CANADA V0V 1H0	604-625-3474 604-625-3246				
RR 1 SITE 27 COMP 60, PRINCE GEORGE, BC	CANADA V2N 2H8	604-963-8451 604-563-9906				
PO BOX 615, LILLOOET, BC	CANADA V0K 1V0	604-256-4118 604-256-4544	X	T	X	
PO BOX 1100, CHASE, BC	CANADA V0E 1M0	604-679-3203 604-679-3220	X	T	X	
PO BOX 1107, CRESTON, BC	CANADA V0B 1G0	604-428-4428 604-428-7686				
RR 1 SITE 17 COMP 18, MERRITT, BC	CANADA V0K 1B0	604-378-5157 604-378-6188		TRA	X	
PO BOX 100, KEREMEOS, BC	CANADA V0X 1N0	604-499-5528 604-499-5335	X	TA	X	
PO BOX 1798, LADYSMITH, BC	CANADA V0R 2E0	604-245-3829			X	
PO BOX 20, LYTTON, BC	CANADA V0K 1Z0	604-455-2304 604-455-2591	X	RA	X	
PO BOX 111, MILL BAY, BC	CANADA V0R 2P0	604-743-3231 604-743-3251			X	
1400 WEIWAKUM RD, CAMPBELL RIVER, BC	CANADA V9W 5W8	604-287-2955 604-287-4655			X	

Legend

1. Lodging - Resort, Motel, RV Park
2. Economic Base - Farming, Fishing, Ranching Operations
3. Tribal Newspaper
4. Museum/Cultural Center

A - Agriculture
F - Fish, Aquaculture
M - Mineral
R - Ranching
RV - Recreational Vehicle
T - Timber
TC - Tribal Contract

HISTORICAL PROFILE

Treaty	Language	Tribal Class	Pop	Acreage*	Nation
				BRITISH COLUMBIA	
			1,870	907.7 h	MASSET FIRST NATION
			110	419.4 h	MATSQUI FIRST NATION
			360		MCLEOD LAKE FIRST NATION
			411	161.8 h	METLAKATLA FIRST NATION
			1,090		MORICETOWN FIRST NATION
			1,361	2,929.1 h	MOUNT CURRIE FIRST NATION
			348	746 h	MOWACHAHT FIRST NATION
			797	254.2 h	MUSQUEAM FIRST NATION
					NADLEH WHUTEN FIRST NATION
			1,159		NAK'AZDLI FIRST NATION
			862	267 h	NANAIMO FIRST NATION
			156	54 h	NANOOSE FIRST NATION
			277	1,844 h	NAZKO FIRST NATION
				1,856 h	NECOSLIE FIRST NATION
					NEE-TAHI-BUHN FIRST NATION
			303	1,383.2 h	NEMAIAH VALLEY FIRST NATION
1877		SALISHAN	434	2,786.7 h	NESKONLITH FIRST NATION

* Note: Some Provinces use hectares, denoted by h. All others are in acres.

BRITISH COLUMBIA

Address		Phone Fax	L[1]	EB[2]	N[3]	M[4]
PO BOX 189, MASSET, BC	CANADA V0T 2M0	604-626-3337 604-626-5440		TFM	X	
31753 HARRIS RD, RR 1 BOX 229, MATSQUI, BC	CANADA V0X 1S0	604-826-6145 604-826-7009				
GENERAL DELIVERY, MCLEOD LAKE, BC	CANADA V0J 2G0	604-750-4415 604-750-4420		TF	X	
PO BOX 459, PRINCE RUPERT, BC	CANADA V8J 3R1	604-628-9294 604-628-9205		TF	X	X
RR 1 SITE 15 BOX 1, SMITHERS, BC	CANADA V0J 2N0	604-847-2133 604-847-9291		TF		
PO BOX 165, MOUNT CURRIE, BC	CANADA V0N 2K0	604-894-6115 604-894-6841		TA		
PO BOX 459, GOLD RIVER, BC	CANADA V0P 1G0	604-283-2532 604-283-7522		T		
6370 SALISH DR, VANCOUVER, BC	CANADA V6N 2C6	604-263-3261 604-263-4212			X	
PO BOX 36, FORT FRASER, BC	CANADA V0J 1N0	604-690-7211 604-690-7316				
PO BOX 1329, FORT ST JAMES, BC	CANADA V0J 1P0	604-996-7171 604-996-8010		T		
1145 TOTEM RD, NANAIMO, BC	CANADA V9R 1H1	604-753-3481 604-753-3492		T	X	
BOX 124 RR 1, LANTZVILLE, BC	CANADA V0R 2H0	604-390-3661 604-390-3365	X		X	
PO BOX 4534, QUESNEL, BC	CANADA V2J 3H8	604-992-9810 604-992-7854		T		
PO BOX 1329, FORT ST JAMES, BC	CANADA V0J 1P0	604-996-7171 604-996-8010				
RR 2 BOX 28, BURNS LAKE, BC	CANADA V0J 1E0	604-694-3301 604-694-3302				
GENERAL DELIVERY, NEMAIAH VALLEY, BC	CANADA V0L 1X0	RADIO N42-6569YJ		TR	X	
PO BOX 608, CHASE, BC	CANADA V0E 1M0	604-679-3295 604-679-5306		A	X	

Legend

1. Lodging - Resort, Motel, RV Park
2. Economic Base - Farming, Fishing, Ranching Operations
3. Tribal Newspaper
4. Museum/Cultural Center

A - Agriculture
F - Fish, Aquaculture
M - Mineral
R - Ranching
RV - Recreational Vehicle
T - Timber
TC - Tribal Contract

HISTORICAL PROFILE

Treaty	Language	Tribal Class	Pop	Acreage*	Nation
					BRITISH COLUMBIA
			83	1,175.6 h	NICOMEN FIRST NATION
			1,235	366 h	NIMPKISH FIRST NATION
	NTLAKYAPUMUK	SALISHAN	142	1,693.4 h	NOOAITCH FIRST NATION
1877		SALISHAN	466	1,521.7 h	NORTH THOMPSON FIRST NATION
					NUCHATLAHT FIRST NATION
			72	404.4 h	OHAMIL FIRST NATION
			432	816 h	OHIAHT FIRST NATION
1877		SALISHAN	1,252	10,603.3 h	OKANAGAN FIRST NATION
					OLD MASSETT VILLAGE FIRST NATION
			183	215 h	OPETCHESAHT FIRST NATION
1878	NTLAKYAPUMUK	SALISHAN	35	822.8 h	OREGON JACK CREEK FIRST NATION
1877		SALISHAN	283	13,052.3 h	OSOYOOS FIRST NATION
			211	712.7 h	OWEEKENO FIRST NATION
			274	174 h	PACHEENAHT FIRST NATION
			228	319 h	PAUQUACHIN FIRST NATION
1861			350	2,111.8 h	PAVILION FIRST NATION
			563	635 h	PENELAKUT FIRST NATION

* Note: Some Provinces use hectares, denoted by h. All others are in acres.

Address		Phone Fax	L[1]	EB[2]	N[3]	M[4]
BRITISH COLUMBIA						
PO BOX 328, LYTTON, BC	CANADA V0K 1Z0	604-455-2279 604-455-2772		A	X	
PO BOX 210, ALERT BAY, BC	CANADA V0N 1A0	604-974-5556 604-974-5900		F	X	
PO BAG 6000, MERRITT, BC	CANADA V0K 2B0	604-378-6141 604-378-9119			X	
PO BOX 220, BARRIERE, BC	CANADA V0E 1E0	604-672-9995 604-672-5858		TA	X	
PO BOX 40, ZEBALLOS, BC	CANADA V0P 2A0	604-761-4520				
C4 SITE 22 RR 2, HOPE, BC	CANADA V0X 1L0	604-869-2627 604-869-9903	X	A		
PO BOX 82 STA A, NANAIMO, BC	CANADA V9R 5K4	604-752-3994 604-726-1222	X			
SITE 8 COMP 20 RR 7, VERNON, BC	CANADA V1T 7Z3	604-542-4326 604-542-4990	X	A		
PO BOX 189, MASSET, BC	CANADA V0T 1M0	604-626-3337				
PO BOX 211, PORT ALBERNI, BC	CANADA V9Y 7M7	604-724-4041 604-724-1232				
PO BOX 940, ASHCROFT, BC	CANADA V0K 1A0	604-453-9098 604-453-9097				
RR 3 SITE 25 COMP 1, OLIVER, BC	CANADA V0H 1T0	604-496-4906 604-496-6577	X	FA	X	
PO BOX 3500, PORT HARDY, BC	CANADA V0N 2P0	604-949-2107 604-949-2107		T		
GENERAL DELIVERY, PORT RENFREW, BC	CANADA V0S 1K0	604-647-5521 604-647-5561	X		X	
PO BOX 517, BRENTWOOD BAY, BC	CANADA V0S 1K0	604-656-0191 604-656-9905			X	
PO BOX 609, CACHE CREEK, BC	CANADA V0K 1H0	604-256-4058 604-256-4058		M	X	
PO BOX 360, CHEMAINUS, BC	CANADA V0R 1K0	604-246-2321 604-246-2725			X	

Legend

1. Lodging - Resort, Motel, RV Park
2. Economic Base - Farming, Fishing, Ranching Operations
3. Tribal Newspaper
4. Museum/Cultural Center

A - Agriculture
F - Fish, Aquaculture
M - Mineral
R - Ranching
RV - Recreational Vehicle
T - Timber
TC - Tribal Contract

HISTORICAL PROFILE

Treaty	Language	Tribal Class	Pop	Acreage*	Nation
					BRITISH COLUMBIA
			620	18,691.5 h	PENTICTON FIRST NATION
1879			91	197.1 h	PETERS FIRST NATION
1879			7	150.9 h	POPKUM FIRST NATION
1889			143		PROPHET RIVER FIRST NATION
			81	77 h	QUALICUM FIRST NATION
					QUATSINO FIRST NATION
			92	683.7 h	RED BLUFF FIRST NATION
			204	182.7 h	SAMAHQUAM FIRST NATION
1889			480		SAULTEAU FIRST NATION
1760			182	236 h	SCOWLITZ FIRST NATION
1979			490	2,140.1 h	SEABIRD ISLAND FIRST NATION
			799	2,572 h	SECHELT FIRST NATION
			50	129.1 h	SEMIAHOO FIRST NATION
					SETON LAKE FIRST NATION
1878	NTLAKYAPUMUK	SALISHAN	111	3,873.7 h	SHACKAN FIRST NATION
			663	476 h	SHESHAHT FIRST NATION
1884		SALISHAN	177	1,106.1 h	SHUSWAP FIRST NATION

* Note: Some Provinces use hectares, denoted by h. All others are in acres.

Address		Phone Fax	L [1]	EB [2]	N [3]	M [4]
BRITISH COLUMBIA						
RR 2 SITE 80 COMP 19, PENTICTON, BC	CANADA V2A 6J7	604-493-0048 604-493-2882		TA	X	
COMP 11 PO BOX 11, 16650 PETERS RD RR 2, HOPE, BC	CANADA V0X 1L0	604-794-7059 604-794-7059		FR	X	
PO BOX 68 RR 1, ROSEDALE, BC	CANADA V0X 1X0	604-794-7924 604-794-5630				
PO BOX 3250, FORT NELSON, BC	CANADA V0C 1R0	604-774-6555				
SITE 347 C-1 RR 3, QUALICUM BEACH, BC	CANADA V0R 1C0	604-773-6555 604-774-2270	X	F	X	
PO BOX 100, COAL HARBOUR, BC	CANADA V0N 1K0	604-949-6245 604-949-6249				
1515 ARBUTUS RD BOX 4693, QUESNEL, BC	CANADA V2J 3J9	604-747-2900 604-747-1341		TA		
PO BOX 3068, MISSION, BC	CANADA V2V 4J3	604-894-5262 604-854-3155			X	
PO BOX 414, CHETWYND, BC	CANADA V0C 1J0	604-788-3955 604-788-9158		RA		
PO BOX 76, LAKE ERROCK, BC	CANADA V0M 1N0	604-826-5813 604-826-5813	X		X	
PO BOX 650, AGASSIZ, BC	CANADA V0M 1A0	604-796-2177 604-796-3729		A		
PO BOX 740, SECHELT, BC	CANADA V0N 3A0	604-688-3017 604-885-3490				
RR 7, 16010 BEACH RD, WHITE ROCK, BC	CANADA V4B 5A8	604-536-1794 604-536-6191			X	
GENERAL DELIVERY, SHALALTH, BC	CANADA V0N 3C0	604-259-8227 604-259-8384				
BAG 6000, MERRITT, BC	CANADA V0K 2B0	604-378-6141 604-378-9119	X	RA	X	
PO BOX 1218, PORT ALBERNI, BC	CANADA V9Y 7M1	604-724-1225 604-724-4385		TF		
PO BOX 790, INVERMERE, BC	CANADA V0A 1K0	604-342-6361 604-342-2948	X	A	X	

Legend

1. Lodging - Resort, Motel, RV Park
2. Economic Base - Farming, Fishing, Ranching Operations
3. Tribal Newspaper
4. Museum/Cultural Center

A - Agriculture
F - Fish, Aquaculture
M - Mineral
R - Ranching
RV - Recreational Vehicle
T - Timber
TC - Tribal Contract

HISTORICAL PROFILE

Treaty	Language	Tribal Class	Pop	Acreage*	Nation
BRITISH COLUMBIA					
1876	SALISH	SALISHAN	168	319.6 h	SISKA FIRST NATION
1879			58	74.9 h	SKAWAHLOOK FIRST NATION
			333	7,908 h	SKEETCHESTN FIRST NATION
			881	670.4 h	SKIDEGATE FIRST NATION
			279	675.8 h	SKOOKUMCHUCK FIRST NATION
			121	68.4 h	SKOWKALE FIRST NATION
			48	211.1 h	SKUPPAH FIRST NATION
1879			327	341.7 h	SKWAH FIRST NATION
1879			104	217.7 h	SKWAY FIRST NATION
			680	1,907.2 h	SLIAMMON FIRST NATION
			258	2,092.7 h	SODA CREEK FIRST NATION
			266	125.5 h	SONGHEES FIRST NATION
			91	68 h	SOOKE FIRST NATION
			233	460.8 h	SOOWAHLIE FIRST NATION
1877			515	3,095.2 h	SPALLUMCHEEN FIRST NATION
			128	636.1 h	SPUZZUM FIRST NATION
			2,231	2,057.7 h	SQUAMISH FIRST NATION

* Note: Some Provinces use hectares, denoted by h. All others are in acres.

Address		Phone Fax	L[1]	EB[2]	N[3]	M[4]
BRITISH COLUMBIA						
PO BOX 358, LYTTON, BC	CANADA V0K 1Z0	604-455-2219 604-455-2565			X	
PO BOX 1668, HOPE, BC	CANADA V0X 1L0	604-796-9877 604-796-9877	X		X	
PO BOX 178, SAVONA, BC	CANADA V0K 2J0	604-373-2493 604-373-2494	X	R	X	
BOX 1301 RR 1, SKIDGATE, BC	CANADA V0T 1S1	604-559-4496 604-559-8247		F	X	
PO BOX 190, PEMBERTON, BC	CANADA V0N 2L0	604-894-6037 604-820-3083				
PO BOX 365, SARDIS, BC	CANADA V2R 1A7	604-792-0730 604-792-0730		F	X	
PO BOX 116, LYTTON, BC	CANADA V0K 1Z0	604-455-2279 604-455-2772		RA	X	
PO BOX 178, CHILLIWACK, BC	CANADA V2P 6H7	604-792-9204 604-792-1093		FA	X	
PO BOX 364, CHILLIWACK, BC	CANADA V2P 6J4	604-858-0662 604-858-4817		TA		
RR 2 SLIAMMON RD, POWELL RIVER, BC	CANADA V8A 4Z3	604-483-9646 604-483-9769		TF	X	
RR 4 SITE 15 COMP 2, WILLIAMS LAKE, BC	CANADA V2G 4M8	604-297-6323 604-297-6300		ARM		
1500 A-ADMIRALS RD, VICTORIA, BC	CANADA V9A 2R1	604-386-1043 604-386-4161			X	
RR 3, 2184 LAZZAR RD, SOOKE, BC	CANADA V0S 1N0	604-642-3957 604-642-7808		T	X	
PO BOX 696, VEDDER CROSSING, BC	CANADA V0X 1Z0	604-858-4603 604-858-2350	X		X	
PO BOX 430, ENDERBY, BC	CANADA V0E 1V0	604-838-6496 604-838-2131		T	X	
RR 1, YALE, BC	CANADA V0K 2S0	604-863-2205 604-455-2772			X	
PO BOX 86131, NORTH VANCOUVER, BC	CANADA V7L 4J5	604-985-7711 604-985-7707	X	T	X	

Legend

1. Lodging - Resort, Motel, RV Park
2. Economic Base - Farming, Fishing, Ranching Operations
3. Tribal Newspaper
4. Museum/Cultural Center

A - Agriculture
F - Fish, Aquaculture
M - Mineral
R - Ranching
RV - Recreational Vehicle
T - Timber
TC - Tribal Contract

HISTORICAL PROFILE

Treaty	Language	Tribal Class	Pop	Acreage*	Nation
BRITISH COLUMBIA					
1879			89	127.7 h	SQUIALA FIRST NATION
1884		KOOTENAYAN	204	7,445.9 h	ST MARY'S FIRST NATION
			282	824.3 h	STELLAQUO FIRST NATION
			227	2,146.4 h	STONE FIRST NATION
			634	3,235.6 h	STONY CREEK FIRST NATION
1879			197	234.6 h	SUMAS FIRST NATION
	TAHLTAN	ATHAPASKAN	229	3,230 h	TAHLTAN FIRST NATION
			452	1,878 h	TAKLA LAKE FIRST NATION
1916			345	1,299 h	TAKU RIVER TLINGITS FIRST NATION
			149	785 h	TANAKTEUK FIRST NATION
			546	220 h	TIA-O-QUI-AHT FIRST NATION
			1,215	2,813.4 h	TL'AZT'EN FIRST NATION (STUART-TREMBLEUR)
			29	8,585 h	TLATLASIKWALA FIRST NATION %WHE-LA-LA-U AREA COUNCIL
			249	464 h	TLOWITSIS-MUMTAGILA FIRST NATION %WHE-LA-LA-U AREA COUNCIL
1884		KOOTENAYAN	116	4,227.5 h	TOBACCO PLAINS FIRST NATION
			186	2,582.5 h	TOOSEY FIRST NATION
			91	196 h	TOQUAHT FIRST NATION

* Note: Some Provinces use hectares, denoted by h. All others are in acres.

Address		Phone Fax	L[1]	EB[2]	N[3]	M[4]
BRITISH COLUMBIA						
PO BOX 392, CHILLIWACK, BC	CANADA V2P 6J7	604-792-8300 604-792-4522		FA	X	
SITE 15 MISSION RD RR 1, CRANBROOK, BC	CANADA V1C 4H4	604-426-5717 604-426-8935		RA	X	X
PO BOX 760, FRASER LAKE, BC	CANADA V0J 1S0	604-699-8747 604-699-6430	X	TA	X	
GENERAL DELIVERY, HANCEVILLE, BC	CANADA V0L 1K0	604-394-4295 604-394-4407		TA		
RR 1 SITE 12 COMP 26, VANDERHOOF, BC	CANADA V0J 3A0	604-567-9293 604-567-9656	X	T	X	
3092 SUMAS MOUNTAIN RD RR 4, ABBOTSFORD, BC	CANADA V2S 4N4	604-852-4040 604-852-3834		RA		
GENERAL DELIVERY, TELEGRAPH CREEK, BC	CANADA V0J 2W0	604-235-3241 604-235-3244			X	
GENERAL DELIVERY, TAKLA LANDING, BC	CANADA V0J 2T0	604-564-3704 604-564-3704		T	X	
PO BOX 132, ATLIN, BC	CANADA V0W 1A0	604-651-7615 604-651-7714	X	T		
PO BOX 330, ALERT BAY, BC	CANADA V0N 1A0	604-974-5489		FM	X	
PO BOX 18, TOFINO, BC	CANADA V0R 2Z0	604-725-3223 604-725-4233		TF	X	
PO BOX 670, FORT ST JAMES, BC	CANADA V0J 1P0	604-648-3212 604-648-3266		T		
PO BOX 150, ALERT BAY, BC	CANADA V0N 1A0	604-974-5501 604-974-5904		F	X	
PO BOX 150, ALERT BAY, BC	CANADA V0L 1A0	604-974-5501 604-974-5904		TFM	X	
PO BOX 21, GRASMERE, BC	CANADA V0B 1R0	604-887-3461 604-887-3424		TAR	X	
GENERAL DELIVERY, RISKE CREEK, BC	CANADA V0L 1T0	604-659-5655 604-659-5601		RA		
PO BOX 759, UCLUELET, BC	CANADA V0R 3A0	604-726-4230 604-726-4403		F		

Legend

1. Lodging - Resort, Motel, RV Park
2. Economic Base - Farming, Fishing, Ranching Operations
3. Tribal Newspaper
4. Museum/Cultural Center

A - Agriculture
F - Fish, Aquaculture
M - Mineral
R - Ranching
RV - Recreational Vehicle
T - Timber
TC - Tribal Contract

Treaty	Language	Tribal Class	Pop	Acreage*	Nation
BRITISH COLUMBIA					
			549	324 h	TSARTLIP FIRST NATION
			382	538 h	TSAWATAINEUK FIRST NATION (CAMPBELL RIVER KINGCOME 5255)
			466	258 h	TSAWOUT FIRST NATION
			142	800 h	TSAWWASSEN FIRST NATION
					TSAY KEH DENE FIRST NATION
			110	28 h	TSEYCUM FIRST NATION
			235	262.1 h	TZEACHTEN FIRST NATION
			121	232 h	UCHUCKLESAHT FIRST NATION
			478	162 h	UCLUELET FIRST NATION
			573	3,213.5 h	ULKATCHO FIRST NATION
1879			72	499.7 h	UNION BAR FIRST NATION
	NTLAKAYAPUMUK	SALISHAN	667	12,503.1 h	UPPER NICOLA FIRST NATION
			40	2,602.5 h	UPPER SIMILKAMEEN FIRST NATION
					WEST MOBERLY FIRST NATION
1860		SALISHAN	404	969 h	WESTBANK FIRST NATION
			91	565.2 h	WHISPERING PINES FIRST NATION
1881		SALISHAN	347	1,927.3 h	WILLIAMS LAKE FIRST NATION

* Note: Some Provinces use hectares, denoted by h. All others are in acres.

Address		Phone Fax	L [1]	EB [2]	N [3]	M [4]

BRITISH COLUMBIA

Address		Phone / Fax	L	EB	N	M
PO BOX 70, BRENTWOOD BAY, BC	CANADA V0S 1A0	604-652-3988 604-652-3788	X		X	
GENERAL DELIVERY, KINGCOME INLET, BC	CANADA V0N 2B0	604-974-3055 604-974-3077		TFA	X	
PO BOX 121, SAANICHTON, BC	CANADA V0S 1M0	604-652-9101 604-652-9114	X		X	
TSAWWASSEN DR BLDG 132N, DELTA, BC	CANADA V4K 3H5	604-943-2112 604-943-9226	X		X	
3845 15TH AVE, PRINCE GEORGE, BC	CANADA V2N 1A4	604-562-8882 604-562-8899				
PO BOX 2596, SIDNEY, BC	CANADA V8L 4C1	604-656-0858 604-656-0868			X	
PO BOX 278, SARDIS, BC	CANADA V2R 1A6	604-858-3888 604-858-7692			X	
PO BOX 157, PORT ALBERNI, BC	CANADA V9Y 7M7	604-724-1832 604-724-1806			X	
PO BOX 699, UCLUELET, BC	CANADA V0R 3A0	604-726-7342 604-726-7552		FM	X	
PO BOX 3430, ANAHIM LAKE, BC	CANADA V0L 1C0	604-742-3260 604-742-3411		TR		
PO BOX 788, HOPE, BC	CANADA V0X 1L0	604-869-9466 604-869-9466		T	X	
PO BAG 3700, MERRITT, BC	CANADA V0K 2B0	604-350-3342 604-350-3319		RA	X	
PO BOX 100, KEREMEOS, BC	CANADA V0X 1N0	604-499-5526 604-499-5335	X	TAR	X	
BOX 90, MOBERLY LAKE, BC	CANADA V0C 1X0	604-788-3663 604-788-9792				
515 HIGHWAY 97 S, KELOWNA, BC	CANADA V1Z 3J2	604-769-5666 604-769-4377		A	X	
RR 1, SITE 8, COMP 4, KAMLOOPS, BC	CANADA V2C 1Z3	604-579-5772 604-579-5772		RA	X	
BOX 4, RR 3, SUGARCANE, WILLIAMS LAKE, BC	CANADA V2G 1M3	604-296-3507 604-296-4750	X	R	X	

Legend

1. Lodging - Resort, Motel, RV Park
2. Economic Base - Farming, Fishing, Ranching Operations
3. Tribal Newspaper
4. Museum/Cultural Center

A - Agriculture
F - Fish, Aquaculture
M - Mineral
R - Ranching
RV - Recreational Vehicle
T - Timber
TC - Tribal Contract

HISTORICAL PROFILE

Treaty	Language	Tribal Class	Pop	Acreage*	Nation
BRITISH COLUMBIA					
			31	19.4 h	YAKWEAKWIOOSE FIRST NATION
1879			105	225.3 h	YALE FIRST NATION
LABRADOR - SEE NEW FOUNDLAND					
MANITOBA					
1906	CREE CHIPEWYAN		559		BARREN LANDS FIRST NATION
1875	OJIBWAY		1,672		BERENS RIVER FIRST NATION
	DAKOTA		457		BIRDTAIL SIOUX FIRST NATION
1875	OJIBWAY		1,086		BLOODVEIN FIRST NATION
1871	OJIBWAY		906		BROKENHEAD OJIBWAY FIRST NATION
1871	OJIBWAY		90		BUFFALO POINT FIRST NATION
1875	CREE		807		CHEMAWAWIN FIRST NATION
1871	OJIBWAY		455		CRANE RIVER FIRST NATION
1875	CREE		3,927		CROSS LAKE FIRST NATION
	DAKOTA		211		DAKOTA PLAINS FIRST NATION
	DAKOTA		202		DAKOTA TIPI FIRST NATION
1871	OJIBWAY		184		DAUPHIN RIVER FIRST NATION

* Note: Some Provinces use hectares, denoted by h. All others are in acres.

Address		Phone Fax	L[1]	EB[2]	N[3]	M[4]
BRITISH COLUMBIA						
7176 CHILLIWACK RIVER RD RR 2, SARDIS, BC	CANADA V2R 1B1	604-858-6726		FA	X	
PO BOX 1869, HOPE, BC	CANADA V0X 1L0	604-863-2423	X	F		
LABRADOR - SEE NEW FOUNDLAND						
MANITOBA						
GENERAL DELIVERY, BROCHET, MB	CANADA R0B 0B0	204-323-2300 204-323-2275				
BERENS RIVER RD PO, BERENS RIVER, MB	CANADA R0B 0A0	204-382-2161 204-382-2297				
PO BOX 22, BEULAH, MB	CANADA R0M 0B0	204-568-4540 204-568-4687				
GENERAL DELIVERY, BLOODVEIN, MB	CANADA R0C 0J0	204-395-2148 204-477-6050				
GENERAL DELIVERY, SCANTERBURY, MB	CANADA R0E 1W0	204-766-2494 204-766-2306				
PO BOX 37, MIDDLEBRO, MB	CANADA R0A 1B0	204-437-2133 204-437-2368				
GENERAL DELIVERY, EASTERVILLE, MB	CANADA R0C 0V0	204-329-2161 204-329-2017				
GENERAL DELIVERY, CRANE RIVER, MB	CANADA R0L 0M0	204-732-2490 204-732-2596				
GENERAL DELIVERY, CROSS LAKE, MB	CANADA R0B 0J0	204-676-2218 204-676-2117				
PO BOX 110, PORTAGE LA PRAIRIE, MB	CANADA R1N 3B2	204-252-2288 204-729-3682				X
PO BOX 1569, PORTAGE LA PRAIRIE, MB	CANADA R1N 3P1	204-857-4381 204-239-6384				
PO BOX 58, GYPSUMVILLE, MB	CANADA R0C 1J0	204-659-6370 204-659-4465				

Legend

1. Lodging - Resort, Motel, RV Park
2. Economic Base - Farming, Fishing, Ranching Operations
3. Tribal Newspaper
4. Museum/Cultural Center

A - Agriculture
F - Fish, Aquaculture
M - Mineral
R - Ranching
RV - Recreational Vehicle
T - Timber
TC - Tribal Contract

HISTORICAL PROFILE

Treaty	Language	Tribal Class	Pop	Acreage*	Nation
					MANITOBA
1871	OJIBWAY		1,115		EBB & FLOW FIRST NATIONS
1871	OJIBWAY		2,284		FAIRFORD FIRST NATION
1875	CREE		2,296		FISHER RIVER FIRST NATION
1871	OJIBWAY CREE		4,266		FORT ALEXANDER FIRST NATION
1910	CHIPEWYAN		506		FORT CHURCHILL FIRST NATION
1910	CREE		566		FOX LAKE FIRST NATION
1874	CREE		97		GAMBLERS FIRST NATION
1909	ISLAND LAKE CREE / OJIBWAY		2,537		GARDEN HILL FIRST NATION
1909	CREE		1,616		GOD'S LAKE FIRST NATION
1909	CREE		413		GOD'S RIVER FIRST NATION
1875	CREE		708		GRAND RAPIDS FIRST NATION
1875	OJIBWAY		779		HOLLOW WATER FIRST NATION
1874	CREE		255		INDIAN BIRCH FIRST NATION
1875	OJIBWAY		466		JACKHEAD FIRST NATION
1871	OJIBWAY		612		KEESEEKOOWENIN FIRST NATION
1871	OJIBWAY		916		LAKE MANITOBA FIRST NATION
1871	OJIBWAY		1,352		LAKE ST MARTIN FIRST NATION

* Note: Some Provinces use hectares, denoted by h. All others are in acres.

Address		Phone Fax	L[1]	EB[2]	N[3]	M[4]

MANITOBA

GENERAL DELIVERY, EBB & FLOW, MB	CANADA R0L 0R0	204-448-2134 204-448-2305				
GENERAL DELIVERY, FAIRFORD, MB	CANADA R0C 0X0	204-659-5705 204-659-2068				
GENERAL DELIVERY, KOOSTATAK, MB	CANADA R0C 1S0	204-645-2171 204-645-2745				
PO BOX 280, FORT ALEXANDER, MB	CANADA R0E 0P0	204-367-2287 204-367-4315				
GENERAL DELIVERY, TADOULE LAKE, MB	CANADA R0B 2C0	204-684-2022 204-684-2336				
PO BOX 369, GILLIAM, MB	CANADA R0B 0L0	204-652-2370 204-486-2503				
PO BOX 250, BINSCARTH, MB	CANADA R0J 0G0	204-532-2464 204-532-2464				
GENERAL DELIVERY, ISLAND LAKE, MB	CANADA R0B 0T0	204-456-2085 204-456-2338				
GENERAL DELIVERY, GOD'S LAKE NARROWS, MB	CANADA R0B 0M0	204-335-2130 204-335-2400				
GENERAL DELIVERY, GODS RIVER, MB	CANADA R0B 0N0	204-366-2011 204-366-2281				
PO BOX 500, GRAND RAPIDS, MB	CANADA R0C 1E0	204-639-2219 204-639-2503				
GENERAL DELIVERY, WANIPIGOW, MB	CANADA R0E 2E0	204-363-7278 204-363-7418				
PO BOX 65, BIRCH RIVER, MB	CANADA R0L 0E0	204-236-4201				
GENERAL DELIVERY, DALLAS, MB	CANADA R0C 0S0	204-394-2366 204-394-2271				
PO BOX 100, ELPHINSTONE, MB	CANADA R0J 0N0	204-625-2004 204-625-2042				
GENERAL DELIVERY, VOGAR, MB	CANADA R0C 3C0	204-768-3492 204-768-3036				
PO BOX 69, GYPSUMVILLE, MB	CANADA R0C 1J0	204-659-4539 204-659-4569				

Legend

1. Lodging - Resort, Motel, RV Park
2. Economic Base - Farming, Fishing, Ranching Operations
3. Tribal Newspaper
4. Museum/Cultural Center

A - Agriculture
F - Fish, Aquaculture
M - Mineral
R - Ranching
RV - Recreational Vehicle
T - Timber
TC - Tribal Contract

HISTORICAL PROFILE

Treaty	Language	Tribal Class	Pop	Acreage*	Nation
					MANITOBA
1875	OJIBWAY		625		LITTLE BLACK RIVER FIRST NATION
1875	OJIBWAY		1,238		LITTLE GRAND RAPIDS FIRST NATION
1871	OJIBWAY		670		LITTLE SASKATCHEWAN FIRST NATION
1871	OJIBWAY		1,791		LONG PLAIN FIRST NATION
1898	CREE		2,015		MATHIAS COLOMB FIRST NATION
1875	CREE		764		MOOSE LAKE FIRST NATION
1908	CREE		3,022		NELSON HOUSE FIRST NATION
1906	DENE		617		NORTHLANDS FIRST NATION
1875	CREE		809		NORWAY HOUSE FIRST NATION
	DAKOTA		503		OAK LAKE SIOUX FIRST NATION
1909	CREE		1,564		OXFORD HOUSE FIRST NATION
1875	OJIBWAY		452		PAUINGASSI FIRST NATION
1871	OJIBWAY CREE		4,870		PEGUIS FIRST NATION
	OJIBWAY		1,410		PINE CREEK FIRST NATION
1875	OJIBWAY		917		POPLAR RIVER FIRST NATION
1909	OJIBWAY CREE		579		RED SUCKER LAKE FIRST NATION
1874	OJIBWAY		526		ROLLING RIVER FIRST NATION

* Note: Some Provinces use hectares, denoted by h. All others are in acres.

Address		Phone Fax	L[1]	EB[2]	N[3]	M[4]

MANITOBA

GENERAL DELIVERY, O'HANLEY, MB	CANADA R0E 1K0	204-367-4411 204-367-2741				
GENERAL DELIVERY, LITTLE GRAND RAPIDS, MB	CANADA R0B 0V0	204-397-2264 204-397-2340				
GENERAL DELIVERY, GYPSUMVILLE, MB	CANADA R0C 1J0	204-659-4584 204-659-2071				
GENERAL DELIVERY, EDWIN, MB	CANADA R0H 0G0	204-252-2731 204-252-2012				
GENERAL DELIVERY, PUKATAWAGAN, MB	CANADA R0B 1G0	204-553-2090 204-553-2419				
GENERAL DELIVERY, MOOSE LAKE, MB	CANADA R0B 0Y0	204-678-2113 204-678-2292				
GENERAL DELIVERY, NELSON HOUSE, MB	CANADA R0B 1A0	204-484-2332 204-484-2392				
GENERAL DELIVERY, LAC BROCHET, MB	CANADA R0B 2E0	204-337-2001 204-337-2110				
PO BOX 218, NORWAY HOUSE, MB	CANADA R0B 1B0	204-359-6786 204-359-6786				
PO BOX 146, PIPESTONE, MB	CANADA R0M 1T0	204-854-2959 204-854-2525				
GENERAL DELIVERY, OXFORD HOUSE, MB	CANADA R0B 1C0	204-538-2156 204-538-2220				
GENERAL DELIVERY, LITTLE GRAND RAPIDS, MB	CANADA R0B 0V0	204-397-2371 204-397-2145				
PO BOX 219, HODGSON, MB	CANADA R0C 1N0	204-645-2359 204-645-2360				
PO BOX 70, CAMPERVILLE, MB	CANADA R0L 0J0	204-524-2478 204-524-2832				
GENERAL DELIVERY, NEGGINAN, MB	CANADA R0B 0Z0	204-244-2267 204-244-2690				
GENERAL DELIVERY, RED SUCKER LAKE, MB	CANADA R0B 1H0	204-469-5041 204-469-5325				
PO BOX 145, ERICKSON, MB	CANADA R0J 0P0	204-636-2211 204-636-7823				

Legend

1. Lodging - Resort, Motel, RV Park
2. Economic Base - Farming, Fishing, Ranching Operations
3. Tribal Newspaper
4. Museum/Cultural Center

A - Agriculture
F - Fish, Aquaculture
M - Mineral
R - Ranching
RV - Recreational Vehicle
T - Timber
TC - Tribal Contract

HISTORICAL PROFILE

Treaty	Language	Tribal Class	Pop	Acreage*	Nation
		MANITOBA			
1871	OJIBWAY		1,436		ROSEAU RIVER FIRST NATION
					SAGKEENG FIRST NATION
1871	OJIBWAY		3,289		SANDY BAY FIRST NATION
1910	CREE		829		SHAMATTAWA FIRST NATION
1874	CREE		927		SHOAL RIVER FIRST NATION
	OJIBWAY SIOUX		1,666		SIOUX VALLEY FIRST NATION
1908	CREE		1,944		SPLIT LAKE CREE FIRST NATION
1909	ISLAND LAKE CREE		2,032		ST THERESA POINT FIRST NATION
1871	OJIBWAY		874		SWAN LAKE FIRST NATION
1876	CREE		2,869		THE PAS FIRST NATION
1874	OJIBWAY		845		VALLEY RIVER FIRST NATION
1908	CREE		178		WAR LAKE CREE FIRST NATION
1909	ISLAND LAKE CREE		1,003		WASAGAMACK FIRST NATION
1871	OJIBWAY		782		WATERHEN FIRST NATION
1874	OJIBWAY		1,433		WAYWAYSEECAPO FIRST NATION
1910	CREE		649		YORK FACTORY FIRST NATION

* Note: Some Provinces use hectares, denoted by h. All others are in acres.

MANITOBA

Address		Phone Fax	L[1]	EB[2]	N[3]	M[4]
PO BOX 30, GINEW, MB	CANADA R0A 2R0	204-427-2312 204-427-2584				
GENERAL DELIVERY, FORT ALEXANDER, MB	CANADA R0E 0P6	204-367-2287 204-367-4315				
GENERAL DELIVERY, MARIUS, MB	CANADA R0H 0T0	204-843-2462 204-843-2706				
GENERAL DELIVERY, SHAMATTAWA, MB	CANADA R0B 1K0	204-565-2340 204-565-2455				
GENERAL DELIVERY, PELICAN RAPIDS, MB	CANADA R0L 1L0	204-587-2012 204-587-2072				
PO BOX 38, GRISWOLD, MB	CANADA R0M 0S0	204-855-2671 204-855-2436				
GENERAL DELIVERY, SPLIT LAKE, MB	CANADA R0B 1P0	204-342-2045 204-342-2270				
GENERAL DELIVERY, ST THERESA POINT, MB	CANADA R0B 1J0	204-462-2106 204-462-2646				
PO BOX 368, SWAN LAKE, MB	CANADA R0G 2S0	204-836-2101 204-836-2255				
PO BOX 297, THE PAS, MB	CANADA R9A 1K4	204-623-5483 204-623-3619			1	
GENERAL DELIVERY, SHORTDALE, MB	CANADA R0L 1W0	204-546-3334 204-546-3218				
GENERAL DELIVERY, ILFORD, MB	CANADA R0B 0S0	204-288-4315 204-288-4371				
GENERAL DELIVERY, WASAGAMACK, MB	CANADA R0B 1Z9	204-457-2337 204-457-2255				
GENERAL DELIVERY, SKOWNAN, MB	CANADA R0L 1Y0	204-628-3373 204-628-3289				
PO BOX 340, ROSSBURN, MB	CANADA R0J 1V0	204-859-2879 204-859-2403				
GENERAL DELIVERY, YORK LANDING, MB	CANADA R0B 2B0	204-341-2180 204-342-2322				

Legend

1. Lodging - Resort, Motel, RV Park
2. Economic Base - Farming, Fishing, Ranching Operations
3. Tribal Newspaper
4. Museum/Cultural Center

A - Agriculture
F - Fish, Aquaculture
M - Mineral
R - Ranching
RV - Recreational Vehicle
T - Timber
TC - Tribal Contract

NEW BRUNSWICK

Treaty	Language	Tribal Class	Pop	Acreage*	Nation
1805	ENGLISH	MICMAC	1,882	4,120	BIG COVE FIRST NATION
1810	ENGLISH	MICMAC	63	154	BOUCTOUCHE FIRST NATION
1802	ENGLISH	MICMAC	1,041	8,241	BURNT CHURCH FIRST NATION
1867	ENGLISH FRENCH	MICMAC	161	766	EDMUNDSTON FIRST NATION
1783	ENGLISH	MICMAC	622	9,464.5	EEL GROUND FIRST NATION
1807	ENGLISH	MICMAC	431	1,338	EEL RIVER BAR FIRST NATION
1969	ENGLISH	MICMAC	75	100	FORT FOLLY FIRST NATION
1948	ENGLISH	MICMAC	119	65	INDIAN ISLAND FIRST NATION
1814	ENGLISH	MALISEET	575	979	KINGSCLEAR FIRST NATION
1895	ENGLISH	MALISEET	335	49	OROMOCTO FIRST NATION
1867	ENGLISH	MICMAC	140	1,053	PABINEAU FIRST NATION
1783	ENGLISH	MICMAC	388	13,359	RED BANK FIRST NATION
1867	ENGLISH FRENCH	MICMAC	161	766	ST BASILE FIRST NATION
1867	ENGLISH	MALISEET	920	327.5	ST MARYS FIRST NATION
1801	ENGLISH	MALISEET	1,384	6,731	TOBIQUE FIRST NATION
1851	ENGLISH	MALISEET	564	220	WOODSTOCK FIRST NATION

* Note: Some Provinces use hectares, denoted by h. All others are in acres.

NEW BRUNSWICK

Address		Phone Fax	L[1]	EB[2]	N[3]	M[4]
BOX 1, SITE 11, RR 1, BIG COVE, NB	CANADA E0A 2L0	506-523-9183 506-523-4901		TFAM		
RR 2, KENT CO, BOUCTOUCHE, NB	CANADA E0A 1G0	506-743-6493 506-743-8995		TAF		
RR 2, LAGACEVILLE, NB	CANADA E0C 1K0	506-776-8331 506-776-3682		TF		
PO BOX 382, EDMUNDSTON, NB	CANADA E3V 3L1	506-739-3379 506-739-7553		T		
BOX 9 SITE 3 RR 1, NEWCASTLE, NB	CANADA E1V 3L8	506-622-2181 506-622-8667		TA		
PO BOX 1444, DALHOUSIE, NB	CANADA 30K 1B0	506-684-2360 506-684-5840		TF		
PO BOX 21 RR 1, DORCHESTER, NB	CANADA E0A 1M0	506-379-6224 506-379-6641		TA		
PO BOX 288 RR 2, REXTON, NB	CANADA E0A 2L0	506-523-9187 506-523-8110	X			
RR 6 BOX 6 COMP 19, FREDERICTON, NB	CANADA E3B 4X7	506-363-9026 506-363-4324	X	T		
PO BOX 417, OROMOCTO, NB	CANADA E2V 2J2	506-357-2083 506-357-2628				
BOX 1 SITE 26 RR 5, BATHURST, NB	CANADA E2A 3Y8	506-548-9211 506-548-9849		TAF		
PO BOX 120, RED BANK, NB	CANADA E0C 1W0	506-836-2366 506-836-7593		TAF		
PO BOX 382, EDMUNSTON, NB	CANADA E0L 1H0	506-739-9765 506-739-7553		T		
247 PAUL, FREDERICTON, NB	CANADA E3A 2V7	506-458-9511 506-453-1793		T		
RR 3, PERTH, NB	CANADA E0J 1V0	506-273-2282 506-273-3035		TAF		
BOX 8 SITE 1 RR 1, WOODSTOCK, NB	CANADA E0J 2B0	506-328-3304 506-328-2420		TA		

Legend

1. Lodging - Resort, Motel, RV Park
2. Economic Base - Farming, Fishing, Ranching Operations
3. Tribal Newspaper
4. Museum/Cultural Center

A - Agriculture
F - Fish, Aquaculture
M - Mineral
R - Ranching
RV - Recreational Vehicle
T - Timber
TC - Tribal Contract

Treaty	Language	Tribal Class	Pop	Acreage*	Nation
NEW FOUNDLAND					
					FIRST NATION COUNCIL OF DAVIS INLET
					FIRST NATION COUNCIL OF NORTH WEST RIVER
1986	ENGLISH	MICMAC	823	640	MIAWPUKEK FIRST NATION
NORTHWEST TERRITORIES					
1921			307		AKLAVIK FIRST NATION
1921			322		ARCTIC RED RIVER FIRST NATION
1921			70		COLVILLE LAKE FIRST NATION
1921			123		DECHILAO'TI COUNCIL DENE (SNARE LAKE)
					DENINOO COMMUNITY COUNCIL FIRST NATION
1921			1,486		DOG RIB RAE FIRST NATION
1899			633	44.7 h	FITZ/SMITH SALT RIVER FIRST NATION # 195 (ALTA-NWT)
1921			653		FORT FRANKLIN FIRST NATION
1921			522		FORT GOOD HOPE FIRST NATION
1922			425		FORT LIARD FIRST NATION (PECHAOT'I K'OE)
1921			1,035		FORT MCPHERSON FIRST NATION
1921			354		FORT NORMAN FIRST NATION

* Note: Some Provinces use hectares, denoted by h. All others are in acres.

Address		Phone Fax	L[1]	EB[2]	N[3]	M[4]
NEW FOUNDLAND (LABRADOR)						
PO BOX 107, LABRADOR, NF	CANADA A0P 1A0	709-478-8999 709-478-8936				
PO BOX 160, SHESHAHT NW RIVER, LABRADOR, NF	CANADA Z0P 1M0	709-497-8522 709-497-8396				
BAIE D'ESPOIR, CONNE RIVER, NF	CANADA A0H 1J0	709-882-2146 709-882-2292		TAF		
NORTHWEST TERRITORIES						
PO BOX 118, KLAVIK, NWT	CANADA X0E 0A0	403-978-2340 403-978-2937		FM		
GENERAL DELIVERY, ARCTIC RED RIVER, NWT	CANADA X0E 0B0	403-953-3901 403-953-3302		F		
GENERAL DELIVERY, FT GOOD HOPE, NWT	CANADA X0E 0H0	MOBILE #2M4486		F		
GENERAL DELIVERY, SNARE LAKE, NWT	CANADA X1A 1C0	403-920-9812 403-920-2836		F		
GENERAL DELIVERY, FT RESOLUTION, NWT	CANADA X0E 0M0	403-394-4556 403-394-5415				
PO BOX 8, FORT RAE, NWT	CANADA X0E 0Y0	403-392-6471 403-392-6150		F		
PO BOX 960, FORT SMITH, NWT	CANADA X0E 0P0	403-872-5101 403-872-3550				
GENERAL DELIVERY, FORT FRANKLIN, NWT	CANADA X0E 0G0	403-589-3151 403-589-4208		FM		
GENERAL DELIVERY, FT GOOD HOPE, NWT	CANADA X0E 0H0	403-598-2231 403-598-2024		FM		
GENERAL DELIVERY, FORT LIARD, NWT	CANADA X0G 0A0	403-770-4141 403-770-3555		F		
PO BOX 100, FORT MCPHERSON, NWT	CANADA X0E 0J0	403-952-2330 403-952-2212		M		
GENERAL DELIVERY, FORT NORMAN, NWT	CANADA X0E 0K0	403-588-3341 403-588-3613		TFM		

Legend

1. Lodging - Resort, Motel, RV Park
2. Economic Base - Farming, Fishing, Ranching Operations
3. Tribal Newspaper
4. Museum/Cultural Center

A - Agriculture
F - Fish, Aquaculture
M - Mineral
R - Ranching
RV - Recreational Vehicle
T - Timber
TC - Tribal Contract

HISTORICAL PROFILE

Treaty	Language	Tribal Class	Pop	Acreage*	Nation
					NORTHWEST TERRITORIES
1921			778		FORT PROVIDENCE DENE FIRST NATION (YAHTI DEWE K'O)
1900			388		FORT RESOLUTION FIRST NATION
1921			942		FORT SIMPSON FIRST NATION
1921			262		FORT WRIGLEY FIRST NATION
1900			388	818 h	HAY RIVER FIRST NATION (XATLO DEHE)
1921			158		INUVIK NATIVE FIRST NATION
1921			60		JEAN MARIE RIVER FIRST NATION (TTHEDZEHK'EDLIK'OE)
1921			37		KAKISA LAKE FIRST NATION (K'AAGEE TU)
1921			371		LAC LA MARTRE FIRST NATION
1922			65		NAHANNI BUTTE DENE FIRST NATION (NAHZAA DEHE)
1921			240		RAE LAKES DENE FIRST NATION
					RAINBOW VALLEY FIRST NATION (YELLOWKNIFE DENE)
1922			78		SAMBAA K'E DENE FIRST NATION (TROUT LAKE)
1900			419		SNOWDRIFT FIRST NATION (LUTSEL K'E DENE)
					TETLIT GWICH'IN COUNCIL FIRST NATION
1900			853		YELLOWKNIFE 'B' FIRST NATION (DETTAH)

* Note: Some Provinces use hectares, denoted by h. All others are in acres.

NORTHWEST TERRITORIES

Address		Phone Fax	L[1]	EB[2]	N[3]	M[4]
GENERAL DELIVERY, FORT PROVIDENCE, NWT	CANADA X0E 0L0	403-699-3401 403-699-4314		F		
GENERAL DELIVERY, FORT RESOLUTION, NWT	CANADA X0E 0M0	403-394-4556 403-394-5415		TF		
PO BOX 469, FORT SIMPSON, NWT	CANADA X0E 0N0	403-695-3131 403-695-2665		T		
GENERAL DELIVERY, FORT WRIGLEY, NWT	CANADA X0E 1E0	403-581-3321 403-581-3229		F		
PO BOX 1638, HAY RIVER, NWT	CANADA X0E 0R0	403-874-6701 403-874-3229		F		
PO BOX 2570, INUVIK, NWT	CANADA X0E 0T0	403-979-3344 403-979-2054		FM		
GENERAL DELIVERY, JEAN MARIE RIVER, NWT	CANADA X0E 0N0	403-695-9801		TF		
PO BOX 419, HAY RIVER, NWT	CANADA X0E 0R0	403-699-9949 403-699-4314		F		
GENERAL DELIVERY, LAC LA MARTRE, NWT	CANADA X0E 1P0	403-573-3012 403-573-3018		F		
PO BOX 376, NAHANNI BUTTE, NWT	CANADA X0E 0N0	403-770-3555				
GENERAL DELIVERY, RAE LAKES, NWT	CANADA X0E 1R0	403-997-3441 403-997-3411		F		
PO BOX 2514, YELLOWKNIFE, NWT	CANADA X1A 2P8	403-873-8952 403-873-8545				
GENERAL DELIVERY, TROUT LAKE, NWT	CANADA X0E 0N0	403-695-9800 403-695-2029		F		
GENERAL DELIVERY, SNOWDRIFT, NWT	CANADA X0E 1A0	403-370-3051 403-370-3010		F		
PO BOX 88, FORT MCPHERSON, NWT	CANADA X0E 0J0	403-952-2330 403-952-2212				
PO BOX 2514, YELLOWKNIFE, NWT	CANADA X1A 2P8	403-873-4307 403-873-5989		FM		

Legend

1. Lodging - Resort, Motel, RV Park
2. Economic Base - Farming, Fishing, Ranching Operations
3. Tribal Newspaper
4. Museum/Cultural Center

A - Agriculture
F - Fish, Aquaculture
M - Mineral
R - Ranching
RV - Recreational Vehicle
T - Timber
TC - Tribal Contract

HISTORICAL PROFILE

NOVA SCOTIA

Treaty	Language	Tribal Class	Pop	Acreage*	Nation
				2,261	ACADIA FIRST NATION
					ACADIA FIRST NATION WILDCAT RESERVE
1820	ENGLISH	MICMAC	368	959	AFTON FIRST NATION
1851	ENGLISH	MICMAC	162	359	ANNAPOLIS VALLEY FIRST NATION CAMBRIDGE RESERVE
1820	ENGLISH	MICMAC	204	1,726	BEAR RIVER FIRST NATION
1792	ENGLISH	MICMAC	401	2,867	CHAPEL ISLAND FIRST NATION
1832	ENGLISH	MICMAC	2,440	10,364	ESKASONI FIRST NATION
1907	ENGLISH	MICMAC	213	423	HORTON FIRST NATION
1833	ENGLISH	MICMAC	694	2,256	MEMBERTOU FIRST NATION
1867	ENGLISH	MICMAC	761	1,129	MILLBROOK FIRST NATION
1865	ENGLISH	MICMAC	338	2,660	PICTOU LANDING FIRST NATION
1820	ENGLISH	MICMAC	1,592	5,175	SHUBENACADIE FIRST NATION
1833	ENGLISH	MICMAC	510	2,389	WAGMATCOOK FIRST NATION
1833	ENGLISH	MICMAC	536	3,281	WHYCOCOMAGH FIRST NATION

* Note: Some Provinces use hectares, denoted by h. All others are in acres.

NOVA SCOTIA

Address		Phone Fax	L[1]	EB[2]	N[3]	M[4]
BOX 5914C RR 4, YARMOUTH, NS	CANADA B5A 4A8	902-682-2150 902-742-8854				
RR 1, SOUTH BROOKFIELD QUEEN CO, NS	CANADA B0T 1X0	902-682-2150 902-682-3112				
AFTON ANTIGONISH CO, ANTIGONISH, NS	CANADA B0H 1A0	902-386-2881 902-386-2043		TF		
PO BOX 89, CAMBRIDGE STA, NS	CANADA B0P 1G0	902-538-7149 902-538-7734				
PO BOX 210, BEAR RIVER, NS	CANADA B0S 1B0	902-467-3802 902-467-4143		TA		
RR 1, BOX 538, ST PETERS, NS	CANADA B0E 3B0	902-535-3317 902-535-3004		TA		
GENERAL DELIVERY, CAPE BRETON, NS	CANADA B0A 1J0	902-379-2800 902-379-2172				
PO BOX 449, HANTSPORT, NS	CANADA B0P 1P0	902-825-4369 902-538-7734		TA		
111 MEMBERTOU, SYDNEY, NS	CANADA B1S 2M9	902-539-6688 902-539-6645		T	X	
PO BOX 634. TRURO, NS	CANADA B2N 5E5	902-895-4365 902-893-4785	X	TA		
PO BOX 249, TRENTON, NS	CANADA B0K 1X0	902-752-4912 902-755-4715		TA		
PO BOX 350, SHUBENACADIE, NS	CANADA B0N 2H0	902-758-2049 902-758-2017		TA		
PO BOX 237, BADDECK, NS	CANADA B0E 1B0	902-295-2596 902-295-3398		TA		
PO BOX 149 WHYCOCOMAGH, CAPE BRETON, NS	CANADA B0E 3M0	902-756-2337 902-756-2060		TM		

Legend

1. Lodging - Resort, Motel, RV Park
2. Economic Base - Farming, Fishing, Ranching Operations
3. Tribal Newspaper
4. Museum/Cultural Center

A - Agriculture
F - Fish, Aquaculture
M - Mineral
R - Ranching
RV - Recreational Vehicle
T - Timber
TC - Tribal Contract

HISTORICAL PROFILE

ONTARIO

Treaty	Language	Tribal Class	Pop	Acreage*	Nation
					ALBANY FIRST NATION (SINCLAIR ISLAND)
					ALBANY FIRST NATION (VILLAGE OF KASHECHEWAN)
	OJIBWAY	ALGONKIAN	712	1,216.1 h	ALDERVILLE FIRST NATION
	ALGONKIN	ALGONKIAN	1,046	688.8 h	ALGONQUIN FIRST NATION (GOLDEN LAKE)
	OJIBWAY	ALGONKIAN			ANISHINABE OF WAUZHUSHK ONIGUM INDIAN BAND
	OJIBWAY	ALGONKIAN	314		AROLAND FIRST NATION
	CREE	ALGONKIAN	2,032	27,144.6 h	ATTAWAPISKAT FIRST NATION
1961	ENGLISH	ALGONKIAN	447	28 h	BARRIERE LAKE FIRST NATION
	OJIBWAY	ALGONKIAN	1,334	2,224.2 h	BATCHEWANA FIRST NATION OF OJIBWAYS
	CREE	ALGONKIAN	558	12,626.3 h	BEARSKIN LAKE FIRST NATION
	OJIBWAY	ALGONKIAN	1,145	5,435.6 h	BEAUSOLEIL FIRST NATION
					BEAVERHOUSE FIRST NATION
	OJIBWAY	ALGONKIAN	391	6,254.1 h	BIG GRASSY FIRST NATION
	OJIBWAY	ALGONKIAN	262	4,330.7 h	BIG ISLAND FIRST NATION
	CREE	ALGONKIAN	964	29,937.6 h	BIG TROUT LAKE FIRST NATION
	OJIBWAY CREE	ALGONKIAN	427	9,314 h	BRUNSWICK HOUSE FIRST NATION
	POTAWATOMI	ALGONKIAN	158		CALDWELL FIRST NATION

* Note: Some Provinces use hectares, denoted by h. All others are in acres.

ONTARIO

Address		Phone Fax	L[1]	EB[2]	N[3]	M[4]
GENERAL DELIVERY, FORT ALBANY, ON	CANADA P0L 1HW	705-278-1044				
GENERAL DELIVERY, KASHECHEWAN, ON	CANADA P0L 1S0	705-275-4440 705-275-4413				
RR 4 BOX 46, ROSENEATH, ON	CANADA K0K 2X0	416-352-2011 416-352-3242				
PO BOX 100, GOLDEN LAKE, ON	CANADA K0J 1X0	613-625-2800 613-625-2332				
PO BOX 1850, KENORA, ON	CANADA P9N 3X8	807-548-5663 807-548-4877				
PO BOX 390, NAKINA, ON	CANADA P0T 2H0	807-329-5970 807-329-5750				
PO BOX 248, ATTAWAPISKAT, ON	CANADA P0L 1A0	705-997-2166 705-997-2116				
RAPID LAKE VIA VAL d'OR, LA VERENDRYE PARK, ON	CANADA J0W 2G0	819-824-1714 819-729-6903				
236 FRONTENAC, SAULT STE MARIE, ON	CANADA P6A 5K9	705-759-0914 705-759-9171				
BEARSKIN LAKE PO, BEARSKIN LAKE, ON	CANADA P0V 1E0	807-363-2518 807-363-1066				
CEDAR POINT PO, CHRISTIAN ISLAND, ON	CANADA L0K 1C0	705-247-2051 705-247-2239				
PO BOX 1092, KIRKLAND LAKE, ON	CANADA P2N 3L4	705-272-4245 705-272-6737				
GENERAL DELIVERY, MORSON, ON	CANADA P0W 1J0	807-488-5552 807-488-5533				
GENERAL DELIVERY, MORSON, ON	CANADA P0W 1J0	807-488-5602 807-488-5942				
GENERAL DELIVERY, BIG TROUT LAKE, ON	CANADA P0V 1G0	807-537-2263 807-537-2574				
PO BOX 1319, CHAPLEAU, ON	CANADA P0M 1K0	705-864-0174 705-864-1960				
PO BOX 163, BOTHWELL, ON	CANADA N0P 1C0	519-695-3642 519-695-2538				

Legend

1. Lodging - Resort, Motel, RV Park
2. Economic Base - Farming, Fishing, Ranching Operations
3. Tribal Newspaper
4. Museum/Cultural Center

A - Agriculture
F - Fish, Aquaculture
M - Mineral
R - Ranching
RV - Recreational Vehicle
T - Timber
TC - Tribal Contract

HISTORICAL PROFILE

Treaty	Language	Tribal Class	Pop	Acreage*	Nation

ONTARIO

Treaty	Language	Tribal Class	Pop	Acreage*	Nation
	CREE	ALGONKIAN	641	9,172.3 h	CARIBOU LAKE FIRST NATION
	OJIBWAY	ALGONKIAN	432	218 h	CAT LAKE FIRST NATION
	CREE	ALGONKIAN	207	108.1 h	CHAPLEAU CREE FIRST NATION
	OJIBWAY	ALGONKIAN	28	1,020 h	CHAPLEAU OJIBWAY FIRST NATION
	OJIBWAY	ALGONKIAN	455	1,353 h	CHIPPEWAS OF GEORGINA ISLAND FIRST NATION
	OJIBWAY	ALGONKIAN	1,476	848.8 h	CHIPPEWAS OF KETTLE & STONY POINT FIRST NATIONS
	OJIBWAY	ALGONKIAN	1,561	7,183.3 h	CHIPPEWAS OF NAWASH FIRST NATION (CAPE CROKER)
	OJIBWAY	ALGONKIAN	926	908.4 h	CHIPPEWAS OF RAMA FIRST NATION
	OJIBWAY	ALGONKIAN	1,380	1,280.5 h	CHIPPEWAS OF SARNIA FIRST NATION
	OJIBWAY	ALGONKIAN	1652	3646.8 h	CHIPPEWAS OF SAUGEEN FIRST NATION
	OJIBWAY	ALGONKIAN	1,173	5,061.5 h	CHIPPEWAS OF THE THAMES FIRST NATION
	OJIBWAY	ALGONKIAN	70	958.3 h	COCKBURN ISLAND FIRST NATION
	CREE	ALGONKIAN	1,073	6,218.5 h	CONSTANCE LAKE FIRST NATION CONSTANCE LAKE INDIAN RESERVE
	OJIBWAY	ALGONKIAN	1,341	6,422.5 h	COUCHICHING FIRST NATION
	OJIBWAY	ALGONKIAN	1,296	875.7 h	CURVE LAKE FIRST NATION
	OJIBWAY	ALGONKIAN	181	3,257 h	DALLES FIRST NATION
	CREE	ALGONKIAN	673	1,654 h	DEER LAKE FIRST NATION

* Note: Some Provinces use hectares, denoted by h. All others are in acres.

Address		Phone Fax	L[1]	EB[2]	N[3]	M[4]
ONTARIO						
GENERAL DELIVERY, WEAGAMOW LAKE, ON	CANADA P0V 2Y0	807-469-5191 807-469-1315				
2 BACK RD, W CAT LAKE, ON	CANADA P0V 1J0	807-347-2100 807-347-2116				
PO BOX 400, CHAPLEAU, ON	CANADA P0M 1K0	705-864-0784 705-864-1760				
PO BOX 279, CHAPLEAU, ON	CANADA P0M 1K0	705-864-1090 705-864-2366				
BOX A3 RR 2, SUTTON WEST, ON	CANADA L0E 1R0	705-437-1337 705-437-4597				
RR 2, FOREST, ON	CANADA N0N 1J0	519-786-2125 519-786-2108				
RR 5, WIARTON, ON	CANADA N0H 2T0	519-534-1689 519-534-2130				
BOX 35 RAMA RD, RAMA, ON	CANADA L0K 1T0	705-325-3611 705-325-0879				
978 TASHMOO AVE, SARNIA, ON,	CANADA N7T 7H5	519-336-8410 591-336-0382				
RR 1, SOUTHAMPTON, ON	CANADA N0H 2L0	519-797-2781 519-797-2978				
RR 1, MUNCEY, ON	CANADA N0L 1Y0	519-264-1526 519-264-2203				
GENERAL DELIVERY, SILVERWATER MANITOULIN ISLD, ON	CANADA P0P 1Y0	705-283-3959 705-674-2372				
GENERAL DELIVERY, CALSTOCK, ON	CAMADA P0L 1B0	705-463-4511 705-463-2222				
C/O PO BOX 723, FORT FRANCES, ON	CANADA P9A 3N1	807-274-3228 807-274-6458				
CURVE LAKE PO BOX 100, CURVE LAKE, ON	CANADA K0L 1R0	705-657-8045 705-657-8708				
PO BOX 1770, KENORA, ON	CANADA P9N 3X7	807-548-1929 807-468-4034				
PO BOX 335, DEER LAKE, ON	CANADA P0V 1N0	705-775-0053 705-775-2220				

Legend

1. Lodging - Resort, Motel, RV Park
2. Economic Base - Farming, Fishing, Ranching Operations
3. Tribal Newspaper
4. Museum/Cultural Center

A - Agriculture
F - Fish, Aquaculture
M - Mineral
R - Ranching
RV - Recreational Vehicle
T - Timber
TC - Tribal Contract

HISTORICAL PROFILE

Treaty	Language	Tribal Class	Pop	Acreage*	Nation
ONTARIO					
	DELAWARE	ALGONKIAN	754	1,281 h	DELAWARE OF THE THAMES FIRST NATION (MORAVIANTOWN)
	OJIBWAY	ALGONKIAN	672	12,262.2 h	DOKIS FIRST NATION
	OJIBWAY	ALGONKIAN	1,449	25,900.3 h	EABAMETOONG FIRST NATION (FORT HOPE)
	OJIBWAY	ALGONKIAN	278	3,592 h	EAGLE LAKE FIRST NATION
	OJIBWAY CREE	ALGONKIAN	96	5,957.1 h	FLYING POST FIRST NATION
	OJIBWAY CREE	ALGONKIAN			FORT ALBANY FIRST NATION
	CREE	ALGONKIAN	392	3,958.7 h	FORT SEVERN FIRST NATION
	OJIBWAY	ALGONKIAN	969	5,815.1 h	FORT WILLIAM FIRST NATION
	OJIBWAY	ALGONKIAN	1,424	14,901.3 h	GARDEN RIVER FIRST NATION
					GIBSON FIRST NATION
	OJIBWAY	ALGONKIAN	522	6,978 h	GINOOGAMING FIRST NATION
	OJIBWAY	ALGONKIAN	825	4,145 h	GRASSY NARROWS FIRST NATION
	OJIBWAY	ALGONKIAN	655	3,940 h	GULL BAY FIRST NATION
	OJIBWAY	ALGONKIAN	349	12,157.8 h	HENVEY INLET FIRST NATION
	OJIBWAY	ALGONKIAN	334	790.4 h	HIAWATHA FIRST NATION
					HORNEPAYNE FIRST NATION
	OJIBWAY	ALGONKIAN	1,109	11,834.3 h	ISLINGTON FIRST NATION

* Note: Some Provinces use hectares, denoted by h. All others are in acres.

Address		Phone Fax	L[1]	EB[2]	N[3]	M[4]
ONTARIO						
RR 3, THAMESVILLE, ON	CANADA N0P 2K0	519-692-3936 519-692-5522				
DOKIS BAY, MONTEVILLE, ON	CANADA P0M 2K0	807-763-2200 705-763-2087				
PO BOX 70 EABMET LAKE, VIA PICKLE LAKE, ON	CANADA P0T 1L0	807-242-7221 807-242-1440				
PO BOX 27, EAGLE RIVER, ON	CANADA P0V 1S0	807-755-5526 807-755-5696				
PO BOX 1027, NIPIGON, ON	CANADA P0T 2J0	807-887-3071 807-887-1138				
GENERAL DELIVERY, FORT ALBANY, ON	CANADA P0L 1H0	705-278-1044 705-278-1193				
GENERAL DELIVERY, FORT SEVERN, ON	CANADA P0V 1W0	807-478-2572 807-478-1103				
PO BOX 786 STATION F, THUNDER BAY, ON	CANADA P7C 4Z2	807-623-9543 807-623-5190				
BOX 7 SITE 5 RR 4, GARDEN RIVER, ON	CANADA P6A 5K9	705-942-4011 705-942-7533				
BALA PO BOX 327, BALA, ON	CANADA P0C 1A0	705-762-3343				
PO BOX 89, LONG LAC, ON	CANADA P0T 2A0	807-876-2242 807-876-4337				
GENERAL DELIVERY, GRASSY MEADOWS, ON	CANADA P0T 2A0	807-925-2201 807-925-2649				
GULL BAY PO, GULL BAY, ON	CANADA P0T 1P0	807-982-2101 807-982-2290				
GENERAL DELIVERY, PICKEREL, ON	CANADA P0G 1J0	705-857-2331 705-857-3021				
RR 2, KEENE, ON	CANADA K0L 2G0	705-295-4421 705-294-4424				
PO BOX 465, SPRUCE HORNEPAYNE, ON	CANADA P0M 1Z0	807-868-2039 807-868-2701				
WHITEDOG PO, WHITEDOG, ON	CANADA P0X 1P0	807-927-2068 807-927-2071				

Legend

1. Lodging - Resort, Motel, RV Park
2. Economic Base - Farming, Fishing, Ranching Operations
3. Tribal Newspaper
4. Museum/Cultural Center

A - Agriculture
F - Fish, Aquaculture
M - Mineral
R - Ranching
RV - Recreational Vehicle
T - Timber
TC - Tribal Contract

Treaty	Language	Tribal Class	Pop	Acreage*	Nation
ONTARIO					
	CREE	ALGONKIAN	545	10,808.5 h	KASABONIKA FIRST NATION
	CREE	ALGONKIAN	476		KEE-WAY-WIN FIRST NATION
	CREE	ALGONKIAN	318	6,962.6 h	KINGFISHER LAKE FIRST NATION
	OJIBWAY	ALGONKIAN	322	4,948 h	LAC DES MILLES LACS FIRST NATION
	OJIBWAY	ALGONKIAN	271	6,214 h	LAC LA CROIX FIRST NATION
	OJIBWAY	ALGONKIAN	1,874	26,821.5 h	LAC SEUL FIRST NATION
	OJIBWAY	ALGONKIAN			LAKE NIPIGON OJIBWAY FIRST NATION
	OJIBWAY	ALGONKIAN	223		LANSDOWNE HOUSE FIRST NATION
1850	OJIBWAY	ALGONKIAN	870	217.3 h	LONG LAKE FIRST NATION # 58
	OJIBWAY	ALGONKIAN	137	4,714.7 h	MAGNETAWAN FIRST NATION
	OJIBWAY	ALGONKIAN	362	7,770.1 h	MARTIN FALLS FIRST NATION
	OJIBWAY CREE	ALGONKIAN	333	4,158.6 h	MATACHEWAN FIRST NATION
	OJIBWAY	ALGONKIAN	236	5,261 h	MATTAGAMI FIRST NATION
	CREE	ALGONKIAN	17		MCDOWELL LAKE FIRST NATION
1850	OJIBWAY	ALGONKIAN	394	3,630.5 h	MICHIPICOTEN FIRST NATION
	CREE	ALGONKIAN	156	87.4 h	MISSANABIE FIRST NATION
	OJIBWAY	ALGONKIAN	677	1,977.2 h	MISSISAUGA FIRST NATION

* Note: Some Provinces use hectares, denoted by h. All others are in acres.

Address		Phone Fax	L[1]	EB[2]	N[3]	M[4]
ONTARIO						
PO BOX 106, KASHECHEWAN, ON	CANADA P0V 1Y0	807-535-2547 807-535-1152				
SANDY LAKE, VIA FAVOURABLE LAKE, ON	CANADA P0V 1V0	807-774-1215 807-737-3501				
GENERAL DELIVERY, KINGFISHER, ON	CANADA P0V 1Z0	807-532-0067 807-532-0063				
905 TUNGSTEN, THUNDER BAY, ON	CANADA P7B 5Z3	807-622-6930 807-468-3908				
PO BOX 640, FORT FRANCES, ON	CANADA P9A 3N9	705-485-2431 807-485-2583				
GENERAL DELIVERY, LAC SEUL, ON	CANADA P0V 2A0	807-582-3211 807-582-3493				
PO BOX 241 ROCKY BAY RESERVE, BEARDMORE, ON	CANADA P0T 2G0	807-885-5441				
LANSDOWNE HOUSE, VIA PICKLE LAKE, ON	CANADA P0T 1Z0	807-479-2570 807-479-1138				
PO BOX 609, LONG LAC, ON	CANADA P0T 2A0	807-876-2292 807-876-2757				
BOX 15 RR 1, BRITT, ON	CANADA P0G 1A0	705-383-2477 705-383-2566				
OGOKI, VIA NAKINA, ON	CANADA P0T 2L0	807-349-2509 807-349-2511				
PO BOX 208, MATACHEWAN, ON	CANADA P0K 1M0	705-565-2288 705-565-2288				
PO BOX 99, GOGAMA, ON	CANADA P0M 1W0	705-894-2072 705-894-2887				
PO BOX 740, RED LAKE, ON	CANADA P0V 2M0	807-727-2803				
BOX 26 SITE 7 RR 1, WAWA, ON	CANADA P0S 1K0	705-856-4455 705-856-1642				
217 JOHN, SAULT STE MARIE, ON	CANADA P6A 1P4	705-942-0123				
PO BOX 1299, BLIND RIVER, ON	CANADA P0R 1B0	705-356-1621 705-356-1740				

Legend

1. Lodging - Resort, Motel, RV Park
2. Economic Base - Farming, Fishing, Ranching Operations
3. Tribal Newspaper
4. Museum/Cultural Center

A - Agriculture
F - Fish, Aquaculture
M - Mineral
R - Ranching
RV - Recreational Vehicle
T - Timber
TC - Tribal Contract

ONTARIO

Treaty	Language	Tribal Class	Pop	Acreage*	Nation
	OJIBWAY	ALGONKIAN	90	321.4 h	MISSISSAUGAS OF SCUGOG FIRST NATION
	OJIBWAY	ALGONKIAN	1,110	2,392.6 h	MISSISSAUGAS OF THE CREDIT FIRST NATION
					MOCREEBEC INDIAN GOVERMENT FIRST NATION
	MOHAWK	IROQUIAN	7,036	3,646.8 h	MOHAWKS OF AKWESASNE FIRST NATION
	MOHAWK	IROQUIAN	485	5,990.7 h	MOHAWKS OF GIBSON FIRST NATION
	MOHAWK	IROQUIAN	5,039	7,274.3 h	MOHAWKS OF THE BAY OF QUINTE FIRST NATION
	OJIBWAY	ALGONKIAN	273	2,505 h	MOOSE DEER POINT FIRST NATION
	CREE	ALGONKIAN	2,394	17,393 h	MOOSE FACTORY FIRST NATION
	DELAWARE	ALGONKIAN	369	1,054 h	MUNSEE-DELAWARE FIRST NATION
	CREE	ALGONKIAN	270	1,939.7 h	MUSKRAT DAM FIRST NATION
	OJIBWAY	ALGONKIAN	235	2,489.3 h	NAICATCHEWENIN FIRST NATION
	CREE	ALGONKIAN	135	2,188 h	NEW POST FIRST NATION
	CREE	ALGONKIAN	131		NEW SLATE FALLS FIRST NATION
	OJIBWAY	ALGONKIAN	288		NIBINAMIK FIRST NATION (SUMMER BEAVER)
	OJIBWAY	ALGONKIAN	160	4,085.7 h	NICICKOUSEMENECANING FIRST NATION
	OJIBWAY	ALGONKIAN	110		NIPIGON OJIBWAY FIRST NATION
	OJIBWAY	ALGONKIAN	1,453	21,007.3 h	NIPISSING FIRST NATION

* Note: Some Provinces use hectares, denoted by h. All others are in acres.

Address		Phone Fax	L [1]	EB [2]	N [3]	M [4]

ONTARIO

RR 5, PORT PERRY, ON	CANADA L9L 1B6	416-985-3337 416-985-8828				
RR 6, HAGERSVILLE, ON	CANADA N0A 1H0	416-768-1133 416-768-1225				
PO BOX 4, MOOSE FACTORY, ON	CANADA P0L 1W0	705-658-4769 705-658-4487				
PO BOX 579, CORNWALL, ON	CANADA K6H 5T3	613-575-2348 613-575-2181				
PO BOX 327, BALA, ON	CANADA P0C 1A0	705-762-3343 705-762-5744				
RR 1, DESERONTO, ON	CANADA K0K 1X0	613-396-3424 613-396-3627				
PO BOX 119, MACTIER, ON	CANADA P0C 1H0	705-375-5209 705-375-0532				
PO BOX 190, MOOSE FACTORY, ON	CANADA P0L 1W0	705-658-4619 705-658-4734				
RR 1, MUNCEY, ON	CANADA N0L 1Y0	519-289-5396 519-289-5156				
GENERAL DELIVERY, MUSKRAT DAM, ON	CANADA P0V 3B0	807-471-2573 807-471-2540				
BOX 12 RR 1, DEVLIN, ON	CANADA P0W 1C0	807-486-3407 807-274-8761				
BOX 2 RR 2 COMP O, COCHRANE, ON	CANADA P0L 1C0	705-272-5685 807-272-3060				
SLATE FALLS, VIA SIOUX LOOKOUT, ON	CANADA P0V 2T0	0920 0120				
SUMMER BEAVER, VIA PICKLE LAKE, ON	CANADA P0T 3B0	807-593-2131 807-593-2270				
PO BOX 68, FORT FRANCES, ON	CANADA P9A 3M5	807-481-2536 807-481-2511				
PO BOX 241, BEARDMORE, ON	CANADA P0T 2B0	807-885-5441 807-885-3231				
RR 1, STURGEON FALLS, ON	CANADA P0H 2G0	705-753-2050 705-753-0207				

Legend

1. Lodging - Resort, Motel, RV Park
2. Economic Base - Farming, Fishing, Ranching Operations
3. Tribal Newspaper
4. Museum/Cultural Center

A - Agriculture
F - Fish, Aquaculture
M - Mineral
R - Ranching
RV - Recreational Vehicle
T - Timber
TC - Tribal Contract

HISTORICAL PROFILE

Treaty	Language	Tribal Class	Pop	Acreage*	Nation

ONTARIO

Treaty	Language	Tribal Class	Pop	Acreage*	Nation
					NORTH CARIBOU LAKE FIRST NATION
	CREE	ALGONKIAN	319	1,816 h	NORTH SPIRIT LAKE FIRST NATION
	OJIBWAY	ALGONKIAN	257	2,586 h	NORTHWEST ANGLE FIRST NATION # 33
	OJIBWAY	ALGONKIAN	175	5,310.4 h	NORTHWEST ANGLE FIRST NATION # 37
	OJIBWAY	ALGONKIAN	436	2,059 h	OJIBWAYS OF ONEGAMING FIRST NATION
	OJIBWAY	ALGONKIAN	693	323.8 h	OJIBWAYS OF PIC RIVER FIRST NATION
	OJIBWAY POTAWATOMI	ALGONKIAN	2,826	15,891.1 h	OJIBWAYS OF WALPOLE ISLAND FIRST NATION
	ONEIDA	IROQUIAN	3,649	2,133.5 h	ONEIDAS OF THE THAMES FIRST NATION
					ONYOTA'A:KA FIRST NATION
	OJIBWAY	ALGONKIAN	976	18,896.4 h	OSNABURG FIRST NATION
1850	OJIBWAY	ALGONKIAN	175	225 h	PAYS PLAT FIRST NATION
					PIC MOBERT FIRST NATION
	OJIBWAY	ALGONKIAN	1,445	1,808 h	PIKANGIKUM FIRST NATION
	OJIBWAY	ALGONKIAN	243	702.2 h	POPLAR HILL FIRST NATION
	OJIBWAY	ALGONKIAN	651	2,463.9 h	RAINY RIVER FIRST NATION (MANITOU)
1850	OJIBWAY	ALGONKIAN	884	197.4 h	RED ROCK FIRST NATION
	OJIBWAY	ALGONKIAN	414	13.4 h	ROCKY BAY FIRST NATION

* Note: Some Provinces use hectares, denoted by h. All others are in acres.

ONTARIO

Address		Phone Fax	L[1]	EB[2]	N[3]	M[4]
BOX 70, WEAGAMOW LAKE, ON	CANADA P0V 2Y0	807-469-5191				
PO BOX 70, NORTH SPIRIT LAKE, ON	CANADA P0V 2G0	0920				
PO BOX 2270, KENORA, ON	CANADA P0X 1N0	807-226-5353 807-226-1164				
GENERAL DELIVERY, SIOUX NARROWS, ON	CANADA P0X 1N0	807-226-5353 807-226-1164				
PO BOX 160, NESTOR FALLS, ON	CANADA P0X 1K0	807-484-2162 807-484-2737				
GENERAL DELIVERY, HERON BAY, ON	CANADA P0T 1R0	807-229-1749 807-229-1944				
RR 3, WALLACEBURG, ON	CANADA N8A 1R0	519-627-1481 519-627-0440				
RR 2, SOUTHWOLD, ON	CANADA N0L 2G0	519-652-3244 519-652-9287				
RR 2, SOUTHWOLD, ON	CANADA N0L 2G0	519-652-3244				
GENERAL DELIVERY, OSNABURG, ON	CANADA P0V 2H0	807-928-2414 807-928-2077				
PO BOX 819, SCHREIBER, ON	CANADA P0T 2S0	807-824-2541 807-824-2206				
MOBERT, ON	CANADA P0M 2J0	807-822-2131 807-822-2134				
GENERAL DELIVERY, PIKANGIKUM, ON	CANADA P0V 2L0	807-773-5578 807-773-5536				
PO BOX 5004, RED HILL, ON	CANADA P0V 2M0	807-772-8838 807-772-8876				
PO BOX 450, EMO, ON	CANADA P0W 1E0	807-482-2479 807-482-2603				
PO BOX 1030, NIPIGON, ON	CANADA P0T 2J0	807-887-2510 807-887-3446				
GENERAL DELIVERY, MACDIAMID, ON	CANADA P0T 2B0	807-885-3401 807-885-3231				

Legend

1. Lodging - Resort, Motel, RV Park
2. Economic Base - Farming, Fishing, Ranching Operations
3. Tribal Newspaper
4. Museum/Cultural Center

A - Agriculture
F - Fish, Aquaculture
M - Mineral
R - Ranching
RV - Recreational Vehicle
T - Timber
TC - Tribal Contract

ONTARIO

Treaty	Language	Tribal Class	Pop	Acreage*	Nation
	CREE	ALGONKIAN	479	8,144.6 h	SACHIGO LAKE FIRST NATION
	OJIBWAY	ALGONKIAN	1,570	11,331.4 h	SAGAMOK ANISHNAWBEK FIRST NATION (SPANISH RIVER)
1850	OJIBWAY	ALGONKIAN	93		SAND POINT FIRST NATION
	CREE	ALGONKIAN	1,435	4,266 h	SANDY LAKE FIRST NATION
					SAUGEEN FIRST NATION
	OJIBWAY	ALGONKIAN	155		SAUGEEN FIRST NATION (SAVANT LAKE)
	OJIBWAY	ALGONKIAN	503	5,152.2 h	SEINE RIVER FIRST NATION
	OJIBWAY	ALGONKIAN	804	10,879 h	SERPENT RIVER FIRST NATION
	OJIBWAY	ALGONKIAN	323	4,508.8 h	SHAWANAGA FIRST NATION
	OTTAWA OJIBWAY	ALGONKIAN	207	2,070.5 h	SHEGUIANDAH FIRST NATION
	OJIBWAY	ALGONKIAN	302	2,023.5 h	SHESHEGWANING FIRST NATION
	OJIBWAY	ALGONKIAN	431	3,824.7 h	SHOAL LAKE FIRST NATION # 39
	OJIBWAY	ALGONKIAN	289	2,579 h	SHOAL LAKE FIRST NATION # 40
	MOHAWK ONEIDA ONANDACA +3	IROQUIAN	16,011	18,174.2 h	SIX NATIONS OF THE GRAND RIVER FIRST NATIONS
	OJIBWAY	ALGONKIAN	54	1,562.6 h	STANJIKOMING FIRST NATION
	OJIBWAY	ALGONKIAN	438	627.3 h	SUCKER CREEK FIRST NATION
					SUMMER BEAVER FIRST NATION

* Note: Some Provinces use hectares, denoted by h. All others are in acres.

ONTARIO

Address		Phone Fax	L[1]	EB[2]	N[3]	M[4]
GENERAL DELIVERY, SACHIGO LAKE, ON	CANADA P0V 2B0	807-595-2577 805-595-1119				
PO BOX 610, MASSEY, ON	CANADA P0P 1P0	705-865-5421 705-865-3307				
104 SYNDICATE AVE N, THUNDER BAY, ON	CANADA P7C 3V7	807-623-4227 807-623-3411				
SANDY LAKE, VIA FAVOURABLE LAKE, ON	CANADA P0V 1V0	807-774-3421 807-774-1040				
RR 1, SOUTHAMPTON, ON	CANADA N0H 2L0	519-797-2218 519-797-2983				
GENERAL DELIVERY, SAVANT LAKE, ON	CANADA P0V 2S0	807-584-2908 807-584-2243				
PO BOX 124, MINE CENTRE, ON	CANADA P0W 1H0	807-599-2224 807-559-2665				
48 VILLAGE RD BOX 14, CUTLER, ON	CANADA P0P 1B0	705-844-2418 705-844-2757				
RR 1, NOBEL, ON	CANADA P0G 1G0	705-366-2526 705-366-2740				
PO BOX 101, SHEGUIANDAH, ON	CANADA P0P 1W0	705-368-2781 705-368-3697				
PO BOX C-1, SHESHEGWANING, ON	CANADA P0P 1X0	705-283-3292 705-283-3481				
GENERAL DELIVERY, KEJICK, ON	CANADA P0X 1E0	807-733-2560 807-733-3106				
GENERAL DELIVERY, KEJICK, ON	CANADA P0X 1E0	807-733-2315 807-733-3115				
PO BOX 1, OSHWEKEN, ON	CANADA N0A 1M0	519-445-2201 519-445-4208				
PO BOX 609, FORT FRANCES, ON	CANADA P9A 3M6	807-274-2188 807-274-8761				
BOX 21 RR 1, LITTLE CURRENT, ON	CANADA P0P 1K0	705-368-2228 705-368-3563				
SUMMER BEAVER, VIA PICKLE LAKE, ON	CANADA P0T 3B0	807-593-2131 807-593-2232				

Legend

1. Lodging - Resort, Motel, RV Park
2. Economic Base - Farming, Fishing, Ranching Operations
3. Tribal Newspaper
4. Museum/Cultural Center

A - Agriculture
F - Fish, Aquaculture
M - Mineral
R - Ranching
RV - Recreational Vehicle
T - Timber
TC - Tribal Contract

Treaty	Language	Tribal Class	Pop	Acreage*	Nation
ONTARIO					
	OJIBWAY CREE	ALGONKIAN	392	293.4 h	TEMAGAMI ANISHNABAI FIRST NATION (BEAR ISLAND)
	OJIBWAY	ALGONKIAN	238	942 h	THESSALON FIRST NATION
					WABASEEMOONG FIRST NATION
	OJIBWAY	ALGONKIAN	124	3,254.5 h	WABAUSKANG FIRST NATION
	OJIBWAY	ALGONKIAN	287	5,209.2 h	WABIGOON LAKE OJIBWAY NATION
	OJIBWAY CREE	ALGONKIAN	118	7,770.1 h	WAHGOSHIG FIRST NATION (ABITIBI #70)
	OJIBWAY	ALGONKIAN	48	1,036 h	WAHNAPITAE FIRST NATION
	OJIBWAY	ALGONKIAN			WALPOLE ISLAND FIRST NATION
	CREE	ALGONKIAN	245	5,631.5 h	WAPEKEKA FIRST NATION (ANGLING LAKE)
	OJIBWAY	ALGONKIAN	722	7,486.8 h	WASAUKSING FIRST NATION (PARRY ISLAND)
	OJIBWAY	ALGONKIAN	161	3,237.5 h	WASHAGAMIS BAY FIRST NATION (MCKENZIE PORTAGE)
	OJIBWAY	ALGONKIAN	346	2,207 h	WAUZHUSHK ONIGUM FIRST NATION (RAT PORTAGE)
	CREE	ALGONKIAN	61		WAWAKAPEWIN FIRST NATION
	OJIBWAY	ALGONKIAN	498		WEBEQUI FIRST NATION
	OJIBWAY CREE	ALGONKIAN	330	5,310 h	WEENUSK FIRST NATION (PEAWANUK)
	OJIBWAY	ALGONKIAN	1,626	3,094.7 h	WEST BAY FIRST NATION
	OJIBWAY	ALGONKIAN	715	4,274.5 h	WHITEFISH BAY FIRST NATION

* Note: Some Provinces use hectares, denoted by h. All others are in acres.

ONTARIO

Address		Phone Fax	L[1]	EB[2]	N[3]	M[4]
GENERAL DELIVERY, BEAR ISLAND, ON	CANADA P0H 2H0	705-237-8943 705-237-8959				
BOX 9 RR 3, THESSALON, ON	CANADA P0R 1L0	705-842-2323 705-842-2332				
WHITEDOG PO, WHITEDOG, ON	CANADA P0X 1P0	807-927-2068 807-927-2146				
PO BOX 1730, KENORA, ON	CANADA P9N 3X7	807-547-2555 807-468-3908				
PO BOX 41, DINORWIC, ON	CANADA P0V 1P0	807-938-6684 807-938-1166				
PO BOX 722, MATHESON, ON	CANADA P0K 1N0	705-567-4891 705-568-4891				
PO BOX 129, WAHNAPITAE, ON	CANADA P0M 3C0	705-694-5632				
RR 3, WALLACEBURG, ON	CANADA N8A 4K9	519-627-1481 519-627-0440				
GENERAL DELIVERY, ANGLING LAKE, ON	CANADA P0V 1B0	807-537-2315 807-537-2396				
PO BOX 253, PARRY ISLAND, ON	CANADA P2A 2X4	705-746-2531 705-746-5984				
PO BOX 625, KEEWATIN, ON	CANADA P0X 1C0	807-543-2532 807-543-2964				
PO BOX 1850, KENORA, ON	CANADA P9N 3X7	807-548-5663 807-548-4877				
GENERAL DELIVERY, LONG DOG LAKE, ON	CANADA P0V 1G0	807-442-2567				
PO BOX 176, WEBEQUI, ON	CANADA P0T 3A0	807-353-6531 807-353-1218				
PO BOX 1, WINISK, ON	CANADA P0L 2H0	705-473-2554 705-473-2503				
PO BOX 2, WEST BAY, ON	CANADA P0P 1G0	705-377-5362 705-377-4890				
PAWITIK PO, PAWITIK, ON	CANADA P0X 1L0	807-226-5411 807-226-5389				

Legend

1. Lodging - Resort, Motel, RV Park
2. Economic Base - Farming, Fishing, Ranching Operations
3. Tribal Newspaper
4. Museum/Cultural Center

A - Agriculture
F - Fish, Aquaculture
M - Mineral
R - Ranching
RV - Recreational Vehicle
T - Timber
TC - Tribal Contract

HISTORICAL PROFILE

Treaty	Language	Tribal Class	Pop	Acreage*	Nation
ONTARIO					
	OJIBWAY CREE	ALGONKIAN	500	17,704.5 h	WHITEFISH LAKE FIRST NATION (NAUGHTON)
	OJIBWAY	ALGONKIAN	680	5,673.4 h	WHITEFISH RIVER FIRST NATION (BIRCH ISLAND)
1850	OJIBWAY	ALGONKIAN	588		WHITESAND FIRST NATION
	OJIBWAY OTTAWA	ALGONKIAN	4,825	46,701.7 h	WIKWEMIKONG FIRST NATION
	CREE	ALGONKIAN	377	9,649.5 h	WUNNUMIN LAKE FIRST NATION
PRINCE EDWARD ISLAND					
	ENGLISH	MICMAC	282	332.96	ABEGWEIT FIRST NATION
1870	ENGLISH	MICMAC	537	1,320	LENNOX ISLAND FIRST NATION
QUEBEC					
1851	ENGLISH	ABENAKI	167	79 h	ABENAKIS DE WOLINAK FIRST NATION RESERVE (INDIENNE DE WOLINAK)
1956	FRENCH	ALGONKIAN	593	88.5 h	ABITIBIWINNI FIRST NATION
		ALGONKIAN			ALGONQUINS OF BARRIERE LAKE FIRST NATION
1906	FRENCH	ALGONKIAN	1,334	771.36 h	ATTIKAMEKS DE MANOUANE FIRST NATION

* Note: Some Provinces use hectares, denoted by h. All others are in acres.

Address		Phone Fax	L[1]	EB[2]	N[3]	M[4]
ONTARIO						
PO BOX 39, NAUGHTON, ON	CANADA P0M 2M0	705-692-3651 705-692-5010				
GENERAL DELIVERY, BIRCH ISLAND, ON	CANADA P0P 1A0	705-285-4335 705-285-4532				
PO BOX 68, ARMSTRONG, ON	CANADA P0T 1A0	807-583-2177 807-583-2170				
PO BOX 112, WIKWEMIKONG, ON	CANADA P0P 2J0	705-859-3122 705-859-3851				
GENERAL DELIVERY, WUNNUMIN LAKE, ON	CANADA P0V 2Z0	807-442-0051 807-442-2627				
PRINCE EDWARD ISLAND						
PO BOX 220, CORNWALL, PEI	CANADA C0A 1H0	902-675-3842 902-368-5544				
GENERAL DELIVERY, LENNOX ISLAND, PEI	CANADA C0B 1P0	902-831-2779 902-831-3153	X	A		
QUEBEC						
4680 BOUL DANUBE, BECANCOUR, PQ	CANADA G0X 1B0	819-294-9835 819-294-6697	X			
PO BOX 86, PIKOGAN AMOS, PQ	CANADA J9T 3A3	819-732-6591 819-732-1569		T	X	
LA VERENDRYE PARK, RAPID LAKE, PQ	CANADA J0W 2G0	819-824-1734 819-824-1734				
331 RUE SIMON OTTAWA, MANOUANE, PQ	CANADA J0K 1M0	819-971-8813 819-971-8848		T	X	

Legend

1. Lodging - Resort, Motel, RV Park
2. Economic Base - Farming, Fishing, Ranching Operations
3. Tribal Newspaper
4. Museum/Cultural Center

A - Agriculture
F - Fish, Aquaculture
M - Mineral
R - Ranching
RV - Recreational Vehicle
T - Timber
TC - Tribal Contract

HISTORICAL PROFILE

Treaty	Language	Tribal Class	Pop	Acreage*	Nation
					QUEBEC
1950	FRENCH	ATTKAMEK	1,391	926.76 h	ATTIKAMEKS OBEDJIWAN FIRST NATION
		CREE			CHIBOUGAMAU FIRST NATION
1974	ENGLISH	CREE	2,225	1,309.56 h	CHISASIBI FIRST NATION
1958	FRENCH	HURON	2,295	111.31 h	CONSEIL DE LA NATION HURONNE-WENDAT
1974	ENGLISH	CREE	411	489.53 sq.k.	EASTMAIN FIRST NATION
	FRENCH	MICMAC	354		GASPE FIRST NATION
	FRENCH	ALGONKIAN	313	12.14 h	GRAND LAC VICTORIA FIRST NATION
1851	ENGLISH	MOHAWK	6,839	12,965.37 h	KAHNAWAKE FIRST NATION
1831	ENGLISH	MOHAWK	1,591	8,866.48 h	KANESATAKE FIRST NATION
		ALGONKIAN			KIPAWA KEBAOWECK FIRST NATION
					KITIGAN ZIBI ANISHINABEG FIRST NATION
1962	ENGLISH	ALGONKIAN	969	275.01 h	LAC SIMON FIRST NATION
	ENGLISH	ALGONKIAN	461	87.84. h	LONG POINT FIRST NATION
1874	FRENCH	MALECITE	229	173.18 h	MALECITES DE VIGER FIRST NATION
1974	ENGLISH	MICMAC	782	182.26 h	MICMACS OF GESGAPEGIAG FIRST NATION-MARIA INDIAN RESERVE
1974	ENGLISH	CREE	2,640	1,380.43 sq.k.	MISTISSINI FIRST NATION
	MOHAWK	MOHAWK			MOHAWKS OF KAHNAWAKE

* Note: Some Provinces use hectares, denoted by h, sq.k. denotes square kilometers. All others are in acres.

QUEBEC

Address		Phone Fax	L[1]	EB[2]	N[3]	M[4]
RESERVE INDIENNE D'OBEDJIWAY, VIA ROBERVAL, PQ	CANADA G0W 3B0	819-974-8837 819-974-8828		T	X	
329 3RD, CHIBOUGAMAU, PQ	CANADA G8P 1N4	418-748-2617 418-748-2061				
PO BOX 150, CHISASIBI, PQ	CANADA J0B 1E0	819-855-2878 819-855-2875	X		X	
255 PL CHEF MICHEL LAVEAU, WENDAKE, PQ	CANADA G0A 4V0	418-843-3767 418-842-1108	X		X	
GENERAL DELIVERY, EASTMAIN, PQ	CANADA J0M 1W0	819-977-0211 819-977-0281	X		X	
BOX 69, FONTENELLE GASPE, PQ	CANADA G0E 1H0	418-368-6005 418-368-1272				
GRAND LAC VICTORIA, VIA LOUVICOURT, PQ	CANADA J0Y 1Y0	819-736-2351 819-736-7311				
PO BOX 720, KAHNAWAKE, PQ	CANADA J0L 1B0	514-632-7500 514-638-5958		M	X	X
PO BOX 607, KANESATAKE, PQ	CANADA J0N 1E0	514-479-8373 514-479-8249		TA	X	
PO BOX 787, TEMISCAMING, PQ	CANADA J0Z 3R0	819-627-3455 819-627-9428				
PO BOX 309, MANIWAKI, PQ	CANADA J9E 3C9	819-449-5170 819-449-5171				
LAC SIMON PO, LAC SIMON, PQ	CANADA J0Y 3M0	819-736-2351 819-736-7311		T	X	
PO BOX 1, WINNEWAY RIVER, PQ	CANADA J0Z 2J0	819-722-2441 819-722-2073		T		
3400 BOUL LOSCH # 39, ST HUBERT, PQ	CANADA J3Y 5T6	514-656-9731 514-656-9735				
PO BOX 368, MARIA, PQ	CANADA G0C 1Y0	418-759-3441 418-759-5856	X			
MISTASSINI LAKE PO, VIA CHIBOUGAMAU, PQ	CANADA G0W 1C0	418-923-3253 418-923-3115	X	T	X	
PO BOX 720, KAHNAWAKE, PQ	CANADA J0L 1B0	514-632-7500 514-638-5958				

Legend

1. Lodging - Resort, Motel, RV Park
2. Economic Base - Farming, Fishing, Ranching Operations
3. Tribal Newspaper
4. Museum/Cultural Center

A - Agriculture
F - Fish, Aquaculture
M - Mineral
R - Ranching
RV - Recreational Vehicle
T - Timber
TC - Tribal Contract

HISTORICAL PROFILE

QUEBEC

Treaty	Language	Tribal Class	Pop	Acreage*	Nation
1861	FRENCH	MONTAGNAIS	2,449	25,536.57 h	MONTAGNAIS DE BETSIAMITES FIRST NATION
1892	FRENCH	MONTAGNAIS	341	38.5 h	MONTAGNAIS DE ESCOUMINS FIRST NATION
1956	FRENCH	MONTAGNAIS			MONTAGNAIS DE LA ROMAINE FIRST NATION
1856	FRENCH	MONTAGNAIS	3,222	3,150.99 h	MONTAGNAIS DE LAC ST-JEAN FIRST NATION
1963	FRENCH	MONTAGNAIS	357	3,887.82 h	MONTAGNAIS DE MINGAN FIRST NATION
1952	FRENCH	MONTAGNAIS	573	20.63 h	MONTAGNAIS DE NATASHQUAN FIRST NATION
1963	FRENCH	MONTAGNAIS	132	4.47 h	MONTAGNAIS DE PAKUA SHIPI FIRST NATION
1960	FRENCH	MONTAGNAIS	546	39.41 h	MONTAGNAIS DE SCHEFFERVILLE FIRST NATION
1949	FRENCH	MONTAGNAIS	2,263	607.59 h	MONTAGNAIS DE UASHAT-MALIOTENAM FIRST NATION
1978	ENGLISH	NASKAPI	430	326.34 sq.k.	NASKAPIS OF QUEBEC FIRST NATION
1974	ENGLISH	CREE	258	152.8 sq.k.	NEMASKA FIRST NATION
					OBEDJIWAN FIRST NATION
1900	ENGLISH	ABENAKIS	1,196	607 h	ODANAK FIRST NATION
		CREE			OLD FACTORY FIRST NATION
1853	ENGLISH	MICMAC	2,262	3,642.12 h	RESTIGOUCHE FIRST NATION
1851	ENGLISH	ALGONKIAN	1,860	10,997.4 h	RIVER DESERT FIRST NATION
1851	ENGLISH	ALGONKIAN	1,007	2,248.08 h	TEMISKAMING FIRST NATION

* Note: Some Provinces use hectares, denoted by h, sq.k. denotes square kilometers. All others are in acres.

QUEBEC

Address		Phone / Fax	L[1]	EB[2]	N[3]	M[4]
20 RUE MESSEK BOX 40, BETSIAMITES, PQ	CANADA G0H 1B0	418-567-2265 418-567-8560		T	X	
27 RUE DE LA RESERVE BOX 820, LES ESCOUMINS, PQ	CANADA G0T 1K0	418-233-2509 418-233-2888	X	TF	X	
GENERAL DELIVERY, LA ROMAINE, PQ	CANADA G0G 1M0	418-229-2110 418-229-2921	X		X	
151 RUE OUIATCHOUAN, POINTE-BLEUE, PQ	CANADA G0W 2H0	418-275-2473 418-275-6212	X		X	X
PO BOX 319, MINGAN, PQ	CANADA G0G 1V0	418-949-2234 418-949-2085	X	T	X	
GENERAL DELIVERY, NATASHQUAN, PQ	CANADA G0G 2E0	418-726-3529 418-726-3606			X	
GENERAL DELIVERY, ST AUGUSTIN, PQ	CANADA G0G 2R0	418-947-2726 418-947-2622			X	
PO BOX 1390, SCHEFFERVILLE, PQ	CANADA G0G 2T0	418-585-2601 418-585-3856		A	X	
1089 RUE DEQUEN BOX 8000, SEPT-ILES, PQ	CANADA G4R 4L9	418-962-0327 418-968-0937	X	T	X	
PO BOX 970, SCHEFFERVILLE, PQ	CANADA G0G 2T0	418-585-2370 418-585-3130			X	
CHAMPION LAKE, VIA POSTE NEMISCAU, PQ	CANADA J0Y 3B0	819-673-2512 819-673-2542	X		X	
GENERAL DELIVERY, VIA ROBERVAL, PQ	CANADA G0W 3B0	819-974-8837 819-974-8828				
58 RUE WABANAKI, ODANAK, PQ	CANADA J0G 1H0	514-568-2810 514-568-7032				X
WEMINDJI, PQ	CANADA J0M 1L0	819-978-0265 819-978-0258				
17 RIVERSIDE W, RESTIGOUCHE, PQ	CANADA G0C 2R0	418-788-2136 418-788-2058	X	T	X	X
PO BOX 309, MANIWAKI, PQ	CANADA J9E 3C9	819-449-5170 819-449-5673		T	X	
PO BOX 336, NOTRE DAME DU NORD, PQ	CANADA J0Z 3B0	819-723-2335 819-723-2353		TA		

Legend

1. Lodging - Resort, Motel, RV Park
2. Economic Base - Farming, Fishing, Ranching Operations
3. Tribal Newspaper
4. Museum/Cultural Center

A - Agriculture
F - Fish, Aquaculture
M - Mineral
R - Ranching
RV - Recreational Vehicle
T - Timber
TC - Tribal Contract

HISTORICAL PROFILE

Treaty	Language	Tribal Class	Pop	Acreage*	Nation
QUEBEC					
				428 h	VIGER FIRST NATION
1974	ENGLISH	CREE	1,572	784.76 h	WASKAGANISH FIRST NATION
1974	ENGLISH	CREE	1,089	598.5 sq.k.	WASWANIPI FIRST NATION
1974	ENGLISH	CREE	916	512.82 sq.k.	WEMINDJI FIRST NATION
					WEYMONTACHIE FIRST NATION
1974	ENGLISH	CREE	482	316.2 sq.k.	WHAPMAGOOSTUI FIRST NATION
	ENGLISH	ALGONKIAN	141	4 h	WOLF LAKE FIRST NATION
SASKATCHEWAN					
1876	CREE	ALGONKIAN	1,799	43,024.95	AHTAHKAKOOP FIRST NATION
1876	CREE	ALGONKIAN	1,809	28,011.91	BEARDY & OKEMASIS FIRST NATION
1899	CHIPEWYAN	ATHAPASKAN	628	23,391.02	BIG C FIRST NATION
1878	CREE	ALGONKIAN	1,659	29,581.4	BIG RIVER FIRST NATION
1899	CHIPEWYAN	ATHAPASKAN	1,177	81,344	BLACK LAKE FIRST NATION
1906	CHIPEWYAN	ATHAPASKAN	711	26,456.2	BUFFALO RIVER FIRST NATION

* Note: Some Provinces use hectares, denoted by h, sq.k. denotes square kilometers. All others are in acres.

Address		Phone Fax	L [1]	EB [2]	N [3]	M [4]
QUEBEC						
8505 RUE CHAUVEAU, MONTREAL, PQ	CANADA H1N 1H5	514-251-1451 514-251-8114				
PO BOX 60, WASKAGANISH, PQ	CANADA J0M 1R0	819-895-8843 819-895-8901	X		X	
WASWANIPI RIVER, WASWANIPI, PQ	CANDA J0Y 3C0	891-753-2587 819-753-2555		T	X	
WEMINDJI, JAMES BAY, PQ	CANADA J0M 1L0	819-978-0254 819-978-0258	X		X	
GENERAL DELIVERY, VIA SANMAUR, PQ	CANADA G0A 4M0	819-666-2237 819-666-2259				
PO BOX 390, HUDSON BAY, PQ	CANADA J0M 1G0	819-929-3503 819-929-3203			X	
PO BOX 1060, TEMISCAMINGUE, PQ	CANADA J0Z 3R0	819-627-3628 819-627-3628	X	T	X	
SASKATCHEWAN						
PO BOX 220, SHELL LAKE, SK	CANADA S0J 2G0	306-468-2326 306-468-2344		TA		
PO BOX 340, DUCK LAKE, SK	CANADA S0K 1J0	306-467-4523 306-467-4404		A		
PO BOX 145, LA LOCHE, SK	CANADA S0M 1G0	306-822-2021 306-822-2250		F		
PO BOX 519, DEBDEN, SK	CANADA S0J 0S0	306-724-4700 306-724-2161		TFA		
GENERAL DELIVERY, BLACK LAKE, SK	CANADA S0J 0H0	306-284-2044 306-284-2101		F		
GENERAL DELIVERY, DILLON, SK	CANADA S0M 0S0	306-282-2033 306-282-2102		TF		

Legend

1. Lodging - Resort, Motel, RV Park
2. Economic Base - Farming, Fishing, Ranching Operations
3. Tribal Newspaper
4. Museum/Cultural Center

A - Agriculture
F - Fish, Aquaculture
M - Mineral
R - Ranching
RV - Recreational Vehicle
T - Timber
TC - Tribal Contract

Treaty	Language	Tribal Class	Pop	Acreage*	Nation
SASKATCHEWAN					
1906	CREE	ALGONKIAN	980	18,130.07	CANOE LAKE FIRST NATION
1877	DAKOTA ASSINIBOINE	SIOUAN	1,445	40,695.57	CARRY THE KETTLE FIRST NATION
1874	OJIBWAY	ALGONKIAN	1,985	22,920	COTE FIRST NATION
1874	CREE	ALGONKIAN	2,125	28,442.5	COWESSESS FIRST NATION
1875	CREE	ALGONKIAN	616	4,639.14	CUMBERLAND HOUSE FIRST NATION
1874	CREE	ALGONKIAN	323	15,360	DAY STAR FIRST NATION
1906	CHIPEWYAN	ATHAPASKAN	814	22,924.43	ENGLISH RIVER FIRST NATION
1876	OJIBWAY	ALGONKIAN	930	7,706.25	FISHING LAKE FIRST NATION
1876	CREE	ALGONKIAN	602	9,269.28	FLYING DUST FIRST NATION
1889	CHIPEWYAN	ATHAPASKAN	1,120	91,677.1	FOND DU LAC FIRST NATION
1874	CREE OJIBWAY	ALGONKIAN	1,888	31,325.42	GORDON FIRST NATION
1907	CHIPEWYAN	ATHAPASKAN	783	27,228	HATCHET LAKE FIRST NATION
1876	CREE	ALGONKIAN	630	17,163.52	ISLAND LAKE FIRST NATION
1876	CREE	ALGONKIAN	1,811	37,184.44	JAMES SMITH FIRST NATION
1876	CREE	ALGONKIAN	835	23,832.3	JOHN SMITH FIRST NATION
1876	CREE	ALGONKIAN	504	11,572.03	JOSEPH BIGHEAD FIRST NATION
1874	CREE	ALGONKIAN	931	19,457	KAHKEWISTAHAW FIRST NATION

* Note: Some Provinces use hectares, denoted by h. All others are in acres.

Address		Phone Fax	L[1]	EB[2]	N[3]	M[4]

SASKATCHEWAN

Address		Phone / Fax	L	EB	N	M
GENERAL DELIVERY, CANOE NARROWS, SK	CANADA S0M 0K0	306-829-2150 306-829-2101		TF		
PO BOX 57, SINTALUTA, SK	CANADA S0G 4N0	306-727-2135 306-727-2149		A		
PO BOX 1659, KAMSACK, SK	CANADA S0A 1S0	306-542-2694 306-542-3735		A		
PO BOX 607, BROADVIEW, SK	CANADA S0G 0K0	306-696-2520 306-696-2767		A		
PO BOX 220, CUMBERLAND HOUSE, SK	CANADA S0E 0S0	306-888-2152 306-888-2084		T		
PO BOX 277, PUNNICHY, SK	CANADA S0A 3C0	306-835-2834 306-835-2724		A		
GENERAL DELIVERY, PATUANAK, SK	CANADA S0M 2H0	306-396-2055 306-396-2155		TFA		
PO BOX 508, WADENA, SK	CANADA S0A 4J0	306-338-3838 306-338-3635		A		
PO BOX 2410, MEADOWLAKE, SK	CANADA S0M 1V0	306-236-4437 306-236-3373		A		
GENERAL DELIVERY, FOND DU LAC, SK	CANADA S0G 0W0	306-686-2102 306-686-2040		F		
PO BOX 248, PUNNICHY, SK	CANADA S0A 3C0	306-835-2232 306-835-2036		A		
GENERAL DELIVERY, WOLLASTON LAKE, SK	CANADA S0J 3C0	306-633-2003 306-633-2040		F		
PO BOX 460, LOON LAKE, SK	CANADA S0M 1L0	306-837-2188 306-837-2266		FA		
PO BOX 1059, MELFORT, SK	CANADA S0E 1A0	306-864-3636 306-864-2404				
PO BOX 9, BIRCH HILLS, SK	CANADA S0J 0G0	306-764-1282 306-764-7272		A		
PO BOX 309, PIERCELAND, SK	CANADA S0M 2K0	306-839-2277 306-839-2323		AM		
PO BOX 609, BROADVIEW, SK	CANADA S0G 0K0	306-696-3291 306-696-3201		A		

Legend

1. Lodging - Resort, Motel, RV Park
2. Economic Base - Farming, Fishing, Ranching Operations
3. Tribal Newspaper
4. Museum/Cultural Center

A - Agriculture
F - Fish, Aquaculture
M - Mineral
R - Ranching
RV - Recreational Vehicle
T - Timber
TC - Tribal Contract

HISTORICAL PROFILE

Treaty	Language	Tribal Class	Pop	Acreage*	Nation
SASKATCHEWAN					
1874	CREE	ALGONKIAN	1,575	19,016	KAWACATOOSE FIRST NATION
1875	OJIBWAY	ALGONKIAN	1,246	11,011	KEESEEKOOSE FIRST NATION
1875	OJIBWAY	ALGONKIAN	724	14,933	KEY FIRST NATION
1876	OJIBWAY	ALGONKIAN	587	11,199.02 h	KINISTIN FIRST NATION
1889	CREE	ALGONKIAN	4,876	104,749.37	LAC LA RONGE FIRST NATION
1874	CREE	ALGONKIAN	302	17,006.38	LITTLE BLACK BEAR FIRST NATION
1879	CREE	ALGONKIAN	1,032	17,267.33	LITTLE PINE FIRST NATION
1879	CREE	ALGONKIAN	73	7,869.4 h	LUCKY MAN FIRST NATION
1876	CREE	ALGONKIAN	792	14,791.94	MAKWA SAHGAIEHCAN FIRST NATION
1876	CREE	ALGONKIAN	1,410	31,110	MISTAWASIS FIRST NATION
1889	CREE	ALGONKIAN	1,863	20,443.4 h	MONTREAL LAKE FIRST NATION
	SIOUX	SIOUAN	270	4,286.67	MOOSE WOODS FIRST NATION
1876	CREE	ALGONKIAN	918	17,261.08	MOOSOMIN FIRST NATION
1876	ASSINIBIONE	SIOUAN		8,679.67	MOSQUITO GRIZZLY BEAR'S HEAD FIRST NATION
1875	OJIBWAY CREE	ALGONKIAN	831	20,634	MUSCOWPETUNG FIRST NATION
1876	CREE	ALGONKIAN	998	17,708.58 h	MUSKEG LAKE FIRST NATION
1874	OJIBWAY	ALGONKIAN	858	16,479	MUSKOWEKWAN FIRST NATION

* Note: Some Provinces use hectares, denoted by h. All others are in acres.

Address		Phone Fax	L[1]	EB[2]	N[3]	M[4]
SASKATCHEWAN						
PO BOX 10, QUINTON, SK	CANADA S0A 3G0	306-835-2125 306-835-2178		A		
PO BOX 1120, KAMSACK, SK	CANADA S0A 1S0	306-542-2516 306-542-2586		A		
PO BOX 70, NORQUAY, SK	CANADA S0A 2V0	306-594-2020 306-594-2020		A		
PO BOX 2590, TISDALE, SK	CANADA S0E 1T0	306-873-5590 306-873-5235				
PO BOX 480, LA RONGE, SK	CANADA S0J 1L0	306-425-2183 306-425-2590		FA		
PO BOX 40, GOODEVE, SK	CANADA S0A 1C0	306-334-2269 306-334-2721		A		
PO BOX 70, PAYNTON, SK	CANADA S0M 2J0	306-398-4942 306-398-2377		A		X
401 PACKHAM PL, SASKATOON, SK	CANADA S7N 2T7	306-374-2828 306-934-2853		A		X
PO BOX 340, LOON LAKE, SK	CANADA S0M 1L0	306-837-2150 306-837-4448		A		X
PO BOX 250, LEASK, SK	CANADA S0J 1M0	306-466-4800 306-466-2299		A		X
GENERAL DELIVERY, MONTREAL LAKE, SK	CANADA S0J 1Y0	306-663-5349 306-663-5320		TF		X
PO BOX 218 RR 5, SASKATOON, SK	CANADA S7K 3J8	306-477-0908 306-374-5899		A		X
PO BOX 45, COCHIN, SK	CANADA S0M 0L0	306-386-2014 306-386-2908		A		X
GENERAL DELIVERY, CANDO, SK	CANADA S0K 0V0	306-937-7707 306-937-7747		A		
PO BOX 1310, FORT QU'APPELLE, SK	CANADA S0G 1S0	306-723-4710 306-723-4710		A		
PO BOX 130, LEASK, SK	CANADA S0J 1M0	306-466-4959 306-466-4951		A		
PO BOX 298, LESTOCK, SK	CANADA S0A 2G0	306-274-2061 306-274-2110		A		X

Legend

1. Lodging - Resort, Motel, RV Park
2. Economic Base - Farming, Fishing, Ranching Operations
3. Tribal Newspaper
4. Museum/Cultural Center

A - Agriculture
F - Fish, Aquaculture
M - Mineral
R - Ranching
RV - Recreational Vehicle
T - Timber
TC - Tribal Contract

HISTORICAL PROFILE

Treaty	Language	Tribal Class	Pop	Acreage*	Nation
		SASKATCHEWAN			
1876	CREE	ALGONKIAN	235	3,037.22	NIKANEET FIRST NATION
1876	OJIBWAY	ALGONKIAN	1,676	14,476.6	NUT LAKE FIRST NATION (YELLOWQUILL BAND)
1874	CREE SAULTEAUX	ALGONKIAN	196	10,201.47 h	OCEAN MAN FIRST NATION
1874	CREE	ALGONKIAN	838	34,624	OCHAPOWACE FIRST NATION
1875	OJIBWAY CREE	ALGONKIAN	336	14,744.7	OKANESE FIRST NATION
					OKEMASIS FIRST NATION
1878	CREE	ALGONKIAN	847	10,209.7	ONE ARROW FIRST NATION
1876	CREE	ALGONKIAN	2,440	43,308.17	ONION LAKE FIRST NATION
1874	OJIBWAY CREE	ALGONKIAN	1,076	22,141	PASQUA FIRST NATION
1874	CREE	ALGONKIAN	1,554	27,180	PEEPEEKISIS FIRST NATION
1889	CREE	ALGONKIAN	632	8,705.01	PELICAN LAKE FIRST NATION
1889	CREE	ALGONKIAN	4,327	33,029.85	PETER BALLANTYNE FIRST NATION
1874	CREE SAULTEAUX	ALGONKIAN	238	19,684.71 h	PHEASANT RUMP NAKOTA FIRST NATION
1875	CREE	ALGONKIAN	1,203	20,536	PIAPOT FIRST NATION
1876	CREE	ALGONKIAN	839	19,204.8	POUNDMAKER FIRST NATION
1876	CREE	ALGONKIAN	741	5,639.95	RED EARTH FIRST NATION
1876	CREE	ALGONKIAN	1,212	24,320	RED PHEASANT FIRST NATION

* Note: Some Provinces use hectares, denoted by h. All others are in acres.

SASKATCHEWAN

Address		Phone Fax	L [1]	EB [2]	N [3]	M [4]
PO BOX 548, MAPLE CREEK, SK	CANADA S0N 1N0	306-662-9196 306-662-4160		A		X
PO BOX 97, ROSE VALLEY, SK	CANADA S0E 1M0	306-322-2281 306-322-2304		A		X
PO BOX 157, STOUGHTON, SK	CANADA S0G 4T0	306-457-2679 306-457-2933		A		X
PO BOX 550, WHITE WOOD, SK	CANADA S0J 5C0	306-696-2637 306-696-3146		A		X
PO BOX 759, BALCARRES, SK	CANADA S0G 0C0	306-334-2532 306-334-2545		A		X
PO BOX 312, DUCK LAKE, SK	CANADA S0J 1J0	306-466-4959 306-466-4951				X
PO BOX 2, BATOCHE, SK	CANADA S0K 0K0	306-423-5900 306-423-5904		A		X
PO BOX 900, LLOYDMINSTER, SK	CANADA S9V 1C3	306-344-2107 306-344-2112		AM		X
PO BOX 968, FORT QU'APPELLE, SK	CANADA S0G 1S0	306-332-5697 306-332-5199		A		X
PO BOX 518, BALCARRES, SK	CANADA S0G 0C0	306-334-2573 306-334-2280		A		X
PO BOX 9, LEOVILLE, SK	CANADA S0J 1N0	306-984-2313 306-984-2029		TAF		X
PO BOX 100, PELICAN NARROWS, SK	CANADA S0P 0E0	306-632-2125 306-632-2275		TF		X
PO BOX 28, KISBY, SK	CANADA S0C 1L0	306-462-2002 306-462-2002		A		
PO BOX 178, CUPAR, SK	CANADA S0G 0Y0	306-781-4848 306-781-4853		A		
PO BOX 220, PAYNTON, SK	CANADA S0M 2J0	306-398-4971 306-398-2522		A		
PO BOX 109, RED EARTH, SK	CANADA S0E 1K0	306-768-3640 306-768-3640		T		
PO BOX 28, CANDO, SK	CANADA S0K 0V0	306-937-7717 306-937-7727		A		

Legend

1. Lodging - Resort, Motel, RV Park
2. Economic Base - Farming, Fishing, Ranching Operations
3. Tribal Newspaper
4. Museum/Cultural Center

A - Agriculture
F - Fish, Aquaculture
M - Mineral
R - Ranching
RV - Recreational Vehicle
T - Timber
TC - Tribal Contract

HISTORICAL PROFILE

SASKATCHEWAN

Treaty	Language	Tribal Class	Pop	Acreage*	Nation
1874	SAULTEAUX	ALGONKIAN	952	21,638.2	SAKIMAY FIRST NATION
				43,000	SANDY LAKE FIRST NATION
1854	OJIBWAY	ALGONKIAN	656	14,386.73	SAULTEAUX FIRST NATION
1876	CREE	ALGONKIAN	448	3,632.1	SHOAL LAKE CREE FIRST NATION
	DAKOTA	SIOUAN	797	5,566.37	STANDING BUFFALO FIRST NATION
1874	CREE	ALGONKIAN	325	13,759.04	STARBLANKET FIRST NATION
1876	CREE	ALGONKIAN	1,420	22,653.94	STURGEON LAKE FIRST NATION
1876	CREE	ALGONKIAN	1,027	42,078.34	SWEETGRASS FIRST NATION
1876	CREE	ALGONKIAN	1,409	16,791.08	THUNDERCHILD FIRST NATION
1906	CHIPEWYAN	ATHAPASKAN	278	6,670	TURNOR LAKE FIRST NATION
	DAKOTA	SIOUAN	193	3,822.01	WAHPETON FIRST NATION
1921	CREE	ALGONKIAN	1,059	19,699.14	WATERHEN LAKE FIRST NATION
1875	CREE OJIBWAY ASSINIBOINE	ALGONKIAN SIOUAN	1,807	42,539	WHITEBEAR FIRST NATION
					WILLIAM CHARLES FIRST NATION
1950	CREE	ALGONKIAN	355	4,224.82	WITCHEKAN LAKE FIRST NATION
	DAKOTA	SIOUAN	131	5,871.62	WOOD MOUNTAIN FIRST NATION
1876	OJIBWAY	ALGONKIAN	1676	14,476.6	YELLOWQUILL FIRST NATION (NUT LAKE)

* Note: Some Provinces use hectares, denoted by h. All others are in acres.

Address		Phone Fax	L[1]	EB[2]	N[3]	M[4]
SASKATCHEWAN						
PO BOX 339, GRENFELL, SK	CANADA S0G 2B0	306-697-2831 306-697-3565		A		
PO BOX 220, SHELL LAKE, SK	CANADA S0J 2G0	306-468-2326 306-468-2344				
PO BOX 1, COCHIN, SK	CANADA S0M 0L0	306-386-2424 306-386-2444		A		
GENERAL DELIVERY, PAKWAW LAKE, SK	CANADA S0E 1G0	306-768-3551 306-768-3486		T		
PO BOX 128, FORT QU'APPELLE, SK	CANADA S0G 1S0	306-332-4685 306-332-5953		A		
PO BOX 456, BALCARRES, SK	CANDA S0G 0C0	306-334-2206 306-334-2606		A		
BOX 5 SITE 12 RR 1, SHELLBROOK, SK	CANADA S0J 2E0	306-764-1872 306-764-1877				
PO BOX 147, GALLIVAN, SK	CANADA S0M 0X0	306-937-2990 306-937-7010		A		
PO BOX 340, TURTLEFORD, SK	CANADA S0M 2Y0	306-845-3424 306-845-3230		A		
GENERAL DELIVERY, TURNOR LAKE, SK	CANADA S0M 3E0	306-894-2030 306-894-2115		F		
PO BOX 128, PRINCE ALBERT, SK	CANADA S6V 5R4	306-764-6649 306-764-6637		A		
GENERAL DELIVERY, WATERHEN LAKE, SK	CANADA S0M 3B0	306-236-6717 306-236-4866		T		
PO BOX 700, CARLYLE, SK	CANADA S0C 0R0	306-577-2461 306-577-2496		AM		
PO BOX 106, MONTREAL LAKE, SK	CANADA S0J 1Y0	306-663-5349 306-663-5320				
PO BOX 879, SPIRITWOOD, SK	CANADA S0J 2M0	306-883-2787 306-883-2008		TAF		
PO BOX 104, WOOD MOUNTAIN, SK	CANADA S0H 4L0	306-266-2027 306-266-2023		A		
PO BOX 97, ROSE VALLEY, SK	CANADA S0E 1M0	306-322-2281 306-322-2304		A		

Legend

1. Lodging - Resort, Motel, RV Park
2. Economic Base - Farming, Fishing, Ranching Operations
3. Tribal Newspaper
4. Museum/Cultural Center

A - Agriculture
F - Fish, Aquaculture
M - Mineral
R - Ranching
RV - Recreational Vehicle
T - Timber
TC - Tribal Contract

HISTORICAL PROFILE

Treaty	Language	Tribal Class	Pop	Acreage*	Nation
SASKATCHEWAN					
1876					YOUNG CHIPPEWAYAN FIRST NATION
YUKON TERRITORY					
	ENGLISH	TAGISH TLINGLIT	360	179.6 h	CARCROSS/TAGISH FIRST NATION
1976	ENGLISH	ATHAPASKAN	477	4,303.5 h	CHAMPAGNE/AISHIHIK FIRST NATION
	ENGLISH	ATHAPASKAN	545	86.33 h	DAWSON FIRST NATION
	ENGLISH	ATHAPASKAN	224	357.2 h	KLUANE FIRST NATION
1900	ENGLISH	TUTEHONE TAGISH	970	19,266 h	KWANLIN DUN FIRST NATION
1961	ENGLISH	ATHAPASKAN	702	263.8 h	LIARD RIVER FIRST NATION
1961	ENGLISH		130		LIARD RIVER INDIAN RESERVE #3 FIRST NATION
	ENGLISH	ATHAPASKAN	398	482 h	LITTLE SALMON/CARMACKS FIRST NATION (TSAWLNJIK DAN)
1904	ENGLISH	ATHAPASKAN	393	461 h	NA-CHO NY'A'K DUN FIRST NATION (MAYO)
1965	ENGLISH	ATHAPASKAN	337	42.2 h	ROSS RIVER FIRST NATION
1898	ENGLISH KUTCHIN	ATHAPASKAN	420	293.38 h	SELKIRK FIRST NATION

* Note: Some Provinces use hectares, denoted by h. All others are in acres.

Address		Phone Fax	L[1]	EB[2]	N[3]	M[4]
SASKATCHEWAN						
409 19TH E, PRINCE ALBERT, SK	CANADA S6V 4A1	306-486-2326				
YUKON TERRITORY						
PO BOX 130, CARCROSS, YT	CANADA Y0B 1B0	403-821-4251 403-821-4811	X	T		
PO BOX 5309, HAINES JUNCTION, YT	CANADA Y0B 1L0	403-634-2288 403-634-2108				
PO BOX 599, DAWSON, YT	CANADA Y0B 1G0	403-993-5385 403-993-5479	X	F		
MILE 1093 ALASKA HWY, BURWASH LANDING, YT	CANADA Y0B 1H0	403-841-4274 403-841-5900	X	F		
PO BOX 1217, WHITEHORSE, YT	CANADA Y1A 2Z1	403-667-6465 403-668-5057				
PO BOX 328, WATSON LAKE, YT	CANADA T0A 1C0	403-536-2131 403-536-2332	X	M		
PO BOX 489, WATSON LAKE, YT	CANADA Y0A 1C0	604-779-3161 604-779-3371				
GENERAL DELIVERY, CARMACKS, YT	CANADA Y0B 1C0	403-863-5576 403-863-5710		M		
PO BOX 220, MAYO, YT	CANADA Y0B 1M0	403-996-2265 403-996-2107	X	M		
GENERAL DELIVERY, ROSS RIVER, YT	CANADA Y0B 1S0	403-969-2278 403-969-2405		TM		
GENERAL DELIVERY, PELLY CROSSING, YT	CANADA Y0B 1P0	403-537-3331 403-357-3902	X	T		

Legend

1. Lodging - Resort, Motel, RV Park
2. Economic Base - Farming, Fishing, Ranching Operations
3. Tribal Newspaper
4. Museum/Cultural Center

A - Agriculture
F - Fish, Aquaculture
M - Mineral
R - Ranching
RV - Recreational Vehicle
T - Timber
TC - Tribal Contract

HISTORICAL PROFILE

Treaty	Language	Tribal Class	Pop	Acreage*	Nation
YUKON TERRITORY					
					TA'AN KWACH'AN COUNCIL FIRST NATION
1941		TLINGIT	442	2,698.83 h	TESLIN TLINGIT FIRST NATION
	ENGLISH	ATHAPASKAN	332	9,135.25 h	VUNTUT GWITCHIN FIRST NATION (OLD CROW)
	ENGLISH	ATHAPASKAN	103	356.2 h	WHITE RIVER FIRST NATION

* Note: Some Provinces use hectares, denoted by h. All others are in acres.

YUKON TERRITORY

Address		Phone Fax	L [1]	EB [2]	N [3]	M [4]
22 NUSUTLIN DR, WHITEHORSE, YT	CANADA Y1A 3S5	403-668-3613 403-668-6577				
GENERAL DELIVERY, TESLIN, YT	CANADA Y0A 1B0	403-390-2532 403-390-2204	X			
GENERAL DELIVERY, OLD CROW, YT	CANADA Y0B 1N0	403-966-3261 403-966-3800		F		
GENERAL DELIVERY, BEAVER CREEK, YT	CANADA Y0B 1A0	403-862-7802 403-862-7806		M		

Legend

1. Lodging - Resort, Motel, RV Park
2. Economic Base - Farming, Fishing, Ranching Operations
3. Tribal Newspaper
4. Museum/Cultural Center

A - Agriculture
F - Fish, Aquaculture
M - Mineral
R - Ranching
RV - Recreational Vehicle
T - Timber
TC - Tribal Contract

ASSEMBLY OF FIRST NATION REGIONAL CHIEFS

Mr. Ovide Mercredi
National Chief
Assembly of First Nations
Branch Office
55 Murray Street
5th Floor
Ottawa, Ontario
K1N 5M3
Telephone: (613) 241-6789
FAX: (613) 241-5808

Mr. Wallace Labillois
Chairman
Council of Elders
R R # 9
Fredericton, New Brunswick
E3B 4X9
Telephone: (506) 457-2129
FAX: (506) 451-9386

PROVINCIAL/TERRITORIAL CHIEFS

ALBERTA REGION

Mr. Mike Beaver
Alberta Regional Chief
c/o First Nations Resource
Council
14601 - 134 Avenue
Edmonton, Alberta
V7P 3J3
Telephone: (403) 453-6114
FAX: (403) 453-6150

BRITISH COLUMBIA REGION

Wendy Grant
B.C. Regional Chief
207 - 1999 Marine Drive
North Vancouver,
British Columbia
V7P 3J3
Telephone: (604) 990-9939
FAX: (604) 990-9949

MANITOBA REGION

Mr. Kenneth B. Young
Manitoba Regional Chief
Assembly of Manitoba Chiefs
400 - 286 Smith Street
Winnipeg, Manitoba
R3C 1K4
Telephone: (204) 956-0610
FAX: (204) 956-2109

NEW BRUNSWICK & PEI REGIONS

Chief Leonard Tomah
Woodstock Indian Band
Box 28, Site 3
Woodstock, New Brunswick
E0J 2B0
Telephone: (506) 328-3303
FAX: (506) 328-2420

NORTH REGION

Mr. Harry Allen
Yukon Regional Chief
Council for Yukon Indians
11 Nisutlin Drive
Whitehorse, Yukon
Y1A 3S4
Telephone: (403) 667-7631
FAX: (403) 668-6577

NORTHWEST TERRITORIES

Bill Erasmus
Interim N.W.T. Regional Chief
Dene Nation
Denendeh National Office
PO Box 2338
4701 Franklin Avenue
Yellowknife,
Northwest Territories
X1A 2P7
Telephone: (403) 873-3310
FAX: (403) 920-2254

NOVA SCOTIA & NEWFOUNDLAND REGIONS

Rick Simon
AFN Regional Chief
PO Box 327
Shubenacadie, Nova Scotia
B0W 2H0
Telephone: (902) 895-4376
FAX: (902) 758-1759

ONTARIO REGION

Mr. Gordon Peters
Ontario Regional Chief
Chiefs of Ontario
22 College Street, 2nd Floor
Toronto, Ontario
M5G 1K2
Telephone: (416) 972-0212
FAX: (416) 972-0217

QUÉBEC / LABRADOR REGION

Mr. Ghislain Picard
Québec/Labrador Regional Chief
430 Koska
Reserve Indienne des Hurons-Wendat
Wendake, Québec
G0A 4V0
Telephone: (418) 842-5020
FAX: (418) 842-2660

SASKATCHEWAN REGION

Chief Blaine Favel
Presidnet, FSIN
FSIN
103-A Packham Avenue
Saskatoon, Saskatchewan
S7N 4K4
Telephone: (306) 665-1215
FAX: (306) 244-4413

A. J. Felix, AFN Vice-Chief
Asimakaniseekan Askly Reserve
Suite 100
103-A Packham Place
Saskatoon, Saskatchewan
S7N 4K4
Telephone: (306) 244-4444
FAX: (306) 244-1391

ASSEMBLY OF FIRST NATIONS

Assembly of First Nations
55 Murray St
5th Floor
Ottawa, Ontario
K1N 5M3
Telephone: (613) 241-6789
FAX: (613) 241-5808

PROVINCIAL/TERRITORIAL ORGANIZATIONS

ALBERTA

Indian Association of Alberta
Stoney Plain Indian
Reserve #135
PO Box 516, Site 2, RR 2
Winterburn, Alberta
T0E 2N0
Telephone: (403) 470-5751
FAX: (403) 470-3077

BRITISH COLUMBIA

Union of British Columbia
Indian Chiefs
342 Water Street, 3rd Floor
Vancouver, British Columbia
V6B 1B6
Telephone: (604) 684-0231
FAX: (604) 684-5726

MANITOBA

First Nations Confederacy
Room 203, 286 Smith Street
Winnipeg, Manitoba
R3C 1K4
Telephone: (204) 944-8245
FAX: (204) 943-1482

Manitoba Keewatinowi
Okimakanak
23 Station Road
Thompson, Manitoba
R8N 0N6
Telephone: (204) 778-4431
FAX: (204) 778-7655

NEW BRUNSWICK

Union of New Brunswick
Indians
385 Wilsey Road, Comp 43
Fredericton, New Brunswick
E3B 5N6
Telephone: (506) 458-9444
FAX: (506) 458-2850

NEWFOUNDLAND

Council of the Conne River Micmacs
Conne River Reserve Micmac Territory
Conne River, Newfoundland
A0H 1J0
Telephone: (709) 882-2470
FAX: (709) 882-2292

NORTHWEST TERRITORIES

Dene Nation
Denedeh National Office
PO Box 2338
4701 Franklin Avenue
Yellowknife,
Northwest Territories
X1A 2P7
Telephone: (403) 873-4081
FAX: (403) 920-2254

NOVA SCOTIA

Union of Nova Scotia Indians
PO Box 961
Sydney, Nova Scotia
B1L 6J4
Telphone: (902) 539-4107
FAX: (902) 565-2137

ONTARIO

Association of Iroquois & Allied Indians
387 Princess Ave
London, Ontario
N6S 2A7
Telephone: (519) 434-2761
FAX: (519) 679-1653

Chiefs of Ontario
2nd Floor, 22 College Street
Toronto, Ontario
M5G 1K2
Telephone: (416) 972-0212
FAX: (416) 972-0217

Grand Council Treaty # 3
PO Box 1720
Kenora, Ontario
P9N 3X7
Telephone: (807) 548-4215
FAX: (807) 548-5041

Nishnawbe-Aski Nation
PO Box 755, Station F
Fort William Reserve
RR 4, Mission Road
Thunder Bay, Ontario
P7C 4W6
Telephone: (807) 623-8228
FAX: (807) 623-7730

Union of Ontario Indians
Branch Office
1813 Danforth Avenue
Toronto, Ontario
M4C 1J2
Telephone: (416) 693-1305
FAX: (416) 693-1620

PRINCE EDWARD ISLAND

Abegweit Band
PO Box 220
Cornwall, Prince Edward Island
C0A 1H0
Telephone: (902) 675-3842
FAX: (902) 892-3420

Lennox Island Indian Band
Box 134
Lennox Island,
Prince Edward Island
C0B 1P0
Telephone: (902) 831-2779
FAX: (902) 831-3153

QUÉBEC

Grand Council of the Crees
(of Québec)
2 Lakeshore Road
Nemaska, Champion Lake
c/o Poste Nemiscau, Québec
J0Y 3B0
Telephone: (819) 673-2600
FAX: (819) 673-2606

Secretariat of First Nations
(of Québec)
430 Koska
Village des Hurons-Wendat
Wendake, Québec
G0A 4V0
Telephone: (418) 842-5020
FAX: (418) 842-2660

SASKATCHEWAN

Federation of Saskatchewan
Indian Nations
Indian Governments of
Saskatchewan
109 Hodsman Road
Regina, Saskatchewan
S4N 5W5
Telephone: (306) 721-2822
FAX: (306) 721-2707

YUKON

Council for Yukon Indians
11 Nisutlin Drive
Whitehorse, Yukon
Y1A 3S5
Telphone: (403) 667-7631
FAX: (403) 668-6577

OBSERVER STATUS

Assembly of Manitoba Chiefs
400 - 286 Smith Street
Winnipeg, Manitoba
R3C 1K4
Telephone: (204) 956-0610
FAX: (204) 956-2109

Federation of Newfoundland
Indians
General Delivery
Benoit's Cove, Newfoundland
A0L 1A0
Telephone: (709) 789-2797
FAX: (709) 789-3308

Innu Nation
PO Box 119
Sheshatsiu, Labrador
A0P 1M0
Telephone: (709) 497-8398
FAX: (709) 497-8398

SUB-OFFICES

Federation of Saskatchewan Indian Nations
201 Robin Crescent
Saskatoon, Saskatchewan
S7L 6M8
Telephone: (306) 244-4444
FAX: (306) 244-1391

Federation of Saskatchewan Indian Nations
222 Cardinal Crescent
Saskatoon, Saskatchewan
S7L 6M8
Telephone: (306) 665-1215
FAX: (306) 244-4413

Grand Council of the Crees (of Québec) / Cree Regional Authority
Ottawa Liaison Office
24 Bayswater Avenue
Ottawa, Ontario
K1Y 2E4
Telephone: (613) 761-1655
FAX: (613) 761-9267

Grand Council Treaty No. 3
45 King Street
2nd Floor
Dryden, Ontario
P8N 1B7
Telephone: (807) 223-4315
FAX: (807) 223-4317

Union of Ontario Indians
Nipissing First Nation
PO Box 711
North Bay, Ontario
P1B 8J8
Telephone: (705) 497-9127
FAX: (705) 497-9135

Provided by: Communications Services Management Directorate Communications Branch Policy and Strategic Direction Sector Indian and Northern Affairs Canada Ottawa, Ontario K1A 0H4

NATIONAL INUIT ORGANIZATIONS

INTERNATIONAL

Inuit Circumpolar of Canada
170 Laurier Ave W
Suite 515
Ottawa, Ontario
K1P 5V5
Telephone: (613) 563-2642
FAX: (613) 565-3089

NATIONAL

Canadian Arctic Resources Committee
1 Nicholas Street
Suite 412
Ottawa, Ontario
K1N 7V7
Telephone: (613) 241-7379
FAX: (613) 241-2244

Inuit Non-Profit Housing Corporation
1208-170 Laurier Avenue W
Ottawa, Ontario
K1P 5V5
Telephone: (613) 594-2810
FAX: (613) 594-8350

Inuit Tapirisat of Canada
170 Laurier Ave W
Suite 510
Ottawa, Ontario
K1P 5V5
Telephone: (613) 238-8181
FAX: (613) 234-1991

REGIONAL INUIT ORGANIZATIONS

NORTHWEST TERRITORIES

Baffin Region Inuit Association
Box 219
Igaluit, Northwest Territories
X0A 0H0
Telephone: (819) 979-5391
FAX: (819) 979-4325

Inuvialuit Development Corporation
Bag Service 7
Inuvik, Northwest Territories
X0E 0T0
Telephone: (403) 979-2419
FAX: (403) 979-3256

Inuvialuit Regional Corporation
PO Box 2120
Inuvik, Northwest Territories
X0E 0T0
Telephone: (403) 979-2737
FAX: (403) 979-2135

Keewatin Inuit Association
Box 340
Rankin Inlet,
Northwest Territories
X0C 0G0
Telephone: (819) 645-2800
FAX: (819) 645-2805

Kitikmeot Inuit Association
Box 18
Cambridge Bay,
Northwest Territories
X0E 0C0
Telephone: (403) 983-2458
FAX: (403) 983-2701

Nunavut Tunngavik Incorporated
4908 - 49th St
Bag 4540
Yellowknife,
Northwest Territories
K1A 1P3
Telephone: (403) 873-9244
FAX: (403) 873-9466

ONTARIO

Inuit Art Foundation
2081 Merivale Road
Nepean, Ontario
K2G 1G9
Telephone: (613) 224-8189
FAX: (613) 224-2907

Inuit Art Showcase
531 Sussex Drive
Ottawa, Ontario
K1N 6Z6
Telephone: (613) 241-1511
FAX: (613) 241-6030

Inuit Broadcasting Corporation
251 Laurier Avenue W
Suite 703
Nepean, Ontario
K2G 1G9
Telephone: (613) 235-1892
FAX: (613) 230-8824

Nunasi Corporation
280 Albert St, Suite 904
Ottawa, Ontario
K1P 5G8
Telephone: (613) 238-4981
FAX: (613) 238-5230

Nunavut Sivuniksavut
336 MacLaren Street
Ottawa, Ontario
K2P 0M6
Telephone: (613) 234-5603
FAX: (613) 233-5565

Nunavut Trust
130 Albert Street
Suite 1510
Ottawa, Ontario
K1T 5G4
Telephone: (613) 238-1096
FAX: (613) 238-4131

Nunavut Tunngavik Incorporated
130 Albert St
Suite 1510
Ottawa, Ontario
K1T 5G4
Telephone: (613) 238-1096
FAX: (613) 238-4131

Pauktuutit
200 Elgin Street
Suite 804
Ottawa, Ontario
K2P 1L5
Telephone: (613) 238-3977
FAX: (613) 238-1787

Tuungasuvvingat Inuit
604 Laurier Avenue W
Ottawa, Ontario
K1R 6L1
Telephone: (613) 563-3546
FAX: (613) 230-8925

Unaaq Fisheries Incorporated
431 Gilmour Street
Suite 200
Ottawa, Ontario
K2P 0R5
Telephone: (613) 234-4550
FAX: (613) 234-4317

QUÉBEC

Makivik Corporation
Box 179
Kuujjuaq, Québec
J0M 1C0
Telephone: (819) 964-2925
FAX: (819) 964-2613

Makivik Corporation
650, 32nd Ave 6th Floor
Lachine, Québec
H8T 3K5
Telephone: (514) 634-8091

NATIVE AND MÉTIS ASSOCIATIONS

Congress of Aboriginal Peoples
384 Bank Street
Suite 200
Ottawa, Ontario
K2P 1Y4
Telephone: (613) 238-3511
FAX: (613) 230-6273

PROVINCIAL/TERRITORIAL ORGANIZATIONS

ALBERTA

Native Council of Canada
(Alberta)
10408 - 124th Street
Suite 306
PO Box 39004
Edmonton, Alberta
T5N 1R5
Telephone: (403) 429-6003
FAX: (403) 428-6964

BRITISH COLUMBIA

United Native Nations
736 Granville Street
8th Floor
Vancouver, British Columbia
V6Z 1G3
Telephone: (604) 688-1821
FAX: (604) 688-1823

LABRADOR

Labrador Métis Association
PO Box 599, Station "B"
Goose Bay, Labrador
A0P 1E0
Telephone: (709) 896-0592
FAX: (709) 896-0594

MANITOBA

Indian Council of First Nations
of Manitoba, Inc.
PO Box 13, Group 10, R R # 2
Ste Anne, Manitoba
R0A 1R0
Telephone: (204) 422-5193
FAX: (204) 422-8860

OR

PO Box 2857
The Pas, Manitoba
R9A 1M6
Telephone: (204) 623-7227
FAX: (204) 623-4041

NEW BRUNSWICK

New Brunswick Aboriginal
Peoples' Council
320 St Mary's Street
Fredericton, New Brunswick
E3A 2S4
Telephone: (506) 458-8422
FAX: (506) 450-3749

NEWFOUNDLAND

Federation of Newfoundland
Indians
General Delivery
Benoit's Cove, Newfoundland
A0L 1A0
Telephone: (709) 789-2797
FAX: (709) 789-3308

NORTHWEST TERRITORIES

Métis Nation Northwest
Territories
PO Box 1375
Yellowknife,
Northwest Territories
X1A 2P1
Telephone: (403) 873-3505
FAX: (403) 873-3995

NOVA SCOTIA

Native Council of Nova Scotia
PO Box 1320
Abenaki Road
Truro, Nova Scotia
B2N 5N2
Telephone: (902) 895-1523
FAX: (902) 895-0024

ONTARIO

Ontario Métis Aboriginal
Association (OMAA)
248 Queen St E, 2nd Floor
Sault Ste Marie, Ontario
P6A 1Y7
Telephone: (807) 767-7887
FAX: (807) 767-7887

PRINCE EDWARD ISLAND

Native Council of Prince
Edward Island
33 Allen Street
Charlottetown,
Prince Edward Island
C1A 3B9
Telephone: (902) 892-5314
FAX: (902) 368-7464

QUÉBEC

Native Alliance of Québec
21 Brodeur Street
Hull, Québec
J8Y 2P6
Telephone: (819) 770-7763
FAX: (819) 770-6070

SASKATCHEWAN

Native Council of
Saskatchewan
PO Box 132
Green Lake, Saskatchewan
S0M 1B0
Telephone: (306) 288-2125
FAX: (306) 832-2117

United Aboriginal Youth
Council of Canada
3355 - 33rd Street West
Saskatoon, Saskatchewan
S7L 4P5
Telephone: (308) 384-3308
FAX: (308) 384-3308

YUKON

Council for Yukon Indians
11 Nisutlin Drive
Whitehorse, Yukon
Y1A 3S4
Telephone: (403) 667-7631
FAX: (403) 668-6577

Yukon Representative
White River First Nations
General Delivery
Beaver Creek, Yukon
Y0B 1A0
Telephone: (403) 862-7806

NATIVE WOMEN'S ASSOCIATIONS

Native Women's Association of Canada
9 Melrose Avenue
Ottawa, Ontario
K1Y 1T8
Telephone: (613) 722-3033
FAX: (613) 722-7687

PROVINCIAL/TERRITORIAL ORGANIZATIONS

ALBERTA

Alberta Aboriginal Women's Society
Box 5168
Peace River, Alberta
T8S 1R8
Telephone: (403) 944-6983
FAX: (403) 423-0176

BRITISH COLUMBIA

British Columbia Native Women's Society
345 Yellowhead Highway
Kamloops, British Columbia
V2H 1H1
Telephone: (604) 828-9796
FAX: (604) 828-9803

LABRADOR

Labrador Native Women's Association
Box 568, Station "C"
Goose Bay, Labrador
A0P 1C0
Telephone: (709) 896-8593
FAX: (709) 896-1732

MANITOBA

Aboriginal Women of Manitoba Inc.
167 Clyde Road
Winnipeg, Manitoba
R2L 2A4
Telephone: (204) 235-3393
FAX: (204) 231-0640

Indigenous Women's Collective of Manitoba
120 - 388 Donald Street
Winnipeg, Manitoba
R3B 2J4
Telephone: (204) 944-8709
FAX: (204) 949-1336

NEW BRUNSWICK

New Brunswick Native Indian Women's Council
65 Brunswick Street Room 258
Fredericton, New Brunswick
E3B 1G5
Telephone: (506) 458-1114
FAX: (506) 451-9386

NORTHWEST TERRITORIES

Native Women's Association of the Northwest Territories
PO Box 2321
Yellowknife,
Northwest Territories
X1A 2P7
Telephone: (403) 873-5509
FAX: (403) 873-3152

NOVA SCOTIA

Nova Scotia Native Women's Association
Box 805
Truro, Nova Scotia
B2N 5E8
Telephone: (902) 893-7402
FAX: (902) 897-7162

ONTARIO

Ontario Native Women's Association
117 North May Street
Thunder Bay, Ontario
P7C 3N8
Telephone: (807) 623-3442
Telephone: 1-800-667-0816
FAX: (807) 623-1104

PRINCE EDWARD ISLAND

Aboriginal Women of Prince Edward Island Inc.
Box 213
Charlottetown,
Prince Edward Island
C1A 7K4
Telephone: (902) 831-2779
FAX: (902) 831-3153

QUÉBEC

Québec Native Women's Association
1450 City Councillors
Suite 440
Montreal, Québec
H3A 2E5
Telephone: (514) 844-9618
Telephone: (800) 363-0322
FAX: (514) 844-2108

SASKATCHEWAN

Aboriginal Women's Council of Saskatchewan
101 - 118, 12th Street East
Prince Albert, Saskatchewan
S6V 1B6
Telephone: (306) 763-6005
FAX: (306) 922-6034

YUKON

Yukon Indian Women's Association
11 Nisutlin Drive
Whitehorse, Yukon
Y1A 3S4
Telephone: (403) 667-6162
FAX: (403) 668-7539

NATIONAL ABORIGINAL ORGANIZATIONS

BRITISH COLUMBIA

British Columbia Aboriginal
Peoples' Fisheries Commission
Suite 204 - 990 Homer Street
Vancouver, British Columbia
V6B 2W7
Telephone: (604) 682-4897
FAX: (604) 682-3550

Native Brotherhood of
British Columbia
200 - 1755 East Hastings Street
Vancouver, British Columbia
V5L 1T1
Telephone: (604) 255-3137
FAX: (604) 251-7107

Native Fishing Association
202 - 1755 East Hasting Street
Vancouver, British Columbia
V5L 1T1
Telephone: (604) 255-5457
FAX: (604) 255-0955

ONTARIO

Aboriginal Nurses Association
of Canada
3rd Floor, 55 Murray St.
Ottawa, Ontario
K1N 5M3
Telephone: (613) 241-1864
FAX: (613) 241-1542

Canadian Native Arts
Foundation
77 Mowat # 508
Toronto, Ontario
M6K 3E3
Telephone: (416) 588-3328
FAX: (416) 588-9198

Congress of Aboriginal Peoples
2nd Floor, 384 Bank St.
Ottawa, Ontario
K2P 1Y4
Telephone: (613) 238-3511
FAX: (613) 230-6273

Cree-Naskapi Commission
Suite 222, Queen St.
Ottawa, Ontario
K1P 5V9
Telephone: (613) 234-4288
FAX: (613) 234-8101

First Nations Education
Counselling Unit
202 - 290 Montreal Rd.
Vanier, Ontario
K1L 6B0
Telephone: (613) 748-0960
FAX: (613) 748-0361

Grand Council of the Crees
24 Bayswater Ave.
Ottawa, Ontario
K1Y 2ER
Telephone: (613) 761-1655
FAX: (613) 761-1388

Indigenous Survival International
298 Elgin, # 105
Ottawa, Ontario
K2P 1M3
Telephone: (613) 230-3616
FAX: (613) 238-5780

Inuit Broadcasting Corporation
703 - 251 Laurier Ave.
Ottawa, Ontario
K1P 5J6
Telephone: (613) 235-1892
FAX: (613) 230-8824

Inuit Tapirisat of Canada
Suite 510,
170 Laurier Ave. West
Ottawa, Ontario
K1P 5H3
Telephone: (613) 238-8181
FAX: (613) 234-1991

Metis National Council
Suite 305, 50 O'Connor St.
Ottawa, Ontario
K1P 6L2
Telephone: (613) 232-3216
FAX: (613) 232-4262

National Aboriginal Forestry Association
PO Box 100
Golden Lake, Ontario
K0J 1X0
Telephone: (613) 233-5563
FAX: (613) 233-4329

National Aboriginal Housing Association
150 Laurier Avenue West
Ottawa, Ontario
Telephone: (613) 237-5066
FAX: (613) 237-5848

National Aboriginal Network on Disabilities
60 - 230 Catherine St.
Ottawa, Ontario
K2P 1C3
Telephone: (613) 563-1066
FAX: (613) 563-4768

National Association of Friendship Centres
Suite 204, 396 Cooper St.
Ottawa, Ontario
K2P 2H7
Telephone: (613) 563-4844
FAX: (613) 594-3428

Native Business Institute
Suite 101, 2055 Carling Ave.
Ottawa, Ontario
K2A 1G6
Telephone: (613) 761-9734
FAX: (613) 725-9031

Native Council of Canada
2 - 384 Bank St.
Ottawa, Ontario
K2P 1Y4
Telephone: (613) 238-3511
FAX: (613) 230-6273

Native Women's Association of
Canada
9 Melrose Ave.
Ottawa, Ontario
K1Y 1T8
Telephone: (613) 722-3033
FAX: (613) 722-7687

Nunavut Tunngavik
Incorporated
Suite 1510, 130 Albert St.
Ottawa, Ontario
K1P 5G4
Telephone: (613) 238-1096
FAX: (613) 238-4131

Pauktuutit (Inuit Women's
Association)
804 - 200 Elgin St.
Ottawa, Ontario
K2P 1L5
Telephone: (613) 238-3977
FAX: (613) 238-1787

Royal Commission on
Aboriginal People
5 - 427 Laurier Ave. West
PO Box 1993, Station "B"
Ottawa, Ontario
K1P 1B2
Telephone: (613) 943-2075
FAX: (613) 943-2073

World Council of Indigenous
Peoples
2 - 100 Argyle St.
Ottawa, Ontario
K2P 1B6
Telephone: (613) 230-9030
FAX: (613) 230-9340

NATIONAL FRIENDSHIP CENTRE

Nat'l Association of Friendship Centres
#204, 396 Cooper St
Ottawa, Ontario K2P 2H7
Canada
Telephone: (613) 563-4844
FAX: (613) 594-3428

PROVINCIAL/TERRITORIAL ASSOCIATIONS

ALBERTA

Alberta Native Friendship
Centres Association
#104, 10534 - 124 Street
Edmonton, Alberta
T5N 1R8
Telphone: (403) 482-5196
FAX: (403) 482-2032

BRITISH COLUMBIA

B.C. Association of Indian
Friendship Centres
#3, 2475 Mt Newton X Road
Saanichton, British Columbia
V0S 1M0
Telephone: (604) 652-0210
FAX: (604) 652-3102

MANITOBA

Manitoba Association of
Friendship Centres
PO Box 716
181 Higgins Avenue, 2nd Floor
Winnipeg, Manitoba
R3C 2K3
Telephone: (204) 942-6299
FAX: (204) 942-6308

NORTHWEST TERRITORIES

Delcho Friendship Centre
PO Box 470
Fort Simpson, NWT
X0E 0N0
Telephone: (403) 695-2577
FAX: (403) 695-2141

ONTARIO

Ontario Federation of Indian
Friendship Centres
290 Shuter Street
Toronto, Ontario
M5A 1W7
Telephone: (416) 956-7575
FAX: (416) 956-7577

QUÉBEC

Le Regroupement des centres
d'amitié autochtone du Québec
Inc.
30 rue de l'Ours
Village-des-Hurons, Québec
G0A 1L4
Telephone: (418) 842-6354
FAX: (418) 842-9795

SASKATCHEWAN

Ilea la Crosse
PO Box 160
Ilea la Crosse, Saskatchewan
S0M 1C0
Telephone: (306) 833-2313
FAX: (306) 833-2216

Information provided by: Nat'l Association of Friendship Centres 1/95

REGIONAL FRIENDSHIP CENTRES

ALBERTA

Athabasca Native Friendship Centre*
Box 1770
Athabasca, Alberta
T0G 0B0
Telephone: (403) 675-3086
FAX: (403) 675-3086

Bonnyville Canadian Native Friendship Centre
PO Box 5399
5106 - 50th Street
Bonnyville, Alberta
T9N 2G5
Telephone: (403) 826-3374
FAX: (403) 826-2540

Calgary Indian Friendship Centre
140 - 2nd Avenue SW
Calgary, Alberta
T3E 6N7
Telephone: (403) 264-1155
FAX: (403) 265-9275

Canadian Native Friendship Centre
11205 - 101 Street
Edmonton, Alberta
T5G 2A4
Telephone: (403) 479-1999
FAX: (403) 479-0043

Edson Friendship Centre*
PO Box 6508
Edson, Alberta
T7E 1T9
Telephone: (403) 723-5494
FAX: (403) 723-4359

Grande Centre Friendship Centre*
PO Box 1978
Grand Centre, Alberta
T0A 1T0
Telephone: (403) 594-7526
FAX: (403) 594-7481

Grande Prairie Friendship Centre
10507 - 98th Avenue
Grande Prairie, Alberta
T8V 4L1
Telephone: (403) 532-5722
FAX: (403) 539-5121

High Level Native Friendship Centre
PO Box 1735
High Level, Alberta
T0H 1Z0
Telephone: (403) 926-3355
FAX: (403) 926-2038

High Prairie Native Friendship Centre
PO Box 1448
4919 - 51st Avenue
High Prairie, Alberta
T0G 1E0
Telephone: (403) 523-4511
FAX: (403) 523-3055

* New and Developing

Lac La Biche Canadian Native
Friendship Centre*
PO Box 2338
10004 - 101 Avenue
Lac La Biche, Alberta
T0A 2C0
Telephone: (403) 623-3249
FAX: (403) 623-1846

Lloydminster Native Friendship
Centre
5010 - 41st Street
Lloydminster, Alberta
T9V 1B7
Telephone: (403) 875-6558
FAX: (306) 875-3812

Mannawanis Native Friendship
Centre Society
PO Box 2519
St Paul, Alberta
T0A 3A0
Telephone: (403) 645-4630
FAX: (403) 645-1980

Napi Friendship Association
PO Box 657
622 Charlotte Street
Pincher Creek, Alberta
T0K 1W0
Telephone: (403) 627-4224
FAX: (403) 627-2564

Nistawoyou Association
Friendship Centre
8310 Manning Avenue
Fort McMurray, Alberta
T9H 1W1
Telephone: (403) 743-8555
FAX: (403) 791-4041

Red Deer Native Friendship
Society
4801 - 49 Street
Red Deer, Alberta
T4N 1T8
Telephone: (403) 340-0020
FAX: (403) 342-1610

Rocky Native Friendship
Society
PO Box 1927
4917 52nd Street
Rocky Mountain House,
Alberta
T0M 1T0
Telephone: (403) 845-2788
FAX: (403) 845-3093

Sagitawa Friendship Centre
PO Box 5083
10108 - 100 Avenue
Peace River, Alberta
T8S 1R7
Telephone: (403) 624-2443
FAX: (403) 624-2728

Sik-Ooh-Kotoki Friendship
Centre
Suite 10, 535 - 13th Street N
Lethbridge, Alberta
T1H 2S6
Telephone: (403) 328-2414
FAX: (403)327-0087

Slave Lake Native Friendship
Centre
416 - 6th Avenue NE
Slave Lake, Alberta
T0G 2A2
Telephone: (403) 849-3039
FAX: (403) 849-2402

* New and Developing

BRITISH COLUMBIA

Cariboo Friendship Society
99 Third Avenue South
Williams Lake, British Columbia
V2G 1J1
Telephone: (604) 398-6831
FAX: (604) 398-6115

Central Okanagan Indian Friendship Society
442 Leon Avenue
Kelowna, British Columbia
V1Y 6J3
Telephone: (604) 763-4905
FAX: (604) 861-5514

Conayt Friendship Centre
PO Box 1989
2067 Quilchena Avenue
Merritt, British Columbia
V0K 2B0
Telephone: (604) 378-5107
FAX: (604) 378-6676

Dze L K'ant Indian Friendship Centre
PO Box 2920
3955 Third Avenue
Smithers, British Columbia
V0J 2N0
Telephone: (604) 847-5211
FAX: (604) 847-5144

First Nations Friendship Centre
2902 - 29 Avenue
Vernon, British Columbia
V1T 1Y7
Telephone: (604) 542-1247
FAX: (604) 542-3707

Fort Nelson-Liard Native Friendship Centre
5012 49th Avenue
PO Box 1266
Fort Nelson, British Columbia
V0C 1R0
Telephone: (604) 774-2993
FAX: (604) 774-2998

Friendship House Association of Prince Rupert
744 Fraser Drive
PO Box 512
Prince Rupert, British Columbia
V8J 3R5
Telephone: (604) 627-1717
FAX: c/o (604) 627-7533

Interior Indian Friendship Society
125 Palm Street
Kamloops, British Columbia
V2B 8J7
Telephone: (604) 376-1296
FAX: (604) 376-2275

Keeginaw Friendship Centre
10208 - 95 Avenue
Fort St John, British Columbia
V1J 1J2
Telephone: (604) 785-8566
FAX: (604)785-1507

Kermode Friendship Centre
3313 Kalum Street
Terrace, British Columbia
V8G 2N7
Telephone: (604) 635-4906
FAX: (604) 635-3013

* New and Developing

Lillooet Friendship Centre Society
PO Box 1270
357 Main Street
Lillooet, British Columbia
V0K 1V0
Telephone: (604) 256-4146
FAX: (604) 256-7928

Mission Indian Friendship Centre
33150 A First Avenue
Mission, British Columbia
V2V 1G4
Telephone: (604) 826-1281
FAX: (604) 826-4056

Nawican Friendship Centre
1320 - 102nd Avenue
PO Box 593
Dawson Creek, British Columbia
V1G 4H4
Telephone: (604) 782-5202
FAX: (604) 782-8411

Port Alberni Friendship Centre
3555 Fourth Avenue
Port Alberni, British Columbia
V9Y 4H3
Telephone: (604) 723-8281
FAX: (604) 723-1877

Prince George Native Friendship Centre
144 George Street
Prince George, British Columbia
V2L 1P9
Telephone: (604) 564-3568
FAX: (604) 563-0924

Quesnel Tillicum Society Friendship Centre
319 North Fraser Drive
Quesnel, British Columbia
V2J 1Y9
Telephone: (604) 992-8347
FAX: (604) 992-5708

Tansi Friendship Centre Society
5301 South Access Road
PO Box 418
Chetwynd, British Columbia
V0C 1J0
Telephone: (604) 788-2996
FAX: (604) 788-2353

Tillicum Haus Native Friendship Centre
927 Haliburton Street
Nanaimo, British Columbia
V9R 6N4
Telephone: (604) 753-8291
FAX: (604) 753-6560

United Native Friendship Centre
2902 29th Ave
Vernon, British Columbia
V1T 1Y7
Telephone: (604) 542-1247
FAX: (604) 542-3707

Valley Native Friendship Centre Society
462 Trans Canada Hwy
PO Box 1015
Duncan, British Columbia
V9L 3Y2
Telephone: (604) 748-2242
FAX: (604) 748-2238

* New and Developing

Vancouver Aboriginal
Friendship Centre Society
1607 East Hasting Street
Vancouver, British Columbia
V5L 1S7
Telephone: (604) 251-4844
FAX: (604) 251-1986

Victoria Native Friendship
Centre
3rd Floor, 531 Yates Street
Victoria, British Columbia
V8W 1K7
Telephone: (604) 384-3211
FAX: (604) 384-1586

LABRADOR
(SEE NEWFOUNDLAND)

MANITOBA

Brandon Friendship Centre
303 - 9th Street
Brandon, Manitoba
R7A 4A8
Telephone: (204) 727-1407
FAX: (204) 726-0902

Dauphin Friendship Centre
210 1st Avenue NE
Dauphin, Manitoba
R7N 1A7
Telephone: (204) 638-5707
FAX: (204) 638-4799

Flin Flon Indian-Metis
Friendship Assoc Inc
PO Box 188
57 Church Street
Flin Flon, Manitoba
R8A 1M7
Telephone: (204) 687-3900
FAX: (204) 687-5328

Indian & Metis Friendship
Centre
45 Robinson Street
Winnipeg, Manitoba
R2W 5H5
Telephone: (204) 586-8441
FAX: (204) 582-8261

Ka-Wawiyak Friendship Centre
Inc.
PO Box 74
Powerview, Manitoba
R0E 1P0
Telephone: (204) 367-2892

Lynn Lake Friendship Centre
PO Box 460
625 Gordon Avenue
Lynn Lake, Manitoba
R0B 0W0
Telephone: (204) 356-2407
FAX: (204) 356-8223

Ma-Mow-We-Tak Friendship
Centre Inc.
122 Hemlock Crescent
Thompson, Manitoba
R8N 0R6
Telephone: (204) 778-7337
FAX: (204) 677-3195

* New and Developing

Portage Friendship Centre
PO Box 1118
Portage La Prairie, Manitoba
R1N 3C5
Telephone: (204) 239-6333
FAX: (204) 239-6534

Riverton & District Friendship Centre Inc.
PO Box 359
Riverton, Manitoba
R0C 2R0
Telephone: (204) 378-2927
FAX: (204) 378-5705

Selkirk Friendship Centre
425 Eveline Street
Selkirk, Manitoba
R1A 2J5
Telephone: (204) 482-7525
FAX: (204) 785-8124

Swan River Indian & Metis Friendship Centre
PO Box 1448
1413 Main Street E
Swan River, Manitoba
R0L 1Z0
Telephone: (204) 734-9301
FAX: (204) 734-3090

The Pas Friendship Centre
PO Box 2638
81 Edwards Avenue
The Pas, Manitoba
R9A 1M3
Telephone: (204) 623-6459
FAX: (204) 623-4268

NEW BRUNSWICK

Fredericton Native Friendship Centre
361 Queen Sreet
Fredericton, New Brunswick
E3B 1B2
Telephone: (506) 459-5283
FAX: (506) 459-1756

NEWFOUNDLAND (LABRADOR)

Labrador Friendship Centre
PO Box 767
Station "B"
Happy Valley-Goose Bay, Labrador (Newfoundland)
A0P 1E0
Telephone: (709) 896-8302
FAX: (709) 896-8731

St John's Native Friendship Centre
61 Cashin Avenue
St John's, Newfoundland
A1E 3B4
Telephone: (709) 726-5902
FAX: (709) 726-3557

NORTHWEST TERRITORIES

Deh Cho Society Centre
PO Box 470
Fort Simpson, Northwest Territories
X0E 0N0
Telephone: (403) 695-2577
FAX: (403) 695-2141

* New and Developing

Ingamo Hall Friendship Centre
PO Box 1293
Inuvik, Northwest Territories
X0E 0T0
Telephone: (403) 979-2166
FAX: (403) 979-2837

Rae-Edzo Friendship Centre
PO Box 85
Rae-Edzo, Northwest Territories
X0E 0Y0
Telephone: (403) 392-6000
FAX: (403) 392-6093

Sappujjijit Friendship Centre
PO Box 429
Rankin Inlet, Northwest Territories
X0C 0G0
Telephone: (819) 645-2488
FAX: (819) 645-2538

Soaring Eagle Friendship Centre
PO Box 396
Hay River, Northwest Territories
X0E 0R0
Telephone: (403) 874-6581
FAX: (403) 874-3362

The Tree of Peace Friendship Centre
PO Box 2667
5009-51 Street
Yellowknife, Northwest Territories
X1A 2P9
Telephone: (403) 873-2864
FAX: (403) 873-5185

Uncle Gabe's Friendship Centre
PO Box 957
Fort Smith, Northwest Territories
X0E 0P0
Telephone: (403) 872-3004
FAX: (403) 872-5313

Zhahti Koe Friendship Centre
General Delivery
Fort Providence, Northwest Territories
X0E 0L0
Telephone: (403) 699-3801
FAX: (403) 699-4355

NOVA SCOTIA

Micmac Native Friendship Centre
2158 Gottingen Street
Halifax, Nova Scotia
B3K 3B4
Telephone: (902) 420-1576
FAX: (902) 423-6130

ONTARIO

Atikokan Native Friendship Centre
PO Box 1510
#307, 309 Main Street
Atikokan, Ontario
P0T 1C0
Telephone: (807) 597-1213
FAX: (807) 597-1473

Barrie Native Friendship Centre*
175 Bayfield Street
Barrie, Ontario
L4M 3B4
Telephone: (705) 721-7689
FAX: (705) 737-4316

Can Am Indian Friendship Centre of Windsor
1684 Ellrose Avenue
Windsor, Ontario
N8Y 3X7
Telephone: (519) 948-8365
FAX: (519) 948-8419

Council Fire Native Cultural Centre Inc*
252 Parliament Street
Lower Level
Toronto, Ontario
M5A 3A4
Telephone: (416) 360-4350
FAX: (416) 360-5978

Dryden Native Friendship Centre*
53 Arthur Street
Dryden, Ontario
P8N 1J7
Telephone: (807) 223-4180
FAX: (807) 223-7136

Fort Erie Native Friendship Centre
796 Buffalo Road
Fort Erie, Ontario
L2A 5H2
Telephone: (905) 871-8931
FAX: (905) 871-9655

Georgian Bay Friendship Centre
175 Yonge Street
Midland, Ontario
L4R 2A7
Telephone: (705) 526-5589
FAX: (705) 526-7662

Hamilton Regional Indian Centre
712 Main Street East
Hamilton, Ontario
L8M 1K8
Telephone: (905) 548-9593
FAX: (905) 545-4077

Indian Friendship Centre
29 Wellington Street E
Sault Ste Marie, Ontario
P6A 6E9
Telephone: (705) 256-5634
FAX: (705) 942-3227

Ininew Friendship Centre
PO Box 1499
190 Third Avenue
Cochrane, Ontario
P0L 1C0
Telephone: (705) 272-4497
FAX: (705) 272-3597

Kapuskasing Indian Friendship Centre*
PO Box 26
62 Riverside
Kapuskasing, Ontario
P5N 1A9
Telephone: (705) 337-1935
FAX: (705) 337-6869

* New and Developing

Katarokwi Friendship Centre*
26 Garrett Street
Kingston, Ontario
K7L 1H6
Telephone: (613) 548-7094
FAX: (613) 530-2111

Moosonee Native Friendship Centre
PO Box 478
Moosonee, Ontario
P0L 1Y0
Telephone: (705) 336-2808
FAX: (705) 336-2929

N-Amerind Friendship Centre
260 Colborne Street
London, Ontario
N6B 2S6
Telephone: (519) 672-0131
FAX: (519) 672-0717

N'Swakamok Native Friendship Centre
110 Elm Street
Sudbury, Ontario
P3C 1T5
Telephone: (705) 674-2128
FAX: (705) 671-3539

Native Canadian Centre of Toronto
16 Spadina Road
Toronto, Ontario
M5R 2S7
Telephone: (416) 964-9087
FAX: (416) 964-6844

Ne-Chee Friendship Centre
PO Box 241
152 Main Street S
Kenora, Ontario
P9N 3X3
Telephone: (807) 468-5440
FAX: (807) 468-5340

Niagara Regional Native Centre*
RR #4
Queenston & Taylor Road
Niagara-on-the-Lake, Ontario
L0S 1J0
Telephone: (902) 688-6484

Nishnawbe-Gamik Friendship Centre
PO Box 1299
52 King Street
Sioux Lookout, Ontario
P8T 1B8
Telephone: (807) 737-1903
FAX: (807) 737-1805

North Bay Indian Friendship Centre
980 Cassells Street
North Bay, Ontario
P1B 4A6
Telephone: (705) 472-2811
FAX: (705) 472-5251

Odawa Native Friendship Centre
396 MacLaren Street
Ottawa, Ontario
K2P 0M8
Telephone: (613) 238-8591
FAX: (613) 238-6106

* New and Developing

Parry Sound Friendship Centre
13 Bowes Street
Parry Sound, Ontario
P2A 2K7
Telephone: (705) 746-5970
FAX: (705) 746-2612

Pine Tree Native Centre of Brant*
25 King Street
Brantford, Ontario
N3T 3C4
Telephone: (519) 752-5132
FAX: (519) 752-5612

Red Lake Indian Friendship Centre*
PO Box 244
Red Lake, Ontario
P0V 2M0
Telephone: (807) 727-2847
FAX: (807) 727-3253

Thunder Bay Indian Friendship Centre
401 N Cumberland Street
Thunder Bay, Ontario
P7A 4P7
Telephone: (807) 345-5840
FAX: (807) 344-8945

Thunderbird Friendship Centre
PO Box 430
301 Beamish Avenue West
Geraldton, Ontario
P0T 1M0
Telephone: (807) 854-1060
FAX: (807) 854-0861

Timmins Native Friendship Centre*
316 Spruce Street S
Timmins, Ontario
P4N 2M9
Telephone: (705) 268-6262
FAX: (705) 268-6266

United Native Friendship Centre
PO Box 752
516 Portage Avenue
Fort Frances, Ontario
P9A 3N1
Telephone: (807) 274-3207
FAX: (807) 274-4110

QUÉBEC

Centre d'amitié autochtone de Québec
234, rue Saint Louis
Lorretteville, Québec
G2B 1L4
Telephone: (418) 843-5818
FAX: (418) 843-8960

Centre d'amitié autochtone de Val d'Or
1101, 6e rue
Val d'Or, Québec
J9P 3W4
Telephone: (819) 825-6857
FAX: (819) 825-7515

* New and Developing

Centre d'amitié autochtone La Tuque
C.P. 335
544, rue St.-Antoine
La Tuque, Québec
G9X 3P3
Telephone: (819) 523-6121
FAX: (819) 523-8637

Centre d'entraide et d'amitié autochtone de Senneterre Inc
C.P. 1769
910, 10e Avenue
Senneterre, Québec
J0Y 2M0
Telephone: (819) 737-2324
FAX: (819) 737-8311

Cree Indian Centre of Chibougamau Inc
95 rue Jaculét
Chibougamau, Québec
G8P 2G1
Telephone: (418) 748-7667
FAX: (418) 748-6954

Native Friendship Centre of Montréal
3730 Côte des Neiges Road
Montréal, Québec
H3H 1V6
Telephone: (514) 937-5338
FAX: (514) 937-4437

SASKATCHEWAN

Battlefords Indian & Métis Friendship Centre
12002 Railway Avenue East
North Battleford, Saskatchewan
S9A 3W3
Telephone: (306) 445-8216
FAX: (306) 445-6863

Buffalo Narrows Friendship Centre
PO Box 189
Buffalo Narrows, Saskatchewan
S0M 0J0
Telephone: (306) 235-4660
FAX: (306) 235-4544

Ile a la Crosse Friendship Centre
PO Box 160
Ile a la Crosse, Saskatchewan
S0M 1C0
Telephone: (306) 833-2313
FAX: (306) 833-2216

Kikinahk Friendship Centre
PO Box 254
320 Boardman Street
LaRonge, Saskatchewan
S0J 1L0
Telephone: (306) 425-2051
FAX: (306) 425-3755

Moose Jaw Native Friendship Centre
42 High Street East
Moose Jaw, Saskatchewan
S6H 0B7
Telephone: (306) 693-6966
FAX: (306) 692-3509

* New and Developing

Moose Mountain Friendship Centre
107 Main Street
Carlyle, Saskatchewan
S0C 0R0
Telephone: (306) 453-2425
FAX: (306) 453-6777

North West Friendship Centre
PO Box 1780
Meadow Lake, Saskatchewan
S0M 1V0
Telephone: (306) 236-3766
FAX: (306) 236-5451

Prince Albert Indian & Métis Friendship Centre
PO Box 2197
1409 - 1st Avenue East
Prince Albert, Saskatchewan
S6V 6Z1
Telephone: (306) 764-3431
FAX: (306) 763-3205

Qu'Appelle Valley Friendship Centre
PO Box 240
Fort Qu'Appelle, Saskatchewan
S0G 1S0
Telephone: (306) 332-5616
FAX: (306) 332-5091

Regina Friendship Centre Corporation
1440 Scarth Street
Regina, Saskatchewan
S4R 2E9
Telephone: (306) 525-5459
FAX: (306) 525-3005

Saskatoon Indian & Métis Friendship Centre
168 Wall Street
Saskatoon, Saskatchewan
S7K 1N4
Telephone: (306) 244-0174
FAX: (306) 664-2536

Yorkton Friendship Centre
108 Myrtle Avenue
Yorkton, Saskatchewan
S3N 1P7
Telephone: (306) 782-2822
FAX: (306) 782-6662

YUKON

Skookum Jim Friendship Centre
3159 - 3rd Avenue
Whitehorse, Yukon
Y1A 1G1
Telephone: (403) 633-7680
FAX: (403) 668-4460

Information provided by:
Nat'l Association of Friendship Centres

* New and Developing

NATIONAL NATIVE CULTURAL/EDUCATIONAL CENTERS

National Association of Cultural Education Centres
RR # 3
Cornwall Island, Ontario
K6H 5R7
Telephone: (613) 932-9452
FAX: (613) 932-0092

Inuit Tapirisat of Canada
510 - 170 Laurier Ave W
Ottawa, Ontario
K1P 5V5
Telephone: (613) 238-8181
FAX: (613) 234-1991

PROVINCIAL/TERRITORIAL ORGANIZATIONS

ALBERTA

Beaver Lake Band
Beaver Lake Cultural Program
Box 960
Lac La Biche, Alberta
T0A 2C0
Telephone: (403) 623-4549
Telephone: (403) 623-4548
FAX: (403) 623-4523
Telephone: (403) 623-4659

Frog Lake Indian Band
Frog Lake, Alberta
T0A 1M0
Telephone: (403) 943-3737
Telephone: (403) 943-3980
FAX: (403) 943-3966

Kehewin Cultural Education Centre
Box 6218
Bonneyville, Alberta
T9N 2G8
Telephone: (403) 826-3333
Telephone: (403) 826-6200
FAX: (403) 826-2355

Maskwachees Cultural College
Box 360
Hobbema, Alberta
T0C 1N0
Telephone: (403) 585-3925
Telephone: (403) 585-3995
FAX: (403) 585-2080

Ninastako Cultural Centre
Box 1299
Cardston, Alberta
T0K 0K0
Telephone: (403) 737-3774
FAX: (403) 737-3786

Oldman River Cultural Centre
PO Box 70
Brocket, Alberta
T0K 0H0
Telephone: (403) 965-3939
FAX: (403) 965-3713

Siksika Cultural Centre
Box 249
Gleichen, Alberta
T0J 1N0
Telephone: (403) 734-5100
Telephone: (403) 264-7250
FAX: (403) 734-5110

Saddle Lake Cultural Education Program
Box 100
Saddle Lake, Alberta
T0A 3T0
Telephone: (403) 726-3829
FAX: (403) 726-3788

Sarcee Cultural Program
Tsut'ina K'osa
Box 135
3700 Anderson Rd SW
Calgary, Alberta
T2W 3C4
Telephone: (403) 238-2677
FAX: (403) 251-5871

Stoney Curriculum Education Centre
Stoney Indian Band
PO Box 40
Morley, Alberta
T0L 1N0
Telephone: (403) 881-3770
Ext. 350
FAX: (403) 881-3909

BRITISH COLUMBIA

Bella Coola Indian Band
Nuxalk Education Authority
PO Box 778
Bella Coola, British Columbia
V0T 1C0
Telephone: (604) 799-5423
FAX: (604) 799-5426

Canoe Creek Indian Band
General Delivery
Dog Creek, British Columbia
V0L 1J0
Telephone: (604) 440-5645
Telephone: (604) 392-2664
FAX: (604) 440-5679

Coqualeetza Education Training Centre
7201 Vedder Road
PO Box 370
Sardis, British Columbia
V2R
Telephone: (604) 858-9431
FAX: (604) 858-8488

Cowichan Band Council
PO Box 880
Duncan, British Columbia
V9L 3Y2
Telephone: (604) 748-3196
FAX: (604) 748-1233

Heiltsuk Cultural Education
Centre (Bella Bella)
Box 880
Waglisla, British Columbia
V0T 1Z0
Telephone: (604) 957-2381
Telephone: (604) 957-2626
FAX: (604) 957-2544

Lake Babine Band
PO Box 879
Burns Lake, British Columbia
V0J 1E0
Telephone: (604) 692-7555
FAX: (604) 692-7559

Mount Currie Band
Ts'zil Board of Education
PO Box 193
Mount Currie, British Columbia
V0N 2K0
Telephone: (604) 894-6131
Telephone: (604) 894-5424
FAX: (604) 894-6841

Nimpkish Band Council
Box 210
Albert Bay, British Columbia
V0N 1A0
Telephone: (604) 974-5591
Telephone: (604) 974-5556
FAX: (604) 974-5900

Okanagan Indian Educational
Resources Society
257 Brunswick Street
Penticton, British Columbia
V2A 5P9
Telephone: (604) 493-7181
FAX: (604) 493-5302

Saanich Cultural Education
Centre
7449 West Saanich Road
PO Box 368
Brentwood Bay,
British Columbia
V0S 1A0
Telephone: (604) 652-1811
FAX: (604) 652-6929

Secwepemc Cultural Education
Society
345 Yellowhead Highway
Kamloops, British Columbia
V2H 1H1
Telephone: (604) 828-0979
FAX: (604) 372-1127

Sliammon Cultural Centre
RR # 2, Sliammon Road
Powell River, British Columbia
V8A 4Z4
Telephone: (604) 483-9317
Telephone: (604) 483-9646
FAX: (604) 483-9769

Stoney Creek Band
Stoney Creek Elders Cultural Society
Site 12, Comp 15, RR 1
Vanderhoof, British Columbia
V0J 3A0
Telephone: (604) 567-4293
FAX: (604) 567-2998

U'Mista Cultural Centre
Box 253
Alert Bay, British Columbia
V0N 1A0
Telephone: (604) 974-5403

LABRADOR

Torngasok Cultural Centre
PO Box 40
Nain, Labrador
A0P 1L0
Telephone: (709) 922-2139
FAX: (709) 922-2863

MANITOBA

Brokenhead Cultural Centre
Brokenhead Cultural Program
Brokenhead Indian Band
Scanterbury, Manitoba
R0E 1W0
Telephone: (204) 766-2494
FAX: (204) 766-2270

Cross Lake Cultural Education Program
PO Box 10
Cross Lake, Manitoba
R0B 0J0
Telephone: (204) 676-2218
FAX: (204) 676-2117

Dakota Ojibway Tribal Council
702 Douglas Street
PO Box 1148
Brandon, Manitoba
R7A 5V2
Telephone: (204) 725-3560
Telephone: (204) 725-3682
FAX: (204) 726-5966

Interlake Reserves Tribal Council
PO Box 580
Ashern, Manitoba
R0C 0E0
Telephone: (204) 659-4465
Telephone: (204) 659-5817
FAX: (204) 659-2147

Manitoba Indian Cultural Education Centre
119 Sutherland Avenue
Winnipeg, Manitoba
R2W 3C9
Telephone: (204) 942-0228
FAX: (204) 947-6564

Cultural Education Centre
Norway House Indian Band Education Authority
PO Box 218
Norway House, Manitoba
R0B 1B0
Telephone: (204) 359-6313
Telephone: (204) 359-6721
FAX: (204) 359-6080

Peguis Cultural Centre
Box 219
Hodgson, Manitoba
R0C 1N0
Telephone: (204) 645-2359

Rolling River Cultural Centre
Rolling River Indian Band
PO Box 145
Erickson, Manitoba
R0J 0P0
Telephone: (204) 636-2211

Sagkeeng Cultural Centre Inc.
Box 749
Pine Falls, Manitoba
R0E 1M0
Telephone: (204) 367-8740
FAX: (204) 943-1482

West Region Tribal Council
Indian Cultural Education Program
21 - 4th Avenue NW
Dauphin, Manitoba
R7N 1H9
Telephone: (204) 638-8225
FAX: (204) 638-8062

NEW BRUNSWICK

Big Cove Cultural Centre
Big Cove Band Council
Site 11, Box 1
Big Cove County,
New Brunswick
E0A 2L0
Telephone: (506) 523-9183
FAX: (506) 523-4901

Buctouche Micmac Band
RR #2, Box 9, Site 1
Buctouche, New Brunswick
E0E 1G0
Telephone: (506) 743-6493

Eel Ground
Eel Ground Indian Band
Box 9, Site 3, RR #1
Newcastle, New Brunswick
E1V 3L8
Telephone: (506) 622-2181
FAX: (506) 622-8667

Eel River Bar Band
Education Committee
PO Box 1444
Dalhousie, New Brunswick
E0K 1B0
Telephone: (506) 684-5268
Telephone: (506) 684-3360
FAX: (506) 684-5840

Fort Folly Indian Band
PO Box 21
Dorchester, New Brunswick
E0A 1M0
Telephone: (506) 379-6224
FAX: (506) 379-6641

Kingsclear Indian Band
RR #6, Comp. 19
Fredericton, New Brunswick
E3B 4X7
Telephone: (506) 363-3028
FAX: (506) 363-4324

Oromocto Nation
PO Box 417
Oromocto, New Brunswick
E2V 2J2
Telephone: (506) 357-2083
FAX: (506) 357-2089

Pabineau Indian Band
Box 1, RR #5, Site 26
Bathurst, New Brunswick
E2A 3Y8
Telephone: (506) 548-9211
FAX: (506) 548-9849

Red Bank Band
PO Box 120
Red Bank, New Brunswick
E0C 1W0
Telephone: (506) 836-2366
FAX: (506) 836-7669

St. Mary's Indian Band
247 Paul Street
Fredericton, New Brunswick
E3A 2V7
Telephone: (506) 458-9511
FAX: (506) 458-2850

Tobique Indian Band
RR #3, PO Box 840
Perth, New Brunswick
E0J 1V0
Telephone: (506) 273-6815
FAX: (506) 273-3035

NORTHWEST TERRITORIES

Dené Cultural Institute
PO Box 570
Hay River, Northwest Territories
X0E 0R0
Telephone: (403) 873-6617
FAX: (403) 873-3867

Inuit Cultural Institute (ICI)
Rankin Inlet,
Northwest Territories
X0C 0G0
Telephone: (819) 645-3021
FAX: (819) 645-3020

NOVA SCOTIA

Micmac Association of Cultural Studies
PO Box 961
Sydney, Nova Scotia
B1P 6J4
Telephone: (902) 539-8037
Telephone: (902) 539-9098
FAX: (902) 539-6645

ONTARIO

Batchewana Indian Band
Rankin Reserve
236 Frontenac Street
R R #4
Sault Ste. Marie, Ontario
P6A 5K9
Telephone: (705) 759-0914
FAX: (705) 759-9171

Lake of the Woods Ojibway Cultural Centre
PO Box 159
Kenora, Ontario
P9N 3X3
Telephone: (807) 548-5744
FAX: (807) 548-1591

North American Indian
Travelling College
Onake Corporation
(N.A.I.T.C.)
R R #3
Cornwall Island, Ontario
K6H 5R7
Telephone: (613) 932-9452
FAX: (613) 932-0092

Ojibway and Cree Cutlural
Centre
84 Elm St. South
Timmins, Ontario
P4N 1W6
Telephone: (705) 267-7911
FAX: (705) 267-4988

Ojibwe Cultural Foundation
PO Box 278
West Bay Indian Reserve
Manitoulin, Ontario
P0P 1G0
Telephone: (705) 377-4902
FAX: (705) 377-5460

Woodland Cultural Centre
PO Box 1506
Brantford, Ontario
N3T 5V6
Telephone: (519) 759-2653
FAX: (519) 759-8912

PRINCE EDWARD ISLAND

Lennox Island Cultural
Educational Centre
Box 134
Lennox Island,
Prince Edward Island
C0B 1P0
Telephone: (902) 831-2779
FAX: (902) 831-3153

QUÉBEC

Avataq Cultural Institute, Inc.
294 Carre St Louis
Montreal, Québec
H2X 1A4
Telephone: (514) 844-0109
FAX: (514) 848-9648

Avataq Cultural Institute, Inc.
Inukjuak, Québec
J0M 1M0
Telephone: (819) 254-8919
FAX: (819) 254-8148

Algonquin Nation Programs &
Services Secretariat
Timiskamingh Reserve
Notre-Dame Du Nord, Québec
J0Z 3B0
Telephone: (819) 723-2019
FAX: (819) 723-2345

Conseil de la Atikamekw
317, St. Joseph, C.P. 848
La Tuque, Québec
G9X 3P6
Telephone: (819) 523-6153
FAX: (819) 523-8706

James Bay Cree Cultural
Education Centre
Box 390
Chisasibi, Québec
J0M 1E0
Telephone: (819) 855-2473
FAX: (819) 733-6271

Institut Culturel et éducatif
montagnais
40, rue Francois Gros-Louis, #7
Wendake (Village des Huron),
Québec
G0A 4V0
Telephone: (418) 843-0258
FAX: (418) 843-7313

Kanesatake Cultural Centre
(Oka)
681 Ste. Philmoene
PO Box 971
Kanesatake, Québec
J0N 1E0
Telephone: (514) 479-8373
FAX: (514) 479-8249

Kanien'kehaka Raotitiohkwa
Kahnawake Indian Band
Box 1988
Kahnawake, Québec
J0L 1B0
Telephone: (514) 638-0880
FAX: (514) 638-0920

Lac Simon Centre Amikwan
Conseil de bande du Lac Simon
Via Louvicourt, Abitibi-Est
Comté Villeneuve, Québec
J0Y 1Y0
Telephone: (819) 736-3161

Maria Band
Micmacs of Maria Band
Maria Reserve
PO Box 1280
Maria, Québec
G0C 1Y0
Telephone: (418) 759-3422
Telephone: (418) 759-3591
FAX: (418) 759-5856

National Huronne-Wendat
Village des Hurons Wendake,
Québec
G0A 4V0
Telephone: (418) 843-3663
Telephone: (418) 843-3767
FAX: (418) 842-1108

Odanak
Reserve Indienne d'Odanak
58, rue Waban-aki
Odanak, Québec
J0C 1H0
Telephone: (514) 568-2810
FAX: (514) 568-3553

Restigouche Institute of
Cultural Education
17 Riverside West
Restigouche, Québec
G0C 2R0
Telephone: (418) 788-2136
Ext. 56
FAX: (418) 788-2058

River Desert Cultural Education Centre
PO Box 309
Maniwaki, Québec
J9E 3B3
Telephone: (819) 449-5039
Telephone: (819) 449-5170
FAX: (819) 449-5673

SASKATCHEWAN

Saskatchewan Indian Cultural Centre
120 - 33rd St. East
Saskatoon, Saskatchewan
S7K 3S9
Telephone: (306) 244-1146
FAX: (306) 665-6520

YUKON TERRITOTY

Champagne/Aishihik First Nations
Box 5309
Haines Junction,
Yukon Territory
Y0B 1L0
Telephone: (403) 634-2288
FAX: (403) 634-2108

Teslin Tlingit Council
General Delivery
Teslin, Yukon Territory
Y0A 1B0
Telephone: (403) 390-2532
Telephone: (403) 390-2560
FAX: (403) 390-2204

Yukon Indian Cultural Education Society
22 Nisutlin Drive
Whitehorse, Yukon Territory
Y1A 3S5
Telephone: (403) 667-7631
FAX: (403) 668-6577

MUSEUMS AND CULTURAL CENTERS (INDIAN OWNED)

ALBERTA

BLACKFOOT MUSEUM
Old Sun Community College
PO Box 1039
Siksika, Alberta T0J 3W0
403-734-3070

FROG LAKE CULTURAL EDUCATION CENTRE
Frog Lake, Alberta T0A 1M0

HEAD-SMASHED-IN BUFFALO JUMP INTERPRETIVE CENTRE
PO Box 1977
Fort McLeod, Alberta T0L 0Z0
403-553-2731

KEHEWIN COMMUNITY EDUCATION CENTRE
Box 218
Bonnyville, Alberta T0A 0L0
403-826-3333

MASKWACHEES CULTURAL COLLEGE
Box 360
Hobbema, Alberta T0C 1N0
403-585-3925

NAKODA INSTITUTE
PO Box 120
Morley, Alberta T0L 1N0
403-881-3770

NINASTAKO CENTRE
Box 1299
Cardston, Alberta T0K 0K0
403-737-3774

OLDMAN RIVER CULTURAL CENTRE
PO Box 70
Brocket, Alberta T0K 0H0
403-965-3939

BRITISH COLUMBIA

COQUALEETZA EDUCATION TRAINING CENTRE
PO Box 370
Sardis, British Columbia V0X 1Y0
604-858-9431

ED JONES CULTURAL/EDUCATIONAL CENTRE
Box 189
Masset, British Columbia V0T 1M0
604-626-5128

HEILTSUK CULTURAL EDUCATION CENTRE
Box 879
Waglisla, British Columbia V0T 1Z0
604-957-2381

'KSAN INDIAN VILLAGE AND MUSEUM
PO Box 326
Hazelton, British Columbia
V0J 1Y0

KWAGIULTH MUSEUM
PO Box 8
Quathiaski Cove,
British Columbia
V0P 1N0

LYTTON HERITAGE SOCIETY
PO Box 117
Lytton, British Columbia
V0K 1Z0

OKANAGAN INDIAN EDUCATIONAL RESOURCES SOCIETY
257 Brunswick St
Penticton, British Columbia
V2A 5P9
604-493-7181

SAANICH INDIAN CULTURAL EDUCATION CENTRE
7449 W Saanich Rd
PO Box 368
Brentwood Bay,
British Columbia V0S 1A0
604-652-1811

SECWEPEMC CULTURAL EDUCATION SOCIETY
345 Yellowhead Highway
Kamloops, British Columbia
V2H 1H1
604-374-0616

SLIAMMON CULTURAL CENTRE
RR # 2, Sliammon Rd
Powell River, British Columbia
V8A 4Z4
604-283-9317

STONEY CREEK ELDERS CULTURAL SOCIETY
Vanderhoof, British Columbia
V0J 3A0
604-567-9293

U'MISTA CULTURAL CENTRE
PO Box 253
Alert Bay, British Columbia
V0N 1A0
604-974-5403

MANITOBA

CROSS LAKE CULTURAL/EDUCATION CENTRE
Cross Lake Indian Reserve
Cross Lake, Manitoba R0B 0J0
204-676-2166

MANITOBA INDIAN CULTURAL EDUCATION CENTRE
119 Sutherland Ave
Winnipeg, Manitoba R2W 3C9
204-942-0228

NORWAY HOUSE INDIAN BAND CULTURAL EDUCATION CENTRE
PO Box 218
Norway House, Manitoba
R0B 1B0
204-359-6313

PEQUIS CULTURAL CENTRE
Box 219
Hodgson, Manitoba R0C 1N0
204-645-2359

SAGKEENG CULTURAL CENTRE
Box 749
Pine Falls, Manitoba R0E 1M0
204-367-8740

NEW BRUNSWICK

BIG COVE CULTURAL CENTRE
Big Cove Reserve
RR # 1
Rexton, New Brunswick
E0A 2L0
506-523-6384

NORTHWEST TERRITORIES

DENE CULTURAL INSTITUTE
PO Box 207
Yellowknife,
Northwest Territories X1A 2N2
403-873-6617

SIPALASEEQUTT MUSEUM SOCIETY
Pangnirtung,
Northwest Territories X0A 0R0

NOVA SCOTIA

MICMAC ASSOCIATION OF CULTURAL STUDIES
PO Box 961
Sydney, Nova Scotia B1P 6J4
902-539-8037

ONTARIO

CHIEFSWOOD MUSEUM
c/o Six Nations Tourism
General Delivery
Ohsweken, Ontario N0A 1M0
519-445-2201

GOLDEN LAKE ALGONQUIN MUSEUM
PO Box 28
Golden Lake, Ontario K0J 1X0

LAKE OF THE WOODS OJIBWAY CULTURAL CENTRE
PO Box 1720
Kenora, Ontario P9N 3X7
807-548-5744

MUSEUM OF THE NORTH AMERICAN INDIAN TRAVELLING COLLEGE
RR 3
Cornwall Island, Ontario
K6H 5R7
613-932-9452

OJIBWAY AND CREE
CULTURAL CENTRE
84 Elm St S
Timmins, ON P4N 1W6
705-267-7911

WOODLAND INDIAN
CULTURAL EDUCATIONAL
CENTRE
184 Mohawk St
PO Box 1506
Brantford, Ontario N3T 5V6
519-759-2650

QUÉBEC

AMIKWAN CENTRE
CONSEIL DE BANDE DU
LAC SIMON
Via Louvicourt, Abitibi-Est
Comte Villeneuve, Québec
J0Y 1M0

AVATAQ CULTURAL
INSTITUTE, INC.
Inukjuak, Québec J0M 1M0
819-254-8919

CREE CULTURAL
EDUCATION CENTRE
Box 291
Chisasibi, Québec J0M 1E0
819-855-2821

HISTORICAL MUSEUM OF
INUIT Povungnituk
Povungnituk, Québec G0M 1P6

INSTITUT EDUCATIF ET
CULTUREL ATTIKAMEK-
MOTAGNAIS
40 rue Francois Gros-Louis
No. 7
Village des Hurons, Québec
G0A 4V0
418-843-0258

KANESATAKE CULTURAL
CENTRE
681 B Ste Philomene
PO Box 640
Kanestake, Québec J0N 1E0
514-479-8524

MASHTEVIATSH POINTE-
BLEUE MUSEUM
406, rue Amisk
Mashteviatsh, Québec
G0W 2H0

MI'GMAQ CULTURE
INTERPRETATION CENTRE
Listuguj Mi'gmaq First Nation
Government
178 Riverside West
Listuguj, Québec G0G 2R0
482-788-2136

MUSEE DES ABENAKIS
108 rue Waban-Aki
Odanak, Québec J0G 1H0
514-568-2600

RESTIGOUCHE INSTITUTE
OF CULTURAL EDUCATION
Retigouche Indian Band
2 Riverside West
Restigouche, Québec G0C 2R0
418-788-2904

RIVER DESERT CULTURAL
EDUCATIONAL CENTRE
River Desert Band
PO Box 309
Maniwaki, Québec J9E 3B3
819-449-5039

SASKATCHEWAN

SASKATCHEWAN INDIAN
CULTURAL CENTRE
120 33rd St East
PO Box 3085
Saskatoon, Saskatchewan
S7K 3S9
306-244-1146

YUKON

YUKON INDIAN CULTURAL
EDUCATION SOCIETY
11 Nisutlin Dr
Whitehorse, Yukon Y1A 3S4
403-667-7631

assistance provided by: Smithsonian Institution
Center for Museum Studies

NATIVE ARTS AND CRAFTS ORGANIZATIONS

BRITISH COLUMBIA

Indian Arts & Crafts Society of British Columbia
530 Hornby Street, Suite 402
Vancouver, British Columbia
V6C 2E7
Telephone: (604) 682-8988
FAX: (604) 682-8994

NORTHWEST TERRITORIES

Northwest Territories Native Arts & Crafts Society
PO Box 2765
Yellowknife,
Northwest Territories
X1A 2R1
Telephone: (403) 920-2854

ONTARIO

Art-I-Crafts Corporation
10 Woodway Trail
Brantford, Ontario
N3R 5Z8
Telephone: (519) 751-0040

QUÉBEC

Les Artisans Indians du Québec
540 Max Gros-Louis Street
Village des Hurons, Québec
G0A 4V0
Telephone: (418) 845-2150

YUKON

Yukon Indian Arts and Crafts Cooperative Ltd.
4230 Fourth Avenue
Whitehorse, Yukon
Y1A 1K1
Telephone: (403) 668-5955

NATIVE AMERICAN DRUMMERS AND MASTER OF CEREMONIES

ALBERTA

BLACKFOOT CROSSING SINGERS
PO Box 222
Cluny, AB

BROKEN KNIFE
Box 11
3700 Anderson Rd SW
Sarcee, AB

HAWK RIVER DRUM
Box 42
Glenevis, AB

LITTLE BOY
Box 305
Duffield, AB
403-967-4032

NAKODA NATION
Box 63
Morley, AB

NORTHERN CREE
PO Box 296
Hobbema, AB
403-585-3258

MARK POUCETTE
PO Box 63
Morley, AB
403-881-3862

RED BULL
Box 197
Saddle Lake, AB T0A 3T0
403-726-3181

STONY PARK
PO Box 82
Exshaw Delta, AB
403-881-2142

BRITISH COLUMBIA

CATHEDRAL LAKES
Box 297
Keremeos, BC

MANITOBA

SIOUX-ASSINIBIONE
PO Box 218
Pipestone, MB
204-854-2219

ONTARIO

MONG SINGERS
PO Box 8
Manitowaning, ON
705-859-3606

SWEET GRASS SINGERS
287 Beaver Cir
Sarnia, ON
519-336-1587

WALPOLE ISLAND DRUM
RR # 3 Wallaceburg
Walpole Island, ON

WHITE EYE SINGERS
RR 3 Wallaceburg
Walpole Island, ON
519-627-2932

WHITE FISH BAY SINGERS
Pawitik, ON
807-226-1155

WOSS NOH DEH DRUM
RR # 1 Wikwemikong
Mantoulin Island, ON

SASKATCHEWAN

BATTLE CREEK
PO Box 162
Cando, SK
306-937-2037

TERRY PASKEMIN
PO Box 125
Gallinan, SK
306-937-7388

STAR BLANKET JRS
PO Box 746
Balcarres, SK S0G 0C0

CANADA

ABORIGINAL MEDIA
NATIONAL ORGANIZATIONS

National Aboriginal Communications Society
15001 - 112nd Ave
Edmonton, Alberta
T5M 2V6
Telephone: (403) 453-6100
FAX: (403) 453-6259
.....to act as a national body for Native Media accross Canada....

Native Journalist Association
R.R. No. 1
Ohsweken, Ontario
N0A 1M0
Telephone: (519) 445-4730
FAX: (416) 205-5945
.....as the Canadian counterpart to the Native American Journalists Association.....

Studio One
9700 Jasper Avenue, Suite 120
Edmonton, Alberta
T5J 4C3
Telephone: (403) 495-5874
FAX: (403) 495-6412
.....to assist Aboriginal people with training in the production of documentaries and films.....distributor for films and videos about Aboriginal people in Canada.....

NATIONAL ABORIGINAL COMMUNICATIONS SOCIETY (NACS)

National Aboriginal Communications Society
Box 2250
Lac La Biche, Alberta
T0A 2C0
Telephone: (403) 623-3301
FAX: (403) 623-3302

PROVINCIAL/TERRITORIAL ORGANIZATIONS

ALBERTA

Aboriginal Multi-Media Society of Alberta (AMMSA)
15001 - 112 Avenue
Edmonton, Alberta
T5M 2V6
Telephone: (403) 455-2700
FAX: (403) 455-7639

The Native Perspective
Box 2250
Lac La Biche, Alberta
T0A 2C0
Telephone: (403) 623-3333
FAX: (403) 623-2811

BRITISH COLUMBIA

Native Communications Society of British Columbia
203 - 540 Burrard Street
Vancouver, British Columbia
V6E 3H4
Telephone: (604) 684-7375
FAX: (604) 684-5375

Northern Native Broadcasting Terrace
Box 1090
Terrace, British Columbia
V8G 4V1
Telephone: (604) 638-8137
FAX: (604) 638-8027

LABRADOR

Okalakatiget Society
Box 160
Nain, Labrador
A0P 1L0
Telephone: (709) 922-2955
FAX: (709) 922-2293

MANITOBA

Native Communications Incorporated
76 Severn Crescent
Thompson, Manitoba
R8N 1M6
Telephone: (204) 778-8343
FAX: (204) 778-6559

NORTHWEST TERRITORIES

Inuvialuit Communications Society
Box 1704
Inuvik, Northwest Territories
X0E 0T0
Telephone: (403) 979-2067
FAX: (403) 979-2744

Native Communications Society of The Western Northwest Territories
Box 1919
N.W.T. Communications Centre
Yellowknife, Northwest Territories
X1A 1P8
Telephone: (403) 873-2661
FAX: (403) 920-4205

NOVA SCOTIA

Native Communications Society of Nova Scotia
Box 344
Sydney, Nova Scotia
B1P 6H2
Telephone: (902) 539-0045
FAX: (902) 564-0430

ONTARIO

Inuit Broadcasting Corporation
251 Laurier Avenue, Suite 703
Ottawa, Ontario
K1P 5J6
Telephone: (613) 235-1892
FAX: (613) 230-8824

Wawatay Native Communications Society
Box 1180, 16 Fifth Avenue
Sioux Lookout, Ontario
P0V 2T0
Telephone: (807) 737-2951
FAX: (807) 737-3224

QUÉBEC

James Bay Cree Communications Society
Lake Mistissini, Québec
G0W 1C0
Telephone: (418) 923-3191
FAX: (418) 923-2088

Société de Communications Atikamekw Montagnais (SOCAM)
80 Boul Bastien
Village des Hurons, Québec
G0A 4V0
Telephone: (418) 843-3873
FAX: (418) 845-9774

Taqramiut Nipingat Inc. (TNI)
185 Dorval Avenue, Suite 501
Dorval, Québec
H9S 3G6
Telephone: (514) 631-1394
FAX: (514) 631-6258

SASKATCHEWAN

Missinipi Broadcasting
Corporation
Box 1529, Laronge Avenue
LaRonge, Saskatchewan
S0J 1L0
Telephone: (306) 425-4003
FAX: (306) 425-3775

Saskatchewan Native
Communications Society
202 - 173 Second Avenue South
Saskatoon, Saskatchewan
S7K 1K6
Telephone: (306) 653-2253
FAX: (306) 664-8551

YUKON

Northern Native Broadcasting -
Yukon
4228 A Fourth Avenue
Whitehorse, Yukon
Y1A 1K1
Telephone: (403) 668-6629
FAX: (403) 668-6612

YE SA TO Communications
Society
11 Nisutlin Drive
Whitehorse, Yukon
Y1A 3S4
Telephone: (403) 667-2774
FAX: (403) 667-6923

ABORIGINAL PRINT MEDIA BY REGION

ALBERTA REGION

Aboriginal Mutli-Media Society of Alberta
15001 - 112 Avenue
Edmonton, Alberta
T5M 2V6
Telephone: (403) 455-2700
FAX: (403) 455-7639

Achimowen
Mikisew Cree First Nation
PO Box 90
Ft. Chipewyan, Alberta
T0P 1B0
Telephone: 403) 697-3740
FAX: (403) 697-3826

Alberta Native News
10036 Jasper Ave Suite 530
Edmonton, Alberta
T5J 2W2
Telephone: (403) 421-7966
FAX: (403) 424-3951

Alberta Sweetgrass
15001 - 112 Avenue
Edmonton, Alberta
T5M 2V6
Telephone: (403) 455-2945
FAX: (403) 455-7639

Blood Tribe Community News
Box 106
Standoff, Alberta
T0L 1Y0
Telephone: (403) 737-2121
FAX: (403) 737-2336

CFWE FM Radio
15001 - 112th Ave
Edmonton, Alberta
T5M 2V6
Telephone: (403) 447-2393
FAX: (403) 454-2820

Cornerstone Press
5B 3911 Brandon Street SE
Calgary, Alberta
T2G 1X5
Telephone: (403) 287-3744
FAX: (403) 287-3714

First Nations Free Press
90 Sioux Rd
Sherwood Park, Alberta
T8A 3X5
Telephone: (403) 449-1803
FAX: (403) 449-1807

The Four Nations Local
PO Box 427
Hobbema, Alberta
T0C 1N0
Telephone: (403) 585-2900

Le Franco
8923, 82 East Ave
Edmonton, Alberta
T6C 0Z2
Telephone: (403) 465-6581

Mawio'mi Journal
10036 Jasper Avenue Suite 240
Edmonton, Alberta
T5J 2W2
Telephone: (403) 990-0303
FAX: (403) 429-7487

Morrow Communications
1612 - 37 Street
Edmonton, Alberta
T6L 2R7
Telephone: (403) 462-1795
FAX: (403) 462-2522

Plains Cree Today
Saddle Lake, First Nations News
PO Box 130
Saddle Lake, Alberta
T0A 3T0
Telephone: (403) 726-2200
FAX: (403) 726-3788

Pow Wow Press
c/o First Nations Resource Council
136 Jasper Avenue Suite 502
Edmonton, Alberta
T5J 2W2
Telephone: (403) 453-6114
FAX: (403) 453-6150

National Aboriginal Communications Society
Box 2250
Lac La Biche, Alberta
Telephone: (403) 623-3301
FAX: (403) 623-3302

Native Cornerstone
(Calgary Native News)
2206 10 Ave SW
Calgary, Alberta
T3C 0K6
Telephone: (403) 245-3690

Native Journal
Box 49039
Edmonton, Alberta
T6E 6H4
Telephone: (403) 448-9693
FAX: (403) 448-9694

Native Network News
13140 St Albert Trail
Edmonton, Alberta
T5L 4R8
Telephone: (403) 454-7076
Telephone: (800) 252-7553
FAX: (403) 452-3468

Native Women's Digest
#3 10032 - 29A Ave
Edmonton, Alberta
T6N 1A8
Telephone: (403) 448-3715
FAX: (403) 448-3721

Newsletter
832 - 220 4th Ave. SE
Calgary, Alberta
T2G 4X3
Telephone: (403) 737-3900
FAX: (403) 737-3901

Northern Lifestyles
Box 1146
High Level, Alberta
T0H 1Z0

Siksika Nation News
PO Box 249
Gleichen, Alberta
T0J 1N0
Telephone: (403) 734-5249
FAX: (403) 734-2355

Tall Cree Tattler
Box 367
Fort Vermilion, Alberta
T0H 1N0
Telephone: (403) 927-3727
FAX: (403) 927-4375

Treaty 7 News
Box 106
Stand Off, Alberta
T0L 1Y0
Telephone: (403) 737-2121
FAX: (403) 737-2336

Western Native News
Suite 330 - 10036 Jasper Ave.
Edmonton, Alberta
T5J 2W2
Telephone: (403) 421-7966
FAX: (403) 424-3951

Windspeaker
15001 - 112 Avenue
Edmonton, Alberta
T5M 2V6
Telephone: (403) 455-2700
Telephone: (800) 661-5469
FAX: (403) 455-7639

ATLANTIC REGION

Kinatuinamot Ilengajuk
Okalakatiget Society
(Print, Radio & Television)
PO Box 160
Nain, Labrador
A0P 1L0
Telephone: (709) 922-2955
FAX: (709) 922-2293

Big Cove Newsletter
Box 11, Site 1
Big Cove, New Brunswick
E0A 2L0
Telephone: (506) 523-9184

Mal-I-Mac News
320 St Marys St
Fredericton, New Brunswick
E3A 2S4
Telephone: (506) 458-8422
FAX: (506) 450-3749

Micmac Maliseet Nation News
PO Box 1590
840 Willow St
Truro, Nova Scotia
B2N 5V3
Telephone: (902) 895-6385
FAX: (902) 893-1520

Micmac News
3 Kateri Street
Sydney, Nova Scotia
Telephone: (902) 539-0045
FAX: (902) 564-0430

Miramichi Leader
Miramichi Indian Agency
65 Jane Street
Newcastle, New Brunswick
E1V 3M6
Telephone: (506) 375-4458
FAX: (506) 722-7422

Miramichi Weekend
139 Duke St
Chatham, New Brunswick
E3V 3K9
Telephone: (506) 622-1600
FAX: (506) 622-7422

Pro Kent
99 Main Street
Richibucto, New Brunswick
E0A 2M0
Telephone: (506) 523-9148
FAX: (506) 523-7556

BRITISH COLUMBIA REGION

CFNR Radio
Northern Native Broadcasting - Terrace
Box 1090
4562B Queensway Dr
Terrace, British Columbia
V8G 3X6
Telephone: (604) 638-8137
FAX: (604) 638-8027

Native Communications Society of British Columbia
203 504 Burrard St
Vancouver, British Columbia
V6E 3H4
Telephone: (604) 684-7375
FAX: (604) 684-5375

Aboriginal Expressions
3359 East 3rd Avenue
Vancouver, British Columbia
V5M 1J9
Telephone: (604) 253-1020

Awa'k'wis Newspaper
109 Tsakis Way
Box 2490
Port Hardy, British Columbia
V0N 2P0
Telephone: (604) 949-9433
FAX: (604) 949-9677

B.C. Native Women's Society Newsletter
345 Yellowhead Hwy
Kamloops, British Columbia
V2H 1H1
Telephone: (604) 828-9796
FAX: (604) 828-9803

Central Okanagan Friendship Center Newsletter
442 Leon Avenue
Kelowna, British Columbia
V1Y 6J3
Telephone: (604) 763-4905
FAX: (604) 861-5514

Coqualeetza Cultural Education Center
7201 Vedder Rd
Box 370
Sardis, British Columbia
V2R 1A7
Telephone: (604) 858-9431
FAX: (604) 858-8488

First Nations Law
Ferguson, Giffords Native Law Group
Suite 500 - 666 Burrard St
Vancouver, British Columbia
V6C 3H3
Telephone: (604) 687-3216

Ha-Shilth-Sa
5001 Mission Road
PO Box 1383
Port Alberni, British Columbia
V9Y 7M2
Telephone: (604) 724-5757
FAX: (604) 723-0463

Kahtou News
c/o K'watamus Publications Inc.
PO Box 192
115A Sinku Drive, SBL # 2
Sechelt, British Columbia
V0N 3A0
Telephone: (604) 885-7391
Telephone: (800) 561-4311
FAX: (604) 885-7397

Penticton Indian Band Newsletter
RR # 1, Suite 80, Comp. 19
Penticton, British Columbia
V2A 6J7
Telephone: (604) 493-0048
FAX: (604) 493-2882

Sqwe'lgwel Tribal Newsletter
Box 310
Sardis, British Columbia
V2R 1A7
Telephone: (604) 858-3366
FAX: (604) 858-4790

Strait Arrow
No. 3 - 1691 Boundary Avenue
Nanaimo, British Columbia
V9S 4P2

Tansai Journal
Louis Riel Metis Council
13565 King George Highway
Surrey, British Columbia
V3T 2V1
Telephone: (604) 581-2522

The Native Voice
200 - 1755 East Hasting St
Vancouver, British Columbia
V5L 1T1
Telephone: (604) 255-3137
FAX: (604) 251-7107

The Rez Magazine
443 West Third St
North Vancouver, British Columbia
V7M 1G9
Telephone: (604) 985-0700
FAX: (604) 980-3861

MANITOBA REGION

Aboriginal Circuit Magazine
Box 2868
Winnipeg, Manitoba
R3C 4B4
Telephone: (204) 663-4543
FAX: (204) 663-3766

CFNC Radio
Box 129
Cross Lake, Manitoba
R0B 0J0
Telephone: (204) 676-2331

CJNC Radio
Box 311 Jack River
Norway House, Manitoba
R0B 1B0
Telephone: (204) 359-6775
FAX: (204) 359-6191

Dakota Times
Box 151
Griswold, Manitoba
R0M 0B0
Telephone: (204) 855-2250
FAX: (204) 855-2436

Native Communications Inc.
76 Severn Crescent
Thompson, Manitoba
R8N 1M6
Telephone: (204) 778-8343
FAX: (204) 778-6559

Indian Life Magazine
PO Box 3765 Station B
Winnipeg, Manitoba
R2W 3R6
Telephone: (204) 661-9333
FAX: (204) 661-3982

First Perspective (The)
c/o Broken Head First Nation
56 Wildwood Park, Section E
Winnipeg, Manitoba
R3T 0C8
Telephone: (204) 766-2686
FAX: (204) 478-9800

Manitoba Association of Native Languages Newsletter
119 Sutherland Avenue
Winnipeg, Manitoba
R2W 3C9
Telephone: (204) 943-3707
FAX: (204) 947-6564

Manitoba Indian Education Association Newsletter
305 - 352 Donald St
Winnipeg, Manitoba
R3B 2H8
Telephone: (204) 947-0421
FAX: (204) 942-3067

Natotawin
Box 297
The Pas, Manitoba
R9A 1K4
Telephone: (204) 623-5483
FAX: (204) 623-5263

Northern Star
Norway House Indian Band Newsletter
PO Box 250
Norway House, Manitoba
R0B 1B0
Telephone: (204) 359-6958
FAX: (204) 359-6080

Weetamah
Box 178
181 Higgins Ave
Winnipeg, Manitoba
R3C 2G9
Telephone: (204) 944-9517
FAX: (204) 944-9521

Whispering Pines
504-63 Albert St
Winnipeg, Manitoba
R3B 1G4
Telephone: (204) 947-2227

WRTC News
West Region Tribal Council
21 - 4th Avenue NW
Dauphin, Manitoba
R7N 1H9
Telephone: (204) 638-8225
FAX: (204) 638-8062

NORTHWEST TERRITORIES

Inuvialuit Communications Society
Box 1704
Inuvik, Northwest Territories
X0E 0T0
Telephone: (403) 979-2067
FAX: (403) 979-2744

Inuvik Drum
65 MacKenzie Road
Box 2719
Inuvik, Northwest Territories
X0E 0T0
Telephone: (403) 979-4545
FAX: (403) 979-4412

Native Communications Society of the Western Northwest Territories
Box 1919
NWT Communications Centre
Yellowknife, Northwest Territories
Telephone: (403) 873-2661
FAX: (403) 920-4205

MacKenzie Times
Box 499
Fort Simpson, Northwest Territories
X0E 0N0
Telephone: (403) 695-3330
FAX: (403) 695-2922

Nunatsiaq News
PO Box 8
Iqaluit, Northwest Territories
X0A 0H0
Telephone: (819) 979-5357
FAX: (819) 979-4763

Tusaayaksat
Box 1704
Inuvik, Northwest Territories
X0E 0T0
Telephone: (403) 979-2320
FAX: (403) 979-2744

ONTARIO REGION

The Aboriginal Voice
158 Sackville Rd
Sault Ste Marie, Ontario
P6B 4T6
Telephone: (705) 949-5161

Anishinabek News
Nipissing First Nation
(Union of Ont. Indians)
PO Box 711
North Bay, Ontario
P1B 8J8
Telephone: (705) 497-9127
FAX: (705) 497-9135

Batchewana First Nation
Newsletter
236 Frontenac St
Sault Ste Marie, Ontario
P6A 5K9
Telephone: (705) 759-0914
FAX: (705) 759-9171

Beedaudjimowin
(Native Peoples Parish)
263 Rocesvatles Ave
Toronto, Ontario
M6H 3Y3

Caribou News
c/o Nortext
14 Colonnade Rd
Nepean, Ontario
K2E 7M6
Telephone: (613) 727-5466
FAX: (613) 727-6910

Chippewa Tribune
978 Tashmoo Ave
Sarnia, Ontario
N7T 7H5
Telephone: (519) 336-8410
FAX: (519) 336-0384

Council Fires
North Shore Tribal Council
1 Industrial Park Rd East
Box 2049
Blind River, Ontario
P0R 1B0
Telephone: (705) 356-1691
FAX: (705) 356-1090

Counciline
Canadian Council for Native
Business
Box 132, Suite 405
Maclean Hunter Building,
College Park
777 Bay St
Toronto, Ontario
M5G 2C8
Telephone: (416) 961-8663
FAX: (416) 961-3995

Holeewas
c/o Oneida of the Thames
RR 2
Southwold, Ontario
N0L 2G0
Telephone: (519) 652-3244
FAX: (519) 652-9287

Inuit Broadcasting Inc
Suite 703
251 Laurier Ave West
Ottawa, Ontario
K1P 5J6
Telephone: (613) 235-1892
FAX: (613) 230-8824

Inuktitut Magazine
170 Laurier Avenue West
Suite 510
Ottawa, Ontario
K1P 5V5
Telephone: (613) 238-8181
FAX: (613) 234-1991

Jibkenyan
Walpole Indian First Nations
RR # 3
Wallaceburg, Ontario
N8A 4K9
Telephone: (519) 627-1481
FAX: (519) 627-0440

Macinigan Community News
c/o Chippewas of Thames
RR #1
Muncy, Ontario
N0L 1Y0
Telephone: (519) 264-1528
FAX: (519) 264-2203

Omushkego Arrow Newspaper
Box 370
Moose Factory, Ontario
P9L 1W0
Telephone: (705) 658-4222
FAX: (705) 658-4250

Native Beat
PO Box 1260
Forest, Ontario
N0N 1J0
Telephone: (519) 786-2142
FAX: (519) 786-6668

Native Canadian
(Friendship Ctr)
16 Spadina Road
Toronto, Ontario
M5R 2S7
Telephone: (416) 964-9087
FAX: (416) 964-2111

N'Amerind Newsletter
260 Colbourne St
London, Ontario
N6B 2S9
Telephone: (519) 672-0131
FAX: (519) 672-0717

Northern Ontario Business
158 Elgin St
Sudbury, Ontario
P3E 3N5
Telephone: (705) 673-5705
FAX: (705) 673-9542

Omusklego Arrow
PO Box 370
Moose Factory, Ontario
P0L 1W0
Telephone: (705) 658-4222
FAX: (705) 658-4250

The Red Eagle
152 Main St S
Kenora, Ontario
P9N 1S9
Telephone: (807) 468-3391
FAX: (807) 468-5340

The Runner Magazine
39 Spadina Road, 2nd Floor
Toronto, Ontario
M5R 2S9
Telephone: (416) 972-0871
FAX: (416) 972-0892

Sequoyah
RR # 4
Niagara-On-The-Lake, Ontario
L0S 1J0
Telephone: (416) 688-6484
FAX: (416) 688-4033

Shoal Lake # 39 Newsletter
c/o Band Office
Kejick Post Office
Kejick, Ontario
P0X 1E0
Telephone: (807) 733-2560
FAX: (807) 733-3106

Smoke Signals
(United Indian Council)
Box A3, RR # 2
Sutton West, Ontario
L0E 1R0
Telephone: (705) 739-8421
FAX: (705) 739-8423

Tekawennake Newspaper
PO Box 1506
Oshweken, Ontario
N0A 1M0
Telephone: (519) 445-2238
FAX: (519) 445-2434

Tyendinaga Territory
Newsletter
c/o Mohawk Band Office
RR # 1
Deseronto, Ontario
K0K 1X0
Telephone: (613) 396-3424

Wawaty News
PO Box 1180
16 - Fifth Ave North
Sioux Lookout, Ontario
P8T 1B7
Telephone: (807) 737-2951
FAX: (807) 737-3224

Wawatay Native
Communications Society
Box 1180, 16 - 5th Avenue
Sioux Lookout, Ontario
P8T 1B7
Telephone: (807) 737-2951
FAX: (807) 737-3224

Wawatay Network Radio
Box 188
Moose Factory, Ontario
P0L 1W1
Telephone: (705) 658-4556

QUÉBEC REGION

Akulivik Community Radio
Nunavik, Québec
J0M 1V0
Telephone: (819) 496-2033

Aupaluk FM Radio Station
Aupaluk, Québec
J0M 1X0
Telephone: (819) 491-7088

Aispich Chakwan
Chisasibi, Québec
J0M 1E0
Telephone: (819) 855-2844
FAX: (819) 855-2867

Akwesasne Notes
Box 189, Hilltop Drive
St Regis, Québec
H0M 1A0
Telephone: (613) 575-2063
FAX: (613) 575-2064

Anngutivik
331 Avenue Mimosa, Poste 230
Dorval, Québec
H9S 3K5
Telephone: (514) 636-8120
FAX: (514) 636-1261

Bulletin Ayimuun
Cree Indian Centre of
Chibougamau
95 Jaculet
Chibougamau, Québec
G8P 2G1
Telephone: (418) 748-7667

Bulletin Du Centre D'Amitie
Autochtone Du Québec
25, rue Saint-Louise
Loretteville, Québec
Q2B 1L4
Telephone: (418) 843-5818

Bulletin Du Centre D'Amitie
Autochtone De Montreal
3730 Chemin Cote des Neiges
Montreal, Québec
H3H 1V6
Telephone: (514) 937-5338

Chewitan
c/o Cree Indian Centre of
Chibougamau
95 Jaculet
Chibougamau, Québec
G8P 2G1
Telephone: (418) 748-7667
FAX: (418) 748-6954

CHRQ
32 Riverside East
Restigouche, Québec
G0C 2R0
Telephone: (418) 788-2449
FAX: (418) 788-2653

Chisasibi Telecommunication
Assoc.
PO Box 420
Chisasibi, Québec
J0M 1E0
Telephone: (819) 855-2619

CHRG Radio
35 rue Principale
Maria, Québec
G0C 1Y0
Telephone: (418) 759-3441

CKHQ
Box 747
505 Center Road
Kanesatake, Québec
J0N 1E0
Telephone: (514) 479-8321

CKON FM Community Radio
Box 309
Akwesasne, Québec
H0M 1A0
Telephone: (613) 938-1113

CKRK - FM Radio
PO Box 1035
Kahnawake, Québec
J0L 1B0
Telephone: (514) 638-1313

CKUJ FM Radio
PO Box 147
Kuujjuaq, Québec
J0M 1C0
Telephone: (819) 964-2921
FAX: (819) 964-2229

CKWE - FM Radio
PO Box 309
Maniwaki, Québec
J9E 3C9
Telephone: (819) 449-5097
FAX: (819) 449-5673

The Eastern Door
Box 326
Kahnawake, Québec
J0L 1B0
Telephone: (514) 635-3050
FAX: (514) 635-8479

Eastmain Community Radio
Eastmain, Québec
J0M 1W0
Telephone: (819) 977-0267

Ekuantshi Kaiamiumistuk
CP 319 Mingan
Mingan,Québec
G0G 1V0
Telephone: (418) 949-2234

Indian Times
Box 189 Hilltop Dr
St Regis, Québec
H0M 1A0
Telephone: (613) 575-2063
FAX: (613) 575-2064

Inukjuak Community Radio
Inukjuak, Québec
J0M 1M0
Telephone: (819) 254-8967

Ivujivik Community Radio
Ivujivik, Québec
J0M 1H0
Telephone: (819) 922-9966

Innipaupik FM Radio
General Delivery
Kangirsuk, Québec
J0M 1A0
Telephone: (819) 935-4258

James Bay Cree
Communications Society
Lake Mistissini, Québec
G0W 1C0
Telephone: (418) 923-3191
FAX: (418) 923-2088

Journal Waskahegan
204 -112 de l'Eglise
Mistassini, Québec
G0W 2C0
Telephone: (418) 276-7551

Kawachikamach Community
FM Radio
Box 939
Kawachikamach, Québec
G0G 2T0
Telephone: (418) 585-2111

K E D G Newsline
Kahnawake Economic
Development Group
General Delivery
Kahnawake, Québec
J0Z 1B0
Telephone: (514) 638-4280

Listuguj Wi'gatign
PO Box 99
Listuguj, Québec
G0C 2R0
Telephone: (418) 788-5544

Long Point First Nations
c/o Radio Station Manager
PO Box 1
Winneway, Québec
J0Z 2J0
Telephone: (819) 722-2441

Makivik News Letter
Inukjuak, Québec
J0M 1M0
Telephone: (819) 254-8878

Matinamatik
Conseil de Bande Grand-
Lac-Victoria
PO Box 35
Grand-Lac-Victoria
Via Louvicourt, Québec
J0Y 1Y0
Telephone: (819) 824-1914
FAX: (819) 824-1931

The Nation (Cree Magazine)
PO Box 48036
5678 Park Avenue
Montreal, Québec
H2V 4S0
Telephone: (514) 272-3077
FAX: (514) 272-9914

Nemiscau Telecommunications
Nemiscau, Québec
J0Y 3B0
Telephone: (819) 673-2512

Pakua Shipu Paushtuk
Kaiamiumistuk
Pakua Shipi, Québec
G0G 2R0
Telephone: (418) 947-2708

Papanassi Kaiamiumist
8 rue Principale
La Romaine, Québec
G0C 1M0
Telephone: (418) 229-2021

Piekougami Kamimkets
99 rue Ouiatchouan
Mashteuiatsh, Québec
G0W 2H0
Telephone: (418) 275-4545
FAX: (418) 275-7064

Pikogan Community Radio
Box 36
Pikogan, Québec
J9T 3A3
Telephone: (819) 727-2180

Radio Communautaire Huronne Wendake
545 Thomas-Martin
Wendake, Québec
G0A 4V0
Telephone: (418) 843-3937

Radio Communautaire Kushapatshaken
Apetaumiss Uasha
CP 338
Sept-Iles-Maliotenam, Québec
G4R 4K6
Telephone: (418) 927-2909

Radio Communautaire Manawan Kitotakan
Manouane, Québec
J0K 1M0
Telephone: (819) 971-8890

Radio Communautaire Montagnais
Les Escoumins, Québec
G0T 1K0
Telephone: (418) 233-2700

Radio Ntetemuk 95.1 FM
8 Lilduit St
Betsiamites, Québec
G0H 1B0
Telephone: (418) 567-4642
FAX: (418) 567-8559

Radio Puvirnituup Tusautinga
Povungnituk, Québec
J0M 1P0
Telephone: (819) 988-2892

Radio Quaqtaq
Quaqtaq, Québec
J0M 1J0
Telephone: (819) 492-9946

Salluit Community Radio
Salluit, Québec
J0M 1S0
Telephone: (819) 255-8910

SOCAM
80 boul Bastien
Village des Huons, Québec
G0A 4V0
Telephone: (418) 843-3873
FAX: (418) 845-9774

Station Manager Committee Radio
General Delivery
Kangiqsujuaq, Québec
J0M 1K0
Telephone: (819) 338-3365

Taqramiut Nipingat Incorporated
185 Dorval Ave, Suite 501
Dorval, Québec
H9S 5J9
Telephone: (514) 631-1394
FAX: (514) 631-6258

Tasiujaq Community Radio
Tasiujaq, Québec
J0M 1T0
Telephone: (819) 633-9915

Tepacimo Kitotakan
Obedjiwan, Québec
G0W 3B0
Telephone: (819) 978-8899

Terres en Vuc
770, Rachel E St
Montreal, Québec
H2J 2H5
Telephone: (514) 521-2714

Tewaterihwareniatha
Kanien kehaka Raotitohkwa
Cultural Center
Case Postale 1988
Kahnawake, Québec
J0L 1B0
Telephone: (514) 688-0880

Umiujaq Community Radio
Umiujaq, Québec
J0M 1Y0
Telephone: (819) 331-7065

Ushashumek Nutashkuaniu
Kaiamiumistuk
Natashquan, Québec
G0G 2E0
Telephone: (418) 726-3327

Waskaganish Radio
Box 69
James Bay, Québec
J0M 1R0
Telephone: (819) 895-8984

Waswanipi Communications
Station
20 Poplar St
Waswanipi, Québec
J0Y 3C0
Telephone: (819) 753-2557

Wemindji Radio Station
Wemindji, Québec
J0M 1L0
Telephone: (819) 978-0330

Wemotaci Kitotakan
Weymontachie, Québec
G0A 4M0
Telephone: (819) 666-2191

Whapmagoostui
Telecommunication Assoc.
Box 189
Whapmagoostui, Québec
J0M 1G0
Telephone: (819) 929-3421
FAX: (819) 929-3203

SASKATCHEWAN REGION

Aboriginal Business Magazine
PO Box 23060
2325 Preston Ave
Saskatoon, Saskatchewan
S7J 2G2
Telephone: (306) 343-6065
FAX: (306) 343-6036

The Aboriginal Woman's
Council of Saskatchewan
62 - 17th Street West
Prince Albert, Saskatchewan
S6V 3X3
Telephone: (306) 763-6005
FAX: (306) 992-6034

Indigenous Times
1223A Idylwyld Drive North
Saskatoon, Saskatchewan
S7L 1A1
Telephone: (306) 975-3969
FAX: (306) 975-3759

Missinipi Broadcasting Corp
Box 1529
La Ronge, Saskatchewan
S0J 1L0
Telphone: (306) 425-4003
FAX: (306) 425-3123

The Northerner
PO Box 1350
La Ronge, Saskatchewan
S0J 1L0
Telephone: (306) 425-3344
FAX: (306) 425-2827

Northwest Eagle
PO Box 2139
205A Third Street East
Meadow Lake, Saskatchewan
S9X 1R2
Telephone: (306) 236-5353
FAX: (306) 236-5962

New Breed
173 - 2nd Avenue South
Bay 202
Saskatoon, Saskatchewan
S7L 1K6
Telephone: (306) 244-7441
FAX: (306) 343-0171

Saskatchewan Indian
1223 Idylwyld Drive North
Saskatoon, Saskatchewan
S7L 1A1
Telephone: (306) 975-3969
FAX: (306) 975-3759

Saskatchewan Native
Communications Corp
202 - 173 Second Avenue South
Saskatoon, Saskatchewan
S7K 1K6
Telephone: (306) 653-2253
FAX: (306) 653-3384

Talking Stick Arts Magazine
2114 College Ave
Regina, Saskatchewan
S4P 1C5
Telephone: (306) 780-9242
FAX: (306) 780-9443

YUKON REGION

Northern Native Broadcasting-
Yukon
4228 A Fourth Avenue
Whitehorse, Yukon
Y1A 1K1
Telephone: (403) 668-6629
FAX: (403) 668-6612

Ye Sa To Communications
Society
11 Nisultlin Drive
Whitehorse, Yukon
Y1A 3S4
Telephone: (403) 667-2774
FAX: (403) 667-6923

Yukon News
211 Wood Street
Whitehorse, Yukon
Y1A 2E4
Telephone: (403) 667-6285
FAX: (403) 668-3755

CANADA

Information Provided by:

Aboriginal Multi-Media Society at Alberta
Missinipi Broadcasting Corporation
Nat'l Aboriginal Communications Society

Editor's Note: Many tribal and organization media are often discontinued in hard financial times but resume after a certain length of time. Others can't publish until enough funds are in hand to print, therefor they are irregular in availability.

ABORIGINAL MAGAZINES

MANITOBA

Aboriginal Circuit Magazine
PO Box 2868
Winnipeg, Manitoba
R3C 4B4
Telephone: (204) 663-4543
FAX: (204) 663-3766

Indian Life Magazine
PO Box 3765, Station B
Winnipeg, Manitoba
R2W 3R6
Telephone: (204) 661-9333
FAX: (204) 661-3982

Neechee Culture Magazine
273 Selkirk Ave
Winnipeg, Manitoba
R2W 2L5
Telephone: (204) 586-3667
FAX: (204) 586-5165

ONTARIO

Inuktitut Magazine
170 Laurier Avenue West
Suite 510
Ottawa, Ontario
K1P 5V5
Telephone: (613) 238-8181
FAX: (613) 234-1991

Native Beat
PO Box 1260
Forest, Ontario
N0N 1J0
Telephone: (519) 786-2142
FAX: (519) 786-6668

The Runner Magazine
39 Spadina Road, 2nd Floor
Toronto, Ontario
M5R 2S9
Telephone: (416) 972-0871
FAX: (416) 972-0892

QUÉBEC

Akwesasne Notes
Box 189, Hilltop Drive
St Regis, Québec
H0M 1A0
Telephone: (613) 575-2063
FAX: (613) 575-2064

The Eastern Door
Box 326
Kahnawake, Québec
J0L 1B0
Telephone: (514) 635-3050
FAX: (514) 635-8479

The Nation (Cree Magazine)
PO Box 48036
5678 Park Avenue
Montreal, Québec
H2V 4S0
Telephone: (514) 272-3077
FAX: (514) 272-5659

SASKATCHEWAN

Aboriginal Business Magazine
PO Box 23060
2325 Preston Ave
Saskatoon, Saskatchewan
S7J 2G2
Telephone: (306) 343-6065
FAX: (306) 343-6036

New Breed
173 - 2nd Avenue South
Bay 202
Saskatoon, Saskatchewan
S7L 1K6
Telephone: (306) 244-7441
FAX: (306) 343-0171

Talking Stick Arts Magazine
2114 College Ave.
Regina, Saskatchewan
S4P 1C5
Telephone: (306) 780-9242
FAX: (306) 780-9443

Fred Synder, Director, Consultant

N.A.²I.I.T.C.

North American Native American Indian Information & Trade Center

Information Provided by:
Aboriginal Multi-Media Society of Alberta
Missinipi Broadcasting Corporation
Nat'l Aboriginal Communications Society

ABORIGINAL RADIO STATIONS/PROGRAMS

ALBERTA REGION

Aboriginal Multi-Media Society of Alberta
15001 - 112 Avenue
Edmonton, Alberta
T5M 2V6
Telephone: (403) 455-2700
FAX: (403) 455-7639

CFWE FM Radio
15001 - 112 Avenue
Edmonton, Alberta
T5M 2V6
Telephone: (403) 447-2393
FAX: (403) 454-2820

National Aboriginal Communications Society
Box 2250
Lac La Biche, Alberta
T0A 2C0
Telephone: (403) 623-3301
FAX: (403) 623-3302

ATLANTIC REGION

Kinatuinamot Ilengajuk Okalakatiget Society
PO Box 160
Nain, Labrador
A0P 1L0
Telephone: (709) 922-2955
FAX: (709) 922-2293

BRITISH COLUMBIA REGION

CFNR Radio
Northern Native Broadcasting - Terrace
Box 1090
4562B Queensway Dr
Terrace, British Columbia
V8G 3X6
Telephone: (604) 638-8137
FAX: (604) 638-8027

Native Communications Society of British Columbia
203 504 Burrard St
Vancouver, British Columbia
V6E 3H4
Telephone: (604) 684-7375
FAX: (604) 684-5375

MANITOBA REGION

CFNC Radio
Box 129
Cross Lake, Manitoba
R0B 0J0
Telephone: (204) 676-2331

CJNC Radio
Box 311 Jack River
Norway House, Manitoba
R0B 1B0
Telephone: (204) 359-6775
FAX: (204) 359-6191

NORTHWEST TERRITORIES REGION

Inuvialuit Communications Society
Box 1704
Inuvik, Northwest Territories
X0E 0T0
Telephone: (403) 979-2067
FAX: (403) 979-2744

Native Communications Society of the Western Northwest Territories
Box 1919
NWT Communications Centre
Yellowknife,
Northwest Territories
X1A 2P8
Telephone: (403) 873-2661
FAX: (403) 920-4205

ONTARIO REGION

Inuit Broadcasting Inc
Suite 703
251 Laurier Ave West
Ottawa, Ontario
K1P 5J6
Telephone: (613) 235-1892
FAX: (613) 230-8824

Wawatay Native Communications Society
Box 1180, 16 - 5th Avenue
Sioux Lookout, Ontario
P8T 1B7
Telephone: (807) 737-2951
FAX: (807) 737-3224

Wawatay Network Radio
Box 188
Moose Factory, Ontario
P0L 1W1
Telephone: (705) 658-4556

QUÉBEC REGION

Akulivik Community Radio
Nunavik, Québec
J0M 1V0
Telephone: (819) 496-2033

Aupaluk FM Radio Station
Aupaluk, Québec
J0M 1X0
Telephone: (819) 491-7088

CHRQ
32 Riverside East
Restigouche, Québec
G0C 2R0
Telephone: (418) 788-2449
FAX: (418) 788-2653

CHRG Radio
35 rue Principale
Maria, Québec
G0C 1Y0
Telephone: (418) 759-3441

CKHQ
Box 747
505 Center Road
Kanesatake, Québec
J0N 1E0
Telephone: (514) 479-8321

CKON FM Community Radio
Box 309
Akwesasne, Québec
H0M 1A0
Telephone: (613) 938-1113

CKRK - FM Radio
PO Box 1035
Kahnawake, Québec
J0L 1B0
Telephone: (514) 638-1313

CKUJ FM Radio
PO Box 147
Kuujjuaq, Québec
J0M 1C0
Telephone: (819) 964-2921
FAX: (819) 964-2229

CKWE - FM Radio
PO Box 309
Maniwaki, Québec
J9E 3C9
Telephone: (819) 449-5097
FAX: (819) 449-5673

Eastmain Community Radio
Eastmain, Québec
J0M 1W0
Telephone: (819) 977-0267

Inukjuak Community Radio
Inukjuak, Québec
J0M 1M0
Telephone: (819) 254-8967

Ivujivik Community Radio
Ivujivik, Québec
J0M 1H0
Telephone: (819) 922-9966

Innipaupik FM Radio
General Delivery
Kangirsuk, Québec
J0M 1A0
Telephone: (819) 935-4258

James Bay Cree
Communications Society
Lake Mistissini, Québec
G0W 1C0
Telephone: (418) 923-3191
FAX: (418) 923-2088

Kawachikamach Community
FM Radio
Box 939
Kawachikamach, Québec
G0G 2T0
Telephone: (418) 585-2111

Pikogan Community Radio
Box 36
Pikogan, Québec
J9T 3A3
Telephone: (819) 727-2180

Radio Communautaire Huronne
Wendake
545 Thomas-Martin
Wendake, Québec
G0A 4V0
Telephone: (418) 843-3937

Radio Communautaire
Kushapatshaken
Apetaumiss Uasha
CP 338
Sept-Iles-Maliotenam, Québec
G4R 4K6
Telephone: (418) 927-2909

Radio Communautaire
Manawan Kitotakan
Manouane, Québec
J0K 1M0
Telephone: (819) 971-8890

Radio Communautaire
Montagnais
Les Escoumins, Québec
G0T 1K0
Telephone: (418) 233-2700

Radio Ntetemuk 95.1 FM
8 Lilduit St
Betsiamites, Québec
G0H 1B0
Telephone: (418) 567-4642
FAX: (418) 567-8559

Radio Puvirnituup Tusautinga
Povungnituk, Québec
J0M 1P0
Telephone: (819) 988-2892

Radio Quaqtaq
Quaqtaq, Québec
J0M 1J0
Telephone: (819) 492-9946

Salluit Community Radio
Salluit, Québec
J0M 1S0
Telephone: (819) 255-8910

SOCAM
80 boul Bastien
Village des Hurons, Québec
G0A 4V0
Telephone: (418) 843-3873
FAX: (418) 845-9774

Station Manager Committee
Radio
General Delivery
Kangiqsujuaq, Québec
J0M 1K0
Telephone: (819) 338-3365

Taqramiut Nipingat
Incorporated
185 Dorval Ave, Suite 501
Dorval, Québec
H9S 5J9
Telephone: (514) 631-1394
FAX: (514) 631-6258

Tasiujaq Community Radio
Tasiujaq, Québec
J0M 1T0
Telephone: (819) 633-9915

Umiujaq Community Radio
Umiujaq, Québec
J0M 1Y0
Telephone: (819) 331-7065

Waskaganish Radio
Box 69
James Bay, Québec
J0M 1R0
Telephone: (819) 895-8984

Wemindji Radio Station
Wemindji, Québec
J0M 1L0
Telephone: (819) 978-0330

SASKATCHEWAN REGION

Missinipi Broadcasting Corp
Box 1529
La Ronge, Saskatchewan
S0J 1L0
Telephone: (306) 425-4003
FAX: (306) 425-3123

Saskatchewan Native
Communications Corp
202 - 173 Second Avenue South
Saskatoon, Saskatchewan
S7K 1K6
Telephone: (306) 653-2253
FAX: (306) 653-3384

YUKON REGION

Northern Native Broadcasting - Yukon
4228 A Fourth Avenue
Whitehorse, Yukon
Y1A 1K1
Telephone: (403) 668-6629
FAX: (403) 668-6612

Information Provided By:
Aboriginal Multi-Media Society of Alberta
Missinipi Broadcasting Corporation
Nat'l Aboriginal Communications Society

ABORIGINAL TELEVISION PROGRAMS

ATLANTIC REGION

Kinatuinamot Ilengajuk
Okalakatiget Society
PO Box 160
Nain, Labrador
A0P 1L0
Telephone: (709) 922-2955
FAX: (709) 922-2293

MANITOBA REGION

Native Communications Inc.
76 Severn Crescent
Thompson, Manitoba
R8N 1M6
Telephone: (204) 778-8343
FAX: (204) 778-6559

ONTARIO REGION

Inuit Broadcasting Inc.
Suite 703
251 Laurier Ave West
Ottawa, Ontario
K1P 5J6
Telephone: (613) 235-1892
FAX: (613) 230-8824

Wawatay Native
Communications Society
Box 1180, 16 - 5th Avenue
Sioux Lookout, Ontario
P8T 1B7
Telephone: (807) 737-2951
FAX: (807) 737-3224

QUÉBEC REGION

Taqramiut Nipingat
Incorporated
185 Dorval Ave, Suite 501
Dorval, Québec
H9S 5J9
Telephone: (514) 631-1394
FAX: (514) 631-6258

Information Provided By:
Aboriginal Multi-Media Society of Alberta
Missinipi Broadcasting Corporation
Nat'l Aboriginal Communications Society

EXPLANATION OF POW WOW CHARTS

MONTH/DAY/ WEEKEND	EVENT	PHONE/FAX	LOCATIONS

DATE	POW WOW	RODEO & FAIR	CAMPING	COST	SOCIAL

CERE -MONY	MARKET	EDUCA-TIONAL	CELE-BRATION	ARTS & CRAFTS	HOST

MONTH/DAY/WEEKEND ...most Indian events always occur on a specific weekend of the month each year. Single date, specific holiday weekends (which move each year) are marked with an asterisk (*) - Easter, Thanksgiving, Veteran's Day, etc.

EVENT ...name of event and full name and address of sponsoring agency

PHONE/FAX ...contact phone number for sponsoring agency with back up phone number to tribe, chamber of commerce, urban group, etc.

LOCATION ...Physical place of event; gym, pow wow grounds and city and state where held

DATE FIRST STARTED ...first year of event

POW WOW ...pow wow event only listing both social and competition

RODEO/FAIR ...cowboy rodeo, amusement rides, commercial entertainment

CAMPING	...overnight camping for dancers, drums, participants; visitors should check with committee for availability of camping
COST	...F - Free $ - Admission fee
SOCIAL	...non competition pow wow, tribal social dances of tribes that do not pow wow
CEREMONIAL	...mostly tribal dances of ceremonial or religious nature ie Sundance, Jumpdance...
MARKET	...usually arts & crafts sales and exhibition only
EDUCATIONAL	...cultural displays by tribes, clubs, organizations and health agencies to educate the public
CELEBRATION	...events that celebrate a treaty signing, chief's birthday or death, significant event of importance to sponsoring group
ARTS & CRAFTS	...exhibit of arts and crafts for sale to the general public by various artists from many tribes
HOST	T - Tribal sponsored event I - Indian organization sponsored event C.- Non-Indian sponsored event

POW WOW PROTOCOL

Ensuring a pleasant experience for both you and the sponsor.

- Pow-wows are <u>not</u> tourist attractions; that is the one basic fact that many visitors fail to grasp.

- The dance will start when the time is right and end when the time is right whether you are there or not.

- Each dance will be held because it is part of the religious life of the Indian - a prayer made visible.

- No alcoholic beverages should be consumed.

- Do not cross, enter, or stand in the sacred areas known as the dance arena for any reason unless asked to participate in a social dance by the master of ceremonies.

- Ask before you take pictures of an individual dancer or drum. Many dancers have items that are not to be photographed. Also, many dancers have items passed down in the family that belong only to certain tribes, clans or individuals.

- Do not interfere with any dancers, and do not touch any drum.

- Commercial use of any photos/video has been a major concern at most pow-wows. So it is the responsibility of the master of ceremonies to let you know when <u>not to shoot.</u>

- Permission for commercial use should be in writing from the pow-wow sponsor for any photos/video.

- Proper courtesy and respect for the event should be shown in dress, mannerisms and cultural differences at each event.

POW WOW NOTES

Additional information:

Some events are one day, some are two and some are three days, still others change each year; we noted most of the single day events and placed them at the beginning of each month. Space is provided after each month of the year for you to add your favorite Indian event in case we missed it. *Remember to send us a copy for our update.*

Remember that the committee for most events is different each year, therefore we have listed at least two phone numbers as back-ups for confirmation of the event. **CALL BEFORE YOU GO !**

MONTH/DAY/ WEEKEND	EVENT	PHONE/FAX	LOCATION	DATE FIRST STARTED	POW WOW	RODEO & FAIR
JANUARY						
2ND WEEKEND	ANNUAL NAPI FRIENDSHIP CENTER POW WOW BOX 657 PINCHER CRK, AB TOK 1NO	403-627-4224 403-627-2564	M.C.C. ARENA MAIN STREET PINCHER CREEK, AB	1976	✓	
12,13,14 1996 10,11,12 1997 9,10,11 1998						
FEBRUARY	***YOUR EVENT CAN BE LISTED! FAX US AT (520) 622-4900***					
MARCH						
2ND WEEKEND	SHOAL LAKE POW WOW GENERAL DELIVERY SHOAL LAKE, ON P0X 1E0	807-226-5411 807-733-2560 807-733-2315	SHOAL LAKE, ON		✓	
9,10,11 1996 7,8,9 1997 6,7,8 1998						
APRIL						
3RD WEEKEND	SASKATCHEWAN INDIAN FEDERATED COLLEGE POW WOW PIAPOT INDIAN RESERVE BOX 9 SITE 3 RR 2 CRAVEN, SK S0G 0W0	306-584-8333 306-584-8334 306-584-0955	AGRIDOME EXHIBITION PARK REGINA, SK	1979	✓	
19,20,21 1996 18,19,20 1997 17,18,19 1998						
MAY						
4TH WEEKEND	RESPECTING THE DRUM ODAWA POW WOW / ODAWA NATIVE FRIENDSHIP CENTER 396 MACLAREN ST OTTAWA, ON K2P 0M8	613-238-8591 613-238-6106	NEPEAN TENT AND PARK NEPEAN, ON	1976	✓	
24,25,26 1996 23,24,25 1997 22,23,24 1998						
	YOUR EVENT CAN BE LISTED ! FAX US AT (520) 622-4900					

CALL BEFORE YOU GO !

POW WOW CALENDAR 1995-1998

CAMPING	COST	SOCIAL	CEREMONY	MARKET	EDUCA-TIONAL	CELE-BRATION	ARTS & CRAFTS	HOST
	$	✓	✓		✓		✓	I
	F	✓					✓	T
	$	✓		✓	✓		✓	I
✓	$			✓			✓	I

T - TRIBAL EVENT I - INDIAN SPONSOR C - NON INDIAN SPONSOR

GUIDE TO CANADA INDIAN COUNTRY

MONTH/DAY/ WEEKEND	EVENT	PHONE/FAX	LOCATION	DATE FIRST STARTED	POW WOW	RODEO & FAIR
JUNE	***YOUR EVENT CAN BE LISTED ! FAX US AT (520) 622-4900***					
1ST WEEKEND	SUCKER CREEK POW WOW BOX 21 RR 1 LITTLE CURRENT, ON P0P 1K0	705-368-2228 705-368-3563	POW WOW GROUNDS CURRENT, ON	1989	✓	
31,1,2 1996 6,7,8 1997 5,6,7 1998						
2ND WEEKEND	BARRIE POWWOW BARRIE NATIVE FRIENDSHIP CENTER 202-105 DUNLOP BARRIE, ON L4M 1A6	705-721-7689			✓	
7,8,9 1996 13,14,15 1997 12,13,14 1998						
3RD WEEKEND	ALEXANDER POW WOW ALEXANDER FIRST NATION PO BOX 510 MORINVILLE, AB T0G 1P0	403-931-3551 403-939-5887	POW WOW GROUNDS ALEXANDER, AB		✓	
	FIRST NATIONS CULTURAL POW WOW 400 EAST AVENUE KITCHNER, ON	519-743-5752 519-744-9592	KITCHENER MEMORIAL COMPLEX KITCHNER, ON		✓	
14,15,16 1996 20,21,22 1997 19,20,21 1998	ROSEAU RIVER POW WOW PO BOX 30 GINEW, MB R0A 2R0	204-427-2139 204-427-2312	HWY 75 3 MILES E HWY 201 ROSSEAU RIVER, MB		✓	
	SARNIA ANNUAL POW WOW 976 TASHMOO AVE SARNIA, ON N7T 7H5	519-336-8410 519-332-1831	COMMUNITY CENTER SARNIA, ON	1961	✓	
	TREATY DAYS CELEBRATION CANOE LAKE FIRST NATION GENERAL DELIVERY CANOE NARROWS, SK S0M 0K0	306-829-2150 306-829-2101	100 MILES N OF MEADOW LAKE, SK		✓	
	WHITESAND TRADITIONAL POW WOW WHITESAND FIRST NATION PO BOX 68 ARMSTRONG, ON P0T 1A0	807-583-2177 807-583-2170	ARMSTRONG, ON		✓	
4TH WEEKEND	ESKASONI ANNUAL POW WOW GENERAL DELIVERY CAPE BRETON, NS B0A 1J0	902-379-2800 902-379-2278			✓	
	MUSKEG LAKE VETERANS TRADITIONAL POW WOW MUSKEG FIRST NATION PO BOX 130 LEASK, SK S0J 1M0	306-466-4959 306-466-4951	POW WOW GROUNDS MUSKEG LAKE, SK		✓	
21,22,23 1996 27,28,29 1997 26,27,28 1998	SADDLE LAKE INDIAN DAYS SADDLE LAKE FIRST NATION PO BOX 100 SADDLE LAKE, AB T0A 3T0	403-726-3829 403-726-3788	POW WOW GROUNDS SADDLE LAKE, AB		✓	
	SIKSIKA NATION FAIR PO BOX 249 GLEICHAN, AB T0J 1N0	403-734-5315 403-264-7250	POW WOW GROUNDS GLEICHAN, AB		✓	

CALL BEFORE YOU GO !

POW WOW CALENDAR 1995-1998

CAMPING	COST	SOCIAL	CEREMONY	MARKET	EDUCA-TIONAL	CELE-BRATION	ARTS & CRAFTS	HOST
✓	F						✓	T
✓							✓	T
✓	F						✓	T
	$						✓	I
✓	F	✓					✓	T
✓	F						✓	T
✓	F	✓					✓	T
✓	F	✓				✓	✓	T
								T
✓	F	✓					✓	T
✓	F	✓				✓	✓	T
✓	F						✓	T

T - TRIBAL EVENT I - INDIAN SPONSOR C - NON INDIAN SPONSOR

MONTH/DAY/ WEEKEND	EVENT	PHONE/FAX	LOCATION	DATE FIRST STARTED	POW WOW	RODEO & FAIR
JULY	*YOUR EVENT CAN BE LISTED ! FAX US AT (520) 622-4900*					
1ST WEEKEND	ABENAKI CULTURAL FESTIVAL ODANAK FIRST NATION 58 RUE WABANAKI ODANAK, PQ J0G 1H0	514-568-5551 514-568-0869	HWY 331 ODANAK, PQ	1964		✓
	ALEXIS COMPETITION POW WOW PO BOX 7 GLENEVIS, AB T0E 0X0	403-967-2225 403-967-5484	POW WOW GROUNDS GLENEVIS, AB	1980	✓	
	ENOCH INDIAN DAYS BOX 2 SITE 2 RR 1 WINTERBURN, AB T0E 2N0	403-470-3202 403-470-4505	CULTURAL GROUNDS ENOCH RESERVE DEVON, AB		✓	
5,6,7 1996 4,5,6, 1997 3,4,5 1998	GOODFISH LAKE TREATY CELEBRATION GENERAL DELIVERY GOODFISH LAKE, AB TOA 1R0	403-636-3622 403-636-2077	POW WOW GROUNDS GOODFISH LAKE, AB		✓	
	N'AMERIND POW WOW N'AMERIND FRIENDSHIP CENTER 260 COLBORNE ST LONDON, ON N6B 2S6	519-451-2800 519-672-0131 519-672-0717	FANSHAWE CONSERVATION AREA, ON		✓	
	POUNDMAKERS NECHI PW POUNDMAKERS LODGE BOX 34007 KINGSWAY MALL P.O. EDMONTON, AB T5G 3G4	403-458-1884	POUNDMAKERS LODGE ST ALBERT, AB	1972	✓	
2ND WEEKEND	BUFFALO DAYS POW WOW ALEXIS FIRST NATION PO BOX 7 GLENEVIS, AB T0E OXO	403-967-2225	FORT MACLEOD, AB	1978		
	CARRY THE KETTLE POW WOW PO BOX 57 SINTALUTA, SK S0G 4N0	306-727-2235 306-727-2135 306-727-2149	POW WOW GROUNDS SINAULTA, SK		✓	
	ECHOES OF A PROUD NATION KAHNAWAKE FIRST NATION PO BOX 720 KAHNAWAKE, PQ J0L 1B0	514-632-8667 514-632-7500 514-638-5958	POW WOW GROUNDS KAWNAWAKE, PQ		✓	
12,13,14 1996 11,12,13 1997 10,11,12 1998	KETTLE & STONEY POINT FIRST NATION POW WOW 53 INDIAN LANE RR 2 FOREST, ON N0N 1J0	519-786-6680 519-786-2125	KETTLE POINT PARK KETTLE POINT, ON		✓	
	MISSION INTERNATIONAL P/W MISSION INDIAN FRIENDSHIP CENTER 33150 FIRST AVE # A MISSION, BC V2V 1G4	604-826-1281 604-826-4056	ST MARY'S GROUN MISSION, BC	1974	✓	
CLOSEST TO 11TH JULY	SPIRITUAL GATHERING POW WOW KANESATAKE FIRST NATION PO BOX 633 KANESATAKE, PQ J0N 1E0	514-479-8811 514-479-8093 514-479-8093	CEREMONIAL GROUNDS KANESATAKE, PQ	1990	✓	
	TEMAGAMI TRADITIONAL POW WOW - BEAR ISLAND TEMAGAMI FIRST NATION GENERAL DELIVERY BEAR ISLAND, ON P0H 2H0	705-237-8980 705-237-8943 705-237-8959	POW WOW GROUNDS LAKE TEMAGAMI, ON		✓	
	WAHPETON DAKOTA NATION ANNUAL POW WOW PO BOX 128 PRINCE ALBERT, SK S6V 5R4	306-764-6649 306-764-6637	T.B.A (NO 1995 EVENT) 1996			

CALL BEFORE YOU GO !

POW WOW CALENDAR 1995-1998

CAMPING	COST	SOCIAL	CEREMONY	MARKET	EDUCA-TIONAL	CELE-BRATION	ARTS & CRAFTS	HOST
✓	F	✓	✓		✓	✓	✓	I
✓	F						✓	T
✓	F					✓	✓	T
✓	F							T
✓	F	✓				✓	✓	I
✓	F		✓	✓			✓	I
								T
✓		✓					✓	T
✓	F	✓					✓	T
✓							✓	T
✓	F	✓					✓	I
✓	$	✓	✓		✓	✓	✓	T
✓	F						✓	T
								T

T - TRIBAL EVENT I - INDIAN SPONSOR C - NON INDIAN SPONSOR

MONTH/DAY/ WEEKEND	EVENT	PHONE/FAX	LOCATION	DATE FIRST STARTED	POW WOW	RODEO & FAIR
JULY						
2ND WEEKEND	WALPOLE ISLAND WEEN-GUSHK CELEBRATION & POW WOW WALPOLE ISLD 1ST NATION RR 3 WALLACEBURG, ON N8A 4K9	519-627-1476 519-622-3439	CEREMONIAL GRO WALPOLE ISLAND ON		✓	
	WHITEFISH BAY ANNUAL POW WOW PAWITIK P.O. PAWITIK, ON P0X 1L0	807-226-5411 807-226-1155	POW WOW GROUNDS WHITEFISH BAY, ON	1970	✓	
	YELLOW QUILL PW PO BOX 97 ROSE VALLEY, SK S0E 1M0	306-322-2281 306-322-2304	YELLOW QUILL RESERVE, SK		✓	
3RD WEEKEND	ENOCH POW WOW ENOCH FIRST NATION BOX 2 SITE 2 RR 1 WINTERBURN, AB T0E 2N0	403-470-4505 403-470-3057	POW WOW GROUNDS WINTERBURN, AB		✓	
	KAINAI INDIAN DAYS BLOOD FIRST NATION PO BOX 60 STANDOFF, AB T0L 1Y0	403-737-3753 403-653-3509	POW WOW GROUNDS STANDOFF, AB	1969	✓	
	ONION LAKE ANNUAL POW WOW DAYS ONION LAKE FIRST NATION ONION LAKE, SK S0M 2E0	306-344-2440 306-344-4530 306-344-2107 306-344-2112	POW WOW GROUN ONION LAKE, SK		✓	
	PEGUIS POW WOW PEGUIS FIRST NATION PO BOX 219 HODGSON, MB R0C 1N0	204-645-2359 204-645-2360	POW WOW GROUN PEGUIS, MB		✓	
	SIOUX VALLEY ANNUAL POW WOW PO BOX 38 GRISWOLD, MB R0M 0S0	205-885-2671 205-885-2547	POW WOW GROUNDS GRISWOLD, MB		✓	
19,20,21 1996 18,19,20 1997 17,18,19 1998	SQUILAX POW WOW LITTLE SHUSWAP FIRST NATION PO BOX 1100 CHASE, BC V0E 1M0	604-679-3203 604-564-3568	LITTLE SHUSWAP RESERVE SQUILAX, BC	1980	✓	
	WAGMATOOK CELEBRATION WAGMATOOK FIRST NATION PO BOX 237 BADDECK, NS B0E 1B0	902-295-2598 902-295-2596 902-295-3398	CEREMONIAL GROUNDS CAPE BRETON, NS	1991	✓	
3RD - 4TH WEEKEND	CREE NATION GATHERING OPASKWAYAK CREE NATION PO BOX 297 THE PAS, MB R9A 1K4	204-623-5483 204-623-4226			✓	
4TH WEEKEND	BIRDTAIL SIOUX CULTURAL WEEK PO BOX 22 BEULAH, MB R0M 0B0	204-568-4540 204-568-4687	SPIRITUAL GROUNDS BEULAH, MB		✓	
	BONAPARTE CROSSROADS GATHERING BONAPARTE RESERVE PO BOX 669 CACHE CREEK, BC V0K 1H0	604-457-9624	3 MI NO CACHE CREEK, BC		✓	
26,27,28 1996 25,26,27 1997 24,25,26, 1998	GRAND RIVER CHAMPION OF CHAMPIONS CONTEST POW WOW SIX NATION RESERVE PO BOX 1 OHSWEKEN, ON N0A 1M0	519-445-4391 519-445-4528	CHIEF WOOD PARK HWY 54 BRANTFORD, ON	1980	✓	

CALL BEFORE YOU GO !

POW WOW CALENDAR 1995-1998

CAMPING	COST	SOCIAL	CEREMONY	MARKET	EDUCA-TIONAL	CELE-BRATION	ARTS & CRAFTS	HOST
✓	F	✓				✓	✓	I
✓							✓	T
✓	F	✓					✓	T
✓	F						✓	T
✓	F	✓					✓	T
✓	F						✓	T
✓	F						✓	T
	F	✓					✓	T
✓	F	✓					✓	T
✓	F					✓	✓	T
✓	F				✓	✓	✓	T
✓	F	✓			✓		✓	T
✓	F	✓					✓	T
✓	F						✓	T

T - TRIBAL EVENT I - INDIAN SPONSOR C - NON INDIAN SPONSOR

MONTH/DAY/ WEEKEND	EVENT	PHONE/FAX	LOCATION	DATE FIRST STARTED	POW WOW	RODEO & FAIR
JULY	*YOUR EVENT CAN BE LISTED ! FAX US AT (520) 622-4900*					
4TH WEEKEND	MOSQUITO ANNUAL POW WOW MOSQUITO FIRST NATION GENERAL DELIVERY CANDO, SK S0K 0V0	306-937-7707 306-937-7747	TRIBAL GROUNDS NORTH BATTLEFORD, SK	1981	✓	
	NAICATCHEWENIN TRADITIONAL POW WOW NAICATCHEWENIN 1ST NATION BOX 12 DEVLIN, ON P0W 1C0	807-486-3407 807-274-8761	POW WOW GROUNDS NORTHWEST BAY, ON		✓	
26,27,28 1996 25,26,27 1997 24,25,26, 1998	OCEAN MAN CELEBRATION OCEAN MAN FIRST NATION PO BOX 157 STOUGHTON, SK S0G 4T0	306-457-2679 306-457-2933	TRIBAL GROUNDS STOUGHTON, SK		✓	
	STURGEON LAKE POW WOW STURGEON LAKE FIRST NATION BOX 5 SITE 12 RR 1 SHELLBROOK, SK S0J 2E0	306-764-1872 306-764-1877	POW WOW GROUNDS STURGEON LAKE, SK		✓	
	WABAMUN LAKE COMPETITION POW WOW PAUL FIRST NATION PO BOX 89 DUFFIELD, AB T0E 0N0	403-892-3453 403-892-2691 403-892-3402	45 MI WEST EDMONTON, AB		✓	
5TH WEEKEND	ANNUAL POW WOW LITTLE PINE FIRST NATION PO BOX 70 PAYNTON, SK S0M 2J0	306-398-4942 306-398-2377	12 MI NO OF CUTKNIFE, SK		✓	
	KAWACATOOSE ANNUAL PW KAWACATOOSE FIRST NATION PO BOX 640 RAYMORE, SK S0A 3J0	306-835-2125 306-835-2178	5 MI NORTH OF QUINTON POW WOW GROUNDS QUINTON, SK		✓	
	OCHAPOWACE TRADITIONAL POW WOW OCHAPOWACE FIRST NATION PO BOX 550 WHITE WOOD, SK S0J 5C0	306-696-3160 306-696-3180 306-696-2637	POW WOW GROUN BROADVIEW, SK		✓	
LAST WEEK-END OF JULY 1996 1997 1998	PAUL BAND POW WOW PAUL BAND FIRST NATION PO BOX 89 DUFFIELD, AB T0E 0N0	403-892-3760 403-892-2691 403-892-3402	POW WOW GROUNDS DUFFIELD, AB		✓	
	PEIGAN ANNUAL CELEBRATION PEIGAN FIRST NATION PO BOX 70 BROCKET, AB T0K 0H0	403-965-3940 403-965-3931	POW WOW GROUNDS BROCKET, AB		✓	
	POW WOW CELEBRATION MONTREAL LAKE CREE FIRST NATION GENERAL DELIVERY MONTREAL LAKE, SK S0J 1YO	306-663-5349 306-922-1994				
	T'SUU T'INA SARCEE INDIAN DAYS SARCEE FOUR NATIONS 3700 ANDERSON RD SW CALGARY, AB T2W 3G4	403-281-4455 403-281-9722	POW WOW GROUNDS BRAGG CREEK, AB		✓	✓
	YOUR EVENT CAN BE LISTED ! FAX US AT (520) 622-4900					

CALL BEFORE YOU GO !

POW WOW CALENDAR 1995-1998

CAMPING	COST	SOCIAL	CEREMONY	MARKET	EDUCA-TIONAL	CELE-BRATION	ARTS & CRAFTS	HOST
✓	F						✓	T
✓	F	✓					✓	T
✓	F					✓	✓	T
✓	F	✓					✓	T
✓	F						✓	T
✓	F						✓	T
✓	F	✓					✓	T
✓	F	✓	✓				✓	T
✓	F	✓					✓	T
✓	F		✓		✓	✓	✓	T
						✓	✓	T
✓	F	✓				✓	✓	T

T - TRIBAL EVENT I - INDIAN SPONSOR C - NON INDIAN SPONSOR

MONTH/DAY/ WEEKEND	EVENT	PHONE/FAX	LOCATION	DATE FIRST STARTED	POW WOW	RODEO & FAIR
AUGUST	*YOUR EVENT CAN BE LISTED ! FAX US AT (520) 622-4900*					
1ST WEEKEND	JOSEPH BIG HEAD CELEBRATION JOSEPH BIG HEAD 1ST NATION PO BOX 309 PIERCELAND, SK S0M 2K0	306-839-2277 306-839-2330	POW WOW GROUNDS PIERCELAND, SK		✓	
	LONG PLAIN POW WOW LONG PLAIN FIRST NATION EDWIN, MB R0H 0G0	204-252-2731 204-252-2012	15 KILOMETERS SOUTHEAST PORTAGE LA PRAIRIE, MB		✓	
	NAKOTA NATION TAOTHA CELEBRATION BIG HORN RESERVE, AB	403-721-2045 403-932-3870	116 KM WEST HWY 11 ROCKY MOUNTAIN HOUSE, AB		✓	✓
4, 5, 6 1995 2, 3, 4 1996 1, 2, 3 1997 31, 1, 2 1998	PEIGAN INDIAN DAYS PEIGAN FIRST NATION PO BOX 70 BROCKET, AB T0K 0H0	403-341-3358 403-965-3940 403-965-3931	POW WOW GROUNDS BROCKET, AB	1957	✓	
	SQUAMISH NATION YOUTH POW WOW 100 MATHIAS RD NORTH VANCOUVER, BC	604-986-2120	CAPILAND PARK NORTH VANCOUVER, BC		✓	
	WIKWEMIKONG ANNUAL PW WIKWEMIKONG HERITAGE ORGANIZATION PO BOX 112 WIKWEMIKONG, ON P0P 2P0	705-859-3122 705-859-3851	POW WOW GROUNDS WIKWEMIKONG, ON	1960	✓	
2ND WEEKEND	DESERONTO TRADITIONAL PW MOHAWKS OF THE BAY OF QUINTE RR 1 DESERONTO, ON K0K 1X0	613-396-2553 613-396-5862 613-396-3424 613-396-3627	POW WOW GROUNDS DESERONTO, ON	1987	✓	
	DRIFTPILE ANNUAL CELEBRATION DRIFTPILE FIRST NATION GENERAL DELIVERY DRIFTPILE, AB T0G 0V0	403-849-4943 403-355-3780 403-355-3650	POW WOW GROUNDS DRIFTPILE, AB	1988	✓	
	ERMINESKIN POW WOW ERMINESKIN FIRST NATION PO BOX 219 HOBBEMA, AB T0C 1N0	403-585-3741 403-585-2550	POW WOW GROUNDS HOBBEMA, AB		✓	
	KAMLOOPA ANNUAL POW WOW 315 YELLOWHEAD HWY KAMLOOPS, BC V2H 1H1 MOVED TO 3RD WEEKEND	604-828-9700 604-828-9819 604-372-8833	CHEF LOUIS WAY KAMLOOPS, BC	1979	✓	
11,12,13 1995 9,10,11 1996 8,9,10 1997 7,8,9 1998	MUSKODAY TRADITIONAL POW WOW	306-764-1282 306-763-1623	19 KILOMETERS SOUTH EAST PRINCE ALBERT, S		✓	
	OAK LAKE SIOUX POW WOW PO BOX 146 PIPESTONE, MB R0M 1T0	204-854-2261 204-854-2959 204-854-2525	POW WOW GROUNDS PIPESTONE, MB		✓	
	PAIMFC ANNUAL CELEBRTN PRINCE ALBERT INDIAN-METIS FRIENDSHIP CENTRE 1409 FIRST AVE PRINCE ALBERT, SK S6V 6Z1	306-764-3431	EXHIBITION GROUNDS PRINCE ALBERT, SK	1987	✓	
	SHESHEGWANING ANNUAL TRADITIONAL SHESHEGWANING 1ST NATION PO BOX C-1 SHESHEGWANING, ON P0P 1X0	705-283-3292 705-283-3481	POW WOW GROUNDS SHESHEGWANING, ON	1992	✓	

CALL BEFORE YOU GO !

POW WOW CALENDAR 1995-1998

CAMPING	COST	SOCIAL	CEREMONY	MARKET	EDUCA-TIONAL	CELE-BRATION	ARTS & CRAFTS	HOST
✓	F					✓	✓	T
✓							✓	T
✓	F						✓	I
✓	F	✓				✓	✓	T
✓	F	✓					✓	T
✓	F	✓					✓	I
✓	F	✓					✓	T
✓	F						✓	T
✓	F					✓	✓	T
✓	F	✓					✓	I
✓	F	✓					✓	I
	F	✓					✓	T
✓	F	✓					✓	I
✓	F	✓					✓	T

T - TRIBAL EVENT I - INDIAN SPONSOR C - NON INDIAN SPONSOR

MONTH/DAY/ WEEKEND	EVENT	PHONE/FAX	LOCATION	DATE FIRST STARTED	POW WOW	RODEO & FAIR
AUGUST	*YOUR EVENT CAN BE LISTED ! FAX US AT (520) 622-4900*					
2ND WEEKEND	STANDING BUFFALO CELEB. STANDING BUFFALO 1ST NATION PO BOX 128 FORT QU'APPELLE, SK SOG 1SO	306-332-4685 306-332-4920 306-332-5953	POW WOW GROUNDS 6 MI WEST OF FORT QU'APPELLE, SK		✓	
2ND-3RD WEEKEND	INTERNATIONAL NATIVE ARTS FESTIVAL PO BOX 502 STA M CALGARY, AB T2P 2J1	403-233-0022 403-233-7681	DOWNTOWN CALGARY, AB	1978	✓	
3RD WEEKEND	ABEGWEIT POW WOW NATIVE COUNCIL OF P.E.I. 33 ALLEN ST CHARLOTTETOWN, PEI C1A 2V6	902-892-5314	PANMURE ISLAND PROVINCIAL PARK, PEI	1992	✓	
	BEARDY'S & OKEMASIS CELEBRATION BEARDY & OKEMASIS 1ST NTN PO BOX 340 DUCK LAKE, SK S0S 1J0	306-467-4523 306-467-2102	POW WOW GROUNDS DUCK LAKE, SK		✓	
	BIG RIVER BAND ANNUAL POW WOW BIG RIVER FIRST NATION PO BOX 519 DEBDEN, SK S0J 0S0	306-724-4700 306-724-2161	DEBDEN, SK		✓	
18,19,20 1995 16,17,18 1996 15,16,17 1997 21,22,23, 1998	CHIPPEWA OF THE THAMES PW CHIPPEWA OF THE THAMES FIRST NATION RR 1 MUNCEY, ON N0L 1Y0	519-264-2284 519-289-5555 519-289-2230	BALL PARK MUNCEY, ON	1976	✓	
	LONG LAKE ANNUAL POW WOW	403-826-3333			✓	
	PIAPOT CELEBRATION PIAPOT FIRST NATION PO BOX 178 CUPAR, SK S0G 0Y0	306-781-4848 306-781-4853	RESERVE POW WOW GROUNDS CUPAR, SK		✓	
	SAUGEEN TRADITIONAL PW SAUGEEN FIRST NATION GENERAL DELIVERY SAVANT LAKE, ON P0V 2S0	519-797-3254 519-797-2781	SOUTHHAMPTON, ON		✓	
4TH WEEKEND	ANNUAL POW WOW CAN AM FRIENDSHIP CTR PO BOX 441 WINDSOR, ON N9A 6L7	519-948-8365 519-252-8331	ST CLAIR COLLEGE GYM WINDSOR, ON	1992	✓	
	FROG LAKE COMPETITION POW WOW FROG LAKE FIRST NATION GENERAL DELIVERY FROG LAKE, AB T0A 1M0	403-943-3737 403-943-3777 403-943-3966	POW WOW GROUNDS FROG LAKE, AB		✓	
25,26,27 1995 30,31,1 1996 29,30,31 1997 28,29,30 1998	THREE FIRES HOMECOMING MISSISSAUGAS 1ST NATION RR 6 HAGERSVILLE, ON N0A 1H0	519-948-8365 416-768-1133 416-768-1225	POW WOW GROUNDS HAGERSVILLE, ON		✓	
	WHITE BEAR POW WOW WHITE BEAR FIRST NATION PO BOX 700 CARLYLE, SK S0C 0R0	306-577-2461 306-577-2496	POW WOW GROUNDS WHITE BEAR, SK		✓	
	YORKTON FRIENDSHIP POW WOW YORKTON FRIENDSHIP CTR 283 MYRTLE AVE YORKTON, SK S3W 1R5	306-782-2822 306-782-6662			✓	

CALL BEFORE YOU GO !

POW WOW CALENDAR 1995-1998

CAMPING	COST	SOCIAL	CEREMONY	MARKET	EDUCA-TIONAL	CELE-BRATION	ARTS & CRAFTS	HOST
✓	F					✓	✓	T
	$	✓	✓	✓	✓	✓	✓	I
✓	F	✓	✓	✓	✓		✓	T
✓	F	✓					✓	T
	F	✓					✓	T
✓	F						✓	T
✓	F						✓	T
✓	F	✓					✓	T
✓	F						✓	I
✓	F						✓	T
✓	F	✓	✓			✓	✓	T
✓	F						✓	T
							✓	I

T - TRIBAL EVENT **I - INDIAN SPONSOR** **C - NON INDIAN SPONSOR**

GUIDE TO CANADA INDIAN COUNTRY

MONTH/DAY/ WEEKEND	EVENT	PHONE/FAX	LOCATION	DATE FIRST STARTED	POW WOW	RODEO & FAIR
SEPTEMBER						
1ST WEEKEND	DELAWARE NTN ANNUAL PW DELAWARE OF THE THAMES FIRST NATION RR 3 THAMESVILLE, ON N0P 2K0	519-692-3936 313-721-4273 519-692-5522	80 MI EAST WINDSOR, ON	1976	✓	
	MORAVIAN POW WOW DELAWARE FIRST NATION RR 3 THAMESVILLE, ON N0P 2K0	519-692-4468 519-692-3936 519-692-5522	TRIBAL GROUNDS THAMESVILLE, ON		✓	
1, 2, 3 1995 6, 7, 8 1996 5, 6, 7 1997 4, 5, 6 1998	NAKOTA ANNUAL CLASSIC PW GOODSTONY FIRST NATION PO BOX 40 MORLEY, AB T0L 1N0	403-881-3939 403-881-3770	CHIEF GOODSTONY COMPLEX MORLEY, AB		✓	
2ND WEEKEND	SIX NATIONS ANNUAL FALL FAIR PO BOX 1 OHSWEKEN, ON N0A 1M0	519-445-4528 519-445-2956 519-445-2201 519-445-4208	FAIRGROUNDS OHSWEKEN, ON	1867	✓	
8,9,10 1995 13,14,15 1996 12,13,14 1997 11,12,13 1998						
3RD WEEKEND	TREATY FOUR PW PO BOX 128 FORT QU'APPELLE, SK S0G 1S0	306-332-1874 306-332-4685 306-332-5953	FORT QU'APPELLE, SK		✓	
15,16,17 1995 20,21,22 1996 19,20,21 1997 18,19,20 1998						
4TH WEEKEND	CURVE LAKE ANNUAL POW WOW CURVE LAKE FIRST NATION PO BOX 100 CURVE LAKE, ON K0L 1R0	705-657-8045 705-657-8708	POW WOW GROUNDS		✓	
22,23,24 1995 27,28,29 1996 26,27,28 1997 25,26,27 1998						
4TH WEEK	NATIVE INDIAN/INUIT PHOTOGRAPHERS ASSOC CONFERENCE (N.I.I.P.A.) 134 JAMES ST SOUTH HAMILTON, ON L8P 2Z4	905-529-7477	VARIES - CANADA			
	YOUR EVENT CAN BE LISTED ! FAX US AT (520) 622-4900					

CALL BEFORE YOU GO !

POW WOW CALENDAR 1995-1998

CAMPING	COST	SOCIAL	CEREMONY	MARKET	EDUCA-TIONAL	CELE-BRATION	ARTS & CRAFTS	HOST
	F	✓					✓	T
✓	F						✓	T
✓	$	✓					✓	T
✓			✓				✓	T
✓	F						✓	T
✓	F						✓	T
	$				✓	✓	✓	I

T - TRIBAL EVENT   I - INDIAN SPONSOR   C - NON INDIAN SPONSOR

MONTH/DAY/ WEEKEND	EVENT	PHONE/FAX	LOCATION	DATE FIRST STARTED	POW WOW	RODEO & FAIR
OCTOBER						
1ST WEEKEND	ANNUAL NATIVE CULTURAL FESTIVAL NATIVE FRIENDSHIP CENTER 3730 COTE DES NEIGES MONTREAL, PQ H3H 1V6	514-937-5338 514-937-4437	VANIER COLLEGE MONTREAL, PQ	1981		
	ANNUAL RAMA THKSGVG CHIPPEWAS OF RAMA FIRST NATION BOX 35, RAMA RD RAMAH, ON L0K 1T0	705-329-1047 705-325-3611 705-325-0879	POW WOW GROUNDS RAMA, ON	1987	✓	
6,7,8 1995 4,5,6 1996 3,4,5 1997 2,3,4 1998	CANADIAN THANKSGIVING POW WOW PO BOX 165 MT CURRY, BC V0N 2K0	604-894-6867 604-894-6115	MT CURRIE, BC	1986	✓	
	NIKANEET ANNUAL PW NIKANEET FIRST NATION PO BOX 548 MAPLE CREEK, SK S0N 1N0	306-662-7513 306-662-9196 306-662-4160	POW WOW GROUNDS MAPLE CREEK, SK		✓	
2ND WEEKEND						
13,14,15 1995 11,12,13 1996 10,11,12 1997 9,10,11 1998						
4TH WEEKEND	INTERNATIONAL POW WOW MANITOBA FIRST NATION PO BOX 1569 PORTAGE LA PRAIRIE, MB R1N 3P1	204-857-4511	WINNIPEG ARENA 1430 MAROONS RD WINNIPEG, MB	1994	✓	
27,28,29 1995 25,26,27 1996 24,25,26 1997 23,24,25 1998						
NOVEMBER	***YOUR EVENT CAN BE LISTED ! FAX US AT (520) 622-4900***					
2ND WEEKEND	VETERANS MEMORIAL PW MONTANA FIRST NATION PO BOX 70 HOBBEMA, AB T0C 1N0	403-585-3741 403-585-3744	AGRICOMPLEX HOBBEMA, AB		✓	
10,11,12 1995 8, 9, 10 1996 7, 8, 9 1997 13,14,15 1998						
DECEMBER						

CALL BEFORE YOU GO !

POW WOW CALENDAR 1995-1998

CAMPING	COST	SOCIAL	CEREMONY	MARKET	EDUCA-TIONAL	CELE-BRATION	ARTS & CRAFTS	HOST
							✓	I
	F	✓	✓			✓	✓	T
		✓				✓	✓	I
✓	F						✓	T
	$			✓	✓			T
							✓	I

T - TRIBAL EVENT I - INDIAN SPONSOR C - NON INDIAN SPONSOR

UNITED STATES

UNITED STATES

Apache
Assiniboine
Blackfeet
Choctaw
Creek
Colville
Delaware
Huron
Hupa
Iowa
Kickapoo
Kiowa
Lumbee
Malisett
Mission
Mohegan
Navajo
Nipmuc
Nez Perce
Paiute
Penobscot
Pequot
Ponca
Potawatomi
Pueblo
Salish
Sac & Fox
Six Nations
Sioux
Tohono-O'odham
Ute
Winnebego
Wintu
Yakima

PRESIDENT'S AMERICAN INDIAN POLICY

On June 14, 1991, President George Bush issued an American Indian policy statement which reaffirmed the government-to-government relationship between Indian tribes and the Federal Government.

The President's policy builds upon the policy of self-determination first announced by President Nixon in 1970, reaffirmed and expanded upon by the Reagan-Bush Administration in 1983. President Bush's policy moves toward a permanent relationship of understanding and trust, and designates a senior staff member as his personal liaison with all Indian tribes. President Bush's policy statement follows:

<u>Reaffirming The Government-to-Government Relationship Between The Federal Government and Tribal Governments</u>

On January 24, 1983, the Reagan-Bush Administration issued a statement on Indian policy recognizing and reaffirming the government-to-government relationship between Indian tribes and the Federal Government. This relationship is the cornerstone of the Bush-Quayle Administration's policy of fostering tribal self-determination. This government-to-government relationship is the result of sovereign and independent tribal governments being incorporated into the fabric of our Nation, of Indian tribes becoming what our courts have come to refer to as quasi-sovereign domestic dependent nations. Over the years the relationship has flourished, grown, and evolved into a vibrant partnership in which over 500 tribal governments stand shoulder to shoulder with the other governmental units that form our Republic.

This is now a relationship in which tribal governments may choose to assume the administration of numerous Federal programs pursuant to the 1975 Indian Self-Determination and Education Assistance Act.

This is a partnership in which an Office of Self-Governance has been established in the Department of the Interior and given the responsibility of working with tribes to craft creative ways of transferring decision-making powers over tribal government functions from the Department to tribal Government.

An office of American Indian Trust will be established in the Department of the Interior and given the responsibility of overseeing the trust responsibility of the Department and of insuring that no Departmental action will be taken that will adversely affect or destroy those physical assets that the Federal Government holds in trust for the tribes.

I take pride in acknowledging and reaffirming the existence and durability of our unique government-to-government relationship.

Within the White House I have designated a senior staff member, my Director of Intergovernmental Affairs, as my personal liaison with all Indian tribes. While it is not possible for a President or his small staff to deal directly with the multiplicity of issues and problems presented by each of the 510 tribal entities in the Nation now recognized by and dealing with the Department of the Interior, the White House will continue to interact with Indian tribes on a intergovernmental basis.

The concepts of forced termination and excessive dependency on the Federal Government must now be relegated, once and for all, to the history books. Today we move forward toward a permanent relationship of understanding and trust, a relationship in which the tribes of the nation sit in positions of dependent sovereignty along with the other governments that compose the family that is America.

American Indians Today third edition, United States Department of the Interior-Bureau of Indian Affairs, MS 2620-MIB, Washington, DC 20240-0001.

Federal Appropriations for Indian Affairs

Over the past decade, the annual budget for the BIA has averaged approximately $1 billion. The fiscal year 1991 appropriation for the BIA is $1.5 billion for the principal program categories of: Education, $554.5 million; Tribal Services (including social services and law enforcement), $338.9 million; Economic Development, $14.6 million; Natural Resources, $139.7 million; Trust Responsibilities, $74.7 million; Facilities Management, $94.2 million; General Administration, $112.0 million; Construction, $167.6 million; Indian Loan Guaranty, $11.7 million; Miscellaneous Payment to Indians, $56.1 million; and Navajo Rehabilitation Trust Fund, $3.0 million.

Under the Indian self-determination policy, tribes may operate their own reservation programs by contracting with the BIA. In fiscal year 1990, tribal governments contracted programs totaling $415 million, over 30 percent of the total BIA budget. Appropriations for other federal agencies with Indian programs, for FY 1991, are: Indian Health Services, $1.4 billion; and Administration for Native Americans, $33.3 million (both agencies of the Department of Health and Human Services); and the Office of Indian Education in the U.S. Department of Education, $75.3 million.

Other federal departments, such as Agriculture, Commerce, and HUD, also receive funds specifically designated for Indian programs.

UNITED STATES

KEY TO TRIBAL GRAPHS ON PAGES 7 TO 84

This graph format is divided into three sections, ie. Historical Profile on the left hand page, Economic Profile on the right hand page and down the middle of each page in the shaded area is the full name, address, state, zip, phone and fax information of each tribal nation. After each state one to several blank spaces are provided to add additional tribes in your state if they have not been included in this publication.

HISTORICAL PROFILE

AREA OFFICE:

The Bureau of Indian Affairs has divided Alaska and the United States into twelve area offices, each is responsible for several Indian tribes/nations. All other boxes represent tribes that are state recognized (STATE) or are independent (IND) and are not recognized by the Federal Government or the State Government.

TREATY/PETITION:

Most tribes have signed treaties more than once for different reasons. We list only the first treaty signing. All listings with only the date of the year are tribes that have signed treaties. All listings with the month, day, and year listed are petitions for government recognition. This process can take several years to meet all requirements. Tribal nations who are not federal or state recognized and who did not apply for recognition is left blank. Some tribes never signed a treaty with the government, others rights were signed by different tribes or bands.

TRIBAL CLASS:

This box includes tribal groups that live within a tribal nation. In many cases several tribes were gathered up by the calvary and all put onto a single land area (reservation). Confederated, United Tribes of..., Six Nations, are just a few of the terms used to denote different tribes living on one reservation.

POPULATION 1990:

The population figures are those reported by the 1990 census and only the figures they report. A census figure is available from the Bureau of Indian Affairs, I.H.S. public health census and the tribal census office. All with great differences in the count.

TRUST ACREAGE:

These figures were reported by the Bureau of Indian Affairs, but one must realize that these figures constantly change. Many tribal nations are checker board land that is both Indian and non-Indian owned. Some nations are buying back lost lands for future use, land claims that take decades to settle have changed some nations, tribes that were terminated have applied and received recognition were given land as part of their settlement, and each tribal nation has their own unique circumstances for adding or deleting their land base.

ECONOMIC PROFILE

G = GAMING/CASINOS

Gaming/Casinos have been a recent economic boom to all tribal nations within the last decade. It is in constant change and difficult to track. We have identified each into three categories ie, T/C designates that a tribal compact has been entered into with the state for gaming which usually allows for video games, card games, keno, and other full scale Las Vegas style gaming; B are bingo operations only; P are pull tabs operation only. We have listed each tribal nation and their respective casino in a separate chapter.

L = LODGING, MOTEL, RESORT, RV PARK

Lodging includes different Motels (M), resorts (R) and recreational vehicle (RV) facilities located on each tribal reservation. Majority of these are Indian/tribal owned but we were unable to identify among them which are individual, tribal, or outside owned/operated.

E. B. = ECONOMIC BASE

This denotes the main economic base that the members of each tribe is involved ie: A - agriculture, F - fish, aquaculture, M - minerals, R - ranching, T - timber. In some cases what the tribe's main source of income and its members source of income varies greatly.

N = NEWSPAPER

This denotes the tribe has a tribal newspaper with an emphasis on its unique culture, tribal meetings, current events, deaths/births and common information important to its members. It must be emphasized that the tribal media is usually the first to be cut during tribal economic hard times. These publications maybe published on an irregular basis. Some may even stop publication for several months or years, then may resume publication.

M = MUSEUM / CULTURAL CENTER

This denotes the tribe has a museum or cultural center with an emphasis on it's unique culture, crafts, oral history and artifacts from that area. These facilities can range from a department within the tribal office complex to a multi-million dollar complex including museum, theater, library, R.V. camping, restaurant, meeting rooms, rodeo and fairgrounds.

Information for the United States graphs provided by:

Bureau of Indian Affairs
Census Bureau
Smithsonian Institution

Format created by:

N. A^2. I. I. T. C.

HISTORICAL PROFILE

Area Office	Treaty Petition [1]	Tribal Class	Pop 1990	Trust Acreage	Tribal Nation
ALABAMA					
	23-SEP-81	CHEROKEE			CHEROKEES OF JACKSON COUNTY AL
STATE		CHEROKEE			CHEROKEES OF NORTHEAST ALABAMA NATION
	27-MAY-88	CHEROKEE			CHEROKEES OF SOUTHEAST ALABAMA
STATE		CHEROKEE			ECHOTA CHEROKEE NATION
STATE	27-JUN-83	CREEK			MACHIS LOWER CREEK INDIAN NATION
STATE	27-MAY-83	CHOCTAW	4,100	300	MOWA BAND OF CHOCTAW INDIAN NATION
EA	1964	CREEK	1,850	600	POARCH BAND OF CREEK INDIANS NATION
	09-NOV-71	CREEK			PRINCIPAL CREEK INDIAN NATION EAST OF THE MISSISSIPPI
STATE		CREEK			STAR CLAN OF MUSCOGEE CREEK NATION
		CHEROKEE			UNITED CHEROKEE OF ALABAMA
ARIZONA					
PHX	1874	TOHONO - O'ODHAM	635	21,840	AK CHIN INDIAN NATION
PHX	1917	YUMAN	758	6,156.3	COCOPAH NATION
PHX	1865	HOPI, CHEMEHUEVI, MOHAVE	2,989	268,917.68	COLORADO RIVER NATIONS
PHX	1936	YAVAPAI, MOHAVE, APACHE	610	24,680	FT. MCDOWELL MOHAVE APACHE NATION

LEGEND:

AREA OFFICES:
ABE - Aberdeen
ABQ - Albuquerque
ANA - Anadarko
BIL - Billings
EA - Eastern
MIN - Minneapolis
MUS - Muskogee
NAV - Navajo
PHX - Phoenix
POR - Portland
SAC - Sacramento
STATE - State Recognized
IND - Independent

1. Date of first Treaty / Date of first Petition

Address	City, State, Zip	Phone Fax	G[2]	L[3]	EB[4]	N[5]	M[6]

ALABAMA

Address	City, State, Zip	Phone Fax	G	L	EB	N	M
PO BOX 41	HIGDON, AL 35979						
222 SLATE ROCK RD	HAZELGREEN, AL 35750	205-881-4475 205-631-6930					
PO BOX 717	DOTHAN, AL 36301	334-578-5390					
PO BOX 20866	BIRMINGHAM, AL 35219	205-663-2196					
RT 1 708 SO JOHN ST	NEW BROCKTON, AL 36351	334-894-5636					
RT 1 BOX 330A	MT VERNON, AL 36560	334-829-5500 334-829-5008		RV	T,A	X	
HCR 69A BOX 85-B	ATMORE, AL 36502	334-368-9136 334-368-4502	B	M			
PO BOX 201	FLORALA, AL 36442	904-834-2728					
PO BOX 126	GOSHEN, AL 36035	334-484-3589					
RT 1 BOX 8	DALEVILLE, AL 36322						

ARIZONA

Address	City, State, Zip	Phone Fax	G	L	EB	N	M
42507 W PETERS & NALL RD	MARICOPA, AZ 85239	520-568-2227 520-254-6133	TC		A	X	X
BOX BIN 'G'	SOMERTON, AZ 85350	520-627-2102 520-627-3173	TC	RV	A		
RT 1 BOX 23 B	PARKER, AZ 85344	520-669-9211 520-669-5675	TC	RV	A		
PO BOX 17779	FOUNTAIN HILLS, AZ 85268	602-837-5121 602-837-1630	TC			X	

2. Gaming / Casino
3. Lodging - Resort, Motel, RV Park
4. Economic Base - Farming, Fishing, Ranching Operations
5. Tribal Newspaper
6. Museum / Cultural Center

A - Agriculture
B - Bingo
F - Fish, Aquaculture
M - Mineral
R - Ranching
RV - Recreational Vehicle

T - Timber
TC - Tribal Contract

HISTORICAL PROFILE

Area Office	Treaty Petition [1]	Tribal Class	Pop 1990	Trust Acreage	Tribal Nation
ARIZONA					
PHX	1859	PIMA	11,000	372,200	GILA RIVER INDIAN NATION
	18-SEP-78	YAQUI			GUADALUPE YAQUI NATION
PHX	1880	HAVASUPAI	594	188,077	HAVASUPAI NATION
PHX	1882	HOPI	6,750	1,561,213	HOPI NATION
PHX	1883	HUALAPAI	1,499	993,083	HUALAPAI NATION
PHX		PAIUTE	214	120,840	KAIBAB PAIUTE NATION
NAVAJO	1868	NAVAJO	219,097	15,432,170	NAVAJO NATION
PHX	18-SEP-78	YAQUI	5,250	892	PASCUA YAQUI NATION
PHX	1884	QUECHAN	2,215	43,622.76	QUECHAN NATION
PHX	1879	PIMA - MARICOPA	4618	52,729	SALT RIVER PIMA-MARICOPA NATION
PHX	1871	APACHE	9,736	1,853,841	SAN CARLOS APACHE NATION
PHX	1989	PAIUTE	190		SAN JUAN SOUTHERN PAIUTE NATION
PHX	1874	TOHONO - O'ODHAM	17,704	2,849,525.7	TOHONO O'ODHAM NATION
PHX	1973	APACHE	85	85	TONTO APACHE NATION
IND		ALLEGHENNY			UNITED SOUTHWESTERN ALLEGHENNY NATION
PHX	1897	APACHE	10,147	1,664,984	WHITE MOUNTAIN APACHE NATION
PHX	1975	APACHE	1,068	635	YAVAPAI-APACHE NATION

LEGEND:

AREA OFFICES:
ABE - Aberdeen
ABQ - Albuquerque
ANA - Anadarko
BIL - Billings
EA - Eastern
MIN - Minneapolis
MUS - Muskogee
NAV - Navajo
PHX - Phoenix
POR - Portland
SAC - Sacramento
STATE - State Recognized
IND - Independent

1. Date of first Treaty / Date of first Petition

Address	City, State, Zip	Phone Fax	G[2]	L[3]	EB[4]	N[5]	M[6]

ARIZONA

Address	City, State, Zip	Phone Fax	G	L	EB	N	M
PO BOX 97	SACATON, AZ 85247	520-562-3311 OR 963-4323 520-562-3422	TC	RV	A	X	X
8619 AVENIDA DEL YAQUI	GUADALUPE, AZ 85283	520-820-8836 800-572-7282				X	X
PO BOX 10	SUPAI, AZ 86435	520-448-2961 520-448-2551		M	A		X
PO BOX 123	KYKOTSMOVI, AZ 86039	520-734-2441 520-734-2435		R	A	X	X
PO BOX 179	PEACH SPRINGS, AZ 86434	520-769-2216 520-769-2343	TC		A	X	X
TRIBAL AFFAIRS BLDG, HC 65 BOX 2	FREDONIA, AZ 86022	520-643-7245 520-643-7260	TC	RV			X
PO BOX 3000	WINDOW ROCK, AZ 86515	520-871-6352 520-871-4025		M	R,A	X	X
7474 S CAMINO DE OESTE	TUCSON, AZ 85746	520-883-2838 520-883-7770	TC		A		
PO BOX 11352	YUMA, AZ 85364	619-572-0213 619-572-2102	TC	RV	A	X	X
RT 1 BOX 216	SCOTTSDALE, AZ 85256	602-941-7277 602-949-2909		RV	A	X	X
PO BOX O	SAN CARLOS, AZ 85550	520-475-2361 520-475-2567	TC	RV	R,T	X	
PO BOX 2656	TUBA CITY, AZ 86045	520-283-4583 OR 4587 520-283-5761					
PO BOX 837	SELLS, AZ 85634	520-383-2221 520-383-3379	TC		R	X	
TONTO RESERVATION #30	PAYSON, AZ 85541	520-474-5000 520-474-9125	B				
PO BOX 1198	FREDONIA, AZ 86022	307-332-2660					
PO BOX 700	WHITERIVER, AZ 85941	520-338-4346 520-338-4778	TC	R	T	X	X
PO BOX 1188	CAMP VERDE, AZ 86322	520-567-3649 520-567-3994	TC	M	RV		X

2. Gaming / Casino
3. Lodging - Resort, Motel, RV Park
4. Economic Base - Farming, Fishing, Ranching Operations
5. Tribal Newspaper
6. Museum / Cultural Center

A - Agriculture
B - Bingo
F - Fish, Aquaculture
M - Mineral
R - Ranching
RV - Recreational Vehicle

T - Timber
TC - Tribal Contract

HISTORICAL PROFILE

Area Office	Treaty Petition [1]	Tribal Class	Pop 1990	Trust Acreage	Tribal Nation

ARIZONA

Area Office	Treaty Petition	Tribal Class	Pop 1990	Trust Acreage	Tribal Nation
PHX	1935	APACHE	115	1,409	YAVAPAI-PRESCOTT NATION

ARKANSAS

Area Office	Treaty Petition	Tribal Class	Pop 1990	Trust Acreage	Tribal Nation
	25-APR-90	OUACHITA			OUACHITA INDIANS OF ARKANSAS & AMERICA

CALIFORNIA

Area Office	Treaty Petition	Tribal Class	Pop 1990	Trust Acreage	Tribal Nation
SAC	1876	CAHUILLA	263	31,610.33	AGUA CALIENTE NATION
SAC		ALTURAS	20	10	ALTURAS RANCHERIA NATION
	18-SEP-90	OHLONE			AMAH BAND OF COASTANOAN/OHLONE DIGGER INDIANS
	24-APR-82	YOSEMITE			AMERICAN INDIAN COUNCIL OF MARIPOSA COUNTY
	09-JUL-76	PAIUTE			ANTELOPE VALLEY PAIUTE TRIBE
		SHOSHONE			ATAHUN SHOSHONES OF SAN JUAN CAPISTRANO
SAC	1875	MISSION	420	5,903.52	BARONA NATION
SAC		PAIUTE	133	320	BENTON PAIUTE INDIAN NATION

LEGEND:

AREA OFFICES:
ABE - Aberdeen
ABQ - Albuquerque
ANA - Anadarko
BIL - Billings
EA - Eastern
MIN - Minneapolis
MUS - Muskogee
NAV - Navajo
PHX - Phoenix
POR - Portland
SAC - Sacramento
STATE - State Recognized
IND - Independent

1. Date of first Treaty / Date of first Petition

Address	City, State, Zip	Phone Fax	G[2]	L[3]	EB[4]	N[5]	M[6]

ARIZONA

Address	City, State, Zip	Phone Fax	G	L	EB	N	M
530 E MERRITT ST	PRESCOTT, AZ 86301	520-445-8790 520-778-9445	B	R			

ARKANSAS

Address	City, State, Zip	Phone Fax	G	L	EB	N	M
PO BOX 34	STORY, AR 71970	501-867-7452 800-831-4810					

CALIFORNIA

Address	City, State, Zip	Phone Fax	G	L	EB	N	M
110 N INDIAN CANYON DR	PALM SPRINGS, CA 92262	619-325-5673 619-325-0593	TC	M			X
PO BOX 360	ALTURAS, CA 96101	916-233-5571 916-233-3055					
789 CANADA RD	WOODSIDE, CA 94062	415-851-7747					
PO BOX 1200	MARIPOSA, CA 95338	209-966-3918					
PO BOX 119	COLEVILLE, CA 96107	916-266-3126					
2352 BAHIA DR	LA JOLLA, CA 92037						
1095 BARONA RD	LAKESIDE, CA 92040	619-443-6612 OR 6613	TC		R		
STAR RT 4 BOX 56A	BENTON, CA 93512	619-933-2321 916-933-2412					

2. Gaming / Casino
3. Lodging - Resort, Motel, RV Park
4. Economic Base - Farming, Fishing, Ranching Operations
5. Tribal Newspaper
6. Museum / Cultural Center

A - Agriculture
B - Bingo
F - Fish, Aquaculture
M - Mineral
R - Ranching
RV - Recreational Vehicle

T - Timber
TC - Tribal Contract

HISTORICAL PROFILE

Area Office	Treaty Petition [1]	Tribal Class	Pop 1990	Trust Acreage	Tribal Nation
					CALIFORNIA
SAC		TYME MAIDU	225	130.08	BERRY CREEK RANCHERIA NATION
SAC		BIG LAGOON	24	9.26	BIG LAGOON RANCHERIA NATION
					BIG MEADOWS LODGE TRIBE
SAC		PAIUTE SHOSHONE	331	558	BIG PINE RESERVATION NATION
SAC		WESTERN MONO	179	239	BIG SANDY RANCHERIA NATION
SAC		POMO	90	106.08	BIG VALLEY RANCHERIA NATION
SAC		PAIUTE	1,016	1,750	BISHOP INDIAN NATION
SAC		SHOSHONE BLUE LAKE	34	4.31	BLUE LAKE RANCHERIA NATION
SAC		PAIUTE	51	80	BRIDGEPORT INDIAN NATION
SAC	1916	MIWOK	1		BUENA VISTA RANCHERIA NATION
SAC	1876	CAHUILLA	25	1,382.28	CABAZON INDIAN NATION OF CALIFORNIA
SAC	1875	CAHUILLA	148	18,884.26	CAHUILLA BAND OF MISSION INDIANS NATION
SAC	1891	DIEGUENO	223	15,480.28	CAMPO BAND OF MISSION INDIAN NATION
SAC		CEDARVILLE	20	17	CEDARVILLE RANCHERIA NATION
PHX		CHEMEHUEVI	541	30,653.87	CHEMEHUEVI NATION
SAC		MI-WUK	6	2.8	CHICKEN RANCH RANCHERIA NATION
SAC					CHICO RANCHERIA NATION

LEGEND:

AREA OFFICES:
ABE - Aberdeen
ABQ - Albuquerque
ANA - Anadarko
BIL - Billings
EA - Eastern
MIN - Minneapolis
MUS - Muskogee
NAV - Navajo
PHX - Phoenix
POR - Portland
SAC - Sacramento
STATE - State Recognized
IND - Independent

1. Date of first Treaty / Date of first Petition

CALIFORNIA

Address	City, State, Zip	Phone Fax	G [2]	L [3]	EB [4]	N [5]	M [6]
5 TYME WAY	OROVILLE, CA 95966	916-534-3859 916-534-1151					
PO BOX 3060	TRINIDAD, CA 95570	707-826-2079 707-826-1737		M			
PO BOX 362	CHESTER, CA 96020						
PO BOX 700	BIG PINE, CA 93513	619-938-2003 619-938-2942					
PO BOX 337	AUBERRY, CA 93602	209-855-4003					
PO BOX 955	LAKEPORT, CA 95453	707-262-0629					
PO BOX 548	BISHOP, CA 93515	619-873-3584 619-873-4143	B				X
PO BOX 428	BLUE LAKE, CA 95525	707-668-5101 707-668-4272					
PO BOX 37	BRIDGEPORT, CA 93517	619-932-7083 619-932-7846					
# GLYNIS FALLS COURT	SACRAMENTO, CA 95831	916-392-5003 916-424-1077					
84-245 INDIO SPRING DR	INDIO, CA 92201	619-342-2593 619-347-7880	TC				
PO BOX 391760	ANZA, CA 92539	909-763-5549 909-763-2808					
1779 CAMPO TRUCK TRL	CAMPO, CA 91906	619-478-9046 619-478-5818					
PO BOX 126	CEDARVILLE, CA 96104	916-279-2270 916-233-2439					
PO BOX 1976	HAVASU LAKE, CA 92363	619-858-4301 619-858-5400		RV			X
PO BOX 1699	JAMESTOWN, CA 95327	209-984-3057	B				
3006 ESPANADE ST STE H & I	CHICO, CA 95926	916-899-8922 916-899-8517					

2. Gaming / Casino
3. Lodging - Resort, Motel, RV Park
4. Economic Base - Farming, Fishing, Ranching Operations
5. Tribal Newspaper
6. Museum / Cultural Center

A - Agriculture
B - Bingo
F - Fish, Aquaculture
M - Mineral
R - Ranching
RV - Recreational Vehicle

T - Timber
TC - Tribal Contract

HISTORICAL PROFILE

Area Office	Treaty Petition [1]	Tribal Class	Pop 1990	Trust Acreage	Tribal Nation

CALIFORNIA

Area Office	Treaty Petition	Tribal Class	Pop 1990	Trust Acreage	Tribal Nation
	14-JUL-88	CHOINUMNI			CHOINUMNI COUNCIL
	09-MAY-85	YOKOTCH			CHUKCHANSI YOKOTCH NATION
	25-MAY-93	CHUKCHANSI			CHUKCHANSI YOKOTCH TRIBE OF MARIPOSA CA
SAC		POMO	7		CLOVERDALE RANCHERIA NATION
SAC	1938	YUROK	73	228	COAST INDIAN NATION RESIGHINI RANCHERIA
	25-MAR-82	CHUMASH			COASTAL BAND & SANTA BARBARA BAND OF CHUMASH INDIANS
	16-SEP-88	MISSION			COASTANOAN BAND OF CARMEL MISSION INDIANS
	09-JUN-89				COASTANOAN/MUTSUN INDIANS OF CALIFORNIA
SAC		COLD SPRINGS	271	309.3	COLD SPRINGS RANCHERIA NATION
SAC	1907	WINTUN	20	546.44	COLUSA RANCHERIA NATION
SAC		WINTUN	115	1,280	CORTINA RANCHERIA NATION
SAC		POMO	225	115.52	COYOTE VALLEY RESERVATION NATION
SAC	1891	DIEGUENO	17	4,102.73	CUYAPAIPE BAND OF MISSION INDIANS NATION
SAC		POMO	163	150	DRY CREEK RANCHERIA NATION
	04-JAN-84	MONO			DUNLAP BAND OF MONO INDIANS
SAC		POMO	155	100	ELEM COLONY OF POMO INDIANS NATION SULPHUR BANK RANCHERIA
SAC		ELK VALLEY	175	17.12	ELK VALLEY RANCHERIA NATION

LEGEND:

AREA OFFICES:
ABE - Aberdeen
ABQ - Albuquerque
ANA - Anadarko
BIL - Billings
EA - Eastern
MIN - Minneapolis
MUS - Muskogee
NAV - Navajo
PHX - Phoenix
POR - Portland
SAC - Sacramento
STATE - State Recognized
IND - Independent

1. Date of first Treaty / Date of first Petition

Address	City, State, Zip	Phone Fax	G [2]	L [3]	EB [4]	N [5]	M [6]

CALIFORNIA

Address	City, State, Zip	Phone Fax	G	L	EB	N	M
2428 N THESTA	FRESNO, CA 93725	209-233-9781					
4962 WATT RD	MARIPOSA, CA 95338	209-742-7060					
C/O MS LYNDA L APPLING / 4962 WATT RD	MARIPOSA, CA 95338-9743	209-742-7060					
555 S CLOVERDALE # 1	CLOVERDALE, CA 94952	707-894-9377					
PO BOX 529	KLAMATH, CA 95548	707-482-2431 707-482-3425		RV		X	
610 DEL MONTE AVE	SANTA BARBARA, CA 93101	805-965-0718					
PO BOX 1657	MONROVIA, CA 91016						
PO BOX 28	HOLLISTER, CA 95024						
PO BOX 209	TOLLHOUSE, CA 93667	209-855-8187 916-855-8359	B				
PO BOX 8	COLUSA, CA 95932	916-458-8231 916-787-4006	B				
PO BOX 7470	CITRUS HEIGHTS, CA 95621	916-726-7118 916-726-3608					
7901 HWY 10 NORTH	REDWOOD VALLEY, CA 95470	707-485-8723 707-468-1247					X
2271 ALPINE BLVD	ALPINE, CA 91901	619-478-5289 714-276-6641					
PO BOX 607	GEYSERVILLE, CA 95441	707-857-3842 916-978-5589					
PO BOX 344	DUNLAP, CA 93621	209-338-2842					
PO BOX 618	CLEARLAKE OAKS, CA 95423	707-998-2549					
PO BOX 1042	CRESCENT CITY, CA 95531	707-464-4680 707-464-4519					

2. Gaming / Casino
3. Lodging - Resort, Motel, RV Park
4. Economic Base - Farming, Fishing, Ranching Operations
5. Tribal Newspaper
6. Museum / Cultural Center

A - Agriculture
B - Bingo
F - Fish, Aquaculture
M - Mineral
R - Ranching
RV - Recreational Vehicle

T - Timber
TC - Tribal Contract

HISTORICAL PROFILE

Area Office	Treaty Petition [1]	Tribal Class	Pop 1990	Trust Acreage	Tribal Nation

CALIFORNIA

Area Office	Treaty Petition [1]	Tribal Class	Pop 1990	Trust Acreage	Tribal Nation
	16-NOV-92	ESSELEN			ESSELEN TRIBE OF MONTEREY COUNCIL
SAC	1871	PAIUTE	190	3,334.97	FORT BIDWELL NATION
SAC	1915	PAIUTE	116	704.48	FORT INDEPENDENCE RESERVATION NATION
PHX		MOJAVE	836	32,679.65	FORT MOJAVE NATION
SAC		MAIDU	7	1	GREENVILLE RANCHERIA NATION
SAC		NOMELAKI, WINTUN, WAILAK	102	160	GRINDSTONE RANCHERIA NATION
SAC					GUIDIVILLE RANCHERIA NATION
	05-JAN-84	WINTU			HAYFORK BAND OF NOR-EL-MUK WINTU INDIANS
SAC	1876	HUPA	1,783	86,674.39	HOOPA VALLEY INDIAN RANCHERIA NATION
SAC		POMO	238	125.3	HOPLAND RESERVATION NATION
SAC	1875	DIEGUENO	17	851.81	INAJA & COSMIT BAND OF MISSION INDIAN NATION
	1916	MIWOK			IONE BAND OF MIWOK INDIANS
SAC		ME-WUK MIWOK	27	661.32	JACKSON RANCHERIA NATION
SAC		MISSION	84	6.03	JAMUL BAND OF MISSION INDIANS
	17-AUG-82	MISSION			JUANENO BAND OF MISSION INDIANS
SAC		KARUK	2,100	271.22	KARUK TRIBE OF CALIFORNIA NATION
	27-FEB-79	PAIUTE			KERN VALLEY INDIAN COMMUNITY

LEGEND:

AREA OFFICES:
ABE - Aberdeen
ABQ - Albuquerque
ANA - Anadarko
BIL - Billings
EA - Eastern
MIN - Minneapolis
MUS - Muskogee
NAV - Navajo
PHX - Phoenix
POR - Portland
SAC - Sacramento
STATE - State Recognized
IND - Independent

1. Date of first Treaty / Date of first Petition

CALIFORNIA

Address	City, State, Zip	Phone Fax	2 G	3	4 EB	5 N	6 M
C/O JOAN DENYS / 301 ROSALIE ST	SAN MATEO, CA 94403	415-570-6496					
PO BOX 129	FORT BIDWELL, CA 96112	916-279-6310 916-279-2233			R		
PO BOX 67	FORT INDEPENDENCE, CA 93526	619-878-2126 619-878-2311		RV	A		
500 MERRIMAN AVE	NEEDLES, CA 92363	619-326-4591 619-326-2468	TC		A		
645 ANTELOPE BL # 15	RED BLUFF, CA 96080	916-528-9000 916-529-9002					
PO BOX 63	ELK CREEK, CA 95939	916-968-5365 916-968-5366					
PO BOX 339	TALMAGE, CA 95481	707-462-3682 707-462-9183					
PO BOX 673	HAYFORK, CA 96041	916-628-5175					
PO BOX 1348	HOOPA, CA 95546	916-625-4211 916-625-4594	B	M			X
PO BOX 610	HOPLAND, CA 95449	707-744-1647 707-744-1506					
PO BOX 186	SANTA YSABEL, CA 92070						
2919 JACKSON VALLEY RD	IONE, CA 95640	209-274-2915					
PO BOX 429	JACKSON, CA 95642	209-223-1935 209-223-5366	B				
PO BOX 612	JAMUL, CA 91935	619-669-4785 619-669-4817					
31742 VIA BELARDES	SAN JUAN CAPISTRANO, CA 92675	714-493-4933					
PO BOX 1016	HAPPY CAMP, CA 96039	916-493-5305 916-493-5322		RV	T		
PO BIN DD	KERNVILLE, CA 93238	619-376-3761					

2. Gaming / Casino
3. Lodging - Resort, Motel, RV Park
4. Economic Base - Farming, Fishing, Ranching Operations
5. Tribal Newspaper
6. Museum / Cultural Center

A - Agriculture
B - Bingo
F - Fish, Aquaculture
M - Mineral
R - Ranching
RV - Recreational Vehicle

T - Timber
TC - Tribal Contract

HISTORICAL PROFILE

Area Office	Treaty Petition [1]	Tribal Class	Pop 1990	Trust Acreage	Tribal Nation

CALIFORNIA

Area Office	Treaty Petition [1]	Tribal Class	Pop 1990	Trust Acreage	Tribal Nation
SAC	1875	LUISENO	239	8541.25	LA JOLLA BAND OF MISSION INDIAN NATION
SAC	1891	MISSION	420	3,556.49	LA POSTA BAND OF MISSION INDIANS NATION
SAC		CAHTO	140	400	LAYTONVILLE RANCHERIA NATION
SAC		PAIUTE SHOSHONE	168	474	LONE PINE RESERVATION NATION
SAC	1889	CAHUILLA	212	25,049.63	LOS COYOTES BAND OF MISSION INDIANS NATION
SAC					LYTTON RANCHERIA
	06-JAN-77	MAIDU			MAIDU NATION
SAC		POMO	621	726.18	MANCHESTER/POINT ARENA RANCHERIA NATION
SAC	1891	KUMEYAAY	84	3,579.38	MANZANITA BAND OF MISSION INDIANS
SAC	1875	MISSION	345	920	MESA GRANDE BAND OF MISSION INDIANS NATION
SAC		POMO		217.40	MIDDLETOWN RANCHERIA NATION
	09-JUL-76	MONO			MONO LAKE INDIAN COMMUNITY
SAC		MAIDU	404		MOORETOWN RANCHERIA NATION
SAC	1877	CAHUILLA	783	32,361.82	MORONGO BAND OF MISSION INDIANS NATION
SAC					NOMLAKI INDIAN NATION
SAC	7-SEP-83	MONO		160	NORTH FORK RANCHERIA NATION
	03-DEC-92	OHLONE COASTANOAN			OHLONE/COASTANOAN - ESSELEN NATION

LEGEND:

AREA OFFICES:
ABE - Aberdeen
ABQ - Albuquerque
ANA - Anadarko
BIL - Billings
EA - Eastern
MIN - Minneapolis
MUS - Muskogee
NAV - Navajo
PHX - Phoenix
POR - Portland
SAC - Sacramento
STATE - State Recognized
IND - Independent

1. Date of first Treaty / Date of first Petition

Address	City, State, Zip	Phone Fax	G[2]	L[3]	EB[4]	N[5]	M[6]

CALIFORNIA

Address	City, State, Zip	Phone Fax	G	L	EB	N	M
STAR RT BOX 158	VALLEY CENTER, CA 92082	619-742-3771 619-742-3772		RV	A		
1064 BARONA RD	LAKESIDE, CA 92040	619-561-9294	B				
PO BOX 1239	LAYTONVILLE, CA 95454	707-984-6197					
1101 S MAIN STAR RT / PO BOX 747	LONE PINE, CA 93545	619-876-5414					
PO BOX 249	WARNER SPRINGS, CA 92086	619-782-3269		RV			
PO BOX 7882	SANTA ROSA, CA 95407	707-537-1655 707-537-1705					
PO BOX 204	SUSANVILLE, CA 96180	916-257-9691					
PO BOX 623	POINT ARENA, CA 95468	707-882-2788 707-882-4142					
PO BOX 1302	BOULEVARD, CA 91905	619-766-4930 619-766-4957		RV			
PO BOX 270	SANTA YSABEL, CA 92070	619-282-9650 619-282-7838					
PO BOX 1035	MIDDLETOWN, CA 95461	707-987-3670 707-987-9615					
PO BOX 237	LEE VINING, CA 93541	619-647-6471					
PO BOX 1842	OROVILLE, CA 95965	916-533-3625 916-533-3680					
11581 POTRERO RD	BANNING, CA 92220	909-849-4697 909-849-4698	TC				X
PO BOX 339	WILLIAMS, CA 95987	916-473-5196					
PO BOX 929	NORTH FORK, CA 93643	209-877-2461					X
C/O LORETTA ESCOBAR-WYER / PO BOX 464	PALO ALTO, CA 94302						

2. Gaming / Casino
3. Lodging - Resort, Motel, RV Park
4. Economic Base - Farming, Fishing, Ranching Operations
5. Tribal Newspaper
6. Museum / Cultural Center

A - Agriculture
B - Bingo
F - Fish, Aquaculture
M - Mineral
R - Ranching
RV - Recreational Vehicle

T - Timber
TC - Tribal Contract

Area Office	Treaty Petition [1]	Tribal Class	Pop 1990	Trust Acreage	Tribal Nation

CALIFORNIA

Area Office	Treaty Petition [1]	Tribal Class	Pop 1990	Trust Acreage	Tribal Nation
	09-MAY-89	OHLONE COASTANOAN MUWEKMA			OHLONE/COASTANOAN MUWEKMA TRIBE
SAC	1875	LUISENO	613	11,892.82	PALA BAND OF MISSION INDIANS NATION
SAC	1891	LUISENO	137	5,877.25	PAUMA BAND OF MISSION INDIANS NATION
SAC	1882	LUISENO	725	4,396.44	PECHANGA BAND OF MISSION INDIANS NATION
SAC	1983	CHUKCHANSI	30	57.52	PICAYUNE RANCHERIA NATION
SAC		POMO		81.48	PINOLEVILLE RANCHERIA NATION
SAC			850	9,567.18	PIT RIVER NATION
SAC		POMO	1		POTTER VALLEY RANCHERIA NATION
SAC	1983	QUARTZ	138	24.02	QUARTZ VALLEY INDIAN NATION
SAC	1891	CAHUILLA	3	560	RAMONA BAND CAHUILLA INDIANS NATION
SAC		REDDING	160	8.35	REDDING RANCHERIA NATION
SAC		POMO	124	354.40	REDWOOD VALLEY RANCHERIA NATION
SAC	1875	LUISENO	671	4,270.02	RINCON BAND OF MISSION INDIANS NATION
SAC	1987	POMO	210	226.06	ROBINSON RANCHERIA NATION
SAC			129	1.0	ROHNERVILLE RANCHERIA NATION
SAC	1870	COVELO	2,699	61,075.02	ROUND VALLEY RESERVATION NATION
SAC	1907	WINTUN	29	370.86	RUMSEY RANCHERIA NATION

LEGEND:

AREA OFFICES:
ABE - Aberdeen
ABQ - Albuquerque
ANA - Anadarko
BIL - Billings
EA - Eastern
MIN - Minneapolis
MUS - Muskogee
NAV - Navajo
PHX - Phoenix
POR - Portland
SAC - Sacramento
STATE - State Recognized
IND - Independent

1. Date of first Treaty / Date of first Petition

CALIFORNIA

Address	City, State, Zip	Phone Fax	G[2]	L[3]	EB[4]	N[5]	M[6]
1845 THE ALAMEDA	SAN JOSE, CA 95113	408-293-9956					
PO BOX 43	PALA, CA 92059	619-742-3784 619-742-1411		RV			X
PO BOX 86	PAUMA VALLEY, CA 92061	619-742-1289 619-742-3422					
PO BOX 1477	TEMECULA, CA 92593	909-676-2768 909-695-1778					
PO BOX 269	COARSEGOLD, CA 93614	209-683-6633 209-683-0599					
367 N STATE # 204	UKIAH, CA 95482	707-463-1454 707-463-6601					
PO DRAWER 1570	BURNEY, CA 96013	916-335-5421 916-335-5241					
417 C TALMAGE RD	UKIAH, CA 95482	707-468-7494 707-468-0874					
9117 SNIKTAW LN	FORT JONES, CA 96032	916-468-5409 916-468-5908					
3940 CARY RD	ANZA, CA 92539	909-763-0371 909-763-0371					
2000 RANCHERIA RD	REDDING, CA 96001	916-225-8979 916-241-1879	B				
PO BOX 499	REDWOOD VALLEY, CA 95470	707-485-0361 707-485-5726					
PO BOX 68	VALLEY CENTER, CA 92082	619-749-1051 619-749-8901	B				X
PO BOX 1119	NICE, CA 95464	707-275-0527 707-275-0235	B				
PO BOX 108	EUREKA, CA 95502	707-443-6150 707-442-6403					
PO BOX 448	COVELO, CA 95428	707-983-6126 707-983-6128			T		
PO BOX 18	BROOKS, CA 95606	916-796-3400 916-796-2143	TC		A		

2. Gaming / Casino
3. Lodging - Resort, Motel, RV Park
4. Economic Base - Farming, Fishing, Ranching Operations
5. Tribal Newspaper
6. Museum / Cultural Center

A - Agriculture
B - Bingo
F - Fish, Aquaculture
M - Mineral
R - Ranching
RV - Recreational Vehicle

T - Timber
TC - Tribal Contract

HISTORICAL PROFILE

Area Office	Treaty Petition [1]	Tribal Class	Pop 1990	Trust Acreage	Tribal Nation
					CALIFORNIA
	10-OCT-89	SALINAN			SALINAN NATION
	18-OCT-84	MISSION			SAN LUIS REY BAND OF MISSION INDIANS
SAC	1891	SERRANO	73	657.93	SAN MANUEL BAND OF MISSION INDIANS NATION
SAC	1891	DIEGUENO	360	1,379.59	SAN PASQUAL NATION
SAC		SANTA ROSA	325	340	SANTA ROSA RANCHERIA NATION
SAC	1891	CAHUILLA	135	11,092.60	SANTA ROSA RESERVATION NATION
SAC	1891	CHUMASH	340	126.63	SANTA YNEZ BAND OF MISSION INDIANS NATION
SAC	1875	DIEGUENO	300	15,526.78	SANTA YSABEL BAND OF MISSION INDIANS NATION
SAC		POMO			SCOTTS VALLEY BAND OF POMO INDIAN NATION
	28-MAY-82				SHASTA INDIAN NATION
SAC	1909	POMO	233	699.94	SHERWOOD VALLEY RANCHERIA NATION
SAC		MIWOK	0	320	SHINGLE SPRINGS RANCHERIA NATION
SAC			360	67.90	SMITH RIVER RANCHERIA NATION
SAC	1883	LUISENO	699	5,915.68	SOBOBA BAND OF MISSION INDIANS NATION
					SONOMA COUNTY INDIAN COUNCIL
SAC		POMO	198	80	STEWARTS POINT RANCHERIA NATION
SAC			111	150.53	SUSANVILLE RANCHERIA NATION

LEGEND:

AREA OFFICES:
ABE - Aberdeen
ABQ - Albuquerque
ANA - Anadarko
BIL - Billings
EA - Eastern
MIN - Minneapolis
MUS - Muskogee
NAV - Navajo
PHX - Phoenix
POR - Portland
SAC - Sacramento
STATE - State Recognized
IND - Independent

1. Date of first Treaty / Date of first Petition

Address	City, State, Zip	Phone Fax	G[2]	L[3]	EB[4]	N[5]	M[6]

CALIFORNIA

Address	City, State, Zip	Phone Fax	G[2]	L[3]	EB[4]	N[5]	M[6]
PO BOX 610546	SAN JOSE, CA 95161	408-923-1315					
360 N MIDWAY # 301	ESCONDIDO, CA 92027	619-741-1996					
PO BOX 266	PATTON, CA 92369	909-864-8933 909-864-3370	TC				
PO BOX 365	VALLEY CENTER, CA 92082	619-749-3200 619-749-3876					
16835 ALKALI DR - PO BOX 8	LEMOORE, CA 93245	209-924-1278 209-924-3583	B				
325 N WESTERN AVE	HEMET, CA 92343	909-849-4761 909-849-5612					
PO BOX 517	SANTA YNEZ, CA 93460	805-688-7997 805-688-8005	B	RV			
PO BOX 130	SANTA YSABEL, CA 92070	619-765-0845 619-765-0320					X
149 N MAIN # 200	LAKEPORT, CA 95453	707-263-4771 707-263-4773					
PO BOX 1054	YREKA, CA 96097	916-842-5654					
190 SHERWOOD HILL DR	WILLITS, CA 95490	707-459-9690 707-459-6936					
PO BOX 1340	SHINGLE SPRINGS, CA 95682	916-676-8010 916-676-8030					
PO BOX 239	SMITH RIVER, CA 95567	707-487-9255 707-487-0930					
PO BOX 487	SAN JACINTO, CA 92581	909-654-2765 909-654-4198	B				
930 PINER RD	SANTA ROSA, CA 95401						
PO BOX 38	STEWARTS POINT, CA 95480	707-528-4267 707-526-1016					
PO DRAWER 410	SUSANVILLE, CA 96130	916-257-6264 916-257-6983					

2. Gaming / Casino
3. Lodging - Resort, Motel, RV Park
4. Economic Base - Farming, Fishing, Ranching Operations
5. Tribal Newspaper
6. Museum / Cultural Center

A - Agriculture
B - Bingo
F - Fish, Aquaculture
M - Mineral
R - Ranching
RV - Recreational Vehicle

T - Timber
TC - Tribal Contract

HISTORICAL PROFILE

Area Office	Treaty Petition [1]	Tribal Class	Pop 1990	Trust Acreage	Tribal Nation

CALIFORNIA

Area Office	Treaty Petition [1]	Tribal Class	Pop 1990	Trust Acreage	Tribal Nation
SAC	1875	DIEGUENO	120	640	SYCUAN NATION
SAC			138	218	TABLE BLUFF RANCHERIA NATION
SAC		YOKUT	95	121.86	TABLE MOUNTAIN RANCHERIA NATION
					TEHATCHAPI INDIAN NATION
SAC	1983	SHOSHONI			TIMBI-SHA SHOSHONE NATION
	31-JAN-83	TOLOWA			TOLOWA NATION
SAC	1876	CAHUILLA	377	14,379.24	TORRES-MARTINEZ BAND OF MISSION INDIANS NATION
SAC	1917	YUROK MWOK TOLOWA	138	47.20	TRINIDAD RANCHERIA NATION
IND					TSNUNGWE INDIAN NATION
SAC	1873	YUKUT	612	110,712	TULE RIVER RESERVATION NATION
SAC	1910	ME-WUK	150	671.54	TUOLUMNE ME-WUK RANCHERIA NATION
SAC	1875	LUISENO	16	240	TWENTY NINE PALMS BAND OF MISSION INDIANS NATION
SAC					UNITED AUBURN INDIAN NATION
	28-APR-80	LUMBEE			UNITED LUMBEE NATION OF NORTH CAROLINA AND AMERICA
SAC		POMO	153	38.96	UPPER LAKE RANCHERIA NATION
SAC	1875	DIEGUENO	202	1,609	VIEJAS NATION
	09-JUL-76	PAIUTE / WASHO			WASHOE/PAIUTE OF ANTELOPE VALLEY

LEGEND:

AREA OFFICES:
ABE - Aberdeen
ABQ - Albuquerque
ANA - Anadarko
BIL - Billings
EA - Eastern
MIN - Minneapolis
MUS - Muskogee
NAV - Navajo
PHX - Phoenix
POR - Portland
SAC - Sacramento
STATE - State Recognized
IND - Independent

1. Date of first Treaty / Date of first Petition

CALIFORNIA

Address	City, State, Zip	Phone Fax	G[2]	3	EB[4]	N[5]	M[6]
5459 DEHESA RD	EL CAJON, CA 92021	619-445-2613 619-445-1927	TC				
PO BOX 519	LOLETA, CA 95551	707-733-5055 707-733-5601					
PO BOX 445	FRIANT, CA 93626	209-822-2587 209-822-2693	B				
219 EAST H ST	TEHATCHAPI, CA 93561						
PO BOX 206	DEATH VALLEY, CA 92328	619-786-2374 619-786-2375					
PO BOX 213	FORT DICK, CA 95538	707-464-7332					
66-725 MARTINEZ RD	THERMAL, CA 92274	619-397-8144 619-397-8146					
PO BOX 630	TRINIDAD, CA 95570	707-677-0211 707-677-3921	B				
PO BOX 373	SALYER, CA 95563	916-629-3356					
PO BOX 589	PORTERVILLE, CA 93258	209-781-4271 209-781-4610				X	
PO BOX 699	TUOLUMNE, CA 95379	209-928-3475 209-928-1677				X	
555 SUNRISE HWY #200	PALM SPRINGS, CA 92264	619-322-0559 619-327-6947					
PO BOX 418	AUBURN, CA 95604						
PO BOX 512	FALL RIVER MILLS, CA 96028	916-336-6701					
PO BOX 245272	SACRAMENTO, CA 95820	916-371-2576 916-371-2576					
PO BOX 908	ALPINE, CA 91903	619-445-3810 619-445-5337	TC	RV			
PO BOX 52	COLEVILLE, CA 96107	916-495-2824					

2. Gaming / Casino
3. Lodging - Resort, Motel, RV Park
4. Economic Base - Farming, Fishing, Ranching Operations
5. Tribal Newspaper
6. Museum / Cultural Center

A - Agriculture
B - Bingo
F - Fish, Aquaculture
M - Mineral
R - Ranching
RV - Recreational Vehicle

T - Timber
TC - Tribal Contract

HISTORICAL PROFILE

Area Office	Treaty Petition [1]	Tribal Class	Pop 1990	Trust Acreage	Tribal Nation

CALIFORNIA

Area Office	Treaty Petition	Tribal Class	Pop 1990	Trust Acreage	Tribal Nation
PHX	1918	SHOSHONE		340	WINNEMUCCA NATION
	26-Oct-84	WINTOON			WINTOON INDIANS
	26-Oct-84	WINTU			WINTU INDIANS OF CENTRAL VALLEY CALIFORNIA
	25-AUG-93	WINTU			WINTU TRIBE OF N CALIFORNIA
PHX		WASHO			WOODFORDS NATION
	22-FEB-88	WUKCHUMNI			WUKCHUMNI COUNCIL
	09-MAR-87	POMO			YOKAYO NATION OF INDIANS
SAC		YUROK		5,373.90	YUROK INDIAN RESERVATION NATION

COLORADO

Area Office	Treaty Petition	Tribal Class	Pop 1990	Trust Acreage	Tribal Nation
	26-JAN-93	WINNEBAGO			COUNCIL FOR THE BENEFIT OF THE COLORADO WINNEBAGO
	22-JUL-77	DELAWARE			MUNSEE THAMES RIVER DELAWARE
ALB	1868	UTE	1,148	307,030.22	SOUTHERN UTE NATION
ALB	1873	UTE	1,674	557,302.29	UTE MOUNTAIN UTE NATION

LEGEND:

AREA OFFICES:
ABE - Aberdeen
ABQ - Albuquerque
ANA - Anadarko
BIL - Billings
EA - Eastern
MIN - Minneapolis
MUS - Muskogee
NAV - Navajo
PHX - Phoenix
POR - Portland
SAC - Sacramento
STATE - State Recognized
IND - Independent

1. Date of first Treaty / Date of first Petition

Address	City, State, Zip	Phone Fax	G[2]	L[3]	EB[4]	N[5]	M[6]
CALIFORNIA							
420 PARDEE	SUSANVILLE, CA 96130	916-257-7093					
1566 PINON AVE	ANDERSON, CA 96007	916-365-0859					
PO BOX 835	CENTRAL VALLEY, CA 96109	916-223-4262					
C/O GENE A MALONE / PO BOX 71036	PROJECT CITY, CA 96079	916-878-4428					
2111 CARSON RIVER RD	MARKLEEVILLE, CA 96120	916-694-2170					
36787 ROAD 197	WOODLAKE, CA 93286	209-625-2449					
1114 HELEN AVE	UKIAH, CA 95482	707-462-4074					
517 3RD ST # 18	EUREKA, CA 95501	800-848-8765 707-444-0437 707-444-0437					
COLORADO							
C/O MS JANICE E STOTT / PO BOX 31397	AURORA, CO 80041						
PO BOX 587	MANITOU SPRINGS, CO 80911						
PO BOX 737	IGNACIO, CO 81137	970-563-0100 970-563-0396	TC	M	A	X	X
PO BOX 52	TOWAOC, CO 81344	970-565-3751 970-565-7412	TC			X	X

2. Gaming / Casino
3. Lodging - Resort, Motel, RV Park
4. Economic Base - Farming, Fishing, Ranching Operations
5. Tribal Newspaper
6. Museum / Cultural Center

A - Agriculture
B - Bingo
F - Fish, Aquaculture
M - Mineral
R - Ranching
RV - Recreational Vehicle

T - Timber
TC - Tribal Contract

HISTORICAL PROFILE

Area Office	Treaty Petition [1]	Tribal Class	Pop 1990	Trust Acreage	Tribal Nation

CONNECTICUT

Area Office	Treaty Petition	Tribal Class	Pop 1990	Trust Acreage	Tribal Nation
	28-JUN-78	PEQUOT			EASTERN PEQUOT INDIANS OF CONNECTICUT
STATE	13-APR-82	PAUGUSSETT		107.25	GOLDEN HILL PAUGUSSETT TRIBE
EA	1667	PEQUOT	250	1,500	MASHANTUCKET PEQUOT NATION
STATE	20-JUN-78	PEQUOT	140	225	PAUCATUCK EASTERN PEQUOT NATION
STATE	14-DEC-81	SHAGHTICOKE		278	SHAGHTICOKE
	06-OCT-92	MOHEGAN			THE MOHEGAN TRIBE & NATION
EA	12-JUL-78	MOHEGAN	900	.5	THE MOHEGAN TRIBE OF INDIANS OF THE STATE OF CONNECTICUT

DELAWARE

Area Office	Treaty Petition	Tribal Class	Pop 1990	Trust Acreage	Tribal Nation
IND		LENAPE			LENAPE NATION OF DELAWARE
IND	08-AUG-78	NANTICOKE			NANTICOKE INDIAN NATION

DISTRICT OF COLUMBIA

Area Office	Treaty Petition	Tribal Class	Pop 1990	Trust Acreage	Tribal Nation
	05-AUG-83	SEMINOLE			SEMINOLE NATION OF FLORIDA INDIAN LAW RESOURCE CENTER

LEGEND:

AREA OFFICES:
ABE - Aberdeen
ABQ - Albuquerque
ANA - Anadarko
BIL - Billings
EA - Eastern
MIN - Minneapolis
MUS - Muskogee
NAV - Navajo
PHX - Phoenix
POR - Portland
SAC - Sacramento
STATE - State Recognized
IND - Independent

1. Date of first Treaty / Date of first Petition

Address	City, State, Zip	Phone Fax	G[2]	L[3]	EB[4]	N[5]	M[6]

CONNECTICUT

Address	City, State, Zip	Phone Fax	G	L	EB	N	M
LANTERN HILL RESERVATION / RFD 7 BOX 941	LEDYARD, CT 06339						
PO BOX 120	TRUMBULL, CT 06611	203-377-4410					
PO BOX 3060	LEDYARD, CT 06339	203 536-2681 203-572-0421	TC				X
939 LANTERN HILL RD	LEDYARD, CT 06339	203-572-9899					
626 WASHINGTON RD	WOODBURY, CT 06798	203-263-0439					
C/O ELEANOR FORTIN / PO BOX 387	NORWICH, CT 06360						
27 CHURCH LN	UNCASVILLE, CT 06382	203-848-9252 203-848-0545					

DELAWARE

Address	City, State, Zip	Phone Fax	G	L	EB	N	M
PO BOX 79	CHESWOOD, DE 19936						
RD 4 BOX 107A	MILLSBORO, DE 19966	302-945-3400					

DISTRICT OF COLUMBIA

Address	City, State, Zip	Phone Fax	G	L	EB	N	M
601 'E' SE	WASHINGTON, DC 20003	202-547-2800					

2. Gaming / Casino
3. Lodging - Resort, Motel, RV Park
4. Economic Base - Farming, Fishing, Ranching Operations
5. Tribal Newspaper
6. Museum / Cultural Center

A - Agriculture
B - Bingo
F - Fish, Aquaculture
M - Mineral
R - Ranching
RV - Recreational Vehicle

T - Timber
TC - Tribal Contract

HISTORICAL PROFILE

FLORIDA

Area Office	Treaty Petition[1]	Tribal Class	Pop 1990	Trust Acreage	Tribal Nation
IND		CHEROKEE			CHEROKEES OF GEORGIA INTER TRIBAL COUNCIL INC
	21-MAR-73	CREEK			CREEKS EAST OF THE MISSISSIPPI
	02-JUN-78	CREEK			FLORIDA TRIBE OF EAST CREEK INDIANS
EA	1962	MICCOSUKEE	375		MICCOSUKEE NATION
		CREEK / MUSKOGEE			NORTH BAY CLAN MUSKOGEE/CREEK NATION
STATE		CREEK			NORTHWEST FLORIDA CREEK NATION INDIAN COUNCIL
IND	12-FEB-90	SEMINOLE			OKLEWAHA BAND SEMINOLE NATION
		CREEK			PRINCIPAL CREEK EAST OF MISSISSIPPI
EA	1953	SEMINOLE	12,000	64,000	SEMINOLE NATION
STATE	05-AUG-83	SEMINOLE			SEMINOLE TRIBAL NATION
					TOPACHULA INDIAN NATION
	19-JAN-79	CHEROKEE			TUSCOLA UNITED CHEROKEE TRIBE OF FLORIDA & ALABAMA INC

LEGEND:

AREA OFFICES:
ABE - Aberdeen
ABQ - Albuquerque
ANA - Anadarko
BIL - Billings
EA - Eastern
MIN - Minneapolis
MUS - Muskogee
NAV - Navajo
PHX - Phoenix
POR - Portland
SAC - Sacramento
STATE - State Recognized
IND - Independent

1. Date of first Treaty / Date of first Petition

FLORIDA

Address	City, State, Zip	Phone Fax	G [2]	[3]	EB [4]	N [5]	M [6]
RT 1 BOX 906	SANDERSON, FL 32087	904-275-2953					
PO BOX 123	MOLINO, FL 32577	904-587-2116					
PO BOX 28	BRUCE, FL 32455	904-835-2078					
PO BOX 440021, TAMIAMI STA	MIAMI, FL 33144	305-223-8380 305-223-1011	B				X
PO BOX 687	LYNN HAVEN, FL 32444	904-265-3345					
3300 N PACE BLVD	PENSACOLA, FL 32505	904-444-8410					
PO BOX 521	ORANGE SPRINGS, FL 32682	904-546-1386					
PO BOX 1331	PAXTON, FL 32538						
6073 STIRLING RD	HOLLYWOOD, FL 33024	305-584-0400 305-581-8917	B	RV	A,R	X	X
RT 6 BOX 718	OKEECHOBEE, FL 33474	202-547-2800					
602 GUNTHER ST	TALLAHASSEE, FL 32308						
PO BOX S	GENEVA, FL 32732	407-349-5257					

2. Gaming / Casino
3. Lodging - Resort, Motel, RV Park
4. Economic Base - Farming, Fishing, Ranching Operations
5. Tribal Newspaper
6. Museum / Cultural Center

A - Agriculture
B - Bingo
F - Fish, Aquaculture
M - Mineral
R - Ranching
RV - Recreational Vehicle

T - Timber
TC - Tribal Contract

HISTORICAL PROFILE

Area Office	Treaty Petition [1]	Tribal Class	Pop 1990	Trust Acreage	Tribal Nation

GEORGIA

Area Office	Treaty Petition [1]	Tribal Class	Pop 1990	Trust Acreage	Tribal Nation
	09-JAN-79	CHEROKEE			CANE BREAK BAND OF EASTERN CHEROKEES
STATE	08-AUG-77	CHEROKEE			CHEROKEE INDIANS OF GEORGIA INC
STATE	27-MAY-88	CHEROKEE			CHEROKEES OF SOUTHEAST ALABAMA
STATE	09-JAN-79	CHEROKEE			GEORGIA TRIBE OF EASTERN CHEROKEES INC
STATE	02-FEB-72	CREEK			LOWER MUSKOGEE CREEK TRIBE EAST OF THE MISSISSIPPI INC
IND	09-MAR-78	CHEROKEE			S E CHEROKEE CONFEDERACY INC

IDAHO

Area Office	Treaty Petition [1]	Tribal Class	Pop 1990	Trust Acreage	Tribal Nation
POR	1873	COEUR D'ALENE	1,216	67,275	COEUR D'ALENE NATION
	26-JUN-79	DELAWARE			DELAWARES OF IDAHO INC
POR	1855	KOOTENAI	82	4,152	KOOTENAI NATION
POR	1855	NEZ PERCE	3,250	170,610	NEZ PERCE NATION
POR	1863	SHOSHONE	406	4,800	NORTHWESTERN BAND OF SHOSHONI NATION
POR	1867	SHOSHONE BANNOCK	6,000	522,510	SHOSHONI BANNOCK NATION

LEGEND:

AREA OFFICES:
ABE - Aberdeen
ABQ - Albuquerque
ANA - Anadarko
BIL - Billings
EA - Eastern
MIN - Minneapolis
MUS - Muskogee
NAV - Navajo
PHX - Phoenix
POR - Portland
SAC - Sacramento
STATE - State Recognized
IND - Independent

1. Date of first Treaty / Date of first Petition

GEORGIA

Address	City, State, Zip	Phone Fax	G[2]	L[3]	EB[4]	N[5]	M[6]
RT 3 BOX 750	DAHLONEGA, GA 30533	404-864-6010					
1809 FULTON AVE	ALBANY, GA 31705	912-436-1605					
1243 LOWER BIG SPRINGS RD	LA GRANGE, GA 30240	706-884-6793					
RT 3 BOX 3162	DAWSONVILLE, GA 30534	404-427-8299					
RT 1, TAMA RESERVATION	CAIRO, GA 31728	912-736-1935					
RT 1 BOX 11	LEESBURG, GA 31763	912-463-9040					

IDAHO

Address	City, State, Zip	Phone Fax	G[2]	L[3]	EB[4]	N[5]	M[6]
PO BOX 238	DESMET, ID 83824	208-686-1800 208-686-1182	TC		A	X	
3677 N MAPLE GROVE RD	BOISE, ID 83704						
PO BOX 1269	BONNERS FERRY, ID 83805	208-267-3519 208-267-2762	TC	M	R	X	
PO BOX 305	LAPWAI, ID 83540	208-843-2253 208-843-7354			R	X	X
PO BOX 637	BLACKFOOT, ID 83221	208-785-7401 208-785-2206	B				
PO BOX 306	FORT HALL, ID 83203	208-238-3700 208-237-0797	TC		A,M	X	X

2. Gaming / Casino
3. Lodging - Resort, Motel, RV Park
4. Economic Base - Farming, Fishing, Ranching Operations
5. Tribal Newspaper
6. Museum / Cultural Center

A - Agriculture
B - Bingo
F - Fish, Aquaculture
M - Mineral
R - Ranching
RV - Recreational Vehicle

T - Timber
TC - Tribal Contract

HISTORICAL PROFILE

Area Office	Treaty Petition [1]	Tribal Class	Pop 1990	Trust Acreage	Tribal Nation

INDIANA

Area Office	Treaty Petition [1]	Tribal Class	Pop 1990	Trust Acreage	Tribal Nation
	02-APR-80	MIAMI			MIAMI NATION OF INDIANS OF THE STATE OF INDIANA INC
	10-APR-91	SHAWNEE			UPPER KISPOKO BAND OF SHAWNEE NATION

IOWA

Area Office	Treaty Petition [1]	Tribal Class	Pop 1990	Trust Acreage	Tribal Nation
MIN	1804	SAC & FOX	1,026	3,485	SAC & FOX NATION

KANSAS

Area Office	Treaty Petition [1]	Tribal Class	Pop 1990	Trust Acreage	Tribal Nation
	19-JUN-78	DELAWARE MUNCIE			DELAWARE-MUNCIE
ANA	1836	IOWA	2,147	1,378	IOWA OF KANSAS AND NEBRASKA NATION
IND	28-APR-80				KAWEAH INDIAN NATION
ANA	1757	KICKAPOO	1,500	6,684	KICKAPOO OF KANSAS NATION
ANA	1789	POTAWATOMI	3,877	21,182	PRAIRIE BAND POTAWATOMI NATION
ANA	1789	SAC & FOX	306	428	SAC & FOX OF KANSAS & NEBRASKA NATIONS

LEGEND:

AREA OFFICES:
ABE - Aberdeen
ABQ - Albuquerque
ANA - Anadarko
BIL - Billings
EA - Eastern
MIN - Minneapolis
MUS - Muskogee
NAV - Navajo
PHX - Phoenix
POR - Portland
SAC - Sacramento
STATE - State Recognized
IND - Independent

1. Date of first Treaty / Date of first Petition

Address	City, State, Zip	Phone Fax	G[2]	L[3]	EB[4]	N[5]	M[6]

INDIANA

Address	City, State, Zip	Phone Fax	G	L	EB	N	M
PO BOX 41	PERU, IN 46970	317-473-9631					
617 S WASHINGTON	KOKOMO, IN 46901	317-457-5376					

IOWA

Address	City, State, Zip	Phone Fax	G	L	EB	N	M
3137 F AVE	TAMA, IA 52339	515-484-4678 515-484-5424	TC		A	X	

KANSAS

Address	City, State, Zip	Phone Fax	G	L	EB	N	M
PO BOX 274	POMONA, KS 66076						
RT 1 BOX 58A	WHITE CLOUD, KS 66094	913-595-3258 913-595-6610	B		A	X	
PO BOX 3121	HUTCHINSON, KS 67501						
PO BOX 271	HORTON, KS 66439	913-486-2131 913-486-2801	TC		A,R	X	
RT 2 BOX 50A / 14880 K RD	MAYETTA, KS 66509	913-966-2255 OR 2771 913-966-2144	B				
RT 1 BOX 60	RESERVE, KS 66434	913-742-7471 913-742-3785			A		

2. Gaming / Casino
3. Lodging - Resort, Motel, RV Park
4. Economic Base - Farming, Fishing, Ranching Operations
5. Tribal Newspaper
6. Museum / Cultural Center

A - Agriculture
B - Bingo
F - Fish, Aquaculture
M - Mineral
R - Ranching
RV - Recreational Vehicle

T - Timber
TC - Tribal Contract

HISTORICAL PROFILE

Area Office	Treaty Petition [1]	Tribal Class	Pop 1990	Trust Acreage	Tribal Nation
LOUISIANA					
STATE	13-SEP-93	CADDO			CADDO ADAIS INDIANS INC
EA	1935	CHITIMACHA	640	283	CHITIMACHA NATION
STATE	02-JUL-78	CHOCTAW APACHE			CHOCTAW-APACHE COMM OF EBARB
STATE	22-MAR-78	CHOCTAW			CLIFTON-CHOCTAW INDIAN NATION
EA	1771	COUSHATTA	570	233	COUSHATTA NATION
STATE		CHOCTAWS			LOUISIANA BAND OF CHOCTAWS NATION
STATE	02-FEB-79	CHOCTAW			JENA BAND OF CHOCTAW NATION
EA	1981	MOUND	440	134	TUNICA-BILOXI INDIAN NATION
STATE		HOUMA			UNITED HOUMA NATION
STATE	10-JUL-79	HOUMA			UNITED HOUMA NATION INC
MAINE					
EA	29-NOV-85	MICMAC	12,000		AROOSTOOK MICMAC NATION
EA		MALISEET			HOULTON MALISEET BAND NATION
EA		PASSAMAQUODDY	350	23,000	INDIAN TOWNSHIP PASSAMAQUODDY NATION
EA	1820	PENOBSCOT	1,900	4,446	PENOBSCOT INDIAN ISLAND NATION
EA	1820	PASSAMAQUODDY		100	PLEASANT POINT PASSAMAQUODDY NATION

LEGEND:

AREA OFFICES:
ABE - Aberdeen
ABQ - Albuquerque
ANA - Anadarko
BIL - Billings
EA - Eastern
MIN - Minneapolis
MUS - Muskogee
NAV - Navajo
PHX - Phoenix
POR - Portland
SAC - Sacramento
STATE - State Recognized
IND - Independent

1. Date of first Treaty / Date of first Petition

Address	City, State, Zip	Phone Fax	G[2]	L[3]	EB[4]	N[5]	M[6]
LOUISIANA							
C/O MR RUFUS DAVIS, JR / RT 2 BOX 246	ROBELINE, LA 71469	318-472-8680					
PO BOX 661	CHARENTON, LA 70523	318-923-7215 318-923-7791	TC			X	
PO BOX 858	ZWOLLE, LA 71486	318-645-2744 318-645-2588					
PO BOX 32	GARDNER, LA 71431	318-793-8796					
PO BOX 818	ELTON, LA 70532	318-584-2261 318-584-2998	TC				X
15212 HUBBS RD	PRIDE, LA 70770						
PO BOX 14	JENA, LA 71432	318-992-2717					
PO BOX 331	MARKSVILLE, LA 71351	318-253-9767 318-253-9791	TC				X
PO BOX 127	DULAC, LA 70353	504-851-1550					
20986 HIGHWAY 1 / STAR RT BOX 95-A	GOLDEN MEADOW, LA 70357	504-475-6640					
MAINE							
PO BOX 722	PRESQUE ISLE, ME 04769	207-764-1972 207-764-7667					
RT 3 BOX 450	HOULTON,ME 04730	207-532-4273 207-532-2660					
PO BOX 301	PRINCETON, ME 04668	207-796-2301 207-796-5256		RV		X	X
COMMUNITY BLDG INDIAN ISLAND	OLD TOWN, ME 04468	207-827-7776 207-827-6042	B				X
PO BOX 343	PERRY, ME 04667	207-853-2600 207-853-6039				X	X

2. Gaming / Casino
3. Lodging - Resort, Motel, RV Park
4. Economic Base - Farming, Fishing, Ranching Operations
5. Tribal Newspaper
6. Museum / Cultural Center

A - Agriculture
B - Bingo
F - Fish, Aquaculture
M - Mineral
R - Ranching
RV - Recreational Vehicle

T - Timber
TC - Tribal Contract

HISTORICAL PROFILE

Area Office	Treaty Petition [1]	Tribal Class	Pop 1990	Trust Acreage	Tribal Nation

MARYLAND

Area Office	Treaty Petition	Tribal Class	Pop 1990	Trust Acreage	Tribal Nation
IND	1974	PISCATAWAY			PISCATAWAY INDIAN NATION
	22-FEB-78	PISCATAWAY CONOY			PISCATAWAY-CONOY CONFEDERACY AND SUB-TRIBES INC.
IND		INTERTRIBAL			THE FREE CHEROKEE NATION
IND	1813	SHAWNEE			YOUGIOGAHENY RIVER BAND OF SHAWNEE INDIAN NATION

MASSACHUSETTS

Area Office	Treaty Petition	Tribal Class	Pop 1990	Trust Acreage	Tribal Nation
STATE	07-JUL-75	WAMPANOAG	1,100	55	MASHPEE-WAMPANOA G INDIAN NATION
STATE		SCHAGTICOKE			NEW ENGLAND COASTAL SCHAGTICOKE INDIAN NATION
STATE	1848	NIPMUC		12	NIPMUC NATION (CHAUBUNAGUNGAMA UG BAND)
	22-APR-80	NIPMUC			NIPMUC TRIBAL COUNCIL OF MASS. (HASSANAMISCO BAND)
EA	06-JULY-81	WAMPANOAG	600	485	WAMPANOAG TRIBE OF GAY HEAD NATION

MICHIGAN

Area Office	Treaty Petition	Tribal Class	Pop 1990	Trust Acreage	Tribal Nation
MIN	1860	CHIPPEWA	915	2,209.47	BAY MILLS CHIPPEWA NATION
STATE	12-SEP-85	OTTAWA CHIPPEWA			BURT LAKE BAND OF OTTAWA & CHIPPEWA NATIONS
	04-DEC-79	OJIBWAY MACKINAC			CONSOLIDATED BAHWETIG OJIBWAY AND MACKINAC NATIONS

LEGEND:

AREA OFFICES:
ABE - Aberdeen
ABQ - Albuquerque
ANA - Anadarko
BIL - Billings
EA - Eastern
MIN - Minneapolis
MUS - Muskogee
NAV - Navajo
PHX - Phoenix
POR - Portland
SAC - Sacramento
STATE - State Recognized
IND - Independent

1. Date of first Treaty / Date of first Petition

Address	City, State, Zip	Phone Fax	G[2]	L[3]	EB[4]	N[5]	M[6]

MARYLAND

Address	City, State, Zip	Phone Fax	G	L	EB	N	M
PO BOX 131	ACCOKEEK, MD 20607	301-932-1704					
PO BOX 48	INDIAN HEAD, MD 20640						
800 OAK DR	MECHANICSVILLE, MD 20659	301-884-5605					
6110 MELVERN DR	BETHESDA, MD 20817	301-770-7912					

MASSACHUSETTS

Address	City, State, Zip	Phone Fax	G	L	EB	N	M
PO BOX 1048 RT 130	MASHPEE, MA 02649	617-477-1825				X	X
PO BOX 551	AVON, MA 02322						
20 SINGLETARY AVE	SUTTON, MA 01527	508-839-7394					X
2 LONGFELLOW RD	NORTHBOROUGH, MA 01532	617-943-4569					
20 BLACK BROOK RD	GAY HEAD, MA 02535	508-645-9265 508-645-3790			F	X	

MICHIGAN

Address	City, State, Zip	Phone Fax	G	L	EB	N	M
RT 1 BOX 313	BRIMLEY, MI 49715	906-248-3241 906-248-3283	TC				
4371 INDIAN RD	BRUTUS, MI 49716	616-529-6564					
PO BOX 697	SAULT ST MARIE, MI 49783	906-635-9521					

2. Gaming / Casino
3. Lodging - Resort, Motel, RV Park
4. Economic Base - Farming, Fishing, Ranching Operations
5. Tribal Newspaper
6. Museum / Cultural Center

A - Agriculture
B - Bingo
F - Fish, Aquaculture
M - Mineral
R - Ranching
RV - Recreational Vehicle

T - Timber
TC - Tribal Contract

HISTORICAL PROFILE

Area Office	Treaty Petition [1]	Tribal Class	Pop 1990	Trust Acreage	Tribal Nation

MICHIGAN

Area Office	Treaty Petition [1]	Tribal Class	Pop 1990	Trust Acreage	Tribal Nation
	24-JUN-92	OTTAWA			GRAND RIVER BAND OF OTTAWA NATION
MIN	1984	OTTAWA / CHIPPEWA	1,702	278	GRAND TRAVERSE BAND OF OTTAWA & CHIPPEWA INDIAN NATIONS
MIN	1913	POTAWATOMI	408	3,410.93	HANNAHVILLE INDIAN NATION
STATE	11-MAR-72	HURON	50	120	HURON POTAWATOMI INC NATION
MIN	1854	CHIPPEWA	2,408	14,643.56	KEWEENAW BAY CHIPPEWA NATION
MIN	1988	CHIPPEWA	201	27.8	LAC VIEUX DESERT BAND OF CHIPPEWA INDIAN NATION
	13-DEC-91	CHIPPEWA			LAKE SUPERIOR CHIPPEWA OF MARQUETTE INC
MIN	04-JUN-91	OTTAWA			LITTLE RIVER BAND OF THE OTTAWA INDIANS
MIN	27-SEP-89	OTTAWA			LITTLE TRAVERSE BAY BANDS OF ODAWA INDIANS
STATE		OTTAWA			NORTHERN MICHIGAN OTTAWA NATION
MIN	23-NOV-81	POTAWATOMI			POKAGON BAND OF POTAWATOMI INDIANS
	03-MAY-81	POTAWATOMI			POTAWATOMI INDIANS OF INDIANA AND MICHIGAN INC
MIN	1864	CHIPPEWA	1,702	1,351.29	SAGINAW CHIPPEWA NATION
MIN	1974	CHIPPEWA	14,870	381.14	SAULT ST MARIE CHIPPEWA NATION
	04-MAY-93	CONFEDERATED			SWAN CREEK BLACK RIVER CONFEDERATED OJIBWA TRIBES INC

LEGEND:

AREA OFFICES:
ABE - Aberdeen
ABQ - Albuquerque
ANA - Anadarko
BIL - Billings
EA - Eastern
MIN - Minneapolis
MUS - Muskogee
NAV - Navajo
PHX - Phoenix
POR - Portland
SAC - Sacramento
STATE - State Recognized
IND - Independent

1. Date of first Treaty / Date of first Petition

MICHIGAN

Address	City, State, Zip	Phone Fax	G[2]	L[3]	EB[4]	N[5]	M[6]
21 GRAND RIVER DR	GRAND LEDGE, MI 48837						
2605 NW BAYSHORE DR	SUTTONS BAY, MI 49682	616-271-3538 616-271-4861	TC	R			
N 14911 HANNAHVILLE BLVD RD	WILSON, MI 49896	906-466-2342 906-466-2933	TC				
2221 1 1/2 MILE RD	FULTON, MI 49052	616-729-5151					
CENTER BLDG / RT 1 BOX 45	BARAGA, MI 49908	906-353-6623 906-353-7540	TC	R			
PO BOX 249	WATERSMEET, MI 49969	906-358-4577 906-358-4785	TC				
%DONALD BRESSETTE /PO BOX 1071	MARQUETTE, MI 49855						
409 WATER ST	MANISTEE, MI 49660	615-723-8288					
PO BOX 246	PETOSKEY, MI 49770	616-348-3410 616-348-2589					
2428 TIMBER LIN	ALPENA, MI 49707	517-354-3442					
53237 TOWN HALL RD	DOWAGIAC, MI 49047	616-782-6323 616-782-9625					
31 WILDWOOD DR CROOKED LAKE	DOWAGIAC, MI 49047	618-424-5553					
7070 E BROADWAY RD	MOUNT PLEASANT, MI 48858	517-772-5700 517-772-3508	TC	RV			
206 GREENOUGH ST	SAULT ST MARIE, MI 49783	906-635-6050 906-722-3508	TC				
C/O MR GERALD GOULD 1312 OAKRIDGE, # 212	EAST LANSING, MI 48823						

2. Gaming / Casino
3. Lodging - Resort, Motel, RV Park
4. Economic Base - Farming, Fishing, Ranching Operations
5. Tribal Newspaper
6. Museum / Cultural Center

A - Agriculture
B - Bingo
F - Fish, Aquaculture
M - Mineral
R - Ranching
RV - Recreational Vehicle

T - Timber
TC - Tribal Contract

HISTORICAL PROFILE

Area Office	Treaty Petition [1]	Tribal Class	Pop 1990	Trust Acreage	Tribal Nation

MINNESOTA

Area Office	Treaty Petition [1]	Tribal Class	Pop 1990	Trust Acreage	Tribal Nation
MIN	1854	CHIPPEWA	2,820	22,196.77	FOND DU LAC CHIPPEWA NATION
MIN	1854	CHIPPEWA	770	46,630.67	GRAND PORTAGE INDIAN NATION
	12-FEB-79	CHIPPEWA			KAH-BAY-KAH-NONG (WARROAD CHIPPEWA)
MIN	1855	CHIPPEWA	6,478	28,725.54	LEECH LAKE INDIAN NATION
MIN	1888	(SIOUX) LAKOTA	620	1,744.93	LOWER SIOUX INDIAN NATION
MIN	1855	CHIPPEWA	2,189	4,029.59	MILLE LACS INDIAN NATION
MIN	1866	CHIPPEWA	2,101	44,050.46	MINNESOTA CHIPPEWA NATION
MIN	1866	CHIPPEWA	2,101	44,405.46	NETT LAKE INDIAN NATION
MIN	1889	(SIOUX) LAKOTA	304	571.20	PRAIRIE ISLAND INDIAN NATION
MIN	1863	CHIPPEWA	7,195	805,722	RED LAKE INDIAN NATION
MIN	1888	(SIOUX) LAKOTA	60	310.25	SHAKOPEE SIOUX NATION
MIN	1938	(SIOUX) LAKOTA		745.65	UPPER SIOUX NATION
MIN	1867	CHIPPEWA	19,895	59,492.05	WHITE EARTH INDIAN NATION

LEGEND:

AREA OFFICES:
ABE - Aberdeen
ABQ - Albuquerque
ANA - Anadarko
BIL - Billings
EA - Eastern
MIN - Minneapolis
MUS - Muskogee
NAV - Navajo
PHX - Phoenix
POR - Portland
SAC - Sacramento
STATE - State Recognized
IND - Independent

1. Date of first Treaty / Date of first Petition

MINNESOTA

Address	City, State, Zip	Phone Fax	G[2]	L[3]	EB[4]	N[5]	M[6]
105 UNIVERSITY RD	CLOQUET, MN 55720	218-879-4593 218-879-4146	TC		F		
PO BOX 428	GRAND PORTAGE, MN 55605	218-475-2279 OR 2277 218-475-2284	TC	R	F,T		
PO BOX 336	WARROAD, MN 56763		TC				
RT 3 BOX 100	CASS LAKE, MN 56633	218-335-8200 218-335-8309	TC		F	X	
RR 1 BOX 308	MORTON, MN 56270	507-697-6185 507-697-6110	TC		A		
HCR 67 BOX 194	ONAMIA, MN 56359	612-532-4181 612-532-4209	TC		F	X	X
PO BOX 217	CASS LAKE, MN 56633	218-335-8581 218-335-6562	TC		F		
PO BOX 16	NETT LAKE, MN 55772	218-757-3261 218-757-3312	TC		A	X	
1158 ISLAND BLVD	WELCH, MN 55089	612-388-2554 612-388-1576	TC				
PO BOX 550	RED LAKE, MN 56671	218-679-3341 218-679-3378	TC	R	T,F	X	
2330 SIOUX TRAIL NW	PRIOR LAKE, MN 55372	612-445-8900 612-445-8906	TC		F		
PO BOX 147	GRANITE FALLS, MN 56241	612-564-2360 612-564-3264	TC				
PO BOX 418	WHITE EARTH, MN 56591	218-983-3285 218-983-3641	TC	R	T,F		

2. Gaming / Casino
3. Lodging - Resort, Motel, RV Park
4. Economic Base - Farming, Fishing, Ranching Operations
5. Tribal Newspaper
6. Museum / Cultural Center

A - Agriculture
B - Bingo
F - Fish, Aquaculture
M - Mineral
R - Ranching
RV - Recreational Vehicle

T - Timber
TC - Tribal Contract

HISTORICAL PROFILE

Area Office	Treaty Petition [1]	Tribal Class	Pop 1990	Trust Acreage	Tribal Nation
MISSISSIPPI					
EA		CHOCTAW	5,000	21,000	MISSISSIPPI BAND CHOCTAW INDIANS NATION
MISSOURI					
MUS		SHAWNEE	1,550		EASTERN SHAWNEE NATION OF OKLAHOMA
	19-FEB-92	CHEROKEE			NORTHERN CHEROKEE NATION OF THE OLD LOUISIANA TERRITORY
	26-JUL-85	CHEROKEE			NORTHERN CHEROKEE TRIBE INDIANS
	05-SEP-91	CHEROKEE			NORTHERN CHICKAMAUGA CHEROKEE NATION OF ARKANSAS & MISSOURI
MONTANA					
		CHIPPEWA			BLACK RIVER CHIPPEWA NATION
BIL	1855	BLACKFEET	13,503	1,256,345	BLACKFEET NATION
BIL	1916	CHIPPEWA CREE	3,968	110,996	CHIPPEWA-CREE NATIONS
POR	1855	SALISH KOOTENAI - PEND D'OREILLES	6,481	619,407.39	CONFEDERATED SALISH & KOOTENAI NATIONS
BIL	1825	CROW	8,020	2,295,092	CROW NATION
BIL	1815	GROS VENTRE ASSINIBOINE	2,799	654,000	FORT BELKNAP NATIONS
BIL	1851	ASSINIBOINE SIOUX	8,794	2,093,318	FORT PECK NATIONS

LEGEND:

AREA OFFICES:
ABE - Aberdeen
ABQ - Albuquerque
ANA - Anadarko
BIL - Billings
EA - Eastern
MIN - Minneapolis
MUS - Muskogee
NAV - Navajo
PHX - Phoenix
POR - Portland
SAC - Sacramento
STATE - State Recognized
IND - Independent

1. Date of first Treaty / Date of first Petition

Address	City, State, Zip	Phone Fax	G[2]	L[3]	EB[4]	N[5]	M[6]

MISSISSIPPI

Address	City, State, Zip	Phone Fax	G	L	EB	N	M
PO BOX 6010 CHOCTAW BRANCH	PHILADELPHIA, MS 39350	601-656-5251 601-656-1992	TC	M		X	X

MISSOURI

Address	City, State, Zip	Phone Fax	G	L	EB	N	M
PO BOX 350	SENECA, MO 64865	918-666-2435 918-666-3325	B				
C/O BEVERLY BAKER NORTHUP / 1502 E BROADWAY # 201	COLUMBIA, MO 65201	314-443-2424					
PO BOX 1121	INDEPENDENCE, MO 64050	816-881-4544 OR 461-6540					
C/O DONALD E COONES / 133 J STREET NW	MIAMI, OK 74354	918-540-1492					

MONTANA

Address	City, State, Zip	Phone Fax	G	L	EB	N	M
PO BOX 197	DIXON, MT 59831						
PO BOX 850	BROWNING, MT 59417	406-338-7276 406-338-7530	TC		R	X	
ROCKY BOY RT PO BOX 544	BOX ELDER, MT 59521	406-395-4282 406-395-4497	TC		R	X	
PO BOX 278	PABLO, MT 59855	406-675-2700 406-675-2806	TC	R	T	X	X
PO BOX 159	CROW AGENCY, MT 59022	406-638-2601 406-638-7283	TC		M	X	X
RT 1 PO BOX 66	HARLEM, MT 59526	406-353-2205 406-353-2797	B	RV			
PO BOX 1027	POPLAR, MT 59255	406-768-5155 406-768-5478	TC				X

2. Gaming / Casino
3. Lodging - Resort, Motel, RV Park
4. Economic Base - Farming, Fishing, Ranching Operations
5. Tribal Newspaper
6. Museum / Cultural Center

A - Agriculture
B - Bingo
F - Fish, Aquaculture
M - Mineral
R - Ranching
RV - Recreational Vehicle

T - Timber
TC - Tribal Contract

HISTORICAL PROFILE

Area Office	Treaty Petition[1]	Tribal Class	Pop 1990	Trust Acreage	Tribal Nation
MONTANA					
	28-APR-78	CHIPPEWA			LITTLE SHELL TRIBE OF CHIPPEWA INDIANS OF MONTANA
BIL	1884	CHEYENNE	5,621	444,775.94	NORTHERN CHEYENNE NATION
NEBRASKA					
IND		PONCA			NORTHERN PONCA NATION
ABE	1854	OMAHA	4,000	26,791.5	OMAHA NATION
ABE		PONCA			PONCA NATION
ABE	1868	(SIOUX) LAKOTA	2,200	9,356.06	SANTEE SIOUX NATION
ABE	1865	WINNEBAGO	3,100	27,537.92	WINNEBAGO NATION
NEVADA					
PHX	1917	SHOSHONE	723	683.30	BATTLE MOUNTAIN BAND NATION
PHX	1917	WASHOE	1,200	156	CARSON COLONY NATION
PHX	1917	WASHOE		40	DRESSLERVILLE NATION
PHX	1940	SHOSHONE	325	3,813.52	DUCKWATER SHOSHONE NATION
PHX	1918	SHOSHONE	761	192.80	ELKO NATION

LEGEND:

AREA OFFICES:
ABE - Aberdeen
ABQ - Albuquerque
ANA - Anadarko
BIL - Billings
EA - Eastern
MIN - Minneapolis
MUS - Muskogee
NAV - Navajo
PHX - Phoenix
POR - Portland
SAC - Sacramento
STATE - State Recognized
IND - Independent

1. Date of first Treaty / Date of first Petition

Address	City, State, Zip	Phone Fax	G[2]	L[3]	EB[4]	N[5]	M[6]

MONTANA

Address	City, State, Zip	Phone / Fax	G	L	EB	N	M
PO BOX 347	HAVRE, MT 59501	406-265-2741					
PO BOX 128	LAME DEER, MT 59043	406-477-8284 406-477-6210	TC		A,R		X

NEBRASKA

Address	City, State, Zip	Phone / Fax	G	L	EB	N	M
2226 LEAVENWORTH	OMAHA, NE 68105	402-341-8471					
PO BOX 368	MACY, NE 68039	402-837-5391 402-837-5308	TC			X	
PO BOX 288	NIOBARA, NE 68760	402-857-3391 402-857-3736					
RT 2	NIOBRARA, NE 68760	402-857-2302 402-857-2307	TC		R	X	
HWY 75 PO BOX 687	WINNEBAGO, NE 68071	402-878-2272 402-878-2963	TC		R	X	

NEVADA

Address	City, State, Zip	Phone / Fax	G	L	EB	N	M
35 MT VIEW DR # 138-13	BATTLE MOUNTAIN, NV 89820	702-635-2004 702-635-8016					
400 SHOSHONE ST	CARSON CITY, NV 89703	702-883-6431			A		
809 P BAUL ST	GARDNERVILLE, NV 89410	702-838-6431 OR 265-5845			A		
PO BOX 140068	DUCKWATER, NV 89314	702-863-0227 702-863-0301		M	R		
PO BOX 748	ELKO, NV 89801	702-738-8889 702-753-5439					

2. Gaming / Casino
3. Lodging - Resort, Motel, RV Park
4. Economic Base - Farming, Fishing, Ranching Operations
5. Tribal Newspaper
6. Museum / Cultural Center

A - Agriculture
B - Bingo
F - Fish, Aquaculture
M - Mineral
R - Ranching
RV - Recreational Vehicle

T - Timber
TC - Tribal Contract

HISTORICAL PROFILE

Area Office	Treaty Petition [1]	Tribal Class	Pop 1990	Trust Acreage	Tribal Nation
			NEVADA		
PHX	1930	SHOSHONE	398	21.0131	ELY COLONY NATION
PHX		PAIUTE	810	5,505	FALLON NATION
PHX	1892	SHOSHONE PAIUTE	689	34,650	FORT MCDERMITT NATION
PHX	1911	SHOSHONE PAIUTE	75	3,884.51	LAS VEGAS COLONY NATION
PHX	1907	PAIUTE	292	20	LOVELOCK NATION
PHX	1873	PAIUTE	257	1,174	MOAPA NATION
	09-NOV-87	PAIUTE			PAHRUMP BAND OF PAIUTES
PHX	1874	PAIUTE	1,720	475,086	PYRAMID LAKE PAIUTE NATION
PHX	1934	WASHOE PAIUTE SHOSHONI	742	2,030	RENO-SPARKS INDIAN NATION
PHX	1863	SHOSHONI PAIUTE	1,850	289,819.3	SHOSHONE PAIUTE NATION
PHX	1941	SHOSHONE	289	9,810.13	SOUTH FORK BAND NATION
PHX	1917	WASHOE		2,877	STEWART NATION
PHX	1913	PAIUTE	111	10,506	SUMMIT LAKE PAIUTE NATION
PHX	1982	SHOSHONE			TE-MOAK TRIBES OF WESTERN SHOSHONE OF NEVADA NATIONS
PHX		PAIUTE	1,325	324,000	WALKER RIVER PAIUTE NATION
PHX		WASHOE	1,423	1,021	WASHOE NATION
PHX	1918	SHOSHONI	194	80	WELLS INDIAN COLONY BAND NATION

LEGEND:

AREA OFFICES:
ABE - Aberdeen
ABQ - Albuquerque
ANA - Anadarko
BIL - Billings
EA - Eastern
MIN - Minneapolis
MUS - Muskogee
NAV - Navajo
PHX - Phoenix
POR - Portland
SAC - Sacramento
STATE - State Recognized
IND - Independent

1. Date of first Treaty / Date of first Petition

NEVADA

Address	City, State, Zip	Phone Fax	G[2]	L[3]	EB[4]	N[5]	M[6]
16 SHOSHONE CIR	ELY, NV 89301	702-289-3013 702-289-3156			R		
8955 MISSION RD	FALLON, NV 89406	702-423-6075 702-423-5202			A	X	
PO BOX 457	FT MCDERMITT, NV 89421	702-532-8259 702-532-8913			A	X	
1 PAIUTE DR	LAS VEGAS, NV 89106	702-386-3926 702-383-4019	TC				
BOX 878	LOVELOCK, NV 89419	702-273-7861 702-273-7861					
PO BOX 340	MOAPA, NV 89025	702-865-2787 702-865 2875	TC		A	X	
PO BOX 73	PAHRUMP, NV 89041	702					
PO BOX 256	NIXON, NV 89424	702-574-1000 702-574-1008		RV	R	X	
98 COLONY RD	RENO, NV 89502	702-329-2936 702-329-8710			A	X	X
PO BOX 219	OWYHEE, NV 89832	702-757-3161 702-757-2219		M		X	
PO BOX B-13	LEE, NV 89829	702-744-4273					
5352 DAT-SO-LA-LEE WAY	CARSON CITY, NV 89701	702-883-7767			A		X
655 ANDERSON	WINNEMUCCA, NV 89445	702-623-5151 702-623-0558			A		
525 SUNSET ST	ELKO, NV 89801	702-738-9251 702-738-2345					
PO BOX 220	SCHURZ, NV 89427	702-773-2306 702-773-2585			A	X	
919 HWY 395 SOUTH	GARDNERVILLE, NV 89410	702-265-4191 OR 883-1446 702-265-6240		M	A	X	
PO BOX 809	WELLS, NV 89835	702-752-3045					

2. Gaming / Casino
3. Lodging - Resort, Motel, RV Park
4. Economic Base - Farming, Fishing, Ranching Operations
5. Tribal Newspaper
6. Museum / Cultural Center

A - Agriculture
B - Bingo
F - Fish, Aquaculture
M - Mineral
R - Ranching
RV - Recreational Vehicle

T - Timber
TC - Tribal Contract

HISTORICAL PROFILE

Area Office	Treaty Petition [1]	Tribal Class	Pop 1990	Trust Acreage	Tribal Nation

NEVADA

Area Office	Treaty Petition [1]	Tribal Class	Pop 1990	Trust Acreage	Tribal Nation
PHX	1918	SHOSHONE		340	WINNEMUCCA COLONY NATION
PHX	1936	PAIUTE	650	1,165.456	YERINGTON PAIUTE NATION
PHX		SHOSHONE	144	4,682	YOMBA NATION

NEW JERSEY

Area Office	Treaty Petition [1]	Tribal Class	Pop 1990	Trust Acreage	Tribal Nation
	03-JAN-92	LENNI-LENAPE			NANTICOKE LENNI-LENAPE INDIANS
	14-AUG-79				RAMAPOUGH MOUNTAIN INDIANS INC

NEW MEXICO

Area Office	Treaty Petition [1]	Tribal Class	Pop 1990	Trust Acreage	Tribal Nation
ALB	1689	PUEBLO	3,995	249,947.95	ACOMA PUEBLO NATION
NAV		NAVAJO	1,100	63,109	ALAMO NAVAJO NATION
NAV	31-JUL-89	NAVAJO	740	76,000	CANONCITO NAVAJO NATION
ALB	1848	PUEBLO	1,057	50,669.36	COCHITI PUEBLO NATION
	18-JAN-71	PIRO MANSO TIWA			INDIAN TRIBE OF THE PUEBLO OF SAN JUAN DE GUADALUPE
ALB	1848	PUEBLO	3,677	211,037.01	ISLETA PUEBLO NATION

LEGEND:

AREA OFFICES:
ABE - Aberdeen
ABQ - Albuquerque
ANA - Anadarko
BIL - Billings
EA - Eastern
MIN - Minneapolis
MUS - Muskogee
NAV - Navajo
PHX - Phoenix
POR - Portland
SAC - Sacramento
STATE - State Recognized
IND - Independent

1. Date of first Treaty / Date of first Petition

Address	City, State, Zip	Phone Fax	G[2]	L[3]	EB[4]	N[5]	M[6]

NEVADA

Address	City, State, Zip	Phone Fax	G	L	EB	N	M
PO BOX 220	WINNEMUCCA, NV 89445						
171 CAMPBELL LN	YERINGTON, NV 89447	702-463-3301 702-463-2416				X	
HC 61 BOX 6275	AUSTIN, NV 89310	702-964-2463 702-964-2443				X	

NEW JERSEY

Address	City, State, Zip	Phone Fax	G	L	EB	N	M
C/O MARK M GOULD / PO BOX 544	BRIDGETON, NJ 08302	609-455-8210 OR 6910					
PO BOX 478	MAHWAH, NJ 07430	201-529-1171 OR 5750					

NEW MEXICO

Address	City, State, Zip	Phone Fax	G	L	EB	N	M
PO BOX 309	ACOMITA, NM 87034	505-552-6604 505-552-6600	B		ARM	X	X
	ALAMO, NM 87825	505-854-2686			A,R		
PO BOX 498	CANONCITO, NM 87026	505-836-7144			R		
PO BOX 70	COCHITI, NM 87072	505-465-2244 505-465-2245			A	X	
4028 SAN YSIDRO DR	SAN YSIDRO, NM 88005	505-526-0790					
PO BOX 1270	ISLETA, NM 87022	505-869-3111 505-869-4236	TC		A,R	X	

2. Gaming / Casino
3. Lodging - Resort, Motel, RV Park
4. Economic Base - Farming, Fishing, Ranching Operations
5. Tribal Newspaper
6. Museum / Cultural Center

A - Agriculture
B - Bingo
F - Fish, Aquaculture
M - Mineral
R - Ranching
RV - Recreational Vehicle

T - Timber
TC - Tribal Contract

HISTORICAL PROFILE

Area Office	Treaty Petition [1]	Tribal Class	Pop 1990	Trust Acreage	Tribal Nation

NEW MEXICO

Area Office	Treaty Petition [1]	Tribal Class	Pop 1990	Trust Acreage	Tribal Nation
ALB	1684	PUEBLO	2,588	89,617.07	JEMEZ PUEBLO NATION
ALB	1887	APACHE	2,764	823,580.24	JICARILLA APACHE NATION
ALB	1848	PUEBLO	6,597	528,684.22	LAGUNA PUEBLO NATION
ALB	1852	APACHE	3,032	460,678.11	MESCALERO APACHE NATION
ALB	1848	PUEBLO	534	19,075.99	NAMBE PUEBLO NATION
ALB	1848	PUEBLO	277	14,947.18	PICURIS PUEBLO NATION
ALB	1848	PUEBLO	132	11,601.69	POJOAQUE PUEBLO NATION
ALB	1848	NAVAJO	1,941	146,953	RAMAH NAVAJO NATION
ALB	1848	PUEBLO	2,516	48,858.86	SAN FELIPE PUEBLO NATION
ALB	1848	PUEBLO	580	26,197	SAN ILDELFONSO PUEBLO NATION
ALB	1848	PUEBLO	2,133	12,237	SAN JUAN PUEBLO NATION
ALB	1848	PUEBLO	368	22,870.91	SANDIA PUEBLO NATION
ALB	1848	PUEBLO	595	61,375.68	SANTA ANA PUEBLO NATION
ALB	1848	PUEBLO	1,493	45,247.18	SANTA CLARA PUEBLO NATION
ALB	1848	PUEBLO	3,503	69,259.82	SANTO DOMINGO PUEBLO NATION
ALB	1848	PUEBLO	2,186	95,341.36	TAOS PUEBLO NATION
ALB	1848	PUEBLO	339	16,813.16	TESUQUE PUEBLO NATION

LEGEND:

AREA OFFICES:
ABE - Aberdeen
ABQ - Albuquerque
ANA - Anadarko
BIL - Billings
EA - Eastern
MIN - Minneapolis
MUS - Muskogee
NAV - Navajo
PHX - Phoenix
POR - Portland
SAC - Sacramento
STATE - State Recognized
IND - Independent

1. Date of first Treaty / Date of first Petition

NEW MEXICO

Address	City, State, Zip	Phone Fax	G [2]	L [3]	EB [4]	N [5]	M [6]
PO BOX 100	JEMEZ PUEBLO, NM 87024	505-834-7359 505-834-7331			A,T	X	
PO BOX 507	DULCE, NM 87528	505-759-3242 505-759-3005	TC	R	A,R	X	X
PO BOX 194	LAGUNA, NM 87026	505-552-6654 505-552-6941			A	X	
PO BOX 176	MESCALERO, NM 88340	505-671-4495 505-671-9191	TC	R	R,A	X	X
RT 1 BOX 117 BB	SANTA FE, NM 87501	505 455-2036 37/38/39 505-455-2038			A		
PO BOX 127	PENASCO, NM 87553	505-587-2519 505-587-1071		R	A,R	X	X
RT 11 BOX 71	SANTA FE, NM 87501	505-455-2278 OR 2279 505-455-2950	TC	R	A		
RT 2 BOX 13	RAMAH, NM 87321	505-775-3533 505-775-3538			R	X	
PO BOX 4339	SAN FELIPE PUEBLO, NM 87001	505-867-3381 505-867-3383	TC		A,R	X	
RT 5 BOX 315A	SANTA FE, NM 87501	505-455-2273 505-455-7351		R	A,R	X	X
PO BOX 1099	SAN JUAN PUEBLO, NM 87566	505-852-4400 OR 4210 505-852-4820	TC			X	
PO BOX 6008	BERNALILLO, NM 87004	505-867-3317 505-867-9235	TC		A,R	X	
2 DOVE RD	BERNALILLO, NM 87004	505-867-3301 505-867-3395	TC		A,M	X	
PO BOX 580	ESPANOLA, NM 87532	505-753-7316 OR 7326/7330 505-753-8988	TC		T,R	X	X
PO BOX 99	SANTO DOMINGO PUEBLO, NM 87052	505-465-2214 505-465-2688			A	X	X
PO BOX 1846	TAOS, NM 87571	505-758-9593 505-758-4604	P		A,R	X	
RT 5 BOX 360T	SANTA FE, NM 87501	505-983-2667 505-982-2331	TC	RV	A		

2. Gaming / Casino
3. Lodging - Resort, Motel, RV Park
4. Economic Base - Farming, Fishing, Ranching Operations
5. Tribal Newspaper
6. Museum / Cultural Center

A - Agriculture
B - Bingo
F - Fish, Aquaculture
M - Mineral
R - Ranching
RV - Recreational Vehicle

T - Timber
TC - Tribal Contract

HISTORICAL PROFILE

Area Office	Treaty Petition [1]	Tribal Class	Pop 1990	Trust Acreage	Tribal Nation

NEW MEXICO

Area Office	Treaty Petition	Tribal Class	Pop 1990	Trust Acreage	Tribal Nation
		PUEBLO			TIWA SAN JUAN NATION
ALB		PUEBLO	708	119,537.89	ZIA PUEBLO NATION
ALB	1848	PUEBLO	7,663	421,481	ZUNI PUEBLO NATION

NEW YORK

Area Office	Treaty Petition	Tribal Class	Pop 1990	Trust Acreage	Tribal Nation
EA		CAYUGA			CAYUGA NATION
		MONTAUK			MONTAUK INDIAN NATION
EA	1500'S	ONEIDA	800	35	ONEIDA NATION OF NY
EA		ONONDAGA	1,300	6,100	ONONDAGA NATION
EA	1794	SENECA	5,000	30,469	SENECA NATION
STATE	08-FEB-78	SHINNECOCK	300	400	SHINNECOCK NATION
EA	1755	MOHAWK	7,000	14,640	ST REGIS MOHAWK NATION
EA	1857	SENECA	850	12,000	TONAWANDA BAND OF SENECAS NATION
EA	1784	TUSCARORA	975	5,700	TUSCARORA NATION
STATE		MONTAUK	100	60	UNKECHAUGE NATION (POOSPATUCK)

LEGEND:

AREA OFFICES:
ABE - Aberdeen
ABQ - Albuquerque
ANA - Anadarko
BIL - Billings
EA - Eastern
MIN - Minneapolis
MUS - Muskogee
NAV - Navajo
PHX - Phoenix
POR - Portland
SAC - Sacramento
STATE - State Recognized
IND - Independent

1. Date of first Treaty / Date of first Petition

Address	City, State, Zip	Phone Fax	G[2]	L[3]	EB[4]	N[5]	M[6]

NEW MEXICO

Address	City, State, Zip	Phone / Fax	G	L	EB	N	M
559 W BROWN RD	LAS CRUCES, NM 88001						
135 CAPITOL SQUARE DR	ZIA PUEBLO, NM 87053	505-867-3304 505-867-3308			A,R	X	
PO BOX 339	ZUNI, NM 87327	505-782-4481 505-782-2700			A	X	X

NEW YORK

Address	City, State, Zip	Phone / Fax	G	L	EB	N	M
PO BOX 11	VERSAILLES, NY 14168	716-532-4847 716-532-5417					
HEMPSTEAD DR	SAG HARBOR, NY 11963						
223 GENNESEE	ONEIDA, NY 13421	315-361-6300 315-361-6333	TC				
RR 1 BOX 270A	NEDROW, NY 13120	315-469-8507					
PO BOX 231	SALAMANCA, NY 14779	716-945-1790 716-532-9132	B	RV	A		X
RT 27A MONTAUK HWY BOX 59	SOUTHAMPTON, NY 11968	516-283-3776 OR 1643			F		
AKWESASNE COMM BLDG RT 37	HOGANSBURG, NY 13655	518-358-2272 518-358-3203	TC		A	X	X
7027 MEADVILLE RD	BASOM, NY 14013	716-542-4244 716-542-9692				X	
5616 WALMORE RD	LEWISTON, NY 14092	716-297-4990	B		T		
PO BOX 86	MASTIC, NY 11950	516-281-6464 OR 399-3843					

2. Gaming / Casino
3. Lodging - Resort, Motel, RV Park
4. Economic Base - Farming, Fishing, Ranching Operations
5. Tribal Newspaper
6. Museum / Cultural Center

A - Agriculture
B - Bingo
F - Fish, Aquaculture
M - Mineral
R - Ranching
RV - Recreational Vehicle

T - Timber
TC - Tribal Contract

HISTORICAL PROFILE

Area Office	Treaty Petition [1]	Tribal Class	Pop 1990	Trust Acreage	Tribal Nation

NORTH CAROLINA

Area Office	Treaty Petition [1]	Tribal Class	Pop 1990	Trust Acreage	Tribal Nation
	20-SEP-83	CHEROKEE			CHEROKEE INDIANS OF HOKE COUNTY INC
	01-FEB-79	CHEROKEE			CHEROKEE INDIANS OF ROBESON & ADJOINING COUNTIES
	07-SEP-84	CHEROKEE POWHATTAN			CHEROKEE - POWHATTAN IND ASSOC
STATE	13-MAR-81	COHARIE			COHARIE INTRATRIBAL NATION
IND	05-AUG-78	COREE	3,000		COREE (FAIRCLOTH) INDIANS
IND	25-FEB-81	TUSCARORA			DROWNING CREEK TUSCARORA NATION
EA	1684	CHEROKEE	6,000	56,573	EASTERN BAND OF CHEROKEE INDIAN NATION
IND		OCCANEECHI			ENO-OCCANEECHI INDIAN NATION
STATE	27-NOV-79	HALIWA - SAPONI	3,000	45	HALIWA-SAPONI NATION
	16-MAR-79	HATTADARE			HATTADARE INDIAN NATION
IND	24-JUN-78	TUSCARORA	900		HATTARAS TUSCARORA INDIAN TRIBE OF EASTERN NORTH CAROLINA
	28-APR-80	KAWEAH			KAWEAH INDIAN NATION INC
IND	07-JAN-80	LUMBEE	40,000		LUMBEE INDIAN NATION OF NORTH CAROLINA
STATE	02-AUG-90	IROQUOIS			MEHERRIN INDIAN NATION
	19-NOV-85	TUSCARORA			TUSCARORA NATION OF NORTH CAROLINA
STATE	27-JUN-83	SIOUX			WACCAMAW SIOUAN DEVELOPMENT ASSOCIATION INC

LEGEND:

AREA OFFICES:
ABE - Aberdeen
ABQ - Albuquerque
ANA - Anadarko
BIL - Billings
EA - Eastern
MIN - Minneapolis
MUS - Muskogee
NAV - Navajo
PHX - Phoenix
POR - Portland
SAC - Sacramento
STATE - State Recognized
IND - Independent

1. Date of first Treaty / Date of first Petition

NORTH CAROLINA

Address	City, State, Zip	Phone Fax	G [2]	L [3]	EB [4]	N [5]	M [6]
RT 1 BOX 129-C	LUMBER BRIDGE, NC 28357	919-323-4848 OR 975-0222					
RT 2 BOX 272-A	RED SPRINGS, NC 28377						
PO BOX 3265	ROXBORO, NC 27573	919-599-6448					
RT 3 BOX 356-B	CLINTON, NC 28328	919-564-6901					
137 NEAL DR	ATLANTIC, NC 28511	919-225-0164					
C/O MR HULL CUMMINGS / RTE 2 BOX 108	MAXTON, NC 28364	919-844-3827					
PO BOX 455	CHEROKEE, NC 28719	704-497-2771 704-497-2952	TC	R		X	X
RT 2 BOX 383	MEBANE, NC 27302	919-563-4640					
PO BOX 99	HOLLISTER, NC 27844	919-586-4017					
RT 1 BOX 85-B	BUNNLEVEL, NC 28232	919-893-2512					
RT 4 BOX 61	MAXTON, NC 28364	919-521-2426					
C/O MR MALCOLM WEBBER / RT 1 BOX 99	ORIENTAL, NC 28571						
PO BOX 68	PEMBROKE, NC 28372	919-521-2401 919-521-8625			R,N,M		
PO BOX 508	WINTON, NC 27986	919-358-4375					
C/O MR ROBERT BREWINGTON / PO BOX 565	PEMBROKE, NC 28372	919-521-2655					
PO BOX 221	BOLTON, NC 28423	919-655-8778					

2. Gaming / Casino
3. Lodging - Resort, Motel, RV Park
4. Economic Base - Farming, Fishing, Ranching Operations
5. Tribal Newspaper
6. Museum / Cultural Center

A - Agriculture
B - Bingo
F - Fish, Aquaculture
M - Mineral
R - Ranching
RV - Recreational Vehicle

T - Timber
TC - Tribal Contract

HISTORICAL PROFILE

Area Office	Treaty Petition [1]	Tribal Class	Pop 1990	Trust Acreage	Tribal Nation
NORTH DAKOTA					
	26-JUN-84	CHIPPEWA			CHRISTIAN PEMBINA CHIPPEWA INDIANS
ABE	1867	(SIOUX) LAKOTA	3,700	53,239.48	DEVILS LAKE SIOUX NATION
	11-NOV-75	CHIPPEWA			LITTLE SHELL BAND OF N DAKOTA
ABE	1868	(SIOUX) LAKOTA	10,109	846,291	STANDING ROCK SIOUX NATION
ABE	1851	GROS VENTRE, MANDAN, ARIKARA	9,200	424,213.42	THREE AFFILIATED NATIONS
ABE	1863	CHIPPEWA	25,000	67,974.22	TURTLE MOUNTAIN NATION
OHIO					
	03-NOV-79	ALLEGHENNY			ALLEGHENNY NATION (OHIO BAND)
	09-APR-79	MIAMI			NORTH EASTERN US MIAMI INTER-TRIBAL COUNCIL
	16-APR-91	SHAWNEE			PIQUA SEPT OF OHIO SHAWNEE INDIANS
IND		SHAWNEE			SHAWNEE NATION OF OHIO
	13-MAR-79	SHAWNEE		135	SHAWNEE NATION UNITED REMNANT BAND
IND		LENAPE			UNITED EASTERN LENAPE NATION

LEGEND:

AREA OFFICES:
ABE - Aberdeen
ABQ - Albuquerque
ANA - Anadarko
BIL - Billings
EA - Eastern
MIN - Minneapolis
MUS - Muskogee
NAV - Navajo
PHX - Phoenix
POR - Portland
SAC - Sacramento
STATE - State Recognized
IND - Independent

1. Date of first Treaty / Date of first Petition

Address	City, State, Zip	Phone Fax	G [2]	L [3]	EB [4]	N [5]	M [6]

NORTH DAKOTA

Address	City, State, Zip	Phone Fax	G	L	EB	N	M
PO BOX 1307	DUNSEITH, ND 58329						
SIOUX COMMUNITY CENTER	FORT TOTTEN, ND 58335	701-766-4221 701-766-4126	TC		R		X
PO BOX 173	ROLETTE, ND 58366						
PO BOX D	FORT YATES, ND 58538	701-854-7201 701-854-7299	TC			X	X
HC 3 BOX 2	NEW TOWN, ND 58763	701-627-4781 701-627-3805	B	M	A,R		X
PO BOX 900	BELCOURT, ND 58316	701-477-5198 701-477-6292	B		R		X

OHIO

Address	City, State, Zip	Phone Fax	G	L	EB	N	M
2239 MAHONING NE	CANTON, OH 44705	216-453-6224					
1535 FLORENCEDALE	YOUNGSTOWN, OH 44505	216-746-4956					
4 W MAIN ST # 828	SPRINGFIELD, OH 45502						
RT 3 BOX 208	RAYLAND, OH 43943						
PO BOX 162	DAYTON, OH 45401	513-275-6685					X
PO BOX 191	FREEPORT, OH 43973						

2. Gaming / Casino
3. Lodging - Resort, Motel, RV Park
4. Economic Base - Farming, Fishing, Ranching Operations
5. Tribal Newspaper
6. Museum / Cultural Center

A - Agriculture
B - Bingo
F - Fish, Aquaculture
M - Mineral
R - Ranching
RV - Recreational Vehicle

T - Timber
TC - Tribal Contract

HISTORICAL PROFILE

Area Office	Treaty Petition [1]	Tribal Class	Pop 1990	Trust Acreage	Tribal Nation
					OKLAHOMA
ANA	1936	SHAWNEE	2,600	11,600	ABSENTEE-SHAWNEE INDIAN NATION
MUS		QUASSARTE			ALABAMA-QUASSARTE NATION
ANA	1882	APACHE	1,186	82	APACHE NATION
ANA		CADDO			CADDO NATION
MUS	1830'S	CHEROKEE	97,000		CHEROKEE NATION OF OKLAHOMA
ANA	1862	CHEYENNE ARAPAHO	9,340	84,152	CHEYENNE-ARAPAHO NATIONS
	05-SEP-91	CHEROKEE			CHICKAMAUGA CHEROKEE INDIAN NATION OF ARKANSAS & MISSOURI
MUS	1830'S	CHICKASAW	12,000		CHICKASAW NATION OF OKLAHOMA
MUS	1830'S	CHOCTAW	49,000	145,920.3	CHOCTAW NATION OF OKLAHOMA
ANA	1789	POTAWATOMI	14,544	4,038	CITIZEN BAND POTAWATOMI NATION
ANA		COMMANCHE			COMMANCHE INDIAN NATION
ANA		DELAWARE			DELAWARE INDIAN NATION OF WESTERN OKLAHOMA
	06-JAN-93	DELAWARE			DELAWARE TRIBE OF EASTERN OKLAHOMA NATION
ANA	1912	APACHE	333	38.75	FORT SILL APACHE NATION
ANA	1890	IOWA	385	1,710.85	IOWA OF OKLAHOMA NATION
ANA	1859	KAW	1,710	1,116	KAW INDIAN NATION
MUS					KIALEGEE NATION

LEGEND:

AREA OFFICES:
ABE - Aberdeen
ABQ - Albuquerque
ANA - Anadarko
BIL - Billings
EA - Eastern
MIN - Minneapolis
MUS - Muskogee
NAV - Navajo
PHX - Phoenix
POR - Portland
SAC - Sacramento
STATE - State Recognized
IND - Independent

1. Date of first Treaty / Date of first Petition

OKLAHOMA

Address	City, State, Zip	Phone Fax	G[2]	L[3]	EB[4]	N[5]	M[6]
2025 S GORDON COOPER DR	SHAWNEE, OK 74801	405-275-4030 405-275-5637	TC			X	
PO BOX 537	HENRYETTA, OK 74437	918-652-8708 918-652-8708	B				
PO BOX 1220	ANADARKO, OK 73005	405-247-9493 405-247-3153	B	M			X
PO BOX 487	BINGER, OK 73009	405-656-2344 405-656-2892					
PO BOX 948	TAHLEQUAH, OK 74465	918-456-0671 918-256-0671	B		A,R	X	X
PO BOX 38	CONCHO, OK 73022	405-262-0345 405-262-0745	B	M		X	
C/O DONALD E COONES / 133 J STREET NW	MIAMI, OK 74354	918-540-1492 OR 1630					
PO BOX 1548	ADA, OK 74820	405-436-2603 405-436-4287	B	R		X	X
PO DRAWER 1210	DURANT, OK 74701	405-924-8280 405-924-1150	B	R		X	
1901 S GORDON COPPER DR	SHAWNEE, OK 74801	405-275-3121 405-275-0198	B	M		X	X
HC 32 BOX 1720	LAWTON, OK 73502	405-492-4988 405-492-4981	B			X	X
PO BOX 825	ANADARKO, OK 73005	405-247-2448 405-247-9393	B				
108 S SENECA	BARTLESVILLE, OK 74003	918-336-5272					
RT 2 BOX 121	APACHE, OK 73006	405-588-2298 405-588-3133					X
RT 1 BOX 721	PERKINS, OK 74059	405-547-2403 405-547-5294	B				
DRAWER 50	KAW CITY, OK 74641	405-269-2552 405-269-2301	B				
PO BOX 332	WETUMKA, OK 74883	405-452-3413					

2. Gaming / Casino
3. Lodging - Resort, Motel, RV Park
4. Economic Base - Farming, Fishing, Ranching Operations
5. Tribal Newspaper
6. Museum / Cultural Center

A - Agriculture
B - Bingo
F - Fish, Aquaculture
M - Mineral
R - Ranching
RV - Recreational Vehicle

T - Timber
TC - Tribal Contract

HISTORICAL PROFILE

Area Office	Treaty Petition [1]	Tribal Class	Pop 1990	Trust Acreage	Tribal Nation

OKLAHOMA

Area Office	Treaty Petition [1]	Tribal Class	Pop 1990	Trust Acreage	Tribal Nation
ANA		KICKAPOO			KICKAPOO NATION OF OKLAHOMA
ANA	1866	KIOWA	9,104	712	KIOWA INDIAN NATION
		SHAWNEE			LOYAL SHAWNEE NATION
MUS		MIAMI			MIAMI NATION OF OKLAHOMA
MUS		MODOC			MODOC NATION OF OKLAHOMA
MUS	1979	YUCHI & CREEK	33,000		MUSCOGEE CREEK NATION
MUS	1906	OSAGE			OSAGE NATION
ANA	1825	OTOE MISSOURI	1,600	1,680	OTOE-MISSOURIA NATION
MUS	1870'S	OTTAWA			OTTAWA INDIAN NATION
ANA	1833	PAWNEE	2,408	726.03	PAWNEE INDIAN NATION
MUS		PEORIA	2,308	500	PEORIA INDIAN NATION
ANA	1817	PONCA	2,164	932.46	PONCA NATION
MUS		QUAPAW	2,300		QUAPAW NATION
ANA	1870	SAC & FOX	2,254	1,000	SAC & FOX NATION OF OKLAHOMA
MUS	1830'S	SEMINOLE	12,000		SEMINOLE NATION OF OKLAHOMA
MUS	1830'S	SENECA CAYUGA	2,500		SENECA-CAYUGA NATION
MUS	1938	CREEK	1,500		THLOPTHLOCCO NATION

LEGEND:

AREA OFFICES:
ABE - Aberdeen
ABQ - Albuquerque
ANA - Anadarko
BIL - Billings
EA - Eastern
MIN - Minneapolis
MUS - Muskogee
NAV - Navajo
PHX - Phoenix
POR - Portland
SAC - Sacramento
STATE - State Recognized
IND - Independent

1. Date of first Treaty / Date of first Petition

Address	City, State, Zip	Phone Fax	G[2]	L[3]	EB[4]	N[5]	M[6]

OKLAHOMA

Address	City, State, Zip	Phone Fax	G	L	EB	N	M
PO BOX 70	MCLOUD, OK 74851	405-964-2075 405-964-2745					
PO BOX 369	CARNEGIE, OK 73015	405-654-2300 405-654-2188	B				X
PO BOX 369	JAY, OK 74346	918-253-4219					X
PO BOX 1326	MIAMI, OK 74355	918-542-1445 918-542-7260					
515 G ST SE	MIAMI, OK 74354	918-542-1190 918-542-5415					
PO BOX 580	OMULGEE, OK 74447	918-756-8700 918-756-2911	B	R	M,R		X
TRIBAL ADM BLDG BOX 779	PAWHUSKA, OK 74056	918-287-1128 918-287-1259	B		M		X
RT 1 BOX 62	RED ROCK, OK 74651	405-723-4466 405-723-4273	B				
PO BOX 110	MIAMI, OK 74355	918-540-1536 918-542-3214					
PO BOX 470	PAWNEE, OK 74058	918-762-3621 918-762-2389	B				X
PO BOX 1527	MIAMI, OK 74355	918-540-2535 918-540-2538				X	X
PO BOX 2 WHITE EAGLE	PONCA CITY, OK 74601	405-762-8104 405-762-7436	B				
PO BOX 765	QUAPAW, OK 74363	918-542-1853 918-542-4694	B				
RT 2 BOX 246	STROUD, OK 74079	918-968-3526 918-968-3887	B	RV	A	X	X
PO BOX 1498	WEWOKA, OK 74884	405-257-6287 405-257-6205	B				X
PO BOX 1283	MIAMI, OK 74355	918-542-6609 918-542-3684	B				X
PO BOX 706	OKEMAH, OK 74859	918-623-2620 918-623-0419	B				

2. Gaming / Casino
3. Lodging - Resort, Motel, RV Park
4. Economic Base - Farming, Fishing, Ranching Operations
5. Tribal Newspaper
6. Museum / Cultural Center

A - Agriculture
B - Bingo
F - Fish, Aquaculture
M - Mineral
R - Ranching
RV - Recreational Vehicle

T - Timber
TC - Tribal Contract

HISTORICAL PROFILE

Area Office	Treaty Petition [1]	Tribal Class	Pop 1990	Trust Acreage	Tribal Nation

OKLAHOMA

Area Office	Treaty Petition [1]	Tribal Class	Pop 1990	Trust Acreage	Tribal Nation
ANA	1855	TONKAWAS	275	160.50	TONKAWA NATION
MUS	1950	CHEROKEE	7,100		UNITED KEETOOWAH NATION
ANA		WICHITA	1,480	2,357.01	WICHITA NATION
MUS		WYANDOTTE			WYANDOTTE NATION OF OK
	05-OCT-90	YUCHI			YUCHI TRIBAL ORGANIZATION

OREGON

Area Office	Treaty Petition [1]	Tribal Class	Pop 1990	Trust Acreage	Tribal Nation
POR	1865	PAIUTE	320	12,130	BURNS-PAIUTE NATION
IND					CHETCO NATION
IND		CHINOOK			CHINOOK INDIAN NATION
POR	1857	CONFEDERATED TRIBES	2,457	9,811	CONFEDERATED GRANDE RONDE NATIONS
POR	1855	COOS LOWER UMPQUA & SIUSLAW	417	6	CONFEDERATED TRIBES OF COOS, LOWER UMPQUA & SIUSLAW INDIANS
POR	1989	COQUILLE			COQUILLE INDIAN NATION
POR	1853	UMPQUA	763	28.71	COW CREEK BAND OF UMPQUA INDIAN NATIONS
POR	1986	KLAMATH	2,477	5	KLAMATH NATION

LEGEND:

AREA OFFICES:
ABE - Aberdeen
ABQ - Albuquerque
ANA - Anadarko
BIL - Billings
EA - Eastern
MIN - Minneapolis
MUS - Muskogee
NAV - Navajo
PHX - Phoenix
POR - Portland
SAC - Sacramento
STATE - State Recognized
IND - Independent

1. Date of first Treaty / Date of first Petition

Address	City, State, Zip	Phone Fax	G[2]	L[3]	EB[4]	N[5]	M[6]

OKLAHOMA

Address	City, State, Zip	Phone Fax	G[2]	L[3]	EB[4]	N[5]	M[6]
PO BOX 70	TONKAWA, OK 74653	405-628-2561 405-628-3375	TC				X
PO BOX 746	TAHLEQUAH, OK 74465	918-456-9462 918-456-3648	B				X
PO BOX 729	ANADARKO, OK 73005	405-247-2425 405-247-2430	B				X
PO BOX 250	WYANDOTTE, OK 74370	918-678-2297 OR 2298 918-678-2944					
30 N WATER	SAPULPA, OK 74067						

OREGON

Address	City, State, Zip	Phone Fax	G[2]	L[3]	EB[4]	N[5]	M[6]
HC 71 PASIGO ST	BURNS, OR 97720	503-573-2088 503-573-2323			R	X	
565 FERN	BROOKINGS, OR 97415	503-469-7131					
5621 ALTAMONT DR	KLAMATH FALLS, OR 97601						
9615 GRANDE RONDE RD	GRAND RONDE, OR 97347	503-879-5211 503-879-5964	TC		T		
455 S 4TH ST	COOS BAY, OR 97420	503-267-5454 503-269-1647	TC				
PO BOX 1435	COOS BAY, OR 97420	503-267-4587 503-269-2573	TC				
2400 STEWART PARKWAY # 300	ROSEBURG, OR 97470	503-672-9405 503-673-0432	TC	M			
PO BOX 436	CHILOQUIN, OR 97624	503-783-2219 503-783-2029 800-524-9787	TC		T		X

2. Gaming / Casino
3. Lodging - Resort, Motel, RV Park
4. Economic Base - Farming, Fishing, Ranching Operations
5. Tribal Newspaper
6. Museum / Cultural Center

A - Agriculture
B - Bingo
F - Fish, Aquaculture
M - Mineral
R - Ranching
RV - Recreational Vehicle

T - Timber
TC - Tribal Contract

HISTORICAL PROFILE

Area Office	Treaty Petition [1]	Tribal Class	Pop 1990	Trust Acreage	Tribal Nation

OREGON

Area Office	Treaty Petition [1]	Tribal Class	Pop 1990	Trust Acreage	Tribal Nation
	09-MAR-78	CHEROKEE			NORTHWEST CHEROKEE WOLF BAND SE CHEROKEE CONFEDERACY INC
POR	1977	CONFEDERATED	1,976	3,689	SILETZ NATION
IND	16-MAY-79	TCHINOUK			TCHINOUK INDIANS
POR	1855	CONFEDERATED	1,249	175,122	UMATILLA NATION
IND	1956	LUMBEE			UNITED LUMBEE NATION WIND RIVER RES
POR	1855	WARM SPRINGS WASO	2,517	643,570.95	WARM SPRINGS INDIAN NATIONS

PENNSYLVANIA

Area Office	Treaty Petition [1]	Tribal Class	Pop 1990	Trust Acreage	Tribal Nation
IND		CHEROKEE			UNITED CHEROKEE NATION OF WV

RHODE ISLAND

Area Office	Treaty Petition [1]	Tribal Class	Pop 1990	Trust Acreage	Tribal Nation
EA	1983	NARRAGANSETT		1,800	NARRAGANSETT INDIAN NATION

LEGEND:

AREA OFFICES:
ABE - Aberdeen
ABQ - Albuquerque
ANA - Anadarko
BIL - Billings
EA - Eastern
MIN - Minneapolis
MUS - Muskogee
NAV - Navajo
PHX - Phoenix
POR - Portland
SAC - Sacramento
STATE - State Recognized
IND - Independent

1. Date of first Treaty / Date of first Petition

Address	City, State, Zip	Phone Fax	G[2]	L[3]	EB[4]	N[5]	M[6]

OREGON

Address	City, State, Zip	Phone Fax	G	L	EB	N	M
PO BOX 592	TALENT, OR 97540	503-535-5406					
PO BOX 549	SILETZ, OR 97380	503-444-2532 OR 2513 503-444-2307	TC		T,F	X	
5621 ALTAMONT DR	KLAMATH FALLS, OR 97601	503-884-3844					
PO BOX 638	PENDLETON, OR 97801	503-276-3165 503-276-3095	TC	M	A,R	X	
PO BOX 1846	BEND, OR 97709	503-382-6564					
PO BOX C	WARM SPRINGS, OR 97761	503-553-1161 503-553-1924	TC	RV	A,F	X	X

PENNSYLVANIA

Address	City, State, Zip	Phone Fax	G	L	EB	N	M
RD 3, 123 TURKEY FOOT RD	SEWICKLEY, PA 15143	412-741-8176					

RHODE ISLAND

Address	City, State, Zip	Phone Fax	G	L	EB	N	M
PO BOX 268	CHARLESTON, RI 02813	401-364-1100 401-364-1104	TC		F		

2. Gaming / Casino
3. Lodging - Resort, Motel, RV Park
4. Economic Base - Farming, Fishing, Ranching Operations
5. Tribal Newspaper
6. Museum / Cultural Center

A - Agriculture
B - Bingo
F - Fish, Aquaculture
M - Mineral
R - Ranching
RV - Recreational Vehicle

T - Timber
TC - Tribal Contract

HISTORICAL PROFILE

Area Office	Treaty Petition [1]	Tribal Class	Pop 1990	Trust Acreage	Tribal Nation

SOUTH CAROLINA

Area Office	Treaty Petition [1]	Tribal Class	Pop 1990	Trust Acreage	Tribal Nation
EA	1763	SIOUX	700	100	CATAWBA NATION
	10-FEB-93	SIOUX			CHICORA INDIAN NATION
STATE	30-DEC-76	EDISTO, NATCHEZ, KUSSO			FOUR HOLE INDIAN ORGANIZATION EDISTO TRIBAL COUNCIL
IND					PEE DEE INDIAN NATION
	04-JUN-79	SANTEE			SANTEE TRIBE WHITE OAK INDIAN COMMUNITY
	16-OCT-92	SIOUX			WACCAMAW - SIOUAN INDIAN ASSOCIATES

SOUTH DAKOTA

Area Office	Treaty Petition [1]	Tribal Class	Pop 1990	Trust Acreage	Tribal Nation
ABE	1868	(SIOUX) LAKOTA	9,841	1,400,614.5	CHEYENNE RIVER SIOUX NATION
ABE	1868	(SIOUX) LAKOTA	3,000	125,483	CROW CREEK SIOUX NATION
ABE	1868	(SIOUX) LAKOTA	544	2,183	FLANDREAU SANTEE SIOUX NATION
ABE	1868	(SIOUX) LAKOTA	1,685	130,239.44	LOWER BRULE SIOUX NATION
ABE	1868	LAKOTA	17,775	1,783,741.1	OGLALA SIOUX NATION
	1981	PONCA			PONCA NATION OF NEBRASKA
ABE	1868	(SIOUX) LAKOTA	15,438	527,640.41	ROSEBUD SIOUX NATION

LEGEND:

AREA OFFICES:
ABE - Aberdeen
ABQ - Albuquerque
ANA - Anadarko
BIL - Billings
EA - Eastern
MIN - Minneapolis
MUS - Muskogee
NAV - Navajo
PHX - Phoenix
POR - Portland
SAC - Sacramento
STATE - State Recognized
IND - Independent

1. Date of first Treaty / Date of first Petition

Address	City, State, Zip	Phone Fax	G[2]	L[3]	EB[4]	N[5]	M[6]

SOUTH CAROLINA

Address	City, State, Zip	Phone Fax	G	L	EB	N	M
PO BOX 11106	ROCK HILL, SC 29731	803-366-4792 803-366-9150					
700-B HIGHWAY 17 N	SURFSIDE, SC 29575						
113 TEE PEE LN	RIDGEVILLE, SC 29472	803-871-2126					
PO BOX 6068	CLIO, SC 29525	803-523-5269					
PO BOX 10603	ROCK HILL, SC 29731						
C/O ROBERT WOLF EAGLE / 1123 3RD AVE	CONWAY, SC 29526						

SOUTH DAKOTA

Address	City, State, Zip	Phone Fax	G	L	EB	N	M
PO BOX 590	EAGLE BUTTE, SD 57625	605-964-4155 605-964-4151	TC		R,A	X	X
PO BOX 50	FORT THOMPSON, SD 57339	605-245-2221 OR 2222 605-245-2470	TC			X	
PO BOX 283	FLANDREAU, SD 57028	605-997-3891 605-997-3878	TC	R			
PO BOX 187	LOWER BRULE, SD 57548	605-473-5561 605-473-5606	TC			X	
PO BOX H 468	PINE RIDGE, SD 57770	605-867-5821 605-867-5659	TC			X	X
GENERAL DELIVERY	WAGNER, SD 57380	605-384-3651					
PO BOX 430	ROSEBUD, SD 57570	605-747-2381 605-747-2243	TC		R	X	X

2. Gaming / Casino
3. Lodging - Resort, Motel, RV Park
4. Economic Base - Farming, Fishing, Ranching Operations
5. Tribal Newspaper
6. Museum / Cultural Center

A - Agriculture
B - Bingo
F - Fish, Aquaculture
M - Mineral
R - Ranching
RV - Recreational Vehicle

T - Timber
TC - Tribal Contract

HISTORICAL PROFILE

Area Office	Treaty Petition [1]	Tribal Class	Pop 1990	Trust Acreage	Tribal Nation

SOUTH DAKOTA

Area Office	Treaty Petition [1]	Tribal Class	Pop 1990	Trust Acreage	Tribal Nation
ABE	1867	(SIOUX) LAKOTA	9,277	108,129.85	SISSETON-WAHPETON SIOUX NATION
ABE	1858	(SIOUX) LAKOTA	5,700	36,561.65	YANKTON SIOUX NATION

TENNESSEE

Area Office	Treaty Petition [1]	Tribal Class	Pop 1990	Trust Acreage	Tribal Nation
STATE	31-DEC-90	CHEROKEE			ETOWAH CHEROKEE NATION
	09-MAR-78	CHEROKEE			RED CLAY INTER-TRIBAL IND BAND SE CHEROKEE CONFEDERACY INC

TEXAS

Area Office	Treaty Petition [1]	Tribal Class	Pop 1990	Trust Acreage	Tribal Nation
ANA	1854	COUSHATTA			ALABAMA-COUSHATTA NATION OF TEXAS
ANA	04-JUN-79	KICKAPOO			KICKAPOO TRADITIONAL NATION OF TEXAS
ALB	1680	PUEBLO	1,113	97.47	YSLETA DEL SUR PUEBLO NATION

LEGEND:

AREA OFFICES:
ABE - Aberdeen
ABQ - Albuquerque
ANA - Anadarko
BIL - Billings
EA - Eastern
MIN - Minneapolis
MUS - Muskogee
NAV - Navajo
PHX - Phoenix
POR - Portland
SAC - Sacramento
STATE - State Recognized
IND - Independent

1. Date of first Treaty / Date of first Petition

Address	City, State, Zip	Phone Fax	G[2]	L[3]	EB[4]	N[5]	M[6]

SOUTH DAKOTA

Address	City, State, Zip	Phone Fax	G	L	EB	N	M
RT 2 BOX 509 AGENCY VILLAGE	SISSETON, SD 57262	605-698-3911 605-698-3708	TC				
PO BOX 248	MARTY, SD 57361	605-384-3804 605-384-5687	TC		F	X	

TENNESSEE

Address	City, State, Zip	Phone Fax	G	L	EB	N	M
PO BOX 5454	CLEVELAND, TN 37320						
7703 GEORGETOWN RD	OOLTEWAH, TN 37363	615-238-9346					

TEXAS

Address	City, State, Zip	Phone Fax	G	L	EB	N	M
RT 3 BOX 640	LIVINGSTON, TX 77351	409-563-4391 409-563-4397					X
PO BOX 972	EAGLE PASS, TX 78853	210-773-2105 210-757-9228					
PO BOX 17579 - YSLETA STN	EL PASO, TX 79917	915-859-7913 915-859-2988					X

2. Gaming / Casino
3. Lodging - Resort, Motel, RV Park
4. Economic Base - Farming, Fishing, Ranching Operations
5. Tribal Newspaper
6. Museum / Cultural Center

A - Agriculture
B - Bingo
F - Fish, Aquaculture
M - Mineral
R - Ranching
RV - Recreational Vehicle

T - Timber
TC - Tribal Contract

HISTORICAL PROFILE

Area Office	Treaty Petition [1]	Tribal Class	Pop 1990	Trust Acreage	Tribal Nation

UTAH

Area Office	Treaty Petition	Tribal Class	Pop 1990	Trust Acreage	Tribal Nation
STATE		(NAVAJO) DINE			BLUE MOUNTAIN DINE NATION
PHX	1863	SHOSHONI	374	77,176.84	GOSHUTE INDIAN NATION
STATE		PAIUTE			KANOSH BAND OF PAIUTE NATION
STATE		PAIUTE			KOOSHAREM BAND OF PAIUTE NATION
		SHOSHONE			N E BAND SHOSHONE INDIAN NATION
PHX	1981	PAIUTE	213	32,458	PAIUTE INDIAN NATION OF UTAH
STATE		PAIUTE			SHIVWITS BAND OF PAIUTE NATION
PHX	1863	GOSHUTE	108	17,444.65	SKULL VALLEY NATION % UINTAH & OURAY AGENCY
PHX	1949	UTE	3,129	1,021,597.8	UINTAH & OURAY NATIONS
STATE		UTE			WHITE MESA UTE NATION

VERMONT

Area Office	Treaty Petition	Tribal Class	Pop 1990	Trust Acreage	Tribal Nation
IND	15-APR-80	ABENAKI			ABENAKI NATION OF MISSIQUOI

LEGEND:

AREA OFFICES:
ABE - Aberdeen
ABQ - Albuquerque
ANA - Anadarko
BIL - Billings
EA - Eastern
MIN - Minneapolis
MUS - Muskogee
NAV - Navajo
PHX - Phoenix
POR - Portland
SAC - Sacramento
STATE - State Recognized
IND - Independent

1. Date of first Treaty / Date of first Petition

Address	City, State, Zip	Phone Fax	G[2]	L[3]	EB[4]	N[5]	M[6]

UTAH

Address	City, State, Zip	Phone Fax	G	L	EB	N	M
388 E 400 SOUTH 101-1	BLANDING, UT 84511	801-678-2950					
PO BOX 6104	IBAPAH, UT 84034	801-234-1136 801-234-6211					
PO BOX 178	KANOSH, UT 84637	801-759-2660					
PO BOX 454	RICHFIELD, UT 84701	801-896-9025					
660 SOUTH 200 WEST	BRIGHAM CITY, UT 84302						
600 NORTH 100 EAST PAIUTE DR	CEDAR CITY, UT 84720	801-586-1112 801-586-7388					
PO BOX 391	SANTA CLARA, UT 84765	801-628-1468					
GENERAL DELIVERY	GRANTSVILLE, UT 84029	801-831-6126 801-722-2406					X
PO BOX 190	FORT DUCHESNE, UT 84026	801-722-5141 801-722-2374	B	R	A,F,M	X	X
PO BOX 340	BLANDING, UT 84511	801-678-3397					

VERMONT

Address	City, State, Zip	Phone Fax	G	L	EB	N	M
PO BOX 276	SWANTON, VT 05488	802-868-2559					

2. Gaming / Casino
3. Lodging - Resort, Motel, RV Park
4. Economic Base - Farming, Fishing, Ranching Operations
5. Tribal Newspaper
6. Museum / Cultural Center

A - Agriculture
B - Bingo
F - Fish, Aquaculture
M - Mineral
R - Ranching
RV - Recreational Vehicle

T - Timber
TC - Tribal Contract

HISTORICAL PROFILE

Area Office	Treaty Petition [1]	Tribal Class	Pop 1990	Trust Acreage	Tribal Nation

VIRGINIA

Area Office	Treaty Petition	Tribal Class	Pop 1990	Trust Acreage	Tribal Nation
IND		CHEROKEE			CHEROKEE NATION OF VIRGINIA
STATE		POWHATTAN	1,000		CHICKAHOMINY INDIAN NATION
STATE		POWHATTAN	150		EASTERN CHICKAHOMINY INDIAN NATION
STATE	1658	POWHATTAN	145	200	MATTAPONI TRIBAL NATION
STATE		POWHATTAN	500		MONACAN INDIAN NATION
STATE		POWHATTAN	100		NANSEMOND INDIAN NATION
STATE	1607	POWHATTAN	515		PAMUNKEY INDIAN NATION
IND		OCCAHANNOK			POCOMOKE-OCCAHAN NOCK NATION
IND		CHEROKEE			UNITED CHEROKEES OF VIRGINIA
STATE	16-NOV-79	POWHATTAN	750		UNITED RAPPAHANNOCK NATION
STATE	26-NOV-79	POWHATTAN	100		UPPER MATTAPONI NATION

WASHINGTON

Area Office	Treaty Petition	Tribal Class	Pop 1990	Trust Acreage	Tribal Nation
IND		LAKE			ARROW LAKE BAND NATION
POR	1939	CHEHALIS	491	2,075.86	CHEHALIS NATION
STATE	23-JUL-79	CHINOOK			CHINOOK INDIAN TRIBE INC

LEGEND:

AREA OFFICES:
ABE - Aberdeen
ABQ - Albuquerque
ANA - Anadarko
BIL - Billings
EA - Eastern
MIN - Minneapolis
MUS - Muskogee
NAV - Navajo
PHX - Phoenix
POR - Portland
SAC - Sacramento
STATE - State Recognized
IND - Independent

1. Date of first Treaty / Date of first Petition

Address	City, State, Zip	Phone Fax	G[2]	L[3]	EB[4]	N[5]	M[6]

VIRGINIA

Address	City, State, Zip	Phone Fax	G[2]	L[3]	EB[4]	N[5]	M[6]
RT 1 BOX 499	RAPIDAN, VA 22733	703-487-5116					
RFD 1 BOX 299	PROVIDENCE FORGE, VA 23140	804-829-2186					
6801 S LOTT CARY RD	PROVIDENCE FORGE, VA 23140	804-745-6508					
BOX 310 RT 2	WEST POINT, VA 23181	804-769-2194					X
PO BOX 173	MONROE, VA 24574	804-745-6508					
3429 GALBERRY RD	CHESAPEAKE, VA 23323	804-929-3289					
RT 2 BOX 360	KING WILLIAM, VA 23086	804-769-4767 804-769-0742					X
	NELSONIA, VA 23414	804-665-4458					
PO BOX 1104	MADISON HEIGHTS, VA 24572	804-845-5606					
C/O A R WINSTON	INDIAN NECK, VA 23077	804-769-3128					X
BOX 12A	ST STEPHENS, VA 23148	804-865-6814					X

WASHINGTON

Address	City, State, Zip	Phone Fax	G[2]	L[3]	EB[4]	N[5]	M[6]
PO BOX 1721	OMAK, WA 98841	509-826-2319 509-826-4120					
PO BOX 536	OAKVILLE, WA 98568	360-273-5911 360-273-5914	B		T,A		
PO BOX 228	CHINOOK, WA 98614	360-777-8303					

2. Gaming / Casino
3. Lodging - Resort, Motel, RV Park
4. Economic Base - Farming, Fishing, Ranching Operations
5. Tribal Newspaper
6. Museum / Cultural Center

A - Agriculture
B - Bingo
F - Fish, Aquaculture
M - Mineral
R - Ranching
RV - Recreational Vehicle

T - Timber
TC - Tribal Contract

HISTORICAL PROFILE

Area Office	Treaty Petition [1]	Tribal Class	Pop 1990	Trust Acreage	Tribal Nation
		WASHINGTON			
POR	1872	CONFEDERATED	7,308	1,300,000	COLVILLE NATION
STATE	17-SEP-75	COWLITZ			COWLITZ TRIBE OF INDIANS
STATE	07-JUN-77	DUWAMISH			DUWAMISH INDIAN TRIBE
POR	1969	HOH	137	443	HOH NATION
POR	1981	S'KLALLAM	228	2.12	JAMESTOWN S'KLALLAM NATION
POR	1914	KALISPEL	211	6,387.12	KALISPEL NATION
STATE					KIKIALLUS INDIAN NATION
POR	1968	LOWER ELWHA	550	427.48	LOWER ELWHA NATION
POR	1855	LUMMI	3,000	7,680.22	LUMMI NATION
POR	1936	MAKAH	1,569	27,265.50	MAKAH NATION
STATE			520		MARIETTA BAND NOOKSACK NATION
POR	1855	MUCKLESHOOT	800	1,274.99	MUCKLESHOOT NATION
POR	1854	NISQUALLY	382	930.06	NISQUALLY INDIAN NATION
POR	1855	NOOKSACK	1,105	2.20	NOOKSACK NATION
POR	1855	S'KALLAM	771	1,303	PORT GAMBLE S'KLALLAM NATION
POR	1854	PUYALLUP	1,450	137.71	PUYALLUP NATION
POR	1936	QUILEUTE	723	814.5	QUILEUTE NATION

LEGEND:

AREA OFFICES:
ABE - Aberdeen
ABQ - Albuquerque
ANA - Anadarko
BIL - Billings
EA - Eastern
MIN - Minneapolis
MUS - Muskogee
NAV - Navajo
PHX - Phoenix
POR - Portland
SAC - Sacramento
STATE - State Recognized
IND - Independent

1. Date of first Treaty / Date of first Petition

WASHINGTON

Address	City, State, Zip	Phone Fax	G[2]	L[3]	EB[4]	N[5]	M[6]
PO BOX 150	NESPELEM, WA 99155	509-634-4711 509-634-4116	B	R	T,R	X	X
PO BOX 2547	LONGVIEW, WA 98632	360-577-8140					
212 WELLS AVE S STE C	RENTON, WA 98055	206-226-5185 206-226-5240					
HC 80 BOX 917 / 2464 LOWER HOH RD	FORKS, WA 98331	360-374-6582 360-374-6549			T,F		
1033 OLD BLYN HWY	SEQUIM, WA 98382	360-683-1109 360-683-4643	TC	R	F	X	X
BOX 39	USK, WA 99180	509-445-1147 509-445-1705	TC	RV	T	X	
3933 BAGLEY AVE N	SEATTLE, WA 98103	206-632-2512					
2851 LOWER ELWHA RD	PORT ANGELES, WA 98362	360-452-8471 360-452-3428	TC				
2616 KWINA RD	BELLINGHAM, WA 98226	360-734-8180 360-384-5521	TC	M	F	X	X
PO BOX 115	NEAH BAY, WA 98357	360-645-2201 360-645-2323	B	R	T,M	X	X
1827 MARINE DR	BELLINGHAM, WA 98226						
39015 172ND ST SE	AUBURN, WA 98002	206-939-3311 206-939-5311	B	M	T	X	
4820 SHE-NAH-NUM DR SE	OLYMPIA, WA 98513	360-456-5221 360-438-8618	B		F	X	
PO BOX 157	DEMING, WA 98244	360-592-5176 360-592-5721	TC		F	X	
31912 LITTLE BOSTON RD	KINGSTON, WA 98346	360-297-2646 360-297-7097				X	
2002 E 28TH ST	TACOMA, WA 98404	206-597-6200 206-272-9514	B	M	T,F		
PO BOX 279	LAPUSH, WA 98350	360-374-6163 360-374-6311		M	F,T	X	

2. Gaming / Casino
3. Lodging - Resort, Motel, RV Park
4. Economic Base - Farming, Fishing, Ranching Operations
5. Tribal Newspaper
6. Museum / Cultural Center

A - Agriculture
B - Bingo
F - Fish, Aquaculture
M - Mineral
R - Ranching
RV - Recreational Vehicle

T - Timber
TC - Tribal Contract

HISTORICAL PROFILE

Area Office	Treaty Petition [1]	Tribal Class	Pop 1990	Trust Acreage	Tribal Nation
WASHINGTON					
POR	28-Jan-05	QUINAULT	2367	129,200.30	QUINAULT NATION
	13-Jun-75	SAMISH	600		SAMISH TRIBE OF INDIANS
POR	1855	SUAK SUIATTLE	210	23.21	SAUK-SUIATTLE NATION
POR	1971	SHOALWATER	130	335	SHOALWATER BAY INDIAN NATION
POR	1980	SKOKOMISH	630	2,986.73	SKOKOMISH INDIAN NATION
STATE	03-MAR-75	SNOHOMISH	871		SNOHOMISH INDIAN NATION
STATE	05-FEB-76	SNOQUALMIE	561		SNOQUALMIE INDIAN NATION
STATE	14-JUN-88	SNOQUALMOO			SNOQUALMOO TRIBE/WHIDBEY ISLAND
POR	1881	SPOKANE	2,025	137,147.42	SPOKANE NATION
POR	1965	CONFEDERATED	380	970.72	SQUAXIN ISLAND INDIAN NATION
STATE	28-AUG-73	STEILACOOM	617		STEILACOOM TRIBE
POR	1855	STILLAQUAMISH	160	21	STILLAGUAMISH NATION
POR	1855	SUQUAMISH	660	8,012	SUQUAMISH INDIAN NATION
POR	1855	SWINOMISH	462	3,601.76	SWINOMISH INDIAN NATION
POR	1855	TULALIP	2,016	10,664.53	TULALIP NATION
POR	1855	UPPER SKAGIT	502	74.17	UPPER SKAGIT INDIAN NATION
POR	1855	YAKIMA	7,724	1,160,456	YAKAMA INDIAN NATION

LEGEND:

AREA OFFICES:
ABE - Aberdeen
ABQ - Albuquerque
ANA - Anadarko
BIL - Billings
EA - Eastern
MIN - Minneapolis
MUS - Muskogee
NAV - Navajo
PHX - Phoenix
POR - Portland
SAC - Sacramento
STATE - State Recognized
IND - Independent

1. Date of first Treaty / Date of first Petition

Address	City, State, Zip	Phone Fax	G[2]	L[3]	EB[4]	N[5]	M[6]

WASHINGTON

Address	City, State, Zip	Phone Fax	G[2]	L[3]	EB[4]	N[5]	M[6]
PO BOX 189	TAHOLAH, WA 98587	360-276-8211 360-276-4191			F,T	X	
PO BOX 217	ANACORTES, WA 98221	360-293-6404					
5318 CHIEF BROWN LN	DARRINGTON, WA 98241	360-436-0131 360-436-1511				X	
PO BOX 130	TOKELAND, WA 98590	360-267-6766 360-267-6778	TC				
N 80 TRIBAL CTR RD	SHELTON, WA 98584	360-426-4232 360-877-5943	B		T,F	X	X
18933 59TH AVE NE #115	ARLINGTON, WA 98223	360-475-7900					
PO BOX 280	CARNATION, WA 98014	206-333-6551 206-333-6553					
PO BOX 463	COUPEVILLE, WA 98239	360-221-8301					
PO BOX 100	WELLPINIT, WA 99040	509-258-4581 OR 838-3465 509-258-9243	TC		F,T	X	X
SE 70 SQUAXIN LN	SHELTON, WA 98584	360-426-9781 360-426-6577	B		F,T		
PO BOX 88419	STEILACOOM, WA 98388	206-584-6308					X
3439 STOLUCKQUAMISH LN	ARLINGTON, WA 98223	360-652-7362 360-435-2204					
PO BOX 498	SUQUAMISH, WA 98392	360-598-3311 360-598-6295	B		T,F	X	X
PO BOX 817	LACONNER, WA 98257	360-466-3163 360-466-5309	TC				
6700 TOTEM BEACH RD	MARYSVILLE, WA 98270	360-653-4585 360-653-0255	TC	M	T,F	X	
2284 COMMUNITY PLAZA	SEDRO WOOLEY, WA 98284	360-856-5501 360-856-3175			F	X	
PO BOX 151	TOPPENISH, WA 98948	509-865-5121 509-865-5528		RV	F	X	X

2. Gaming / Casino
3. Lodging - Resort, Motel, RV Park
4. Economic Base - Farming, Fishing, Ranching Operations
5. Tribal Newspaper
6. Museum / Cultural Center

A - Agriculture
B - Bingo
F - Fish, Aquaculture
M - Mineral
R - Ranching
RV - Recreational Vehicle

T - Timber
TC - Tribal Contract

HISTORICAL PROFILE

Area Office	Treaty Petition [1]	Tribal Class	Pop 1990	Trust Acreage	Tribal Nation

WISCONSIN

Area Office	Treaty Petition [1]	Tribal Class	Pop 1990	Trust Acreage	Tribal Nation
MIN	1854	CHIPPEWA	4,664	56,652.87	BAD RIVER INDIAN NATION
STATE	1982	CONFEDERATED MOHIGAN			BROTHERTON INDIAN NATION
	15-APR-80				BROTHERTON INDIANS OF WISCONSIN
MIN	1913	POTAWATOMI	283	11,692.35	FOREST COUNTY POTAWATOMI NATION
MIN	1854	CHIPPEWA	5,217	48,317.36	LAC COURTE OREILLES NATION
MIN	1854	CHIPPEWA	2,706	44,874.33	LAC DU FLAMBEAU NATION
MIN	1817	MENOMINEE	6,380	235,033	MENOMINEE INDIAN NATION OF WISCONSIN
MIN	1838	ONEIDA	11,000	65,430	ONEIDA INDIAN NATION
MIN	1854	CHIPPEWA	2,830	7,856,393	RED CLIFF INDIAN NATION
MIN	1934	CHIPPEWA	1,399	1,694	SOKAOGON CHIPPEWA NATION
MIN	1938	CHIPPEWA	759	1,943.96	ST CROIX NATION
MIN	1856	STOCKBRIDGE -MUNSEE	1,653	15,602.75	STOCKBRIDGE - MUNSEE NATION
MIN		WINNEBAGO	3,970	4,245.50	WISCONSIN WINNEBAGO INDIAN NATION

LEGEND:

AREA OFFICES:
ABE - Aberdeen
ABQ - Albuquerque
ANA - Anadarko
BIL - Billings
EA - Eastern
MIN - Minneapolis
MUS - Muskogee
NAV - Navajo
PHX - Phoenix
POR - Portland
SAC - Sacramento
STATE - State Recognized
IND - Independent

1. Date of first Treaty / Date of first Petition

WISCONSIN

Address	City, State, Zip	Phone Fax	G[2]	L[3]	EB[4]	N[5]	M[6]
PO BOX 39	ODANAH, WI 54861	715-682-7111 715-682-7118	TC		A		X
RT 4 BOX 90-1	ARBOR VITAE, WI 54510	414-923-3173					
2848 WITCHES LAKE RD	WOODRUFF, WI 54568	715-542-3913					
PO BOX 340	CRANDON, WI 54520	715-478-2903 715-478-5280	TC			X	
RT 2 BOX 2700	HAYWARD, WI 54843	715-634-8934 715-634-4797	TC		T	X	X
PO BOX 67	LAC DU FLAMBEAU, WI 54538	715-588-3303 715-588-7930	TC	RV	F,A		X
PO BOX 910	KESHENA, WI 54135	715-799-5100 715-799-4525	TC		T	X	
PO BOX 365	ONEIDA, WI 54155	414-869-2772 OR 2214 414-869-2894	TC	R	T	X	X
PO BOX 529	BAYFIELD, WI 54814	715-779-3701 715-779-3704	TC	RV	F		X
RT 1 BOX 625	CRANDON, WI 54520	715-478-2604 715-478-5275	TC				
PO BOX 287	HERTEL, WI 54845	715-349-2195 715-349-5768	TC		F		X
N 8476 MOH CON NUCK RD	BOWLER, WI 54416	715-793-4111 715-793-4299	TC		T		X
PO BOX 667	BLACK RIVER FALLS, WI 54615	715-284-9343 715-284-9805	TC		T	X	

2. Gaming / Casino
3. Lodging - Resort, Motel, RV Park
4. Economic Base - Farming, Fishing, Ranching Operations
5. Tribal Newspaper
6. Museum / Cultural Center

A - Agriculture
B - Bingo
F - Fish, Aquaculture
M - Mineral
R - Ranching
RV - Recreational Vehicle

T - Timber
TC - Tribal Contract

HISTORICAL PROFILE

WYOMING

Area Office	Treaty Petition [1]	Tribal Class	Pop 1990	Trust Acreage	Tribal Nation
BIL	1878	ARAPAHOE	3,826	584,140.34	ARAPAHOE INDIAN NATION
BIL	1863	SHOSHONE	2,479	584,140.34	EASTERN SHOSHONE NATION

LEGEND:

AREA OFFICES:
ABE - Aberdeen
ABQ - Albuquerque
ANA - Anadarko
BIL - Billings
EA - Eastern
MIN - Minneapolis
MUS - Muskogee
NAV - Navajo
PHX - Phoenix
POR - Portland
SAC - Sacramento
STATE - State Recognized
IND - Independent

1. Date of first Treaty / Date of first Petition

Address	City, State, Zip	Phone Fax	G[2]	L[3]	EB[4]	N[5]	M[6]

WYOMING

Address	City, State, Zip	Phone / Fax	G	L	EB	N	M
PO BOX 217	FORT WASHAKIE, WY 82514	307-332-6120 307-332-7543		RV	R	X	X
PO BOX 217	FORT WASHAKIE, WY 82514	307-332-3532 307-332-3055		RV	R,T	X	X

INFORMATION PROVIDED BY:
B.I.A.
CENSUS BUREAU
SMITHSONIAN INSTITUTION

FORMAT CREATED BY:
N.A2.I.I.T.C.
NORTH AMERICAN NATIVE AMERICAN INDIAN
INFORMATION AND TRADE CENTER

2. Gaming / Casino
3. Lodging - Resort, Motel, RV Park
4. Economic Base - Farming, Fishing, Ranching Operations
5. Tribal Newspaper
6. Museum / Cultural Center

A - Agriculture
B - Bingo
F - Fish, Aquaculture
M - Mineral
R - Ranching
RV - Recreational Vehicle

T - Timber
TC - Tribal Contract

INTRODUCTION TO NEO-INDIAN TRIBES

The list of Indian Tribes and groups to follow is offered without comment as to what they are doing, or any opinions on how authentic they may be or supposed to be. They range from Boy-Scout like activities to great swelling "one and only real authentic" bluster. The Reader is reminded that each and every one has a legal right to exist. S/he should approach them carefully and judge them on their merits. This is not intended to be an endorsement of any particular group.

The Tribes are listed by states so the Reader can choose one or more near to them to contact for possible fellowship, participation in their activities, and so on. Persons with heritage from so-called extinct or no longer recognized tribes may scan the organizations to find one that is reviving and celebrating his/her ancient heritage.

While some of these tribes have, or are planning to, petition for State and/or Federal Acknowledgement, many have no intention to place themselves in the morass of constantly changing politics. They are simply desiring recognition for whatever they are and wish to forge their own futures just as the tribes did before the Concentration camps were established.

We mail the Pan-Am News to this list regularly and trust the Post Office to supply us with changes of address, but this bulletin is a living entity with constantly changing parameters. *Additions and corrections from readers are greatly appreciated and should be addressed to:*

The Pan-American Indian Association, Inc.
Nocatee FL 33864-0244

and

Indian Information and Trade Center
P.O. Box 27626
Tucson AZ 85726

Let's work together to keep this an accurate list of groups formed to help seekers revive their personal Indian heritage. We are not interested in any jealous evaluations as to how authentic any of them are. They all believe they are doing the right thing and we trust they are doing the best they can. It is their Constitutional and Civil Right to assemble and to enjoy the free pracitice of religion. These rights are not subject to outside revision or changing laws.

Persons wishing to organize an Indian Revival Group are invited to contact the Pan-American Indian Association, Inc., Nocatee FL 33864-0244.

Yours as long as the grass grows and the water flows!

Chief Piercing Eyes/Penn
CPE/P:ck

UNITED STATES

ALABAMA

Cherokees of Southeast Alabama
2221 Rocky Ridge Rd
Hoover AL 35216
(205) 979-7019

The Free Cherokees
Eagle Bear Band
Rt 2 Box 310
Hamilton AL 35570
(205) 921-2589

ALASKA

Southeastern Cherokee Confederacy
POB 520348
Big Lake AK 99652-0348
(907) 892-8203

Southeastern Cherokee Confederacy
POB 54
Soldotna AK 99669-0054
Last # (907) 283-8119

ARIZONA

Deer Tribe Metis Medicine Society
11259 E Via Linda #100-142
Scottsdale AZ 85259-4706

United Lumbee Nation
Eagle Clan
POB 306
Quartzsite AZ 85346-0306
(520) 927-4288

United Lumbee Nation
Eagle Clan
3441 Blacklidge # 14
Tucson AZ 85716-1706

ARKANSAS

The Free Cherokees
POB 641
Helena AR 72342-0641
(501) 388-7966

The Free Cherokees
Ark Bear Tribe Band
Rt 1 Box 184
Mountain Home AR 72653
(501) 481-5394

The Free Cherokees
Dung Beetle Society
Rt 1 Box 256
Portland AR 71663
(501) 737-2381

The Free Cherokees
Good Medicine Band
HC 62 Box 378
Old Joe AR 72658
(501) 297-8083

The Revived Ouachita Indians
HC 67 Box 48
Norman AR 71860

The Revived Ouachita Indians
216 Virginia St
Hot Springs AR 71901

The Revived Ouachita Indians
1100 Emory St
Hot Springs AR 71901

The Revived Ouachita Indians
2156 Higdon Ferry Rd
Hot Springs AR 71913

The Revived Ouachita Indians
POB 137
Donaldson AR 71941-0137

The Revived Ouachita Indians
POB 162
Jessyville AR 71949-0162

The Revived Ouachita Indians
POB 587
Mt Ida AR 71957-0587

CALIFORNIA

Ani-Yun-Wiya Society
POB 1921
Bakersfield CA 93301-1921

The Free Cherokees
Box 1599
Sutter Creek CA 95685-1599
Home: (209) 267-0507
Work: (209) 267-0519
FAX: (209) 267-5144

Hownonquet Community Assoc
POB 239
Smith River CA 95567-0239

Miwok Indian Band
Star Rt 1
West Point CA 95255

Northern Maidu Tribe
POB 217
Greenville CA 95947-0217

Pan-American Indian Assoc
#19
Thunderbird Clan
111 Orchard Lane
Carlotta CA 95528
(707) 768-3226

The Revived Ouchita Indians
470 Derby Lane
Santa Rosa CA 95404

Shadowlight Medicine Clan
4021 N F St
San Bernardino CA 92407-3409
(909) 883-1212

United Lumbee Nation
POB 512
Fall River Mills CA 96028
(916) 336-6701

United Lumbee Nation
Bear Clan
3427 West Monte Vista
Visalia CA 93277

COLORADO

Pan-Am Indians
Little Bear Tribe
2056 Odin Drive
Silt CO 81652
(303) 876-5896

CONNECTICUT

The Free Cherokees, Moon
Band
168 Hornbeam Rd
Groton, CT 06340
(203) 445-1923

The Free Cherokees, Snake Band
68 Bushnell Ave.
Oakville CT 06797
Home: (203) 945-6379
Work: (203) 945-0623

FLORIDA

Apalachicola Creek Indians Blount Band
c/o Mary Blount
476 Highpoint Lane
Tallahassee FL 32301
(904) 942-3741

Cherokee/Creek
6944 Cox Road
Bascom FL 32423
(904) 592-4401

Cherokees of Florida
Rt 1 Box 100 A-1
Bowling Green FL 33834
(813) 773-3393

Cherokees of Georgia
Rt 2 Box 394J
Hilliard FL 32046
(904) 275-2953

The Conastoga/Susquehannock Tribe
POB 244
Nocatee FL 33864-0244
(813) 494-6930

E-Chota Cherokee Tribe of Florida
#5 N 24th St
Defuniak Springs FL 32433
(904) 892-5870

E-Chota Cherokee Tribe of Florida
2304 Cornsilk Road
Marianna FL 32446
(904) 592-2025

Earth Mother Indian Council
51 North Federal Hwy # 19
Pompano Beach FL 33062
(305) 941-0263 or 792-6818

The Evans Clan
POB No 1
Point Washington FL 32454
(904) 231-4324

Full Moon Ceremony
5503 N US Hwy 98
Dade City FL 33525-6651
(park) (305) 247-2044

The Full Moon Ceremony
8040 Park Byrd Rd
Lakeland FL 33809
(813) 859-1087

Minquass Susquannanooks
12850 SE 7th St
Silver Springs FL 32688
(904) 625-3589

Muskogee Creek Nation
Ancilla Clan
Rt 5 Box 423
Perry FL 32347

The Free Cherokees
N Georgia Chickamaugan Circle
POB 291
Flintstone GA 30725-0291
(706) 820-0458

The Free Cherokees
Turtle Clan
235 Cherokee Village Drive
Ball Ground GA 30107
(706) 735-4197

The Free Cherokees
Turtle Clan
c/o Santinka
POB 1231
Lilburn GA 30226-1231
(404) 381-0628

Southeastern Cherokee Confederacy
318 Crestview Dr
Valdosta GA 31602
(912) 244-9104

Southeastern Cherokee Confederacy
Bear Clan
Rt 3 Box 291
Adel GA 31620

Southeastern Cherokee Confederacy
3895 Shelton Rd
Lake Park GA 31636
(912) 242-3504

Southeastern Cherokee Confederacy
Rt 4 Box 120
Albany GA 31705
(912) 787-5722

South Eastern Cherokee Confederacy
POB 367
Ochlocknee GA 31773-0367
(912) 574-5497

Southeastern Cherokee Confederacy
1448 Minton Rd
Sylvester GA 31791
(912) 776-7538

Southeastern Cherokee Confederacy
Deer Clan
POB 1784
Thomasville GA 31799-1784
(912) 574-5497

United Eastern Lenape Band
927 Gunter Circle
Lawrenceville GA 30243

IDAHO

The Revived Ouachita Indians
226 Adams St
Chubbuck ID 83202

ILLINOIS

The Shadow Nation
403 E Hanover
New Baden IL 62265-1903
(618) 588-4590

Pan-Am Indians
Red Path Works
POB 881
Englewood FL 34295-0881
(813) 474-0261

Pan-Am Indians
Shadow Oak Clan # 14
10622 Shadow Oak Trail
Clermont FL 34711
(904) 394-3823

Pan-American Assoc
Mockingbird Clan
2227 Tulip
Sarasota FL 34239
(813) 922-7839 or 955-2724

Pan-American Indian Assoc
Rainbow Moon Clan
8335 Sevigny Drive
North Ft Myers FL 33917-1705
(813) 731-7029

The Sacred Tree Circle
2954 Calvin St
Ft Myers FL 33901
(813) 334-1373

SE Cherokee Confederacy
5452 N Dean Rd
Orlando FL 32817
(407) 657-0704

Shawnees
POB 964
Crawfordville FL 32326-0964

Southeastern Cherokee
Confederacy
2119 Garden View Rd
Sebring FL 33870
(813) 385-0705 OR
(813) 385-4836

Southeastern Cherokee
Confederacy
3530 Schrock St
Sarasota FL 34239-3427
(813) 365-6054

The Willow Pond
Rt 2 Box 106-2
Webster FL 33597
(904) 793-2104

GEORGIA

Cherokee Nation of Texas
POB 1324
Clayton GA 30525-1324
(706) 746-2448

Cherokees of Georgia
3291 Church St
Scottsdale GA 30079
(404) 299-2940
FAX (404) 294-5313

The Free Cherokees
264 Timber Creek Lane
Marietta GA 30060
Home: (404) 433-8441
Work: (404) 331-1436

The Free Cherokees
Good Medicine Band
2170 Poplar Trail
Cumming GA 30131-4894

INDIANA

Big Horn Lenape Nation
1261 E Naomi
Indianapolis IN 46203

Miami Indian Council
641 Buchanan St
Huntington IN 46750

KENTUCKY

Southeastern Cherokee
Confederacy
POB 424
Kenvir KY 40847-0424
(606) 837-2222

Southeastern Cherokee
Confederacy
Black Wolf Band and Warrior
Society
POB 221
Wallins Creek KY 40873-0221
(606) 573-9350

MARYLAND

The Free Cherokees
800 Oak Drive
Mechanicville MD 20659
(301) 884-5605

The Free Cherokees
Bird Band
Rt 1 Box 303-E
Lexington Park MD 20653
Home: (301) 862-1305
Work: (301) 862-2111

The Free Cherokees
Wild Potato Band
577 Joy Lane
Hollywood MD 20636
(301) 373-8584

Piscataway Indian Tribe
Maryland Indian Heritage
Society
POB 905
Waldorf MD 20601-0905

MASSACHUSETTS

The Free Cherokees
Eagle Council
21 Shackford Rd
Reading MA 01867
(617) 944-3243

Free Cherokees
Wild Potato Band
POB 385
Feeding Hill MA 01030-0385
(413) 785-5912

MICHIGAN

The Free Cherokees
Rebus Clan
4575 Sycamore
Holt MI 48842
(517) 694-7914

Grand River Ottawa Nation
200 Peach Ave
Hart MI 49420

MISSISSIPPI

The Free Cherokees
Star Hawk Band
1926 Catalina Drive
Jackson MS 39204
(602) 371-8242

MISSOURI

Amonsoquath Tribe
1731 W Florida
Springfield MO 65803
(417) 865-4136

Amonsoquath Tribe of Cherokee
6248 State Hwy W
Ozark MO 65721
(417) 865-4136

Chickamunga Cherokee Nation
4021 W Gardenia St
Brookline MO 65619
(417) 886-0675

Chickamunga Cherokee Nation AR/MO
Tribal Office
217 Forest Lane
Republic MO 65738
(417) 732-2100

The Free Cherokees
Dogwood Band
Rt 1-1151 Nashville Church Rd
Ashland MO 65010
(314) 657-9004

Spirit of the Four Winds Tribe
Pan-Am Indians no 22
715 South Monroe St
Lebanon MO 65536
(417) 588-1412

NEW HAMPSHIRE

Mettanokit
Medicine Story
173 Merriam Hill Rd
Greenville NH 03048
(603) 878-3201

NEW JERSEY

The Free Cherokees,
Osprey Band
POB 673
Mays Landing NJ 08330
(609) 625-4129

Native Delaware Indians
New Jersey Indian Office
300 Main St # 3F
Orange NJ 07050
(201) 675-0694

Powhatan Renape Nation
POB 225
Rancocas NJ 08073-0225
(609) 261-4747

Weequahic Band
POB 386
East Orange NJ 07019
Home: (201) 672-1978
Work: (201) 648-4235

Southeastern Cherokee
Confederacy
WESA
36 Overlook Drive
Mastic NY 11950-4913
(516) 281-6343

United Eastern Lenape Band
4952 Williams St
Lancaster NY 14086

United Indian Group
9 Harold St
Port Jarvis NY 12771

NORTH CAROLINA

Northern Tsalagi Tribe of SW
Virginia
1813 Chandler St
Burlington NC 27217
(919) 584-4834

Person County Indians
Rt 6 Box 104
Roxboro NC 27573

Southeastern Cherokee
Confederacy
9114 NC49 North
Cedar Grove NC 27231
(919) 562-4222

Southeastern Cherokee
Confederacy
108 Third St
Haw River NC 27258
(919) 578-0995

Tuscarora Nation of N Carolina
Rt 4 Box 172
Maxton NC 28364
(919) 844-3352

OHIO

Big Horn Lenape Nation
c/o Mess
1056 West Rd
Martinsville OH 45146-9550

Big Horn Lenape Nation
Village of Rising Wings
193 E Main St # 228
Chillicothe OH 45601

The Free Cherokees
Hokshichankiya Band
Rt 1 Box 91
Creola OH 45622-9727
(614) 596-5371

Munsee Thames River
Delaware Tribe
4133 Dundee Ave # D
c/o Bungard
Columbus OH 43227

United Eastern Allegheny
Nation
7797 Millersburg Rd
Wooster OH 44691
(216) 264-1646

United Eastern Lenape Band
960 Orchard St
Zanesville OH 43701

Weequahic Band
POB 1855
Newark NJ 07101-1855
(201) 622-6314

NEW MEXICO

San Juan de Guadalupe Tiwa Tribe
559 West Brown Rd
Las Cruces NM 88001

NEW YORK

Big Horn Lenape Nation
Box 73
Chemung NY 14825-0073

Big Horn Lenape Nation
332 S Glen Ave
Watkins Glen NY 14891

Big Horn Lenape Nation
Wolf Clan
408 ½ Hudson St
Ithaca NY 14850

The Free Cherokees
Box 62
North Hudson NY 12855-0062
(518) 532-0570

The Free Cherokees
Eagle Deer Band
146-16 220th St
Rosedale, Queens NY 11413
(718) 723-0921

The Free Cherokees
Many Walks Council
POB 54
Stony Creek NY12878-0054
(518) 696-3180

The Free Cherokees
Wolf Council
75 Robert Quigley Drive
Scottsville NY 14546
(716) 889-7272

NorthEastern Native American Assoc.
198-04 120th Ave
St Albans NY 11412
(718) 978-7057

NorthEastern Native Amer. Assoc.
POB 266
Jamaica NY 11423-0266
(718) 297-6464

NorthEastern Native American Assoc.
POB 230266
Hollis NY 11423-0266
(718) 297-6464

NorthEastern Native American Assoc.
114-12 175th St
St Albans NY 11434
(718) 297-7632

NorthEastern Native American Assoc.
163-49 130th Ave # 4A-13E
Jamaica NY 11434
(718) 276-6697

United Eastern Lenape Nation
Big House Peoples Band
98 N High Street
Gahanna OH 43230
(614) 337-9494

OKLAHOMA

Northern Cherokee Tribe
412 7th St
Weatherford OK 73096-4712

PENNSYLVANIA

The Bear Tribe
East Coast Office
POB 199
Devon PA 19333-0199
(215) 993-3344
FAX (215) 993-3345

Big Horn Lenape Nation
Rt 3 Box 240A
Gillett PA 16925

Cherokee of Virginia
4167 Timberline Dr
Allison Park PA 15101
(412) 487-7093

League of Separated Tribes
POB 68
Saltsburg PA 15681-0068

League of Separated Tribes
(LOST)
122 N 4th St
Youngwood PA 15697

Lenape Homeland Band
252 E Summit St
Souderton PA 18964

Mingo Tribe
Box 99 Walnut Valley Farm
Loganville PA 17342-5099

United Eastern Lenape Band
81 E Main St
Norristown PA 19401

United Eastern Munsee Band
Rt 1 Box 1129
Forksville PA 18616

SOUTH CAROLINA

Chicora-Siouan Indian People
700-B Highway 17 N
Surfside Beach SC 29575

Santee Tribe
White Oak Indian Community
Rt 1 Box 34-M
Holly Hill SC 29059

TENNESSEE

Cherokee Nation of Texas
4646 Almo
Memphis TN 38118
(901) 365-1192

The Eighth Arrow Tribe
POB 352
Lafayette TN 37083-0352

Etowah Cherokee Nation
POB 5454
Cleveland TN 37320-5454

5 Nations
690 Crownover Rd
Sherwood TN 37376
(615) 598-0489

The Free Cherokees
615 Jolly Rd
Grandview TN 37337
(615) 365-9965

The Free Cherokees
Chickamaungan Circle
9001 Bill Reed Road # 6
Ooltewah TN 37363
(615) 855-2909

The Original Cherokee Nation
POB 9808
Chattanooga TN 37412-9808
(615) 842-2823

Tennessee Band of Cherokees
405 East Red Bud Drive
Knoxville TN 37920-5139
(615) 577-9559

United Eastern Lenape Band
Middle Division
Rt 1 Box 22
Winfield TN 37892

TEXAS

The Algonquin Confederacy
Iron Thunderhorse # 624391
9601 NE 24th Ave
Clements Unit
Amarillo TX 79107-9601

Cherokee Nation of Texas
505 East McKay
Troup TX 75789
(903) 842-3329

Court of the Golden Eagle
8115 Buford Drive
Dallas TX 75241
(214) 224-6881

The Free Cherokees
Hummingbird Clan
c/o Griffith
5221 Bonita
Dallas TX 75206-6750
(214) 828-0349

Sovereign Cherokee Nation
Tejas
POB 360217
Dallas TX 75336-0217
(214) 288-8538

VERMONT

The Free Cherokees
Tribal Council
77 Main St
Springfield VT 05156
Work: (802) 885-5728
Home: (802) 886-8452

Green Mountain Band of
Cherokees
91 North F Street
Bristol VT 05443
(802) 453-2750

VIRGINIA

The Free Cherokees
Spider Clan
POB 11472
Richmond VA 23230-1472
Home: (804) 358-8345
Work: (804) 355-0529

Ouichita Indians
Rt 3 Box 373
Edinburg VA 22824

Turtle Band of Cherokee
Rt 3 Box 194
Evington VA 24550

WASHINGTON

The Free Cherokees
4 Directions Council
175 Smokey Valley Rd
Toledo WA 98591
(206) 864-4601

QUICK NOTES !

**Information for this page is only available in the Library Edition.

Fred Synder, Director, Consultant

N.A.²I.I.T.C.

North American Native American Indian Information & Trade Center

QUICK NOTES !

**Information for this page is only available in the Library Edition.

Fred Synder, Director, Consultant

N.A.²I.I.T.C.

North American Native American Indian Information & Trade Center

QUICK NOTES !

**Information for this page is only available in the Library Edition.

Fred Synder, Director, Consultant

N.A.²I.I.T.C

North American Native American
Indian Information & Trade Center

QUICK NOTES !

**Information for this page is only available in the Library Edition.

Fred Synder, Director, Consultant

N.A.²I.I.T.C.

North American Native American Indian Information & Trade Center

QUICK NOTES !

**Information for this page is only available in the Library Edition.

Fred Synder, Director, Consultant

N.A.²I.I.T.C.

North American Native American
Indian Information & Trade Center

QUICK NOTES !

**Information for this page is only available in the Library Edition.

Fred Synder, Director, Consultant

N.A.²I.I.T.C

North American Native American Indian Information & Trade Center

QUICK NOTES !

**Information for this page is only available in the Library Edition.

Fred Synder, Director, Consultant

N.A.²I.I.T.C

North American Native American
Indian Information & Trade Center

QUICK NOTES !

**Information for this page is only available in the Library Edition.

QUICK NOTES !

**Information for this page is only available in the Library Edition.

Fred Synder, Director, Consultant

N.A.[2]I.I.T.C

North American Native American
Indian Information & Trade Center

QUICK NOTES !

**Information for this page is only available in the Library Edition.

QUICK NOTES !

**Information for this page is only available in the Library Edition.

Fred Synder, Director, Consultant

N.A.[2]I.I.T.C

North American Native American Indian Information & Trade Center

QUICK NOTES !

**Information for this page is only available in the Library Edition.

Fred Synder, Director, Consultant

N.A.²I.I.T.C. **North American Native American Indian Information & Trade Center**

QUICK NOTES !

**Information for this page is only available in the Library Edition.

QUICK NOTES !

**Information for this page is only available in the Library Edition.

Fred Synder, Director, Consultant

N.A.²I.I.T.C.

North American Native American Indian Information & Trade Center

POPULATION TOTALS FOR AMERICAN INDIANS, ESKIMOS & ALEUTS

The American Indian, Eskimo, or Aleut population exceeded 100,000 in four states in 1990

Oklahoma had the largest American Indian, Eskimo, or Aleut population in 1990 (252,000), followed by California, Arizona, and New Mexico (Figure 1). Seven states had American Indian, Eskimo, or Aleut populations between 50,000 and 100,000: the last six States shown in figure 1 and South Dakota with 51,000. (The term American Indian is used also in this report to include Eskimo and Aleut).

With the exception of New York replacing South Dakota, the 10 states with the largest American Indian populations in 1990 were the same as in 1980. Oklahoma rose to first, exchanging ranks with California, and North Carolina fell from fifth to seventh as Alaska and Washington moved up in rank to fifth and sixth, respectively.

The American Indian population is more concentrated than the total population. A majority lived in 6 states in 1990 compared to 9 states for the total population. Sixty-five percent of the American Indian population resides in the 10 states with the largest American Indian Population compared to 54 percent of the total population in the 10 most populous States.

The largest increase in American Indian population in the 1980-90 decade was in Oklahoma (83,000), followed by Arizona and California (figure 2). Oklahoma accounted for 15 percent of the American Indian population growth in the United States during the decade while the 10 states with the largest American Indian growth together accounted for 61 percent of the national increase.

The American Indian, Eskimo, or Aleut percentage is highest in Alaska. American Indians, Eskimos, and Aleuts represented 15.6 percent of Alaska's population in 1990, down slightly from 16.0 percent in 1980. There were five other States in which this group represented at least 5 percent of the total population in 1990: New Mexico (8.9 percent, up from 8.1 percent in 1980), Oklahoma (8.0, up from 5.6) South Dakota (7.3, up from 6.5), Montana (6.0, up from 4.7), and Arizona (5.6, unchanged from 1980). There were 35 states in which American

Indians represented less than one percent of the population in 1990.

U.S. CENSUS REPORTS

WASHINGTON(AP)-More Native Americans relocated away from their reservations and tribal lands in the last decade, the Census Bureau reported, and many of them are looking for jobs. The 1990 census found 35% of the nations 2 million Native Americans, Eskimos and Aleuts lived in areas governed by tribes. That's down from 37% in 1980.

The Navajo Nation is the most populous in the U.S. with 143,405 Native Americans living there, the Census Bureau said.

The census found 685,464 Native Americans, Eskimos, and Aleuts lived on tribal lands. Nearly 1.3 million lived outside tribal lands and reservations.

The reservations with the largest Native American population, after the Navajo Nation are:

Pine Ridge, SD -	11,182
Fort Apache, AZ -	9,825
Gila River, AZ -	9,116
Papago, AZ -	8,480
Rosebud, SD -	8,043
San Carlos, AZ -	7,110
Zuni Pueblo, NM -	7,073
Hopi, AZ -	7,061
Blackfoot, MT -	7,025

Urban areas with the greatest Native American populations are:

Los Angeles -	87,487
Tulsa -	48,196
New York City -	46,191
Oklahoma City -	45,720
San Francisco -	40,847
Phoenix -	38,017
Seattle - Tacoma -	32,071
Tucson -	20,330
San Diego -	20,066

Since the 1950's more than 200,000 Native Americans have moved from reservations and tribal lands with government assistance.

INDIAN POPULATIONS BY STATE

POPULATION:
According to U.S. Census Bureau Figures, there were 1,959,234 American Indians and Alaska Natives living in the United States in 1990 (1,878,285 American Indians, 57,152 Eskimos, and 23,797 Aleuts). This is a 37.9 percent increase over the 1980 recorded total of 1,420,400. The increase is attributed to improved census taking and more self-identification during the 1990 count. The BIA's 1990 estimate is that almost 950,000 individuals of this total population lived on or adjacent to federal Indian reservations. This is the segment of the total U.S. Indian and Alaska Native Population served by the BIA through formal, on-going relations.

RESERVATIONS:
The number of Indian land areas in the U.S. administered as Federal Indian reservations (reservations, pueblos, rancherias, communities, etc.) total 527. The largest is the Navajo Reservation of some 16 million acres of land in Arizona, New Mexico and Utah. Many of the smaller reservations are less than 1,000 acres with the smallest less than 100 acres. On each reservation, the local governing authority is the tribal government. The states in which the reservations are located have limited powers over them, and only as provided by federal law. On some reservations, however, a high percentage of the land is owned and occupied by non-Indians. Some 140 reservations have entirely tribally-owned land.

TRUST LANDS:
A total of 56.2 million acres of land are held in trust by the United States for various Indian tribes and individuals. Much of this reservation land; however, not all reservations land is trust land. On behalf of the United States, the Secretary of the Interior serves as trustee for such lands with many routine trustee responsibilities delegated to BIA officials.

INDIAN TRIBES:
There are 510 federal recognized tribes in the United States, including about 200 village groups in Alaska. "Federally-recognized" means these tribes and groups have a special, legal relationship to the U.S. Government and its agent, the BIA, depending upon the particular situation of each tribe.

URBAN AND OFF-RESERVATION INDIAN POPULATIONS:
Members of federal tribes who do not reside on their reservations have limited relations with the BIA, Since BIA programs are primarily administered for members of federally-recognized tribes <u>who live on or near</u> reservations.

NON-FEDERAL TRIBES AND GROUPS:
A number of Indian tribes and groups in the U.S. do not have a federally-recognized status, although some are state-recognized. This means they have no relations with the BIA or the programs it operates. A special program of the BIA, however, works with those seeking federal recognition and status. Of 126 petitions for federal recognition received by the BIA since 1978, eight have received acknowledgment of tribal status through the BIA process through action by the U.S. Congress.

 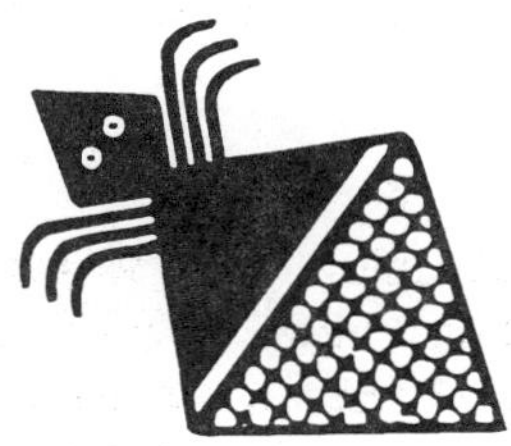

<u>American Indians Today</u> third edition, United States Department of the Interior-Bureau of Indian Affairs, MS 2620-MIB, Washington, DC 20240-0001

AMERICAN INDIAN POPULATION BY STATE

Based on 1990 Census

RANK	STATE	POPULATION
26	Alabama	16,506
5	Alaska	85,698
3	Arizona	203,527
33	Arkansas	12,773
2	California	242,164
17	Colorado	27,776
42	Connecticut	6,654
49	Delaware	2,019
51	District of Columbia	1,466
16	Florida	36,335
31	Georgia	13,348
45	Hawaii	5,099
30	Idaho	13,780
21	Illinois	21,836
34	Indiana	12,720
41	Iowa	7,349
20	Kansas	21,965
44	Kentucky	5,769
25	Louisiana	18,541
43	Maine	5,998
32	Maryland	12,972
36	Massachusetts	12,241
10	Michigan	55,638
12	Minnesota	49,909
39	Mississippi	8,525

Figure 2

AMERICAN INDIAN POPULATION BY STATE

Based on 1990 Census

RANK	STATE	POPULATION
23	Missouri	19,835
13	Montana	47,679
35	Nebraska	12,410
24	Nevada	19,637
48	New Hampshire	2,134
28	New Jersey	14,970
4	New Mexico	134,355
9	New York	62,651
7	North Carolina	81,155
18	North Dakota	25,917
22	Ohio	20,358
1	Oklahoma	252,420
15	Oregon	38,496
29	Pennsylvania	14,733
46	Rhode Island	4,071
40	South Carolina	8,246
11	South Dakota	50,575
37	Tennessee	10,039
8	Texas	65,877
19	Utah	24,283
50	Vermont	1,696
27	Virginia	15,282
6	Washington	81,483
47	West Virginia	2,458
14	Wisconsin	39,387
38	Wyoming	9,479

Figure 2

AMERICAN INDIAN POPULATION BY RANK

Based on 1990 Census

RANK	STATE	POPULATION
1	Oklahoma	252,240
2	California	242,164
3	Arizona	203,527
4	New Mexico	134,355
5	Alaska	85,698
6	Washington	81,483
7	North Carolina	81,155
8	Texas	65,877
9	New York	62,651
10	Michigan	55,638
11	South Dakota	50,575
12	Minnesota	49,909
13	Montana	47,679
14	Wisconsin	39,387
15	Oregon	38,496
16	Florida	36,335
17	Colorado	27,776
18	North Dakota	25,917
19	Utah	24,283
20	Kansas	21,965
21	Illinois	21,836
22	Ohio	20,358
23	Missouri	19,835
24	Nevada	19,637
25	Louisiana	18,541

Figure 1

AMERICAN INDIAN POPULATION BY RANK

Based on 1990 Census

RANK	STATE	POPULATION
26	Alabama	16,506
27	Virginia	15,282
28	New Jersey	14,970
29	Pennsylvania	14,733
30	Idaho	13,780
31	Georgia	13,348
32	Maryland	12,972
33	Arkansas	12,773
34	Indiana	12,720
35	Nebraska	12,410
36	Massachusetts	12,241
37	Tennessee	10,039
38	Wyoming	9,479
39	Mississippi	8,525
40	South Carolina	8,246
41	Iowa	7,349
42	Connecticut	6,654
43	Maine	5,998
44	Kentucky	5,769
45	Hawaii	5,099
46	Rhode Island	4,071
47	West Virginia	2,458
48	New Hampshire	2,134
49	Delaware	2,019
50	Vermont	1,696
51	District of Columbia	1,466

Figure 1

QUESTIONS & ANSWERS -- U.S. CENSUS REPORTS

Why can't tribes and villages do their own count?

The U.S. Constitution states that the census shall be used for apportioning seats in the House of Representatives and Title 13 of the U.S. Code assigns the responsibility to conduct the census to the Census Bureau. This assures that the results will be consistent from area to area. Also, to maintain the strict confidentiality required by law, the Census Bureau uses employees sworn to uphold the confidentiality of the census data.

How does the census bureau count American Indians who have moved off the reservation?

They will receive questionnaires at the housing units or group quarters where they reside or they will be enumerated during special operations conducted in colleges and universities, hospitals, shelters and the like. They will have the opportunity to identify themselves as American Indians and to identify their tribe.

Has the American Indians and Alaska Natives population been under counted in the past?

Limitations of Census Bureau methodology prevent accurate estimates of coverage errors for the American Indian and Alaskan Native population. The Census Bureau does not know that, for a number of reasons, about 2.2 million people were not counted in the last census (about 1 percent). This is called an undercount. Among minority population as a whole, the figure was higher, about 6 percent.

Why do the tribes have to work with the Bureau of Indian Affairs to certify the boundary lines for reservations?

The Federal Office of Management and Budget determined that the BIA is the central custodian of boundary information for all federally-recognized reservations and related trust lands. The OMB directed the Census Bureau to obtain certified boundary maps from the BIA for use in the 1990 decennial census. The OMB also recommended that the

Census Bureau work with appropriate state officials to obtain the boundaries for state-recognized reservations.

Why does the Census Bureau let people identify themselves as American Indians when they may not be?

The concept of race, as used by the Census Bureau, reflects self-identification; it does not denote any clear-cut scientific definition of biological stock.

How should American Indians with multiple tribal affiliations list themselves on the census questionnaire?

American Indians should list the complete name of their enrolled or principal tribe where it asks on the census questionnaire. If a person lists more than one tribe, only the first tribe written will be used.

Footnotes In Census History

- American Indians were first enumerated as a separate group in the 1860 census.
- Indians living in Indian Territory and on reservations were not included in population counts until the 1890 census.
- Special efforts were made to secure complete enumeration of persons with Indian ancestry beginning in the 1910 census.

STATE COMMISSIONS ON INDIAN AFFAIRS

ALABAMA

ALABAMA INDIAN
AFFAIRS COMMISSION
669 S Lawrence St
Montgomery, AL 36130
334-631-1510
334-980-0005
334-631-1514 FAX

ARKANSAS

LIAISON FOR INDIAN
AFFAIRS
PO Box 26
Norman, AR 71960
501-334-2400

ARIZONA

ARIZONA COMMISSION ON
INDIAN AFFAIRS
1645 W Jefferson #127
Phoenix, AZ 85007
602-542-3123
602-542-3223 FAX

CALIFORNIA

NATIVE AMERICAN
HERITAGE COMMISSION
915 Capitol Mall # 364
Sacramento, CA 95814
916-653-4080

COLORADO

COLORADO COMMISSION
ON INDIAN AFFAIRS
130 State Capitol, Rm 144
Denver, CO 80203
303-866-3027
303-866-2003 FAX

CONNECTICUT

D. E. T. OFFICE OF INDIAN
AFFAIRS
Dept Environmental Protection
165 Capitol Ave, Rm 249
Hartford, CT 06106
203-238-3874

DELAWARE

HUMAN RELATIONS
DIVISION
Indian Affairs
820 N French, 4th Fl
Wilmington, DE 19801
302-571-3716

NANTICOKE INDIAN
ASSOC
RT 4 Box 107A
Millsboro, DE 19966
302-945-7022

FLORIDA

FLORIDA GOVERNORS
COUNCIL ON INDIAN
AFFAIRS
PO Box 10449 (32302)
521 E College Ave
Tallahassee, FL 32301
904-488-0730
800-322-9186
904-488-5875 FAX

GEORGIA

STATE OFFICE OF INDIAN
HERITAGE
330 Capitol Ave, SE
Atlanta, GA 30334
404-651-9115

HAWAII

OFFICE OF HAWAIIAN
AFFAIRS
711 Kapiolani Blvd, Suite 500
Honolulu, HI 96813
808-586-3777

DEPT OF HAWAIIAN HOME
LANDS
PO Box 1879
Honolulu, HI 96805
808-586-3806
808-586-6450
808-586-3835 FAX

IDAHO

HUMAN RIGHTS
COMMISSION
450 W State
Boise, ID 83720
208-334-2873

ILLINOIS

None

INDIANA

CIVIL RIGHTS
COMMISSION
32 E Washington #900
Indianapolis, IN 46204
317-232-2612

IOWA

OFFICE OF THE GOVERNOR
Indian Affairs
1001 N Dakota
State Capitol
Ames, IA 50010
515-239-1982 FAX

KANSAS

OFFICE OF THE GOVERNOR
Federal & State Affairs
State Capitol, 2nd Fl
Topeka, KS 66612-1590
913-296-3232
913-296-7973 FAX

KENTUCKY

OFFICE OF THE GOVERNOR
Indian Affairs Liaison
700 Capitol Ave
Frankfort, KY 40601
502-564-2611

LOUISIANA

GOVERNORS COMMISSION
ON INDIAN AFFAIRS
PO Box 44072 (70804)
1885 Wooddale Blvd, #1100
Baton Rouge, LA 70806
504-925-4509
504-925-4508 FAX

MAINE

MAINE INDIAN TRIBAL-
STATE COMMISSION
PO Box 87
Hallowell, ME 04347
207-622-4815

MARYLAND

MARYLAND COMMISSION
ON INDIAN AFFAIRS
100 Community Place
Crownsville, MD 21032
410-514-7651
410-987-4071 FAX

MASSACHUSETTS

MASSACHUSETTS
COMMISSION ON INDIAN
AFFAIRS
1 Ashburton Place #1001
Boston, MA 01208
617-727-6394

MICHIGAN

MICHIGAN COMMISSION
ON INDIAN AFFAIRS
PO Box 30026 (48909)
611 W Ottawa, 3rd Fl
Lansing, MI 48933
517-373-0654

MINNESOTA

MINNESOTA INDIAN
AFFAIRS COUNCIL
1819 Bemidji Ave
Bemidji, MN 56601
218-775-3875

MISSISSIPPI

None

MISSOURI

None

MONTANA

MONTANA INDIAN
COMMISSION
Office Of The Governor
State Capitol Bldg
1424 9th Ave, Rm 202
Helena, MT 59620-0401
406-444-3702
406-444-1350 FAX

NEBRASKA

NEBRASKA INDIAN COMMISSION
State Capitol Bldg
PO Box 94981
Lincoln, NE 68509-4981
402-471-3475
402-471-3392 FAX

NEVADA

NEVADA INDIAN COMMISSION
3100 Mill #206
Reno, NV 89502
702-688-1347
702-688-1113 FAX

NEW HAMPSHIRE

None

NEW JERSEY

ETHNIC ADVISORY COMMISSION INDIAN AFFAIRS
State House C N 300
Trenton, NJ 08625
609-261-4747

NEW MEXICO

OFFICE OF INDIAN AFFAIRS
228 E Palace Ave
LaVilla Bldg
Santa Fe, NM 87501
505-827-6440
505-827-6445 FAX

NEW YORK

NEW YORK SATE DEPT OF INDIAN AFFAIRS
40 N Pearl, State Capitol
Albany, NY 12243
518-474-9319
518-474-9556 FAX

NORTH CAROLINA

NORTH CAROLINA COMMISSION OF INDIAN AFFAIRS
PO Box 27228
325 N Salisbury St #579
Raleigh, NC 27603-5940
919-733-5998
919-733-1207 FAX

NORTH DAKOTA

NORTH DAKOTA INDIAN AFFAIRS COMMISSION
600 E Boulevard 1st Floor, Judicial Wing
Bismarck, ND 58505
701-328-2428
701-328-3000 FAX

OHIO

N/A INDIAN CULTURAL CENTERS
1062 Triplett Blvd
Akron, OH 44306
216-724-1280

OKLAHOMA

OKLAHOMA INDIAN AFFAIRS COMMISSION
4545 N Lincoln #282
Oklahoma City, OK 73105
405-521-3828
405-521-0902 FAX

OREGON

COMMISSION ON INDIAN AFFAIRS
167 State Capitol
Salem, OR 97310
503-986-1067
503-986-1071 FAX

PENNSYLVANIA

PENNSYLVANIA HERITAGE AFFAIRS COMMISSION
309 Forum Bldg
Harrisburg, PA 17120
717-783-8625

RHODE ISLAND

GOVERNOR'S INDIAN POLICY OFFICE
State House Rm 128
Providence, RI 02903

SOUTH CAROLINA

SOUTH CAROLINA COUNCIL ON NATIVE AMERICANS
Office of The Governor
1205 Pendleton St
Columbia, SC 29201
803-734-0395

SOUTH DAKOTA

SOUTH DAKOTA INDIAN AFFAIRS OFFICE
118 W Capitol, Rm 305
Pierre, SD 57501-2017
605-773-3415

TENNESSEE

TENNESSEE COMMISSION ON INDIAN AFFAIRS
401 Church St
Nashville, TN 37243-0459
423-532-0745
423-867-4658

TEXAS

CLIENT SELF-SUPPORT SERVICES
Texas DHS
PO Box 149030, E-311
Austin, TX 78714
512-450-3399
512-450-3017

UTAH

UTAH DIVISION OF INDIAN AFFAIRS
324 S State St, Suite 103
Salt Lake City, UT 84114
801-538-8808
801-538-8809
801-538-8888 FAX

VERMONT

NATIVE AMERICAN COMMISSION
Pavilion Office Building
Office of The Governor
Montpelier, VT 05609
802-828-3333

VIRGINIA

VIRGINIA COUNCIL ON INDIANS
121 S Boggs Ave
Virginia Beach, VA 23452
804-431-2230

WASHINGTON

OFFICE OF INDIAN AFFAIRS
1515 S. Cherry St
Olympia, WA 98504-0909
360-753-2411

WEST VIRGINIA

None

WISCONSIN

D.C.S. TRIBAL PROGRAMS
Health & Social Services
PO Box 7851
Madison, WI 53707
608-266-5862

WYOMING

GOVERNOR'S LIAISON TO THE TRIBES
PO Box 248
Ft Washakie, WY 82514

WYOMING INDIAN AFFAIRS COUNCIL
115 N 5th Street E
Riverton, WY 82501
307-856-9828

Information provided by: Governor's Interstate Indian Council
Montana Indian Commission
Florida's Council on Indian Affairs

NATIONAL INDIAN ORGANIZATIONS

ALASKA

A.F.N.
ALASKA FEDERATION OF NATIVES
1577 C St # 100
Anchorage, AK 99501
907-274-3611
907-276-2989 FAX

...advocate for Alaskan Eskimos, Indians, and Aleuts before Congress...
FOUNDED 1966

I.A.N.A.
INSTITUTE OF ALASKA NATIVE ARTS
455 Third Avenue #117
PO Box 70769
Fairbanks, AK 99707
907-456-7491
907-451-7268 FAX

...to foster the continuation of Alaska Native traditions in crafts, dance, story telling, cultural preservation...
FOUNDED 1976

I.B.C.
INDIGENOUS BROADCAST CENTER, ALASKA PUBLIC RADIO NETWORK
810 E Ninth Avenue
Anchorage, AK 99501
907-263-7409
907-263-7497 FAX

...national training center...for Native participation in the media...
FOUNDED 1995

I.C.C.
INUIT CIRCUMPOLAR CONFERENCE
C/O 1577 C St # 100
Anchorage, AK 99501
907-258-6917

...committed to upholding rights of indigenous peoples across the Arctic rim...
FOUNDED 1966

N.A.R.F.
NATIVE AMERICAN RIGHTS FUND
310 K Street #708
Anchorage, AK 99501
907-276-0680

See Colorado Listing

N.N.N.
NATIONAL NATIVE NEWS
ALASKA PUBLIC RADIO NETWORK
810 E Ninth Avenue
Anchorage, AK 99501
907-263-7409
907-263-7497 FAX

...programing over public radio stations...
FOUNDED

* additional listings in Alaska Section

ARIZONA

A.T.L.A.T.L.
2303 North Central #104
Phoenix, AZ 85004
602-253-2731
602-256-6385 FAX

...promote professional Indian artists thru research, newsletters, exhibits and conferences...
FOUNDED 1977

N.A.^{2}I.I.T.C.
NORTH AMERICAN NATIVE AMERICAN INDIAN INFORMATION AND TRADE CENTER
2830 S Thrasher Avenue
Tucson, AZ 85713
520-622-4900
520-622-4900 FAX

...clearinghouse on North American Indians, Native, First Peoples, organizations, events, media, etc....
FOUNDED 1991

N.C.A.I.E.D.
NAT'L CENTER FOR AMERICAN INDIAN ENTERPRISE DEVLPT
953 E Juanita Avenue
Mesa, AZ 85204
602-831-7524
800-423-0452
602-491-1332 FAX

...promote business and economic development among American Indians and tribes...
FOUNDED 1969

N.C.T.A.
NAVAJO CODE TALKERS ASSOCIATION
PO Box 416
Fort Defiance, AZ 86504
520-729-2728

...association of WWII marines responsible for winning WWII for America...
FOUNDED

N.I.T.R.C.
NATIONAL INDIAN TRAINING AND RESEARCH CENTER
2121 S Mill Avenue #216
Tempe, AZ 85282
602-967-9484
800-528-6425
602-921-1015 FAX

...training and research projects for the social and economic betterment of Indian people...
FOUNDED 1969

N.N.A.C.
NATIONAL NATIVE AMERICAN COOPERATIVE
PO Box 1000
San Carlos, AZ 85550
520-622-4900
520-292-0779

...provides incentives to Native Americans to encourage the preservation of their culture...
FOUNDED 1969

ARKANSAS

A.N.P.R.A.
AMERICAN NATIVE PRESS RESEARCH ASSOCIATION
2801 S University Avenue
Little Rock, AR 72204
501-569-3160

...promote and foster academic research concerning the American native press...
FOUNDED 1984

O.I.W.
ORDER OF THE INDIAN WARS
PO Box 7401
Little Rock, AR 72217
501-225-3996
501-225-5167

...documents and records historical events and places of Native American importance...
FOUNDED 1979

CALIFORNIA

A.I.F.
AMERICAN INDIAN FILM FESTIVAL
333 Valencia Street #212
San Francisco, CA 94103
415-554-0525
415-554-0542 FAX

...dedicated to the preservation of Native Americans in cinema...
FOUNDED

A.I.L.C.
AMERICAN INDIAN LIBERATION CRUSADE
4009 S Halldale Avenue
Los Angeles, CA 90062
213-299-1810

...radio broadcasts...publicizing the physical and spiritual needs of Americans...
FOUNDED 1952

A.I.R.I.
AMERICAN INDIAN RESOURCES INSTITUTE
319 Mac Arthur Blvd
Oakland, CA 94610
510-834-9333
510-834-3836 FAX

..training resources to Indian attorneys, law students...serving the legal need of Indian people...
FOUNDED 1975

I.I.T.C.
INTERNATIONAL INDIAN TREATY COUNCIL
54 Mint Street #400
San Francisco, CA 94103
415-512-1501
415-512-1507 FAX

..formed to draw attention to Indian problems and Indian rights...
FOUNDED 1974

N.N.A.A.P.C.
NATIONAL NATIVE AMERICAN AIDS PREVENTION CENTER
2100 Lake Shore Ave, Suite A
Oakland, CA 94606
510-444-2051
800-283-2437
510-444-1593 FAX

...national clearinghouse on AIDS and the American Indian...
FOUNDED 1987

S.A.I.I.C.
SOUTH AMERICAN INDIAN INFORMATION CENTER
PO Box 28703
Oakland, CA 94604
510-834-4263
510-834-4263 FAX

...collection, desimination, and publication of Indian concerns of Central and South America...
FOUNDED 1983

S.G.F.
THE SEVENTH GENERATION FUND FOR INDIAN DEVELOPMENT
PO Box 4569
Arcata, CA 95521
707-825-7650
707-825-7639 FAX

...provides seed grants and technical assistance in order to increase self-reliance in Indian communities and decrease government dependency...
FOUNDED 1977

COLORADO

A.I.H.C.A.
AMERICAN INDIAN HEALTH CARE ASSOCIATION
1999 Broadway # 2530
Denver, CO 80202-5726
303-295-3757
800-473-1926
303-295-3390 FAX

...to develop, promote, and support culturally sensitive health services...
FOUNDED 1975

A.I.S.E.C.
AMERICAN INDIAN SCIENCE AND EDUCATION CENTER
1085 14th #1506
Boulder, CO 80302
303-492-8658

...provides training and educational opportunities to American Indian college students and tribal leaders...
FOUNDED 1960

A.I.S.E.S.
AMERICAN INDIAN SCIENCE AND ENGINEERING SOCIETY
1085 14th #1506
Boulder, CO 80302
303-492-8658
303-492-7090

...seeks to motivate and encourage students to pursue graduate studies in science, engineering, and technology...
FOUNDED 1977

C.E.R.T.
COUNCIL OF ENERGY RESOURCE TRIBES
1999 Broadway #2600
Denver, CO 80202-5726
303-297-2378
303-296-5690 FAX

...American Indian tribes owning energy resources...(ie) oil, coal, natural gas, uranium, geothermal, oil shale, and other resources to building healthy communities...
FOUNDED 1975

N.A.F.W.S.
NATIVE AMERICAN FISH & WILDLIFE SOCIETY
750 Burbank Street
Broomfield, CO 80020
303-466-1725
303-466-5414 FAX

...to encourage Indian youth to pursue careers in the fish and wildlife fields...
FOUNDED 1982

N.A.R.F.
NATIVE AMERICAN RIGHTS FUND
1506 Broadway
Boulder, CO 80302
303-447-8760
303-443-7776 FAX

...represents Indians and tribes in legal matters of national significance for protection of Indian rights...
FOUNDED 1970

N.I.H.B.
NATIONAL INDIAN HEALTH BOARD
1385 S Colorado Blvd #708A
Denver, CO 80222
303-759-3075

...advocates the improvement of health conditions which affect American Indians...
FOUNDED 1969

DISTRICT OF COLUMBIA

ARROW INCORPORATED
1000 Connecticut Ave NW #1206
Washington, DC 20036
202-296-0685
202-659-4377 FAX

...seeks to help the American Indian achieve a better educational, cultural, and economic standard and provide needy individuals with health care...
FOUNDED 1949

B.C.I.M.
BUREAU OF CATHOLIC INDIAN MISSIONS
2021 "H" St NW
Washington, DC 20006
202-331-8542
202-331-8544 FAX

...to conduct religious, charitable, and education activities at American Indian and Eskimo missions...
FOUNDED 1874

F.C.N.L.
FRIENDS COMMITTEE ON NATIONAL LEGISLATION
245 2nd Street NE
Washington, DC 20002
202-547-6000
202-547-6019 FAX

...reporting on legislative issues affecting Native Americans...
FOUNDED 1877

I.L.R.C.
INDIAN LAW RESOURCE CENTER
601 E St SE
Washington, DC 20003
202-547-2800
202-547-2803 FAX

See Montana Listing
OPENED

MORNINGSTAR FOUNDATION
403 10th Street, SE
Washington, DC 20003
202-547-5531
202-546-6724 FAX

...activities for protection of Native sacred sites and religious freedoms...
FOUNDED 1984

N.A.C.I.E.
NATIONAL ADVISORY COUNCIL ON INDIAN EDUCATION
600 Independence Ave SW
The Portals # 6211
Washington, DC 20202-7556
202-205-8353
202-205-9446 FAX

...advise Congress and secretary of education to education programs affecting Indian children...
FOUNDED 1972

N.A.I.C.C.A.
NATIONAL AMERICAN INDIAN COURT CLERKS ASSOCIATION
1000 Connecticut NW #1206
Washington, DC 20036
202-296-0685
202-659-4377 FAX

...improve the efficiency and provide for the upgrading of the American Indian court system...
FOUNDED 1980

N.A.I.H.C.
NATIONAL AMERICAN INDIAN HOUSING COUNCIL
900 2nd St NE # 220
Washington, DC 20002
202-789-1754
800-284-9165
202-789-1758 FAX

...to provide training and technical assistance to members (of) tribal housing authorities...
FOUNDED 1974

N.A.I.C.J.A.
NATIONAL AMERICAN INDIAN COURT JUDGES ASSOCIATION
1000 Connecticut Ave NW
#1206
Washington, DC 20036
202-296-0685
202-659-4377 FAX

...to improve the American Indian court system throughout the United States...
FOUNDED 1968

N.A.R.F.
NATIVE AMERICANS RIGHTS FUND
1712 N Street NW
Washington, DC 20036
202-785-4166
202-822-0068 FAX

See Colorado Listing
OPENED 1971

N.C.A.I.
NATIONAL CONGRESS OF AMERICAN INDIANS
2010 Massachusetts Ave NW
2nd Fl
Washington, DC 20036
202-446-7767
202-546-3741 FAX

...seeks to protect, conserve, and develop Indian natural and human resources...
FOUNDED 1944

N.I.G.C.
NATIONAL INDIAN GAMING COMMISSION
1850 M St # 250
Washington, DC 20036
202-632-7003

...consortium of American Indian gaming facilities...
FOUNDED 1992

N.I.P.C.
NATIONAL INDIAN POLICY CENTER
2136 Pennsylvania Ave NW
Washington, DC 20052
202-994-1446
202-994-4405 FAX

...commission Native American research and policy analysis...publications, conferences, seminars...
FOUNDED

FLORIDA

N.A.P.N.
NATIVE AMERICAN POLICY NETWORK
Barry University
11300 2nd Ave, NE
Miami, FL 33161
305-899-3473

...foster research in all areas of Native American policy...
FOUNDED 1979

ILLINOIS

A.I.L.A.
AMERICAN INDIAN LIBRARY ASSOCIATION
50 E Huron St
Chicago, IL 60611
312-944-6780

...promoting the development, maintenance and improvement of libraries, library systems, and cultural information services on reservations...
FOUNDED 1979

IOWA

I.Y.A.
INDIAN YOUTH OF AMERICA
609 Badgerow Bldg, Box 2786
Sioux City, IA 51106
712-252-3230

...dedicated to improving the lives of Indian children...
FOUNDED 1978

KANSAS

LEONARD PELTIER DEFENSE COMMITTEE
PO Box 583
Lawrence, KS 66044
913-842-5774

...obtain justice for Leonard Peltier and all political prisoners...
FOUNDED 1978

MARYLAND

N.A.I.W.A.
NORTH AMERICAN INDIAN WOMEN'S ASSOCIATION
9602 Maestor's Lane
Gaithersburg, MD 20879
301-330-0397

...to protect and preserve historic sites related to those (Indian) wars...
FOUNDED 1970

MINNESOTA

A.I.L.A.
AMERICAN INDIAN LIBRARY ASSOC.
C/o Joan Howland
Law Library, Univ. Of Minn.
229 S 19th Ave
Minneapolis, MN 55455
612-625-5526
612-625-3478 FAX

...promoting the development, maintenance and improvement of libraries, library systems, and cultural information services on reservations...
FOUNDED 1979

A.I.M.
AMERICAN INDIAN MOVEMENT
PO Box 13521
Minneapolis, MN 55414
612-721-3914
612-721-7826 FAX

...to encourage self-determination among American Indians...to establish international recognition of American Indian treaty rights...
FOUNDED 1968

I.W.N.
INDIGENOUS WOMEN'S NETWORK
PO Box 174
Lake Elmo, MN 55042
612-770-3861

...increase visibility of the indigenous women of the Western Hemisphere...
FOUNDED 1989

NATIONAL COALITION ON RACISM IN SPORTS & MEDIA
PO Box 13521
Minneapolis, MN 55414
612-721-3914
612-721-7826 FAX

...provide cultural awareness and sensitivity on names affecting Native Americans...
FOUNDED 1994

N.A.J.A.
NATIVE AMERICAN
JOURNALIST ASSOCIATION
1433 E Franklin #11
Minneapolis, MN 55404
612-874-8833
612-874-9007 FAX

...organization of American Indian newspapers, radio, television writers...
FOUNDED 1984

MONTANA

I.A.C.
INTERTRIBAL
AGRICULTURAL COUNCIL
100 W 27th Street #500
Billings, MT 59101
406-259-3525

...consortium of tribes for better management of agricultural resources...
FOUNDED 1987

I.L.R.C.
INDIAN LAW
RESOURCE CENTER
602 N Ewing St
Helena, MT 59601
406-449-2006
406-449-2031 FAX

...works to enable Indian people to survive as distinct peoples with unique cultures...
FOUNDED 1978

T.C.N.C.
TEKAKWITHA
CONFERENCE
NATIONAL CENTER
PO Box 6759
Great Falls, MT 59406
406-727-0147
406-452-9845 FAX

...develope Catholic evangelization...among Native American Ministry...catechesis, liturgy, family life, spirituality...
FOUNDED 1939

NEBRASKA

N.A.P.B.C.
NATIVE AMERICAN
PUBLIC BROADCASTING
CONSORTIUM
PO Box 83111
Lincoln, NE 68501
402-472-3522
402-472-8675

...promoting the production and distribution of high-quality programming by, for and about Native Americans...
FOUNDED 1977

NEW MEXICO

A.I.G.C.
AMERICAN INDIAN
GRADUATE CENTER
4520 Montgomery Blvd NE
#1B
Albuquerque, NM 87109
505-881-4584

...provides scholarship and fellowship assistance for Native American students...at the graduate and professional school...
FOUNDED 1969

A.I.L.A.
AMERICAN INDIAN
LAW CENTER
PO Box 4456 Sta A
Albuquerque, NM 87196
505-277-5462

...to render services, primarily research and training, of a broad legal and governmental nature...
FOUNDED 1967

A.I.P.C.
ALL INDIAN PUEBLO
COUNCIL
PO Box 3256
Albuquerque, NM 87190
505-881-1992

...advocate on behalf of 19 Pueblo Indian Tribes on education, health, social, and economic issues...
FOUNDED 1958

AMERICANS FOR INDIAN
OPPORTUNITY
681 Juniper Hill Road
Bernalillo, NM 87004
505-867-0278
505-867-0441

...promotes economic self-sufficiency for American Indian Tribes and individuals...
FOUNDED 1970

C.I.A.
COALITION FOR INDIAN EDUCATION
8200 Mountain NE # 203
Albuquerque, NM 87110
505-266-6510
505-262-0534 FAX

...ensure that education, health and other programs for Native Americans are effective and outstanding in their performance...
FOUNDED 1987

I.A.C.A.
INDIAN ARTS AND CRAFTS ASSOCIATION
122 La Veta Drive NE #B
Albuquerque, NM 87108
505-265-9149

...to promote, preserve, protect and enhance the understanding of authentic American Indian arts and crafts...
FOUNDED 1974

I.A.I.A.
INSTITUTE OF AMERICAN INDIAN ARTS
PO Box 20007
Santa Fe, NM 87504
505-988-6463

...offers learning opportunities in the arts and crafts to Native American youth...
FOUNDED 1962

N.C.B.I.A.E.
NATIONAL COUNCIL OF BIA EDUCATORS
8009 Mountain Rd Place NE
Albuquerque, NM 87110
505-266-6638

...to protect the rights and interests of teachers in Indian education...
FOUNDED 1967

NATIONAL INDIAN BUSINESS ASSOCIATION
2820 Central Ave SE #D-2
Albuquerque, NM 87106
505-256-0589
505-266-9498

...promote Indian business development...education, communication, advocacy...
FOUNDED 1992

N.I.C.O.A.
NATIONAL INDIAN COUNCIL ON AGING
6400 Uptown Blvd NE #510W
Albuquerque, NM 87110
505-888-3302
505-888-3276 FAX

...to act as a focal point for the ariculation of the needs of the Indian elderly...
FOUNDED 1976

N.I.S.W.A.
NATIONAL INDIAN SOCIAL WORKERS ASSOCIATION
PO Box 27463
Albuquerque, NM 87125

...advocates for the rights of American Indians in social service areas...
FOUNDED 1970

N.I.Y.C.
NATIONAL INDIAN YOUTH COUNCIL
318 Elm SE
Albuquerque, NM 87102
505-247-2251
505-247-4251 FAX

...advocate for Native American youth betterment...
FOUNDED 1961

NEW YORK

A.A.I.A.
ASSOCIATION ON AMERICAN INDIAN AFFAIRS
245 5th Avenue # 1801
New York, NY 10016
212-689-8720
212-685-4692 FAX

...provides legal and technical assistance to Indian Tribes throughout the US...
FOUNDED 1923

A.I.C.F.
AMERICAN INDIAN COLLEGE FUND
21 W 68th Street #1F
New York, NY 10023
212-787-6312
212-496-1050
800-766-FUND

...raises funds to support tribally-controlled colleges...
FOUNDED 1989

M.L.C.I.M.
MARQUETTE LEAGUE FOR THE CATHOLIC INDIAN MISSIONS
1011 1st Avenue
New York, NY 10022
202-371-1000

...provides financial support for the material welfare of Catholic Indian missions in the US...
FOUNDED 1904

NORTH DAKOTA

I.N.M.E.D.
INDIANS INTO MEDICINE
Univ of ND School of
Medical Education
501 N Columbia Road
Grand Forks, ND 58203
701-777-3037
701-777-3277 FAX

...recruit and enroll American Indians into health care at Univ of ND School of Medicine... programs...
FOUNDED 1973

NATIONAL RESOURCE
CENTER ON NATIVE
AMERICAN AGING
Univ of North Dakota
PO Box 7090
Grand Forks, ND 58202
701-777-3766
800-896-7628

...collection and desimination of statistics and resources for senior Native Americans...
FOUNDED 1994

OHIO

C.C.A.I.
CONTINENTAL
CONFEDERATION OF
ADOPTED INDIANS
960 Walhonding Avenue
Logan, OH 43138
614-385-7136

...non-Indians who have been presented with honorary tribal chieftainship...
FOUNDED 1950

OKLAHOMA

AMERICAN INDIAN
INSTITUTE
555 Constitution Ave
Norman, OK 73072
405-325-4127
800-523-7363 xx 4127
405-325-7757 FAX

...training and research...promoting education, training, career development...
FOUNDED 1951

A.A.I.P.
ASSOC OF AMERICAN INDIAN PHYSICIANS
1235 Sovereign Row # C-7
Oklahoma City, OK 73108
405-946-7072
405-946-7621 FAX

..physicians (M.D. or D.O.) of American Indian descent...recruit, policy, recommendation on Indian health concerns...
FOUNDED 1971

C.N.H.S.
CHEROKEE NATIONAL HISTORICAL SOCIETY
PO Box 515
Tahlequah, OK 74465
918-456-6007
918-456-6165 FAX

...preserving the history and tradition of the Cherokee Indian Nation...
FOUNDED 1963

I.D.I.L.
INSTITUTE FOR THE DEVLPT OF INDIAN LAW
2501 N Blackwelder
Oklahoma City, OK 73106
405-521-5188

...a research training center on federal Indian law...
FOUNDED 1971

N.A.C.E.
NATIVE AMERICANS FOR A CLEAN ENVIRONMENT
PO Box 1671
Tahlequah, OK 74465
918-458-4322
918-458-0322 FAX

...devoted to halting contamination of the environment...
FOUNDED 1985

U.N.I.T.Y.
UNITED NATIONAL INDIAN TRIBAL YOUTH INC
PO Box 25042
4010 Lincoln Blvd # 202
Oklahoma City, OK 73125
405-424-3010
405-424-3018 FAX

...empower Indian youth...spiritually, mentally, physically, socially...
FOUNDED 1976

OREGON

A.I.C.A.E.
AMERICAN INDIAN
COUNCIL OF ARCHITECTS
AND ENGINEERS
11675 SW 66th Ave
Portland, OR 97223
503-620-2743

...enhance and improve the professional skills of American Indians in architecture and engineering...
FOUNDED 1976

I.S.T.A.I.A.
INSTITUTE FOR THE
STUDY OF TRADITIONAL
A/I ARTS
PO Box 66124
Portland, OR 97266
503-233-8131

...promotes traditional Native American arts through publications, lectures and seminars...
FOUNDED 1982

I.T.C.
INTERTRIBAL TIMBER
COUNCIL
PO Box C
Warm Springs, OR 97761
503-553-1161

...promote conservation and development of tribal timber resources...
FOUNDED 1977

NATIONAL INDIAN CHILD
WELFARE ASSOCIATION
3611 SW Hood St # 201
Portland, OR 97201
503-222-4044
503-222-4007 FAX

...comprehensive program for Indian children promoting safety, health, self esteem...
FOUNDED 1987

SOUTH DAKOTA

C.H.M.F.
CRAZY HORSE
MEMORIAL FOUNDATION
Avenue of the Chiefs
Crazy Horse, SD 57730
605-673-4681

...seeks completion of the memorial to North American Indians...
FOUNDED 1948

D.W.A.R.N.
DAKOTA WOMEN OF ALL RED NATIONS
PO Box 423
Rosebud, SD 57570

...grass roots organization of American Indian women seeking to advance the Native American Movement...
FOUNDED 1978

INTERTRIBAL BISON COOPERATIVE
520 Kansas City St # 209
Rapid City, SD 57701
605-394-9730
605-394-7742 FAX

...reestablish buffalo herds on Indian lands...
FOUNDED 1992

TENNESSEE

U.S.E.T.
UNITED SOUTH AND EASTERN TRIBES
1101 Kermit Drive #302
Nashville, TN 37217
615-361-8700

...alliance of 19 Eastern tribes...
FOUNDED 1969

TEXAS

AMERICAN INDIAN HORSE REGISTRY
Rt 3 Box 64
Lockhart, TX 78644
512-398-6642

...owners of America Indian horses...collect, record, preserve, pedigrees...
FOUNDED 1961

VIRGINIA

A.I.H.F.
AMERICAN INDIAN HERITAGE FOUNDATION
6051 Arlington Boulevard
Falls Church, VA 22044
202-463-4267

...to inform and educate non-Indians concerning the culture and heritage of the American Indian...

FALMOUTH INSTITUTE
3918 Prosperity Ave # 302
Fairfax, VA 22031
703-641-9100
703-641-1558
800-992-4489

...provide training, technical assistance, consulting...Indians and their communities...
FOUNDED 1980

F.N.D.I.
FIRST NATIONS
DEVELOPMENT INSTITUTE
11917 Main Street
Fredericksburg, VA 22408
703-371-5615
703-371-3505 FAX

...aims to help tribes achieve self-sufficiency...
FOUNDED 1980

N.I.E.A.
NATIONAL INDIAN
EDUCATION ASSOCIATION
121 Oronoco St
Alexandria, VA 22314-2015
703-838-2870

...advocates educational programs to improve the social and economic well-being of American Indians and Alaskan natives...
FOUNDED 1970

WASHINGTON

C.T.E.R.
COUNCIL OF TRIBAL
EMPLOYMENT RIGHTS
19450 Pacific Hwy S #102
Seattle, WA 98188

...provides technical assistance and training to Indian tribes, organizations, and government agencies...
FOUNDED

NATIONAL ASSOC FOR
NATIVE AMERICAN
CHILDREN OF
ALCOHOLICS
1402 3rd Ave # 1110
Seattle, WA 98101
206-467-7686
800-322-5601
206-467-7689 FAX

...promote, awareness, development of resources for Indian children of alcoholics...
FOUNDED 1988

N.W.I.F.C.
NORTHWEST INDIAN
FISHERIES COMMISSION
6730 Martin Way E
Olympia, WA 98506
360-438-1180

...consortium of tribes to reestablish salmon preservation...
FOUNDED 1976

WISCONSIN

H.O.N.O.R.
HONOR OUR NEIGHBORS
ORIGINS & RIGHTS
2647 North Stowell Avenue
Milwaukee, WI 53211
414-963-1324
414-963-0137 FAX

...treaty support group of Native Americans, citizens and church groups...
FOUNDED 1988

* To list your organization send full details including newsletter, phone, fax, zip code, mission statement, and add us to your mailing list:

N.A.^{2}I.I.T.C.
National Organizations Dept.
PO Box 27626
Tucson, AZ 85726
520-292-0779 FAX

QUICK NOTES !

**Information for this page is only available in the Library Edition.

Fred Synder, Director, Consultant

N.A.²I.I.T.C.

North American Native American Indian Information & Trade Center

QUICK NOTES !

**Information for this page is only available in the Library Edition.

Fred Synder, Director, Consultant

N.A.²I.I.T.C.

North American Native American Indian Information & Trade Center

QUICK NOTES !

**Information for this page is only available in the Library Edition.

Fred Synder, Director, Consultant

N.A.²I.I.T.C.

North American Native American
Indian Information & Trade Center

MUSEUMS AND CULTURAL CENTERS (INDIAN OWNED)

ALABAMA

POARCH CREEK INDIAN HERITAGE CENTER
HC 69 Box 85B
Atmore, AL 36502-8940
205-368-9136

ARIZONA

AK-CHIN HIM DAK
Route 2, Box 635
Maricopa, AZ 85239
520-568-2221

COLORADO RIVER INDIAN TRIBES MUSEUM
Rt 1, PO Box 23-B
Parker, AZ 85344
520-669-9211
Founded 1970

FORT MCDOWELL MOHAVE-APACHE CULTURAL CENTER
PO Box 1779
Fountain Hills, AZ 85202
602-837-5121

FORT YUMA QUECHAN MUSEUM
PO Box 11352
Yuma, AZ 85366
619-572-0661

GILA RIVER ARTS AND CRAFTS MUSEUM
PO Box 457
Sacaton, AZ 85247
520-963-3981

HAVASUPAI MUSEUM
PO Box 10
Supai, AZ 86435
520-448-2731

HOO-HOOGAM KI MUSEUM
SALT RIVER PIMA-MARICOPA CULTURAL CENTER
Route 1, Box 216
Scottsdale, AZ 85256
602-941-7379

HOPI CULTURAL CENTER MUSEUM
PO Box 8
Second Mesa, AZ 86043
520-734-6650
Opened 1970

HUALAPAI TRIBAL MUSEUM
PO Box 179
Peach Springs, AZ 86434
520-769-2216

NAVAJO COMMUNITY COLLEGE MUSEUM
NED HATATHLI CULTURAL CENTER
Tsalie, AZ 86556
520-724-3311
520-724-3327 FAX

NAVAJO NATION MUSEUM
PO Box 308/Highway 264
Window Rock, AZ 86515-9000
520-871-6673
Est. 1961

N.A^2.I.I.T.C.
NORTH AMERICAN NATIVE AMERICAN INDIAN INFORMATION AND TRADE CENTER
PO Box 27676
Tucson, AZ 85726
520-622-4900
520-622-4900 FAX
Est. 1990

WHITE MOUNTAIN APACHE CULTURAL CENTER
PO Box 507
Fort Apache, AZ 85926
520-338-4625
Fort built in 1870; center opened 1970, expanded 1976

CALIFORNIA

AGUA CALIENTE CULTURAL MUSEUM
219 S Palm Canyon Dr
Palm Springs, CA 92260-6310
619-325-5673

CHAW SE REGIONAL INDIAN MUSEUM
14881 Pinegrove Volcano Rd
Pine Grove, CA 95665
209-296-7488

CUPA CULTURAL CENTER
Temecula Rd Box 1
Pala, CA 92059

HOOPA TRIBAL MUSEUM
PO Box 1245
Hoopa, CA 95546
916-625-4110

INTERTRIBAL FRIENDSHIP HOUSE/GALLERY
523 E 14th St
Oakland, CA 94606
415-452-1235

KERN VALLEY INDIAN COMMUNITY
NATIVE AMERICAN INTERPRETIVE CENTER
PO Box 168
Kernville, CA 93238
619-376-4240

MALKI MUSEUM INC
Morongo Indian Reservation
11-895 Fields Rd
Banning, CA 92220
714-849-7289
Founded 1964

OWENS VALLEY PAIUTE-SHOSHONE MUSEUM
PO Box 1281
Bishop, CA 93514
619-873-4478

RINCON TRIBAL LIBRARY AND MUSEUM
PO Box 1147
Valley Center, CA 92082

SHERMAN INDIAN MUSEUM
910 Magnolia Ave
Riverside, CA 92503
714-276-6332

SIERRA MONO MUSEUM
PO Box 275
North Fork, CA 93643
206-877-2115

COLORADO

SOUTHERN UTE INDIAN CULTURAL CENTER
17253 Chipeta Dr
Montrose, CO 81402
303-249-3098
303-563-0396 FAX
Founded 1972

UTE MOUNTAIN TRIBAL PARK/MUSEUM
General Delivery
Towaoc, CO 81334

CONNECTICUT

MASHANTUCKET PEQUOT TRIBAL MUSEUM
PO Box 3060
Ledyard, CT 06339-3060
203-536-7200

TANTAQUIDGEON INDIAN MUSEUM
1819 New London Turnpike
Uncasville, CT 06382
203-848-9145

DELAWARE

NANTICOKE INDIAN ASSOC MUSEUM
Route 4, Box 170B
Millsboro, DE 19966
302-847-3544

FLORIDA

MICCOUSUKEE CULTURAL CENTER
PO Box 440021
Tamiami Station
Miami, FL 33144
305-223-8388

SEMINOLE TRIBAL MUSEUM
5221 N Orient Rd
Tampa, FL 33610

SEMINOLE TRIBAL MUSEUM
3240 N 64th Ave
Hollywood, FL 33042
305-967-8997

GEORGIA

TAMA MUSEUM
Lower Creek Muskogee Tribe
Rt 2, Box 370
Whigham, GA 31797
912-762-3165

HAWAII

LANA'I CULTURAL AND HERITAGE CENTER
PO Box 774
Lana'i City, HI 96763
808-565-4545

IDAHO

SHOSHONE-BANNOCK TRIBAL MUSEUM
PO Box 306
Fort Hall, ID 83203
208-237-9791
208-237-0797 FAX

INDIANA

NATIVE AMERICAN MUSEUM
5050 E Popular St
Terre Haute, IN 47803

KANSAS

INDIAN CENTER MUSEUM
MID-AMERICA ALL-INDIAN CENTER
650 N Seneca
Wichita, KS 67203
316-262-5221
Founded 1975

KAW INDIAN MISSION
500 N Mission
Council Grove, KS 66846
316-767-5410

LOUISIANA

COUSHATTA INDIAN CULTURAL CENTER
PO Box 818
Elton, LA 70582
318-584-2262

TUNICA-BILOXI REGIONAL INDIAN CENTER & MUSEUM
PO Box 31
Marksville, LA 71351
318-253-8174

MAINE

PENOBSCOT NATIONAL HISTORICAL SOCIETY
PO Box 313
Indian Island, ME 04468
207-827-6545

WABANAKI MUSEUM AND RESOURCE CENTER
Pleasant Point Reservation
PO Box 295
Perry, ME 04667
207-853-2551

MARYLAND

PISCATAWAY INDIAN MUSEUM
AMERICAN INDIAN CULTURAL CENTER
PO Box 1024
White Plains, MD 20695
301-372-1932

MASSACHUSETTS

WAMPANOAG INDIAN PROGRAM OF PLIMOTH PLANTATION
PO Box 1620
Plymouth, MA 02360
617-746-1622

WAMPANOAG TRIBE OF GAY HEAD
RR 1 Box 137
Gay Head, MA 02535-9701
617-645-9265

MICHIGAN

MUSEUM OF OJIBWA CULTURE
500 N State St
St Ignace, MI 49781

SAGINAW CHIPPEWA INDIAN TRIBE
Facility Task Force Planning Office
913 E Pickard, Ste J
Mt Pleasant, MI 48858
517-775-3232

MINNESOTA

LEECH LAKE HERITAGE SITES
RR 3 Box 100
Cass Lake, MN 56633
218-335-8200
218-335-8309 FAX

MILLE LACS INDIAN MUSEUM
HCR 67 Box 194
Onamia, MN 56359

RED LAKE NATIONS TRIBAL ARCHIVES AND LIBRARY
PO Box 297
Red Lake, MN 56671
218-679-3341

LOWER SIOUX AGENCY HISTORY CENTER
RR 1 Box 125
Morton, MN 56270
507-697-6321

UPPER MIDWEST INDIAN CULTURAL CENTER AT PIPESTONE NATIONAL MONUMENT
PO Box 727
Pipestone, MN 56164
507-825-5464

MISSISSIPPI

CHOCTAW MUSEUM OF SOUTHERN INDIANS
PO Box 6010
Philadelphia, MS 39350
601-656-5251

MONTANA

CROW TRIBE HISTORICAL AND CULTURAL COMMISSION
PO Box 173
Crow Agency, MT 59022
406-638-2328

FLATHEAD INDIAN MUSEUM
PO Box 460
St Ignatius, MT 59865
406-745-2951

FORT PECK TRIBAL MUSEUM
PO Box 115
Poplar, MT 59255
406-768-5155

KOOTENAI CULTURE PROGRAM
PO Box 155
Elmo, MT 59915
406-849-5541
406-849-5888 FAX

MUSEUM OF THE PLAINS INDIAN
Box 400, US Hwy 89 & 2
Browning, MT 59417
406-338-2230
Federal with Indian Staffing

NORTHERN CHEYENNE TRIBAL MUSEUM
PO Box 128
Lame Deer, MT 59043

PEOPLE'S CENTER SQELIX'W/AQLSMAKNIK CULTURAL CENTER
Box 278
Pablo, MT 59855
406-675-4800
406-675-2806 FAX

NEBRASKA

PLAINS INDIAN CULTURAL CENTER
1100 Military Rd
Lincoln, NE 68508-1089
402-438-5236
402-438-5236 FAX

NEVADA

STEWART INDIAN MUSEUM ASSOCIATION
5366 Snyder Ave
Carson City, NV 89701
702-882-1808

NEW MEXICO

ACOMA TOURIST AND VISITATION CENTER
PO Box 309
Pueblo of Acoma, NM 87034
505-252-1139
800-747-0181
Founded 1978

INDIAN PUEBLO CULTURAL CENTER INC
2401 12th St NW
Albuquerque, NM 87102
505-242-4943/843-7270
Founded 1976

INSTITUTE OF AMERICAN INDIAN ARTS MUSEUM
PO Box 20007
Santa Fe, NM 87504
505-988-6603
Founded 1962

JICARILLA ARTS AND CRAFTS MUSEUM
PO Box 507
Dulce, NM 87528
505-759-3242

MESCALERO APACHE CULTURAL CENTER/MUSEUM
PO Box 176
Mescalero, NM 88340
505-671-4495

A:SHIWI AWAN, ZUNI ECO-MUSEUM AND HERITAGE CENTER
PO Box 339 Hwy 53
Zuni, NM 87327
505-782-4814/4403
Opened 1990

PICURIS PUEBLO MUSEUM
PO Box 228
Penasco, NM 87553

POEH CENTER
Pueblo of Pojoaque
Rt 11 Box 27E
Santa Fe, NM 87501
505-455-3334

SAN IDELFONSO PUEBLO MUSEUM
Route 5 Box 315-A
Santa Fe, NM 87501
505-455-2424

SANTA CLARA PUYE CLIFFS
PO Box 580
Espanola, NM 87532
505-753-7326

NEW YORK

AKWESASNE MUSEUM
St Regis Mohawk Reservation
Route 37
Hogansburg, NY 13655
518-358-2272
Founded 1972

GANONDAGAN STATE HISTORIC SITE
Box 239
Victor, NY 14564
716-924-5848
Founded 1972

IROQUOIS INDIAN MUSEUM
PO Box 7 Caverns Rd
Howes Cave, NY 12092
518-234-8319
Founded 1980

MOHAWK-CAUGHANWAGA MUSEUM
Rt 5 Box 554
Fonda, NY 12068
518-853-3678

NATIVE AMERICAN CENTER FOR THE LIVING ARTS
25 Rainbow Mall
Niagara Falls, NY 14303
716-284-2427
Founded 1970

SENECA INDIAN HISTORICAL SOCIETY
12199 Brant Reservation Rd
Irving, NY 14081

SENECA-IROQUOIS
NATIONAL MUSEUM
Allegany Indian Reservation
PO Box 442
Broad St Ext
Salamanca, NY 14779
716-945-1738
Founded 1977

SHINNECOCK NATION
CULTURAL CENTER
PO Box 59
Southampton, NY 11969
516-283-1643 / 516-287-4923

SIX NATIONS INDIAN
MUSEUM
HC 1 Box 10
Onchiota, NY 12968
518-891-0769
Founded 1955

NORTH CAROLINA

MUSEUM OF THE
CHEROKEE INDIAN
PO Box 770A, US Hwy 441 N
Cherokee, NC 28719
704-497-3481
Founded 1948

NATIVE AMERICAN
RESOURCE CENTER
Pembroke State University
Pembroke, NC 28372
910-521-4214

NORTH CAROLINA INDIAN
CULTURAL CENTER
PO Box 2410
Pembroke, NC 28372
910-521-2433
910-521-0394 FAX

NORTH DAKOTA

STANDING ROCK
RESERVATION MUSEUM
PO Box D
Fort Yates, ND 58538
701-854-7231

THREE AFFILIATED TRIBES
MUSEUM
Fort Berthold Reservation
PO Box 220
New Town, ND 58763
701-627-4781

TURTLE MOUNTAIN
CHIPPEWA HERITAGE
CENTER
Box 257
Belcourt, ND 58316
701-477-6451
Founded 1985

OKLAHOMA

AMERICAN INDIAN
HERITAGE CENTER
Harwelden
2210 S Main
Tulsa, OK 74114
918-585-8444
918-585-5554 FAX

APACHE TRIBE OF
OKLAHOMA
PO Box 1220
Anadarko, OK 73005
405-247-9493

ATALOA LODGE MUSEUM
BACONE COLLEGE
MUSEUM
East Shawnee
Muskogee, OK 74402
918-683-4581
Founded 1932

CADDO TRIBAL MUSEUM
PO Box 487
Binger, OK 73009
405-656-2344

CHEROKEE NATIONAL
MUSEUM
TSA-LA-GI CHEROKEE
HERITAGE CENTER
PO Box 515
Tahlequah, OK 74465
918-456-6007
Founded 1963

CHEYENNE CULTURAL
CENTER
RR 1 Box 3130
Clinton, OK 73601
405-323-6224

CHICKASAW COUNCIL
HOUSE MUSEUM
PO Box 717
Tishomingo, OK 73460
405-371-3351

CHICKASAW NATION
CULTURAL CENTER
PO Box 1548
Ada, OK 74820
405-436-2603

CHOCTAW NATION
MUSEUM
Route 1 Box 105AAA
Tuskahoma, OK 74574
918-569-4465

CITIZEN BAND
POTAWATOMI TRIBAL
MUSEUM
1901 S Gordon Cooper Dr
Shawnee, OK 74801
405-275-3121

CREEK COUNCIL HOUSE
MUSEUM
Creek Council House
Okmulgee, OK 74447
918-756-2324
Founded 1923
Municipal with Indian Staff

COMANCHE CULTURAL
CENTER
PO Box 908
Lawton, OK 73502
405-429-1990

COMANCHE CULTURAL
CENTER MUSEUM
PO Box 606
Cache, OK 73527

DELAWARE TRIBAL MUSEUM
PO Box 369
Anadarko, OK 73005

FIVE CIVILIZED TRIBES MUSEUM
Agency Hill, Honor Heights Dr
Muskogee, OK 74401
918-683-1701

FORT SILL APACHE TRIBAL MUSEUM
Route 2 Box 121
Apache, OK 73006
405-588-2298

INDIAN CITY USA
Box 695, Hwy 8
Anadarko, OK 73005
405-247-5661

KIOWA TRIBAL MUSEUM & RESOURCE CENTER
PO Box 369
Carnegie, OK 73015
405-654-2300

NATIONAL HALL OF FAME FOR FAMOUS AMERICAN INDIANS
PO Box 808 Hwy 62
Anadarko, OK 73005
405-247-5795

NE OKLAHOMA NATIVE AMERICAN CULTURAL CENTER
PO Box 1308
Miami, OK 74355
918-542-1235

OSAGE TRIBAL MUSEUM
PO Box 779
Pawhuska, OK 74056
918-287-2495

PAWNEE TRIBAL MUSEUM
PO Box 470
Pawnee, OK 74058
918-762-3621

POTAWATOMI INDIAN NATION ARCHIVES AND MUSEUM
Route 5 Box 151
Shawnee, OK 74801

SAC & FOX TRIBAL RV PARK AND MUSEUM
Route 2 PO Box 246
Stroud, OK 74079
918-968-3526

SEMINOLE NATION MUSEUM
Box 1532
524 Wewoka S
Wewoka, OK 74884
405-257-5580

SOUTHERN PLAINS INDIAN MUSEUM
PO Box 749
Anadarko, OK 73005
405-247-6221
Federal with Indian staffing

TONKAWA TRIBAL MUSEUM
PO Box 95
Tonkawa, OK 74653
405-628-2561

WHITE HAIR MEMORIAL
PO Box 185
Ralston, OK 74650

WICHITA TRIBAL
CULTURAL CENTER
PO Box 729
Anadarko, OK 73005
405-247-2425

OREGON

COQUILLE INDIAN TRIBE
PO Box 1435
Coos Bay, OR 97420
503-267-4587
503-269-2573 FAX

MUSEUM AT WARM
SPRINGS
PO Box C
Warm Springs, OR 97761
503-553-3331

UMATILLA INDIAN
RESERVATION MUSEUM
PO Box 638
Pendleton, OR 97801
503-276-3165

PENNSYLVANIA

LENNI LENAPE
HISTORICAL SOCIETY
Rt 2, Fish Hatchery Rd
Allentown, PA 18103-9801
610-797-2121

NATIVE AMERICAN
CULTURAL CENTER
927 N 6th St
Philadelphia, PA 19123

UNITED INDIANS OF
DELAWARE
VALLEY/MUSEUM
225 Chestnut St
Philadelphia, PA 19106
215-574-9020

RHODE ISLAND

TOMAQUAG INDIAN
MEMORIAL MUSEUM
Summit Rd
Exeter, RI 02822
401-539-7213

SOUTH DAKOTA

BUECHEL MEMORIAL
LAKOTA MUSEUM
PO Box 499
St Francis, SD 57572
605-747-2361
Church-affiliated with Indian
staffing
Founded 1915

HARRY V JOHNSTON
AMERICAN INDIAN
CULTURAL CENTER
Cheyenne River Reservation
Box 590
Eagle Butte, SD 57625
605-964-2542

HERITAGE CENTER
Red Cloud Indian School
Pine Ridge, SD 57770
605-857-5491

OGLALA SIOUX MUSEUM
Wounded Knee, SD 57794

OGLALA SIOUX
COMMUNITY COLLEGE
RESOURCE CENTER
PO Box 490
Kyle, SD 57752
605-455-2321

SINTE GLESKA COLLEGE
AHIANPA
PO Box 490
Rosebud, SD 57570
605-747-2263

SIOUX INDIAN MUSEUM
PO Box 1504
Rapid City, SD 57709
605-348-0557

YANKTON SIOUX MUSEUM
Box 244
Marty, SD 57361
605-384-3804

TENNESSEE

SEQUOYAH BIRTHPLACE
MUSEUM
PO Box 69 Citico Rd
Vonore, TN 37885
615-884-6246

TEXAS

ALABAMA-COUSHATTA
TRIBAL MUSEUM
Route 3 Box 640
Livingston, TX 77351
409-563-4391
800-444-3507
Founded 1965

TIGUA PUEBLO MUSEUM
Texas Indian Reservation
119 S Old Pueblo Rd
El Paso, TX 79917
915-859-7913

UTAH

UTE TRIBAL MUSEUM
PO Box 190
Fort Duchesne, UT 84026
801-722-4992
801-722-2083 FAX
Founded 1976

VERMONT

ABENAKI CULTURAL
CENTER
HCR 1 Box 110
Morrisville, VT 05661
802-888-5605

VIRGINIA

AMERICAN INDIAN
HERITAGE
FOUNDATION/MUSEUM
6051 Arlington Blvd
Falls Church, VA 22044
703-237-7500

MATTAPONI INDIAN
MUSEUM
Mattaponi Indian Reservation
West Point, VA 23181
804-769-2194

MONACAN INDIAN
ACESTRIAL MUSEUM
Rt 6 Box 26 Kenmore Rd
Amherst, VA 24521
804-929-6929

PAMUNKEY INDIAN
VILLAGE & CULTURAL
MUSEUM
Rt 1 PO Box 217-AA
King William, VA 23806
804-843-4792

WASHINGTON

COLVILLE
CONFEDERATED TRIBES
MUSEUM
PO Box 233
Coulee Dam, WA 99116
509-634-4711

COQUILLE INDIAN TRIBE
1400 Talbot Rd S Ste 100
Renton, WA 98055-4282

DAYBREAK STAR ARTS
CENTER/MUSEUM
PO Box 99253
Seattle, WA 98199
206-285-4425

LUMMI INDIAN BUSINESS
COUNCIL
2616 Kwina Rd
Bellingham, WA 98226-9298
360-734-8180
360-647-6234 FAX

MAKAH CULTURAL AND
RESEARCH CENTER
PO Box 160
Neah Bay, WA 98357
360-645-2711
360-645-2711 FAX

PUYALLUP TRIBAL
MUSEUM
2215 E 22nd St
Tacoma, WA 98404
206-597-6479

QUILEUTE TRIBE
PO Box 279
LaPush, WA 98350
360-374-6163
360-374-6311 FAX

SPOKANE TRIBAL
MUSEUM
Box 100
Wellpinit, WA 99040
509-258-4581

SKOKOMISH MUSEUM
N 80 Tribal Center Rd
Shelton, WA 98584
360-426-4232

STEILACOOM CULTURAL
CENTER
1515 Lafayette
Steilacoom, WA 98388
206-584-6308

SUQUAMISH MUSEUM
PO Box 498
15838 Sandy Hook NE
Suquamish, WA 98392
360-598-3311
Founded 1983

TULALIP TRIBE MUSEUM
6700 Totem Beach Rd
Marysville, WA 98270
360-653-4585

YAKAMA NATION MUSEUM
PO Box 151
Toppenish, WA 98948
509-865-2800
509-865-4664 FAX
Founded 1980

WISCONSIN

BAD RIVER HERITAGE CENTER
PO Box 39
Odanah, WI 54861
715-682-9119

CHIEF OSHKOSH MUSEUM
7631 Egg Harbor Rd
Egg Harbor, WI 54209
414-868-3240

LAC DE FLAMBEAU CHIPPEWA MUSEUM & CULTURE CENTER
PO Box 804
Lac de Flambeau, WI 54538
715-588-3333

MENOMINEE LOGGING CAMP MUSEUM
PO Box 910
Keshena, WI 54135
715-799-3757
715-799-4525 FAX

ARVID E MILLER MEMORIAL LIBRARY MUSEUM
Stockbridge-Munsee Historical Society
Route 1 Box 300
Bowler, WI 54416
715-793-4270

ONEIDA NATION MUSEUM
PO Box 365
Oneida, WI 54155
414-869-2768

RED CLIFF ARTS AND CRAFTS CULTURAL CENTER
PO Box 529
Bayfield, WI 54814
715-779-5609

WYOMING

ARAPAHO CULTURAL MUSEUM
Wind River Reservation
PO Box 127
Ethete, WY 82520
307-332-6120

NORTH AMERICAN INDIAN HERITAGE CENTER
PO Box 275
Saint Stephens, WY 82624
307-856-6688

PLAINS INDIAN MUSEUM
BUFFALO BILL
HISTORICAL CENTER
720 Sheridan Ave
PO Box 1000
Cody, WY 82414
307-587-4771
Founded 1917

SHOSHONE TRIBAL
CULTURAL CENTER
PO Box 903
Fort Washakie, WY 82514
307-332-3532

Fred Synder, Director, Consultant

N.A.²I.I.T.C.

North American Native American
Indian Information & Trade Center

Assistance provided by: Smithsonian Institution
Center for Museum Studies
North American Indian Information
and Trade Center

UNITED STATES

MUSEUMS AND CULTURAL CENTERS (NON-INDIAN OWNED AND OPERATED)

ARKANSAS

KA-DO-HA INDIAN VILLAGE
PO Box 669, Rt 1
Murfreesboro, AR 71958
501-285-3736

ARIZONA

CANYON DE CHELLY NATIONAL MONUMENT
PO Box 588
Chinle, AZ 86503
520-674-5436

CASA GRANDE RUINS NATIONAL MONUMENT
PO Box 518
Coolidge, AZ 85228
602-723-3172

THE HEARD MUSEUM
22 E Monte Vista Rd
Phoenix, AZ 85004
602-252-8840

MONTEZUMA CASTLE NATIONAL MONUMENT
PO Box 219
Camp Verde, AZ 86322
520-567-3322

MUSEUM OF NORTHERN ARIZONA
RT 4 , Box 720
Flagstaff, AZ 86001
520-774-5211

PUEBLO GRANDE MUSEUM
4619 E Washington
Phoenix, AZ 85034
602-275-3452

TUZIGOOT NATIONAL MONUMENT
PO Box 68
Clarkdale, AZ 86324
520-634-5564

CALIFORNIA

CALIFORNIA STATE INDIAN MUSEUM
2618 K ST
Sacramento, CA 95816
916-324-0971

CHARLES W BOWERS MEMORIAL MUSEUM
2002 N Main
Santa Ana, CA 92706
714-972-1900

EASTERN CALIFORNIA MUSEUM
200 South H
Independence, CA 93526
619-878-2411

MARIN MUSEUM OF THE AMERICAN INDIAN
2200 Novato Blvd
Novato, CA 94947
415-897-4064

NATURAL HISTORY MUSEUM
900 Exposition Blvd
Los Angeles, CA 90007
213-744-3382

SAN DIEGO MUSEUM OF MAN
1350 El Prado, Balboa Park
San Diego, CA 92101

SOUTHWEST MUSEUM
234 Museum Dr
Los Angeles, CA 90042
213-221-2164

COLORADO

DENVER ART MUSEUM
100 W 14th Ave Pky
Denver, Co 80204
303-575-2256

DENVER MUSEUM OF NATURAL HISTORY
City Park
Denver, CO 80205
303-370-6357

MESA VERDE NATIONAL PARK MUSEUM
Mesa Verde, CO 81330
303-529-4475

CONNECTICUT

AMERICAN INDIAN ARCHAEOLOGICAL INSTITUTE
PO Box 260, Curtis Rd
Washington, CT 06793
203-868-0518

DISTRICT OF COLUMBIA

MUSEUM STUDIES/ SMITHSONIAN
Office of Museum Programs
Arts & Sci Bldg 2235, Stop 427
Washington, DC 20560
202-357-3101

NATIONAL MUSEUM OF AMERICAN HISTORY
American Indian Program
Smithsonian Instit, Rm 5119
Washington, DC 20560
202-357-1534

NATIONAL ANTHROPOLOGICAL ARCHIVES
Smithsonian Institution
Washington, DC 20560
202-357-1976

NATIONAL MUSEUM OF NATURAL HISTORY
-Nation Museum of Man
NHB 112, Smithsonian Instit.
Washington, DC 20560
202-357-4760

SMITHSONIAN INSTITUTION
Native American Museums Program
Arts & Industries Bldg.
Rm. 2235
Washington, DC 20560
202-357-3101

US DEPT OF THE INTERIOR MUSEUM
18th & C St, NW
Washington, DC 20240
202-343-2743

FLORIDA

INDIAN TEMPLE MOUND MUSEUM
139 Miracle Strip Pky
Fort Walton Beach, FL 32548
904-243-6521

ILLINOIS

CAHOKIA MOUNDS ST. HISTORIC
Site & Museum
7850 Collinsville Rd
East St. Louis, IL 62201
618-344-5268

FIELD MUSEUM OF NATURAL HISTORY
Roosevelt Rd at Lake Shore Dr
Chicago, Il 60605
312-922-9410

HAUBERG INDIAN MUSEUM
Black Hawk State Park
Rock Island, IL 61201
309-788-9536

NEWBERRY LIBRARY
Ctr For History of American Indian
60 W Walton
Chicago, IL 60610
312-943-9090

INDIANA

MUSEUM OF INDIAN HERITAGE
500 W Washington
Indianapolis, IN 46204
317-293-4488

NATIVE AMERICAN MUSEUM
Terre Haute Parks Dept
5050 E Poplar St
Terre Haute, IN 47803

THE POTAWATOMI MUSEUM
PO Box 486, N Wayne & City Limits
Fremont, IN 46737

MASSACHUSETTS

PEABODY MUSEUM OF ARCHAEOLOGY & ETHNOLOGY
11 Divinity Ave
Cambridge, MA 02138
617-495-2248

WAMPANOAG INDIAN
PROGRAM OF PLYMOUTH
PLANTATION
PO Box 1620
Plymouth, MA 02360
617-746-1622

MISSISSIPPI

THE GRAND VILLAGE
OF NATCHEZ INDIANS
400 Jefferson Davis Blvd
Natchez, MS 39120
601-446-6502

MONTANA

CUSTER BATTLEFIELD
NATIONAL MONUMENT
PO Box 39
Crow Agency, MT 59022
406-638-2621

MUSEUM OF THE PLAINS
INDIAN
PO Box 400, Hwy 89
Browning, MT 59417
406-338-2230

NORTH CAROLINA

INDIAN MUSEUM OF THE
CAROLINAS
607 Turnpike Rd
Laurinburg, NC 28352
919-276-5880

SCHIELE MUSEUM
REFERENCE LIBRARY
& Cntr for SE N/A Studies
1500 E Garrison Blvd
Gastonia, NC 28053
704-865-6131

TOWN CREEK INDIAN
MOUND ST. HISTORIC
SITE
Rt 3, Box 50
Mt. Gilead, NC 27306
919-439-6802

NEVADA

NEVADA STATE MUSEUM
Carson City, NV 89701

NORTHEASTERN NEVADA
MUSEUM
1515 Idaho
Elko, NV 89801

NEW MEXICO

AZTEC RUINS NATIONAL
MONUMENT
PO Box 640
Aztec, NM 87410
505-334-6174

MILLICENT ROGERS
MUSEUM
PO Box A
Taos, NM 87571
505-758-2462

RED ROCK MUSEUM
PO Box 328, Red Rock St Park
Church Rock, NM 87311
505-722-6196

THE WHEEL WRIGHT MUSEUM OF AMERICAN INDIAN
704 Camino Lejo
Sante Fe, NM 87502
505-982-4636

NEW YORK

MUSEUM OF THE AMERICAN INDIAN
1 Bowling Green
New York, NY 10032
212-283-2420

OKLAHOMA

BACONE COLLEGE MUSEUM
Ataloa Art Lodge
East Shawnee
Muskogee, OK 74403
918-683-4581

SOUTH DAKOTA

AMERICAN INDIAN CULTURE
Research Center
Blue Cloud Abbey
Marvin, SD 57251
605-432-5528

FATHER BUECHEL MEMORIAL
Lakota Museum
PO Box 499
St. Francis, SD 57572
605-747-2361

INDIAN MUSEUM OF NORTH AMERICA
Avenue of the Chiefs
The Black Hills
Crazy Horse, SD 57730
605-573-4681

TENNESSEE

C.H. NASH MUSEUM-CHUCALISSA
1987 Indian Village Dr
Memphis, TN 38109
901-785-3160

WASHINGTON

LELOOSKA FAMILY MUSEUM
5618 Lewis River Rd
Ariel, WA 98603

MUSEUM OF NATIVE AMERICAN CULTURES
E 200 Cataldo
Spokane, WA 99220
509-324-4550

WASHINGTON STATE MUSEUM
Thomas Burke Memorial
University of Washington
Seattle, WA 98195
206-543-5590

WISCONSIN

WISCONSIN PUBLIC INDIAN MUSEUM
PO Box 441
Wisconsin Dells, WI 53965
608-254-2268

WYOMING

NORTH AMERICAN INDIAN
HERITAGE CENTER
PO Box 275
St. Stephens, WY 82624
307-856-6688

PLAINS INDIAN MUSEUM
720 Sheridan Ave
Cody, WY 82414
307-587-4771

Fred Synder, Director, Consultant
N.A.²I.I.T.C
North American Native American
Indian Information & Trade Center

UNITED STATES

INDIAN HEAD START PROGRAMS

PROJECT HEAD START ADMIN.
CHILDREN, YOUTH AND FAMILIES DEPT.
HEALTH & HUMAN SERVICES
330 C ST SW ROOM 2231 (ZIP 20201)
PO BOX 1182
WASHINGTON, DC 20013
202-205-8437
202-401-5916 FAX

ARIZONA

*Chinle Head Start
PO Box 797
Chinle, AZ 86503
520-674-2141
520-674-2147 FAX

Cocopah Head Start
PO Box Bin G
Somerton, AZ 85350
520-627-2811
520-627-8626 FAX

Colorado River Head Start
Route 1 Box 39-X
Parker, AZ 85344
520-662-4311
520-662-4322 FAX

*Fort Defiance Head Start
PO Drawer 260
Fort Defiance, AZ 86504
520-729-4221
520-729-4213 FAX

Gila River Head Start and Disabilities Program
PO Box A
Sacaton, AZ 85247
520-562-3423
520-562-3422 FAX

Havasupai Head Start
PO Box 10
Supai, AZ 86435
520-448-2821
520-448-2551

Hopi Head Start
PO Box 123
Kykotsmovi, AZ 86039
520-734-2441
520-734-2435 FAX

Hualapai Head Start
PO Box 119
Peach Springs, AZ 86434-0119
520-769-2399
520-769-2343 FAX

* NAVAJO DEPT OF HEAD START

NAVAJO DEPT OF HEAD START*
Div. Of Child Development
PO Drawer 2919
Window Rock, AZ 86515
520-871-6902
520-871-7866 FAX

*Alamo Head Start
PO Box 907
Magdalena, NM 87825
505-854-2694
505-854-2545 FAX

*Chinle Head Start
PO Box 797
Chinle, AZ 86503
520-674-2141
520-674-2147 FAX

*Crownpoint Head Start
PO Box 2079
Crownpoint, NM 87313
505-786-5841
505-786-5502 FAX

*Fort Defiance Head Start
PO Drawer 260
Fort Defiance, AZ 86504
520-729-4221
520-729-4213 FAX

*Ramah Head Start
PO Box 37
Pine Hill, NM 87357
505-775-3355

*Shiprock Head Start
PO Drawer 310
Shiprock, NM 87420
505-368-5146
505-368-4599 FAX

Pascua Yaqui Tribal Head Start
7474 S Camino de Oeste
Tucson, AZ 85746
520-883-5189
520-883-5014 FAX

Quechan Tribal Head Start
PO Box 11352
Yuma, AZ 85366
619-572-0264
619-572-2102 FAX

Salt River Pima-Maricopa
Indian Community - Head Start
Rt 1 Box 216
Scottsdale, AZ 85256
602-941-7253
602-949-2909 FAX

San Carlos Apache Tribe
Head Start
PO Box 278
San Carlos, AZ 85550
520-475-2740
520-475-2881 FAX

Tohono O'odham Nation
Early Childhood Head Start
PO Box 837
Sells, AZ 85634
520-383-2221
520-383-2417

Tuba City Head Start
PO Box 157
Tuba City, AZ 86045
520-283-5136
520-283-4830 FAX

*NAVAJO DEPT OF HEAD START

White Mountain Apache
Head Start
White Mountain Apache
Reservation
PO Box 738
Whiteriver, AZ 85941
520-338-4938
520-338-1598 FAX

CALIFORNIA

California Rural Indian Health
Board , Inc.
Head Start
650 Howe Ave Ste 200
Sacramento, CA 95825
916-929-9761
916-929-7246 FAX

Covelo Indian Community
Head Start
PO Box 856
Covelo, CA 95428
707-983-6919
707-983-6128 FAX

Hoopa Valley Business Council
Head Start
PO Box 1287
Hoopa, CA 95546
916-625-4408
916-625-4594 FAX

Inter-Tribal Council of
California
Head Start
2755 Cottage Way Ste 14
Sacramento, CA 95825
916-973-9581
916-973-0117 FAX

Inyo Child Care Services, Inc.
Head Start
Rte 3 Box B75
Bishop, CA 93514
619-872-3911
619-872-4857 FAX

Karuk Head Start
PO Box 1016
Happy Camp, CA 96039
916-842-5280
916-842-1646 FAX

La Jolla Head Start
1871 Rosewood St
La Verne, CA 91750
909-596-7454

Morongo Band of Mission
Indians Head Start
11581 Potrero Rd
Banning, CA 92220
909-849-1058
909-849-4425 FAX

Redding Head Start
2000 Rancheria Rd
Redding, CA 96001
916-225-8979
916-241-1879 FAX

Rincon Indian Reservation
Head Start
PO Box 68
Valley Center, CA 92082
619-751-9821
619-749-8901 FAX

Yurok Tribe Head Start
PO Box 218
Klamath, CA 95548
707-482-2811
707-482-9465 FAX

COLORADO

Southern Ute Head Start
PO Box 400
Ignacio, CO 81137
303-563-4566
303-563-4380 FAX

Ute Mountain Ute Tribe
Head Start
General Delivery
Towaoc, CO 81334
303-565-3751 xx 222
303-565-7412 FAX

FLORIDA

Miccosukee Head Start
PO Box 440021
Tamiami Station
Miami, FL 33144
305-223-8380 xx 362
305-223-1011 FAX

Seminole Tribe of Florida
Head Start
3006 Josie Billie Ave
Hollywood, FL 33024
305-962-1866
305-966-2809 FAX

IDAHO

Coeur D'Alene Tribal
Head Start
PO Box 219
Desmet, ID 83824
208-274-3224
208-274-2001

Nez Perce Tribe Head Start
PO Box 365
Lapwai, ID 83540-0365
208-843-7330
208-843-2223 FAX

Shoshone-Bannock Tribes
Head Start
Fort Hall Reservation
PO Box 306
Fort Hall, ID 83203
208-238-3986
208-237-0797

KANSAS

Kickapoo Tribe of Kansas
Head Start
PO Box 271
Horton, KS 66439
913-486-3685
913-486-2198

Prairie Band of Potawatomi
Indians Head Start
15392 K Rd
Mayetta, KS 66509-9114
913-966-2255
913-966-2144 FAX

MAINE

Aroostook Band of Micmac
Head Start
521 D Main St
Presque Isle, ME 04769
207-764-6536
207-764-7667 FAX

Passamaquoddy Maine Indian
Education Head Start
PO Box 412
Calais, ME 04619
207-454-2128
207-454-3772 FAX

MICHIGAN

Grand Traverse Band of Ottawa
and Chippewa Indians
Head Start
2631 NW Bayshore Dr
Suttons Bay, MI 49682
616-271-6302
616-271-4861 FAX

Inter-Tribal Council of
Michigan, Inc.
Head Start
405 E Easterday Ave
Sault Ste Marie, MI 49783
906-632-6896
906-632-1810 FAX

Inter-Tribal Council of
Michigan, Inc.
Parent Child Center
405 E Easterday Ave
Sault Ste Marie, MI 49783
906-248-5820
906-632-1810 FAX

Sault Ste Marie Tribe of
Chippewa Indians Head Start
2303 Ashmun St
Sault Ste Marie, MI 49783
906-635-6080
906-635-3805 FAX

MINNESOTA

Boise Forte Reservation
Business Committee Head Start
PO Box 16
Nett Lake, MN 55772
218-757-3265
218-757-3312 FAX

Fond Du Lac Head Start
105 University Rd
Cloquet, MN 55720
218-879-0943
218-879-4146 FAX

Grand Portage Reservation
Business Committee Head Start
PO Box 428
Grand Portage, MN 55605
218-475-2234
218-475-2284 FAX

Leech Lake Head Start
Rt 3 Box 100
Cass Lake, MN 56633
218-335-8257
218-335-8309 FAX

Mille Lacs Band of Chippewa
Indians Head Start
HCR 67 Box 194
Onamia, MN 56359
612-532-4720
612-532-4209 FAX

Red Lake Reservation
Head Start
PO Box 53
Red Lake, MN 56671
218-679-3396
218-679-3378 FAX

White Earth Tribal Council
Head Start
PO Box 418
White Earth, MN 56591
218-983-3285 xx 260
218-983-3641 FAX

MISSISSIPPI

Mississippi Band of Choctaw
Indians Head Start
PO Box 6010 - Choctaw Branch
Philadelphia, MS 39350
601-656-5251
601-656-1992 FAX

MONTANA

Blackfeet Tribe Head Start
Program
PO Box 518
Browning, MT 59417
406-338-7370
406-338-7030 FAX

Blackfeet Tribe Parent Child
Center Head Start
PO Box 1805
Browning, MT 59417
406-338-5606
406-338-7838 FAX

Confederated Salish &
Kootenai Tribes Head Start
PO Box 266
St Ignatius, MT 59865
406-745-4509
406-745-4210 FAX

Crow Tribe Head Start Program
PO Box 249
Crow Agency, MT 59022
406-638-2697
406-638-2364 FAX

Fort Belknap Reservation
Head Start
RR 1 Box 65
Harlem, MT 59526
406-353-2827
406-353-2797 FAX

Fort Peck Tribe's Project
Head Start
PO Box 1027
Poplar, MT 59255
406-768-5155 xx 347
406-768-5478 FAX

Northern Cheyenne
Head Start Program
PO Box 128
Lame Deer, MT 59043
406-477-6346
406-477-6210 FAX

Rocky Boy's Chippewa Cree
Head Start
Box 620 Route 1
Box Elder, MT 59521
406-395-4666
406-395-4829 FAX

NEBRASKA

Omaha Tribe of Nebraska
Head Start
PO Box 459
Macy, NE 68039
402-837-5334
402-837-5308 FAX

Santee Sioux Reservation
Head Start
Route 2
Niobrara, NE 68760
402-857-2738
402-857-2307 FAX

Winnebago Tribe of Nebraska
Head Start
PO Box 747
Winnebago, NE 68071
402-878-2200
402-878-2963 FAX

NEVADA

Inter-Tribal Council of Nevada
Head Start
680 Greenbrae Dr Ste 280
Sparks, NV 89431
702-355-0600
702-355-0648 FAX

NEW MEXICO

Acoma Pueblo Head Start
PO Box 428
Acoma, NM 87034
505-552-6959
505-552-9455 FAX

*Alamo Head Start
PO Box 907
Magdalena, NM 87825
505-854-2694
505-854-2545 FAX

*Crownpoint Head Start
PO Box 2079
Crownpoint, NM 87313
505-786-5841
505-786-5502 FAX

Eight Northern Indian Pueblos
Council Head Start
PO Box 969
San Juan Pueblo, NM 87566
505-852-4265
505-852-4835 FAX

Five Sandoval Indian Pueblos,
Inc. - Head Start
PO Box 580
Bernalillo, NM 87004
505-867-3351 xx 27
505-867-3514 FAX

Jicarilla Apache Tribe
Head Start
PO Box 506
Dulce, NM 87528
505-759-3343
505-759-3098 FAX

Mescalero Apache Tribe
Head Start
PO Box 776
Mescalero, NM 88340
505-671-9183
505-671-4822 FAX

*NAVAJO DEPT OF HEAD START

Pueblo of Isleta Head Start
PO Box 579
Isleta, NM 87022
505-869-3700
505-869-4236 FAX

Pueblo of Jemez Head Start
PO Box 9
Jemez Pueblo, NM 87024
505-834-7366
505-834-7331 FAX

Pueblo of Laguna Head Start
PO Box 207
Laguna, NM 87026
505-552-6008
505-552-6398 FAX

Pueblo of Zuni Head Start
PO Drawer 449
Zuni, NM 87327
505-782-5750
505-782-2700 FAX

*Ramah Head Start
PO Box 37
Pine Hill, NM 87357
505-775-3355 FAX

San Felipe Pueblo Inc.
Head Start
PO Box 4346
San Felipe Pueblo, NM 87001
505-867-2816
505-867-5055 FAX

Santo Domingo Tribe
Head Start
PO Box 40
Santo Domingo Pueblo, NM
87052
505-465-2728
505-465-2688 FAX

*Shiprock Head Start
PO Drawer 310
Shiprock, NM 87420
505-368-5146
505-368-4599 FAX

Taos Pueblo Tribe Head Start
PO Box SS
Taos, NM 87571
505-758-5819
505-758-8831 FAX

NEW YORK

Seneca Nation of Indians
Head Start
1530 Route 438
Irving, NY 14081
716-532-5576
716-532-4255 FAX

St. Regis Mohawk Tribal
Council Head Start
Route 37
Hogansburg, NY 13655
518-358-2988
518-358-3203 FAX

*NAVAJO DEPT OF HEAD START

NORTH CAROLINA

Eastern Band of Cherokees
Head Start
PO Box 1178
Cherokee, NC 28719
704-497-9416
704-497-4212 FAX

NORTH DAKOTA

Little Hoop Head Start
PO Box 269
Fort Totten, ND 58335
701-766-4827
701-766-4077 FAX

Standing Rock Sioux Tribe
Head Start
PO Box 473
Fort Yates, ND 58538
701-854-3457
701-854-7221 FAX

Three Affiliated Tribes
Head Start
Box 687
New Town, ND 58763
701-627-4820
701-627-3805 FAX

Turtle Mountain Chippewa
Head Start
PO Box 900
Belcourt, ND 58316
701-477-6451 xx 144
701-477-6836 FAX

OKLAHOMA

Caddo Tribe of Oklahoma
Head Start
PO Box 487
Binger, OK 73009
405-656-9286
405-656-2892 FAX

Central Tribes of Shawnee
Area, Inc. Head Start
526 N Kimberly
Shawnee, OK 74801
405-275-4870
405-275-9684 FAX

Cherokee Nation Head Start
PO Box 948
Tahlequah, OK 74465
918-458-4393
918-458-5799 FAX

Cheyenne-Arapahoe Tribes of
Oklahoma Head Start
PO Box 38
Concho, OK 73022
405-262-0345
405-262-0745 FAX

Chickasaw Nation Head Start
PO Box 1548
Ada, OK 74820
405-436-7262
405-436-7265 FAX

Choctaw Nation of Oklahoma
Head Start
PO Drawer 1210
Durant, OK 74702-1210
405-924-8280 xx 212
405-924-4136 FAX

Creek Nation of Oklahoma
Head Start
PO Box 580
Okmulgee, OK 74447
918-756-8700
918-756-1450 FAX

Kickapoo Head Start, Inc.
PO Box 399
McLoud, OK 74851
405-964-3676
405-964-3417 FAX

Kiowa Tribe of Oklahoma
Head Start
PO Box 369
Carnegie, OK 73015
405-654-2300 xx 273
405-654-2188 FAX

Osage Nation Head Start
PO Box 1389
Pawhuska, OK 74056
918-287-1246
918-287-3416 FAX

Otoe-Missouria Tribe
Head Start
Rt 1 Box 62
Red Rock, OK 74651
405-268-3016
405-723-4273 FAX

Seminole Nation of Oklahoma
Head Start
PO Box 1498
Wewoka, OK 74884-1498
405-257-6663
405-257-3704 FAX

OREGON

Confederated Tribes of Siletz
Head Start
PO Box 549
Siletz, OR 97380
503-444-4233
503-444-2307 FAX

Confederated Tribes of Warm
Springs Head Start
PO Box C
Warm Springs, OR 97761
503-553-3241
503-553-1924 FAX

Confederated Tribes of
Umatilla Head Start
PO Box 638
Pendleton, OR 97801
503-278-5306
503-276-3095 FAX

SOUTH DAKOTA

Cheyenne River Sioux Tribe
Head Start
PO Box 590
Eagle Butte, SD 57625
605-964-8710
605-964-4151 FAX

Crow Creek Sioux Tribe
Head Start
PO Box 78
Fort Thompson, SD 57339
605-245-2337
605-245-2366 FAX

Dakota Transitional Head Start
919 Main St Ste 112
Rapid City, SD 57701
605-341-3163
605-341-2314 FAX

Tokahe Waonspe Parent Child Center Head Start
919 Main St Ste 112
Rapid City, SD 57701
605-343-4741
605-341-2314 FAX

Lower Brule Sioux Tribe Head Start
PO Box 804
Lower Brule, SD 57548
605-473-5878
605-473-5606 FAX

Oglala Sioux Tribe
Early Childhood Component Head Start
PO Box 279
Porcupine, SD 57772
605-867-5170
605-867-5030 FAX

Oglala Sioux Tribe Parent Child Center Head Start
PO Box 279
Porcupine, SD 57772
605-867-5170
605-867-5030 FAX

Rosebud Sioux Tribe Head Start
PO Box 269
Mission, SD 57555
605-856-2391
605-856-2039 FAX

Sisseton-Wahpeton Dakota Nation Head Start
PO Box 749
Agency Village, SD 57262
605-698-3103
605-698-3708 FAX

UTAH

Ute Indian Tribe Head Start
PO Box 265
Fort Duchesne, UT 84026
801-722-4506
801-722-2083 FAX

WASHINGTON

Chehalis Indian Head Start
PO Box 536
Oakville, WA 98568
206-273-5514
206-273-6230 FAX

Colville Confederated Tribe Head Start
PO Box 150
Nespelem, WA 99155
509-634-4711
509-634-8799 FAX

Lower Elwha Head Start
463 Stratton Rd
Port Angeles, WA98363
360-452-8471
360-452-3428 FAX

Lummi Indian Business Council Head Start
2616 Kwina Rd
Bellingham, WA 98226
360-647-6260
360-384-5521 FAX

Makah Tribal Council
Head Start
PO Box 115
Neah Bay, WA 98357
360-645-2336
360-645-2685 FAX

Muckleshoot Tribe Head Start
39015 172nd Ave SE
Auburn, WA 98092
206-939-3311
206-939-5311 FAX

Nisqually Tribe Head Start
4818 She-Nah-Num Dr SE
Olympia, WA 98513
360-459-9602
360-438-8618 FAX

Nooksack Indian Tribe
Head Start
PO Box 157
Deming, WA 98244
360-592-5176 xx 219
360-592-5721 FAX

Port Gamble S'Klallam
Head Start
31912 Little Boston Rd NE
Kingston, WA 98346
360-297-6258
360-297-7097 FAX

Port Gamble S'Kallam PCC
Head Start
31912 Little Boston Rd NE
Kingston, WA 98346
360-297-4634
360-297-7097 FAX

Quileute Tribe Head Start
PO Box 279
La Push, WA 98350
360-374-2061
360-374-9608 FAX

Quinault Tribal Council
Head Start
HC 80 Box 1480
Forks, WA 98331
360-962-2071
360-962-2460 FAX

Skokomish Tribe Head Start
North 80, Tribal Center Rd
Shelton, WA 98584
360-426-4232
360-877-5943 FAX

Spokane Tribal Head Start
Project
PO Box 217
Wellpinit, WA 99040
509-258-7229
509-258-9347 FAX

Yakama Tribal Council
Head Start
PO Box 151
Toppenish, WA 98948
509-865-5121 xx 516
509-865-6092 FAX

WISCONSIN

Bad River Tribal Council
Head Start
PO Box 39
Odanah, WI 54861
715-682-7144
715-682-7118 FAX

Forest County Potawatomi
Tribe Head Start
PO Box 340
Crandon, WI 54520
715-478-7350
715-478-7360 FAX

Lac Courte Oreilles Head Start
Rte 2 Box 2700
Hayward, WI 54843
715-634-8934
715-634-4797 FAX

Lac Du Flambeau Public
School/Head Start
2899 Hiway 47
Lac du Flambeau, WI 54538
715-588-9291
715-588-3243 FAX

Oneida Tribe of Indians of
Wisconsin Head Start
PO Box 365
Oneida, WI 54155
414-869-4369
414-869-2194 FAX

Red Cliff Band of Lake
Superior Chippewa Head Start
PO Box 529
Bayfield, WI 54814
715-779-5030
715-779-5046 FAX

Stockbridge-Munsee Head Start
W 13429 Cherry St
Bowler, WI 54416
715-793-4100
715-793-4529 FAX

Ho-Chunk Nation Head Start
PO Box 667
Black River Falls, WI 54615
715-284-4915
715-284-1760 FAX

WYOMING

Shoshone & Arapaho Tribes
Head Start
Wind River Indian Reservation
PO Box 308
Fort Washakie, WY 82514
307-332-7163
307-332-3055 FAX

INDIAN TRIBES OPERATING INDIAN COMMUNITY COLLEGES

CANADA

RED CROW COLLEGE
PO Box 1258
Cardston, Alberta T0K 0K0
403-737-2400
403-737-2361 FAX

SASKATCHEWAN INDIAN FEDERATED COLLEGE
127 College West
Univ. Of Regina
Regina, Saskatchewan S4S 0A2
306-584-8333
306-584-0955 FAX

ARIZONA

NAVAJO COMMUNITY COLLEGE
Tsaile Rural PO
Tsaile, AZ 86556
520-724-3311
520-724-3327 FAX

CALIFORNIA

D-Q UNIVERSITY
PO Box 409
Davis, CA 95617
916-758-0470
916-758-4891

KANSAS

HASKELL INDIAN NATIONS UNIVERSITY
155 Indian Avenue
Lawrence, KS 66046
913-749-8450
913-749-8406 FAX

MICHIGAN

BAY MILLS COMMUNITY COLLEGE
Rt 1, Box 315A
Brimley, MI 49715
906-248-3354
906-248-3351 FAX

MINNESOTA

FOND DU LAC COMMUNITY COLLEGE
2101 14th Street
Cloquet, MN 55720
218-879-0800
218-879-0814

LEECH LAKE COMMUNITY COLLEGE
Rt 3, Box 100
Cass Lake, MN 56633
218-335-2828
218-335-8309

UNITED STATES

MONTANA

BLACKFEET COMMUNITY COLLEGE
PO Box 819
Browning, MT 59417
406-338-7755
406-338-7808 FAX

DULL KNIFE MEMORIAL COLLEGE
PO Box 98
Lame Deer, MT 59043
406-477-6215
406-477-6219

FORT BELKNAP COMMUNITY COLLEGE
PO Box 159
Harlem, MT 59526
406-353-2607
406-353-2829

FORT PECK COMMUNITY COLLEGE
PO Box 398
Poplar, MT 59255
406-768-5551
406-768-5552

LITTLE BIG HORN COLLEGE
PO Box 370
Crow Agency, MT 59022
406-638-2228
406-638-7213 FAX

SALISH KOOTENAI COLLEGE
PO Box 117
Pablo, MT 59855
406-675-4800
406-675-4801

STONE CHILD COMMUNITY COLLEGE
Rocky Boy Rt, Box 1082
Box Elder, MT 59521
406-395-4375
406-395-4836 FAX

NEBRASKA

NEBRASKA INDIAN COMMUNITY COLLEGE
PO Box 752
Winnebago, NE 68071
402-878-2414
402-878-2522 FAX

NEW MEXICO

INSTITUTE OF AMERICAN INDIAN ARTS
PO Box 20007
Santa Fe, NM 87504
505-988-6463

CROWPOINT INSTITUTE OF TECHNOLOGY
PO Box 849
Crownpoint, NM 87313
505-786-5851
505-786-5644 FAX

SOUTHWEST INDIAN POLYTECHNIC INSTITUTE
PO Box 10146
Albuquerque, NM 87184
505-897-5347
505-897-5343 FAX

NORTH DAKOTA

FT. BERTHOLD COMMUNITY COLLEGE
PO Box 490
New Town, ND 58763
701-627-3665
701-627-3609

LITTLE HOOP COMMUNITY COLLEGE
PO Box 269
Ft. Totten, ND 58335
701-766-4415
701-766-4077

STANDING ROCK COLLEGE
HC 1, Box 4
Ft. Yates, ND 58538
701-854-3861
701-854-3403 FAX

TURTLE MOUNTAIN COMMUNITY COLLEGE
PO Box 340
Belcourt, ND 58316
701-477-5605
701-477-5028

UNITED TRIBES TECHNICAL COLLEGE
3315 University Dr
Bismarck, ND 58501
701-255-3285
701-255-1844 FAX

OKLAHOMA

BACONE COLLEGE
2299 Old Bacone Road
Muskogee, OK 74403-1597
918-683-4581
918-687-5913 FAX

SOUTH DAKOTA

CHEYENNE RIVER COMMUNITY COLLEGE
PO Box 220
Eagle Butte, SD 57625
605-964-8635
605-964-1144 FAX

OGLALA LAKOTA COLLEGE
PO Box 490
Kyle, SD 57752
605-455-2321
605-455-2787 FAX

SINTE GLESKA UNIVERSITY
PO Box 490
Rosebud, SD 57570
605-747-2263
605-747-2098

SISSETON-WAHPETON COMMUNITY COLLEGE
CPO Box 689, Agency Village
Sisseton, SD 57262
605-698-3966
605-698-3132

UNITED STATES

WASHINGTON

NORTHWEST INDIAN COLLEGE
2522 Kwina Road
Bellingham, WA 98226
360-676-2772
360-738-0136

WISCONSIN

LAC COURTE OREILLES OJIBWA COMMUNITY COLLEGE
Rural Rt 2, Box 2357
Hayward, WI 54843
715-634-4790
715-634-5049

COLLEGE OF THE MENOMINEE NATION
PO Box 1179
Keshena, WI 54135
715-799-5208
715-799-1308

NATIVE AMERICAN UNIVERSITY PROGRAMS

KEY

2Y - 2 year program
4Y - 4 year program
G - graduate program

ARIZONA

NAVAJO COMMUNITY COLLEGE
N/A Studies Program
PO Box 126
Tsaile, AZ 86556
2Y
520-724-3311

SCOTTSDALE COMMUNITY COLLEGE
N/A Studies
9000 E Chaparral Rd
Scottsdale, AZ 85256
2Y
602-423-6139

UNIV OF ARIZONA/ARTS & SCIENCES
American Indian Studies Program
Tucson, AZ 85721
G
520-621-7108

CALIFORNIA

CALIFORNIA STATE UNIVERSITY
N/A Studies Program-Sacramento
6435 Crystalaire Dr
Sacramento, CA 95819
4Y
916-278-3901

PALOMAR COMMUNITY COLLEGE
N/A Studies Program
San Marcos, CA 92069
2Y
619-744-1150

SAN DIEGO STATE UNIVERSITY
N/A Studies Program
San Diego, CA 92182
4Y
619-594-5384

SAN FRANCISCO STATE UNIVERSITY
American Indian Studies Program
San Francisco, CA 94132
G
415-338-1693

SANTA BARBARA CITY COLLEGE
N/A Studies Program
Santa Barbara, CA 93109
2Y
805-965-0581

SONOMA STATE UNIVERSITY
N/A Studies Program
Rohnert Park, CA 94928
4Y
707-664-2458

UNIV OF CAL/COLLEGE LETTERS & SCIENCE
American Indian Studies Program
Los Angeles, CA 90024
G
213-825-7420

UNIVERSITY OF CALIFORNIA
N/A Studies Program
Berkeley, CA 94720
4Y
510-642-2261

UNIVERSITY OF CALIFORNIA
N/A Studies Program
Tecumseh Center
Davis, CA 95616
4Y
800-523-2847
916-752-7097 FAX

UNIVERSITY OF CALIFORNIA
Ethnic Studies Graduate Program
Berkeley, CA 94720
G
510-642-2261

HAWAII

UNIVERSITY OF HAWAII SCHL PUBLIC HEALTH
A/I & Alaska Native Supp Program
Honolulu, HI 96822
G
800-927-3927

IOWA

CORNELL UNIVERSITY
N/A Studies Program
Mt Vernon, IA 52314
4Y
800-747-1112

MORNINGSIDE COLLEGE
N/A Studies Program
Sioux City, IA 51106
4Y
800-831-0806

MASSACHUSETTS

HAMPSHIRE COLLEGE
N/A Studies Program
Amherst, MA 01002
4Y
413-549-4600

MINNESOTA

BEMIDJI STATE
UNIVERSITY
N/A Studies Program
Bermidji, MN 56601
4Y
218-755-2027

COLLEGE OF ST
SCHOLASTICS
N/A Studies Program
Duluth, MN 55811
4Y
218-723-6046

UNIVERSITY OF
MINNESOTA
TWIN CITIES
N/A Studies Program
Minneapolis, MN 55455
4Y
800-826-0750

MONTANA

DULL KNIFE MEMORIAL
COLLEGE
N/A Studies Program
PO Box 98
Lame Deer, MT 59043
2Y
406-477-6215

FORT PECK COMMUNITY
COLLEGE
N/A Studies Program
PO Box 575
Poplar, MT 59255
406-768-5553

SALISH KOOTENAI
COLLEGE
N/A Studies Program
PO Box 117
Pablo, MT 59855
2Y
406-675-4800

NORTH CAROLINA

PEMBROKE STATE
UNIVERSITY
N/A Studies Program
Pembroke, NC 28372
4Y
919-521-4214

NORTH DAKOTA

STANDING ROCK COLLEGE
N/A Studies Program
HC 1 Box 4
Fort Yates, ND 58538
2Y
701-854-3862

UNIVERSITY OF NORTH
DAKOTA
N/A Studies Program
Grand Forks, ND 58202
4Y
800-437-5379

UNIVERSITY OF NORTH
DAKOTA
Indians Into Medicine Program
501 N Columbia Rd
Grand Forks, ND 58203
G
701-777-3037

NEBRASKA

NEBRASKA INDIAN COMMUNITY COLLEGE
N/A Studies Program
PO Box 752
Winnebago, NE 68071
2Y
402-878-2414

UNIVERSITY OF NEBRASKA, LINCOLN
N/A Studies Program
Lincoln, NE 68588
4Y
800-742-8800

NEW HAMPSHIRE

DARTMOUTH COLLEGE
N/A Studies Program
Hanover, NH 03755
4Y
603-646-2875

NEW JERSEY

RUTGERS UNIVERSITY
North American Indian Stud Prog
25 Bishop Place
New Brunswick, NJ 08903
G
908-932-7908

NEW YORK

COLGATE UNIVERSITY
N/A Studies Porgram
Hamilton, NY 13346
4Y
315-824-1000

FRIENDS WORLD COLLEGE
N/A Studies Program
Huntington, NY 11743
4Y
516-549-1102

STATE UNIVERSITY OF NEW YORK
N/A Studies Program
Hayes Annex A Main
Buffalo, NY 14214
4Y
716-831-2111

STATE UNIVERSITY OF NEW YORK
N./A Studies Program
Hayes Annex A Main
Buffalo, NY 14214
G
716-831-2111

OHIO

UNION INSTITUTE
N/A Studies Program
Cincinnati, OH 45202
4Y
513-621-6400

UNION INSTITUTE
N/A Studies Program
Cincinnati, OH 45202
G
513-621-6400

OKLAHOMA

NORTHEASTERN STATE UNIVERSITY
N/A Studies Program
Talequah, OK 74464
4Y
800-722-9614

ROGERS STATE COLLEGE
N/A Studies Program
Claremore, OK 74017
2Y
918-341-7510

ROSE STATE COLLEGE
N/A Studies Program
Midwest City, OK 73110
2Y
405-733-7308

UNIVERSITY OF SCIENCE & ARTS OF OKLAHOMA
N/A Studies Program
Chickasha, OK 73018
4Y
405-224-3140

SOUTH DAKOTA

BLACK HILLS STATE UNIVERSITY
N/A Studies Program
Spearfish, SD 57783
4Y
800-255-2487

DAKOTA WESLEYAN UNIVERSITY
N/A Studies Program
Mitchell, SD 57301
4Y
605-995-2650

OGLALA LAKOTA COLLEGE
Native American Studies
PO Box 490
Kyle, SD 57752
4Y
605-455-2321

OGLALA LAKOTA COLLEGE
N/A Studies Graduate Program
PO Box 490
Kyle, SD 57752
G
605-455-2321

SINTE GLESKA COLLEGE
Native American Studies
PO Box 490
Rosebud, SD 57570
4Y
605-747-2263

UTAH

UTAH STATE UNIVERSITY
N/A Studies Program
Logan, UT 84322
4Y
801-750-1106

VERMONT

GODDARD COLLEGE
N/A Studies Program
Plainfield, VT 05667
4Y
802-454-8311

GODDARD COLLEGE
N/A Studies Program
Plainfield, VT 05667
G
802-454-8311

WASHINGTON

EVERGREEN STATE
COLLEGE
N/A Studies Program
Olympia, WA 98505
4y
206-866-6000

UNIVERSITY OF
WASHINGTON
N/A Studies Program
Seattle, WA 98195
4Y
206-543-9686

WASHINGTON STATE
UNIVERSITY
N/A Studies Program
Pullman, WA 99164
4Y
509-335-5586

WISCONSIN

LAC COURTE OREILLES
OJIBWA COMM COLLEGE
N/A Studies Program
R R 2, Box 2357
Hayward, WI 54843
2Y
715-634-4719

MOUNT SENARIO
COLLEGE
N/A Studies Program
Ladysmith, WI 54848
4Y
715-532-5511

NORTHLAND COLLEGE
N/A Studies Program
Ashland, WI 54806
4Y
715-682-1224

*To list your University Native American Program forward all details and fax to : Indian Information and Trade Center
University Native American Programs
PO Box 27626
Tucson, AZ 85726

520-292-0779 FAX

QUICK NOTES !

**Information for this page is only available in the Library Edition.

Fred Synder, Director, Consultant

N.A.2I.I.T.C

North American Native American Indian Information & Trade Center

QUICK NOTES !

**Information for this page is only available in the Library Edition.

Fred Synder, Director, Consultant

N.A.²I.I.T.C

North American Native American
Indian Information & Trade Center

BUREAU OF INDIAN AFFAIRS -- A SHORT HISTORY

The Bureau of Indian Affairs (BIA) in the U.S. Department of the Interior, is the federal agency with primary responsibility for working with federally-recognized Indian tribal governments and with Alaska Native village communities. Other federal, state, county and local government agencies may work with Indians or Alaska Natives as members of ethnic groups or as U.S. Citizens. The BIA relates its work to federal tribal governments in what is termed a "government-to-government relationship".

It must be made clear at this point that the BIA does not run Indian reservations. "Elected tribal governments run Indian Reservations, working with BIA whenever trust resources or Bureau programs are involved.

Under a U.S. policy of Indian self-determination, the Bureau's main goal is to support tribal efforts to govern their own reservation communities by providing them with technical assistance, as well as programs and services, through 12 area offices and 109 agencies and special offices.

A principal BIA responsibility is administering and managing some 56.2 million acres of land held in trust by the United States for Indians. Developing forest lands, increasing mineral rights, directing agricultural programs and protecting water and land rights are a part of this responsibility in cooperation with the tribes, who have a greater decision-making role in these matters now than in the past.

Most Indian students (about 89 percent) attend public, private or parochial schools. BIA augments these through funding of 180 Bureau education facilities, many of which are operated by tribes under contract with the Bureau. The BIA also provides assistance for Indian College students; vocational training; adult education; a solo parent program and a gifted and talented students program.

A part of the Bureau's work is also to assist tribes with local governmental services such as road construction and maintenance, social services, police protection, economic development, and enhancement of governance and administrative skills.

The BIA was established in 1824 in the War Department. It became an agency of the Department of the Interior when the Department was created in 1849. Until 1980, BIA was headed by a Commissioner who by law was a presidential appointee requiring confirmation by the U.S. Senate. The post remained vacant until 1991 when the post of

Deputy Commissioner was filled by David J. Matheson, an enrolled member of the Coeur d'Alene Tribe of Idaho, who is responsible for the day-to-day operations of the Bureau. His post as Deputy Commissioner does not require senate confirmation. From 1980 to 1991, the BIA was administered by an Assistant Secretary - Indian Affairs (or his deputy), a post that was created in 1977 by the Interior Secretary. Five successive Indians have been appointed by the President to the Office. Since 1989, Eddie F. Brown, an enrolled member of the Pasqua Yaqui Tribe of Arizona, has held the post. He sets policy for the BIA. Ada Deer, the first female to hold this office currently, is a member of the Menominee Nation of Wisconsin.

About 87 percent of BIA employees are Indian through Indian preference in hiring. Under federal law, a non-Indian cannot be hired for a vacancy if a qualified Indian has applied for the position. To qualify for preference status, a person must be a member of a federally-recognized Indian tribe or be of at least one-half Indian blood of tribes indigenous to the U.S.

BIA EDUCATION PROGRAMS

Legislation - Since the 1970's, two major laws restructured the BIA education program. In 1975, the Indian Self-Determination and Education Assistance Act (P.L. 98-511, 99-89 and 100-297) mandated major changes in both Bureau-operated and tribal contracted schools, including decision-making powers for Indian school boards, local hiring of teachers and staff, direct funding to schools, and increased authority to the director of Indian Education Programs within the Bureau.

Federal Schools - In 1990-91, the BIA is funding 180 education facilities including 48 day schools, 39 on-reservation boarding schools, five off-reservation boarding schools and eight dormitories operated by the Bureau. Additionally, under "638" contracting, tribes operate 62 day schools, 11 on-reservation boarding schools, one off-reservation boarding school and six dormitories. The dormitories enable Indian students to attend public schools.

Indian Children in Federal Schools - Enrollment in schools and dormitories funded by the BIA for 1991 is about 40,841 including 39,092 instructional and 1,749 dormitory students.

PUBLIC SCHOOL ASSISTANCE (JOHNSON-O'MALLEY PROGRAM) - The BIA provides funds to public school districts under the Johnson-O'Malley Act of 1934 to meet the special educational needs of about 225,871 eligible Indian students in public schools.

Indians in College - Approximately 15,000 Indian students received scholarship grants from the BIA in the 1990-91 school year to enable them to attend colleges and universities. About 432 students receiving BIA assistance are in law school and other graduate programs. The total number of Indian college students is not known, but is estimated to be more than 70,000. Total appropriations provided through the BIA for Indian higher education was about $30.2 million in fiscal year 1991.

Tribal Controlled Colleges - Currently, the BIA provides grants for the operation of 22 tribally controlled community colleges. The number of Indian students enrolled in these colleges in school year 1990-91 was approximately 7,050 with a total funding of $23.3 million.

BIA Post-Secondary Schools - The BIA operates two post secondary schools: Haskell Indian Junior College in Lawrence, Kansas, with an enrollment of about 816 students, and Southwest Indian Polytechnic Institute at Albuquerque, New Mexico, with about 427 students.

Handicapped Children's Program - Under the Handicapped Children's Act (P.L. 94-142), the Bureau provides financial support for the education costs of an average of 226 such children annually in some 28 different facilities.

Substance/Alcohol Abuse Education Program - BIA education programs in substance and alcohol abuse provide Bureau schools with curriculum materials and technical assistance in developing and implementing identification, assessment, prevention, and crisis intervention programs through referrals and added counselors at the schools.

BIA HOUSING

The BIA Housing Program administers the Housing Improvement Program (HIP), a grant program to which Indians may apply who are unable to obtain housing assistance from other sources, to repair and renovate existing housing. In some special cases, HIP provides for the construction of new homes. It also provides financial help to qualified Indians for down payments in the purchase of new homes. The grants are made only to those Indians who do not have the income to qualify for loans from tribal, federal or other sources of credit.

The 1989 BIA inventory of housing needs on reservations and in Indian communities shows that of a total of 155,539 existing dwellings, 100,037 meet standards and 55,502 needed replacement (39,516 of which can be renovated). With the numbers of dwellings needing total replacement (15,986) and families needing housing (35,886), the BIA Housing Program estimates that a total of 51,872 new homes are required. The program budget for fiscal year 1991 is $20.1 million.

The program works cooperatively with the Indian Health Services which provides water and sewage facilities for the homes, and the Housing and Urban Development (HUD) program which builds new homes.

American Indians Today third edition, United States Department of the Interior-Bureau of Indian Affairs, MS 2620-MIB, Washington, DC 20240-0001

B.I.A. AREA OFFICES

ALASKA

Junea Area Office
Bureau of Indian Affairs
PO Box 25520
Juneau, AK 99802
907-586-7177
907-586-7169 FAX

ARIZONA

Phoenix Area Office
Bureau of Indian Affairs
PO Box 10
Phoenix, AZ 85001
602-379-6600
602-379-4413 FAX

CALIFORNIA

Sacramento Area Office
Bureau of Indian Affairs
2800 Cottage Way
Sacramento, CA 95825
916-979-2600
916-979-2569 FAX

MINNESOTA

Minneapolis Area Office
Bureau of Indian Affairs
331 S 2nd Ave
Minneapolis, MN 55401
612-373-1000
612-373-1186 FAX

MONTANA

Billings Area Office
Bureau of Indian Affairs
316 N 26th St
Billings, MT 59101
406-657-6315
406-657-6559 FAX

NEW MEXICO

Albuquerque Area Office
Bureau of Indian Affairs
PO Box 26567
Albuquerque, NM 87125
505-766-3754
505-766-1964 FAX

Navajo Area Office
Bureau of Indian Affairs
PO Box 1060
Gallup, NM 87301
505-863-8314
505-863-8324 FAX

OKLAHOMA

Anadarko Area Office
Bureau of Indian Affairs
W.C.D. Office Complex
PO Box 368
Anadarko, OK 73005
405-247-6673
405-247-2242 FAX

Muskogee Area Office
Bureau of Indian Affairs
Old Federal Bldg
101 N 5th St
Muskogee, OK 74401
918-687-2296
918-687-2571 FAX

OREGON

Portland Area Office
Bureau of Indian Affairs
Federal Building
911 NE 11th Ave
Portland, OR 97232
503-231-6702
503-231-2201 FAX

SOUTH DAKOTA

Aberdeen Area Office
Bureau of Indian Affairs
115 4th Ave SE
Aberdeen, SD 57401
605-226-7343
605-226-7446 FAX

VIRGINIA

Eastern Area Office
Bureau of Indian Affairs
3701 N Fairfax Dr
Mailstop VASQ 260
Arlington, VA 22203
703-235-3006
703-235-8610 FAX

B.I.A. AREA OFFICES AND TRIBAL AGENCIES

ALASKA

Anchorage Agency
Bureau of Indian Affairs
1675 C St
Anchorage, AK 99501
907-271-4088
907-271-4083 FAX

Bethel Agency
Bureau of Indian Affairs
PO Box 347
Bethel, AK 99559
907-543-2727
907-543-3574 FAX

Fairbanks Agency
Bureau of Indian Affairs
101 12th Ave
Box 16
Fairbanks, AK 99701
907-456-0222
907-456-0225 FAX

★JUNEAU AREA OFFICE
Bureau of Indian Affairs
PO Box 25520
Juneau, AK 99802
907-586-7177
907-586-7169 FAX

Metlakatla Field Station
Bureau of Indian Affairs
PO Box 450
Metlakatla, AK 99926
907-886-3791
907-886-7738 FAX

Nome Agency
Bureau of Indian Affairs
PO Box 1108
Nome, AK 99762
907-443-2284
907-443-2317 FAX

ARIZONA

Chinle Agency
Bureau of Indian Affairs
PO Box 7H
Chinle, AZ 86503
520-674-5201 xx 101
520-674-5201 xx 105 FAX

Colorado River Agency
Bureau of Indian Affairs
Rt 1 Box 9C
Parker, AZ 85344
520-669-7111
520-669-7187 FAX

Fort Apache Agency
Bureau of Indian Affairs
PO Box 560
Whiteriver, AZ 85941
520-338-5353
520-338-5383 FAX

Fort Defiance Agency
Bureau of Indian Affairs
PO Box 619
Fort Defiance, AZ 86504
520-729-7221
520-729-7225 FAX

★AREA OFFICES HEADQUARTERS

Fort Yuma Agency
Bureau of Indian Affairs
PO Box 1591
Yuma, AZ 85364
619-572-0248
619-572-0895 FAX

Hopi Agency
Bureau of Indian Affairs
PO Box 158
Keams Canyon, AZ 86034
520-738-2228
520-738-5522 FAX

Papago Agency
Bureau of Indian Affairs
PO Box 578
Sells, AZ 85634
520-383-3286
520-383-2087 FAX

★PHOENIX AREA OFFICE
Bureau of Indian Affairs
PO Box 10
Phoenix, AZ 85001
602-379-6600
602-379-4413 FAX

Pima Agency
Bureau of Indian Affairs
PO Box 8
Sacaton, AZ 85247
520-562-3326
520-562-3543 FAX

Salt River Agency
Bureau of Indian Affairs
Rt 1 PO Box 117
Scottsdale, AZ 85256
602-640-2168
602-650-2809 FAX

San Carlos Agency
Bureau of Indian Affairs
PO Box 209
San Carlos, AZ 85550
520-475-2321
520-475-2783 FAX

Truxton Canyon Agency
Bureau of Indian Affairs
PO Box 37
Valentine, AZ 86437
520-769-2286
520-769-2444 FAX

Western Navajo Agency
Bureau of Indian Affairs
PO Box 127
Tuba City, AZ 86045
520-283-4531 xx 205
520-283-4531 xx 215 FAX

CALIFORNIA

Central California Agency
Bureau of Indian Affairs
1824 Tribute Rd # J
Sacramento, CA 95815
916-566-7121
916-566-7510 FAX

Northern California Agency
Bureau of Indian Affairs
1900 Churn Creek Rd # 300
PO Box 494879
Redding, CA 96049
916-246-5141
916-246-5167 FAX

★AREA OFFICES HEADQUARTERS

Palm Springs Field Agency
Bureau of Indian Affairs
441 S Calle Encilla # 8
PO Box 2245
Palm Springs, CA 92263
619-322-3086
619-322-2031 FAX

★SACRAMENTO AREA OFFICE
Bureau of Indian Affairs
2800 Cottage Way
Sacramento, CA 95825
916-979-2600
916-979-2569 FAX

Southern California Agency
Bureau of Indian Affairs
3600 Lime # 722
Riverside, CA 92501
909-276-6624
909-276-6641 FAX

COLORADO

Southern Ute Agency
Bureau of Indian Affairs
PO Box 315
Ignacio, CO 81137
970-563-4511
970-563-9321 FAX

Ute Mountain Ute Agency
Bureau of Indian Affairs
General Delivery
Towaoc, CO 81334
970-565-8471
970-454-8906 FAX

FLORIDA

Seminole Agency
Bureau of Indian Affairs
6075 Stirling Rd
Hollywood, FL 33024
305-581-7050
305-792-7340 FAX

IDAHO

Fort Hall Agency
Bureau of Indian Affairs
PO Box 220
Fort Hall, ID 83203
208-238-2301
208-237-0466 FAX

Nothern Idaho Agency
Bureau of Indian Affairs
PO Box 277
Lapwai, ID 83540
208-843-2300
208-843-7142 FAX

Plummer Field Office
Bureau of Indian Affairs
Agency Rd
Plummer, ID 83851
208-686-1277
208-686-1908 FAX

IOWA

Sac & Fox Area Field Office
Bureau of Indian Affairs
1657 320th St
Tama, IA 52339
515-484-4041
515-484-6518 FAX

★AREA OFFICES HEADQUARTERS

KANSAS

Horton Agency
Bureau of Indian Affairs
PO Box 31
Horton, KS 66439
913-486-2161
913-486-2515 FAX

MICHIGAN

Michigan Agency
Bureau of Indian Affairs
2901.5 I-75 Spur
Sault St Marie, MI 49783
906-632-6809
906-632-0689 FAX

MINNESOTA

★MINNEAPOLIS AREA OFFICE
Bureau of Indian Affairs
331 S 2nd Ave
Minneapolis, MN 55401
612-373-1000
612-373-1186 FAX

Minnesota Agency
Bureau of Indian Affairs
Rt 3 Box 112
Cass Lake, MN 56633
218-335-6913
218-335-2819 FAX

Red Lake Agency
Bureau of Indian Affairs
Red Lake, MN 56671
218-679-3361
218-679-3691 FAX

MISSISSIPPI

Choctaw Agency
Bureau of Indian Affairs
421 Powell
Philadelphia, MS 39350
601-656-1521
601-656-2350 FAX

MONTANA

★BILLINGS AREA OFFICE
Bureau of Indian Affairs
316 N 26th St
Billings, MT 59101
406-657-6315
406-657-6559 FAX

Blackfeet Agency
Bureau of Indian Affairs
PO Box 880
Browning, Mt 59417
406-338-7544
406-338-7716 FAX

Crow Agency
Bureau of Indian Affairs
Crow Agency, MT 59022
406-638-2672
406-638-2380 FAX

Flathead Agency
Bureau of Indian Affairs
PO Box A
Pablo, MT 59855
406-675-7200
406-675-2805 FAX

★AREA OFFICES HEADQUARTERS

Fort Belknap Agency
Bureau of Indian Affairs
PO Box 98
Harlem, MT 59526
406-353-2901
406-353-2886 FAX

Fort Peck Agency
Bureau of Indian Affairs
PO Box 637
Poplar, MT 59255
406-768-5312
406-768-3405 FAX

Northern Cheyenne Agency
Bureau of Indian Affairs
Lame Deer, MT 59043
406-477-8242
406-477-6636 FAX

Rocky Boy's Agency
Bureau of Indian Affairs
Box Elder, MT 59521
406-395-4476
406-395-4382 FAX

NEBRASKA

Winnebago Agency
Bureau of Indian Affairs
Rt 1 Box 18
Winnebago, NE 68071
402-878-2502
402-878-2943 FAX

NEVADA

Eastern Nevada Agency
Bureau of Indian Affairs
PO Box 5400
Elko, NV 89802
702-738-0569
702-738-4710 FAX

Western Nevada Agency
Bureau of Indian Affairs
1677 Hot Springs Rd
Carson City, NV 89706
702-887-3500
702-887-3531 FAX

NEW MEXICO

★ALBUQUERQUE AREA OFFICE
Bureau of Indian Affairs
PO Box 26567
Albuquerque, NM 87125
505-766-3754
505-766-1964 FAX

Eastern Navajo Agency
Bureau of Indian Affairs
PO Box 328
Crownpoint, NM 87313
505-786-6100
505-786-6107 FAX

Jicarilla Agency
Bureau of Indian Affairs
PO Box 167
Dulce, NM 87528
505-759-3951
505-759-3948 FAX

★AREA OFFICES HEADQUARTERS

Laguna Agency
Bureau of Indian Affairs
PO Box 1448
Laguna, NM 87026
505-552-6001/6002
505-552-7497 FAX

Mescalero Agency
Bureau of Indian Affairs
PO Box 189
Mescalero, NM 88340
505-671-4423
505-671-4215 FAX

★NAVAJO AREA OFFICE
Bureau of Indian Affairs
PO Box 1060
Gallup, NM 87301
505-863-8314
505-863-8324 FAX

Northern Pueblos Agency
Bureau of Indian Affairs
PO Box 4269
Fairview Stn
Espanola, NM 87523
505-753-1400
505-753-1404 FAX

Ramah-Navajo Agency
Bureau of Indian Affairs
Rt 2 Box 14
Ramah, NM 87321
505-775-3235
505-775-3387 FAX

Shiprock Agency
Bureau of Indian Affairs
PO Box 966
Shiprock, NM 87420
505-368-4427 xx 301
505-368-4321 FAX

Southern Pueblos Agency
Bureau of Indian Affairs
PO Box 1667
Albuquerque, NM 87103
505-766-3021
505-766-3023 FAX

Zuni Agency
Bureau of Indian Affairs
PO Box 369
Zuni, NM 87327
505-782-5591
505-782-5715 FAX

NEW YORK

New York Liaison Office
Bureau of Indian Affairs
100 S Clinton St Rm 523
PO Box 7366
Syracuse, NY 13261
315-448-0620
315-448-0624 FAX

NORTH CAROLINA

Cherokee Agency
Bureau of Indian Affairs
Cherokee, NC 28719
704-497-9131
704-497-6715 FAX

NORTH DAKOTA

Fort Berthold Agency
Bureau of Indian Affairs
PO Box 370
New Town, ND 58763
701-627-4707
701-627-3601 FAX

★AREA OFFICES HEADQUARTERS

Fort Totten Agency
Bureau of Indian Affairs
PO Box 270
Fort Totten, ND 58335
701-766-4545
701-766-4854 FAX

Standing Rock Agency
Bureau of Indian Affairs
PO Box E
Fort Yates, ND 58538
701-854-3433
701-854-7541 FAX

Turtle Mountain Agency
Bureau of Indian Affairs
PO Box 60
Belcourt, ND 58316
701-477-3191
701-477-6628 FAX

OKLAHOMA

★ANADARKO AREA OFFICE
Bureau of Indian Affairs
W.C.D. Office Complex
PO Box 368
Anadarko, OK 73005
405-247-6673
405-247-2242 FAX

Anadarko Agency
Bureau of Indian Affairs
PO Box 309
Anadarko, OK 73005
405-247-6673
405-247-9232 FAX

Chickasaw Agency
Bureau of Indian Affairs
PO Box 2240
Ada, OK 74821
405-436-0784
405-436-3215 FAX

Concho Agency
Bureau of Indian Affairs
PO Box 96
El Reno, OK 73036
405-262-7481
405-262-3140 FAX

Miami Agency
Bureau of Indian Affairs
PO Box 391
Miami, OK 74355
918-542-3396
918-542-7202 FAX

★MUSKOGEE AREA OFFICE
Bureau of Indian Affairs
Old Federal Bldg
101 N 5th St
Muskogee, OK 74401
918-687-2296
918-687-2571 FAX

Okmulgee Agency
Bureau of Indian Affairs
PO Box 370
Okmulgee, OK 74447
918-756-3950
918-756-9626 FAX

★AREA OFFICES HEADQUARTERS

Osage Agency
Bureau of Indian Affairs
PO Box 1539
Pawhuska, OK 74056
918-287-1032
918-287-4320 FAX

Pawnee Agency
Bureau of Indian Affairs
PO Box 440
Pawnee, OK 74058
918-762-2585
918-762-3201 FAX

Shawnee Agency
Bureau of Indian Affairs
624 W Independence # 114
Shawnee, OK 74801
405-273-0317
405-273-0072 FAX

Talihina Agency
Bureau of Indian Affairs
PO Drawer H
Talihina, OK 74571
918-567-2207
918-567-2061 FAX

Wewoka Agency
Bureau of Indian Affairs
PO Box 1060
Wewoka, OK 74884
405-257-6259
405-257-6748 FAX

OREGON

★PORTLAND AREA OFFICE
Bureau of Indian Affairs
Federal Building
911 NE 11th Ave
Portland, OR 97232
503-231-6702
503-231-2201 FAX

Chiloquin Sub-Agency
Bureau of Indian Affairs
PO Box 360
Chiloquin, OR 97624
503-783-2189
503-783-2946 FAX

Siletz Agency
Bureau of Indian Affairs
PO Box 569
Siletz, OR 97380
503-444-2679
503-444-2513 FAX

Umatilla Agency
Bureau of Indian Affairs
PO Box 520
Pendleton, OR 97801
503-278-3786
503-278-3791 FAX

Warm Springs Agency
Bureau of Indian Affairs
PO Box 1239
Warm Springs, OR 97761
503-553-2411
503-553-2426 FAX

★AREA OFFICES HEADQUARTERS

SOUTH DAKOTA

★ABERDEEN AREA OFFICE
Bureau of Indian Affairs
115 4th Ave SE
Aberdeen, SD 57401
605-226-7343
605-226-7446 FAX

Cheyenne River Agency
Bureau of Indian Affairs
PO Box 325
Eagle Butte, SD 57625
605-964-6611
605-964-4060 FAX

Crow Creek Agency
Bureau of Indian Affairs
PO Box 139
Fort Thompson, SD 57339
605-245-2311
605-245-2343 FAX

Lower Brule Agency
Bureau of Indian Affairs
PO Box 190
Lower Brule, SD 57548
605-473-5512
605-473-5491 FAX

Pine Ridge Agency
Bureau of Indian Affairs
PO Box 1203
Pine Ridge, SD 57770
605-867-5125
605-867-1141 FAX

Rosebud Agency
Bureau of Indian Affairs
PO Box 550
Rosebud, SD 57570
605-747-2224
605-747-2805 FAX

Sisseton Agency
Bureau of Indian Affairs
PO Box 688
Agency Village, SD 57262
605-698-7676
605-698-7784 FAX

Yankton Agency
Bureau of Indian Affairs
PO Box 577
Wagner, SD 57380
605-384-3651
605-384-3876 FAX

UTAH

Uintah & Ouray Agency
Bureau of Indian Affairs
PO Box 130
Fort Duchesne, UT 84026
801-722-2406
801-722-2406 xx 61

VIRGINIA

★EASTERN AREA OFFICE
Bureau of Indian Affairs
3701 N Fairfax Dr
MS VASQ 260
Arlington, VA 22203
703-235-3006
703-235-8610 FAX

★AREA OFFICES HEADQUARTERS

WASHINGTON

Colville Agency
Bureau of Indian Affairs
PO Box 111
Nespelem, WA 99155
509-634-4901
509-634-8751 FAX

Makah Agency
Bureau of Indian Affairs
PO Box 115
Neah Bay, WA 98357
360-645-2201
360-645-2788 FAX

Olympic Peninsula Agency
Bureau of Indian Affairs
Office Bldg
PO Box 120
Hoquiam, WA 98550
360-533-9100
360-533-9141 FAX

Puget Sound Agency
Bureau of Indian Affairs
3006 Colby Fed Bldg
Everett, WA 98201
206-258-2651
206-258-1254 FAX

Spokane Agency
Bureau of Indian Affairs
PO Box 389
Wellpinit, WA 99040
509-258-4561
509-258-7542 FAX

Yakima Agency
Bureau of Indian Affairs
PO Box 632
Toppenish, WA 98948
509-865-2255
700-446-8198 FAX

WISCONSIN

Great Lake Agency
Bureau of Indian Affairs
615 Main St
Ashland, WI 54806
715-682-4527
715-682-8897 FAX

WYOMING

Wind River Agency
Bureau of Indian Affairs
Fort Washakie, WY 82514
307-332-7810
307-332-4578 FAX

UNITED STATES

BOARDING SCHOOLS OPERATED BY THE BUREAU OF INDIAN AFFAIRS

US DEPT OF THE INTERIOR
BUREAU OF INDIAN AFFAIRS
OFFICE OF INDIAN EDUCATION
MS 3512 MIB CODE OIE-3
1849 C St NW
Washington, DC 20240
202-208-6123
202-208-3271 FAX

ARIZONA

Black Mesa Community
RRDS Box 215
Chinle, AZ 86503
520-674-3632

Blackwater Community
Rt 1 Box 95
Coolidge, AZ 85228
520-215-5859

Casa Blanca Day
PO Box 940
Bapchule, AZ 85221
520-315-3489

Chilchinbeto Day
PO Box 547
Kayenta, AZ 86033
520-697-3448

Chinle Boarding
PO Box 70
Many Farms, AZ 86538
520-781-6221

Cibecue Community
PO Box 80068
Cibecue, AZ 85911
520-332-2444

Cottonwood Day
Navajo Rt 4
Chinle, AZ 86503
520-725-3256

Dennehotso Boarding
PO Box LL
Dennehotso, AZ 86535
520-658-3201

Dilcon Boarding
Star Route Hwy 61
Winslow, AZ 86047
520-657-3211

Flagstaff Dormitory
PO Box 609
Flagstaff, AZ 86002
520-774-5270

Gila Crossing Day
PO Box 10
Laveen, AZ 85339
520-550-4834

Greasewood Boarding
Ganado, AZ 86505
520-654-3331

Greyhills High School
PO Box 160
Tuba City, AZ 86045
520-283-6271

Havasupai
PO Box 40
Supai, AZ 86435
520-448-2901

Holbrook Dormitory
PO Box 758
Holbrook, AZ 86025
520-524-6222

Hopi Day
PO Box 42
Kykotsmovi, AZ 86039
520-734-2468

Hopi High School
PO Box 337
Keams Canyon, AZ 86034
520-738-5111

Hotevilla Bacavi Community
PO Box 48
Hotevilla, AZ 86030
520-734-2462

Hunters Point Boarding
PO Box 99
St Michaels, AZ 86511
520-871-4439

John F. Kennedy Day
PO Box 130
White River, AZ 85941
520-338-4593

Kaibeto Boarding
Hwy 160 E
Kaibeto, AZ 86053
520-673-3480

Kayenta Boarding
PO Box 188
Kayenta, AZ 86033
520-697-3439

Keams Canyon Boarding
PO Box 397
Keams Canyon, AZ 86034
520-738-2385

Kinlichee Boarding
Ganado, AZ 86505
520-755-3439

Leupp Schools, Inc.
PO Box HC-61
Winslow, AZ 86047
520-686-6211

Little Singer Community
HC 61 Box 239
Winslow, AZ 86047
520-526-6680

Low Mountain Boarding
Navajo Rt 65
Chinle, AZ 86503
520-725-3308

Lukachukai Boarding
Navajo Rt 12
Lukachukai, AZ 86507
520-787-2301

Many Farms High School
PO Box 307
Many Farms, AZ 86538
520-781-6226

Moencopi Day
PO Box 185
Tuba City, AZ 86045
520-283-5361

Navajo Mountain Boarding
PO Box 10010
Tonalea, AZ 86044
520-672-2851

Nazlini Boarding
Navajo Rt 27
Ganado, AZ 86505
520-755-6125

Pine Springs Boarding
PO Box 198
Houck, AZ 86506
520-871-4311

Pinon Dormitory
PO Box 159
Pinon, AZ 86510
520-725-3250

Polacca Day
PO Box 750
Polacca, AZ 86042
520-737-2581

Red Lake Day
PO Box 39
Tonalea, AZ 86044
520-283-6325

Red Rock Day
PO Box Drawer 10
Red Valley, AZ 86544
520-653-4456

Rock Point Community
Hwy 191
Rock Point, AZ 86545
520-659-4224

Rocky Ridge Boarding
PO Box 299
Kykotsmovi, AZ 86039
520-725-3415

Rough Rock Demonstration
RRDS Box 217
Chinle, AZ 86503
520-728-3311

Salt River Day
10000 E McDowell Rd
Scottsdale, AZ 85256
602-640-2810

San Simon
HC 02 Box 92
Sells, AZ 85634
520-362-2231

Santa Rosa Ranch
HC 04 #7570
Tucson, AZ 85735
520-383-2359

Santa Rosa Boarding
HC 02 Box 400
Sells, AZ 85634
520-361-2331

Seba Dalkai Boarding
HC 63
Winslow, AZ 86047
520-657-3208

Second Mesa Day
PO Box 98
Second Mesa, AZ 86043
520-737-2571

Shonto Boarding
Shonto, AZ 86054
520-672-2652

Teecnospos Boarding
PO Box 102
Teecnospos, AZ 86514
520-656-3451

Theodore Roosevelt
PO Box 567
Fort Apache, AZ 85926
520-338-4464

Tohono O'odham High School
HC 02 PO Box 513
Sells, AZ 85634
520-362-2400

Tuba City Boarding
PO Box 187
Tuba City, AZ 86045
520-283-2334

Wide Ruins Boarding
PO Box 309
Chambers, AZ 86502
520-652-3251

Winslow Dormitory
600 N Alfred Ave
Winslow, AZ 86047
520-289-4483

CALIFORNIA

Noli School
PO Box 487
San Jacinto, CA 92581
909-654-5596

Sherman Indian High School
9010 Magnolia Ave
Riverside, CA 92503
909-276-6327

FLORIDA

Ahfachkee Day
Star Rt Box 40
Clewiston, FL 33440
813-983-6348

Miccosukee Indian
PO Box 440021 Tamiami Sta
Miami, FL 33144
305-223-8380

IDAHO

Coeur D'Alene Tribal
PO Box 338
DeSmet, ID 83834
208-274-6921

ShoBan School District 512
PO Box 790
Fort Hall, ID 83203
208-238-3975

IOWA

Sac & Fox Settlement
1657 320th St
Tama, IA 52339
515-484-4990

KANSAS

Haskell Indian Nations University
155 University Ave # 1305
Lawrence, KS 66046
913-749-8404

Kickapoo Nation
PO Box 106
Powhattan, KS 66527
913-474-3550

LOUISIANA

Chitimacha Day
3613 Chitimacha Trl
Jeanerette, LA 70544
318-923-9960

MAINE

Beatrice Rafferty
Pleasant Point Reservation
RR 1 Box 338
Perry, ME 04667
207-853-6085

Indian Island
1 River Rd/Box 566
Old Town, ME 04468
207-827-4285

Indian Township
Peter Dana Point
Princeton, ME 04668
207-796-2362

MICHIGAN

Hannahville Indian
14911 N Hannahville B1 Rd
Wilson, MI 49896
906-466-2952

MINNESOTA

Chief Bug-O-Nay-Ge-Shig
Rt 3 Box 100
Cass Lake, MN 56633
218-665-2282

Circle of Life Survival
PO Box 447
White Earth, MN 56591
218-983-3285 xx 269

Fond du Lac Ojibway
105 University Rd
Cloquet, MN 55720
218-879-0241

Nay-Ah-Shing
HC 67 Box 242
Onamia, MN 56359
612-532-4695

MISSISSIPPI

Bogue Chitto
Rt 2 Box 274
Philadelphia, MS 39350
601-656-8611

Choctaw Central High School
Rt 7 Box 72
Philadelphia, MS 39350
601-656-8870

Choctaw Central Middle School
Rt 7 Box 72
Philadelphia, MS 39350
610-656-8938

Conehatta
Rt 1 Box 343
Conehatta, MS 39057
601-775-8254

Pearl River Elementary
Rt 7 Box 19-H
Philadelphia, MS 39350
601-656-9051

Red Water
Rt 4 Box 30
Carthage, MS 39051
601-267-8500

Standing Pine
Rt 2 Box 236
Walnut Grove, MS 39189
601-267-9225

Tucker
Rt 4 Box 351
Philadelphia, MS 39350
601-656-8775

MONTANA

Blackfeet Dormitory
Blackfeet Agency
PO Box 820
Browning, MT 59417
406-338-7441

Busby
PO Box 38
Busby, MT 59016
406-592-3646

Rocky Boy Tribal
Box 620 Rocky Boy Rt
Box Elder, MT 59521
406-395-4291

Two Eagle River
PO Box 362
Pablo, MT 59855
406-675-0292

NEVADA

Duckwater Shoshone
PO Box 140038
Duckwater, NV 89314
702-863-0242

Pyramid Lake High School
PO Box 256
Nixon, NV 89424
705-574-1016

NEW MEXICO

Alamo Navajo
PO Box 907
Magdalena, NM 87825
505-854-2635

Aztec Dormitory
1600 Lydia Rippey Rd
Aztec, NM 87410
505-334-6565

Baca Community
PO Box 509
Prewitt, NM 87045
505-876-2769

Beclabito Day
PO Box 1146
Shiprock, NM 87420
520-656-3555

Bread Springs Day
PO Box 1117
Gallup, NM 87305
505-778-5665

Chi-Ch'il-Tah/Jones Ranch
Commmunity
PO Box 278
Vanderwagon, NM 87326
505-778-5573

Chuska Boarding
PO Box 321
Tohatchi, NM 87325
505-733-2280

Cove Day
PO Box 3537
Shiprock, NM 87420
520-653-4457

Crownpoint Community
PO Box 178
Crownpoint, NM 87313
505-786-6160

Crystal Boarding
Navajo, NM 87328
505-777-2385

Dibe Yazhi Habitiin Olta Inc
PO Box 679
Crownpoint, NM 87313
505-786-5237

Dlo'Ay Azhi Community
PO Box 789
Thoreau, NM 87323
505-862-7525

Dzilth-na-o-dith-hle
Community
Star Rt 4 Box 5003
Bloomfield, NM 87413
505-632-1697

Huerfano Dormitory
PO Box 639
Bloomfield, NM 87413
505-325-3411

Isleta
PO Box 550
Isleta, NM 87022
505-869-2321

Jemez Day
PO Box 139
Jemez Pueblo, NM 87024
505-834-7304

Jicarilla Dormitory
PO Box 1009
Dulce, NM 87528
505-759-3101

Laguna Elementary
PO Box 191
Laguna, NM 87026
505-552-9200

Laguna Middle School
PO Box 268
Laguna, NM 87026
505-552-9091

Lake Valley Navajo
PO Box 748
Crownpoint, NM 87313
505-786-5392

Mariano Lake Community
PO Box 498
Crownpoint, NM 87313
505-786-5265

Mescalero
210 Central Mescalero Ave
Mescalero, NM 88340
505-671-4431

Na'Neelzhiin Ji'Olta (Torreon)
HCR 79 Box 9
Cuba, NM 87013
505-731-2272

Navajo Mission Academy
1220 W Apache
Farmington, NM 87401
505-326-6571

Nenahnezad Boarding
PO Box 337
Fruitland, NM 87416
505-598-6922

Ojo Encino Day
HCR 79 Box 7
Cuba, NM 87013
505-731-2333

Pine Hill
PO Box 202
Pine Hill, NM 87357
505-775-3242

Pueblo Pintado Community
HCR 79 Box 80
Cuba, NM 87013
505-655-3341

San Felipe
PO Box 4343
San Felipe Pueblo, NM 87001
505-867-3364

San Ildefonso Day
Rt 5 Box 308
Santa Fe, NM 87501
505-455-2366

San Juan Day
PO Box 1077
San Juan Pueblo, NM 87566
505-852-2154

Sanostee Day
PO Box 159
Sanostee, NM 87461
505-723-2476

Santa Clara Day
PO Box HHH
Espanola, NM 87532
505-753-4406

Santa Fe Indian
1501 Cerrillos Rd
PO Box 5340
Santa Fe, NM 87501
505-989-6300

NORTH DAKOTA

Dunseith Day
PO Box 759
Dunseith, ND 58329
701-263-4636

Four Winds Community
Tate Topa Tribal School
PO Box 199
Fort Totten, ND 58335
701-766-4161

Mandaree Day
PO Box 488
Mandaree, ND 58757
701-759-3311

Ojibwa Indian
PO Box 600
Belcourt, ND 58316
701-477-3108

Standing Rock Community
PO Box 377
Fort Yates, ND 58538
701-854-3865

Theodore Jamerson
3315 University Dr
Bismarck, ND 58504
701-255-3285

Turtle Mountain Elementary
PO Box 440
Belcourt, ND 58316
701-477-6471 xx 314

Turtle Mountain High School
PO Box 440
Belcourt, ND 58316
701-477-6471 xx 222

Turtle Mountain Middle School
PO Box 440
Belcourt, ND 58316
701-477-6471 xx 270

Twin Buttes Day
Rt 1 Box 65
Halliday, ND 58636
701-938-4396

Circle of Nations
Wahpeton Indian Boarding
832 8th St N
Wahpeton, ND 58075
701-642-3796

White Shield
HC 1 Box 45
Roseglen, ND 58775
701-743-4355

OKLAHOMA

Eufaula Dormitory
Swadley Dr
Eufaula, OK 74432
918-689-2522

Carter Seminary
2400 Chickasaw Blvd
Ardmore, OK 73401
405-223-8547

Jones Academy
HCR 74 Box 102-5
Hartshorne, OK 74547
918-297-2518

Riverside Indian
Route 1
Anadarko, OK 73005
405-247-6673

Shiprock Reservation Dormitory
PO Box 1180
Shiprock, NM 87420
505-368-5113

Shiprock Alternative High School
PO Box 1799
Shiprock, NM 87420
505-368-5144

Shiprock Alternative Elementary
1879 Pinon St
Shiprock, NM 87420
505-368-5170

S.W. Indian Poly. Inst.
PO Box 10146
Albuquerque, NM 87184
505-897-5347

Sky City Community
PO Box 349
Acoma, NM 87034
505-552-6671

Taos Day
PO Drawer X
Taos, NM 87571
505-758-3652

Tesuque Day
Rt 11 Box 2
Santa Fe, NM 87501
505-982-1516

To'Hajiilee-He (Canoncito)
PO Box 438
Laguna, NM 87026
505-831-6426

Toadlena Boarding
PO Box 9857
Newcomb, NM 87455
505-789-3201

Tse'ii'ahi' Community
PO Box 828
Crownpoint, NM 87313
505-786-5389

Wingate
PO Box 1
Fort Wingate, NM 87316
505-488-6470

Wingate High School
PO Box 2
Fort Wingate, NM 87316
505-488-6400

Zia Day
350 Riverside Dr
San Ysidro, NM 87053
505-867-3553

NORTH CAROLINA

Cherokee Central High School
PO Box 134
Cherokee, NC 28719
704-497-6370

Cherokee Elementary
PO Box 134
Cherokee, NC 28719
704-497-6370

Sequoyah High School
PO Box 948
Tahlequah, OK 74465
918-456-0631

OREGON

Chemawa Indian
3700 Chemawa Rd NE
Salem, OR 97305
503-399-5721

SOUTH DAKOTA

American Horse
PO Box 660
Allen, SD 57714
605-455-2480

Cheyenne-Eagle Butte
PO Box 672
Eagle Butte, SD 57625
605-964-8777

Crazy Horse
PO Box 260
Wanblee, SD 57577
605-462-6511

Crow Creek Sioux Tribal Elementary
PO Box 469
Fort Thompson, SD 57339
605-245-2372

Crow Creek Reservation High School
PO Box 12
Stephan, SD 57346
605-852-2455

Enemy Swim Day
RR 1 Box 87
Waubay, SD 57273
605-947-4605

Flandreau Indian
1000 N Crescent
Flandreau, SD 57028
605-997-2724

Fort Thompson
PO Box 139
Fort Thompson, SD 57339
605-245-2372

Little Eagle Day
PO Box 26
Little Eagle, SD 57639
605-823-4235

Little Wound Day
PO Box 500
Kyle, SD 57752
605-455-2461

Loneman Day
PO Box 50
Oglala, SD 57764
605-867-5633

Lower Brule Day
PO Box 245
Lower Brule, SD 57548
605-473-5510

Marty Indian
PO Box 187
Marty, SD 57361
605-384-5431

Pierre Indian Learning Ctr
HC 31 Box 148
Pierre, SD 57501
605-224-8661

Pine Ridge
PO Box 1202
Pine Ridge, SD 57770
605-867-5198

Porcupine Day School
PO Box 180
Porcupine, SD 57772
605-867-5336

Promise Day
HCR 30 Box 10
Mobridge, SD 57601
605-733-2148

Rock Creek Day
PO Box 127
Bullhead, SD 57621
605-823-4971

Rosebud Dormitories
PO Box 669
Mission, SD 57555
605-856-4486

St Francis Indian
PO Box 379
St Francis, SD 57572
605-747-2299

Swift Bird Day
HCR 3 Box 119
Gettysburg, SD 57442
605-733-2143

Takini
HC 77 Box 537
Howes, SD 57748
605-538-4399

Tiospa Zina
PO Box 719
Agency Village, SD 57262
605-698-3953

White Horse Day
PO Box 7
White Horse, SD 57661
605-733-2183

Wounded Knee District
PO Box 350
Manderson, SD 57756
605-867-5433

UTAH

Aneth Community
PO Box 600
Montezuma Creek, UT 84534
801-651-3271

Richfield Dormitory
PO Box 638
Richfield, UT 84701
801-896-5101

WASHINGTON

Lummi High School
2522 Kwina Rd
Bellingham, WA 98226
360-738-2330

Lummi Tribal School System
2530 Kwina Rd
Bellingham, WA 98226
360-647-6275

Muckleshoot Tribal
39015 172nd Ave SE
Auburn, WA 98092
206-939-3311

Paschal Sherman Indian
Omak Lake Rd
Omak, WA 98841
509-826-2097

Puyallup Nation Education
System (Chief Leschi)
2002 E 28th St
Tacoma, WA 98404
206-593-0218

Quileute Tribal School
PO Box 39
La Push, WA 98350
360-374-2061

Wa He Lut Indian
11110 Conine Ave SE
Olympia, WA 98513
360-456-1311

Yakama Tribal
PO Box 151
Toppenish, WA 98948
509-865-5121

WISCONSIN

Lac Courte Oreilles Ojibwa
Rt 2 Box 2800
Hayward, WI 54843
715-634-8924

Menominee Tribal
Menominee Indian Tribe
PO Box 39
Neopit, WI 54150
715-756-2354

Oneida Tribal
PO Box 365
Oneida, WI 54155
414-869-1676

WYOMING

Saint Stephens Indian
PO Box 345
St Stephens, WY 82524
307-856-4147

Information provided by: Office of Indian Programs
Education Directory 1995-1996

ANSWERS TO FREQUENTLY ASKED QUESTIONS

Who is an Indian?

No single federal or tribal criterion establishes a person's identity as an Indian. Government agencies use differing criteria to determine who is an Indian eligible to participate in their programs. Tribes also have varying eligibility criteria for membership. To determine what the criteria might be for agencies or tribes, you must contact them directly.

For its purposes, the Bureau of Census counts anyone an Indian who declares himself or herself to be such.

To be eligible for Bureau of Indian Affairs services, an Indian must (1) be a member of a tribe recognized by the federal government and (2) must, for some purposes, be of one-fourth or more Indian ancestry. By legislative and administrative decision, the Aleuts, Eskimos and Indians of Alaska are eligible for BIA services. Most of the BIA's services and programs, however, are limited to Indians living on or near federal reservations.

What is an Indian Tribe?

Originally, an Indian tribe was a body of people bound together by blood ties who were socially, politically, and religiously organized, who lived together in a defined territory and who spoke a common language or dialect.

The establishment of the reservation system created some new tribal groupings when two or three tribes were placed on one reservation, or when members of one tribe were spread over two or three reservations.

How does an Indian become a member of a tribe?

A tribe sets up its own membership criteria, although the U.S. Congress can also establish tribal membership criteria. Becoming a member of a particular tribe requires meeting its membership rules, including adoption. Except for adoption, the amount of blood quantum needed varies, with some tribes requiring only a trace of Indian blood (of the tribe) while others require as much as one-half.

What is a reservation?

In the U.S. there are only two kinds of reserved lands that are well known - military and Indian. An Indian reservation is land a tribe reserved for itself when it relinquished its other land areas to the U.S. through treaties. More recently, Congressional acts, executive orders and administrative acts have created reservations. Some reservations, today, have non-Indian residents and land owners.

Are Indians required to stay on reservations?

No. Indians are free to move about like all other Americans.

Did all Indians speak one Indian language?

No. At the end of the 15th century, more than 300 languages were spoken by the native population of what is now the United States. Some were linked by "linguistic stocks" which meant that widely scattered tribal groups had some similarities in their languages. Today, some 250 tribal languages are still spoken, some by only a few individuals and others by many. Most Indians now use English as their main language for communicating with non-tribal members. For many, it is a second language.

Do Indians serve in the Armed Forces?

Indians have the same obligations for military service as other U.S. citizens. They have fought in all American wars since the Revolution. In the Civil War, they served on both sides. Eli S. Parker, Seneca from New York, was at Appamattox as aide to Gen. Ulyssess S. Grant when Lee surrendered, and the unit of Confederate Brigadier General Stand Watie, Cherokee, was the last to surrender. It was not until World War I that Indians' demonstrated patriotism (6,000 of more than 8,000 who served were volunteers) moved congress to pass the Indian Citizenship Act of 1924. In World War II, 25,000 Indian men and women, mainly enlisted Army personnel, fought on all fronts in Europe and Asia, winning (according to an incomplete count) 71 Air Medals, 51 Silver Stars, 47 Bronze Stars, 34 Distinguished Flying Crosses, and two Congressional Medals of Honor. The most famous Indian exploit of World War II was the use by Navajo Marines of their language as a battlefield code, the only such code which the enemy could not break. In the Korean conflict, there was one Indian Congressional medal of Honor winner. In the Vietnam War, 41,500 Indians served in the military forces. In 1990, prior to Operation Desert Storm, some 24,000 Indian men and women were in the military. Approximately

3,000 served in the Persian Gulf with three among those killed in action. One out of every four Indian males is a military veteran and 45 to 47 percent of tribal leaders today are military veterans.

Are Indians wards of the government?

No. The federal government is a trustee of Indian property, it is not a guardian of individual Indians. The Secretary of the Interior is authorized by law, in many instances, to protect the interests of minors and incompetents, but this protection does not confer a guardian-ward relationship.

Do Indians get payments from the government?

No individual is automatically paid for being an Indian. The federal government may pay a tribe or an individual in compensation for damages for losses resulting from treaty violations, for encroachments on Indian lands, or for other past or present wrongs. A tribe or an individual may also receive a government check for payment of income from their lands and resources, but his is only because their resources are held in trust by the Secretary of the Interior and payment for their use has been collected from users by the federal government in their behalf. Fees from oil or grazing leases are an example.

Are Indians U.S. Citizens?

Yes. Before the U.S. Congress extended American citizenship in 1924 to all Indians born in the territorial limits of the United States, citizenship has been conferred upon approximately two-thirds of the Indian population through treaty agreements, statutes, naturalization proceedings, and by "service in the Armed Forces with an honorable discharge" in World War I. Indians are also members of their respective tribes.

Can Indians Vote?

Indians have the same right to vote as other U.S. Citizens. In 1948, the Arizona supreme court declared unconstitutional disenfranchising interpretations of the state constitution and Indians were permitted to vote as in most other states. A 1953 Utah state law stated that persons living on Indian reservation were not residents of the state and could not vote. That law was subsequently repealed. In 1954, Indians in Maine who were not then federally recognized were given the right to vote, and in 1962, New Mexico extended the right to vote to Indians.

Indians also vote in state and local elections and in the elections of the tribes of which they are members. Each tribe, however, determines which of its members is eligible to vote in its elections and qualifications to do so are not related to the individual Indian's right to vote in national, state, or local (non-Indian) elections.

Do Indians have the right to hold federal, state and local government offices?

Indians have the same right as other citizens to hold public office, and Indian men and women have held elective and appointive offices at all levels of government. Charles Curtis, a Kaw Indian from Kansas, served as Vice President of the United States under President Herbert Hoover.

Indians have been elected to the U.S. Congress from time to time for more than 80 years. Ben Reifel, a Sioux Indian from South Dakota, served five terms in the U.S. House of Representatives. Ben Nighthorse Campbell, a member of the Northern Cheyenne Tribe of Montana, was elected to the U.S. House of Representatives in 1986 from the Third District of Colorado, and is currently serving in his third term. He is the only American Indian currently serving in Congress. Indians also served and now hold office in a number of state legislatures. Others currently hold or have held elected or appointed positions in state judiciary systems and in county and city governments including local school boards.

Do Indians have the right to own land?

Yes. As U.S. citizens, Indians can buy and hold title to land purchased with their own funds. Nearly all lands of Indian tribes, however, are held in trust for them by the United States and there is no general law that permits a tribe to sell its land. Individual Indians also own trust land which they can sell, but only upon the approval of the Secretary of the Interior or his representative. If an Indian wants to extinguish the trust title of his land and hold title like any other citizen (with all the attendant responsibilities such as paying taxes), he can do so if the Secretary of the Interior or his authorized representative, determines that he is able to manage his own affairs. This is a protection for the individual.

Do Indians pay taxes?

Yes. They pay the same taxes as other citizens with the following exceptions applying to those Indians living on federal reservations: (1) federal income taxes are not levied on income from trust lands held for them by the United States; (2) state income taxes are not paid on income earned on a federal reservation; (3) state sales tax are not paid on transactions made on a federal reservation, and (4) local property taxes are not paid on reservation or trust land.

Do laws that apply to non-Indians also apply to Indians?

Yes. As U.S. citizens, Indians are generally subject to federal, state, and local laws. On federal reservations, however, only federal and tribal laws apply to members of the tribe unless the Congress provides otherwise. In federal law, the Assimilative Crimes Act makes any violation of state criminal law a federal offense on reservations.

Most tribes now maintain tribal court systems and facilities to detain tribal members convicted of certain offenses within the boundaries of the the reservation. A recent U.S. Supreme Court decision restricted the legal jurisdiction of federal tribes on their reservations to members only, meaning that an Indian tribe could not try in its tribal court a member of another tribe even though that person might be a resident on the reservation and have violated its law. There currently are bills in the Congress that would restore tribes' rights to prosecute any Indian violating laws on an Indian reservation.

Does the United States still make treaties with Indians?

Congress ended treaty-making with Indian tribes in 1871. Since then, relations with Indian groups are by congressional acts, executive orders, and executive agreements. The treaties that were made often contain obsolete commitments which have either been fulfilled or superseded by congressional legislation., The provision of educational, health, welfare, and other services by the government to tribes often has extended beyond treaty requirements. A number of large Indian groups have no treaties, yet share in the many services for Indians provided by the federal government.

The specifics of particular treaties signed by government negotiators with Indians are contained in one volume (Vol.II) of the publication, "Indian Affairs, Laws, and Treaties", compiled, annotated and edited by Charles Kappler. Published by the Government Printing Office in 1904, it is now out of print, but can be found in most large law libraries. More recently, the treaty volume has been published privately under the title, "Indian Treaties, 1778-1883". Originals of all the treaties are maintained by the National Archives and Records Service of the General Services Administration. A duplicate of a treaty is available upon request for a fee. The agency will also answer questions about specific Indian treaties. Write to: Diplomatic Branch, National Archives and Records Service, Washington, D.C. 20408.

How do Indian tribes govern themselves?

Most tribal governments are organized democratically, that is, with an elected leadership. The governing body is generally referred to as a "council" and is comprised of persons elected by vote of the eligible adult tribal members. The presiding official is the "chairman", although some tribes use other titles such as "principal chief", "president" or "governor". An elected tribal council, recognized as such by the Secretary of the Interior, has authority to speak and act for the tribe and to represent it in negotiations with federal, state, and local governments.

Tribal governments generally define conditions of membership, regulate domestic relations of members, prescribe rules of inheritance for reservation property not in trust status, levy taxes, regulate property under tribal jurisdiction, control conduct of members by tribal ordinances, and administer justice.

Many tribes are organized under the Indian Reorganization Act (IRA) of 1934, including a number of Alaskan Native villages, which adopted formal governing documents (Constitutions) under the provisions of a 1936 amendment to the IRA. The passage in 1971 of the Alaska Native Claims Settlement Act, however, provided for the creation of village and regional corporations under state law to manage the money and lands granted by the Act. The Oklahoma Indian Welfare Act of 1936 provided for the organization of Indian tribes within the State of Oklahoma. Some tribes do not operate under any of these acts, but are nevertheless organized under documents approved by the Secretary of the Interior. Some tribes continue their traditional forms of government.

Prior to reorganization, the tribes maintained their own, often highly developed, systems of self-government.

Do Indians have special rights different from other citizens?

Any special rights that Indian tribes or members of those tribes have are generally based on treaties or other agreements between the United States and tribes. The heavy price Indians paid to retain certain "sovereign" rights was to relinquish much of their land to the United States. The inherent rights they did not relinquish are protected by U.S.

law. Among those may be hunting and fishing rights and access to religious sites.

How do I trace my Indian ancestry and become a member of a tribe?

The first step in tracing Indian ancestry is basic genealogical research if you do not already have specific family information and documents that identify tribal ties. Some information to obtain is; names of ancestors; dates of birth, marriages and death; places where they lived; their brothers and sisters, if any, and most importantly, tribal affiliations. Among family documents to check are bibles, wills, and other such papers. The next step is to determine whether any of your ancestors are on an official tribal roll or census. For this there are several sources. Contact the National Archives and Records Administration, Natural Resources Branch, Civil Archives Division, 8th and Pennsylvania Ave. N.W., Washington, D.C. 20408. Also, you may contact the tribal enrollment officer of the tribe of which you think your ancestors may have been members. Another source is the Bureau of Indian Affairs, Branch of Tribal Enrollment, 1849 C St. N.W., Washington, D.C. 20240. The key in determining your Indian ancestry is identification of a specific tribal affiliation.

Becoming a member of a tribe is determined by the enrollment criteria of the tribe from which your Indian blood may be derived, and this varies with each tribe. Generally, if your linkage to an identified tribal member is far removed, you would not qualify for membership, but it is the tribe, not the BIA, which makes the determination.

What does tribal sovereignty mean to Indians?

When Indian tribes first encountered Europeans, they were dealt with from strength of numbers and were treated as sovereigns with whom treaties were made. When tribes gave up lands to the U.S., they retained certain sovereignty over the lands they kept. While such sovereignty is limited today, it is nevertheless jealously guarded by the tribes against encroachments by other sovereign entities such as states. Tribes enjoy a direct government-to-government relationship with the U.S. government wherein no decisions about their lands and people are made without their consent.

What does the term "federally-recognized" mean?

Indian tribes that have a legal relationship to the U.S. government through treaties, Acts of Congress, executive orders, or other administrative actions are "recognized" by the federal government as official entities and receive services from the state. Others have neither federal or state recognition and may not seek such recognition. Any tribe or group is eligible to seek federal recognition by a process administered by a program of the Bureau of Indian Affairs or through direct petition to the U.S. Congress. Only the congress has the power to terminate a tribe from federal recognition. In that case, a tribe no longer has its lands held in trust by the U.S. nor does it receive services from the BIA.

Do all Indians live on reservations?

No. Indians can and do live anywhere in the United States that they wish. Many leave their home reservations for educational and employment purposes. Over half of the total U.S. Indian and Alaska Native population now lives away from reservations. Most return home often to participate in family and tribal life and sometimes to retire.

Why are Indians sometimes referred to as Native Americans?

The term, "Native American", came into usage in the 1960s' to denote the groups served by the Bureau of Indian Affairs: American Indians and Alaska Natives (Indians, Eskimos and Aleuts of Alaska). Later the term also included Native Hawaiians and Pacific Islanders in some federal programs. It, therefore, came into disfavor among some Indian groups. The Eskimos and Aleuts in Alaska are two culturally distinct groups and are sensitive about being included under the "Indian" designation. They prefer, "Alaska Native".

Does the BIA provide scholarships for all Indians?

The Bureau provides some higher education scholarship assistance for eligible members of federally-recognized tribes. For information, contact the Indian Education Program, Bureau of Indian Affairs, 1849 C St. N.W., Washington, D.C. 20240.

American Indians Today third edition, United States Department of the Interior-Bureau of Indian Affairs, MS 2620-MIB, Washington, D.C. 20240-0001.

QUICK NOTES !

**Information for this page is only available in the Library Edition.

Fred Synder, Director, Consultant

N.A.²I.I.T.C.

North American Native American Indian Information & Trade Center

QUICK NOTES !

**Information for this page is only available in the Library Edition.

Fred Synder, Director, Consultant

N.A.²I.I.T.C.

North American Native American Indian Information & Trade Center

QUICK NOTES !

**Information for this page is only available in the Library Edition.

Fred Synder, Director, Consultant

N.A.²I.I.T.C.

North American Native American Indian Information & Trade Center

UNITED STATES

INDIAN HEALTH SERVICE PROJECTS

Indian Health Services

The primary Federal health resource for American Indians and Alaska Natives is the Indian Health Service (IHS), an agency of the Public Health Service of the U.S. Department of Health and Human Services. The IHS operates hospitals and clinics on reservations and provides related health services for Indian communities. Like the BIA, the IHS contracts with tribes to operate some of its programs. Some of the significant statistics related to the state of Indian health in 1991 are as follows:

Birth Rate - Birth rates were 28.0 births per 1,000 in 1986-88. The U.S. all races rate was 15.7 births per 1,000 in 1987.

Infant Death Rate - The infant death rate was 9.7 per 1,000 live births in 1986-88, while the U.S. all races was 10.1 per 1,000 births in 1987.

Life Expectancy - In 1979-81, life expectancy was 71.1 years (males, 67.1 years and females 75.1 years). These figures are based on 1980 census information.

Causes of Death - Diseases of the heart and accidents continue to be the two major causes of death among American Indians and Alaska Natives. The 1988 age-adjusted death rate for diseases of the heart was 138.1 per 100,000 of the population and 166.3 per 100,000 for all U.S. races. In the same period, the age-adjusted death rate from accidents was 80.8 per 100,000, including 44.7 related to motor vehicle accidents and 36.1 from other accidents. The U.S. all races 1988 age-adjustment rate was 35.0 per 100,000, including 19.7 related to motor vehicle accidents and 15.3 related to other accidents.

Suicide Rate - The age-adjusted suicide death rate for the population has decreased 29 percent since its peak in 1975 (21.1 deaths per 100,000 population). The Indian rate for 1988 was 14.5 compared to the U.S. all races rate of 11.4.

HIV/AIDS - The numbers of AIDS cases among American Indians and Alaska Natives is, as yet, relatively low (236 in the period 1982-1990). There are, however, no firm statistics on the numbers of those who may be HIV-positive. The IHS is, therefore, directing its attention to education/prevention, surveillance, and treatment programs in cooperation with the BIA in its school systems, with tribal leaders, and local and state health departments. The Centers for Disease Control (CDS) provides some funding support toward the total fiscal year 1991 budget for this work of $3.1 million.

American Indians Today third edition, United States Department of the Interior-Bureau of Indian Affairs, MS 2620-MIB, Washington, DC 20240-0001.

INDIAN HEALTH SERVICE HEADQUARTERS

US DEPT. OF HEALTH &
HUMAN SERVICES
PUBLIC HEALTH SERVICE
PARKLAWN BUILDING
5600 FISHERS LANE
ROCKVILLE MD 20857
301-443-0658
1-800-638-3986
301-443-0507 FAX

ALBUQUERQUE -
HEADQUARTERS WEST
5300 HOMESTEAD RD NE
ALBUQUERQUE NM 87110
505-837-4101
505-837-4415 FAX

ALASKA: * SEE ALASKA SECTION*

INDIAN HEALTH SERVICE REGIONAL HEADQUARTERS

Aberdeen Area Indian
Health Services
Federal Building
115 Fourth Ave SE
Aberdeen SD 57401
605-226-7581
605-226-7670 FAX
States Served: ND, SD, IA, NE
Office Hours: 7:45AM - 4:30PM Central Time

Alaska Area Indian
Health Service
250 Gambell St
Anchorage AK 99501
907-257-1363
907-257-1168 FAX
States Served: AK
Office Hours: 7:30AM - 4:30PM Pacific Time

Albuquerque Area Indian
Health Service
505 Marquette NW Ste 1502
Albuquerque NM 87102-2163
505-766-2334
505-766-2157 FAX
States Served: NM, CO, TX
Office Hours: 8:00AM - 4:30PM Mountain Time

Bemidji Area Indian
Health Service
127 Federal Building
Bemidji MN 56601
218-759-3378
218-759-3511 FAX
States Served: MN, MI, WI
Office Hours: 8:00AM - 4:30PM Central Time

Billings Area Indian
Health Service
PO Box 2143
711 Central Ave
Billings MT 59103
406-657-6403
406-657-6333 FAX
States Served: MT, WY
Office Hours: 8:00AM -
4:30PM Mountain Time

California Area Indian
Health Service
1825 Bell St Ste 200
Sacramento CA 95825-1097
916-978-4202
916-978-4216 FAX
States Served: CA
Office Hours: 8:00AM -
4:30PM Pacific Time

Nashville Area Indian
Health Service
711 Stewarts Ferry Pike
Nashville TN 37214-2634
615-736-2440
615-736-2391
States Served: Eastern
Office Hours: 8:00AM -
4:30PM Central Time

Navajo Area Indian
Health Service
PO Box 9020
Hwy 264 - St Michaels
Window Rock AZ 86515
520-871-5811
520-871-5896
States Served: AZ, NM, UT
Office Hours: 8:00AM -
4:45PM Mountain Time

Oklahoma City Area Indian
Health Service
Five Corporate Plaza
3625 NW 56 St
Oklahoma City OK 73112
405-945-6890
405-945-6870
States Served: OK, KS, TX
Office Hours: 8:00AM -
4:45PM Central Time

Phoenix Area Indian
Health Service
3738 N 16th St Ste A
Phoenix AZ 85016-5981
602-640-2061
602-640-2557
States Served: AZ, NV, UT
Office Hours: 8:00AM -
4:30PM Mountain Time

Portland Area Indian
Health Service
1220 SW Third Ave Rm 476
Portland OR 97204-2892
503-326-2009
503-326-7280
States Served: ID, OR, WA
Office Hours: 8:00AM -
4:45PM Pacific Time

Office of Health Program
Research & Development
Indian Health Service
7900 S "J" Stock Rd
Tucson AZ 85746-9352
520-295-2406
States Served: AZ
Office Hours: 8:00AM -
4:30PM Mountain Time

IHS HOSPITALS, CLINICS, CONSORTIUMS

ARIZONA

Bylas Health Center
PO Box 208
San Carlos, AZ 85550
520-485-2686

Chinle PHS Indian Hospital
PO Drawer PH
Chinle, AZ 86503
520-674-5282

Cibecue PHS Indian Health Center
Cibecue, AZ 85941
520-332-2560

Fort Defiance PHS Indian Hospital
PO Box 649
Ft. Defiance, AZ 86504
520-729-5741

Fort Yuma PHS Indian Hospital
PO Box 1368
Yuma, AZ 85364
619-572-0217

Havasupai Indian Health Station
Supai, AZ 86435
520-448-2641

Huhukam Memorial Hospital
PO Box 38
Sacaton, AZ 85247
520-562-3321

Inscription House PHS Indian Health Center
Inscription House, AZ 86054
520-672-2611

Kayenta PHS Indian Health Center
PO Box 368
Kayenta, AZ 86033
520-697-3211

Keams Canyon PHS Indian Hospital
PO Box 98
Keams Canyon, AZ 86034
520-738-2211

★NAVAJO AREA INDIAN HEALTH SERVICE
PO Box 9020
Window Rock, AZ 86515
520-871-5811
520-871-5866 FAX

Parker PHS Indian Hospital
Rt 1 Box 12
Parker, AZ 85344
520-669-2137

Peach Springs PHS Indian Health Center
PO Box 190
Peach Springs, AZ 86434
520-769-2204

Phoenix Indian Medical Center
4212 N 16th
Phoenix, AZ 85016
602-263-1200

★PHOENIX AREA INDIAN HEALTH SERVICE
3738 N 16th # A
Phoenix, AZ 85016
602-640-2061
602-640-2557 FAX

*TRIBAL OPERATION ★AREA OFFICE

San Carlos PHS Indian Hospital
PO Box 208
San Carlos, AZ 85550
520-475-2371

San Xavier PHS Indian Health Center
7900 S "J" Stock Rd
Tucson, AZ 85746
520-295-2550

Santa Rosa PHS Indian Health Center
Star Rt Box 71
Sells, AZ 85634
520-361-2261

Scottsdale Salt River Clinic
Rt 1 Box 215
Scottsdale, AZ 85256
602-379-4281

Second Mesa PHS Indian Health Center
PO Box 98
Keams Canyon, AZ 86034
520-738-2297

Sells PHS Indian Hospital
PO Box 548
Sells, AZ 85634
520-383-7251

Tsaile PHS Indian Health Center
Tsaile, AZ 86556
520-724-3391

Tuba City PHS Indian Med. Ctr.
PO Box 600
Tuba City, AZ 86045
520-283-6211

Whiteriver PHS Indian Hospital
PO Box 860
Whiteriver, AZ 85941
520-338-4911

Winslow PHS Indian Health Center
PO Drawer 40
Winslow, AZ 86047
520-289-4646

CALIFORNIA

American Indian Health Council - Central CA
2210 Chester Ave
Bakersfield, CA 93301
805-327-2207
805-327-4533 FAX

American Indian Free Clinic
9500 E Artesia Blvd
Bellflower, CA 90708
310-920-7272
310-920-5677 FAX

★CALIFORNIA AREA INDIAN HEALTH SERVICE
1825 Bell # 200
Sacramento, CA 95821
916-978-4202
916-978-4216 FAX

Central Valley Health Program
20 N Dewitt
Clovis, CA 93612
209-299-2578
209-299-0245 FAX

Chapa-De Indian Health Program
11670 Atwood Rd
Auburn, CA 95603
916-887-2800
916-887-2819 FAX

Consolidated Tribal Health Program
564 S Dora
Ukiah, CA 95482
707-468-5341
707-468-8610 FAX

Feather River Indian Health
2167 Montgomery St
Oroville, CA 95965
916-534-6135
916-534-3820 FAX

Fresno Indian Health Assoc
4991 E McKinley Ste 109
Fresno, CA 93727
209-255-0261

*Greenville Rancheria Tribal Health
PO Box 279
Greenville, CA 95947
916-284-6135
916-284-7135 FAX

*Hoopa Health Association
PO Box 1288
Hoopa, CA 95546
916-625-4261
916-625-4781 FAX

Indian Health Center of Santa Clara Valley
1333 Meridan Ave
San Jose, CA 95125
408-294-7553
408-294-6452 FAX

Indian Health Council
PO Box 406
Pauma Valley, CA 92061
619-749-1410
619-749-1564 FAX

Karuk Tribal Health
PO Box 1016
Happy Camp, CA 96039
916-493-5304
916-493-5322 FAX

Lake County Tribal Health
5124 Hill Rd E
Lakeport, CA 95453
707-263-8322
707-263-0329 FAX

Modoc Indian Health Program
PO Box 251
Alturas, CA 96101
916-233-4591
916-233-3055 FAX

Native American Health
56 Julian Ave
San Francisco, CA 94103
415-621-8051
415-621-3985 FAX

Northern Valley Indian Health Program
827-A S Tehema
Willows, CA 95988
916-934-9293
916-534-6140 FAX

Pi-Ma-Pa Lassen Indian Health Center
745 Joaquin St
Susanville, CA 96130
916-257-2541
916-257-6983 FAX

Pit River Health Services
PO Box 2720
Burney, CA 96013
916-335-5091
916-335-5241 FAX

*TRIBAL OPERATION ★AREA OFFICE

Redding Rancheria Health
3184 Churn Creek Rd
Redding, CA 96002
916-224-2700
916-224-2738 FAX

Riverside/San Bernardino Co. Indian Health Program
11555 1/2 Potrero Rd
Banning, CA 92220
909-849-4761
909-849-5612 FAX

Round Valley Indian Health Program
PO Box 247
Covelo, CA 95428
707-983-6181
707-983-6842 FAX

Sacramento Urban Indian Health
801 Broadway
Sacramento, CA 95819
916-441-0918
916-441-1261

San Diego American Indian Health
2561 1st Ave
San Diego, CA 92103
619-234-2158
619-234-0206

Santa Barbara Urban
1919 State
Santa Barbara, CA 93105
805-682-6701

Santa Ynez Indian Health Program
PO Box 539
Santa Ynez, CA 93460
805-688-4886
805-688-2060 FAX

Shasta-Trinity Indian Health Program
2110 North St
Anderson, CA 96007
916-365-9191

Sherman School Health Center
8934 Magnolia
Riverside, CA 92503
909-276-6321

Sonoma County Indian Health
PO Box 7308
Santa Rosa, CA 95407
707-544-4056
707-526-1015 FAX

Southern Indian Health Council
PO Box 2128
Alpine, CA 91903
619-445-1188
619-445-4131 FAX

Sycuan Medical/Dental Center
5442 Denesa Rd
El Cajon, CA 92019
619-445-0707
619-445-0988 FAX

Toiyabe Indian Health Program
PO Box 1296
Bishop, CA 93514
619-837-8464
619-873-3935 FAX

Tule River Indian Health Program
PO Box 768
Porterville, CA 93258
209-784-2316
209-781-6514 FAX

*TRIBAL OPERATION ★AREA OFFICE

Tuolumne River Indian Health
PO Box 577
Tuolumne, CA 95379
209-928-4277
209-928-1295

United Indian Health Services
PO Box 420
Trinidad, CA 95570
707-677-3693
707-677-3170 FAX

Urban Indian Health Board
3124 E 14th
Oakland, CA 94601
510-261-0524
510-261-6438 FAX

Warner Mt Indian Health
PO Box 127
Ft Bidwell, CA 96112
918-279-6194
918-279-2233 FAX

COLORADO

Ignacio PHS Indian Health Center
PO Box 889
Ignacio, CO 81137
303-563-4581

Southern Colorado
Ute Service Unit
PO Box 778
Ignacio, CO 81137
303-563-9447
303-563-9447 FAX

Towaoc PHS Indian Health
Center
General Delivery
Towaoc, CO 81334
303-565-4441
303-565-4945 FAX

IDAHO

Northern Idaho PHS Indian
Health Center
PO Drawer 367
Lapwai, ID 83540
208-843-2271

Not-Tsoo Gah-Nee Indian Health
Center
PO Box 717
Ft. Hall, ID 83203
208-238-2400

KANSAS

Haskell PHS Indian Health Center
2415 Massachusetts Ave
Lawrence, KS 66044
913-843-3750
913-843-8815 FAX

Holton PHS Indian Health Center
100 W 6th
Holton, KS 66436
913-364-2177
913-364-3691 FAX

Kickapoo Health Center
PO Box 271
Horton, KS 66439
913-486-2822

MICHIGAN

*Bay Mills Indian Community
Rt 1 Box 313
Brimley, MI 49751
906-248-3204

*TRIBAL OPERATION

★AREA OFFICE

*Grand Traverse
Ottawa/Chippewa
Rt 1 Box 135
Suttons Bay, MI 49682
616-271-3882

*Hannahville Indian Community
14911 N Hannahville Blvd Rd
Wilson, MI 49896
906-466-2782

Keweenaw Bay Indian Community
Route 1
Baraga, MI 49908
906-353-6671

*Lac Vieux Desert Band
PO Box 446
Watersmeet, MI 49969
906-358-4577

*Min-no-aya-win Clinic
927 Trettel Ln
Cloquet, MI 55720
218-879-1227

*Nimkee Memorial
Wellness Center
2591 S Leaton Rd
Mt Pleasant, MI 48858
517-773-9887

Saginaw Chippewa Indian
Community
7070 E Broadway Rd
Mt. Pleasant, MI 48858
517-773-9887

*Sault St. Marie Tribal Clinic
Wilson Road, Bld 312
Kincheloe, MI 49788
906-495-5615

MINNESOTA

★BEMIDJI AREA INDIAN HEALTH SERVICE
127 Federal Bldg
Bemidji, MN 56601
218-759-3378
218-759-3511 FAX

*Bois Forte Tribal Clinic
PO Box 16
Nett Lake, MN 55772
218-757-3296

*Grand Portage Band
PO Box 428
Grand Portage, MN 55605
218-475-2235

Leech Lake PHS
Indian Hospital
PO Box 60
Cass Lake, MN 56633
218-335-2293

Leech Lake Band
Rt 3 Box 100
Cass Lake, MN 56633
218-335-8851

*Lower Sioux Community
Council
PO Box 308 Rt 1
Morton, MN 56270
507-697-6185

*Ne-ia-shing Clinic
HCR 67 Box 241
Onamia, MN 56359
615-532-4163

*TRIBAL OPERATION

★AREA OFFICE

*Prairie Island Community Council
1158 Island Blvd
Welch, MN 55089
612-385-2554

Red Lake Comp Health Service
Red Lake, MN 56671
218-679-3316
218-679-3390 FAX

Red Lake PHS Indian Hospital
Red Lake, MN 56671
218-679-3912

*Shakopee Mdewakanton Business Council
2320 Sioux Trail NW
Prior Lake, MN 55372
612-445-8900

*Upper Sioux Board of Trustees
PO Box 147
Granite Falls, MN 56241
612-564-2360

White Earth Service Unit
PHS Indian Health Center
White Earth, MN 56591
218-983-3221

White Earth PHS Indian Health Center
PO Box 418
White Earth, MN 56591
218-983-3285

MISSISSIPPI

Philadelphia Choctaw Health Center
Rt 7 Box R-50
Philadelphia, MS 39350
601-656-2211

*TRIBAL OPERATION

MONTANA

★BILLINGS AREA INDIAN HEALTH SERVICE
711 Central Ave
Billings, MT 59103
406-657-6403
406-657-6333

Box Elder PHS Indian Health Center
Box Elder, MT 59521
406-395-4486

Browning PHS Indian Hospital
Browning, MT 59417
406-338-6100

Crow Agency PHS Indian Health Hospital
Crow Agency, MT 59022
406-638-2626

*Flathead Tribal Health & Human Services
Indian Health Center
PO Box 280
St. Ignatius, MT 59865
406-745-2411

Harlem PHS Indian Hospital
Harlem, MT 59526
406-353-2651

Lame Deer PHS Indian Health Center
Lame Deer, MT 59043
406-477-6201

Lodge Grass PHS Indian Health Center
Lodge Grass, MT 59050
406-639-2317

★AREA OFFICE

Poplar PHS Indian Health Center
Poplar, MT 59255
406-768-3491

Wolf Point PHS Indian Health Center
Wolf Point, MT 59201
406-653-1641

NEBRASKA

*Carl T. Curtis Health Center
Macy, NE 68039
402-837-5381
402-837-5303

Winnebago PHS Indian Hospital
Winnebago, NE 68071
402-878-2231
402-878-2535 FAX

NEVADA

Elko Southern Band Clinic
515 Shoshone Circle
Elko, NV 89801
702-738-2252

Fallon Community Health Service
PO Box 1980
Fallon, NV 89406
702-423-3634

McDermitt Tribal Health Center
PO Box 457
McDermitt, NV 89421
702-532-8259

Owyhee PHS Indian Hospital
PO Box 212
Owyhee, NV 89832
702-757-2415
800-642-6999

Pyramid Lake Health Department
PO Box 227
Nixon, NV 89424
702-574-1018

Reno Tribal Health Station
34 Reservation Rd
Reno, NV 89502
702-329-5162

Schurz Indian Health Center
Drawer A
Schurz, NV 89427
702-773-2345

*Walker River Paiute
Tribal Health Center
PO Drawer C
Schurz, NV 89427
702-773-2005

Washoe Tribal Health Center
919 Hwy 395 S
Gardnerville, NV 89410
702-883-4137

Yerington Health Department
171 Campbell Ln
Yerington, NV 89447
702-463-3301

NEW MEXICO

Acomita Canoncito Laguna PHS
Indian Hospital
PO Box 130
San Fidel, NM 87049
505-552-6634
505-552-7363 FAX

*TRIBAL OPERATION

★AREA OFFICE

Alamo Navajo Health Station
PO Box 907
Magdalena, NM 87825
505-854-2626
505-854-2545 FAX

Albuquerque PHS Indian Hospital
801 Vassar Dr NE
Albuquerque, NM 87106
505-256-4000
505-256-4088 FAX

★ALBUQUERQUE INDIAN HEALTH SERVICE-HEADQUARTERS WEST
5300 Homestead NE
Albuquerque, NM 87110
505-837-4101
505-837-4115 FAX

Albuquerque Area Indian Health Service
505 Marquette NW # 1502
Albuquerque, NM 87102
505-766-2151
505-766-2157 FAX

Crownpoint Comprehensive Health Care Facility
PO Box 358
Crownpoint, NM 87313
505-786-5291

Dulce PHS Indian Health Center
PO Box 187
Dulce, NM 87528
505-759-3291
505-759-3532

Dzilth-Na-O-Dith-Hle PHS Indian Health Center
Star Rt 4 Box 5400
Bloomfield, NM 87413
505-632-1801

Gallup Indian Medical Center
PO Box 1337
Gallup, NM 87301
505-722-1000

Mescalero PHS Indian Hospital
PO Box 210
Mescalero, NM 88340
505-671-4441
505-671-4422

New Sunrise Regional Treatment Center
PO Box 219
San Fidel, NM 87049
505-552-6091
505-552-6527

Pine Hill PHS Indian Health Center
PO Box 310
Pine Hill, NM 87357
505-775-3271
505-775-3240

Santa Clara PHS Indian Health Center
RR 1 Box 446
Espanola, NM 87532
505-753-9421
505-753-5039 FAX

Santa Fe PHS Indian Hospital
1700 Cerrillos Rd
Santa Fe, NM 87501
505-988-9821
505-983-6243

Shiprock PHS Indian Hospital
PO Box 160
Shiprock, NM 87420
505-368-4971

*TRIBAL OPERATION

★AREA OFFICE

Southwestern Indian Polytechnic
Institute Dental Center
PO Box 25927
Albuquerque, NM 87125
505-897-5306
505-897-5311 FAX

Taos PHS Indian Health Center
PO Box 1956
Taos, NM 87571
505-758-4224
505-758-1822

Tohatchi PHS Indian Health
Center
PO Box 142
Tohatchi, NM 87325
505-733-2244

Zuni PHS Indian Hospital
PO Box 467
Zuni, NM 87327
505-782-4431
505-782-5723 FAX

NORTH CAROLINA

Cherokee PHS Indian Hospital
Cherokee, NC 28719
704-497-9163
704-497-9163 xx 225

Unity Regional Youth
Treatment Center
PO Box C-201
Cherokee, NC 28719
704-497-3958
704-497-6826 FAX

NORTH DAKOTA

Belcourt PHS Indian Hospital
PO Box 160
Belcourt, ND 58316
701-477-6112

Fort Berthold PHS Indian Health
Center
PO Box 400
New Town, ND 58763
701-627-4701
701-627-3902 FAX

Fort Totten PHS Indian Health
Center
PO Box 200
Fort Totten, ND 58335
701-766-4291
701-766-4295 FAX

Fort Yates PHS Indian Hospital
PO Box J
Fort Yates, ND 58538
701-854-3831
701-854-7399 FAX

*Trenton-Williston Indian
Service Area
PO Box 210
Trenton, ND 58853
701-774-0461
701-572-0124 FAX

OKLAHOMA

Anadarko PHS Indian
Health Center
PO Box 828
Anadarko, OK 73005
405-247-2458
405-247-7052 FAX

*TRIBAL OPERATION

★AREA OFFICE

*Ardmore Chickasaw Health Clinic
2510 Chickasaw Blvd
Ardmore, OK 73401
405-226-8181

Blackhawk Health Center
Sac and Fox Nation of OK
Rt 2 Box 246
Stroud, OK 73079
918-968-9531

Carl Albert Indian Hospital
1001 N Country Club Dr
Ada, OK 74820
405-436-3980
405-332-1421 FAX

Carnegie Indian Health Center
PO Box 1120
Carnegie, OK 73015
405-654-1100

*Cherokee Nation Health Clinic
Rt 2 Box 5
Stillwell, OK 74960
918-696-6911

*Choctaw Nation Health Services Authority
Rt 2 Box 1725
Talihina, OK 74571
918-567-2211
918-567-2211 xx 319 FAX

*Choctaw Nation Health Center
PO Box 190
Broken Bow, OK 74728
405-584-2740
405-584-2073 FAX

Claremore Indian Hospital
West Will Rogers & Moore
Claremore, OK 74017
918-342-6200
918-342-6585

Clinton PHS Indian Hospital
PO Box 279
Clinton, OK 73601
405-323-2884
405-323-2884 xx 211 FAX

Concho PHS Indian Health Clinic
PO Box 150
Concho, OK 73022
405-262-7631

*Creek Nation Community Hospital
PO Box 228
Okemah, OK 74859
918-623-1424

El Reno PHS Indian Health Clinic
1631A E. Hwy 66
El Reno, OK 73036
405-262-7631
405-262-8099 FAX

Eufala Health Center
Creek Nation of OK
800 Forest Ave
Eufala, OK 74432
918-689-2547

*Hugo Health Center
PO Box 340
Hugo, OK 74743
405-326-7561

*TRIBAL OPERATION ★AREA OFFICE

Lawton PHS Indian Health Center
Lawton, OK 73501
405-353-0350
405-353-0350 xx 206 FAX

*McAlester Health Center
903 E Monroe
McAlester, OK 74501
918-423-8440

Miami PHS Indian Health Center
PO Box 1498
Miami, OK 74355
918-542-1655
918-540-1685 FAX

*Nowata Indian Health Clinic
Cherokee Nation of OK
304 E. Cherokee
Nowata, OK 74048
918-273-0192

Okemah Indian Health Center
PO Box 429
Okemah, OK 74859
918-623-0555

★OKLAHOMA AREA INDIAN HEALTH SERVICE
5 Corporate Plaza
3625 N.W. 56th St.
Oklahoma City, OK 73112
405-945-6890
405-945-6870 FAX

Pawhuska PHS Indian Health Center
715 Grandview
Pawhuska, OK 74056
918-287-4491

Pawnee PHS Indian Health Center
Rural Rt 2 Box 1
Pawnee, OK 74058
918-762-2517
918-762-2517 xx 200 FAX

*Redbird Smith Health Center
301 J. T. Stitkes Ave.
Sallisaw, OK 74955
918-775-9159
918-775-4778 FAX

*Salina Community Clinic
PO Box 936
Salina, OK 74365
918-434-5397

*Sam Hider Jay Community Clinic
PO Box 350
Jay, OK 74346
918-253-4271
918-434-5397 FAX

*Sapulpa Health Center
Creek Nation of OK
1125 E Cleveland
Sapulpa, OK 74066
918-224-9310

Shawnee PHS Indian Health Center
2001 S Gordon Cooper Dr
Shawnee, OK 74801
405-275-4270
405-275-4270 xx 268 FAX

*Tishomingo Chickasaw Health Center
815 E 6th
Tishomingo, OK 73460
405-371-2392
405-371-9323 FAX

*TRIBAL OPERATION

★AREA OFFICE

W.W. Hastings Indian Hospital
100 S Bliss
Tahlequah, OK 74464
918-458-3100
918-458-3262 FAX

Watonga PHS Indian Health Center
PO Box 878
Watonga, OK 73772
405-623-4991
405-623-5490 FAX

Wewoka PHS Indian Health Center
PO Box 1475
Wewoka, OK 74884
405-257-6281
405-257-2696 FAX

White Eagle PHS Indian Health Center
PO Box 2071
Ponca City, OK 74601
405-765-2501
405-765-6348 FAX

OREGON

Chemawa Indian Health Center
3750 Chemawa Rd NE
Salem, OR 97305
503-399-5937

★PORTLAND AREA INDIAN HEALTH SERVICE
1220 SW 3rd Ave Rm 476
Portland, OR 97204
503-326-3288
503-326-7280 FAX

Warm Springs PHS Indian Health Center
PO Box 1209
Warm Springs, OR 97761
503-553-1196

Yellowhawk PHS Indian Health Center
PO Box 160
Pendleton, OR 97801
503-278-3870

SOUTH DAKOTA

★ABERDEEN AREA INDIAN HEALTH SERVICE
115 4th Ave SE
Aberdeen, SD 57401
605-226-7581
605-226-7670 FAX

Eagle Butte PHS Indian Hospital
PO Box 1012
Eagle Butte, SD 57625
605-964-7030
605-964-1110 FAX

Fort Thompson PHS Indian Health Center
PO Box 200
Fort Thompson, SD 57339
605-245-2285
605-245-2399 FAX

Kyle PHS Health Center
PO Box 540
Kyle, SD 57752
605-455-2451
605-455-2808 FAX

*TRIBAL OPERATION ★AREA OFFICE

Lower Brule PHS Indian
Health Center
PO Box 248
Lower Brule, SD 57548
605-473-5544

McLaughlin PHS Indian
Health Center
PO Box 879
McLaughlin, SD 57642
605-823-4459
605-823-4755 FAX

Pine Ridge PHS Indian Hospital
Pine Ridge, SD 57770
605-867-5131
605-867-1018 FAX

Rapid City PHS Indian
Health Hospital
3200 Canyon Lake Dr
Rapid City, SD 57702
605-348-1900
605-348-7150 FAX

Rosebud PHS Indian Hospital
Rosebud, SD 57570
605-747-2231
605-747-2216

Sisseton PHS Indian Hospital
PO Box 189
Sisseton, SD 57262
605-698-7606
605-698-4270 FAX

Wagner PHS Indian Hospital
110 Washington
Wagner, SD 57380
605-384-3621
605-384-5229 FAX

TENNESSEE

★NASHVILLE AREA INDIAN HEALTH SERVICE
711 Stewarts Ferry Pike
Nashville, TN 37214
615-736-2441
615-736-2391 FAX

TEXAS

Ysleta Del Sur Service Unit
119 S Old Pueblo Rd
El Paso, TX 79907
915-859-7913
915-859-2988 FAX

UTAH

Fort Duchesne PHS Indian
Health Center
PO Box 160
Roosevelt, UT 84026
801-722-5122

WASHINGTON

Colville PHS Indian Health
Center
PO Box 71, Agency Campus
Nespelem, WA 99155
509-634-4771

David C. Wynecoop Memorial
Clinic
PO Box 357
Wellpinit, WA 99040
509-258-4517

Lummi PHS Indian Health Center
2592 Kwina Rd
Bellingham, WA 98226
206-676-8373

*TRIBAL OPERATION

★AREA OFFICE

Puget Sound PHS Indian
Health Station
2201 6th Ave Rm 300
Seattle, WA 98121
206-615-2781

Sophie Trettevick Indian
Health Center
PO Box 410
Neah Bay, WA 98357
206-645-2233

Taholah PHS Indian Health
Center
PO Box 219
Tahloah, WA 98587
206-276-4405

Yakima PHS Indian Health Center
401 Buster Rd.
Toppenish, WA 98948
509-865-2102

WISCONSIN

*Bad River Health Services
PO Box 39
Odanah, WI 54861
715-682-7137

*Peter Christensen
Chippewa Health Center
450 Old Adobe Rd
Lac du Flambeau, WI 54538
715-588-3371

Forest Co., Potawatomi
Community
PO Box 346
Crandon, WI 54520
715-478-3431

*LacCourte Oreilles Tribal Clinic
Rt 2 Box 2750
Hayward, WI 54843
715-634-4153

*Menominee Tribal Clinic
PO Box 970
Keshena, WI 54135
715-799-3361

*Oneida Community Health
Center
PO Box 365
Oneida, WI 54155
414-869-2711

*Red Cliff Health Services
PO Box 529
Bayfield, WI 54814
715-779-3707

*Sokaogan Chippewa Community
PO Box 616
Crandon, WI 54520
715-478-5180

*St. Croix Health Services
PO Box 287
Hertel, WI 54845
715-349-2195

*Stockbridge-Munsee
Health Center
PO Box 86
Bowler, WI 54416
715-793-4144

*Wisconsin Winnebago
Health Dept.
PO Box 636
Black River Falls, WI 54615
715-284-7548

*TRIBAL OPERATION ★AREA OFFICE

WYOMING

Arapahoe PHS Indian
Health Center
Arapahoe, WY 82510
307-856-9281

Fort Washakie PHS Indian
Health Center
Ft. Washakie, WY 82514
307-332-9416
307-332-9418 FAX

INFORMATION PROVIDED BY: I.H.S DIRECTORY 1994.

*TRIBAL OPERATION ★AREA OFFICE

URBAN INDIAN CENTERS IN MAJOR METROPOLITAN AREAS

ARIZONA

NATIVE AMERICANS FOR COMMUNITY ACTION, INC.
2717 N Steves Blvd Ste 11
Flagstaff, AZ 86004
520-526-2968
520-526-0708 FAX

PHOENIX INDIAN CENTER
2601 N 3rd St Ste 100
Phoenix, AZ 85004
602-263-1017
602-263-7822 FAX

ST. NICHOLAS INDIAN CENTER
349 W 31st
Tucson, AZ 85713
520-622-5363

TRADITIONAL INDIAN ALLIANCE
2925 S 12th Ave
Tucson, AZ 85713
520-882-0555
520-623-6529 FAX

TUCSON AMERICAN INDIAN ASSOC.
131 E Broadway Blvd (85701)
PO Box 2307
Tucson, AZ 85702
520-884-7131
520-884-0240 FAX

WINSLOW INDIAN CENTER
PO Box 670
Winslow, AZ 86047
520-289-4525

ARKANSAS

AMERICAN INDIAN CENTER ARKANSAS
1100 N University # 133
Little Rock, AR 72207
501-666-9032
501-666-5875 FAX

AMERICAN INDIAN CENTER AR-FORT SMITH
235 N Greenwood
Fort Smith, AR 72901
501-785-5149

CALIFORNIA

AMERICAN ASSOC. SAN BERNARDINO
IANNA Central Office
443 W 4th
San Bernardino, CA 92401
909-889-2444

AMERICAN INDIAN CENTER OF CENTRAL CA
32980 Auberry Rd # 607
PO Box 607
Auberry, CA 93602
209-855-2695

FONTANA NATIVE
AMERICAN INDIAN
CENTER INC.
PO Box 1258
Fontana, CA 92334
714-823-6150

INDIAN CENTER OF
SAN JOSE
SANTA CLARA VALLEY
919 The Alameda
San Jose, CA 95126
408-971-9622

INTERTRIBAL FRIENDSHIP
HOUSE
523 E 14th St
Oakland, CA 94606
510-452-1235

MENDOCINO COUNTY
INDIAN CENTER
PO Box 495
Hwy 101 S
Hopland, CA 95449

MENDOCINO COUNTY
INDIAN CENTER
1621 Talmadge Rd
Ukiah, CA 95482

MEXI'CAYOTL INDIO
CULTURAL CENTER
PO Box 4052
Chula Vista, CA 91909
619-691-1044

ORANGE COUNTY
INDIAN CENTER
12755 Brookhurst St
Garden Grove, CA 92643
714-530-0221

RIVERSIDE AME[illegible]
INDIAN CENTER
2060 University Av[illegible]
Riverside, CA 92507
909-682-1637

SACRAMENTO INDIAN
CENTER
2729 P St
Sacramento, CA 95816

SAN DIEGO HUMAN
RESOURCE CENTER
(San Diego Indian Center)
4040 30th # A
San Diego, CA 92104
619-281-5964

SANTA BARBARA
INDIAN CENTER
1236 Chapala # 302
Santa Barbara, CA 93101
805-965-4688

SOUTH AND MESO
AMERICAN INDIAN INFO.
CENTER
PO Box 28703
Oakland, CA 94604
510-834-4263
510-834-4264 FAX

SO CALIF INDIAN CENTER
500 E Carson Plaza Dr # 101
Carson, CA 90746
213-329-9595

SO CALIF INDIAN CENTER
5900 S Eastern Ave # 104
City of Commece, CA 90040
213-728-8844

SO CALIF INDIAN CENTER
6320 Van Nuys Blvd # 104
Van Nuys, CA 91401
818-782-1191

SO CALIF INDIAN CENTER
12755 Brookhurst St
PO Box 2550
Garden Grove, CA 92642
714-530-0221
714-636-4226 FAX

SO CALIF INDIAN CENTER
LOS ANGELES
2500 Wilshire Blvd # 750
Los Angeles, CA 90057
213-387-5772

COLORADO

DENVER NATIVE
AMERICANS UNITED, INC.
4407 Morrison Rd
Denver, CO 80219
303-937-0401

CONNECTICUT

AMERICAN INDIANS FOR
DEVELOPMENT
236 W Main St
PO Box 117
Meridan, CT 06450
203-238-4009

GEORGIA

NATIVE AMERICAN
CENTER OF GEORGIA INC
110 S Main St # 203
PO Box 2249
Woodstock, GA 30188
404-924-3738

ILLINOIS

AMERICAN INDIAN
CENTER
1630 W Wilson
Chicago, IL 60640
312-275-5871

ST. AUGUSTINE'S CENTER
4512 N Sheridan Rd
Chicago, IL 60640
312-784-1050

INDIANA

INDIAN AWARENESS
CENTER
Fulton Co. Historical Soc. Inc.
37 E 375 N
Rochester, IN 46975
219-223-4436

MINNETRISTA CULTURAL
CENTER
1200 N Minnetrista Pky
PO Box 1527
Muncie, IN 47308-1527
317-282-4848
317-288-5520

IOWA

NATIVE AMERICAN
CULTURAL CENTER
216 S 8th St
Fort Dodge, IA 50501
515-576-3867

SIOUX CITY AMERICAN
INDIAN CENTER
619 6th St
Sioux City, IA 51102
712-255-8957

KANSAS

MID-AMERICA
ALL-INDIAN CENTER, INC.
650 N Seneca
Wichita, KS 67203
316-262-5221

THE INDIAN CENTER
OF LAWRENCE
1423 Haskell Ave
PO Box 1016
Lawrence, KS 66044
913-841-7202

WICHITA INDIAN
HEALTH CENTER
2318 E Central
Wichita, KS 67214
316-262-2415

MARYLAND

MARYLAND AMERICAN
INDIAN HERITAGE SOC.
INC.
PO Box 950
Waldorf, MD 20601
301-372-1932

BALTIMORE AMERICAN
INDIAN CENTER
113 S Broadway
Baltimore, MD 21231
410-675-3535

MASSACHUSETTS

MASSACHUSETTS CENTER
FOR NATIVE AMERICAN
AWARENESS INC
PO Box 5885
Boston, MA 02114
617-884-4227

NORTH AMERICAN INDIAN
CENTER OF BOSTON INC
105 S Huntington
Jamaica Plain, MA 02130
617-232-0343
617-232-3863 FAX

MICHIGAN

ALL TRIBES
INDIAN CENTER
118 W Pine
Ironwood, MI 39938

AMERICAN INDIAN
SERVICE INC
25351 5 Mile Rd
Redford, MI 48239-3703

GENESSE INDIAN CENTER
609 W Court St
Flint, MI 48503
313-239-6621

LANSING NORTH AMERICAN INDIAN CENTER
1235 Center St
Lansing, MI 48906

LUCY COUNTY INTERTRIBAL CENTER
PO Box 155
Newberry, MI 49868
906-293-3491
906-293-3001 FAX

NORTH AMERICAN INDIAN ASSOC. DETROIT, INC.
22720 Plymouth Rd
Detroit, MI 48239
313-535-2966
313-535-8060 FAX

SAGINAW INTER-TRIBAL ASSOCIATION, INC.
3239 Christy Way
Saginaw, MI 48603
517-792-4610

SOUTH EASTERN MICHIGAN INDIANS, INC.
PO Box 861
Warren, MI 48090
313-756-1350

MINNESOTA

DIVISION OF INDIAN WORK
1001 E Lake St
Minneapolis, MN 55407-1616
612-722-8722
612-722-8669 FAX

INDIAN CENTER
5633 Regent Ave N
Minneapolis, MN 55440

MINNEAPOLIS AMERICAN INDIAN CENTER
1530 E Franklin Ave
Minneapolis, MN 55404
612-879-1760
612-879-1795

UPPER MIDWEST AMERICAN INDIAN CENTER
113 W Broadway
Minneapolis, MN 55411
612-522-4436

MISSOURI

AMERICAN INDIAN CENTER OF MID-AMERICA
4115 Connecticut
St Louis, MO 63116
314-773-3316
314-773-7160 FAX

AMERICAN INDIAN SOCIETY ST LOUIS, INC.
6651 Gravois # 112
St Louis, MO 63113
314-351-0669

HEART OF AMERICA
INDIAN CENTER
1340 E Admiral Blvd
Kansas City, MO 64124
816-421-7608
816-421-6493 FAX

SOUTHWEST MISSOURI
INDIAN CENTER
2422 W Division
Springfield, MO 65802
417-869-9550

MONTANA

BILLINGS AMERICAN
INDIAN COUNCIL
PO Box 853
Billings, MT 59103
406-248-1648

GREAT FALLS
INDIAN CENTER
700 S 10th
PO Box 2612
Great Falls, MT 59403
406-761-3165

HELENA INDIAN
ALLIANCE
436 N Jackson
Helena, MT 59601
406-442-9334

MISSOULA INDIAN
CENTER
2300 Regent St # A
Missoula, MT 59801
406-329-3373

NORTH AMERICAN
INDIAN ALLIANCE
12 E Galena
PO BOX 286
Butte, MT 59701
406-723-4361

NEBRASKA

LINCOLN INDIAN
CENTER, INC.
1100 Military Rd
Lincoln, NE 68508
402-474-5231

NATIVE AMERICAN
COMMUNITY
DEVELOPMENT CORP
2451 St Marys Ave
Omaha, NE 68105
402-341-8471
402-341-3160 FAX

NEVADA

LAS VEGAS
INDIAN CENTER
2300 W Bonanza Rd
Las Vegas, NV 89106
702-647-5842

NEVADA URBAN
INDIANS, INC.
2100 Capurro Way # A
Sparks, NV 89431
702-365-8111

NEW JERSEY

NANTICOKE LENNI
LENAPE CENTER OF NJ
18 E Commerce
PO Box 553
Bridgeton, NJ 08302
609-455-6910

NEW JERSEY AMERICAN
INDIAN CENTER
21 Village Rd
Morganville, NJ 07751
908-591-8335

NEW YORK

AMERICAN INDIAN
COMMUNITY HOUSE
404 Lafayette, 2nd Floor
New York, NY 10003
212-598-0100
212-598-4909 FAX

NATIVE AMERICAN
COMMUNITY SERVICES-
BUFFALO
1047 Grant St
PO Box 86
Buffalo, NY 14207
716-874-4990
716-874-0967 FAX

NATIVE AMERICAN
COMMUNITY SERVICES-
NIAGARA FALLS
561 Portage Rd
Niagara Falls, NY 14301
716-282-5441
716-282-5454 FAX

THE TURTLE
25 Rainbow Mall
Niagara Falls, NY 14303
716-284-2427

NORTH CAROLINA

CUMBERLAND CO. ASSOC.
OF INDIAN PEOPLE
102 Indian Dr
Fayetteville, NC 28301
919-483-8442

GUILFORD NATIVE
AMERICAN ASSOC.
400 Prescott
Greensboro, NC 27403
919-273-8686

METROLINA NATIVE
AMERICAN ASSOCIATION
2601 E 7th # A
Charlotte, NC 28204
704-331-4818

NORTH DAKOTA

FARGO-MOORHEAD
INDIAN CENTER
PO Box 1914
Fargo, ND 58107
701-293-6863

OHIO

CLEVELAND AMERICAN
INDIAN CENTER
5500-02 Loraine Ave
Cleveland, OH 44102
216-961-3490

LIMA COUNCIL FOR
NATIVE AMERICANS
466 N McDonel St
Lima, OH 45801
419-228-1097

NATIVE AMERICAN
INDIAN CENTER
PO Box 07705
Columbus, OH 43207
614-443-6120

NORTH AMERICAN INDIAN
CULTURAL CENTER
1062 Triplett Blvd
Akron, OH 44306
216-724-1280
216-724-9298 FAX

OHIO AMERICAN
INDIAN COUNCIL
5076 ½ Center Rd
Lowellville, OH 44436
216-536-6852

XENIA INDIAN CENTER
2110 Drake Dr
Xenia, OH 45385
216-724-1280

OKLAHOMA

AMERICAN INDIAN
CENTER
1608 NW 35th
Oklahoma City, OK 73117

KOWETA INDIAN
COMMUNITY CENTER
PO Box 22
Coweta, OK 74429-9998

NATIVE AMERICAN
COALITION OF TULSA, INC.
1740 W 41st St
Tulsa, OK 74107
918-446-8432

RED EARTH INDIAN
CENTER
2100 NE 52nd St
Oklahoma City, OK 73111
405-427-4228

OREGON

ORGANIZATION OF
FORGOTTEN AMERICAN
PO Box 1257
Klamath Falls, OR 97601
503-882-4441

PENNSYLVANIA

COUNCIL OF THREE
RIVERS AMERICAN INDIAN
CENTER, INC.
200 Charles
Pittsburgh, PA 15238
412-782-4457
412-767-4808 FAX

UNITED AMERICAN
INDIANS OF THE
DELAWARE VALLEY
225 Chestnut
Philadelphia, PA 19106
215-574-9020

RHODE ISLAND

RHODE ISLAND INDIAN COUNCIL, INC.
444 Friendship
Providence, RI 02907
401-331-4440
401-331-4494 FAX

TEXAS

AMERICAN INDIAN CENTER
818 E Davis
Grand Prairie, TX 75050
214-262-1349

DALLAS INTER-TRIBAL CENTER, INC.
209 E Jefferson Blvd
Dallas, TX 75203
214-941-1050
214-941-6537 FAX

UTAH

INDIAN WALK IN CENTER
120 W 1300 South
Salt Lake City, UT

VERMONT

ABENAKI SELF-HELP ASSOCIATION
PO Box 276
Swanton, VT 05488

WASHINGTON

AMERICAN INDIAN COMMUNITY CENTER
905 E 3rd
Spokane, WA 99202
509-535-0886
509-534-7210 FAX

DAYBREAK STAR UNITED INDIAN ALL-TRIBES
PO Box 99100
Seattle, WA 98199
206-285-4425

KITSAP COUNTY INDIAN CENTER
22222 NW Bucklin Hill Rd
Silverdale, WA 98383
360-692-7460
360-692-2344 FAX

SEATTLE INDIAN CENTER, INC.
616 12th Ave S # 300
Seattle, WA 98144
206-329-8700

WEST VIRGINIA

PARKERSBURG NATIVE AMERICAN CENTER
3400 A Dudley Ave
Parkersburg, WV 26101

WISCONSIN

NATIVE AMERICAN CENTER
012 Old Main, Univ of WI
Stevens Point, WI 54481
715-346-2004

URBAN INDIAN HEALTH CARE PROJECTS

URBAN INDIAN HEALTH PROGRAMS
INDIAN HEALTH SERVICE, OHP
Parklawn Bldg., Rm. 5A-41
5600 Fishers Ln.
Rockville, MD 20857
301-443-4680

AMERICAN INDIAN HEALTH
CARE ASSOCIATION
1550 Larimer St. # 225
Denver, CO 80202
303-607-1048
303-825-0610 FAX

ARIZONA

INDIAN COMMUNITY
HEALTH SERVICE INC
1427 N 3rd # 100
Phoenix, AZ 85004
602-254-0456
602-254-2488 FAX

NATIVE AMERICANS FOR
COMMUNITY ACTION
2717 N Steves Blvd # 11
Flagstaff, AZ 86004
520-526-2968
520-526-0708 FAX

NATIVE AMERICANS FOR
COMMUNITY ACTION
SATELLITE CLINIC
1355 N. Beaver # 160
Flagstaff, AZ 86004
520-773-1245
520-773-9429 FAX

TRADITIONAL INDIAN
ALLIANCE
2925 S 12th Ave
Tucson, AZ 85713
520-882-0555
520-623-6529 FAX

CALIFORNIA

AMERICAN INDIAN FREE
CLINIC
9500 E. Artesia Blvd.
Bellflower, CA 90706
310-920-7227
310-920-5677 FAX

AMERICAN INDIAN COUNCIL
OF CENTRAL CALIF. INC.
PO Box 3341
2210 Chester Ave. # A
Bakersfield, CA 93301
805-327-2207
805-327-4533 FAX

FRESNO INDIAN HEALTH ASSOCIATION
4991 E. McKinley # 109
Fresno, CA 93727
209-255-0261
209-255-2149 FAX

INDIAN HEALTH CENTER OF SANTA CLARA
1333 Meridian
San Jose, CA 95125
408-445-3415
408-269-9273 FAX

S.F. OAKLAND INDIAN HEALTH BOARD
56 Julian Ave.
San Francisco, CA 94103
415-621-8051
415-621-3985 FAX

S.F. OAKLAND INDIAN HEALTH BOARD
3124 E 14th
Oakland, CA 94601
510-261-0524
510-261-0646 FAX

SACRAMENTO URBAN INDIAN HEALTH PROJECT INC
801 Broadway # B
Sacramento, CA 95818
916-441-0918
916-441-1261 FAX

SAN DIEGO AMERICAN INDIAN HEALTH CENTER
2561 1st Ave
San Diego, CA 92103
619-234-2158
619-234-0206 FAX

SANTA BARBARA URBAN INDIAN HEALTH
1919 State # 109
Santa Barbara, CA 93101
805-682-6701

COLORADO

DENVER INDIAN HEALTH & FAMILY SERVICES
3749 S King St
Denver, CO 80236
303-781-4050
303-781-4333 FAX

ILLINOIS

AMERICAN INDIAN HEALTH SERVICES OF CHICAGO
838 W Irving Park Rd
Chicago, IL 60613
312-883-9100
312-883-0005 FAX

IOWA

SATELLITE CLINIC
1000 W 6th
Sioux City, IA 51102
712-252-5730

KANSAS

HUNTER HEALTH CLINIC
2318 E Central
Wichita, KS 67214
316-262-3611
316-262-0741 FAX

MASSACHUSETTS

NORTH AMERICAN INDIAN
CENTER OF BOSTON INC
105 S Huntington Ave
Jamaica Plains, MA 02130
617-232-0343
617-232-3863 FAX

MICHIGAN

DETROIT AMERICAN INDIAN
HEALTH & FAMILY
SERVICES
4880 Lawndale
Detroit, MI 48210
313-846-3718
313-846-0150 FAX

MINNESOTA

INDIAN HEALTH BOARD OF
MINNEAPOLIS
1315 E 24th
Minneapolis, MN 55404
612-721-9800
612-721-2904 FAX

MONTANA

HELENA INDIAN ALLIANCE
436 N Jackson
Helena, MT 59601
406-442-9244
406-449-5371 FAX

INDIAN HEALTH BOARD
OF BILLINGS
915 Broadwater Square
Billings, MT 59102
406-245-7372
406-245-8872 FAX

MISSOULA INDIAN CENTER
Urban I.H. Clinic
2300 Regent St. # A
Missoula, MT 59801
406-329-3373
406-329-3398 FAX

NATIVE AMERICAN
CENTER INC
700 S 10th
PO Box 2612
Great Falls, MT 59405
406-761-3165
406-727-7423 FAX

NORTH AMERICAN INDIAN
ALLIANCE
100 E Galena
Butte, MT 59701
406-723-4361
406-782-7435 FAX

NEBRASKA

NEBRASKA URBAN INDIAN
HEALTH COALITION
140 S 27th St
Lincoln, NE 68510
402-434-7177
402-434-7180 FAX

NEVADA

NEVADA URBAN INDIANS INC
2100 Capurros Ln. #A
Sparks, NV 89431
702-356-8111
702-356-8080 FAX

SATELLITE CLINIC
Nevada Urban Indians
675 Fairview #222
Carson City, NV 89707
702-329-4439

NEW MEXICO

ALBUQUERQUE URBAN INDIAN HEALTH CENTER
4100 Silver St. #B
Albuquerque, NM 87108
505-262-2481
505-262-0781 FAX

NEW YORK

AMERICAN INDIAN COMMUNITY HOUSE
404 Lafayette 2nd Flr
New York, NY 10003
212-598-4842
212-598-4909 FAX

OKLAHOMA

INDIAN HEALTH CARE RESOURCE CENTER
915 S Cincinnati
Tulsa, OK 74119
918-582-7225
918-582-6405 FAX

OKLAHOMA CITY INDIAN CLINIC
1214 N Hudson
Oklahoma City, OK 73103
405-232-1526
405-235-5877 FAX

OREGON

NATIVE AMERICAN REHABILITATION ASSOC. OF N.W. INC.
2022 N.W. Division
Gresham, OR 97030
503-669-7889
503-669-8141 FAX

NORTHWEST INDIAN HEALTH CLINIC
2901 E. Burnside
Portland, OR 97214
503-230-9875
503-230-9877 FAX

SOUTH DAKOTA

SOUTH DAKOTA URBAN INDIAN HEALTH
122 E Dakota
Pierre, SD 57501
605-224-8841
605-224-6852 FAX

TEXAS

DALLAS INTERTRIBAL CENTER
209 E Jefferson
Dallas, TX 75203
214-941-1050
214-941-6537 FAX

UTAH

INDIAN HEALTH CARE
CLINIC
146 E 600 South
Salt Lake City, UT 84111
801-359-6906
801-328-9040 FAX

WASHINGTON

SEATTLE INDIAN HEALTH
BOARD
PO Box 3364 (98114)
611 12th Ave S # 200
Seattle, WA 98144
206-324-9360
206-324-8910 FAX

SPOKANE URBAN INDIAN
HEALTH
PO Box 4598
E 905 Third Ave.
Spokane, WA 99202
509-535-0868
509-535-3230 FAX

WISCONSIN

MILWAUKEE INDIAN
HEALTH CENTER
930 N 27th St.
Milwaukee, WI 53208
414-931-8111
414-931-0443 FAX

UNITED AMERINDIAN
HEALTH CENTER INC.
409 Dousman
PO Box 2248
Green Bay, WI 54303
414-437-2161
414-433-0121 FAX

LIST PROVIDED BY: I.H.S. 1/94

INDIAN CHAMBERS OF COMMERCE

ARIZONA

AMERICAN INDIAN
TRADE CENTER
CHAMBER OF
COMMERCE OF NORTH
AMERICA
PO Box 27626
Tucson, AZ 85726
520-622-4900
520-622-4900 FAX

COLORADO

WESTERN AMERICAN
INDIAN CHAMBER OF
COMMERCE
1600 17th #200
Denver, CO 80202
303-620-9292

MINNESOTA

MINNEAPOLIS INDIAN
CHAMBER OF COMMERCE
1433 Franklin Ave #3C
Minneapolis, MN 55404
612-871-2157
612-871-0021 FAX

NEW MEXICO

ALL INDIAN PUEBLO
COUNCIL
P O Box 3256
Albuquerque, NM 87190
505-881-1992

NATIONAL INDIAN
BUSINESS ASSOC
1605 Carlisle NE # A-1
Albuquerque, NM 87117
505-256-0589

TEXAS

AMERICAN INDIAN
CHAMBER OF COMMERCE
P O Box 153409
Irving, TX 75015
817-429-1866
817-332-5103 FAX

Note: To be listed send all details, including, phone, fax, newsletter, and add us to your mailing list !

N.A.^{2}I.I.T.C.
Chambers of Commerce
PO Box 27626
Tucson, AZ 85726
520-292-0779 FAX

UNITED STATES

INDIAN CRAFTS GUILDS AND COOPERATIVES

ALASKA

MUSK OX PRODUCERS
CO OPERATIVE
604 H St
Anchorage, AK 99501
907-272-9225

ST LAWRENCE ISLAND
IVORY COOPERATIVE LTD
PO Box 189
Gambell, AK 99742
907-985-5112
907-985-5649 FAX

TAHETA ARTS AND
CULTURAL GROUP
605 A St
Anchorage, AK 99501
907-272-5829

ARIZONA

ATLATL
2303 N Central # 104
Phoenix, AZ 85004
602-253-2731
602-256-6385 FAX

HOPI ARTS & CRAFTS
Co-Operative Guild
PO Box 37
Second Mesa, AZ 86043
520-734-2463

NATIONAL NATIVE
AMERICAN CO-OPERATIVE
PO Box 1000
San Carlos, AZ 85550
520-622-4900
520-622-4900 FAX

NAVAJO ARTS & CRAFTS
ENTERPRISE
PO Drawer A
Window Rock, AZ 86515
520-871-4090/3340

SAN JUAN SO PAIUTE
YINGUP WEAVERS ASSOC
PO Box 1336
Tuba City, AZ 86045
520-526-7143

CALIFORNIA

HOOPA VALLEY NATIVE
AMERICAN CO-OP
PO Box 1304
Hoopa, CA 95546

DISTRICT OF COLUMBIA

INDIAN ARTS & CRAFTS
BOARD
US Dept of Int # 4004 - M1B
Washington, DC 20240
202-208-3773

MICHIGAN

NATIVE AMERICAN ARTS AND CRAFTS COUNCIL
PO Box 1049 Goose Creek Rd
Grayling, MI 49738
517-348-3190

MINNESOTA

IKWE MARKETING COLLECTIVE
Rt 1 Box 286
Ponsford, MN 56575
218-573-3411

MONTANA

BLACKFEET CRAFTS ASSOC
PO Box 51
Browning, MT 59417

NORTHERN CHEYENNE ARTS AND CRAFTS ASSOC
Carol A. White Wolf
General Delivery
Lame Deer, MT 59043

NORTHERN PLAINS INDIAN CRAFTS ASSOCIATION
PO Box E
Browning, MT 59417
406-338-5661

NEW MEXICO

CROWNPOINT RUG WEAVERS ASSOC INC
PO Box 1630
Crownpoint, NM 87313
505-786-8713

O'KE OWEENGE
PO Box 1095
San Juan Pueblo, NM 87566
505-852-2372

PUEBLO OF ZUNI ARTS & CRAFTS
PO Box 425
Zuni, NM 87327
505-782-5531/2136

TA-MA-YA CO OP ASSOC
St Rt 37
Bernalillo, NM 87004
505-867-3301

ZUNI CRAFTSMAN CO-OP
PO Box 426
Zuni, NM 87327
505-782-4425

NEW YORK

MEDICINE STAR CO-OP
1116 Flatbush Ave #116
Brooklyn, NY 11226

NORTH CAROLINA

HALIWA SAPONI TRIBAL POTTERY AND ARTS
PO Box 99
Hollister, NC 27844
919-586-4017

QUALLA ARTS & CRAFTS MUTUAL INC
PO Box 310
Cherokee, NC 28719
704-497-3103

OKLAHOMA

OKLAHOMA CHEROKEE
ARTIST ASSOC
PO Box 182
Rose, OK 74354
918-868-3345
918-868-2933 FAX

OKLAHOMA INDIAN ARTS
& CRAFTS COOPERATIVE
PO Box 966
Anadarko, OK 73005
405-247-3486

SOUTH DAKOTA

BRULE SIOUX ARTS &
CRAFTS CO-OP
PO Box 230
St Francis, SD 57572
605-747-2361

INTERTRIBAL BISON
COOPERATIVE
520 Kansas City St # 209
Rapid City, SD 57701
605-394-9730
605-394-7742 FAX

Note: To list your cooperative or craft guild send full details including newsletter, phone, fax, zip code and add us to your mailing list:

N.A.^{2}I.I.T.C.
Attn: Craft Guilds/Coop
PO Box 27626
Tucson, AZ 85726
520-292-0779 FAX

EXHIBITION NATIVE AMERICAN DANCERS

ARIZONA

LILLIAN ASHLEY
SWEETHEARTS OF NAVAJO LAND
Box 366
Chinle, AZ 86503

ALFRED BURDETTE
MOUNTAIN SPIRIT DANCERS
PO Box 14
Peridot, AZ 85542

FORREST CHIMERICA
HOPI SOCIAL DANCERS
4721 N 27th Dr
Phoenix, AZ 85017
602-249-0701

R T CODY
TREE CODY RED CEDAR WHISTLE
4539 N 10th Ave
Phoenix, AZ 85013
602-248-8777

DOROTHY LEWIS
SALT RIVER PIMA/MARICOPA BASKET DANCERS
PO Box 1224
Scottsdale, AZ 85251

C B MANUEL
814 Walnut
Prescott, AZ 86301
520-776-9237

ROGER MASE
HOPI DANCE GROUP
PO Box 658
Keams Canyon, AZ 86034

CARLOS NAKAI
PO Box 86477
Tucson, AZ 85754-6477

ERNIE NORTHRUP
HOPI FLUTE
414 E Glenn
Tucson, AZ 85705

EDGAR PERRY
WHITE MOUNTAIN FORT APACHE CROWN DANCERS
PO Box 507
Fort Apache, AZ 85926
520-338-4625

HART PRESTON
APACHE CROWN DANCERS
General Delivery
San Carlos, AZ 85550

THEODORE SMITH SR
YAVAPAI/TONTO APACHE TRIBE
PO Box 2429
Camp Verde, AZ 86322

FRANCIS TSOSIE
NAVAJO FIRELIGHTERS
General Delivery
Chinle, AZ 86503

CALIFORNIA

MARIO AGUILAR
AZTECA DANCERS -
DANZA MEXI'CAYOTL
988 Barrett Ave
Chula Vista, CA 92011
619-691-1044

CLARENCE ATWELL JR
16835 Alkali Dr
Lemoore, CA 93245

LORENZO BACA
TOULUMNE BAND OF
CALIFORNIA MIWOK
PO Box 4353
Sonora, CA 95370

KEN FLYING EAGLE
PO Box 12067
El Cajon, CA 92022
619-491-1812

ELISE RICKLIFF
PO Box 1348
Hoopa, CA 95546

ERIC RUNNINGPATH
PO Box 12067
El Cajon, CA 92022
619-390-1743

ALVINO SIVA
CAUILLA BIRD SINGERS
2934 W Westward
Banning, CA 92220
714-849-3450

COLORADO

KEN EDWARDS
STORYTELLER
8383 N 87th St
Longmont, CO 80503
303-772-9119

FLORIDA

GEORGE MCMULLEN
Miccosukee Tribe
PO Box 440021
Miami, FL 33144

MONTANA

GLADYS JEFFERSON
CROW DANCE GROUP
PO Box 151
Crow Agency, MT 59055

NEW MEXICO

PAT AGUINO
SAN JUAN PUEBLO
DANCERS
PO Box 928
San Juan Pueblo, NM 87556

EDWARD BAUTISTA SR
LAGUNA DANCE GROUP
PO Box 929
Paguate, NM 87040

CORNELIA BOWANNIE
ZUNI OLLA MAIDENS
PO Box 1123
Zuni, NM 87327

NATHANIEL CHEE
MESCALERO APACHE
DANCE GROUP
General Delivery
Mescalero, NM 88340

ARTHUR COMETSEVAH
CHEYENNES OF
OKLAHOMA
PO Box 353
Fort Wingate, NM 87316

LESLIE FRANCISCO
NAVAJO DANCE GROUP
PO Box 1203
Navajo, NM 87328

EVAN RILEY
LAGUNA PUEBLO
DANCERS
PO Box 255
Old Laguna, NM 87026

JOE SHUNKAMOLA
OSAGE DANCE GROUP
PO Box 151
New Laguna, NM 87038

ANDREW THOMAS
INUVIK NATIVE BAND
Indian Pueblo Cultural Ctr
2401 12th NW
Albuquerque, NM 87102

ADAM TRUJILLO/G
FLYING EAGLE
TAOS DANCE GROUP
PO Box 1321
Taos, NM 87581

VAL WHITE CLOUD
JEMEZ PUEBLO DANCERS
PO Box 111
Jemez Pueblo, NM 87024

OKLAHOMA

LUPE GOODAY
BIA AREA OFFICE
Rt 1
Anadarko, OK 73005

BILL KOOMSA SR
KIOWA DANCE GROUP
Rt 3
Carnegie, OK 73015

TOM MAUCHAHTY-WARE
COMANCHE DANCE
GROUP
PO Box 1771
Anadarko, OK 73005

FRANKLIN RILEY
SAC & FOX DANCE GROUP
508 N Roosevelt
Shawnee, OK 74801

OREGON

ART MITCHELL SINGERS
PO Box 124
Warm Springs, OR 97761

SOUTH DAKOTA

WHITNEY RENCOUNTER
RED MEDICINE
CULTURAL SURVIVAL
GROUP
PO Box 573
Fort Thompson, SD 57339

VIRGINIA

RAPPAHANNOCK-
MATTAPONI DANCERS
Rt 1 Box 522
Rappahannock, VA 23023

RISING WATERS DANCERS
Rt 2 Box 107-B
Bruington, VA 23023

Fred Synder, Director, Consultant

N.A.²I.I.T.C

North American Native American
Indian Information & Trade Center

Note: To list your dance group forward all information:
Indian Information and Trade Center
Dance Groups
PO Box 27626
Tucson, AZ 85726
520-292-0779 FAX

NATIVE AMERICAN DRUMMERS AND MASTERS OF CEREMONIES

ARIZONA

RED ROCK CREEK SINGERS
Dennis Alley
PO Box 33053
Phoenix, AZ 85067
602-973-2026

ANTELOPE WATER DRUM
PO Box 1933
Snowflake, AZ 85937

PAUL BEMORE
PO Box 170
Fort Defiance, AZ 86504

BIG SOLDIGER
224-B Tashquinth Dr
Laveen, AZ 85339
520-550-2042

BLU SPRINGS
PO Box 866
Kykotsmovi, AZ 86039
520-734-9260

DESERT BEAR HEEL SINGERS
7665 E Ranch Vista Dr
Scottsdale, AZ 85251
602-946-3478

DINÉ NATION
Jim Tso
PO Box 583
Tuba City, AZ 86045

DINÉH SINGERS
6932 E 4th
Tucson, AZ 85710
520-886-7651

EAGLE CREEK
Box 629
San Carlos, AZ 85550

EAGLE SKY
PO Box 5206
Leupp, AZ 86035

EARTH SPIRIT
PO Box 4314
Tuba City, AZ 86045

INTERTRIBAL SINGERS
PO Box 1267
Window Rock, AZ 86515
520-871-5202

IRONWATER DRUM
PO Box 1035
Keams Canyon, AZ 86034
520-736-2414

IRONWATER SINGERS
PO Box 383
Keams Canyon, AZ 86034

MEDICINE SHIELD
Freddie Johnson
PO Box 166
Rockpoint, AZ 86545

MOTEL 6 SINGERS
Box 2079
Tuba City, AZ 86045

NATIVE BOYS
Venson Bahe
PO Box 302
Keams Canyon, AZ 86034

PIMA AGENCY SINGERS
PO Box 833
Bapchule, AZ 85221

RED ANTELOPE SINGERS
Box 1262
Kayenta, AZ 86033

RED SAND
PO Box 629
Polacca, AZ 86042

REDHORSE SINGERS
PO Box 2667
Window Rock, AZ 86515

REX REDHOUSE SINGERS
6932 E 4th St
Tucson, AZ 85710

ROAMING BUFFALO
PO Box 1011
Sedona, AZ 86336
520-282-0586

ROCKY PARK
PO Box 2013
Flagstaff, AZ 86003

SACRED STAR SINGERS
PO Box 330
Second Mesa, AZ 86043
520-734-2484

SALT RIVER SINGERS
10004 N Central Ave # C
Phoenix, AZ 85020
602-389-5510

SHADOW PREY
T E Yazzie
PO Box 1272
Ganado, AZ 86505

SKYHAWK
4758 E Moreland
Phoenix, AZ 85008
602-844-2729

SOARING EAGLE
1325 W Ironwood Dr
Phoenix, AZ 85021
602-263-1528

SOUTHERN MEDICINE
Box 33
Fort Defiance, AZ 86504
520-871-4941

SOUTHERN SPIRIT
Dwayne Tofpi
541 W Stella Ln
Phoenix, AZ 85013

STAR EAGLE DRUM
PO Box 2004
Kayenta, AZ 86033

SUN LODGE DRUM
PO Box 2877
Tuba City, AZ 86045

SAMMY TONEI WHITE
Master of Ceremonies
PO Box 9522
Scottsdale, AZ 85252
602-946-7407

WHITERIVER DRUM
Dilcon School
Winslow, AZ 86047

WINTER HAWK TAIL SINGERS
Damon Polk
PO Box 10373
Yuma, AZ 85366

YOEM
5370 S Pin Oak Dr
Tucson, AZ 85746
520-889-9985

CALIFORNIA

L A NATION
227 E 67th
Long Beach, CA 90809
213-763-1968

L A NATION
8329 Lavilla
Downey, CA 90241
213-869-1902

TRADITIONAL ANDEAN MOUNTAIN MUSIC
San Diego, CA
619-235-1942

WHITECLOUD SINGERS
1174 W Chateau
Anaheim, CA 92802
714-635-3570

COLORADO

CATCHING EAGLE
PO Box 116
Towaoc, CO 81334
303-565-3267

MICHIGAN

ALL NATIONS SINGERS
1187 Buckingham Rd
Halsett, MI 48840
517-339-1069

BLUE LAKE SINGERS
130 Stevens Dr # 304
Ypsilanti, MI 48197
313-482-8211

EAGLE FEATHER SINGERS
17340 Oak
Spring Lake, MI 49456
616-846-0582

FOUR WINDS DRUM
PO Box 249
Sault Ste Marie, MI 49783
906-632-3460

KEWEENAW BAY SINGERS
PO Box 385
Baraga, MI 49908
906-353-6285

LANSING SINGERS
820 N Pennsylvania
Lansing, MI 48906

NORTHERN SKY DRUM
405 W Trail # 4
Jackson, MI 49201
906-353-6957

RED EAGLE SINGERS
3124 Dear Lake Ave
Grand Rapids, MI 49505
616-361-0687

STAR SINGERS
2055 Jefferson
Sturgis, MI 49091
517-772-5700

TWO HAWK SINGERS
Grand Rapids Intertribal
45 Lexington Ave
Grand Rapids, MI 49504
616-774-8331

MONTANA

EAGLE WHISTLE
Box 453
Frazer, MT 59225

MC
Box 676
Crow Agency, MT 59022

ROCKY BOY SINGERS
PO Box 917
Box Elder, MT 59521
406-395-4707

SOUTHERN CREE
Harlan Gopher
PO Box 474
Box Elder, MT 59521

SPOTTED EAGLE SINGERS
PO Box 961
Browning, MT 59417
406-338-5545

NEVADA

RAINBOW SHIELD SINGERS
Herbert McCabe
4663 E Patterson
Las Vegas, NV 89104

THREE NATIONS DRUM
1719 Sagebrush Dr
Elko, NV 89801

NEW MEXICO

KNIFEWING SINGERS
PO Box 83
Zuni, NM 87327

MC
PO Box 553
Zuni, NM 87327

NORTH CLOUD
Jemez Pueblo
PO Box 459
Jemez, NM 87024
505-867-5073

RED EAGLE WING DRUM
PO Box 2870
Shiprock, NM 87420

RED SKY
Melvin Mills
5101 Cargo
Farmington, NM 87402
505-325-1650

SEVEA STAR
PO Box 713
Algodomes, NM 87001
505-867-4524

SPOTTED EAGLE
8 Rd # 3942
Farmington, NM 87501
505-327-7416

ZUNI BEAR
PO Box 103
Zuni, NM 87327
505-782-2265

NEW YORK

YOUNG NATION SINGERS
7128 Meadville Rd
Basom, NY 14013
716-542-9942

OKLAHOMA

GENE RAY AHBOAH
Po Box 991
Anadarko, OK 73005

BLACKBIRD
Graham Primeaux
961 Barkley Cir
Norman, OK 73071
405-360-6312

COZAD FAMILY SINGERS
PO Box 683
Hominy, OK 74035

FORT OAKLAND RAMBLERS
Don Patterson
PO Box 95
Tonkawa, OK 74653

GRAY HORSE
Box 581241
Tulsa, OK 74158
918-742-6432
918-749-1697 FAX

ARCHIE MASON, M.C.
2541 W 53rd
Tulsa, OK 74107
918-446-5116

O-HO-MAH
PO Box 6038
Moore, OK 73153
405-799-9030

SCREAMING EAGLE
PO Box 517
Apache, OK 73006

YELLOW HAMMER RANGERS
PO Box 161
Red Rock, OK 74651

OREGON

ART MITCHELL SINGERS
PO Box 124
Warm Springs, OR 97761

SOUTH DAKOTA

IRONWOOD
PO Box 612
Rosebud, SD 52520
605-747-2967

UTAH

WHITE RIDGE SINGERS
Darren Etsitty
PO Box 417
Bluff, UT 84512
602-697-3620

VIRGINIA

ROBERT WHITEAGLE, M.C.
PO Box 305
Clincho, VA 24226
703-835-8823

WASHINGTON

BLACK LODGE SINGERS
Kenny Scabbyrobe
PO Box 626
White Swan, WA 98952
509-874-2844

BLACKLODGE DRUM NORTHERN
PO Box 626
White Swan, WA 98952

EAGLE SPIRIT DRUM
2240 Schuster Rd
Granger, WA 98932

INDIAN NATION
PO Box 398
Granger, WA 98932

WISCONSIN

BEAR CLAN SINGERS
RR 2 Box 136
Osseo, WI 54758
414-549-4201

SMOKEYTOWN SINGERS
PO Box 188
Neopit, WI 54150
715-634-8401

THREE FIRES SOCIETY SINGERS
Mole Lake Indian Reservation
Crandon, WI 54502
715-478-5180

WISCONSIN DELLS SINGERS
PO Box 184
Wisconsin Dells, WI 53965

WYOMING

17 MILE SINGERS
PO Box 132
Riverton, WY 82501
307-857-6816

*To list your drum or master of ceremonies send us your details:
Indian Information Center
PO Box 27627
Tucson, AZ 85726
520-292-0779 FAX

UNITED STATES

PERSONAL QUICK NOTES

NATIVE AMERICAN MUSIC PRODUCERS

CANADA

FIRST NATIONS MUSIC INC
3025 Kennedy Rd # 3A
Scarborough, ON M1V 1S3
CANADA
415-291-7651
415-291-8962 FAX

LITTLE BUFFALO
RECORDS
3142 33rd St W
Saskatoon, SK S7L 6V5
CANADA
306-382-5775

SUNSHINE RECORDS LTD
228 Selkirk Ave
Winnipeg, MB
CANADA
204-586-8057
204-582-8397 FAX

SWEETGRASS RECORDS
PO Box 23002
Saskatoon, SK S7L 6V5
306-343-7053

ARKANSAS

VIP PUBLISHING CO
1507 Wesley
Springdale, AR 72764
501-750-2803
501-751-4102 FAX

ARIZONA

R C NAKAI
PO Box 86477
Tucson, AZ 85754
520-743-9902
520-743-9902 FAX

CANYON RECORDS
4143 N 16th
Phoenix, AZ 85016
602-266-4823
602-265-2402 FAX

IDAHO

JOHN MININICK
PO Box 120
Lenore, ID 83541

NEW MEXICO

HIGH STAR PRODUCTIONS
PO Box 3069
Taos, NM 87571

INDIAN HOUSE
PO Box 472
Taos, NM 87571
505-776-2953

SOAR
PO Box 8606
Albuquerque, NM 87198
505-268-6110

UNITED STATES

OKLAHOMA

INDIAN RECORDS
PO Box 47
Fay, OK 73646

INDIAN SOUNDS
PO Box 6038
Moore, OK 73153
405-793-1442

SOUTH DAKOTA

FEATHERSTONE
PO Box 487
Brooking, SD 57006

assistance by: Jim Bond I.T., Indian Trader

NATIVE AMERICAN FILM MAKERS, PRODUCERS, WRITERS & DIRECTORS

CANADA

GARY FARMER
LAUGHING DOG PLAYS
PO Box 270
Tamworth, ON
CANADA

ARIZONA

VICTOR MASAYESVA JR
PO Box 747
Hotevilla, AZ 86030
520-734-2324

CALIFORNIA

ARLENE BOWMAN
2318 ½ 4th Ave
Los Angeles, CA 90018
213-734-7881

BOB HICKS
3740 Evans # 208C
Los Angeles, CA 90027
213-664-3962

BOB SCHOENHUT
PO Box 27957
Los Angeles, CA 90027
213-664-8218

HANAY GEIOGAMAH
1750 Wilcox # 223
Los Angeles, CA 90028
213-463-8535

PHYLLIS WOLFCHILD
47080 Pala Rd
Temecula, CA 92390
714-699-3825

SHELDON WOLFCHILD
47080 Pala Rd
Temecula, CA 92390
714-699-3825

ROBERT LABATTE
CENTER FOR AMERICAN INDIAN NEWS & TELEVISION
PO Box 77
Fairfax, CA 94930

GERALDINE KEAMS
HOZHONI FILMS
5152 La Vista Ct
Hollywood, CA 90004
213-464-3666

JUNE LEGRAND
KKUP RADIO / THE LIVING SPIRIT
PO Box 160328
Cupertino, CA 95016

RUSSELL MOORE
NEW BREED PRODUCTIONS
2401 Santa Fe Ave
Los Angeles, CA 90058

GEORGE BURDEAU
RALEIGH STUDIOS
650 N Bronson Ave # 215
Hollywood, CA 90004
213-871-8689

COLORADO

AVA HAMILTON
6393 S Boulder Rd
Boulder, CO 80203
303-494-8308

STELLA LOGAN
WYLDFYRE VIDEO INC
PO Box 1256
Boulder, CO 80306
303-530-9440

DISTRICT OF COLUMBIA

SUSAN HARJO
MORNING STAR
FOUNDATION
403 10th SE
Washington, DC 20003
202-547-5531
202-546-6727 FAX

IOWA

MARY GOOSE
4118 51st
Des Moines, IA 50310

MINNESOTA

MONA SMITH
2116 16th Ave S
Minneapolis, MN 55404
612-872-7886

CHRIS SPOTTED EAGLE
SPOTTED EAGLE
PRODUCTIONS
2524 Hennepin Ave S
Minneapolis, MN 55405
612-377-4212

MONTANA

WILLIAM YELLOW
ROBE JR
PO Box 394
Arlee, MT 59821

RUBIE SOOTKIS
MORNING STAR
PRODUCTIONS
PO Box 671
Lame Deer, MT 59043
406-477-8315

FRANK TYRO
SALISH KOOTENAI
COLLEGE
PO Box 117
Pablo, MT 59855
405-675-4800

NEBRASKA

ANNA ROMERO
5015 Poppleton Ave # 3
Omaha, NE 68106

FRANK BLYTHE
N/A PUBLIC
BROADCASTING
CONSORTIUM
PO Box 83111
Lincoln, NE 68501
402-472-3522

MATTHEW JONES
N/A PUBLIC
BROADCASTING
CONSORTIUM
PO Box 83111
Lincoln, NE 68501
402-472-3522

NEW MEXICO

LARRY LITTLEBIRD
PO Box 2900
Santa Fe, NM 87501
505-455-3196

JOY HARJO
PO Box 4999
Albuquerque, NM 87196

CARRIE H HOUSE
PO Box 127
Thoreau, NM 87323
505-862-7543

FIDEL MORENO
PO Box 856
Toadlena, NM 87324
505-789-3246/3221

FILEBERTO KURV'ES
RR Box 74K
Tesuque, NM 87574

DIANE REYNA
PO Box 15222
Santa Fe, NM 87506
505-471-8820
505-988-6319

BEVERLY MORRIS
1901 Calle Miquela
Santa Fe, NM 87505
505-988-6319

LENA CARR
K-KARR PRODUCTIONS
10705 Benito SW
Albuquerque, NM 87121
505-836-1336

GARY ROBINSON
PHIL LUCAS PRODUCTIONS
1007 Bishops Lodge Rd
Santa Fe, NM 87501
505-984-2365

KAREN ROBERTS-STRONG
SEAGULL WOMAN
PUBLICATION
2442 Cerrillos Rd # 270
Santa Fe, NM 87501

OKLAHOMA

DAN JONES
PO Box 421
Stillwater, OK 74076
405-372-8859
405-372-7571 FAX

JACKSON WRIGHT
1117 S Grand Ave
Cherokee, OK 73728

RICHARD R WHITMAN
3223 12th Ave NW
Norman, OK 73069

BILLY T WILLIAMSON
PO Box 3239
Oklahoma City, OK 73123
405-789-4300

DIANE FRAHER
% CELIA WALKER
5153 S Utica Ave # 1
Tulsa, OK 74105

KATHRYN BELL
AIMS INC
PO Box 274
Okmulgee, OK 74447
918-267-4033

OREGON

RONALD FOSS
PO Box 91151
Portland, OR 97292
503-647-5796

SOUTH DAKOTA

GEMMA LOCKHART
% WHIRLWIND SOLDIER
PO Box 154
Rosebud, SD 57570
605-747-2835

GARY GARRISON
SDPTV-KUSD TV
414 E Clark
Vermillion, SD 57069
605-677-5861

TENNESSEE

CAROL CORNSILK
WDCN
PO Box 120609
Nashville, TN 37212
615-259-9325

TEXAS

PRESTON THOMPSON
EAGLE KING
PRODUCTIONS
2601 S Braeswood # 1505
Houston, TX 77025

UTAH

L FLINT ESQUERRA
PO Box 1753
Salt Lake City, UT 84110

LARRY CESSPOOCH
UTE INDIAN TRIBE
Audio-Visual
PO Box 190
Fort Duchesne, UT 84026
801-722-5141

WASHINGTON

ROBERT W REDEAGLE
2240 E Sherman
Tacoma, WA 98404
206-272-9391

GLENN RAYMOND
INDIAN VISION
PO Box 43
100 Rima Ave
Inchelium, WA 99138
509-722-5969
509-633-2193

SANDY OSAWA
UPSTREAM PRODUCTIONS
420 1st Ave W
Seattle, WA 98119
206-524-8879

Note: To be listed forward all information including, phone, fax and zip code to:

N.A.[2]I.I.T.C.
Film Makers
PO Box 27627
Tucson, AZ 85726
520-292-0779 FAX

LEONARD PELTIER NETWORK

CANADA

LEONARD PELTIER
CANADIAN
Defense Committee
43 Chandler Dr
Scarbourough, ON
CANADA
416-439-1893

CALIFORNIA

INDIGENOUS RESISTANCE
RESOURCE NETWORK
733 Pacific Ave
Long Beach, CA 90813
213-437-8340

INTERNATIONAL INDIAN
TREATY COUNCIL
54 Mint St # 400
San Francisco, CA 94103
415-512-1501

L P S G
11525 Everston
Norwalk, CA 90650
213-864-1661

L P S G
PO Box 1307
Redway, CA 95560

LEONARD PELTIER
ALLIANCE
53 N Keeble Ave # 7
San Jose, CA 95126
408-279-2389

COLORADO

L P S G
PO Box 7489
Boulder, CO 80306
303-786-9589

L P S G
PO Box 18717
Denver, CO 80218

FLORIDA

FIRST NATIONS RESOURCE
NETWORK INC
PO Box 59
St Petersburg, FL 33731
813-821-6604

INDIANA

GRAYWOLF
RR 2 Box 81
Monrovia, IN 46157
317-342-1962

L P S G
5501 N Indianola
Indianapolis, IN 46220
317-255-5429

KANSAS

LEONARD PELTIER
DEFENSE COMMITTEE
PO Box 583
Lawrence, KS 66044
913-842-5774
913-842-5796 FAX

MASSACHUSETTS

L P S G
204 Butler
Fall River, MA 02724
508-674-4084

L P S G
PO Box 1396
Mashpee, MA 02649

MARYLAND

AMERICAN INDIAN
SUPPORT GROUP
Univ of Maryland
PO Box 242
College Park, MD 20742

L P S G
PO Box 312
Port Tobacco, MD 20677
301-932-1704

MISSOURI

L P S G / B M S G
611 W Broadway
Columbia, MO 65203
314-443-5985

L P S G ST LOUIS
438 N Skinker
St Louis, MO 63130
314-531-3356

L P S G KANSAS CITY
5016 N Lawn
Kansas City, MO 64119
816-455-3014

NEW HAMPSHIRE

SEVEN GENERATIONS
PO Box 126
Warner, NH 03278

NEW YORK

PROTECT INDIGENOUS
CULTURE & TRADITION
PO Box 4364
Brick, NY 08723
201-477-7443

OKLAHOMA

G MACHELL
5412 N Hudson
Oklahoma City, OK 73118

E FULKERSON
3225 S Troost
Tulsa, OK 74105

PENNSYLVANIA

L P S G / B M S G
PO Box 8411
Philadelphia, PA 19101
215-623-2018

SOUTH CAROLINA

L P S G
PO Box 124
Clemson, SC 29633
803-885-0760

TEXAS

L P S G
3314 N Central Expwy # 1
Plano, TX 75074
214-422-1422

UTAH

L P S G SALT LAKE CITY
PO Box 9401
Salt Lake City, UT 84109
801-272-9128

WASHINGTON

L P S G / B M S G
PO Box 2104
Seattle, WA 98101

L P S G BELLINGHAM
PO Box 1394
Bellingham, WA 98225
206-734-0727

INDIAN HOBBYIST ORGANIZATIONS

ALABAMA

ECHOTA CHEROKEE TRIBE
PO Box 190103
Birmingham, AL 35219

SOUTHEASTERN
INTERTRIBAL ASSN
Rt 3 Box 110e
Atmore, AL 36502

CALIFORNIA

CALIFORNIA INDIAN
HOBBYIST ASSN
3825 Dixon Pl
San Diego, CA 92107

CENTRAL CA INDIAN
TRIBAL COUNCILS
PO Box 1861
Stockton, CA 95201

ORDER OF INDIAN SCOUTS
OF AMERICA
PO Box 1686
Placerville, CA 95667

FLORIDA

AMERICAN INDIAN ASSN
OF FLORIDA
PO Box 43
Winter Park, FL 32790

FLORIDA INDIAN
HOBBYIST ASSN
1006 Bermuda Ave
Fort Pierce, FL 33482

NORTH FLORIDA INDIAN
CULTURAL SOCIETY
11372 Timber Ln
Brooksville, FL 34601

STRONG BEAR CLAN
Rt 2 Box 331
Interlachen, FL 32148

GEORGIA

CHEROKEES OF GEORGIA
3291 Church
Scottsdale, GA 30079

ILLINOIS

MASCOUTIN SOCIETY OF
CHICAGOLAND
PO Box 179
Elmwood Park, IL 60635

MIKES GROUP INC
SOUTHERN DRUM
107 White
Troy, IL 62294

WHITE BEAR SOCIETY
9709 Bianco Tr # C
Des Plaines, IL 60016

INDIANA

AMERICAN INDIAN
COUNCIL INC
1302 Victoria Dr
Lebannon, IN 46052

FOUR WINDS INDIAN
CULTURAL ASSN
1054 E 100s
Hartford, IN 47348

KUNIEH SOCIETY
RR 3 Box 260
Nashville, IN 47448

TECUMSEH LODGE
15160 Cherry Tree Rd
Noblesville, IN 46060

KENTUCKY

RED ROAD INDIAN
COUNCIL INC
Route 1
Hardinsburg, KY 40143

LOUISIANA

LOUISIANA INDIAN
HERITAGE ASSN
8009 Wales
New Orleans, LA 70126

TWIN EAGLES INDIAN
ASSN
520 E Kings Hwy
Shreveport, LA 71105

MARYLAND

AMERICAN INDIAN INTER-
TRIBAL CULTURAL
ORGANIZATION
PO Box 775
Rockville, MD 20848

RED SHIELD INDIAN
DANCERS
511 S Clinton
Baltimore, MD 21224

MASSACHUSETTS

AMERICAN INDIANISTS
SOCIETY
15 Mattson Ave
Worcester, MA 01606

FRIENDS OF NATIVE
AMERICANS
206 Massachusetts Ave
Arlington, MA 02174

MISSISSIPPI

SEBOONEY OKASUCCA
POW WOW CLUB
855 Riverside Dr
Jackson, MS 39202

MISSOURI

AMERICAN INDIAN
SOCIETY OF ST LOUIS
6651 Gravois
St Louis, MO 63116

NEW HAMPSHIRE

LACONIA INDIAN
HISTORICAL ASSN
295 Court
Laconia, NH 03246

NEW MEXICO

NEW MEXICO INDIANS
POW WOW ASSN
9205 Hagerman NE
Albuquerque, NM 87109

NEW YORK

AIS MAN DANCE
ORGANIZATION
35 Ferry Blvd
So Glen Falls, NY 12803

CALICO DANCERS
Rd 2 Box 2538
Fort Edward, NY 12828

COASTAL PLAINS SINGERS
1439 Brooklyn Blvd
Bay Shore, NY 11706

NIGHTHAWK DANCERS
PO Box 128
Little Falls, NY 13365

OHIO

MSI-KAH MI-QUI LODGE
5040 E Kemper Rd
Cincinnati, OH 45241

OGLEWANAGI INDIAN
DANCERS
1003 Shoshone Trail
Macedonia, OH 44056

OREGON

OREGON INDIAN
HOBBYIST ASSN
1805 2nd Ave SE
Albany, OR 97321

SCISSORTAIL SINGERS &
DANCERS
35696 Phillips Ln
Philomath, OR 97370

PENNSYLVANIA

CHINQUALIPPA INDIAN
DANCERS
855 Gainsway Rd
Yardley, PA 19067

LENNI LENAPE
HISTORICAL SOCIETY
2825 Fish Hatchery Rd
Allentown, PA 18103

PENNSYLVANIA INDIAN
HOBBYIST ASSOCIATION
4617 Newhall
Philadelphia, PA 19144

WESTERN PA POW WOW
CLUB
RR 04 Box 4104
Mercer, PA 16137

SOUTH DAKOTA

OGLALA LAKOTA
ARCHIVAL SOCIETY
PO Box 490
Kyle, SD 57752

TENNESSEE

NATIVE AMERICAN INTERTRIBAL ASSOCIATION
PO Box 11473
Memphis, TN 38111

NATIVE AMERICAN INDIAN ASSN OF TENN
211 Union # 404
Nashville, TN 37201

TEXAS

INTER-TRIBAL COUNCIL OF HOUSTON
PO Box 7973
Houston, TX 77270

KWAHADI DANCERS
PO Box 7606
Amarillo, TX 79109

NATIVE AMERICAN INTERTRIBAL ASSOCIATION
Rt 2 Box 198
Kingland, TX 78639

TEXAS GULF COAST TIA-PIAH SOC
8926 Woodlyn
Houston, TX 77078

TEXAS INDIAN HOBBYIST ASSN
5105 Bob Dr
No Richland Hills, TX 76180

WISCONSIN

WISCONSIN INDIAN SOCIETY
N81W14038 Eastwood Dr
Menominee Falls, WI 53051

List provided by: Louisiana Indian Heritage Association.

EUROPEAN INDIAN SUPPORT GROUPS

AUSTRIA

GESELLSCHAFT FÜR BEDROHTE
Volker
Mariahilfer Str 105/11/1/13
A-1060 Wien
AUSTRIA

WORKING CIRCLE HOPI-AUSTRIA
Obersdorf 35
A8983 Bad Mittefndorf
AUSTRIA

BELGIUM

BOOBEJAANLAND
PARC & INDIAN MUSEUM
Steenweg 45
2451 Lichtaat
BELGIUM
014/557811

CENTRO ANDINO VZW
Doornstraat 32
2610 Wilrijk
BELGIUM
03/8272405

FLEMISH INSTITUTE FOR AMERICAN CULTURE
Nieuwe Beggaardenstraat 15
2800 Mechelen 2
BELGIUM
015-41-98-37

KANTO DE LA TIERRA MEDICINE EAGLES GATHERING
Blaarstraat 82
3700 Tongeren
BELGIUM

LATIJNS AMERIKA KOMITEE
Ter Lo 49
8310 Brugge
BELGIUM
050/355199

PATER DE SMET KOMITEE
Vlasmarkt 23
9330 Dendermonde
BELGIUM

SOLIDARIDAD (LATIN AMERICA)
Lange Lozannastraat 14
2018 Antwerpen
BELGIUM
03/2375730

STUDY CENTRE FOR AMERICAN INDIANS
Tolbareel 60
2130 Brasschaat
BELGIUM
03/6515744

VLAAMSE WERKGROEP INDIANEN
Zuid Amerika (Vlaamse Wiza)
Rood Kruisstraat 43
D-8800 Roeselare
BELGIUM
051/228849

WALK IN SPIRIT
Weggevoerdenstraat 120
310 Wilsele-Leuven
BELGIUM
016/448342

ZUNI AMERICAN INDIAN
ART & JEWELRY
Groentenmarkt
9000 Gent
BELGIUM
091/242342

DENMARK

INTERNATIONAL WORK
GROUP FOR INDIGENOUS
AFFAIRS
Fiolstraede 10
Dk-1171 Copenhagen K
DENMARK
45 01 12 47 24

ENGLAND

THE MINORITY RIGHTS
GROUP
379 Brixton Rd
London SW9 7DE
ENGLAND
01-978-9498

SURVIVAL
INTERNATIONAL
11-15 Emerald St
London WC1N 3QL
ENGLAND
UNITED KINGDOM
0171-242-1441
0171-242-1771 FAX

FRANCE

NITASSINAN
B P 101
75623 Paris Cedex 13
FRANCE

SURVIVAL
INTERNATIONAL
45 rue du Faubourg du Temple
Paris 75010
FRANCE
42-41-47-62

GERMANY

BIG MOUNTAIN
AKTIONSGRUPPE
Klenzestr. 5
8000 Munchen 5
GERMANY

GESELLSCHAFT FÜR
BEDROHTE
Volker
Postfach 2024
D-3400 Gottingen
GERMANY

GLOBAL NETWORK E.V.
Oberou 63
1800 Freiburg
GERMANY
011-49-761-31193/381282

INDIANER
KUNSTGEWERBE
Burgplatz 2
4000 Dusseldorf 1
GERMANY
0211-326944

INDIANERKUNST FRANK STOP
PO Box 202342
2000 Hamburg 20
GERMANY
1-49-4101-26550

KARL MAY FESTSPIELE ELSPE
5940 LENNESTADT
12-Elspe
GERMANY
2721/1451

NORDAMERIKANISHER INDIANER
Senfgtenberger Ring 40g
1000 Berlin 26
GERMANY
030-4165792

SUPPORT GROUP FOR NATIVE PEOPLE
Islandische Str 6
1071 Berlin
GERMANY
44-88-997

TAKINI
Lowengasse I
9000 St Gallen
GERMANY

TRAMPS
Spandauestraße 2
4019 Monheim
GERMANY

ITALY

CALUMET
Via Fiume 60
53036
Poggibonsi (Si)
ITALY
0577/936288

COOP SOLIDARIETA BOTEGA
Terzo Meno
Piazza Palestro 17
25038 Rovato (BS)
ITALY

SOCONAS INCOMINDIOS
Corso Vittorio Emanele 59
10128 Torino
ITALY
010/2099835
010/2099826 FAX

SURVIVAL INTERNATIONAL
Casella Postale 1194
20101 Milan
ITALY
02-89000671

NETHERLANDS

DE KIVA
c/o Mw S C Helsloot
Pijnackerstraat 4-1
1072 Jt Amsterdam
NETHERLANDS
020-6625655

INDIAANSE VROUWEN EN GEZONDHEIDSZORG
Polsbroekstr 67-69
2546 Rl Den Haag
NETHERLANDS
070-293967

KIVA WERKGROEP NOORD-AMERIKAANSE INDIANEN IN NEDERLAND
En Belgie
Carpinistraat 8
5665 H.S. Geidrop
NETHERLANDS
040-852552

NEDERLANDSE AKTIEGROEP NOORD-AMERIKAANSE INDIANEN (NANAI)
Kamgras 23
3068 Cb Rotterdam
NETHERLANDS
010-20 98 44

STICHTING TUNA SARAPA SURINAME
Postbus 10497
1001 El Amsterdam
NETHERLANDS

THER GERONIMO MUSIC SALOON
Noorderkanaalweg 100
Rotterdam
NETHERLANDS
47656650

TURTLE SPIRIT IMPORT
N Makato
Postbus 31007
6503 Ca Nijmegenen
NETHERLANDS
080-240710

NORWAY

WORLD COUNCIL OF INDIGENOUS PEOPLES
PO Box 213
N-9520 Gouvdageaidnu
NORWAY
084-56767
084-56483 FAX

POLAND

AMERICAN INDIAN FRIENDS ASSOC
Sovereign Bldg
Roman Bala V1
Kickiego 9
POLAND
(22)12(20-39) EXT 27

SPAIN

SURVIVAL INTERNATIONAL
Calle Principe 12
Piso 3, Oficina 3
Madrid 28012
SPAIN
1-521-7283

SWITZERLAND

INCOMINDIOS
Postfach 321
Ch-8820 Wadenswil
SWITZERLAND
01-780 59 22
07-780 60 41 FAX

U.S.S.R.

BYELORUSSIAN-
AMERICAN INDIAN
SOCIETY
PO Box 114
Gomel 246049 Byelorussia
U.S.S.R.

Fred Synder, Director, Consultant
N.A.²I.I.T.C
North American Native American
Indian Information & Trade Center

information provided by: Study Center for
American Indians, Belgium
North American Indian Information
And Trade Center, USA

TRIBAL GAMING OPERATIONS

ALABAMA

CREEK BINGO PALACE
PO Box 09, Highway 21
Atmore, AL 36504
800-826-9121
205-368-8007
202-368-8590 FAX
sponsored by the Poarch Creek Indians

ARIZONA

AK CHIN HARRAH'S
Rt 2 PO Box 27
Maricopa, AZ 85007
520-568-2618
520-254-6133 FAX
sponsored by AK CHIN Indian Community

APACHE GOLD CASINO
PO Box 1210
San Carlos, AZ 85550
800-APACHE
sponsored by San Carlos Apache Nation

THE ARIZONA CLUB CASINO OF THE SUN
7406 S Camino De Oeste
Tucson, AZ 85746
800-344-9435
520-883-1700
520-883-0983 FAX
sponsored by the Pascua Yaqui Indians

COCAPAH BINGO & CASINO
15136 South Avenue B
Somerton, AZ 85350
602-726-8066
602-344-8010 FAX
sponsored by the Cocapah Indian Tribe

FORT MCDOWELL GAMING
Route 1, Box 798
Scottsdale, AZ 85264
602-837-1424
602-837-0844 FAX
sponsored by the Fort McDowell Mohave-Apache Tribe

GILA RIVER CASINO
PO Box 97
Sacaton, AZ 85247
520-963-4323
520-562-3422 FAX
sponsored by Gila River Indian Community

HON-DA CASINO
PO Box 700
Whiteriver, AZ 85941
sponsored by White Mountain Apache Nation

MAZATZAL CASINO
Tonto Reservation # 30
Payson, AZ 85541
520-474-6044
520-474-4238 FAX
sponsored by Tonto Apache Nation

PAPAGO BINGO /
DESERT DIAMOND CASINO
7350 S Old Nogales Hwy
PO Box 22230
Tucson, AZ 85734
520-294-7777
520-294-9955 FAX
sponsored by the Tohono O'dham Nation

YAVAPAI GAMING CENTER
1500 & 1505 East Hwy 69
Prescott, AZ 86301
520-778-7909
520-778-9854 FAX
sponsored by the Yavapai Prescott Indian Tribe

CALIFORNIA

BARONA CASINO
1000 Wild Cat Canyon Rd
Lakeside, CA 92040
619-443-2300
619-443-6977 FAX
sponsored by the Barona Group of the Capitan Grande Band of Mission Indians

CACHE CREEK INDIAN BINGO
PO Box 65
Brooks, CA 95606
916-796-3118
916-796-2112 FAX
sponsored by the Rumsey Rancheria Tribe

CASINO MORONGO
49750 Seminole Drive
Cabazon, CA 92230
909-849-3080
sponsored by the Morongo Band of Mission Indians

CHER-AE HEIGHTS BINGO
27 Cher-ae Lane
Trinidad, CA 95570
707-677-3611
707-677-1653 FAX
sponsored by the Cher-ae Heights Community of the Trinidad Racheria

CHICKEN RANCH BINGO
PO Box 1699
Jamestown, CA 95327
209-984-3000
800-752-4646 (CA Only)
209-984-4158 FAX
sponsored by the Chicken Ranch Rancheria Band of Miwuk Indians

COLUSA INDIAN BINGO
PO Box 1267
Colusa, CA 95932
916-458-8844
916-458-2018 FAX
sponsored by Colusa Wintu Community

GOLD FEATHER CASINO
1940 Feather River Blvd
Oroville, CA 95965
916-534-9484
sponsored by Mooretown Rancheria Community

HOOPA VALLEY BINGO
PO Box 176
Hoopa, CA 95546
916-625-4809
sponsored by Hoopa Tribal Nation

INDIO BINGO PALACE & CASINO
84-245 Indio Springs Drive
Indio, CA 92201
619-345-9000
619-347-7880 FAX
sponsored by the Cabazon Band of Mission Indians

JACKSON INDIAN BINGO & CASINO
16000 Bingo Way
Jackson, CA 95642
209-223-1677
209-223-3424 FAX
sponsored by the Miwuk Tribe

KABITAN II INDIAN BINGO
390 Forbes St
Lakeport, CA 95453
707-275-3140
sponsored by Pomo Indian Nations

MOJAVE CASINO
500 Merriman Avenue
Needles, CA 92363
619-326-4591 FAX

PALACE BINGO
PO Box 308
17225 Jersey Avenue
Lemoore, CA 93245
209-924-7751
209-924-8949 FAX
sponsored by the Tachi Tribe/ Santa Rosa Rancheria

QUECHAN INDIAN BINGO
350 Picacho Rd
Winterhaven, CA 92283
619-572-0678
sponsored by Quechan Tribal Nation

ROBINSON RANCHERIA BINGO AND CASINO
1545 E Highway 20
Nice, CA 95464
707-275-9000
707-275-9440 FAX
sponsored by Robinson Rancheria Community

SAN MANUEL INDIAN BINGO & CASINO
5797 North Victoria Avenue
Highland, CA 92346
800-359-BINGO
909-862-3405 FAX
sponsored by the San Manuel Band if Mission Indians

SYCUAN GAMING CENTER
5469 Dehesa Road
El Cajon, CA 92019
619-445-6002
619-445-1961 FAX
sponsored by the Kumeyaay Band of Mission Indians

TABLE MOUNTAIN RANCHERIA CASINO & BINGO
PO Box 445
Friant, CA 93626
209-822-2485
209-822-3555 FAX
sponsored by the Chichansi & Mono Tribes

VIEJAS CASINO
PO Box 2208
Alpine, CA 91901
sponsored by Viejas Tribal Nation

WIN-RIVER CASINO BINGO
2000 Rancheria Road
Redding, CA 96001
916-225-8979
916-241-1879 FAX
sponsored by the Redding Rancheria

COLORADO

SKY UTE BINGO
PO Box 550
Ignacio, CO 81137
303-563-9583
sponsored by the Southern Ute Tribe

UTE MOUNTAIN CASINO
PO Drawer V
Cortez, CO 81334
303-565-8800
303-565-7276 FAX
sponsored by Ute Mountain Ute Nation

CONNECTICUT

FOXWOODS HIGH-STAKES BINGO & CASINO
PO Box 410
Ledyard, CT 06339
203-885-3000
800-442-1000
203-599-2849 FAX
sponsored by the Mashantucket Pequot Tribal Nation

FLORIDA

MICCOSUKEE INDIAN BINGO
PO Box 651737
Miami, FL 33265
305-222-4600
305-226-9254 FAX
sponsored by the Miccosukee Tribe

SEMINOLE INDIAN BINGO OF HOLLYWOOD
4150 North State Road 7
Hollywood, FL 33021
305-961-3220
sponsored by the Seminole Tribe of Florida

SEMINOLE BINGO OF BRIGHTON
Rt 6 Box 611
Okechobee, FL 34974
305-792-1021
305-583-4369 FAX
sponosred by Seminole Tribe of Florida

SEMINOLE BINGO OF TAMPA
5223 North Orient Road
Tampa, FL 33610
813-621-1302
800-282-7016 (Florida Only)
sponsored by the Seminole Tribe of Florida

IDAHO

COEUR D'ALENE TRIBAL BINGO
PO Box 236 Hwy 95
Worley, ID 83876
800-523-2464
208-686-1503 FAX
sponsored by Coeur d'Alene Tribal nation

KOOTENAI RIVER INN CASINO
Kootenai River Plaza
Bonner's Ferry, ID 83805
208-267-8511
800-346-5668
208-267-8511 FAX
sponsored by Kootenai Tribal Nation

SHOSHONE-BANNOCK GAMING ENTERPRISES
PO Box 868
Fort Hall, ID 83203
208-237-8774
208-237-8207 FAX
sponsored by the Shonone-Bannock Tribes

IOWA

CASINO OMAHA
1 Blackbird Bend
PO Box 89
Onawa, IA 51040
800-858-UBET
712-423-3700
712-423-3128 FAX
sponsored by the Omaha Tribe of Nebraska and Iowa

MESQUAKI BINGO & CASINO
1504 305th Street
Tama, IA 52339
800-728-GAME
515-484-2108
515-484-3218 FAX
sponsored by the Sac & Fox Tribe of the Mississippi in Iowa/Mesquaki

WINNA VEGAS CASINO
1500 - 330 Street
Sloan, IA 51055
712-428-9466
sponsored by Ho Chuck Tribe of Nebraska

KANSAS

IOWA TRIBE PARTY GAMES
Rt 1 Box 58A
White Cloud, KS 66094
913-595-3258
919-595-6610 FAX
sponsored by Iowa Nation

KICKAPOO BINGO HALL
Rt 1 Box 157A
Horton, KS 66439
913-486-2131
913-486-2801
sponsored by Kickapoo Tribal Nation

PRAIRIE BAND POTAWATOMI BINGO HALL
Rt 2 Box 50-A
Mayetta, KS 66509
913-966-2771
sponsored by Prairie Band Potawatomi Nation

LOUISIANA

COUSHATTA GAMING OPERATION
PO Box 818
Elton, LA 70532
318-584-2209
sponsored by Coushatta Tribal Nation

CYPRESS BAYOU CASINO
PO Box 519
Charenton, LA 70523
800-284-4386
318-923-7882
sponsored by Chitimacha Tribal Nation

TUNICA-BILOXI GAMING OPERATION
PO Box 311
Mansura, LA 71351
318-253-9767
sponsored by Tunica-Biloxi Tribal Nation

MICHIGAN

BAY MILLS INDIAN BINGO/ KINGS CLUB CASINO
Route 1, Box 313
Brimley, MI 49715
906-248-3241
906-248-3283 FAX
sponsored by the Bay Mills Chippewa Indian Community

BIG BUCKS BINGO/OJIBWA CASINO
PO Box 284A
Baraga, MI 49908
800-323-8045
906-353-7618 FAX
sponsored by the Keweenaw Bay Indian Community

GRAND TRAVERSE BAND VIDEO PALACE
Route 1 Box 157-A
Suttons, Bay, MI 49682
616-271-6477
616-271-4230 FAX
sponsored by Grand Traverse Band of Ottawa/Chippewa Indians

HANNAHVILLE BINGO & CHIP-IN CASINO
PO Box 351
W 399 Hwys 2 & 41
Harris, MI 49845
800-682-6040
906-466-2941
906-466-2945 FAX
sponsored by the Hannahville Tribe

KEWADIN SHORES CASINO
3039 Mackinac Trail
St. Ignace, MI 49781
906-643-7071
sponsored by Sault Ste. Marie Tribe of Chippewa Indians

LAC VIEUX DESERT CASINO
PO Box 249, Choate Rd
Watersmeet, MI 49969
906-358-4423
906-358-4785 FAX
sponsored by the Lac Vieux Desert Band of Lake Superior Chippewa Indians

LEELANAU SANDS CASINO
2521 N West-Bay Shore Dr
Suttons Bay, MI 49682
616-271-4104
616-271-4136 FAX
sponsored by Grand Traverse Tribal Nation

SAGINAW CHIPPEWA CASINO
7070 East Broadway
Mt. Pleasant, MI 48858
517-772-8900
517-772-0827 FAX
sponsored by the Saginaw Chippewa Tribe

SAGINAW CHIPS CARD ROOM AND CASINO
7498 E Broadway
Mt. Pleasant, MI 48858
517-772-5700
517-772-2982 FAX
sponsored by the Saginaw Chippewa Tribe

SOARING EAGLE CASINO
2395 S Leaton Rd
Mt. Pleasant, MI 48858
517-772-8900
517-772-7759 FAX
sponsored by the Saginaw Chippewa Tribe

SUPER GAMING PALACE
Rt 1 Box 157-A
Suttons Bay, MI 49652
616-271-6852
616-271-4208 FAX
sponsored by Grand Traverse Tribal Nation

VEGAS KEWADIN CASINO
2186 Shunk Road
Saulte Ste Marie, MI 49783
800-626-9878
906-632-8300 FAX
sponsored by the Sault Ste. Marie Tribe of Chippewa Indians

MINNESOTA

FIREFLY CREEK CASINO
Route 2, PO Box 96
Granite Falls, MN 56241
612-564-2121
800-232-1439
612-564-2547 FAX
sponsored by the Upper Sioux Community

FOND DU LAC BIG BUCKS CASINO
105 University Rd
Cloquet, MN 55720
218-879-4691
218-879-7839 FAX
sponsored by Fond du Lac Reservation Business Committee

FOND-DU-LUTH GAMING CASINO
129 East Superior Street
Duluth, MN 55802
218-722-0280
218-722-7505 FAX
sponsored by the Fond Du Lac Band of Lake Superior Chippewa

FORTUNE BAY CASINO
1430 Bois Forte Road
Tower, MN 55790
800-992-PLAY
218-753-6400
218-753-6404 FAX
sponsored by the Bois Forte Band of Chippewa

GOLDEN EAGLE BINGO LODGE
PO Box 418
Highway 59
Mahnomen, MN 56557
218-935-5385
sponsored by the White Earth Band of Chippewa Indians

GRAND CASINO HINCKLEY
777 Lady Luck Drive
Route 3, Box 15
Hinckley, MN 55037
800-GRAND 21
612-384-7771
612-449-7757 FAX
sponsored by the Mille Lacs Band of Ojibwe/Minnesota Chippewa

GRAND CASINO MILLE LACS
PO Box 240
Onamia, MN 56359
800-626-LUCK
612-449-5992 FAX
sponsored by Mille Lacs Band of Ojibwe

GRAND PORTAGE LODGE & CASINO
Highway 61 & Marina Road
PO Box 307
Grand Portage, MN 55605
800-543-1384
218-475-2401
218-475-2309 FAX
sponsored by the Grand Portage Chippewa

JACKPOT JUNCTION CASINO
PO Box 420
Morton, MN 56270
800-WIN-CASH
507-644-2645 FAX
sponsored by the Lower Sioux Indian Community

LAKE OF THE WOODS CASINO
1012 Lake Street
Warroad, MN 56763
800-386-3846
218-386-3381
218-386-2969 FAX
sponsored by the Red Lake Band of Chippewa

LITTLE 6 BINGO
2400 Mystic Lake Blvd
Prior Lake, MN 55372
612-445-9000
612-496-7280 FAX
sponsored by Red Lake Band of Chippewa Indians

MYSTIC LAKE BINGO & CASINO
2400 Mystic Lake Boulevard
Prior Lake, MN 55372
800-262-7799
612-445-9000
612-496-7280 FAX
sponsored by the Shakopee Mdewakanton Dakota

NORTHERN LIGHTS CASINO
HCR 73, Box 1003
Walker, MN 56484
800-252-7529
218-547-2744
218-547-1368 FAX
sponsored by the Leech Lake Reservation Tribal Council

PALACE BINGO & CASINO
Route 3, Box 3
Bingo Palace Drive
Cass Lake, MN 56633
218-335-6787
800-228-6676 (MN Only)
218-335-6899 FAX
sponsored by the Leech Lake Reservation Tribal Council

RED LAKE TRIBAL BINGO
PO Box 550
Red Lake, MN 56671
218-679-3941
218-679-3378 FAX
sponsored by the Red Lake Tribe

RIVER ROAD CASINO
RR 3 Box 168A
Thief River Falls, MN 56701
218-681-4062
218-681-8370 FAX
sponsored by Red Lake Band of Chippewa Indians

SHOOTING STAR CASINO
777 Casino Road, Box 401
Mahnomen, MN 56557
218-935-2711
218-935-2206 FAX
sponsored by White Earth Band of Chippewa Indians

TREASURE ISLAND BINGO & CASINO
PO Box 75
Red Wing, MN 55066
800-222-7077
612-385-2560 FAX
sponsored by the Prairie Island Mdewakanton Dakota

MISSISSIPPI

MISSISSIPPI BAND OF CHOCTAW GAMING OPERATION
PO Box 6010
Philadelphia, MS 39350
601-656-5251
sponsored by Mississippi Band of Choctaw Indians

MISSOURI

EASTERN SHAWNEE TRIBAL BINGO
PO Box 350
Seneca, MO 64865
918-666-8702
918-666-3325
sponsored by the Eastern Shawnee Tribe of Oklahoma

MONTANA

BLACKFEET BINGO
PO Box 837
Browning, MT 59417
406-338-5751
sponsored by Blackfeet Tribal Business Council

FORT BELKNAP BINGO ENTERPRISE
PO Box 338
Harlem, MT 59526
406-353-2965
800-343-6107 (MT Only)
406-353-4923 FAX
sponsored by the Fort Belknap Agency-Gros Ventre & Assininboine

4 C'S CAFE & CASINO
Rocky Boy Route
PO Box 544
Box Elder, MT 59521
406-395-4863
sponsored by Chippewa Cree Tribe of the Rocky Boy's Reservation

LITTLE BIG HORN CASINO
PO Box 580
Crow Agency, MT 59022
406-638-4444
sponsored by Crow Indian Tribe

NORTHERN CHEYENNE BINGO
Box 130
Lame Deer, MT 59043
406-477-6677
sponsored by Northern Cheyenne Tribe

WPCO CASINO/SILVER WOLF CASINO
Highway 13 West
PO Box 726
Wolf Point, MT 59201
406-653-3476
406-653-3181 FAX
sponsored by the Fort Peck Tribes

NEBRASKA

CASINO OMAHA BINGO
PO Box 387
Macy, NE 68039
800-368-8248
sponsored by Omaha Tribal Council

NEW MEXICO

ACOMA GAMING
OPERATION
PO Box 309
Acomita, NM 87034
505-552-6017
sponsored by Pueblo of Acoma

BINGO OF MESCALERO
PO Box 190
Mescalero, NM 88340
505-257-9268
505-257-2945 FAX
sponsored by the Mescalero Apache Tribe

INN OF THE MOUNTAIN
GODS
PO Box 269
Mescalero, NM 88340
505-257-5141
505-257-6173
sponsored by the Mescalero Apache Tribe

ISLETA GAMING PALACE
11000 Broadway, SE
Albuquerque, NM 87105
505-869-2614
505-869-0152 FAX
sponsored by the Pueblo of Isleta

JICARILLA INN BINGO
PO Box 233
Dulce, NM 87528
505-759-3663
800-742-1938
505-759-3170 FAX
sponsored by the Jicarilla Apache Tribe

POJOAQUE GAMING, INC.
Route 11, Box 21-B
Santa Fe, NM 87501
800-455-3313
505-455-3313
505-455-3363 FAX
sponsored by the Pojoaque Pueblo Tribe/Tewa

SAN JUAN PUEBLO
VIDEO/BINGO
PO Box 1099
San Juan Pueblo, NM 87566
505-747-1668
sponsored by Pueblo of San Juan

SANDIA INDIAN BINGO
PO Box 10188
Albuquerque, NM 87184
505-897-2173
800-526-9366
505-897-1117 FAX
sponsored by the Pueblo of Sandia

SANTA ANA STAR CASINO
Box 9201
54 Jemez Canyon Dam Road
Bernalillo, NM 87004
505-867-0000
505-867-1472 FAX
sponsored by the Santa Ana Pueblo

TAOS PUEBLO PULL TAB
OPERATION
PO Box 1846
Taos, NM 87571
505-758-4460
sponsored by Taos Pueblo

TESUQUE PUEBLO BINGO
CAMEL ROCK GAMING
Route 11, Box 3A
Santa Fe, NM 87501
505-984-8414
800-GO-CAMEL
505-989-9234 FAX
sponsored by the Tesuque Pueblo

NEW YORK

BILLY'S BINGO HALL
PO Box 366
Hogansburg, NY 13655
518-358-2106
800-532-7855
518-358-3203 FAX
sponsored by Seneca Nation of Indians

MOHAWK BINGO PALACE
PO Box 480
Hogansburg, NY 13655
518-358-2246
518-358-2249 FAX
Sponsored by the St. Regis Mohawk Tribe

ONEIDA INDIAN NATION BINGO
PO Box 388
4 Territory Road
Oneida, NY 13421
800-782-1938
315-363-7771
315-361-1961 FAX
sponsored by the Oneida Indian Nation of New York

SENECA BINGO
PO Box 231
Salamanaca, NY 14779
716-945-4080
800-421-2464 (NY Only)
716-945-3354
sponsored by the Seneca Nation of Indians

NORTH CAROLINA

CHEROKEE BINGO
PO Box 1629
Cherokee, NC 28719
704-497-4320
800-410-1254
704-497-4321 FAX
sponsored by the Cherokee Nation

TRIBAL BINGO & CASINO
PO Box 1897
Cherokee, NC 28719
704-497-7554
704-497-4320
800-410-1254
704-497-4321 FAX
sponsored by Eastern Band of Cherokee Indians

NORTH DAKOTA

DAKOTAH BINGO PALACE
PO Box 165
St. Michaels, ND 58370
701-766-4433
sponsored by Devils Lake Sioux Tribe

PRAIRIE KNIGHTS CASINO
HC 1 Box 26A
Fort Yates, ND 58538
701-854-7777
701-854-7785 FAX
sponsored by Standing Rock Sioux Tribe

TURTLE MOUNTAIN CHIPPEWA CASINO
PO Box 1449
Belcourt, ND 58316
701-477-3281
701-477-5331 FAX
sponsored by the Turtle Mountain Band of Chippewa Indians

OKLAHOMA

ARROWHEAD BINGO
HC 67 Box 5
Canadian, OK 74425
800-422-2711
918-339-6562 FAX
sponsored by Choctaw Nation of Oklahoma

BRISTOW INDIAN BINGO
PO Box 955
121 West Lincoln
Bristow, OK 74010
918-367-9168
sponsored by the Creek Indians

CHECOTAH COMMUNITY INDIAN BINGO
830 N Broadway
PO Box 554
Checotah, OK 74426
918-473-5200
sponsored by Muscogee (Creek) Nation

CHEROKEE NATION'S BINGO OUTPOST
PO Box 1000
Roland, OK 74954
918-427-7491
918-427-6805 FAX
sponsored by the Cherokee Nation

CHEYENNE & ARAPAHO BINGO
PO Box 95
Concho, OK 73022
405-262-8245
405-262-6350 FAX
sponsored by the Cheyenne and Arapaho Tribes

CHOCTAW INDIAN BINGO PALACE
PO Box 1909
Durant, OK 74702
800-788-BINGO
405-920-0024
sponsored by the Choctaw Nation of Oklahoma

CIMARRON BINGO CASINO
PO Box 190
Perkins, OK 74059
405-547-5352
sponsored by the Iowa Tribe of Oklahoma

COMANCHE NATION GAMES
PO Box 347
Lawton, OK 73502
405-492-4982
sponsored by the Comanche Tribe-Anadarko Agency

CREEK NATION
HOLDENVILLE BINGO
416 E Poplar
PO Box 315
Holdenville, OK 74848
sponsored by Muscogee (Creek) Nation

CREEK NATION
OKMULGEE BINGO
PO Box 790
Okmulgee, OK 74447
918-756-8400
918-756-8938 FAX
sponsored by the Muscogee (Creek) Nation

CREEK NATION TULSA BINGO
PO Box 70083
Tulsa, OK 74170
918-299-8518
918-299-0867 FAX
sponsored by the Creek Nation

EAST GORE BINGO
2325 E Gore Blvd
Lawton, OK 73502
405-248-5905
sponsored by Fort Sill Apache Tribe of Oklahoma

EUFAULA INDIAN
COMMUNITY BINGO
806 Forest Ave
Eufaula, OK 74432
918-689-9191
sponsored by Muscogee (Creek) Nation

GOLD NUGGET GAMES
PO Box 806
Anadarko, OK 73005
405-247-6979
sponsored by Delaware Tribe of Oklahoma

GOLDSBY GAMING CENTER
1500 N Country Club
Ada, OK 74820
405-436-4311
405-436-1152 FAX
sponsored by Chickasaw Nation of Oklahoma

GOLDSBY GAMING CENTER
Route 1, Box 104P
Norman, OK 73072
405-329-5447
sponsored by the Chickasaw Nation

GRAYHORSE INDIAN VILLAGE
504 W 45th
Sand Springs, OK 74063
sponsored by Osage Tribe of Indians

HOMINY INDIAN VILLAGE BINGO
PO Box 2585
Stillwater, OK 74076
405-743-1278
405-743-1280 FAX
sponsored by Osage Tribe of Indians

KAW NATION BINGO
PO Box 171
Newkirk, OK 74647
405-362-2578
405-362-2726 FAX
sponsored by the Kaw Nation

LUCKY STAR BINGO
7777 North Highway 81
PO Box 150
Concho, OK 73022
800-81-LUCKY
405-262-7612
405-262-4429 FAX
sponsored by the Cheyenne and Arapaho Tribes of Oklahoma

MUSKOGEE BINGO
PO Box 1249
Muskogee, OK 74401
918-683-1825
sponsored by Muscogee (Creek) Nation

NA-I-SHA GAMES
PO Box 1220
620 East Colorado Street
Anadarko, OK 73005
405-247-9331
405-247-2951 FAX
sponsored by the Apache Tribe of Oklahoma

O-GAH-PAG BINGO
Route 2 Box 17B
Miami, OK 74354
918-542-1085
sponsored by Quapaw Tribe of Oklahoma

OKLAHOMA INDIAN COUNTRY BINGO INC.
C/O Sac & Fox Tax Commission
Route 2 Box 246
Stroud, OK 74079
918-968-3526
918-968-3887 FAX
sponsored by Sac & Fox Nation of Oklahoma

OTOE-MISSOURIA TRIBAL BINGO
PO Box 2585
Stillwater, OK 74076
405-743-1278
sponsored by Otoe-Missouria Tribe of Oklahoma

OUTPOST BINGO
PO Box 948
Tahlequah, OK 74465
918-456-0671
918-456-6485 FAX
sponsored by the Cherokee Nation of Oklahoma

PAWHUSKA INDIAN VILLAGE
Box 60
Pawhuska, OK 74056
sponsored by Osage Tribe of Indians

PAWNEE TRIBAL BINGO
Box 69
Pawnee, OK 74058
918-762-3301
sponsored by Pawnee Business Council

PONCA GAMING
OPERATION
Box 2 White Eagle
Ponca City, OK 74601
405-762-8104
sponsored by Ponca Tribe of Oklahoma

POTAWATOMI BINGO/
FIRELAKE
ENTERTAINMENT CENTER
1901 South Gordon Cooper Dr
Shawnee, OK 74801
405-273-2242
405-273-0686 FAX
sponsored by the Citizen Band Potawatomi Tribe of Oklahoma

SEMINOLE NATION BINGO
PO Box 1019
Wewoka, OK 74884
405-382-7920
sponsored by by Seminole Nation of Oklahoma

SENECA-CAYUGA GAMING
OPERATION
PO Box 1283
Miami, OK 74355
918-542-6609
sponsored by Seneca-Cayuga Tribe of Oklahoma

SULPHUR GAMING
CENTER
West First & Muskogee
Sulphur, OK 73086
405-622-2156
405-622-3094 FAX
sponsored by the Chickasaw Nation

THLOPTHLOCO BINGO
Box 706
Okemah, OK 74859
918-623-2620
918-623-2620 FAX (Call First)
sponsored by the Thlopthloco Tribal Town

THUNDERBIRD
ENTERTAINMENT CENTER
15700 East SH9
Norman, OK 73071
405-360-9270
405-360-9288 FAX
sponsored by Absentee-Shawnee Tribe of Oklahoma

TONKAWA TRIBAL BINGO
PO Box 2585
Stillwater, OK 74076
405-743-1278
sponsored by Tonkawa Business Committee

TOUSA ISHTO-CHICKASAW
GAMING CENTER
Exit 1, Highway I-35
Thackerville, OK 73459
405-276-4229
405-276-2164 FAX
sponsored by the Chickasaw Nation

UNITED KEETOOWAH
BINGO
PO Box 746
Tahlequah, OK 74465
918-456-5491
918-456-9601 FAX
sponsored by the United Keetoowah Band of Cherokees

OREGON

CHINOOK WINDS
2120 NW 44th St # A
Lincoln City, OR 97367
503-996-5508
800-863-3314
503-996-5491 FAX
sponsored by Confederated Tribes of Siletz Indians of Oregon

COW CREEK INDIAN BINGO
1476 Chief Miwaleta Ln
Canyonville, OR 97417
503-839-1111
503-839-4300 FAX
sponsored by the Cow Creek Band of the Umpqua Tribe

MISSION BINGO
PO Box 638
Pendleton, OR 97801
503-276-3873
503-276-3262 FAX
sponsored by the Confederated Tribes of the Umatilla Indian Reservation (Cayuse, Umatilla, Walla Walla)

WILD HORSE GAMING RESORT
PO Box 638
Pendleton, OR 97801
503-276-3873
503-276-3262
sponsored by the Confederated Tribes of the Umatilla Indian Reservation (Cayuse, Umatilla, Walla Walla)

SOUTH DAKOTA

AGENCY BINGO & CASINO
PO Box 569
Veterans Memorial Drive
Agency Village, SD 57262
800-542-2876
605-698-4273
605-698-3551 FAX
sponsored by Sisseton-Wahpeton Sioux Tribe

BEAR SOLDIER JACKPOT BINGO
PO Box 876
McLaughlin, SD 57642
605-823-4364
605-823-4987
605-823-4273 FAX
sponsored by the Standing Rock Sioux Tribe, Bear Soldier District

DAKOTA SIOUX CASINO
Sioux Valley Road
PO Box 290
Watertown, SD 57201
800-658-4717
605-882-2185 FAX
sponsored by the Sisseton-Wahpeton Dakota Nation

FORT RANDALL CASINO & HOTEL
West Highway 46
PO Box 756
Wagner, SD 57380
800-553-3003
605-487-7871
605-487-7354 FAX
sponsored by the Yankton Sioux Tribe

GOLDEN BUFFALO CASINO
321 Sitting Bull Street
PO Box 204
Lower Brule, SD 57548
605-473-5577
605-473-9270 FAX
sponsored by the Lower Brule Sioux Tribe

LONE STAR CASINO
PO Box 658
Fort Thompson, SD 57339
605-245-2221
605-245-2470 FAX
sponsored by Crow Creek Sioux Tribe

OGLALA SIOUX BINGO
PO Box H
Pine Ridge, SD 57770
605-867-5821
605-867-5582 FAX
sponsored by Oglala Sioux Tribe

ROSEBUD CASINO
PO Box 430
Rosebud, SD 57570
605-747-2381
605-747-2243 FAX
sponsored by Rosebud Sioux Tribe

ROYAL RIVER CASINO
PO Box 326
Flandreau, SD 57028
800-234-2WIN
605-276-3262 FAX
sponsored by the Santee Sioux Tribe

TEXAS

SPEAKING ROCK CASINO & ENTERTAINMENT CENTER
PO Box 17579
El Paso, TX 79917
915-858-6934
915-859-4240 FAX
sponsored by Ysleta Del Sur Pueblo Indian Tribe

WASHINGTON

B.J.'S BINGO
4411 Pacific Highway East
Tacoma, WA 98424
206-922-0430
206-922-1590 FAX
sponsored by the Puyallup Nation

CHEHALIS BINGO
PO Box 536
Oakville, WA 98568
206-273-8066
sponsored by Confederated Tribes of the Chehalis Reservation

COLVILLE TRIBAL BINGO
Rt 2, 7 Apple Way
Okanogan, WA 98840
sponsored by Confederated Tribes of the Colville Reservation

LANDRY'S MUSEUM BINGO
Star Route Box 493
Tokeland, WA 98590
206-267-6766
sponsored by Shoalwater Bay Tribal Council

LOWER ELWHA BINGO
2851 Lower Elwha Rd
Port Angeles, WA 98362
206-452-8471
206-452-3428 FAX
sponsored by Lower Elwha S'Klallam Tribe

THE LUMMI CASINO
2559 Lummi View Drive
Bellingham, WA 98225
360-758-7559
360-758-7545 FAX
sponsored by the Lummi Indian Nation

MAKAH BINGO
PO Box 115
Neah Bay, WA 98357
206-645-2201
sponsored by Makah Tribal Council

MICRO DOME INC
PO Box 1074
Milton, WA 98354
206-922-1931
sponsored by Puyallup Tribe of Indians

MUCKLESHOOT INDIAN BINGO
2602 Auburn Way South
Auburn, WA 98002
206-735-2404
206-735-0384 FAX
sponsored by the Muckleshoot Indian Tribe

MUCKLESHOOT INDIAN CASINO
39105 172nd Street SE
Auburn, WA 98002
206-939-3311
206-939-5311 FAX

NISQUALLY INDIAN TRIBE
12819 Yelm Highway SE
Olympia, WA 98513
800-497-0113
206-456-6034 FAX
sponsored by Nisqually Indian Tribe

NOOKSACK RIVER CASINO
PO Box 157
Deming, WA 98244
360-592-5176
360-592-5753
sponsored by Nooksack Indian Tribe

PORT MADISON ENTERPRISES
PO Box 797
Suquamish, WA 98392
206-598-3399
sponsored by Suquamish Tribe

PUYALLUP TRIBAL BINGO PALACE
2002 East 28th Street
Tacoma, WA 98404
800-876-2464
206-383-1572
206-382-0774 FAX
sponsored by the Puyallup Tribe of Indians

QUILEUTE BINGO
PO Box 279
Lapush, WA 98350
206-374-6163
206-374-6311 FAX
sponsored by Quileute Indian Tribe

SPOKANE INDIAN BINGO
U.S. Highway 395, Smith Road
Chewelah, WA 99109
509-935-6167
509-935-8052
sponsored by the Spokane Tribe

SWINOMISH INDIAN BINGO
PO Box 1075
Anacortes, WA 98221
360-293-4687
800-877-7529 (WA & Canada Only)
360-299-9556 FAX
sponsored by the Swinomish Tribal Community

TRIBAL SITTY HALL
5803 N Levee Rd E
Tacoma, WA 98424
206-922-5513
206-922-9197 FAX
sponsored by Puyallup Tribe of Indians

TULALIP BINGO & CASINO
6330 33rd Avenue NE (Bingo)
6410 33rd Avenue NE (Casino)
Marysville, WA 98271
360-653-7395 (Bingo)
360-651-1111 (Casino)
360-651-2234 FAX
sponsored by the Tulalip Tribe

WISCONSIN

BAD RIVER CASINO
PO Box 39
Odanah, WI 54861
715-682-7131 (Casino)
715-682-7147 (Bingo)
715-682-7149 FAX
sponsored by the Bad River Band of Lake Superior Chippewa

GOLDEN NICKEL BINGO & CASINO
PO Box 131
S-3214 Highway 12
Baraboo, WI 53913
800-362-8404 (Bingo)
800-647-3132 (Casino)
608-356-9193
608-356-1899 FAX (Bingo)
608-356-2121 FAX (Casino)
sponsored by the Ho Chunk Nation

HOLE IN THE WALL CASINO
PO Box 98
Danbury, WI 54830
715-656-3444
715-656-3434 FAX
sponsored by St. Croix Chippewa Indians

ISLE VISTA CASINO
PO Box 1167
Bayfield, WI 54814
715-759-3739
715-779-3715
sponsored by the Red Cliff Band of Lake Superior Chippewa

LAC DU FLAMBEAU TRIBAL BINGO
LAKE OF THE TOURCHS CASINO
PO Box 67, 408 Little Pines
Lac du Flambeau, WI 54538
715-588-3305 (Bingo)
715-588-7070 (Casino)
715-588-7930 FAX
sponsored by the Lake Superior Band of Chippewa Indians Lac du Flambeau Tribe

LCO BINGO PALACE
Route 2, Box 2400
Hayward, WI 54843
800-422-2175
715-634-4422
715-634-8110 FAX
sponsored by the Lac Courte Oreilles

MAJESTIC PINES CASINO
PO Box 433-G
Route 5, Highway 54
Black River Falls, WI 54615
800-657-4621
715-284-2721
715-284-7700 FAX
sponsored by the Ho Chunk Nation

MENOMINEE NATION CASINO - CRYSTAL PALACE
PO Box 760
Highways 47 & 55
Keshena, WI 54135
715-799-5284
715-799-4051 FAX
sponsored by the Menominee Indian Tribe of Wisconsin

MOHICAN NORTH STAR CASINO & BINGO
W12180A County Road A
Bowler, WI 54416
715-787-3110
800-952-0195 (WI Only)
715-787-3129 FAX
sponsored by the Stockbridge-Munsee Community of Mohican Indians

NORTHERN LIGHTS CASINO
PO Box 140 Hwy 32
Wabeno, WI 54566
715-473-2021
sponsored by the Stockbridge-Munsee Community of Mohican Indians

ONEIDA BINGO & CASINO
PO Box 365
Oneida, WI 54155
800-238-4263
414-497-8118
414-496-2019 FAX
sponsored by the Oneida Tribe of Indians of Wisconsin

POTAWATOMI BINGO
1721 W Canal St
Milwaukee, WI 53233
800-755-6171
414-645-6888
414-645-6866 FAX
sponsored by the Forest County Potawatomi Tribe

RAINBOW BINGO & CASINO
949 CTY TRK G
Nekoosa, WI 54457
715-886-4560
715-886-4551 FAX
sponsored by the Ho Chunk Nation

REGENCY RESORT CASINOS
Mole Lake, Grand Royale, Regency
Route 1, Box 625
Crandon, WI 52450
715-478-5565 (Grand Royale)
715-478-5290 (Regency)
715-886-4551 FAX
sponsored by Sokaogon Chippewa Tribe of Wisconsin

SAND LAKE BINGO & CASINO
PO Box 287
Hertel, WI 54845
715-349-2195
715-349-5768 FAX
sponsored by the St. Croix Chippewa

ST. CROIX CASINO & HOTEL
777 Highway 8
Turtle Lake, WI 54889
715-986-4777
715-986-2800 FAX
sponsored by the St. Croix Chippewa of Wisconsin

WYOMING

789 BINGO
Northern Arapaho Trust
407 E Main St
Riverton, WY 82501
307-856-3964
307-856-0741 FAX
sponsored by Northern Arapaho Tribe

Information provided by: Nat'l Indian Gaming Commission - Indian Gaming Magazine

UNITED STATES

NATIVE AMERICAN MEDIA: AN OVERVIEW

American Indian media (for example, newsletters, newspapers, tabloids) are some of the most misunderstood functions in Indian country. All are designed to inform their tribal or organization members of current events, tribal business and social activities. Yet the first cut by tribal officials or Indian organizations who feel the financial pinch, is their written media.

There also has been no continuous source nationally for these media to receive timely news stories on a regular basis without hooking up to an expensive wire service.

Many newspapers report only local news plus articles forwarded by the Bureau of Indian Affairs Bi-weekly , "Indian News Notes" from Washington, D.C., at this time, 1995, it too has been discontinued.

Only a small percentage belong to the Native American Journalist Association, which itself has had four addresses in five/six years.

Most directories of media such as Gale Research publications, Oxbridge Directory or Grebbie, don't even list Indian newspapers.

Due to these situations, many Indian newspapers have an on again off again printing cycle. Some are only available within their tribal communities. Others, like "Akwasasne Notes" print when the funds are available. These we have indicated by "I" for irregular publishing.

...personal observation of the editor over twenty years

NATIVE AMERICAN PRINT MEDIA							
PUBLICATION	**INDIVIDUAL**	**TRIBE**	**ORGANIZATION**	**INDEPENDENT**	**OFF RESERVATION**	**MAJOR**	**FREQUENCY**
ALABAMA							
DRUMS ACROSS ALABAMA NEWSLETTER ALABAMA INDIAN AFFAIRS COMMISSION 669 S LAWRENCE ST MONTGOMERY, AL 36130 334-242-2831 800-436-8261 334-240-3408 FAX			X				Q
POARCH CREEK NEWS HC 69, BOX 85-B ATMORE, AL 36502 334-368-9136 334-368-4502 FAX		X					M
ALASKA							
AFN NEWSLETTER 1577 C STREET #100 ANCHORAGE, AK 99501 907-274-3611 907-276-2989 FAX			X				M

KEY

B - BI-MONTHLY	**W - WEEKLY**
U - BI-WEEKLY	**M - MONTHLY**
Q - QUARTERLY	**D - DAILY**
Y - YEARLY	**I - IRREGULAR**

NATIVE AMERICAN PRINT MEDIA							
PUBLICATION	INDIVIDUAL	TRIBE	ORGANIZATION	INDEPENDENT	OFF RESERVATION	MAJOR	FREQUENCY
COASTAL CROSSINGS KETCHIKAN MUSEUMS TOTEM HERITAGE CENTER 629 DOCK STREET KETCHIKAN, AK 99901 907-228-5600 907-228-5602 FAX			X		X		M
HAN ZAADLITL GE PO BOX 309 NANANA, AK 99760			X				M
JOURNAL OF ALASKA NATIVE ARTS INSTITUTE OF ALASKA NATIVE ARTS PO BOX 70769 FAIRBANKS, AK 99707 907-456-7491 907-451-7268 FAX			X		X		Q
MANILLAQ ASSOCIATION PO BOX 256 KOTZEBUE, AK 99742			X				Q
NEWSLETTER INDIGENOUS BROADCAST CENTER 810 EAST 9TH AVENUE ANCHORAGE, AK 99501 907-263-7409 907-263-7497 FAX			X		X		Q

NATIVE AMERICAN PRINT MEDIA							
PUBLICATION	INDIVIDUAL	TRIBE	ORGANIZATION	INDEPENDENT	OFF RESERVATION	MAJOR	FREQUENCY
NEWSLETTER SEALASKA HERITAGE FOUNDATION ONE SEALASKA PLAZA #201 JUNEAU, AK 99801 907-463-7491			X				M
THE TCC COUNCIL 122 FIRST AVENUE FAIRBANKS, AK 99701 907-452-8251 907-459-3851 FAX			X				M
TUNDRA TIMES PO BOX 92247 ANCHORAGE, AK 99509-2247 907-274-2512 800-764-2512 907-277-7217 FAX			X		X		U

NATIVE AMERICAN PRINT MEDIA							
PUBLICATION	INDIVIDUAL	TRIBE	ORGANIZATION	INDEPENDENT	OFF RESERVATION	MAJOR	FREQUENCY
ARIZONA							
AK-CHIN O'ODHAM RUNNER 42507 W PETERS AND NALL ROAD MARICOPA, AZ 85239 520-568-2228 520-254-6133 FAX		X					U
AMERICAN INDIAN ART MAGAZINE 7314 E OSBORN DRIVE SCOTTSDALE, AZ 85251 602-994-5445				X	X		Q
AMERICAN INDIAN REHABILITATION NAU CAMPUS BOX 5630 FLAGSTAFF, AZ 86001 520-523-4791 800-553-0714 520-523-9127 FAX	X		X				Q
AU-AUTHM ACTION NEWS SALT RIVER TRIBAL NATION RT 1 BOX 216 SCOTTSDALE, AZ 85256 602-941-7277 602-949-2909 FAX		X					M
CANYON SHADOWS PO BOX 10 SUPAI, AZ 86435 520-448-2961		X					

NATIVE AMERICAN PRINT MEDIA							
PUBLICATION	**INDIVIDUAL**	**TRIBE**	**ORGANIZATION**	**INDEPENDENT**	**OFF RESERVATION**	**MAJOR**	**FREQUENCY**
CAPITOL DRUMBEAT AZ COMM OF INDIAN AFFAIRS 1400 W JEFFERSON #300 PHOENIX, AZ 85007 602-542-3123 602-542-3223 FAX			X				Q
COCOPAH NEWSLETTER BOX G SOMERTON, AZ 85350 520-627-2102 520-627-3173 FAX		X					
COLORADO RIVER SIGNAL RT 1 BOX 23-A PARKER, AZ 85344 520-669-9211 520-669-5675 FAX		X					
DINEH TRIBUNE PO DRAWER 490 WINDOW ROCK, AZ 86515 520-871-4325				X			M
DISCOVER NAVAJOLAND NAVAJOLAND TOURISM DEPT PO BOX 663 WINDOW ROCK, AZ 86515 520-871-6436 800-806-2825 520-871-7381 FAX		X	X				Y

NATIVE AMERICAN PRINT MEDIA							
PUBLICATION	INDIVIDUAL	TRIBE	ORGANIZATION	INDEPENDENT	OFF RESERVATION	MAJOR	FREQUENCY
DNA UPDATE D.N.A. LEGAL SERVICES PO BOX 898 WINDOW ROCK, AZ 86515 520-871-4151 520-871-5036 FAX			X				Q
EDUCATION UPDATE SW RES & EVAL RES CENTER NATIONAL INDIAN TRAINING 2121 S MILL AVENUE #216 TEMPE, AZ 85282 602-967-9428 800-528-6425 602-921-1015 FAX			X		X		M
FORT APACHE SCOUT PO BOX 898 WHITERIVER, AZ 85941 520-338-4813 520-338-1894 FAX		X					U
FORT MCDOWELL BAJA NEWS PO BOX 17779 FOUNTAIN HILLS, AZ 85269 602-990-0995		X					
FOUR RIVERS ADVOCATE RT 1 BOX 215X SCOTTSDALE, AZ 85256 602-949-5512			X				

NATIVE AMERICAN PRINT MEDIA

PUBLICATION	INDIVIDUAL	TRIBE	ORGANIZATION	INDEPENDENT	OFF RESERVATION	MAJOR	FREQUENCY
GILA RIVER INDIAN NEWS PO BOX 459 SACATON, AZ 85247 520-562-3311 520-562-3422 FAX		X					M
GUM-U HUALAPAI TRIBAL NATION BOX 179 PEACH SPRINGS, AZ 86425 520-769-2216 520-769-2343 FAX		X					
HOPI TUTUVENI HOPI TRIBAL NEWSLETTER PO BOX 123 KYKOTSMOVI, AZ 86039 520-734-2441 X 190 520-734-6648		X					U
ICHS HEALTH REPORT INDIAN COMM HEALTH SERV INC 1427 N 3RD #100 PHOENIX, AZ 85004 602-254-0456 602-254-2488 FAX			X				M
INDIAN AMERICA CARD DECK N.A^2.I.I.T.C. PO BOX 27626 TUCSON, AZ 85726 502-622-4900 502-622-4900 FAX			X	X			2Y

NATIVE AMERICAN PRINT MEDIA							
PUBLICATION	INDIVIDUAL	TRIBE	ORGANIZATION	INDEPENDENT	OFF RESERVATION	MAJOR	FREQUENCY
INDIAN BUSINESS & MGMT NCAID 953 E JUANITA AVE MESA, AZ 85204 602-831-7524 800-423-0452 602-491-1332			X				B
INDIAN COUNTRY TODAY (SOUTHWEST) 10415 N SCOTTSDALE RD SCOTTSDALE, AZ 85253 602-443-9100 602-443-4002 FAX	X			X	X		W
INDIAN NOTES INDIAN DEL DIST OF ARIZ 5150 N 16TH ST #A-116 PHOENIX, AZ 85016 602-274-6151 602-274-7633 FAX			X				M
INDIAN QUEST COOK COLLEGE & THEO SCHOOL 2121 S MILL #E 210c PO BOX 2037 TEMPE, AZ 85280 602-968-9354 602-968-9357 FAX	X			X	X		
INTERCOM 1515 E OSBORN RD #ANNEX PHOENIX, AZ 85014			X				

NATIVE AMERICAN PRINT MEDIA							
PUBLICATION	INDIVIDUAL	TRIBE	ORGANIZATION	INDEPENDENT	OFF RESERVATION	MAJOR	FREQUENCY
LAND AND LIFE TECHQUA IKACHI BOX 174 HOTEVILLA, AZ 86030					X		I
NACCD CLIPS PO BOX 1281 SCOTTSDALE, AZ 85252							
NATIVE AMERICAN DIRECTORY PO BOX 27626 TUCSON, AZ 85726 520-622-4900 520-622-4900 FAX			X	X	X		Y
NATIVE AMERICAN SMOKE SIGNALS PO BOX 515 MAYER, AZ 86333-0515	X			X	X		M
NATIVE ARTS UPDATE ATLATL 2303N CENTRAL #104 PHOENIX, ARIZONA 85004 602-253-2731 602-256-6385 FAX			X				Q
NATIVE DIRECTIONS TUCSON INDIAN CENTER PO BOX 2307 TUCSON, AZ 85702 520-884-7131 520-884-0240 FAX			X		X		I

NATIVE AMERICAN PRINT MEDIA							
PUBLICATION	INDIVIDUAL	TRIBE	ORGANIZATION	INDEPENDENT	OFF RESERVATION	MAJOR	FREQUENCY
NATIVE DISCIPLESHIP MAGAZINE CHIEF 1644 E CAMPO BELLO DR PHOENIX, AZ 85022 602-482-0828 602-482-0860 FAX			X		X		Q
NATIVE PEOPLES MAGAZINE 5333 N 7TH ST #C224 PHOENIX, AZ 85014 602-252-2236 602-265-3113 FAX			X	X	X		Q
NAVAJO TIMES PO BOX 310 WINDOW ROCK, AZ 86515 520-871-6641		X					W
NAVAJO-HOPI OBSERVER 2608 N STEVES BLVD FLAGSTAFF, AZ 86004 520-526-3881 520-527-0217 FAX				X	X	X	W
NEWSLETTER TREES FOR MOTHER EARTH PO BOX 1491 CHINLE, AZ 86503 520-674-3258	X		X				Q

NATIVE AMERICAN PRINT MEDIA							
PUBLICATION	**INDIVIDUAL**	**TRIBE**	**ORGANIZATION**	**INDEPENDENT**	**OFF RESERVATION**	**MAJOR**	**FREQUENCY**
PASCUA PUEBLO NEWS 7474 S CAMINO DE OESTE TUCSON, AZ 85746 520-883-2838 520-883-7770 FAX		X					I
RED HILLS NEWSLETTER KAIBAB PAIUTE NATION TRIBAL AFFAIRS BLDG HC 65 BOX 2 FREDONIA, AZ 86022 520-643-7245 520-643-7260 FAX		X					
RED INK AMERICAN INDIAN GRADUATE CTR UNIV OF ARIZONA 1621 E 7TH ST TUCSON, AZ 85719 520-621-7989 520-623-3233 FAX			X		X		I
ROUGH ROCK NEWS DINE'BIOLTA'DAAHANI ROUGH ROCK DEMONSTRATION SCHOOL RRDS BOX 217 ROUGH ROCK, AZ 86503 520-728-3311			X				

NATIVE AMERICAN PRINT MEDIA							
PUBLICATION	INDIVIDUAL	TRIBE	ORGANIZATION	INDEPENDENT	OFF RESERVATION	MAJOR	FREQUENCY
SAN CARLOS APACHE MOCCASSIN PO BOX 31 294 N PINE ST GLOBE, AZ 85501 520-425-7001		X		X	X		W
SAN CARLOS WILDLIFE MGMT PROGRAM PO BOX 97 SAN CARLOS, AZ 85550 520-475-2361		X					M
SCC TRIBAL MGMT PROGRAM 9000 E CHAPARRAL RD SCOTTSDALE, AZ 85256 602-423-6139			X				I
THE SEEDHEAD NEWS NATIVE SEEDS/SEARCH 2509 N CAMPBELL AVE #325 TUCSON, AZ 85719 520-327-9123 520-327-5821 FAX			X	X	X		Q
SOUTHWEST SCENE PO BOX 580 WINDOW ROCK, AZ 86515 505-371-5392 520-491-1331	X			X			M

NATIVE AMERICAN PRINT MEDIA							
PUBLICATION	INDIVIDUAL	TRIBE	ORGANIZATION	INDEPENDENT	OFF RESERVATION	MAJOR	FREQUENCY
SUN TRACKS UNIV OF ARIZONA DEPARTMENT OF LINGUISTICS DOUGLAS 200 EAST TUCSON, AZ 85721 520-621-1836 520-621-7397 FAX			X		X		
SUNDEVIL ROUNDUP ROUGH ROCK COMM HIGH SCHOOL STAR RT 1 ROUGH ROCK, AZ 86503			X				I
THE THUNDERER AMERICAN INDIAN BIBLE COLLEGE 10002 N 15TH AVE PHOENIX, AZ 85021 602-944-3335 602-943-8299 FAX			X		X		
TOHONO'ODHAM RUNNER PO BOX 837 SELLS, AZ 85634 520-383-2221 520-383-3379 FAX	X	X		X			M
VALLEY SPIRIT NEWS PO BOX 3122 SCOTTSDALE, AZ 85271 602-941-3169	X			X			

NATIVE AMERICAN PRINT MEDIA							
PUBLICATION	**INDIVIDUAL**	**TRIBE**	**ORGANIZATION**	**INDEPENDENT**	**OFF RESERVATION**	**MAJOR**	**FREQUENCY**
WA:AK NEWSLETTER SAN XAVIER DISTRICT 2018 W SAN XAVIER RD TUCSON, AZ 85726 520-294-5727 520-294-0613 FAX		X					M
YOIDA NAVA INDIAN CLUB AZ WESTERN COLLEGE YUMA, AZ 85364			X				
ARKANSAS							
LODGE TALES A.I.C. OF ARKANASAS, INC 1100 N UNIVERSITY #133 LITTLE ROCK, AR 72207 501-666-9032 501-666-5875 FAX			X				M

NATIVE AMERICAN PRINT MEDIA							
PUBLICATION	INDIVIDUAL	TRIBE	ORGANIZATION	INDEPENDENT	OFF RESERVATION	MAJOR	FREQUENCY
THE FLOWERING TREE THE GOOD MEDICINE SOCIETY PO BOX 449 NORFOLK, AR 72658 501-297-8083			X				Q
NATIVE AMERICAN PRESS U OF A LITTLE ROCK STABLER HALL 502 2801 S UNIVERSITY AVENUE LITTLE ROCK, AR 72204 501-569-3161			X				Q
ORDER OF THE INDIAN'S WARS PO BOX 7401 LITTLE ROCK, AR 72217 501-225-3996 501-225-5167 FAX			X				M

PUBLICATION	INDIVIDUAL	TRIBE	ORGANIZATION	INDEPENDENT	OFF RESERVATION	MAJOR	FREQUENCY
CALIFORNIA							
AGUA COUNCIL LETTER 110 N INDIAN CANYON DR PALM SPRINGS, CA 92262 619-325-5673 619-325-0593 FAX		X					
AMER INDIAN CULTURE & RESEARCH JOURNAL 3220 CAMPBELL HALL - UCLA 405 HILGARD AVE LOS ANGELES, CA 90024 310-206-7508 310-206-7060 FAX			X		X		Q
AMER INDIAN GRADUATE PROGRAM UNIVER OF CAL - BERKELEY 140 WARREN HALL BERKELEY, CA 94720 510-642-3228 510-843-8661 FAX			X		X		Q
AMERICAN INDIAN RELIGIONS CENTER FOR ACADEMIC PUBLICATION STANFORD UNIVERSITY BOX 5097 STANFORD, CA 94309			X		X		Q

NATIVE AMERICAN PRINT MEDIA							
PUBLICATION	INDIVIDUAL	TRIBE	ORGANIZATION	INDEPENDENT	OFF RESERVATION	MAJOR	FREQUENCY
ANTELOPE INDIAN CIRCLE INDIAN ARCHIVES BOX 790 SUSANVILLE, CA 96130	X		X				
ARROW GAZETTE BUREAU OF INDIAN AFFAIRS 2800 COTTAGE WAY SACRAMENTO, CA 95825 916-978-4691			X				M
BARONA NEWSLETTER 1095 BARONA RD LAKESIDE, CA 92040 619-443-6612		X					
BIG PINE NEWSLETTER PO BOX 700 BIG PINE, CA 93513 619-938-2942 619-938-2942 FAX		X					
BISHOP NEWSLETTER PO BOX 548 BISHOP, CA 93515 619-873-3584 619-873-4143 FAX		X					
CABAZON NEWSLETTER 84-245 INDIO SPRINGS DR INDIO, CA 92201 619-342-2593 619-347-7880 FAX		X					

NATIVE AMERICAN PRINT MEDIA							
PUBLICATION	**INDIVIDUAL**	**TRIBE**	**ORGANIZATION**	**INDEPENDENT**	**OFF RESERVATION**	**MAJOR**	**FREQUENCY**
CAHUILLA COUNCIL LETTER PO BOX 391760 ANZA, CA 92539 909-763-5549 909-763-2808 FAX		X					
CAMPO NEWSLETTER 1779 CAMPO TRUCK TRAIL CAMPO, CA 91906 619-478-9046 619-478-5818 FAX		X					
CHRISTIAN HOPE INDIAN LIFE ESKIMO FELLOWSHIP BOX 2600 ORANGE, CA 92669			X		X		
THE CLAPPER STICK CHAW-SE ASSOC 14881 PINE GROVE - VOLCANO RD PINE GROVE, CA 95665 209-296-7488			X		X		Q
COMMUNITY NEWSLETTER INDIAN HUMAN RES CENTER INC 4040 30TH #A SAN DIEGO, CA 92104 619-281-5964			X		X		M

NATIVE AMERICAN PRINT MEDIA							
PUBLICATION	INDIVIDUAL	TRIBE	ORGANIZATION	INDEPENDENT	OFF RESERVATION	MAJOR	FREQUENCY
CUYAPAIPE COUNCIL LETTER 2271 ALPINE BLVD #D ALPINE, CA 91901 619-478-5289 714-276-6641 FAX		X					M
DAUGHTERS OF ABYA YALA SAIIC - WOMEN'S COMMITTEE PO BOX 28703 OAKLAND, CA 94604 510-834-4263 510-834-4264			X				Y
EARLY AMERICAN - NEWSLETTER CALIF INDIAN EDUC ASSOC PO BOX 2250 DAVIS, CA 95617			X				Q
ECH-KA-NAV-CHA FORT MOHAVE NATION 500 MERRIMAN NEEDLES, CA 92363 619-326-4591 619-326-2468 FAX		X					
HEALTH PATHWAYS HEALTH PROFESSIONS CAREER PROGRAM 1600 9TH #441 SACRAMENTO, CA 95814 916-654-1730 916-654-3138 FAX	X		X		X		Q

NATIVE AMERICAN PRINT MEDIA							
PUBLICATION	INDIVIDUAL	TRIBE	ORGANIZATION	INDEPENDENT	OFF RESERVATION	MAJOR	FREQUENCY
I.C.E. MAGAZINE AMERICAN INDIAN FILM INSTITUTE 333 VALENCIA #322 SAN FRANCISCO, CA 94103 415-554-0525 415-554-0542 FAX	X		X		X		Q
INDIAN CRUSADER AMERICAN INDIAN LIBERATION CRSD 4009 S HALLDALE AVE LOS ANGELES, CA 90062 213-299-1810			X		X		Q
INDIAN HEALTH COUNCIL INC PO BOX 406 PAUMA VALLEY, CA 92061	X		X				
INDIAN HEALTH NEWSLETTER RIVERSIDE - SAN BERNARDINO 11555 1/2 POTRERO RD BANNING, CA 92220 714-849-4761			X		X		
INDIAN HEALTH UNIT NEWSLETTER 2141 BERKELEY WAY BERKELEY, CA 94704			X		X		

NATIVE AMERICAN PRINT MEDIA							
PUBLICATION	INDIVIDUAL	TRIBE	ORGANIZATION	INDEPENDENT	OFF RESERVATION	MAJOR	FREQUENCY
INDIAN LAW REPORTER 319 MACARTHUR BLVD OAKLAND, CA 94610 510-834-9333 510-834-3836 FAX			X	X	X		
INDIAN NATIONS VOICE CALIFORNIA ADVISORY COUNCIL ON INDIAN POLICY 1771 TRIBUTE RD #B SACRAMENTO, CA 95815 916-568-5196 800-489-1994			X		X		M
JAMUL COUNCIL LETTER PO BOX 612 JAMUL, CA 91935 619-669-4785 619-669-4817 FAX		X					
LA JOLLA NEWSLETTER STAR RT BOX #158 VALLEY CENTER, CA 92082 619-742-3771 619-742-3772 FAX		X					
LA POSTA COUNCIL LETTER 1064 BARONA RD LAKESIDE, CA 92040 619-561-9294		X					

NATIVE AMERICAN PRINT MEDIA							
PUBLICATION	INDIVIDUAL	TRIBE	ORGANIZATION	INDEPENDENT	OFF RESERVATION	MAJOR	FREQUENCY
LAND OF TWO ASSOC STUDENTS DQU BOX 409 DAVIS, CA 95617 916-758-0470 916-758-4891 FAX			X	X	X		
LONE PINE NEWSLETTER STAR RT #1 1101 S MAIN PO BOX 747 LONE PINE, CA 93545 619-876-5414		X					
LOS COYOTES COUNCIL LETTER PO BOX 249 WARNER SPRINGS, CA 92086 619-782-3269		X					
LUMBEE NATION TIMES - UNITED LUMBEE NATION OF NC PO BOX 512 FALL RIVER MILLS, CA 96028 916-336-6701		X		X			3X
MANZANITA COUNCIL LETTER PO BOX 1302 BOULEVARD, CA 91905 619-766-4930 619-766-4957 FAX		X					

NATIVE AMERICAN PRINT MEDIA							
PUBLICATION	**INDIVIDUAL**	**TRIBE**	**ORGANIZATION**	**INDEPENDENT**	**OFF RESERVATION**	**MAJOR**	**FREQUENCY**
MESA GRANDE COUNCIL LETTER PO BOX 270 SANTA YSABEL, CA 92070 619-282-9650 619-282-7838 FAX		X					
MULTI-CULTURAL PUBLISHER'S EXCHANGE 2280 GRASS VALLEY HWY 181 AUBURN, CA 95603 916-889-4438 916-888-0690 FAX			X				B
N.A.S.A. NEWSLETTER UNIV OF CALIF - RIVERSIDE 2333 LIBRARY SOUTH RIVERSIDE, CA 92521 909-787-4143			X		X		Q
NA TINI XWE HOOPA TRIBAL NATION PO BOX 1348 HOOPA, CA 95546 916-625-4211 916-625-4594 FAX		X					

NATIVE AMERICAN PRINT MEDIA							
PUBLICATION	INDIVIDUAL	TRIBE	ORGANIZATION	INDEPENDENT	OFF RESERVATION	MAJOR	FREQUENCY
NATIVE AMERICAN ART MUSEUM NEWS SANTA ROSA JUNIOR COLLEGE 1501 MENDOCINO AVE SANTA ROSA, CA 95401 707-527-4800 707-527-4816 FAX			X				
NATIVE AMERICAN CONNECTIONS YEARBOOK PO BOX 579 32818 GRAND AVE WINCHESTER, CA 92596 909-926-2119	X			X	X		Y
THE NATIVE MAGAZINE 835 KLEIN WAY SACRAMENTO, CA 95831 916-421-5121	X				X		M
NATIVE SELF-SUFFICIENCY PO BOX 4569 ARCATA, CA 95521-8519 707-825-7650 707-825-7639 FAX			X	X	X		
NEW WORLD TIMES 625 ASHBURY #14 SAN FRANCISCO, CA 94117 415-864-0487 415-864-0455 FAX	X			X	X		I

NATIVE AMERICAN PRINT MEDIA							
PUBLICATION	**INDIVIDUAL**	**TRIBE**	**ORGANIZATION**	**INDEPENDENT**	**OFF RESERVATION**	**MAJOR**	**FREQUENCY**
NEWS FORT INDEPENDENCE COUNCIL PO BOX 67 FT INDEPENDENCE, CA 93526 619-878-2126 619-878-2311 FAX		X					M
NEWS SOUTHERN CALIFORNIA INDIAN CENTER PO BOX 2550 GARDEN GROVE, CA 92642 714-530-0221 714-636-4226 FAX			X		X		M
NEWS FROM NATIVE CALIFORNIA PO BOX 9145 BERKELEY, CA 94709 510-549-3564	X			X	X		Q/B
NEWSLETTER AMER INDIAN EDUCATION CTR BOX 43 PALA, CA 92059 619-742-3784			X				
NEWSLETTER AMERICAN INDIAN RESOURCE CENTER 6518 MILES AVE HUNTINGTON PK, CA 90255 213-585-1461			X		X		

NATIVE AMERICAN PRINT MEDIA							
PUBLICATION	INDIVIDUAL	TRIBE	ORGANIZATION	INDEPENDENT	OFF RESERVATION	MAJOR	FREQUENCY
NEWSLETTER AMER INDIAN STUDENT ASSOC 18111 S NORDHOFF #218 NORTHRIDGE, CA 91330			X				
NEWSLETTER IND TEACHER & EDUC PRSNNL PROG HUMBOLDT STATE UNIVERSITY ARCATA, CA 95521			X				6X
NEWSLETTER OWENS VALLEY INDIAN EDUCATION CTR BOX 1648 BISHOP, CA 93514	X		X				
NEWSLETTER SOUTH & MESO AMERICAN INDIAN INFORMATION CENTER PO BOX 28703 OAKLAND, CA 94604 510-834-4263 510-834-4264 FAX	X		X	X			Q
PAUMA NEWSLETTER PO BOX 86 PAUMA VALLEY, CA 92061 619-742-1289 619-742-3422 FAX		X					

NATIVE AMERICAN PRINT MEDIA							
PUBLICATION	INDIVIDUAL	TRIBE	ORGANIZATION	INDEPENDENT	OFF RESERVATION	MAJOR	FREQUENCY
PECHANGA COUNCIL LETTER PO BOX 1477 TEMECULA, CA 92595 909-676-2768 909-695-1778 FAX		X					
RINCON NEWSLETTER PO BOX 68 VALLEY CENTER, CA 92082 619-749-1051 619-749-8901 FAX		X					
SAN MANUEL COUNCIL LETTER PO BOX 266 PATTON, CA 92369 909-864-8933 909-864-3370 FAX		X					
SAN PASQUAL COUNCIL LETTER PO BOX 365 VALLEY CENTER, CA 92082 619-749-3200 619-749-3876 FAX		X					
SANTA ROSA COUNCIL LETTER 16835 ALKALI DR PO BOX 8 LEMOORE, CA 93245 209-924-1278 209-924-3583 FAX		X					

NATIVE AMERICAN PRINT MEDIA							
PUBLICATION	INDIVIDUAL	TRIBE	ORGANIZATION	INDEPENDENT	OFF RESERVATION	MAJOR	FREQUENCY
SANTA YSABEL NEWSLETTER PO BOX 130 SANTA YSABEL, CA 92070 619-765-0845 619-765-0320		X					
SEASONS AIDS PREVENTION NATIVE AMERICAN AIDS PREVENTION CENTER 2100 LAKE SHORE AVE #A OAKLAND, CA 94606 510-444-2051 800-283-2437 510-444-1593 FAX			X				Y
SHAMAN'S DRUM A JOURNAL OF EXPERIMENTAL SHAMANISM PO BOX 311 ASHLAND, OR 97520 503-552-0839	X		X	X	X		Q
SIGNAL NEWSPAPER 24000 CREEKSIDE RD VALENCIA, CA 91355							
SOBOBA NEWSLETTER PO BOX 487 SAN JACINTO, CA 92581 909-654-2765 909-654-4198		X					

NATIVE AMERICAN PRINT MEDIA							
PUBLICATION	INDIVIDUAL	TRIBE	ORGANIZATION	INDEPENDENT	OFF RESERVATION	MAJOR	FREQUENCY
THE SPEAKING LEAVES AM INDIAN CULT CTR BOX 2000 VACAVILLE, CA 95688			X	X			
SYCUAN COUNCIL LETTER 5459 DEHESA RD EL CAJON, CA 92021 619-445-2613 619-445-1927 FAX		X					
TALKING LEAF AMERICAN INDIAN COMM ARTS INC 145 S BERKELEY AVE PASADENA, CA 91107 818-584-9481	X			X	X		I
TEEPEE TALK TULE RIVER TRIBAL NATION BOX 589 PORTERSVILLE, CA 93258 209-781-4271 209-781-4610 FAX		X					
TEHIPITE TOPICS PO BOX 5369 FRESNO, CA 93755				X	X		

NATIVE AMERICAN PRINT MEDIA							
PUBLICATION	INDIVIDUAL	TRIBE	ORGANIZATION	INDEPENDENT	OFF RESERVATION	MAJOR	FREQUENCY
TIMBA-SHA COUNCIL LETTER TIMBI-SHA SHOSHONE NATION PO BOX 206 DEATH VALLEY, CA 92328 619-786-2374 619-786-2375 FAX		X					
TORRES-MARTINEZ COUNCIL LETTER 66-725 MARTINEZ RD THERMAL, CA 92274 619-397-0300		X					
TREATY COUNCIL NEWS INTERNATIONAL INDIAN TREATY COUNCIL 54 MINT ST #400 SAN FRANCISCO, CA 94103 415-512-1501 415-512-1507 FAX			X	X	X		Q/I
TRIBAL NEWSLETTER CHEMEHUEVI NATION PO BOX 1976 HAVASU LAKE, CA 92363 619-858-4531 619-858-5400 FAX		X					
TRIBE OF FIVE FEATHERS NEWS PO BOX W LOMPOC, CA 93436	X			X			

NATIVE AMERICAN PRINT MEDIA							
PUBLICATION	**INDIVIDUAL**	**TRIBE**	**ORGANIZATION**	**INDEPENDENT**	**OFF RESERVATION**	**MAJOR**	**FREQUENCY**
TWENTY-NINE PALMS COUNCIL LETTER 555 SUNRISE HWY #200 PALM SPRINGS, CA 92264 619-322-0559		X					
VIEJAS NEWSLETTER PO BOX 908 ALPINE, CA 91903 619-445-3810 619-445-5337 FAX		X					
YA-KA-AMA NEWSLETTER 6215 EASTSIDE RD FORESTVILLE, CA 95436 707-887-1541							
COLORADO							
C.E.R.T. REPORT COUNCIL OF ENERGY RESOURCE TRIBES 1999 BROADWAY #2600 DENVER, CO 80202 303-297-2378 303-296-5690 FAX			X	X	X		Q

NATIVE AMERICAN PRINT MEDIA							
PUBLICATION	**INDIVIDUAL**	**TRIBE**	**ORGANIZATION**	**INDEPENDENT**	**OFF RESERVATION**	**MAJOR**	**FREQUENCY**
C.S.E.R.A CTR FOR STUDIES - ETHNICITY & RACE IN AMERICA UNIV OF COLORADO - BOULDER KETCHUM 30, C. BOX 339 BOULDER, CO 80309 303-492-8852 303-492-5105			X		X		M
D.C. UPDATE C.E.R.T. 1999 BROADWAY #2600 DENVER, CO 80202 303-297-2378 303-296-5690 FAX			X				M
ECHO UTE MOUNTAIN TRIBE PO BOX 52 TOWAOC, CO 81344 970-565-3751 970-565-7412 FAX		X					M
EDUCATION NEWSLETTER A.I.S.E.S. 1085 14TH ST # 1506 BOULDER, CO 80302 303-492-8658 303-492-7090 FAX			X	X	X		

NATIVE AMERICAN PRINT MEDIA							
PUBLICATION	INDIVIDUAL	TRIBE	ORGANIZATION	INDEPENDENT	OFF RESERVATION	MAJOR	FREQUENCY
FOURTH WORLD BULLETIN UNIV OF COLORADO - DENVER CAMPUS BOX 190 POLITICAL SCIENCE PO BOX 173364 DENVER, CO 80217 303-556-2850 303-556-6041 FAX			X		X		3X
HEALTH REPORTER NATIONAL INDIAN HEALTH BOARD 1385 SO COLORADO BLVD, #708 A DENVER, CO 80222 303-759-3075 303-759-3674 FAX			X				I
INTERTRIBAL NEWS INTERCULTURAL CENTER CENTENNIAL 3002 FT LEWIS COLLEGE DURANGO, CO 81301 970-247-7221			X		X		9X

NATIVE AMERICAN PRINT MEDIA							
PUBLICATION	INDIVIDUAL	TRIBE	ORGANIZATION	INDEPENDENT	OFF RESERVATION	MAJOR	FREQUENCY
JOURNAL OF THE NATIONAL CENTER A/I A/N MENTAL HEALTH RESEARCH UNIVERSITY PRESS OF COLORADO PO BOX 849 NIWOT, CO 80544 303-530-5337 303-530-5306 FAX			X		X		
KOSHARE NEWS BOY SCOUT TROOP #232 PO BOX 580 LA JUNTA, CO 81050 719-384-4411			X		X		2X
MINORITY NOTES WILLARD ADM CTR #203 UNIVERSITY OF COLORADO BOX 138 BOULDER, CO 80309			X				
NARF LEGAL REVIEW 1506 BROADWAY BOULDER, CO 80302 303-447-8760 303-443-7776 FAX			X				Q
NATIVE MONTHLY READER BOX 217 CRESTONE, CO 81131 719-256-4848 719-256-4849 FAX			X	X	X		8X

NATIVE AMERICAN PRINT MEDIA							
PUBLICATION	INDIVIDUAL	TRIBE	ORGANIZATION	INDEPENDENT	OFF RESERVATION	MAJOR	FREQUENCY
NEWSLETTER COLORADO COMMISSION ON INDIAN AFFAIRS STATE CAPITAL #144 130 STATE STREET DENVER, CO 80203 303-866-3027			X		X		I
NEWSLETTER NATIVE AMERICAN FISH & WILDLIFE SOCIETY 750 BURBANK BROOMFIELD, CO 80020 303-466-1725 303-466-5414 FAX			X		X		
OYATE NEWS UNIV OF COLORADO CAMPUS BOX 135 BOULDER, CO 80309			X				I
SOUTHERN UTE DRUM PO BOX 737 IGNACIO, CO 81137 970-563-4525		X					M
VISIONS A.I.S.E.S. 1630 30TH ST #301 BOULDER, CO 80301 303-492-8658 303-492-3400 FAX			X		X		

NATIVE AMERICAN PRINT MEDIA							
PUBLICATION	INDIVIDUAL	TRIBE	ORGANIZATION	INDEPENDENT	OFF RESERVATION	MAJOR	FREQUENCY
WESTERN AMERICAN INDIAN CHAMBER NEWSLETTER 1660 17TH ST #200 DENVER, CO 80202 303-620-9292			X		X		M
WINDS OF CHANGE A.I.S.E.S. PUBLISHING CO 1630 30TH ST #301 BOULDER, CO 80301 303-939-0023 303-939-8150 FAX			X		X		Q
CONNECTICUT							
EAGLE WING PRESS PO BOX 579-M O NAUGATUCK, CT 06770 203-238-4009				X	X		B

NATIVE AMERICAN PRINT MEDIA							
PUBLICATION	INDIVIDUAL	TRIBE	ORGANIZATION	INDEPENDENT	OFF RESERVATION	MAJOR	FREQUENCY
MAY WUTCHE AUQE'NE NEWSLETTER AMERICAN INDIANS FOR DEVELOPMENT 236 W MAIN PO BOX 117 MERIDEN, CT 06450 203-238-4009			X		X		
WUSKUSU YERTUM PO BOX 160 LEDYARD, CT 06339 203-536-2681	X		X				
DELAWARE							
CRAFTS REPORT PO BOX 1992 WILMINGTON, DE 19899 302-656-2209			X	X	X		M

NATIVE AMERICAN PRINT MEDIA							
PUBLICATION	**INDIVIDUAL**	**TRIBE**	**ORGANIZATION**	**INDEPENDENT**	**OFF RESERVATION**	**MAJOR**	**FREQUENCY**
DISTRICT OF COLUMBIA							
ACCESS OFFICE/MINORITY BUS ENTRPRS DEPT OF COMMERCE WASHINGTON, DC 20230			X		X		
AMERICAN INDIAN COURTLINE A. R. R. O. W. 1000 CONSITUTION AVE NW #1206 WASHINGTON, DC 20036 202-296-0685 202-659-4377 FAX			X	X	X		
AMERICAN INDIAN EDUCATION NEWS BIA/OIEP MS 3512 MIB CODE 0IE-13 1849 "C" STREET NW WASHINGTON, D.C. 20240 202-208-6364			X	X	X		M
BIA INDIAN NEWS NOTES 1849 "C" ST NW MS 4140 MIB WASHINGTON, DC 20240 202-219-4152			X		X		I

PUBLICATION	INDIVIDUAL	TRIBE	ORGANIZATION	INDEPENDENT	OFF RESERVATION	MAJOR	FREQUENCY
NATIVE AMERICAN PRINT MEDIA							
C.R.M. MAGAZINE CULTURAL RESOURCES MGMT US DEPT INTERIOR NATIONAL PARK SERVICES PO BOX 37127 WASHINGTON, DC 20013-7127 202-343-3395			X		X		Q
FEDERAL ARCHEOLOGY NATIONAL PARK SERVICE ARCHEOLOGICAL ASSISTANCE DIVISION PO BOX 37127 WASHINGTON, DC 20013-7127 202-343-4101 202-523-1547 FAX			X		X		Q
HUMAN DEVELOPMENT NEWS HHH BLDG 200 INDEPENDENCE NW #305G WASHINGTON, DC 20201			X		X		
INDIAN REPORT F.C.N.L. 245 SECOND ST NE WASHINGTON, DC 20002 202-547-6000 202-547-6019 FAX			X	X	X		Q

NATIVE AMERICAN PRINT MEDIA							
PUBLICATION	INDIVIDUAL	TRIBE	ORGANIZATION	INDEPENDENT	OFF RESERVATION	MAJOR	FREQUENCY
N.A.I.H.C. PATHWAY NEWS NAT'L AMERICAN INDIAN HOUSING COUNCIL 900 SECOND ST NE #220 WASHINGTON, DC 20002 202-789-1754 800-284-9165 202-789-1758 FAX			X		X		M
NACIE NEWSLETTER NAT'L ADVISORY COUNCIL ON INDIAN EDUCATION 600 INDEPENDENCE AVE SW THE PORTALS, STE 6211 WASHINGTON, DC 20202-7556 202-205-8353 202-205-9446 FAX			X	X	X		Q
NATIVE AMERICAN DEVELOPMENT ASSOCIATION 1000 CONN AVE, NW #1206 WASHINGTON, DC 20036 202-296-0685 202-659-4377 FAX			X		X		
NEWSLETTER BUREAU OF CATHOLIC INDIAN MISSIONS 2021 H ST N W WASHINGTON, DC 20006 202-331-8542 202-331-8544 FAX			X		X		M

NATIVE AMERICAN PRINT MEDIA							
PUBLICATION	INDIVIDUAL	TRIBE	ORGANIZATION	INDEPENDENT	OFF RESERVATION	MAJOR	FREQUENCY
NEWSLETTER MORNING STAR FOUNDATION 403 10TH SE WASHINGTON, DC 20003 202-547-5531 202-546-6724 FAX	X		X		X		
NEWSLETTER NATIONAL INDIAN POLICY CENTER 2136 PENNSYLVANIA AVE NW WASHINGTON, DC 20052 202-994-1446 202-994-4404 FAX			X		X		
SENTINEL NATIONAL CONGRESS OF AMERICAN INDIANS 2010 MASSACHUSETTS AVE NW 2ND FL WASHINGTON, DC 20036 202-466-7767			X	X	X		I
SMITHSONIAN RUNNER SMITHSONIAN INSTITUTION A & I BLDG, ROOM #2410, MRC 421 WASHINGTON, DC 20560 202-357-2627 800-242-NMAI 202-786-2377 FAX			X		X		B

NATIVE AMERICAN PRINT MEDIA							
PUBLICATION	INDIVIDUAL	TRIBE	ORGANIZATION	INDEPENDENT	OFF RESERVATION	MAJOR	FREQUENCY
SOURCE DIRECTORY INTERIOR INDIAN ARTS & CRAFTS BOARD US DEPT OF INTERIOR, RM 4004 WASHINGTON, DC 20240 202-208-3773			X		X		I
FLORIDA							
ALLIGATOR TIMES SEMINOLE TRIBE 6073 STIRLING RD HOLLYWOOD, FL 33024 305-582-8917		X					
INDIGENOUS THOUGHT 6802 SW 13TH ST GAINESVILLE, FL 32608 904-378-3246	X			X	X		

NATIVE AMERICAN PRINT MEDIA							
PUBLICATION	INDIVIDUAL	TRIBE	ORGANIZATION	INDEPENDENT	OFF RESERVATION	MAJOR	FREQUENCY
MICCOSUKEE EVERGLADES NEWS TAMIAMI STATION PO BOX 440021 MIAMI, FL 33144 305-223-8380 305-223-1011 FAX		X					
NATIVE AMERICAN ANCESTRY HUNTING NEWSLETTER 3308 ACAPULO DR RIVERVIEW, FL 33569 813-653-0015	X			X	X		M
NEWSLETTER NATIVE AMERICAN POLICY NETWORK BARRY UNIVERSITY-SOC SCI DEPT 11300 NE 2ND AVE MIAMI SHORES, FL 33161 305-899-3473	X				X		Q
PRISON LEGAL NEWS PO BOX 1684 LAKE WORTH, FL 33460				X	X		M
REDSTICKS PRESS FIRST NATIONS RESOURCE NETWORK, INC PO BOX 59 ST PETERSBURG, FL 33731 813-821-6604 813-821-8804 FAX	X		X		X		Q

NATIVE AMERICAN PRINT MEDIA							
PUBLICATION	INDIVIDUAL	TRIBE	ORGANIZATION	INDEPENDENT	OFF RESERVATION	MAJOR	FREQUENCY
SEMINOLE TRIBUNE 6333 NW 30TH ST HOLLYWOOD, FL 33024 305-964-1875 305-983-4205 FAX		X					U
GEORGIA							
THE ECHO PO BOX 537 VILLA RICA, GA 30180 404-459-2677	X				X		
INDIAN AMERICAN NEWS L&R PUBLISHING 1807 OVERLOOK DR MOULTRIE, GA 31768 912-890-9102	X			X	X		M
HAWAII							
KA-WAI-OLA-O-OHA OFFICE OF HAWAIIAN AFFAIRS 711 KAPIOLANI BLVD 5TH FL HONOLULU, HI 96813 808-586-3777			X	X	X		M

NATIVE AMERICAN PRINT MEDIA							
PUBLICATION	INDIVIDUAL	TRIBE	ORGANIZATION	INDEPENDENT	OFF RESERVATION	MAJOR	FREQUENCY
NEWSLETTER ALU LIKE INC 1624 MAPUNAPUNA HONOLULU, HI 96819 808-836-8940			X	X			M
IDAHO							
COUNCIL FIRES TRIBAL HEADQUARTERS COEUR D'ARLENE NATION PO BOX 238 DESMET, ID 83824 208-686-1800 208-686-1182		X					
FORT HALL NEWSLETTER BIA STAFF FT HALL, ID 83203 208-238-3710			X				
SHO-BAN NEWS PO BOX 900 FORT HALL, ID 83203 208-238-3888 208-238-3702 FAX		X					U

NATIVE AMERICAN PRINT MEDIA							
PUBLICATION	**INDIVIDUAL**	**TRIBE**	**ORGANIZATION**	**INDEPENDENT**	**OFF RESERVATION**	**MAJOR**	**FREQUENCY**
ILLINOIS							
AMERICAN INDIAN BUSINESS NATIONAL INDIAN BUSINESS ASSOCIATION 206 SO GALENA AVE FREEPORT, IL 61032 815-232-5176 815-232-1363 FAX			X		X		B
INTER-COM 2838 W PETERSON AVE CHICAGO, IL 60659			X	X	X		
MEETING GROUND THE NEWBERRY LIBRARY 50 W WALTON CHICAGO, IL 60610 312-943-9090			X		X		Q
NEWSLETTER AMERICAN INDIAN LIBRARIES C/O LAW LIBRARY ATTN: JOAN HOWLAND UNIV OF MINN 229 S 19TH AVE MINNEAPOLIS, MN 55455 612-625-5526 612-625-3478 FAX			X		X		Q
SPRING CREEK PACKET 1945 S SPRING ST SPRINGFIELD, IL 62704 217-525-2698	X				X		M

NATIVE AMERICAN PRINT MEDIA							
PUBLICATION	**INDIVIDUAL**	**TRIBE**	**ORGANIZATION**	**INDEPENDENT**	**OFF RESERVATION**	**MAJOR**	**FREQUENCY**
THE WARRIOR AMERICAN INDIAN CENTER 1630 W WILSON AVE CHICAGO, IL 60640 312-275-5871			X		X		M
WILDWEST PO BOX 385 MOUNT MORRIS, IL 61054 815-734-6309	X			X	X		M
INDIANA							
INDIAN PROGRESS HAROLD SMUCK, ED PO BOX 1661 100 GUNTER HILL DR RICHMOND, IN 47374 317-962-9169				X	X		

NATIVE AMERICAN PRINT MEDIA							
PUBLICATION	**INDIVIDUAL**	**TRIBE**	**ORGANIZATION**	**INDEPENDENT**	**OFF RESERVATION**	**MAJOR**	**FREQUENCY**
NEWSLETTER AMERICAN INDIAN COUNCIL INC 1302 VICTORIA DR LEBANON, IN 46052 317-482-3315			X	X	X		M
NEWSLETTER BROTHERS OF THE WIND OF INDIANA 54755 BEECH RD OSCEOLA, IN 46561			X	X	X		M
NEWSLETTER INDIAN AWARENESS CENTER 37 E 375 N ROCHESTER, IN 46975-9412 219-223-4436			X	X	X		Q
NEWSLETTER NATIVE AMERICAN MUSEUM 5050 E POPLAR ST TERRE HAUTE, IN 47803 812-877-6007			X		X		B
NEWSLETTER THE TECUMSEH LODGE 15160 CHERRYTREE RD NOBLESVILLE, IN 46060 317-773-4233	X		X	X	X		M

NATIVE AMERICAN PRINT MEDIA							
PUBLICATION	INDIVIDUAL	TRIBE	ORGANIZATION	INDEPENDENT	OFF RESERVATION	MAJOR	FREQUENCY
IOWA							
INDIAN YOUTH OF AMERICA PO BOX 2786 SIOUX CITY, IA 51106 712-252-3230			X		X		Q
INDIAN COUNTRY SAC & FOX SETTLEMENT 3137 F AVE TAMA, IA 52339 515-484-4678 515-484-5424 FAX		X					
KANSAS							
INDIAN DRUM BEAT N/A INDIAN CULTURE GROUP PO BOX 1000 LEAVENWORTH, KS 66048			X		X		

NATIVE AMERICAN PRINT MEDIA							
PUBLICATION	INDIVIDUAL	TRIBE	ORGANIZATION	INDEPENDENT	OFF RESERVATION	MAJOR	FREQUENCY
INDIAN LEADER NAVARRE HALL 155, INDIAN AVE HASKELL INDIAN NATIONS COLLEGE LAWRENCE, KS 66044 913-749-8477 913-749-8406 FAX			X		X		M
ITZA VOICE AMERICAN INDIAN DEFENSE NEWS KAWEAH INDIAN NATION PO BOX 3121 HUTCHINSON, KS 67501 316-665-3614	X		X		X		M
NEWSLETTER LITTLE INDIAN CENTER BOX 1016 LAWRENCE, KS 66044 913-841-7202			X		X		
NEWSLETTER MID-AMERICA ALL INDIAN CENTER 650 N SENECA WICHITA, KS 67203 316-262-5221			X		X		M
NISH-NA-BA AMERICAN INDIAN CULTURE GROUP PO BOX 2 LANSING, KS 66043			X		X		

NATIVE AMERICAN PRINT MEDIA							
PUBLICATION	INDIVIDUAL	TRIBE	ORGANIZATION	INDEPENDENT	OFF RESERVATION	MAJOR	FREQUENCY
SPIRIT OF CRAZY HORSE PELTIER DEFENSE COMMITTEE PO BOX 583 LAWRENCE, KS 66044 913-842-5774			X	X	X		
VOICE OF THE SPIRIT KEEPER GREAT PLAINS DELEGATION ALCATRAZ 6424 W PARK VIEW DR WICHITA, KS 67219 316-744-0465	X		X	X	X		I
KENTUCKY							
IRON HOUSE DRUM NAPRRP 2848 PADDOCK LANE VILLA HILLS, KY 41017			X	X	X		Q

NATIVE AMERICAN PRINT MEDIA							
PUBLICATION	INDIVIDUAL	TRIBE	ORGANIZATION	INDEPENDENT	OFF RESERVATION	MAJOR	FREQUENCY
LOUISIANA							
WHISPERING WIND MAGAZINE 8009 WALES NEW ORLEANS, LA 70126 504-241-5886	X			X	X		B
MAINE							
MAWIW-KILUN INDIAN TOWNSHIP NATION PO BOX 301 PRINCETON, ME 04668 207-796-2301 207-796-5256 FAX		X					
NATION NOTES PENOBSCOT INDIAN NATION 6 RIVER RD INDIAN ISLAND OLDTOWN, ME 04468 207-827-7776 207-827-6042 FAX		X					

NATIVE AMERICAN PRINT MEDIA							
PUBLICATION	**INDIVIDUAL**	**TRIBE**	**ORGANIZATION**	**INDEPENDENT**	**OFF RESERVATION**	**MAJOR**	**FREQUENCY**
SIPAYIK NIES PLEASANT PT PASSAMAQUODDY NATION BOX 343 PERRY, ME 04667 207-853-2551		X					
MARYLAND							
CHR, PROGRAM UPDATE PUBLIC HEALTH SERVICE INDIAN HEALTH SERVICE ROCKVILLE, MD 20857			X	X	X		
INDIAN HEALTH COMMUNICATOR 5600 FISHERS LANE #5A-39 ROCKVILLE, MD 20857 301-443-3593			X	X	X		
NETWORK NEWSLETTER INDIAN HEALTH 8609 2ND AVE #506 SILVER SPRINGS, MD 20910			X	X	X		
NEWSLETTER AMERICAN INDIAN STUDY CENTER 211 S BROADWAY BALTIMORE, MD 21231 410-675-3535			X		X		I

NATIVE AMERICAN PRINT MEDIA							
PUBLICATION	INDIVIDUAL	TRIBE	ORGANIZATION	INDEPENDENT	OFF RESERVATION	MAJOR	FREQUENCY
RATTLE & DRUM NEWSLETTER AMERICAN INDIAN INTER-TRIBAL CULTURAL ORG PO BOX 775 TWINBROOK STA ROCKVILLE, MD 29848 301-869-9381			X	X	X		B
SMOKE SIGNALS NEWSLETTER BALTIMORE AMERICAN INDIAN CENTER 113 S BROADWAY BALTIMORE, MD 21231 410-675-3535			X		X		
TRIBAL COLLEGE PO BOX 898 CHESTERTOWN, MD 21620 410-778-5628 410-778-5897			X		X		Q

NATIVE AMERICAN PRINT MEDIA							
PUBLICATION	INDIVIDUAL	TRIBE	ORGANIZATION	INDEPENDENT	OFF RESERVATION	MAJOR	FREQUENCY
MASSACHUSETTS							
THE CIRCLE NORTH AMERICAN INDIAN CENTER OF BOSTON 105 S HUNTINGTON AVE JAMAICA PLAIN, MA 02130 617-232-0343 617-232-3863 FAX			X		X		I
FRIENDS OF NATIVE AMERICANS 206 MASSACHUSETTS AVE ARLINGTON, MA 02174				X	X		
HARVARD INDIAN NEWSLETTER HARVARD GRAD SCHOOL OF EDUC READ HOUSE APPIAN WAY CAMBRIDGE, MA 02138 617-495-4923			X				
NASHAUONK WAMPANOAG TRIBAL NATION BOX 1048 RT 130 MASHPEE, MA 02649 617-447-0208 617-447-1218 FAX		X					
NEWSLETTER GREATER LOWELL INDIAN CULTURAL ASSOCIATION 551 TEXTILE AVE DRACUT, MA 01826				X	X		

NATIVE AMERICAN PRINT MEDIA							
PUBLICATION	**INDIVIDUAL**	**TRIBE**	**ORGANIZATION**	**INDEPENDENT**	**OFF RESERVATION**	**MAJOR**	**FREQUENCY**
MICHIGAN							
AMERICAN INDIAN UNLIMITED NEWSLETTER 240 MICHIGAN UNION 530 STATE- UM ANN ARBOR, MI 48104			X		X		
ANISHNABEG MOM-WEH NEWSLETTER COMMUNITY CENTER 1219 1ST AVE SOUTH ESCANABA, MI 49829 906-786-0556			X				M
BEAR TALK SAGINAW INTERTRIBAL ASSOCIATION PO BOX 7005 SAGINAW, MI 48603 517-792-4610			X		X		
COLLEGE NEWS BAY MILLS COMMUNITY COLLEGE RT 1 BOX 315-A BRIMLEY, MI 49715 906-248-3354 906-248-3351 FAX			X		X		
COUNCIL DRUM NEWS 2512 UNION AVE NE GRAND RAPIDS, MI 49505			X				

NATIVE AMERICAN PRINT MEDIA							
PUBLICATION	INDIVIDUAL	TRIBE	ORGANIZATION	INDEPENDENT	OFF RESERVATION	MAJOR	FREQUENCY
FEATHER FLYER LUCEY COUNTY INTERTRIBAL CENTER PO BOX 155 317 NEWBERRY AVENUE NEWBERRY, MI 49868 906-293-3491 906-293-3001 FAX			X		X		M
GREAT LAKES PATHFINDER 460 W SPRUCE SAULT STE MARIE, MI 49783		X					
INDIAN EDUCATION NEWSLETTER PORT HURON AREA SCHOOL DIST 1925 LAPEER AVE PO BOX 5013 PORT HURON, MI 48061 810-984-3101 X337 810-984-6606 FAX			X		X		
THE MICHIGAN INDIAN MICHIGAN COMMISSION OF INDIAN AFFAIRS PO BOX 30026 611 W OTTAWA - 3RD FL LANSING, MI 48913 517-373-0654 517-335-1642 FAX			X	X	X		Q

NATIVE AMERICAN PRINT MEDIA							
PUBLICATION	**INDIVIDUAL**	**TRIBE**	**ORGANIZATION**	**INDEPENDENT**	**OFF RESERVATION**	**MAJOR**	**FREQUENCY**
NATIVE SON NORTH AMERICAN INDIAN ASSOC OF DETROIT INC 22720 PLYMOUTH RD DETROIT, MI 48239 313-535-2966 313-535-8060 FAX			X		X		Q
NEWS BEAT 405 E EASTERDAY AVE SAULT STE MARIE, MI 49783							
NEWSLETTER AMERICAN INDIAN COMMUNITIES LEADERSHIP COUNCIL 5315 RAVENSWOOD KIMBALL, MI 48074			X		X		
THE TALKING PEACE PIPE S E MICHIGAN INDIANS INC PO BOX 861 WARREN, MI 48090 313-756-1350			X	X	X		Q
TRIBAL NEWSLETTER GRAND TRAVERSE OTTAWA/CHIPPEWA NATIONS 2605 NW BAYSHORE DRIVE SUTTONS BAY, MI 49682 616-271-3538 616-271-4861 FAX		X					M

NATIVE AMERICAN PRINT MEDIA							
PUBLICATION	INDIVIDUAL	TRIBE	ORGANIZATION	INDEPENDENT	OFF RESERVATION	MAJOR	FREQUENCY
TRIBAL OBSERVER SAGINAW CHIPPEWA NATION 7070 E BROADWAY MT. PLEASNT, MI 48858 517-772-5700 517-772-3508 FAX		X					
TRIBAL TRAILS 1391 TERRACE MUSKEGON, MI 49442							
TURTLE TALK NEWSLETTER NATIVE AMERICAN PREVENTION SERVICES 45 LEXINGTON NW GRAND RAPIDS, MI 49504 616-458-4078 616-774-2810 FAX			X	X	X		M
WASSO-GEE-WAD-NEE COUNCIL AMERICAN INDIAN PROGRAMS OFFICE 1102 UNIVERSITY CENTER MARQUETTE, MI 49855			X		X		
WIN-A WENEN NISITUNG RT 2, BOX 267 2218 SKUNK RD SAULT STE MARIE, MI 49783 906-635-6050 906-635-6064 FAX		X					M

NATIVE AMERICAN PRINT MEDIA							
PUBLICATION	**INDIVIDUAL**	**TRIBE**	**ORGANIZATION**	**INDEPENDENT**	**OFF RESERVATION**	**MAJOR**	**FREQUENCY**
MINNESOTA							
AMERIND CLUB BOX 1000 SANDSTONE, MN 55072			X				
ANISHNABE DEE-BAH-GEE-MO-WIN WHITE EARTH RESV TRIBAL NATION PO BOX 418 WHITE EARTH, MN 56591 218-982-3285 X 206 218-983-3641 FAX		X					M
ANISHNAWBE JOURNAL PINE POINT SCHOOL PONSFORD, MN 56575			X		X		
THE BEAVER TAIL TIMES PO BOX 721 CASS LAKE, MN 56633	X			X			M
BOIS FORTE NEWS BOIS FORTE CHIPPEWA BOX 16 NETT LAKE, MN 55772 218-757-3261 218-757-3312 FAX		X					M
THE CIRCLE NEWSPAPER MINNEAPLIS AM INDIAN CTR 1530 E FRANKLIN AVE MINNEAPOLIS, MN 55404 612-879-1760 612-879-1712 FAX			X		X		M

NATIVE AMERICAN PRINT MEDIA							
PUBLICATION	INDIVIDUAL	TRIBE	ORGANIZATION	INDEPENDENT	OFF RESERVATION	MAJOR	FREQUENCY
THE COMMUNICATOR MIGIZI COMMUNICATIONS 3123 E LAKE #200 MINNEAPOLIS, MN 55406 612-721-6631 612-721-3936 FAX	X		X	X	X		Q
DE-BAH-JI-MON LEECH LAKE RESERVATION RT 3, BOX 100 CASS LAKE, MN 56633 218-335-8200 218-335-8309 FAX		X					M
FOCUS: INDIAN EDUCATION MINN DEPT OF EDUCATION 736 CAPITOL SQUARE BLDG 550 CEDAR STREET ST PAUL, MN 55101 612-296-6458 612-297-7895 FAX			X		X		
FON DU LAC RESERVATION NEWS 105 UNIVERSITY DR CLOQUET, MN 55720 218-879-4593 218-879-4146 FAX		X					M
INDIGENOUS WOMAN INDIAN WOMAN NETWORK PO BOX 174 LAKE EDMO, MN 55042 612-770-3861 612-728-2000 FAX			X		X		

NATIVE AMERICAN PRINT MEDIA							
PUBLICATION	**INDIVIDUAL**	**TRIBE**	**ORGANIZATION**	**INDEPENDENT**	**OFF RESERVATION**	**MAJOR**	**FREQUENCY**
INDIAN VOICE AMERICAN INDIAN FOLKLORE GROUP BOX 55 STILLWATER, MN 55082			X		X		
MILLE LAC NEWS HC 67, BOX 195 OMANIA, MN 56395 612-532-4181 612-532-4209 FAX		X					
MOCCASIN TELEGRAPH GRAND PORTAGE RESERVATION PO BOX 428 GRAND PORTAGE, MN 55605 218-475-2279 218-475-2284 FAX		X					M
NAJA NEWS NATIVE AMERICAN JOURNALISTS ASSOC 1433 E FRANKLIN #11 MINNEAPOLIS, MN 55404 612-874-8833 612-874-9007 FAX			X	X	X		Q
NETT LAKE NEWS PO BOX 16 NETT LAKE, MN 55772 218-757-3261 218-757-3312 FAX		X					

NATIVE AMERICAN PRINT MEDIA							
PUBLICATION	INDIVIDUAL	TRIBE	ORGANIZATION	INDEPENDENT	OFF RESERVATION	MAJOR	FREQUENCY
NEWSLETTER ARCHDIOCESE OF ST PAUL & MINNEAPOLIS 1308 E FRANKLIN AVE MINNEAPOLIS, MN 55404			X		X		
OJIBEWA NEWS 1819 BERMIDJI AVE BEMIDJI, MN 56601 218-751-1655 218-751-0650 FAX		X					W
OSHKABEWIS INDIAN STUDIES PROGRAM BEMIDJI STATE UNIV BEMIDJI, MN 56601							
RED LAKE NEWSLETTER NEIGHBORHOOD CTR NEWSLETTER RED LAKE RESERVATION RED LAKE, MN 56671 218-679-3341 218-679-3378 FAX		X					
SPEAKING OF OURSELVES MINN CHIPPEWA TRIBE PO BOX 217 CASS LAKE, MN 56633 218-335-8581 X68 218-335-6562 FAX		X					M

NATIVE AMERICAN PRINT MEDIA							
PUBLICATION	**INDIVIDUAL**	**TRIBE**	**ORGANIZATION**	**INDEPENDENT**	**OFF RESERVATION**	**MAJOR**	**FREQUENCY**
VISION ON THE WIND - D.I.W. MINNEAPOLIS COUNCIL OF CHURCHES 1001 E LAKE ST MINNEAPOLIS, MN 55407 612-722-8722 612-722-8669 FAX			X		X		Q
WINNEBAGO MINN NEWSLETTER ST PAUL URBAN LEAGUE 401 SELBY AVE ST PAUL, MN 55102			X		X		
MISSISSIPPI							
CHOCTAW COMMUNITY NEWS PO BOX 6010 PHILADELPHIA, MS 39350 601-656-5251 601-656-1992 FAX		X					B
U.S.E.T. GAMING M.B.C.I. PO BOX 6010 PHILADELPHIA, MS 39350 601-650-9574 601-656-6696 FAX			X				Q

NATIVE AMERICAN PRINT MEDIA							
PUBLICATION	**INDIVIDUAL**	**TRIBE**	**ORGANIZATION**	**INDEPENDENT**	**OFF RESERVATION**	**MAJOR**	**FREQUENCY**
MISSOURI							
EYAPAHA NEWSLETTER A.I.C. MID-AMERICA 4115 CONNECTICUT ST LOUIS, MO 63116 314-773-3316 314-773-7160 FAX			X				M
INTERTRIBAL TRIBUNE NEWSLETTER HEART OF A.I.C. 1340 E ADMIRAL BLVD KANSAS CITY, MO 64106 816-421-7608 816-421-6493 FAX			X		X		M
RISING SUN NEWS SW MISSOURI INDIAN CENTER 2422 W DIVISION SPRINGFIELD, MO 65802 417-869-9550			X		X		M

NATIVE AMERICAN PRINT MEDIA							
PUBLICATION	**INDIVIDUAL**	**TRIBE**	**ORGANIZATION**	**INDEPENDENT**	**OFF RESERVATION**	**MAJOR**	**FREQUENCY**
MONTANA							
AN-CHI-MO-WIN CHIPPEWA CREE NATION ROCKY BOY ROUTE, BOX 544 BOX ELDER, MT 59521 406-395-4421 406-395-4497 FAX		X					
ARROW ST LABRE'S INDIAN SCHOOL ASHLAND, MT 59003			X				
BILLINGS INDIAN CENTER NEWSLETTER PO BOX 853 BILLINGS, MT 59103 406-248-1648	X		X				
BLACKFEET MEDIA PO BOX 850 BROWNING, MT 59417 406-338-7276 406-338-7530 FAX		X					
BUFFALO GRASS NEWS NATIVE AMERICAN SERVICES 2300 REGENT ST #A MISSOULA, MT 59801			X		X		

NATIVE AMERICAN PRINT MEDIA							
PUBLICATION	INDIVIDUAL	TRIBE	ORGANIZATION	INDEPENDENT	OFF RESERVATION	MAJOR	FREQUENCY
CAMP CRIER FORT BELKNAP NATIONS RR 1, BOX 66 HARLEM, MT 59526 406-353-2205 406-353-2797 FAX		X					
CHAR-KOOSTA NEWS SALISH/KOOTENAI NATIONS PO BOX 278 PABLO, MT 59855 406-675-3000		X					W
COLLEGE NEWS FORT BELNAP COMMUNITY COLLEGE PO BOX 159 HARLEM, MT 59526 406-353-2607 406-353-2829 FAX			X				
COLLEGE NEWS LITTLE BIG HORN COLLEGE PO BOX 370 CROW AGENCY, MT 59022 406-638-2260 406-638-7213 FAX			X				

NATIVE AMERICAN PRINT MEDIA							
PUBLICATION	INDIVIDUAL	TRIBE	ORGANIZATION	INDEPENDENT	OFF RESERVATION	MAJOR	FREQUENCY
COLLEGE NEWS STONE CHILD COMMUNITY COLLEGE ROCKY BOY ROUTE BOX 1082 BOX ELDER, MT 59521 406-395-4313 406-395-4836 FAX			X				
COUNCIL SIGNALS MONTANA INDIAN AFFAIRS HELENA, MT 59620 406-444-3702			X		X		
CROSS AND FEATHER TEKAKWITHA CONFERENCE NATIONAL NEWSLETTER PO BOX 6759 GREAT FALLS, MT 59406 406-727-0147 406-452-9845 FAX			X		X		B
CROW TRIBE NEWSLETTER PUBLIC RELATIONS OFFICE PO BOX 159 CROW AGENCY, MT 59022 406-638-2601		X					
EYAPI OAYE ASSINIBOINE & SIOUX NATIONS PO BOX 1027 POPLAR, MT 59255 406-768-5155 406-768-5478		X					

NATIVE AMERICAN PRINT MEDIA							
PUBLICATION	INDIVIDUAL	TRIBE	ORGANIZATION	INDEPENDENT	OFF RESERVATION	MAJOR	FREQUENCY
FORT PECK COMMUNITY COLLEGE NEWS FORT PECK COMMUNITY COLLEGE PO BOX 398 POPLAR, MT 59255 406-768-5551 406-768-5552 FAX			X				
GLACIER REPORTER BOX R BROWNING, MT 59417 406-338-2090						X	W
HO GEGCANA BROCKTON HIGH SCHOOL BROCKTON, MT 59213			X				
THE HUNTER NORTH AMERICAN INDIAN LEAGUE BOX 7 DEER LODGE, MT 59772			X				
INDIAN RIGHTS-HUMAN RIGHTS INDIAN LAW RESOURCE CENTER 602 N EWING ST HELENA, MT 59601 406-449-2006 406-449-2031 FAX			X		X		Q

NATIVE AMERICAN PRINT MEDIA							
PUBLICATION	INDIVIDUAL	TRIBE	ORGANIZATION	INDEPENDENT	OFF RESERVATION	MAJOR	FREQUENCY
IAC NEWSLETTER INTERTRIBAL AGRICULTURE COUNCIL 100 W 27TH ST # 500 BILLINGS, MT 59101 406-259-3525			X	X	X		Q
NORTHERN CHEYENNE TRIBAL NEWSLETTER NORTHERN CHEYENNE NATION PO BOX 128 LAME DEER, MT 59043 406-477-8283		X					
SALISH KOOTENAI COLLEGE NEWS SALISH KOOTENAI COLLEGE PO BOX 117 PABLO, MT 59855 406-675-4800 406-675-4801 FAX			X				
SPIRIT TALK NEWS POSTAL DRAWER V BROWNING, MT 59417 406-338-2882 406-338-2882 FAX	X			X			Q
TSISTSISTAS PRESS PO BOX 128 LAME DEER, MT 59043 406-477-8283	X						

NATIVE AMERICAN PRINT MEDIA							
PUBLICATION	**INDIVIDUAL**	**TRIBE**	**ORGANIZATION**	**INDEPENDENT**	**OFF RESERVATION**	**MAJOR**	**FREQUENCY**
WINTER COUNT CTR FOR NATIVE AMERICAN STUDIES 2-152 WILSON HALL -MSU BOZEMAN, MT 59717			X		X		
WOTANIN WOWAPI FORT PECK NATIONS PO BOX 1027 POPLAR, MT 59255 406-768-5155 406-768-5478 FAX		X					W
NEBRASKA							
NEB INDIAN COMMUNITY COLLEGE NEWS PO BOX 752 WINNEBAGO, NE 68071 402-878-2414 402-878-2522 FAX			X		X		
NEBRASKA INDIAN PRESS BOX 128 MACY, NE 68039	X		X				

NATIVE AMERICAN PRINT MEDIA							
PUBLICATION	**INDIVIDUAL**	**TRIBE**	**ORGANIZATION**	**INDEPENDENT**	**OFF RESERVATION**	**MAJOR**	**FREQUENCY**
THE NEWS U OF NEBRASKA AT OMAHA MULTICULTURAL AFFAIRS OMAHA, NE 68182 402-554-2248			X		X		
NEWSLETTER NEBRASKA COMMISSION ON INDIAN AFFAIRS STATE CAPITOL PO BOX 94981 6TH FLOOR E LINCOLN, NE 68509 402-471-3475			X		X		
THE TRUMPET CALL ST AUGUSTINE'S INDIAN MISSION WINNEBAGO, NE 68071			X				
WINNEBAGO INDIAN NEWS HWY 75, BOX 687 WINNEBAGO, NE 68071 402-878-2272 402-878-2963 FAX		X					

NATIVE AMERICAN PRINT MEDIA							
PUBLICATION	INDIVIDUAL	TRIBE	ORGANIZATION	INDEPENDENT	OFF RESERVATION	MAJOR	FREQUENCY
NEVADA							
DESERT BREEZE PYRAMID LAKE PAIUTE NATION PO BOX 256 NIXON, NV 89424 702-574-1000 702-574-1008 FAX		X					
ELKO COMMUNITY NEWS TE MOAK TRIBAL NATION 525 SUNSET ELKO, NV 89801 702-738-9251 702-738-2345 FAX		X					
MOAPA NATION PO BOX 340 MOAPA, NV 89025 702-865-2787 702-865-2875 FAX		X					
NEWS NOTES WALKER RIVER PAIUTE TRIBAL NATION PO BOX 220 SCHURZ, NV 89427 702-773-2306 702-773-2585 FAX		X					

NATIVE AMERICAN PRINT MEDIA							
PUBLICATION	**INDIVIDUAL**	**TRIBE**	**ORGANIZATION**	**INDEPENDENT**	**OFF RESERVATION**	**MAJOR**	**FREQUENCY**
NEWSLETTER WESTERN SHOSHONE DEFENSE PROJECT PO BOX 211106 CRESCENT VALLEY, NV 89821 702-468-0230 702-468-0237 FAX			X				Q
NEWSLETTER INTERTRIBAL COUNCIL OF NEVADA 48 RESERVATION RD RENO, NV 89502			X				
NEWSLETTER SACRED RAINBOW CIRCLE 2735 LAKESIDE DR #C RENO, NV 89509 702-826-5226				X			M
NUMA NEWS FALLON TRIBAL NATION 8955 MISSION RD FALLON, NV 89406 702-423-6075 702-423-5202 FAX		X					
SHO-PAI NEWS SHOSHONE PAIUTE NATION BOX 219 OWYHEE, NV 89832 702-757-3102 702-757-2219 FAX		X					M

NATIVE AMERICAN PRINT MEDIA							
PUBLICATION	**INDIVIDUAL**	**TRIBE**	**ORGANIZATION**	**INDEPENDENT**	**OFF RESERVATION**	**MAJOR**	**FREQUENCY**
SHOSHONE VOICES SHOSHONE HISTORIC PRESERVATION SOCIETY 1545 SILVER EAGLE DR ELKO, NV 89801			X				I
NEW HAMPSHIRE							
LIHA NEWS LACONIA INDIAN HISTORICAL SOCIETY 245 COURT LACONIA, NH 03246	X		X				M

NATIVE AMERICAN PRINT MEDIA							
PUBLICATION	**INDIVIDUAL**	**TRIBE**	**ORGANIZATION**	**INDEPENDENT**	**OFF RESERVATION**	**MAJOR**	**FREQUENCY**
NEW JERSEY							
ATTAN-AKAMIK RANKOKUS ROAD PO BOX 225 RANKOKUS, NJ 08073	X		X		X		I
DINESH D'SOUVA PO BOX 343 HANOVER, NJ 08754				X	X		
NEWSLETTER INTER-TRIBAL INDIANS OF NJ 22 VILLAGE RD MORGANVILLE, NJ 07751 908-591-8335			X		X		
NEWSLETTER NEW JERSEY AMERICAN INDIAN CTR 1301 HIGHWAY 9 NORTH OLD BRIDGE, NJ 08857 908-525-0066			X		X		
SPIKE PO BOX 368 MILLTOWN, NJ 08850 908-545-2349	X			X	X		M

NATIVE AMERICAN PRINT MEDIA							
PUBLICATION	INDIVIDUAL	TRIBE	ORGANIZATION	INDEPENDENT	OFF RESERVATION	MAJOR	FREQUENCY
NEW MEXICO							
AMERICAN INDIAN NEWS SOUTHWEST ASSOCIATION FOR INDIAN ARTS 317 OLD SANTA FE TRAIL SANTA FE, NM 87501 505-983-5220			X				M
ARTWINDS - IAIA INSTITUTE OF AMERICAN INDIAN ARTS PO BOX 1836 SANTA FE, NM 87504 505-988-2200			X		X		3X
COCHITI LAKE SUN PO BOX 70 COCHITI, NM 87072 505-465-2244		X					
DRUMBEATS INSTITUTE OF AMERICAN INDIAN ARTS PO BOX 20007 SANTA FE, NM 87501 505-988-6463			X		X		
ELDER VOICES NATIONAL INDIAN COUNCIL ON AGING 6400 UPTOWN BLVD NE CITY CENTER 510-W ALBUQUERQUE, NM 87110 505-888-3302 505-888-3276 FAX			X		X		Q

NATIVE AMERICAN PRINT MEDIA							
PUBLICATION	INDIVIDUAL	TRIBE	ORGANIZATION	INDEPENDENT	OFF RESERVATION	MAJOR	FREQUENCY
FARMINGTON DAILY TIMES PO BOX 450 FARMINGTON, NM 87499 505-325-4545						X	D
FOUR DIRECTIONS KIVA CLUB 1812 LOS LOMAS NE ALBUQUERQUE, NM 87106				X	X		
INDIAN EXTENSION NEWS NEW MEXICO STATE UNIVERSITY LAS CRUCES, NM 87001			X		X		
INDIAN FORERUNNER EIGHT NORTHERN PUEBLO NEWS PO BOX 969 SAN JUAN PUEBLO, NM 87566 505-852-4265 505-852-4835 FAX			X				
THE INDIAN TRADER ARTS CRAFTS & CULTURE PUBLICATION 311 E AZTEC AVE BOX 1421 GALLUP, NM 87305 505-722-6994 800-748-1624	X			X	X		M
JICARILLA CHIEFTAN BOX 507 DULCE, NM 87528 505-759-3242		X					

NATIVE AMERICAN PRINT MEDIA							
PUBLICATION	INDIVIDUAL	TRIBE	ORGANIZATION	INDEPENDENT	OFF RESERVATION	MAJOR	FREQUENCY
KACHINA MESSENGER PO BOX 1210 GALLUP, NM 87301 505-863-6811						X	W
LAW NEWSLETTER AMERICAN INDIAN LAW CENTER 1117 STANFORD DR NE BOX 4456 STATION A ALBUQUERQUE, NM 87196 505-277-5462			X		X		
NEWSLETTER AMERICAN INDIAN GRADUATE CENTER 4520 MONTGOMERY BLVD, NE #1B ALBUQUERQUE, NM 87109 505-881-4584			X				
NEWSLETTER AMERICANS FOR INDIAN OPPORTUNITY 681 JUNIPER HILL RD BERNALILLO, NM 87004 505-867-0278 505-867-0441 FAX			X	X	X		I

NATIVE AMERICAN PRINT MEDIA							
PUBLICATION	**INDIVIDUAL**	**TRIBE**	**ORGANIZATION**	**INDEPENDENT**	**OFF RESERVATION**	**MAJOR**	**FREQUENCY**
NEWSLETTER NATIONAL COALITION FOR INDIAN EDUCATION 8200 MOUNTAIN RD NE #203 ALBUQUERQUE, NM 87110 505-266-6510 505-262-0534			X		X		3X
NEWSLETTER ZUNI LEGAL AID PO BOX 368 ZUNI, NM 87327			X				
NINETEEN PUEBLOS NEWS 1000 INDIAN SCHOOL RD BOX 6053 ALBUQUERQUE, NM 87107			X				
PAN AMERICAN INDIAN ASSOCIATION NEWS PO BOX 58 MONTEZUMA, NM 87731 505-454-9413				X	X		M
PUEBLO HORIZON INDIAN PUEBLO CULTURAL CENTER 2401 12TH ST NW ALBUQUERQUE, NM 87102 505-881-1992			X	X	X		

NATIVE AMERICAN PRINT MEDIA							
PUBLICATION	INDIVIDUAL	TRIBE	ORGANIZATION	INDEPENDENT	OFF RESERVATION	MAJOR	FREQUENCY
THE SOURCE NM OFFICE OF INDIAN AFFAIRS 228 E PALACE AVE SANTE FE, NM 87501 505-827-6440			X		X		I
SOUTHERN PUEBLOS AGENCY BULLETIN BIA 1000 INDIAN SCHOOL RD NW ALBUQUERQUE, NM 87103			X		X		
SOUTHWEST INDIAN TOURISM AND GAMING NEWS MULTI-VISION PUBLISHING 7805 HERMANSON N.E. ALBUQUERQUE, NM 87110 505-888-3500 505-888-3501 FAX	X			X	X		Q
SOUTHWIND NATIVE NEWS PO BOX 40176 ALBUQUERQUE, NM 87196 505-296-6981							
TRUST NEWSLETTER U.S.D.I. - B.I.A. OFFICE OF TRUST FUNDS MANAGEMENT 505 MARQUETTE AVE NW ALBUQUERQUE, NM 87102			X		X		

NATIVE AMERICAN PRINT MEDIA							
PUBLICATION	INDIVIDUAL	TRIBE	ORGANIZATION	INDEPENDENT	OFF RESERVATION	MAJOR	FREQUENCY
TWIN LIGHT TRAIL 11024 MONTGOMERY NE #166 ALBUQUERQUE, NM 87111 505-764-5563 505-299-9031 FAX	X			X	X		B
UPDATE/QUARTERLY NATIONAL INDIAN COUNCIL ON AGING 6400 UPTOWN BLVD NE #510W ALBUQUERQUE, NM 87110 505-888-3302 505-888-3276 FAX			X				Q
ZUNI TRIBAL NEWSLETTER ZUNI TRIBAL OFFICE BOX 339 ZUNI, NM 87327 505-782-4881		X					W

NATIVE AMERICAN PRINT MEDIA							
PUBLICATION	**INDIVIDUAL**	**TRIBE**	**ORGANIZATION**	**INDEPENDENT**	**OFF RESERVATION**	**MAJOR**	**FREQUENCY**
NEW YORK							
AKWESASNE NOTES MOHAWK NATION PO BOX 196 ROOSEVELTOWN, NY 13683 518-358-9531 613-575-2935 FAX			X	X			I
CLAN DESTINY SENECA INDIAN HISTORICAL SOCIETY 12199 BRANT RESERVATION IRVING, NY 14081 716-549-3889			X	X			
DAYBREAK PO BOX 315 WILLIAMSVILLE, NY 14231 716-636-3678				X	X		
I.P.N. NATIONAL BUREAU 3 RR BOX 136 2226 BLACKMAN HILL RD BERKSHIRE, NY 13736			X	X	X		
IKHANA - NEWSLETTER ALASKAN/NATIVE MINISTRY 815 2ND AVE NEW YORK, NY 10017 800-334-7626			X		X		Q

NATIVE AMERICAN PRINT MEDIA							
PUBLICATION	INDIVIDUAL	TRIBE	ORGANIZATION	INDEPENDENT	OFF RESERVATION	MAJOR	FREQUENCY
INDIAN AFFAIRS ASSN OF AMERICAN INDIAN AFFAIRS 245 5TH AVE #1801 NEW YORK, NY 10016 212-689-8720 212-689-4692 FAX			X		X		Q
INDIAN TIMES BOX 196 ROOSEVELTOWN, NY 13683 518-358-9531 613-575-2935	X		X	X			M
KARIWENHAWI NEWSLETTER C/O AKWESASNE LIBRARY RR 1 BOX 14 C ST REGIS RESERVATION HOGANSBURG, NY 13655 518-358-2240			X				M
KINZUA PLANNING NEWSLETTER SENECA NAT OF INDIANS BOX 231 SALAMANCA, NY 14081 716-945-1790		X					

NATIVE AMERICAN PRINT MEDIA							
PUBLICATION	INDIVIDUAL	TRIBE	ORGANIZATION	INDEPENDENT	OFF RESERVATION	MAJOR	FREQUENCY
LEAGUE OF NATIONS PAN-AM INDIANS TUSCARORA INDIAN RESERVATION 5616 WALMORE RD LEWISTON, NY 14092 716-297-4990		X					
NAEP NEWSLETTER 234 W 109TH #507 NEW YORK, NY 10025			X				
NATIVE AMERICAN (AKWE: KON) AMERICAN INDIAN PROGRAM 300 CALDWELL HALL CORNELL UNIVERSITY ITHACA, NY 14853 607-255-4308 607-255-0185 FAX			X		X		Q
NEWSLETTER AMERICAN INDIAN COMMUNITY HOUSE 404 LAFAYETTE - 2ND FLOOR NEW YORK, NY 10003 212-598-0100 212-598-4909 FAX			X		X		Q
RESERVATION TIMES 1500 RTE 438 IRVING, NY 14081		X					

NATIVE AMERICAN PRINT MEDIA							
PUBLICATION	INDIVIDUAL	TRIBE	ORGANIZATION	INDEPENDENT	OFF RESERVATION	MAJOR	FREQUENCY
STUDIES IN AMER INDIAN LITERATURE COLUMBIA UNIVERSITY 602 PHILOSOPHY HALL NEW YORK, NY 10027			X		X		
TONAWANDA INDIAN NEWS 7027 MEADVILLE RD BASOM, NY 14013 716-542-9943		X					
TURTLE QUARTERLY MAGAZINE 25 RAINBOW MALL NIAGARA FALLS, NY 14303 716-284-2427			X	X	X		Q
THE WEB NEWSLETTER AMERICAN INDIAN PROGRAM 300 CALDWELL HALL ITHACA, NY 14853 607-225-4308 607-225-6246 FAX			X		X		Q

NATIVE AMERICAN PRINT MEDIA							
PUBLICATION	**INDIVIDUAL**	**TRIBE**	**ORGANIZATION**	**INDEPENDENT**	**OFF RESERVATION**	**MAJOR**	**FREQUENCY**
NORTH CAROLINA							
CAROLINA CIRCLE NEWS 1204 E FRANKLIN GASTONIA, NC 28054			X		X		B
CAROLINA INDIAN VOICE BOX 1075 304 NORMAL ST PEMBROKE, NC 28372 910-521-2826 910-521-1975 FAX				X			W
CHEROKEE ONE FEATHER PO BOX 501 CHEROKEE, NC 28719 704-497-5513 704-497-4810 FAX		X					W
CHEROKEE TIMES BOX 105 CHEROKEE, NC 28719		X					
EARTHKEEPER PO BOX 242 WHITTIER, NC 28789 704-497-5963	X			X			Q
JOURNAL MUSEUM OF CHEROKEE INDIANS CHEROKEE STUDIES BOX 1599 CHEROKEE, NC 28719 704-497-3481			X				

NATIVE AMERICAN PRINT MEDIA							
PUBLICATION	INDIVIDUAL	TRIBE	ORGANIZATION	INDEPENDENT	OFF RESERVATION	MAJOR	FREQUENCY
LUMBEE OUTREACH PO BOX 68 PEMBROKE, NC 28372 919-521-9761			X				
NEWSLETTER CHEROKEE BOYS CLUB, INC PO BOX 507 CHEROKEE, NC 28719			X				2X
SPIRIT NATIVE AMERICAN RESOURCE CTR PEMBROKE STATE UNIVERSITY PEMBROKE, NC 28372 919-521-6282			X				M
TIP OF THE FEATHER 511 LATIMER HILLSBOROUGH, NC 27278 919-732-8512	X			X	X		Q

NATIVE AMERICAN PRINT MEDIA							
PUBLICATION	INDIVIDUAL	TRIBE	ORGANIZATION	INDEPENDENT	OFF RESERVATION	MAJOR	FREQUENCY
NORTH DAKOTA							
THE ACTION NEWS BOX 605 NEW TOWN, ND 58763		X					
ARROW NEWS MANDAREE HIGH SCHOOL MADAREE, ND 58737			X				
BELLS OF ST ANNE ST ANNE'S INDIAN MISSION BELCOURT, ND 58316			X				
COLLEGE NEWS FORT BETHOLD COMMUNITY COLLEGE PO BOX 490 NEW TOWN, ND 58763 701-627-3665 701-627-3609 FAX			X				
DACOTAH NEWS FORT TOTTEN, ND 58335		X					
DAKOTA STUDENT UNIVERSITY STATION PO BOX 8177 GRAND FORKS, ND 58202		X					
DEVILS LAKE NEWSLETTER SIOUX COMMUNITY CENTER FORT TOTTEN, ND 58335 701-766-4221 701-766-4126 FAX		X					

NATIVE AMERICAN PRINT MEDIA							
PUBLICATION	**INDIVIDUAL**	**TRIBE**	**ORGANIZATION**	**INDEPENDENT**	**OFF RESERVATION**	**MAJOR**	**FREQUENCY**
E'YANAPAHA PUBLIC INFORMATION OFFICE FORT TOTTEN, ND 58335 701-766-4221		X					
FT BERTHOLD NEWS BULLETIN PO BOX 370 FT BERTHOLD AGENCY NEW TOWN, ND 58763 701-627-4707		X					
INDIAN LIFE MAGAZINE PO BOX 32 PEMBINA, ND 58271 204-661-9333 204-661-3982			X		X		B
LITTLE HOOP COMMUNITY COLLEGE NEWS PO BOX 269 FORT TOTTEN, ND 58335 701-766-4415 701-766-4077 FAX	X		X				
MANDAN-HIDATSA-ARIKARA TIMES PO BOX 669 NEW TOWN, ND 58763 701-627-3333		X					M

NATIVE AMERICAN PRINT MEDIA							
PUBLICATION	INDIVIDUAL	TRIBE	ORGANIZATION	INDEPENDENT	OFF RESERVATION	MAJOR	FREQUENCY
NATIVE AGING VISIONS NAT'L RESOURCE CTR ON NATIVE AMERICAN AGING UNIV OF NORTH DAKOTA PO BOX 7090 GRAND FORKS, ND 58202 701-777-3766 800-896-7628 701-777-4257 FAX			X		X		Q
NEWSLETTER NORTHERN PLAINS RESOURCE & EVALUATION CTR II 3315 UNIVERSITY DR BISMARCK, ND 58504 701-258-0437	X		X		X		M
SERPENT, STAFF & DRUM INDIANS INTO MEDICINE UND SCHOOL OF MEDICINE 501 N COLUMBIA RD GRAND FORKS, ND 58203 701-777-3037 701-777-3277 FAX			X				Q
TRIBAL NEWSLETTER STANDING ROCK SIOUX PO BOX D FORT YATES, ND 58538 701-854-7231 701-854-7299 FAX		X					

NATIVE AMERICAN PRINT MEDIA							
PUBLICATION	**INDIVIDUAL**	**TRIBE**	**ORGANIZATION**	**INDEPENDENT**	**OFF RESERVATION**	**MAJOR**	**FREQUENCY**
UNITED TRIBES NEWS 3315 UNIVERSITY DR BISMARCK, ND 58501 701-255-3285 701-255-1844 FAX			X		X		
WAHPETON HIGHLIGHTS WAHPETON INDIAN SCHOOL WAHPETON, ND 58075 701-642-3796			X				
OHIO							
NEWSLETTER CLEVELAND AMERICAN INDIAN CENTER 5500-5502 LORAIN AVE CLEVELAND, OH 44102 216-961-3490			X		X		

NATIVE AMERICAN PRINT MEDIA							
PUBLICATION	INDIVIDUAL	TRIBE	ORGANIZATION	INDEPENDENT	OFF RESERVATION	MAJOR	FREQUENCY
NEWSLETTER UNITED INTER-TRIBAL INDIAN COUNCIL 1785 ST RD 28 #358 GOSHEN, OH 45122 513-528-5265 513-722-3887 FAX	X		X		X		
NONNE 1251 S REYNOLDS RD #499 TOLEDO, OH 43615 419-389-1034							
SMOKE & FIRE NEWS PO BOX 166 GRAND RAPIDS, OH 43522 419-832-0303	X			X	X		M
TALKING LEAVES NATIVE AMERICAN INDIAN CENTER 2565 VILLA LN CINCINNATI, OH 45208			X		X		
TOSAN AMERICAN INDIAN PEOPLES NEWS PO BOX 162 DAYTON, OH 45401			X		X		

NATIVE AMERICAN PRINT MEDIA							
PUBLICATION	INDIVIDUAL	TRIBE	ORGANIZATION	INDEPENDENT	OFF RESERVATION	MAJOR	FREQUENCY
OKLAHOMA							
AAIP NEWSLETTER AMERICAN ASSOCIATION OF INDIAN PHYSICIANS 1235 SOVEREIGN ROW #C7 OKLAHOMA CITY, OK 73108 405-946-7072 405-946-7651 FAX			X		X		Q
THE AMER IND BAPT VOICE 1724 E 9TH OKMULGEE, OK 74447			X		X		
AMERICAN INDIAN QUARTERLY UNIVERSITY OF OKLAHOMA - ANTHO NORMAN, OK 73019 405-325-2491			X		X		Q
BISHINIK NEWSPAPER CHOCTAW NATION PO DRAWER 1210 DURANT, OK 74701 405-924-8280 405-924-1150 FAX		X					M
THE BUCKSKIN ROUTE 3 EUFAULA, OK 74432							

NATIVE AMERICAN PRINT MEDIA							
PUBLICATION	**INDIVIDUAL**	**TRIBE**	**ORGANIZATION**	**INDEPENDENT**	**OFF RESERVATION**	**MAJOR**	**FREQUENCY**
CHEROKEE ADVOCATE PO BOX 948 TAHLEQUAH, OK 74465 918-456-0671 918-456-6485 FAX		X					M
CHEROKEE OBSERVER PO BOX 1301 JAY, OK 74346 918-253-8752	X			X			M
CHEYENNE-ARAPAHO BULLETIN C & A TRIBES OF OKLAHOMA PO BOX 38 CONCHO, OK 73022 405-262-0345 405-262-0745 FAX		X					M
CHICKASAW TIMES CHICKASAW NATION PO BOX 1548 ADA, OK 74820 405-436-2603 405-436-4287 FAX		X					
CHILOCCO NEWSLETTER OKLAHOMA CITY, OK			X		X		M
COLUMNS NEWSLETTER CHEROKEE NATIONAL HISTORICAL SOCIETY PO BOX 515 TAHLEQUAH, OK 74465 918-456-6007 918-456-6165 FAX			X	X			M

NATIVE AMERICAN PRINT MEDIA							
PUBLICATION	INDIVIDUAL	TRIBE	ORGANIZATION	INDEPENDENT	OFF RESERVATION	MAJOR	FREQUENCY
COMANCHE HC 32 BOX 1720 LAWTON, OK 73502 405-492-4988 405-492-4981 FAX		X					M
CREEK COMMUNICATIONS CREEK NATION PO BOX 580 OKMULGEE, OK 74447 918-756-8700 918-756-0824 FAX		X	X				
DELAWARE INDIAN NEWS DELAWARE TRIBE OF INDIANS 108 S SENECA BARTLESVILLE, OK 74003 918-336-5272 918-336-5513 FAX		X					M
DELAWARE NEWSLETTER PO BOX 825 ANADARKO, OK 73005 405-247-2448		X					M
FEATHER REVIEW PO BOX 149 MOUNTAIN VIEW, OK 73062		X					M

NATIVE AMERICAN PRINT MEDIA							
PUBLICATION	INDIVIDUAL	TRIBE	ORGANIZATION	INDEPENDENT	OFF RESERVATION	MAJOR	FREQUENCY
HOWNIKAN ABSENTEE SHAWNEE NEWS 2025 S GORDON COOPER BOX 1714 SHAWNEE, OK 74801 405-275-4030 405-275-5637 FAX		X					
INDIAN JOURNAL BOX 689 EUFAULA, OK 74432							
INDIGENOUS EYE PO BOX 612 TAHLEQUAH, OK 74465 918-696-3335							
INTER-TRIBAL VOICE NATIVE AMERICAN COALITION OF TULSA 1740 W 41ST TULSA, OK 74107 918-446-8432				X	X		
KANZA NEWS KAW TRIBAL NATION DRAWER 50 KAW CITY, OK 74641 405-269-2301 405-269-2552 FAX		X					Q

NATIVE AMERICAN PRINT MEDIA							
PUBLICATION	INDIVIDUAL	TRIBE	ORGANIZATION	INDEPENDENT	OFF RESERVATION	MAJOR	FREQUENCY
THE MUSCOGEE NATION NEWS PO BOX 580 OKMULGEE, OK 74447 918-756-8700 918-758-0824 FAX		X					M
NEWS SOUTHERN PLAINS INDIAN MUSEUM 715 E CENTRAL ANADARKO, OK 73005			X				
OSAGE NATION NEWS OSAGE NATION MEDIA CENTER OSAGE AGENCY CAMPUS PO BOX 779 PAWHUSKA, OK 74056 918-287-2496		X					
PHOENIX PO BOX 19668 MUSKOGEE, OK 74402							
SAC & FOX NEWS SAC & FOX INDIAN NATION RT 2, BOX 246 STROUD, OK 74079 918-968-3526		X					B

NATIVE AMERICAN PRINT MEDIA							
PUBLICATION	INDIVIDUAL	TRIBE	ORGANIZATION	INDEPENDENT	OFF RESERVATION	MAJOR	FREQUENCY
SAY YES NEWSLETTER INST FOR DEVELOPMENT OF INDIAN LAW 2501 N BLACKWELDER OKLAHOMA CITY, OK 73106 405-521-5188			X	X	X		
SMOKE DREAMS RIVERSIDE HIGH SCHOOL ANADARKO, OK 73005			X				
SMOKE SIGNALS BACONE COLLEGE 99 BACONE RD MUSKOGEE, OK 74401 918-683-4581 918-687-5913 FAX			X		X		
THE STORYTELLER RED EARTH INC 2100 NE 52ND ST OKLAHOMA CITY, OK 73111 405-427-5228			X		X		Q
TRIBAL COURT NEWS-BRIEFS OKLAHOMA CITY UNIVERSITY SCHOOL OF LAW, NALRC 2501 BLACKWELDER OKLAHOMA CITY, OK 73106 405-521-5017			X				B

NATIVE AMERICAN PRINT MEDIA							
PUBLICATION	**INDIVIDUAL**	**TRIBE**	**ORGANIZATION**	**INDEPENDENT**	**OFF RESERVATION**	**MAJOR**	**FREQUENCY**
U.K.B. NEWSLETTER UNITED KEETOWAH BAND OF CHEROKEE INDIANS BOX 746 TAHLEQUAH, OK 74465 918-456-5491		X					M
UNITED NAT'L INDIAN TRIBAL YOUTH INC PO BOX 25042 OKLAHOMA CITY, OK 73125 405-524-2031			X				I
OREGON							
AMERICAN INDIAN CULTURAL RESOURCE OREGON COMMISSION ON INDIAN SERVICES 167 STATE CAPITOL SALEM, OR 97310 503-986-1067			X		X		Y

NATIVE AMERICAN PRINT MEDIA							
PUBLICATION	**INDIVIDUAL**	**TRIBE**	**ORGANIZATION**	**INDEPENDENT**	**OFF RESERVATION**	**MAJOR**	**FREQUENCY**
CHEMAWA CHATTER CHEMAWA INDIAN HEALTH CENTER 3750 CHEMAWA RD NE SALEM, OR 97305 503-399-5931			X		X		Q
CONFEDERATED UMATILLA JOURNAL BOX 638 PENDLETON, OR 97801 503-276-3165 503-278-5390 FAX		X					M
DRUMBEAT SILETZ TRIBES 3789 RIVER RD N #D KEIZER, OR 97303 503-390-9494		X					M
E.O.P. EXTRA NEWSLETTER EDUCATIONAL OPPORTUNITIES PROGRAM OREGON STATE UNIVERSITY WALDO HALL, RM 337 CORVALLIS, OR 97331 503-737-3628			X		X		Q
HEALTH NEWS & NOTES N.W. PORTLAND AREA INDIAN HEALTH BOARD 520 SW HARRISON #335 PORTLAND, OR 97201 503-228-4185			X		X		Q

NATIVE AMERICAN PRINT MEDIA							
PUBLICATION	INDIVIDUAL	TRIBE	ORGANIZATION	INDEPENDENT	OFF RESERVATION	MAJOR	FREQUENCY
HONORING THE CHILDREN NAT'L INDIAN CHILD WELFARE ASSOC 3611 SW HOOD ST #201 PORTLAND, OR 97201 503-222-4044 503-222-4007 FAX			X		X		Y
INDIAN BUSINESS REVIEW N/A BUSINESS ALLIANCE 8435 SE 17TH PORTLAND, OR 97202 503-233-4841			X		X		M
INDIAN EDUCATION NEWSLETTER COOS CO. INDIAN EDUCATION 9140 CAPARAGO HWY COOS BAY, OR 97420 503-888-4584			X		X		
INDIAN EDUCATION PROGRAM PORTLAND PUBLIC SCHOOLS 8020 NE TILLAMOOK PORTLAND, OR 97213 503-331-3141			X		X		
ISSUES - THE OFFICE OF MULTICULTURAL AFFAIRS 1255 OREGON HALL UNIVERSITY OF OREGON EUGENE, OR 97403 503-346-3479			X		X		Q

NATIVE AMERICAN PRINT MEDIA							
PUBLICATION	INDIVIDUAL	TRIBE	ORGANIZATION	INDEPENDENT	OFF RESERVATION	MAJOR	FREQUENCY
KLAMATH NEWS THE KAMATH NATION PO BOX 436 CHILOQUIN, OR 97624 503-783-2219 800-524-9787 503-783-2029 FAX		X					M
LAKOTA OYATE-KO OREGON STATE PENITENTIARY 2605 STATE ST SALEM, OR 97310			X				
LEGIS UPDATE COMM ON INDIAN SVCS 167 STATE CAPITOL SALEM, OR 97310 503-986-1067			X				Y
MOCCASIN TELEGRAPH 525 MILL SPRINGFIELD, OR 97477				X			
MUKLUKS HEMCUNGA ORG OF THE FORGOTTEN AMERICAN BOX 1257 KLAMATH FALLS, OR 97601 503-882-4442			X				

NATIVE AMERICAN PRINT MEDIA							
PUBLICATION	INDIVIDUAL	TRIBE	ORGANIZATION	INDEPENDENT	OFF RESERVATION	MAJOR	FREQUENCY
N.I.C.W.A. NEWS NATIONAL INDIAN CHILD WELFARE ASSOC 3611 SW HOOD ST #201 PORTLAND, OR 97201 503-222-4044 503-222-4007 FAX			X		X		Q
NATIVE NEWS PROGRAM EUGENE PUBLIC SCHOOLS 200 N MONROE EUGENE, OR 97402 503-687-3489			X		X		
NEWSLETTER INTERNATIONAL TIMBER COUNCIL PO BOX C WARM SPRINGS, OR 97761 503-553-1161			X				
NEWSLETTER INTERTRIBAL TIMBER COUNCIL 4370 NE HALSY ST PORTLAND, OR 97213			X				
NEWSLETTER INSTITUTE FOR STUDY TRAD AM IND ART PO BOX 66124 PORTLAND, OR 97266 503-233-8131			X		X		

NATIVE AMERICAN PRINT MEDIA							
PUBLICATION	INDIVIDUAL	TRIBE	ORGANIZATION	INDEPENDENT	OFF RESERVATION	MAJOR	FREQUENCY
O-SI-YO CHEROKEE - WOLF BAND PO BOX 592 TALENT, OR 97540 503-535-5406		X					
OREGON INDIAN EDUCATION NEWSLETTER 720 NANTUCKET EUGENE, OR 97404 503-687-3489			X		X		Q
OYATE WO'WAPI TAHANA WHITECROW FOUNDATION PO BOX 18181 SALEM, OR 97305			X		X		Q
SILETZ NEWSLETTER CONF TRIBES OF SILETZ INDIANS PO BOX 549 SILETZ, OR 97380 503-444-2532 X 134 800-922-1399		X					M
SMOKE SIGNALS CONFED TRIBES OF GRAND RONDE 9615 GRAND RONDE RD GRAND RONDE, OR 97347 503-879-2254 800-422-0232		X					M

NATIVE AMERICAN PRINT MEDIA							
PUBLICATION	INDIVIDUAL	TRIBE	ORGANIZATION	INDEPENDENT	OFF RESERVATION	MAJOR	FREQUENCY
SPILYAY TYMOO PO BOX 870 WARM SPRINGS, OR 97761 503-553-1644 503-553-3539 FAX		X					U
SPRINGFIELD AREA OFFICE NEWS CONF. TRIBES OF SILETZ 188 W B ST, BLDG P SPRINGFIELD, OR 97477 503-746-9658			X		X		M
TRIBAL NEWSLETTER CONFEDERATED TRIBES OF COOS, UMPQUA, SIUSLAW 455 S 4TH ST COOS BAY, OR 97420 503-267-5454 503-269-1647		X					M
TU'KWA HONE NEWSLETTER BURNS PAIUTE TRIBE HC 71 100 PA'SI'GO BURNS, OR 97720 503-573-2088		X					W
WANA CHINOOK TYMO RIVER REPORT - CRITFC 729 NE OREGON ST #200 PORTLAND, OR 97232 503-238-0667			X	X	X		Q

NATIVE AMERICAN PRINT MEDIA							
PUBLICATION	**INDIVIDUAL**	**TRIBE**	**ORGANIZATION**	**INDEPENDENT**	**OFF RESERVATION**	**MAJOR**	**FREQUENCY**
PENNSYLVANIA							
AMERICAN INDIAN LEADERSHIP PROGRAM PENN STATE UNIV #320 RACKLEY BLDG UNIVERSITY PARK, PA 16802			X		X		
ECHO OF THE FOUR WINDS UNITED METHODIST CHURCH 1305 SUNNY AYR WAY LANSDALE, PA 19446			X	X			B
INDIAN ARTIFACT MAGAZINE RD 1, BOX 240 TUBOTVILLE, PA 17772	X			X	X		Q
LENAPE OLAM MUSEUM OF INDIAN CULTURE 2825 FISH HATCHERY RD ALLENTOWN, PA 18103-9801 610-797-2121			X		X		Q
NEWSLETTER MINA-WIHE NATIVE AMERICAN HISTORICAL PO BOX 59072 PITTSBURGH, PA 15210 512-431-9050	X			X	X		B

NATIVE AMERICAN PRINT MEDIA							
PUBLICATION	INDIVIDUAL	TRIBE	ORGANIZATION	INDEPENDENT	OFF RESERVATION	MAJOR	FREQUENCY
RISING SUN NEWSLETTER UNITED AMERICAN INDIANS OF DELAWARE VALLEY 225 CHESTNUT ST PHILADELPHIA, PA 19106 215-574-9020			X		X		Q
ROOTS AWAKENING NATIVE AMERICAN HERITAGE COMMITTEE 406 FEDERAL BLDG 1000 LIBERTY AVE PITTSBURGH, PA 15222 412-885-5097			X		X		M
SINGING WINDS NEWSLETTER COUNCIL OF THREE RIVERS 200 CHARLES DORSEYVILLE, PA 15238 412-782-4457 412-767-4808 FAX			X		X		I
SPIRIT WALKER NEWSLETTER NATIVE AMERICAN INDIAN COMMUNITY RD 2, BOX 247-A KITTANNING, PA 16201 412-548-7335 412-548-8332 FAX	X	X					

NATIVE AMERICAN PRINT MEDIA							
PUBLICATION	**INDIVIDUAL**	**TRIBE**	**ORGANIZATION**	**INDEPENDENT**	**OFF RESERVATION**	**MAJOR**	**FREQUENCY**
WALKS BY DAY - NEWSLETTER LEAGUE OF SEPARATED TRIBES 1809 FRANKLIN GREENSBURG, PA 15601	X		X	X	X		
WILDFIRE MAGAZINE BEAR TRIBE PO BOX 199 DEVON, PA 19333 215-993-3344 215-993-3345	X		X		X		Q
RHODE ISLAND							
THE CORNPLANTER RHODE ISLAND INDIAN COUNCIL INC 444 FRIENDSHIP PROVIDENCE, RI 02907 401-331-4440 401-331-4494 FAX			X		X		Q

NATIVE AMERICAN PRINT MEDIA							
PUBLICATION	INDIVIDUAL	TRIBE	ORGANIZATION	INDEPENDENT	OFF RESERVATION	MAJOR	FREQUENCY
INDIAN COMMUNICATIONS 386 SUMMIT RD EXETER, RI 02822		X					
NEWSLETTER NARRAGANSETT INDIAN NATION PO BOX 268 CHARLESTOWN, RI 02813 401-364-1100 401-364-1104 FAX		X					
SOUTH DAKOTA							
THE BLUE CLOUD QUARTERLY BLUE CLOUD ABBEY MARVIN, SD 57251			X				Q

NATIVE AMERICAN PRINT MEDIA							
PUBLICATION	INDIVIDUAL	TRIBE	ORGANIZATION	INDEPENDENT	OFF RESERVATION	MAJOR	FREQUENCY
BUFFALO TRACKS INTERTRIBAL BISON COOPERATIVE PO BOX 8105 520 KANSAS CITY ST # 209 RAPID CITY, SD 57701 605-394-9730 605-394-7742 FAX			X		X		Q
THE BULLETIN INSTITUTE OF AMERICAN INDIAN STUDIES 414 E CLARK ST VERMILLION, SD 57069-2390 605-677-5209 605-677-5073 FAX			X				Q
CAP NEWSLETTER ROSEBUD SIOUX NATION PO BOX 430 ROSEBUD, SD 57570 605-747-2381 605-747-2243 FAX		X					
COLLEGE NEWS CHEYENNE RIVER COMMUNITY COLLEGE PO BOX 220 EAGLE BUTTE, SD 57625 605-964-8635 605-964-1144 FAX			X				

NATIVE AMERICAN PRINT MEDIA							
PUBLICATION	INDIVIDUAL	TRIBE	ORGANIZATION	INDEPENDENT	OFF RESERVATION	MAJOR	FREQUENCY
COLLEGE NEWS SISSETON-WAHPETON COMMUNITY COLLEGE AGENCY VILLAGE CPO BOX 689 SISSETON, SD 57262 605-698-3966 605-698-3132 FAX			X				
CRAZY HORSE PROGRESS THE BLACK HILLS AVENUE OF THE CHIEFS CRAZY HORSE, SD 57730 605-673-4681 605-673-2185 FAX	X		X		X		Q
DAKOTA WOWAPIPHI YANKTON SIOUX NATION PO BOX 248 MARTY, SD 57361 605-384-3641		X					
DRUMBEAT CROW CREEK HIGH SCHOOL PO BOX 12 STEPHAN, SD 57346 605-852-2455			X				
EAGLE BUTTE NEWS PO BOX 210 EAGLE BUTTE, SD 57625 605-964-2100	X			X			

NATIVE AMERICAN PRINT MEDIA							
PUBLICATION	INDIVIDUAL	TRIBE	ORGANIZATION	INDEPENDENT	OFF RESERVATION	MAJOR	FREQUENCY
FLANDREAU SPIRIT FLANDREAU HIGH SCHOOL FLANDREAU, SD 57028 605-997-2724			X	X			
GREAT PLAINS OBSERVER 218 S EGAN MADISON, SD 57042 605-256-4555				X	X		
INDIAN COUNTY TODAY (LAKOTA TIMES) 1920 LOMBARDY DR PO BOX 2180 RAPID CITY, SD 57701 605-341-0011 605-341-6940 FAX	X			X	X		W
INDIAN EDUCATION NEWSLETTER UNITED TRIBES OF SO. DAKOTA PO BOX 1193 PIERRE, SD 57501			X	X	X		
LITTLE SIOUX ST FRANCIS INDIAN MISSION BOX 149 ST FRANCIS, SD 57572 605-747-2299			X				

NATIVE AMERICAN PRINT MEDIA							
PUBLICATION	**INDIVIDUAL**	**TRIBE**	**ORGANIZATION**	**INDEPENDENT**	**OFF RESERVATION**	**MAJOR**	**FREQUENCY**
MUSTANG NEWS LITTLE WOUND SCHOOL BOARD PO BOX 500 KYLE, SD 57752 605-455-2461			X				
NEWS BULLETIN CHEYENNE RIVER AGENCY PO BOX 590 EAGLE BUTTE, SD 57625 605-964-4155			X				
NEWSLETTER CENTER FOR WESTERN STUDIES AUGUSTANA COLLEGE BOX 727 SIOUX FALLS, SD 57197 605-336-4007			X		X		
NEWSLETTER SINTE GLESKA COLLEGE CENTER PO BOX 490 ROSEBUD, SD 57570 605-747-2263 605-747-2098 FAX			X				
OGLALA LAKOTA COLLEGE NEWS PO BOX 490 KYLE, SD 57752 605-455-2321 605-455-2787 FAX			X				

NATIVE AMERICAN PRINT MEDIA							
PUBLICATION	INDIVIDUAL	TRIBE	ORGANIZATION	INDEPENDENT	OFF RESERVATION	MAJOR	FREQUENCY
PAHA SAPA WAHOSI INDIAN CLUB BLACK HILLS STATE COLLEGE SPEARFISH, SD 57783 800-255-2487			X		X		
PILC NEWS PIERRE INDIAN LEARNING CENTER STAR RT #3 PIERRE, SD 57501			X		X		
RED CLOUD COUNTRY RED CLOUD INDIAN SCHOOL PINE RIDGE, SD 57770			X	X			
SCOUT EPISCOPAL CHURCH LOWER BUTTE, SD 57578			X	X			
SICANGU SUN-TIMES PO BOX 750 ROSEBUD, SD 57570 605-747-2058 605-747-2058 FAX	X			X			W
SIOUX SAN SUN PHS INDIAN HOSPITAL 3200 CANYON LAKE DR RAPID CITY, SD 57702 605-348-1900			X		X		

NATIVE AMERICAN PRINT MEDIA							
PUBLICATION	**INDIVIDUAL**	**TRIBE**	**ORGANIZATION**	**INDEPENDENT**	**OFF RESERVATION**	**MAJOR**	**FREQUENCY**
SISSETON AGENCY NEWS SISSETON BIA AGENCY PO BOX 688 AGENCY VILLAGE, SD 57262 605-698-7676			X				
SOTA IYA YE YAPI SISSETON-WAHPETON SIOUX NATION RT 2 BOX 509 SISSETON, SD 57262 605-698-3911		X					
SPEARHEAD LUTHERAN SOCIAL SVCS 600 W 12TH SIOUX FALLS, SD 57104			X		X		
TEPEE TALK BIA AGENCY PO BOX 550 ROSEBUD, SD 57570 605-747-2224			X				
TODD COUNTY TRIBUNE & EYAPAHA PO BOX 229 MISSION, SD 57555 605-856-4469	X			X		X	
UTSD NEWSLETTER UNITED TRIBES OF SOUTH DAKOTA PO BOX 1193 PIERRE, SD 57501			X	X	X		

PUBLICATION	INDIVIDUAL	TRIBE	ORGANIZATION	INDEPENDENT	OFF RESERVATION	MAJOR	FREQUENCY
WOYAKAPI ST FRANCIS MISSION PO BOX 379 ST FRANCIS, SD 57572 605-747-2299			X	X			
YANKTON SIOUX MESSENGER PO BOX 248 MARTY, SD 57361 605-384-3804 605-384-5687 FAX			X				
TENNESSEE							
INDIAN NEWS PO BOX 72711 CHATTANOOGA, TN 37407 615-821-1508	X		X	X	X		

NATIVE AMERICAN PRINT MEDIA							
PUBLICATION	INDIVIDUAL	TRIBE	ORGANIZATION	INDEPENDENT	OFF RESERVATION	MAJOR	FREQUENCY
INDIAN READER PO BOX 59 STRAWBERRY PLAINS, TN 37871 615-933-6246	X		X	X	X		I
NATIVE AMERICAN VOICES UNITED METHODIST COMMUNICATIONS PO BOX 320 NASHVILLE, TN 37202 605-742-5414 605-742-5413 FAX	X		X		X		U
SACRED EARTH NEWS X.A.T. MEDICINE SOCIETY 1404 GALE LN NASHVILLE, TN 37212 615-298-9932			X	X	X		I

NATIVE AMERICAN PRINT MEDIA							
PUBLICATION	**INDIVIDUAL**	**TRIBE**	**ORGANIZATION**	**INDEPENDENT**	**OFF RESERVATION**	**MAJOR**	**FREQUENCY**
TEXAS							
FIRST AMERICAN PO BOX 153409 IRVING, TX 75015 817-429-1866 817-332-5103 FAX				X	X		
NATIVE AMERICAN NEWS OF TEXAS 1200 LANTANA PO BOX 2369 CORPUS CHRISTI, TX 78403			X		X		
SMOKE SIGNALS DALLAS INTERTRIBAL CTR NEWSLETTER 209 E JEFFERSON BLVD DALLAS, TX 75203 214-941-1050 214-941-6537 FAX			X		X		Q

NATIVE AMERICAN PRINT MEDIA							
PUBLICATION	INDIVIDUAL	TRIBE	ORGANIZATION	INDEPENDENT	OFF RESERVATION	MAJOR	FREQUENCY
UTAH							
THE EAGLE'S EYE BRIGHAM YOUNG UNIVERSITY 128 ELWC PROVO, UT 84602			X		X		3X
NEWSLETTER PAIUTE INDIAN NATION 600 N 100 EAST CEDAR CITY, UT 84720 805-586-1112 805-586-7388 FAX		X					
NEWSLETTER ST CHRISTOPHER'S MISSION BLUFF, UT 84512			X		X		
UTE BULLETIN PO BOX 400 FORT DUCHESNE, UT 84026 801-722-5141 801-722-2374 FAX		X					B

NATIVE AMERICAN PRINT MEDIA							
PUBLICATION	INDIVIDUAL	TRIBE	ORGANIZATION	INDEPENDENT	OFF RESERVATION	MAJOR	FREQUENCY
VIRGINIA							
AMERICAN INDIAN SOCIETY OF WASHINGTON, DC PO BOX 6431 FALLS CHURCH, VA 22040 703-914-0548			X	X	X		
BEAR TRACKS FIRST NATION ARTS PROGRAM 11917 MAIN ST FREDERICKSBURG, VA 22408 703-371-5615 703-371-3505 FAX			X		X		
BUSINESS ALERT FIRST NATION DEVELOPMENT INSTITUTE 11917 MAIN ST FREDERICKSBURG, VA 22408 703-371-5615 703-371-3505 FAX			X		X		B
PATHFINDER AMERICAN INDIAN HERITAGE CTR 6051 ARLINGTON BLVD FALLS CHURCH, VA 22044 202-463-4267			X		X		

NATIVE AMERICAN PRINT MEDIA							
PUBLICATION	**INDIVIDUAL**	**TRIBE**	**ORGANIZATION**	**INDEPENDENT**	**OFF RESERVATION**	**MAJOR**	**FREQUENCY**
WASHINGTON							
AMER INDIAN PROG NEWSLETTER MULTICULTURAL CTR 107 WASH ST UNIV PULLMAN, WA 99164-2328 509-335-8676 509-335-8368 FAX			X		X		
AQUOL QUOL LUMMI TRIBAL OFFICE 2616 KWINA RD BELLINGHAM, WA 98226 360-734-8180 360-384-5521 FAX		X					M
CHINOOK WESTERN WASH UNIV 215 VIKING UNION BELLINGHAM, WA 98225			X		X		
COYOTE TRACKS HUB 208, BOX 160 NACO SEATTLE, WA 98195 206-685-4147			X		X		M
DAYBREAK STAR INDIAN READER 1945 YALE PLACE E SEATTLE, WA 98102 206-325-0070			X	X	X		M

NATIVE AMERICAN PRINT MEDIA							
PUBLICATION	**INDIVIDUAL**	**TRIBE**	**ORGANIZATION**	**INDEPENDENT**	**OFF RESERVATION**	**MAJOR**	**FREQUENCY**
THE DREAMERS CHEROKEE PRODUCTIONS PO BOX 16101 SEATTLE, WA 98116 206-608-0876 800-484-6660 206-361-6312 FAX	X			X	X		Q
DRUM BEAT SEATTLE INDIAN HEALTH BOARD PO BOX 3364 612 12TH AVE SO #200 SEATTLE, WA 98114 206-324-9360			X		X		M
DSUQ-WUB SIATSUB SUQUAMISH TRIBAL CENTER BOX 498 SUQUAMISH, WA 98392 360-598-3311 360-598-6295 FAX		X					M
HUCHOOSEDAH NEWSLETTER SEATTLE PUBLIC SCHOOL INDIAN EDUCATION PROGRAM 815 FOURTH AVE N SEATTLE, WA 98109 206-298-7945			X		X		Q

NATIVE AMERICAN PRINT MEDIA							
PUBLICATION	INDIVIDUAL	TRIBE	ORGANIZATION	INDEPENDENT	OFF RESERVATION	MAJOR	FREQUENCY
INDIAN AFFAIRS NEWSLETTER GOVERNOR'S OFFICE OF INDIAN AFFAIRS 1515 S CHERRY PO BOX 40909 OLYMPIA, WA 98504 360-753-2411 360-586-3653 FAX			X		X		
INDIAN HERITAGE NEWSLETTER RAINIER BEACH HIGH SCHOOL 8815 SEWARD PK AVE SOUTH SEATTLE, WA 98109			X		X		
INDIANS OF ALL TRIBES CLUB BOX 777 MONROE, WA 98272	X		X	X			
KEE-YOKA PO BOX 817 LA CONNER, WA 98257 360-466-3163 360-466-5309 FAX		X					
KLAH-CHE-MIN SKOKOMISH TRIBAL NATION 80 TRIBAL CENTER SHELTON, WA 98584 360-426-4232 360-877-5943 FAX		X					

NATIVE AMERICAN PRINT MEDIA							
PUBLICATION	INDIVIDUAL	TRIBE	ORGANIZATION	INDEPENDENT	OFF RESERVATION	MAJOR	FREQUENCY
KUMTUX 4759 15TH AVE NE SEATTLE, WA 98105 206-528-2421 206-525-1218	X			X	X		M
MAKAH NEWSLETTER MAKAH TRIBAL COUNCIL BOX 115 NEAH BAY, WA 98357 360-645-2201 360-645-2323 FAX		X					
MUCKLESHOOT HEALTH NEWS 39015 172ND ST AUBURN, WA 98092 206-939-3311 X 157 206-939-5311 FAX			X				M
N.A.T.I.V.E. NEWSLETTER 1803 W MAXWELL SPOKANE, WA 99201 509-325-5502 509-325-9839			X		X		B
N.W.I.F. COMMISSION NEWS NORTHWEST INDIAN FISHERIES COMMISSION 6730 MARTIN WY E OLYMPIA, WA 98506 360-438-1180			X		X		M

NATIVE AMERICAN PRINT MEDIA							
PUBLICATION	**INDIVIDUAL**	**TRIBE**	**ORGANIZATION**	**INDEPENDENT**	**OFF RESERVATION**	**MAJOR**	**FREQUENCY**
NEWSLETTER AMERICAN INDIAN COMMUNITY CENTER 905 E THIRD SPOKANE, WA 99202 509-535-0886 X222 509-534-7210 FAX			X		X		
NEWSLETTER AMERICAN INDIAN STUDENT COMMISSION HUB 204 U, FK-30 UNIV OF WASHINGTON SEATTLE, WA 98195 206-685-4147			X		X		I
NISQUALLY INDIAN NATION 4820 SHE-NAH-NUM DR SE OLYMPIA, WA 98513 360-456-5221 360-438-8618 FAX		X					M
NORTHWEST INDIAN COLLEGE NEWS 2522 KWINA RD BELLINGHAM, WA 98226 360-676-2772 360-738-0136 FAX			X				
OCEAN EDGE:A JOURNAL OF APPLIED STORYTELLING PO BOX 98228 TACOMA, WA 98498 360-564-8350			X	X	X		

NATIVE AMERICAN PRINT MEDIA							
PUBLICATION	INDIVIDUAL	TRIBE	ORGANIZATION	INDEPENDENT	OFF RESERVATION	MAJOR	FREQUENCY
OLYMPIAN PO BOX 407 OLYMPIA, WA 98507					X	X	D
ON INDIAN LAND - NATIVE SOVEREIGNTY PO BOX 2104 SEATTLE, WA 98111 206-525-5086				X	X		Q
PORT GAMBLE TRIBAL NEWSLETTER PO BOX 280 KINGSTON, WA 98346 360-297-2646 360-297-7097 FAX		X					
PUYALLUP TRIBAL NEWS PUYALLUP TRIBAL NATION 2002 E 28TH ST TACOMA, WA 98404 360-597-6200 360-272-9514 FAX		X					M
QUILEUTE INDIAN NEWS BOX 279 LAPUSH, WA 98350 360-374-6163 360-374-6311 FAX		X					

NATIVE AMERICAN PRINT MEDIA							
PUBLICATION	**INDIVIDUAL**	**TRIBE**	**ORGANIZATION**	**INDEPENDENT**	**OFF RESERVATION**	**MAJOR**	**FREQUENCY**
QUINAULT STREET JOURNAL NUGGUAM QUINAULT TRIBAL AFFAIRS PO BOX 189 TAHOLAH, WA 98587 360-276-8211 360-276-4191 FAX			X	X			
RAVEN CHRONICALS PO BOX 95918 SEATTLE, WA 98145					X		Q
S'KLALLAM NEWS PO BOX 280 KINGSTON, WA 98346 360-297-4450 360-297-7097 FAX		X					M
SHOALWATER NEWSLETTER SHOALWATER BAY NATION PO BOX 130 TOKELAND, WA 98590 360-267-6766 360-267-6778 FAX		X					
SMOKE SIGNAL KALISPEL NATION PO BOX 39 USK, WA 99180 509-445-1147 509-445-1705 FAX		X					M

NATIVE AMERICAN PRINT MEDIA							
PUBLICATION	INDIVIDUAL	TRIBE	ORGANIZATION	INDEPENDENT	OFF RESERVATION	MAJOR	FREQUENCY
SNEE NEE CHUM NOOKSACK NATION BOX 157 DEMING, WA 98244 360-592-5176 360-592-5721		X					
SOVEREIGN NATIONS LUMMI INDIAN BUSINESS COUNCIL 2616 KWINA RD BELLINGHAM, WA 98226 360-738-2301 360-647-6298 FAX			X	X			M
SPIPA INTER TRIBAL NEWS SE 2750 OLD OLYMPIC HWY HOODSPORT, WA 98548 360-426-3990 360-427-8003 FAX			X		X		B
THE SQUAW'S MESSAGE SISTERHOOD OF AMERICAN INDIANS BOX 17 GIG HARBOR, WA 98335			X		X		
SQUOL QUOL LUMMI TRIBAL OFFICE 2616 KWINA RD BELLINGHAM, WA 98226 360-734-8180 360-384-5521 FAX			X				M

PUBLICATION	INDIVIDUAL	TRIBE	ORGANIZATION	INDEPENDENT	OFF RESERVATION	MAJOR	FREQUENCY
NATIVE AMERICAN PRINT MEDIA							
STOWW INDIAN VOICE BOX 578 SUMNER, WA 98390		X					
THE TALKING STICK SEATTLE NATIVE AMERICAN MINISTRY 302 N 78TH SEATTLE, WA 98103				X	X		
TRIBAL NEWS FOR REGION 10 C/O DEPT OF ECOLOGY PV-11 OLYMPIA, WA 98504			X				M
TRIBAL TRIBUNE COLVILLE TRIBE BOX 150 NESPELEM, WA 99155 509-634-8835 509-634-4617 FAX		X					M
UNITED INDIAN NEWS ALL TRIBES FOUNDATION BOX 99100 SEATTLE, WA 98199 206-285-4425			X		X		
WICAZO SA REVIEW INDIAN STUDIES JOURNAL EASTERN WASHINGTON UNIV MS 188 CHENEY, WA 99004 509-359-2441							

NATIVE AMERICAN PRINT MEDIA							
PUBLICATION	INDIVIDUAL	TRIBE	ORGANIZATION	INDEPENDENT	OFF RESERVATION	MAJOR	FREQUENCY
YAKAMA NATION REVIEW YAKAMA TRIBE PO BOX 310 TOPPENISH, WA 98948 509-865-5121 509-865-2794 FAX		X					B
WEST VIRGINIA							
ERIC/CRESS BULLETIN APPALACHIA EDUCATION LABORATORY PO BOX 1348 CHARLESTON, WV 25325 304-347-0400 800-624-9120 304-347-0487 FAX			X	X	X		Q
WISCONSIN							
BOARD IN BRIEF 124 S WEBSTER BOX 7841 MADISON, WI 53707							

NATIVE AMERICAN PRINT MEDIA							
PUBLICATION	**INDIVIDUAL**	**TRIBE**	**ORGANIZATION**	**INDEPENDENT**	**OFF RESERVATION**	**MAJOR**	**FREQUENCY**
DEPT OF MASS COMMUNIC-IND BOX 413 UNIVERSITY OF WISCONSIN MILWAUKEE, WI 53201			X				I
EXPLORE INDIAN COUNTRY RT 2, BOX 2900 HAYWARD, WI 54843 715-634-5226 715-634-3243 FAX	X			X			B
GREAT LAKES IND NEWS BUREAU RT 5 LARSON RD HAYWARD, WI 54843				X			
HO-CHUNK WO-LDUK HO-CHUNK NATION PUBLIC RELATIONS DEPT 133 MAIN ST BLACK RIVER FALLS, WI 54615 715-284-7824 800-331-7824 715-284-7634 FAX		X					U
HONOR DIGEST 2647 N STOWELL AVE MILWAUKEE, WI 53211 414-963-1324 414-963-0137 FAX			X	X	X		8X

NATIVE AMERICAN PRINT MEDIA							
PUBLICATION	INDIVIDUAL	TRIBE	ORGANIZATION	INDEPENDENT	OFF RESERVATION	MAJOR	FREQUENCY
KALIHWISAKS ONEIDA NATION NEWSPAPER PO BOX 365 ONEIDA, WI 54155 414-869-2772 414-869-2894 FAX		X					M
LAC COURTE OREILLES OJIBWA COLLEGE NEWS RR 2 BOX 2357 HAYWARD, WI 54843 715-634-4790 715-634-5049 FAX			X				W
LAC DU FLAMBEAU NEWS PO BOX 67 LAC DU FLAMBEAU, WI 54538 715-588-3303 715-588-9408 FAX		X					M
MASINAIGAN GREAT LAKES FISH & WILDLIFE COMMISSION PO BOX 9 ODANAH, WI 54861 715-682-6619 715-682-9294 FAX			X				B
MENOMINEE TRIBAL NEWS MENOMINEE TRIBAL NATION PO BOX 910 KESHENA, WI 54135 715-799-5167 715-799-4525 FAX		X					B

NATIVE AMERICAN PRINT MEDIA							
PUBLICATION	INDIVIDUAL	TRIBE	ORGANIZATION	INDEPENDENT	OFF RESERVATION	MAJOR	FREQUENCY
MIGIZI EXPRESS MILWAUKEE INDIAN COMM SCHOOL 3126 W KILBOURN AVE MILWAUKEE, WI 53208 414-345-3078 414-345-3079 FAX			X	X	X		M
NATIVE AMERICAN COUNCIL UNIVERSITY OF WISCONSIN 204 HAGESTAD STUDENT CENTER RIVER FALLS, WI 54022			X		X		
NEWS FROM INDIAN COUNTRY RT 2 BOX 2900-A HAYWARD, WI 54843 715-634-5226 715-634-3243 FAX	X			X			B
NEWS FROM THE SLOUGHS BAD RIVER CHIPPEWA NATION PO BOX 51 ODANAH, WI 54861 715-682-7893 715-682-7894 FAX		X					M
NORTHLAND NATIVE AMERICAN NEWS NORTHLAND COLLEGE ASHLAND, WI 54806 715-682-1224			X		X		

NATIVE AMERICAN PRINT MEDIA							
PUBLICATION	**INDIVIDUAL**	**TRIBE**	**ORGANIZATION**	**INDEPENDENT**	**OFF RESERVATION**	**MAJOR**	**FREQUENCY**
QUIN-A-MONTH-A STOCKBRIDGE-MUNSEE NATION RT 1 BOX 300 BOWLER, WI 54416 715-793-4111 715-793-4299 FAX		X					
RED CLIFF NEWSLETTER PO BOX 529 BAYFIELD, WI 54814 715-779-5805		X					
SHENANDOAH NEWSLETTER LALIHWISKAS 736 W OKLAHOMA APPLETON, WI 54914 414-832-9525	X			X	X		M
ST CROIX HEALTH NOTES TRIBAL HEALTH DEPT BOX 287 HERTEL, WI 54845		X	X				
TRAIL OF VISIONS N 3RD BLACK RIVER FALLS, WI 54615				X			

PUBLICATION	INDIVIDUAL	TRIBE	ORGANIZATION	INDEPENDENT	OFF RESERVATION	MAJOR	FREQUENCY
NATIVE AMERICAN PRINT MEDIA							
WYOMING							
AMERICAN INDIAN NEWS BOX 217 FT WASHAKIE, WY 82514 307-332-6120				X			
ARAPAHOE AGENCY COURIER ARAPAHOE, WY 82510 307-332-7812		X					
SMOKE SIGNALS ALL AMERICAN INDIAN DAYS BOX 451 SHERIDAN, WY 82801			X		X		
THUNDER CHILD NEWS THUNDER CHILD TREATMENT CTR BLDG 24 V.A.M.C. SHERIDAN, WY 82801 307-672-3484 307-672-0571 FAX			X		X		Q
WIND RIVER NEWS PO BOX 900 LANDER, WY 82520 307-332-2323 307-332-9332 FAX				X		X	W

NATIVE AMERICAN PRINT MEDIA								
PUBLICATION	INDIVIDUAL	TRIBE	ORGANIZATION	INDEPENDENT	OFF RESERVATION	MAJOR	FREQUENCY
THE WIND RIVER RENDEZVOUS ST STEPHENS INDIAN MISSION FOUNDATION PO BOX 278 ST STEPHENS, WY 82524 307-856-6797			X	X			Q

QUICK NOTES !

**Information for this page is only available in the Library Edition.

Fred Synder, Director, Consultant

N.A.²I.I.T.C

North American Native American Indian Information & Trade Center

QUICK NOTES !

**Information for this page is only available in the Library Edition.

Fred Synder, Director, Consultant

N.A.[2]I.I.T.C

North American Native American Indian Information & Trade Center

QUICK NOTES !

**Information for this page is only available in the Library Edition.

QUICK NOTES !

**Information for this page is only available in the Library Edition.

Fred Synder, Director, Consultant

N.A.²I.I.T.C

North American Native American Indian Information & Trade Center

QUICK NOTES !

**Information for this page is only available in the Library Edition.

Fred Synder, Director, Consultant

N.A.²I.I.T.C.

North American Native American Indian Information & Trade Center

QUICK NOTES !

**Information for this page is only available in the Library Edition.

Fred Synder, Director, Consultant

N.A.²I.I.T.C.

North American Native American Indian Information & Trade Center

QUICK NOTES !

**Information for this page is only available in the Library Edition.

Fred Synder, Director, Consultant

N.A.²I.I.T.C

North American Native American
Indian Information & Trade Center

QUICK NOTES !

**Information for this page is only available in the Library Edition.

Fred Synder, Director, Consultant

N.A.²I.I.T.C.

North American Native American Indian Information & Trade Center

QUICK NOTES !

**Information for this page is only available in the Library Edition.

QUICK NOTES !

**Information for this page is only available in the Library Edition.

Fred Synder, Director, Consultant

N.A.²I.I.T.C.

North American Native American
Indian Information & Trade Center

QUICK NOTES !

**Information for this page is only available in the Library Edition.

Fred Synder, Director, Consultant

N.A.²I.I.T.C.

North American Native American Indian Information & Trade Center

USA EVENTS CALENDAR

FAIRS

RODEOS

POW-WOWS

CONFERENCES

CONVENTIONS

CEREMONIALS

CELEBRATIONS

RUG AUCTIONS

PUEBLO EVENTS

INDIAN MARKETS

ARTS & CRAFTS SHOWS

EXPLANATION OF POW WOW CHARTS

MONTH/DAY/ WEEKEND	EVENT	PHONE/FAX	LOCATIONS

DATE STARTED	POW WOW	RODEO & FAIR	CAMPING	COST	SOCIAL

CEREMONY	MARKET	EDUCA-TIONAL	CELE-BRATION	ARTS & CRAFTS	HOST

MONTH/DAY/WEEKEND ...most Indian events always occur on a specific weekend of the month each year. Single date, specific holiday weekends (which move each year) are marked with an asterisk (*) - Easter, Thanksgiving, Veteran's Day, etc.

EVENT ...name of event and full name and address of sponsoring agency

PHONE/FAX ...contact phone number for sponsoring agency with back up phone number to tribe, chamber of commerce, urban group, etc.

LOCATION ...Physical place of event; gym, pow wow grounds and city and state where held

DATE FIRST STARTED ...first year of event

POW WOW ...pow wow event only listing both social and competition

RODEO/FAIR ...cowboy rodeo, amusement rides, commercial entertainment

CAMPING	...overnight camping for dancers, drums, participants; visitors should check with committee for availability of camping
COST	...F - Free $ - Admission fee
SOCIAL	...non competition pow wow, tribal social dances of tribes that do not pow wow
CEREMONIAL	...mostly tribal dances of ceremonial or religious nature ie Sundance, Jumpdance...
MARKET	...usually arts & crafts sales and exhibition only
EDUCATIONAL	...cultural displays by tribes, clubs, organizations and health agencies to educate the public
CELEBRATION	...events that celebrate a treaty signing, chief's birthday or death, significant event of importance to sponsoring group
ARTS & CRAFTS	...exhibit of arts and crafts for sale to the general public by various artists from many tribes
HOST	T - Tribal sponsored event I - Indian organization sponsored event C - Non-Indian sponsored event

POW WOW PROTOCOL

Ensuring a pleasant experience for both you and the sponsor.

- Pow-wows are <u>not</u> tourist attractions; that is the one basic fact that many visitors fail to grasp.

- The dance will start when the time is right and end when the time is right whether you are there or not.

- Each dance will be held because it is part of the religious life of the Indian - a prayer made visible.

- No alcoholic beverages should be consumed.

- Do not cross, enter, or stand in the sacred areas known as the dance arena for any reason unless asked to participate in a social dance by the master of ceremonies.

- Ask before you take pictures of an individual dancer or drum. Many dancers have items that are not to be photographed. Also, many dancers have items passed down in the family that belong only to certain tribes, clans or individuals.

- Do not interfere with any dancers, and do not touch any drum.

- Commercial use of any photos/video has been a major concern at most pow-wows. So it is the responsibility of the master of ceremonies to let you know when <u>not to shoot.</u>

- Permission for commercial use should be in writing from the pow-wow sponsor for any photos/video.

- Proper courtesy and respect for the event should be shown in dress, mannerisms and cultural differences at each event.

POW WOW NOTES

Additional information:

Some events are one day, some are two and some are three days, still others change each year; we noted most of the single day events and placed them at the beginning of each month. Space is provided after each month of the year for you to add your favorite Indian event in case we missed it. *Remember to send us a copy for our update.*

Remember that the committee for most events is different each year, therefore we have listed at least two phone numbers as back-ups for confirmation of the event. **CALL BEFORE YOU GO !**

APACHE

Apache Sunrise Dances (Puberty Dances) are held every weekend throughout the year on the San Carlos, White Mountain, Mescalero, Jicarilla and other Apache Reservations. Contact the tribal office of each nation listed in the Native American Directory.

HOPI

Traditional Hopi Dances are held thru late winter, spring and summer each weekend but check with the tribal office to see if visitors are allowed! Sometimes these dances are not open to the public.

NAVAJO

Traditional dances, games, and events are held on the Navajo Reservation all year! Check with the Navajo Tourism office at 602-871-6659 or 602-871-6436 for more information.

NORTHWEST COAST

Potlatch and water canoe races are held sporadically by the Northwest Coast tribes by various canoe clubs, but a list is not available at this time.

MONTH/DAY/ WEEKEND	EVENT	PHONE/FAX	LOCATION	DATE FIRST STARTED	POW WOW	RODEO & FAIR
JANUARY	*YOUR EVENT CAN BE LISTED ! FAX US AT (520) 622-4900*					
1ST	TURTLE, CORN & VARIOUS DANCES (MOST PUEBLOS)	505-843-7270 800-288-0721	TAOS, SANTO DOMINGO SAN FELIPE, COCHITI,PICURIS NEW MEXICO	∞		
6TH	THREE KING'S DAY & INSTALLATION OF NEW GOVERNORS & OFFICIALS - DEER, BUFFALO, EAGLE, ELK DANCES	505-843-7235 800-288-0721	MOST NORTHERN & SOUTHERN PUEBLOS, NEW MEXICO	∞		
1ST WEEKEND	INDIAN AMERICA NEW YEAR'S COMPETITION POW WOW 2830 S THRASHER AVE TUCSON, AZ 85713	520-622-4900 520-292-0779	AMIGOS INDOOR COMPLEX TUCSON, ARIZONA	1989	✓	
5,6,7 '96 3,4,5 '97 2,3,4 '98 1,2,3 '99	NEW YEARS ANNUAL P/W LCO TRIBAL NATION RT 2 BOX 2700 HAYWARD, WI 54843	715-634-4795 715-634-8934	TRIBAL GROUNDS HAYWARD, WISCONSIN		✓	
2ND WEEKEND	SANTA MONICA INDIAN CEREMONIAL SHOW & P/W 8921 CARBURTON ST LONG BEACH, CA 90808	310-430-5112	SANTA MONICA CIVIC AUDITORIUM SANTA MONICA, CALIFORNIA		✓	
12-14 '96 10-12 '97 9-11 '98 8-10 '99	*"1200 INDIAN EVENTS"* *POW WOW ON THE RED ROAD*					
3RD WEEKEND	LIHA SOCIAL, SEMINAR... LACONIA INDIAN HIST ASSN 295 COURT ST LACONIA, NH 03246	603-783-9922 603-539-4386	V.F.W. LACONIA, NEW HAMPSHIRE			
19-21 '96 17-19 '97 16-18 '98 15-17 '99						
FEBRUARY						
1ST WEEKEND	LINCOLN'S BIRTHDAY & SELF-GOV'T SOVEREIGNTY POW WOW PO BOX C WARM SPRINGS, OR 97761	503-553-2282	LONGHOUSE WARM SPRINGS, OREGON		✓	
2,3,4 '96 31- 2 '97 30- 1 '98 5,6,7 '99	SAN MATEO AMERICAN INDIAN EXPO AMER IND TRADERS GUILD 3876 E FEDORA AVE FRESNO, CA 93726	209-221-4355 209-221-0844	SAN MATEO EXPO CENTER SAN MATEO, CALIFORNIA	1991	✓	
	WASHINGTON'S BIRTHDAY WEEKEND POW WOW PO BOX 151 TOPPENISH, WA 98948	509-865-5121	TOPPENISH COMM CTR TOPPENISH, WASHINGTON		✓	
2ND WEEKEND	PLEASANTON AMERICAN INDIAN EXPO AMER IND TRADERS GUILD 3876 E FEDORA AVE FRESNO, CA 93726	209-221-4355 209-221-0844	ALAMEDA FAIRGROUNDS PLEASANTON, CALIFORNIA	1989		
9-11 '96 7- 9 '97 6- 8 '98 12-14 '99	SEMINOLE TRIBAL FAIR & RODEO SEMINOLE NATION 6073 STIRLING RD HOLLYWOOD, FL 33024	305-584-0400 305-321-1051	TRIBAL FAIR GROUNDS HOLLYWOOD, FLORIDA	1971	✓	✓

CALL BEFORE YOU GO! ∞ OLDER THAN RECORDED HISTORY

POW WOW CALENDAR 1996-1999

CAMPING	COST	SOCIAL	CEREMONY	MARKET	EDUCA-TIONAL	CELE-BRATION	ARTS & CRAFTS	HOST
	F		✓			✓		T
	F		✓			✓		T
	$			✓	✓		✓	I
	F	✓					✓	T
	$			✓			✓	C
	F	✓			✓		✓	C
✓	F	✓				✓	✓	T
				✓			✓	C
✓	F	✓		✓		✓	✓	I
				✓			✓	C
✓	$	✓		✓	✓		✓	T

T - TRIBAL EVENT **I - INDIAN SPONSOR** **C - NON INDIAN SPONSOR**

MONTH/DAY/ WEEKEND	EVENT	PHONE/FAX	LOCATION	DATE FIRST STARTED	POW WOW	RODEO & FAIR
FEBRUARY	***YOUR EVENT CAN BE LISTED ! FAX US AT (520) 622-4900***					
3RD WEEKEND	NATIVE AMERICAN HERITAGE RADFORD UNIV RADFORD, VA 24141	703-633-1871	PETERS GYM RADFORD, VIRGINIA	1988	✓	
16-18 '96 14-16 '97 20-22 '98 19-21 '99	O'ODHAM TASH INDIAN FESTIVAL PO BOX 11165 CASA GRANDE, AZ 85230	520-836-4723 520-836-2125	CITY WIDE CASA GRANDE, ARIZONA	1967	✓	✓
	TONY WHITE CLOUD COMPETITION HOOP DANCE THE HEARD MUSEUM 22 E MONTE VISTA RD PHOENIX, AZ 85004	602-251-0212	AMPHITHEATER PHOENIX, ARIZONA	1991		
	TULSA INDIAN ARTS FESTIVAL & POW WOW PO BOX 52694 TULSA, OK 74152	918-583-2253	EXPO STATE PAVILION TULSA, OKLAHOMA		✓	
4TH WEEKEND	AMERICAN INDIAN WESTERN ART ANTIQUE SHOW & SALE 2320 W 25TH ST LOS ANGELES, CA 90018	714-732-8605	CONVENTION CENTER PASADENA, CALIFORNIA	1990		
23-25 '96 21-23 '97 27- 1 '98 26-28 '99						
MARCH	***"1200 INDIAN EVENTS"*** ***<u>POW WOW ON THE RED ROAD</u>***					
EASTER *	* BASKET AND CORN DANCES VARIOUS DANCES	505-843-7270 800-288-0721	MOST PUEBLOS NEW MEXICO	∞		
1ST WEEKEND	GATHERING OF CLANS METLAKATLA INDIAN CMTY PO BOX 8 METLAKATLA, AK 99780	907-886-4441 907-886-7997	METLAKATLA, ALASKA			
1,2,3 '96 31,1,2 '97 6,7,8 '98 5,6,7 '99	HEARD MUSEUM GUILD INDIAN FAIR & MARKET HEARD MUSEUM 22 E MONTE VISTA RD PHOENIX, AZ 85004	602-252-8840	THE HEARD MUSEUM PHOENIX, ARIZONA	1958		
	OKLAHOMA FED INDIAN WOMEN P/W / JR MISS INDIAN OKLAHOMA 515 SE 45TH OKLAHOMA CITY, OK 73129	405-632-5227	STATE FAIRGROUNDS OKLAHOMA CITY, OKLAHOMA		✓	
2ND WEEKEND	EH-PAH-TAS POW WOW NEZ PERCE INDOOR CELEB. NEZ PERCE NATION PO BOX 305 LAPWAI, ID 83540	208-843-2267 208-843-2253	LAPWAI, IDAHO		✓	
8,9,10 '96 7,8,9 '97 13-15 '98 12-14 '99	SAN DIEGO STATE UNIV. ANNUAL POW WOW AMERICAN INDIAN STUDIES COLLEGE ARTS & LETTERS SAN DIEGO, CA 92182-0387	619-594-6991 619-594-2764	MONTEZUMA HALL, AZTEC CTR SAN DIEGO, CALIFORNIA	1971	✓	
	WA:AK POW WOW WA:AK POW WOW COMMITTEE 2018 W SAN XAVIER RD TUCSON, AZ 85746	520-294-5727	BALL PARK, SAN XAVIER MISSION TUCSON, ARIZ	1983	✓	

CALL BEFORE YOU GO !

POW WOW CALENDAR 1996-1999

CAMPING	COST	SOCIAL	CEREMONY	MARKET	EDUCA-TIONAL	CELE-BRATION	ARTS & CRAFTS	HOST
		✓						I
✓	$	✓	✓	✓			✓	C
	$	✓	✓		✓	✓	✓	C
	$	✓		✓			✓	I
	$			✓			✓	C
	F		✓			✓		I
	$	✓	✓	✓	✓		✓	T
	$	✓		✓			✓	C
		✓				✓		I
	F	✓	✓			✓	✓	T
	F						✓	I
✓	$	✓					✓	I

T - TRIBAL EVENT I - INDIAN SPONSOR C - NON INDIAN SPONSOR

MONTH/DAY/ WEEKEND	EVENT	PHONE/FAX	LOCATION	DATE FIRST STARTED	POW WOW	RODEO & FAIR
MARCH	*YOUR EVENT CAN BE LISTED ! FAX US AT (520) 622-4900*					
2ND WEEKEND	WINTERHAVEN POW WOW PO BOX 11352 YUMA, AZ 85364	619-572-0222 619-572-0213	SAN PASQUAL HIGH SCHOOL WINTERHAVEN CALIFORNIA	1980	✓	
3RD WEEKEND	DENVER MARCH POW WOW PO BOX 19178 DENVER, CO 80219	303-936-4826	DENVER COLISEUM DENVER, COLORADO	1974	✓	
15-17 '96 14-16 '97 20-22 '98 19-21 '99	GREAT FALLS NATIVE AMERICAN ART ASSN PO BOX 2429 GREAT FALLS, MT 59403	406-791-2212 406-761-6251	PONDEROSA INN GREAT FALLS, MONTANA	1982		
	TRADITIONAL PEOPLE'S GATHERING CRAFTON HILLS COLLEGE 11711 SAND CANYON RD YUCAIPA, CA 92399	909-389-3358 909-389-9141	CAMPUS WIDE CRAFTON COLLEGE YUCAIPA CALIFORNIA	1991	✓	
4TH WEEKEND	DOUG ALLARD AUCTIONS MILLION DOLLAR INDIAN AUCTION PO BOX 460 ST IGNATIUS, MT 59865	406-745-2951 800-821-3318 406-745-2961	HOLIDAY INN PHOENIX, ARIZONA	1989		
22-24 '96 21-23 '97 27-29 '98 26-28 '99	EDISTO INDIAN CULTURAL FESTIVAL EDISTO TRIBAL COUNCIL 113 TEEPEE RIDGEVILLE, SC 29472	803-871-2126 803-871-3453	SUMMERVILLE, SOUTH CAROLINA		✓	
	NATCHEZ ANNUAL POW WOW 150 JEFFERSON DAVIS HWY NATCHEZ, MS 39120	601-446-6502 601-466-5117 601-445-0210	GRAND VILLAGE OF NATCHEZ INDIANS NATCHEZ, MISSISSIPPI		✓	
APRIL	*"1200 INDIAN EVENTS"* ***POW WOW ON THE RED ROAD***					
1ST WEEKEND	BLACKLODGE CELEBRATION YAKIMA INDIAN NATION PO BOX 151 TOPPENISH, WA 98948	509-865-5121 509-865-5528	WHITE SWAN PAVILION WHITE SWAN, WASHINGTON		✓	
5,6,7 '96 4,5,6 '97 3,4,5 '98 2,3,4 '99	D.Q. CULTURAL DAYS D.Q. UNIVERSITY POW WOW COMMITTEE PO BOX 409 DAVIS, CA 95617	916-758-0470 916-758-2518	U.C. DAVIS CAMPUS DAVIS, CALIFORNIA	1969	✓	
	Y-M SALMON FEAST & POW WOW PO BOX 365 THE DALLES, OR 97058	503-298-1559	CEULO VILLAGE, OREGON	1800	✓	

CALL BEFORE YOU GO !

POW WOW CALENDAR 1996-1999

CAMPING	COST	SOCIAL	CEREMONY	MARKET	EDUCA-TIONAL	CELE-BRATION	ARTS & CRAFTS	HOST
	$						✓	I
	$			✓	✓		✓	I
	F			✓			✓	C
✓	F	✓			✓		✓	I
	$			✓	✓		✓	I
✓	$	✓				✓	✓	T
✓	$						✓	I
	F	✓						I
	F	✓		✓	✓	✓	✓	I
✓	F	✓	✓				✓	I

T - TRIBAL EVENT I - INDIAN SPONSOR C - NON INDIAN SPONSOR

MONTH/DAY/ WEEKEND	EVENT	PHONE/FAX	LOCATION	DATE FIRST STARTED	POW WOW	RODEO & FAIR
APRIL	*YOUR EVENT CAN BE LISTED ! FAX US AT (520) 622-4900*					
2ND WEEKEND	ARIZONA STATE UNIV. SPRING COMPETITION ASU POW WOW COMMITTEE PO BOX 248 TEMPE, AZ 85280	602-965-5224	ASU BAND PRACTICE FIELD 6TH & RURAL RD TEMPE, ARIZONA	1986	✓	
12-14 '96 11-13 '97 10-12 '98 9-11 '99	CHEYENNE-ARAPAHO CELEBRATION PO BOX 38 CONCHO, OK 73022	405-832-3538 405-262-0345	CORDELL, OKLAHOMA		✓	
	NAVAJO COMMUNITY COLLEGE POW WOW PO BOX 126 TSAILE, AZ 86556	520-724-6219 520-724-3311	TSAILE, ARIZONA	1971	✓	
	TEWAQUACHI POW POW NATIVE AMERICAN STUDIES CSU FRESNO FRESNO, CA 93726	209-266-3277	CALIFORNIA STATE UNIV. FRESNO, CALIFORNIA	1982	✓	
3RD WEEKEND	GATHERING OF NATIONS POW WOW UNIV. OF NEW MEXICO PO BOX 75102, STA. 14 ALBUQUERQUE, NM 87194	505-836-2810	UNIV. OF NEW MEXICO ARENA (THE PIT) ALBUQUERQUE, NEW MEXICO	1984	✓	
14-16 '96 19-21 '97 17-19 '98 16-18 '99	HALIWA SAPONI POW WOW HALIWA SAPONI NATION PO BOX 99 HOLLISTER, NC 27844	919-586-4017	HALIWA SCHOOL HOLLISTER, NC	1965	✓	
	SHERMAN INDIAN HIGH SCHOOL ANNUAL P/W SHERMAN INDIAN SCHOOL 9010 MAGNOLIA AVE RIVERSIDE, CA 92503	714-351-6315 714-276-6309	SCHOOL CAMPUS RIVERSIDE, CALIFORNIA		✓	
	WESTERN WASHINGTON UNIV. ANNUAL POW WOW NASO 516 HIGH BELLINGHAM, WA 98225	360-676-3000	WESTERN WASHINGTON UNIVERSITY BELLINGHAM, WASHINGTON	1985	✓	
4TH WEEKEND	MAPLE SYRUP FESTIVAL G.L.I.C.A. PO BOX 1181 BEDFORD, MA 01730	508-453-7182	TYNGSBOROUGH STATE FOREST LOWELL, MASSACHUSETTS			
26-28 '96 25-27 '97 24-26 '98 23-25 '99	TIA-PIAH POW WOW TEXAS GULF ASSN 8926 WOODLYN HOUSTON, TX 77078	713-423-0583	SALLAS COUNTY PARK NEW CANEY, TEXAS		✓	
5TH WEEKEND	BACONE COLLEGE SPRING POW WOW NASO 99 BACONE RD MUSKOGEE, OK 74403	918-683-4581	MUSKOGEE, OKLAHOMA		✓	
LAST WEEKEND	TATE HOUSE INDIAN FESTIVAL & POW WOW PO BOX 33 TATE, GA 30177	800-342-7515 404-735-3122	TATE HOUSE, HWY 53 TATE, GEORGIA		✓	

CALL BEFORE YOU GO !

POW WOW CALENDAR 1996-1999

CAMPING	COST	SOCIAL	CEREMONY	MARKET	EDUCA-TIONAL	CELE-BRATION	ARTS & CRAFTS	HOST
✓	$				✓		✓	I
	F	✓				✓	✓	T
	F	✓					✓	I
	F	✓					✓	I
	$	✓		✓				I
✓	$	✓			✓		✓	T
	$	✓		✓	✓		✓	I
	$	✓			✓		✓	I
	F	✓		✓		✓		I
✓	F	✓					✓	C
	F	✓						I
	$					✓	✓	I

T - TRIBAL EVENT I - INDIAN SPONSOR C - NON INDIAN SPONSOR

MONTH/DAY/ WEEKEND	EVENT	PHONE/FAX	LOCATION	DATE FIRST STARTED	POW WOW	RODEO & FAIR
MAY	*YOUR EVENT CAN BE LISTED ! FAX US AT (520) 622-4900*					
VARIES	BLESSING OF THE FIELDS, CORN OR FLAG DANCE PUEBLO OF TESUQUE RT 11 BOX 1 SANTA FE, NM 87501	505-983-2667	TESUQUE PUEBLO PLAZA TESUQUE, NEW MEXICO	∞		
1ST WEEKEND	CHAUBUNAGUNGA NIPMUCKS PLANTING MOON CEREMONY 20 SINGLETARY AVE SUTTON, MA 01527	508-943-4569	NIPMUCK RESERVATION SCHOOL WEBSTER, MASSACHUSETTS		✓	
3,4,5 '96 2,3,4 '97 1,2,3 '98 30,1,2 '99	SOUTHERN UTE TRIBAL BEAR DANCE SOUTHERN UTE NATION PO BOX 737 IGNACIO, CO 81137	970-563-4525 970-563-4033	CEREMONIAL GROUNDS IGNACIO, COLORADO	∞		
	TURTLE POW WOW NATIVE AMERICAN CENTER FOR LIVING ARTS PO BOX 945 NIAGARA FALLS, NY 14302	716-284-2427 716-284-0477	NATIVE AMERICAN CTR FOR LIVING ARTS NIAGARA FALLS, NEW YORK	1981	✓	
2ND WEEKEND	DARTMOUTH COLLEGE P/W NATIVE AMERICAN PROGRAM 323 COLLEGE HALL HANOVER, NH 03755	603-646-2110 603-646-2875	DARTMOUTH CAMPUS HANOVER, NEW HAMPSHIRE		✓	
10-12 '96 9-11 '97 8-10 '98 7- 9 '99	HASKELL INDIAN NATIONS UNIV. SPRING POW WOW N.A.S.A. PO BOX H1304 LAWRENCE, KS 66044	913-749-8461 913-749-8448	HASKELL INDIAN NATIONS UNIV. CAMPUS LAWRENCE, KANSAS	1925	✓	
	MAY-ALYMA ROOT FESTIVAL NEZ PERCE NATION PO BOX 305 LAPWAI, ID 83540	208-843-2253 208-843-2036	KAMIAH, IDAHO	1900		
	STANFORD POW WOW STANFORD UNIVERSITY AMERICAN INDIAN ORG. PO BOX 2990 STANFORD, CA 94309	415-723-4078 415-725-6944	STANFORD UNIV. CAMPUS STANFORD, CALIFORNIA	1971	✓	
3RD WEEKEND	BLACK LEGGINS CEREMONY KIOWA INDIAN NATION PO BOX 369 CARNEGIE, OK 73015	405-247-6651 405-247-3987	INDIAN CITY DANCE GROUNDS ANADARKO, OKLAHOMA		✓	
17-19 '96 16-18 '97 15-17 '98 14-16 '99	CHEHAW NATIONAL INDIAN FESTIVAL PO BOX 3492 ALBANY, GA 31706	912-436-1625	CHEHAW PARK ALBANY, GEORGIA		✓	
	DE ANZA COLLEGE SPRING POW WOW & INDIAN ARTS 21250 STEVENS CREEK BLVD CUPERTINO, CA 95014	408-864-5448 408-733-8315	DE ANZA COLLEGE CAMPUS CUPERTINO, CALIFORNIA	1981	✓	
	SAN DIEGO AMERICAN INDIAN CULTURAL DAYS INDIAN HUMAN RESOURCE 4040 30TH # A SAN DIEGO, CA 92104	619-281-5964	BALBOA PARK PARK BLVD & PRESIDENTS WAY SAN DIEGO, CA	1990	✓	
	"1200 INDIAN EVENTS" *POW WOW ON THE RED ROAD*					

CALL BEFORE YOU GO !

POW WOW CALENDAR 1996-1999

CAMPING	COST	SOCIAL	CEREMONY	MARKET	EDUCA-TIONAL	CELE-BRATION	ARTS & CRAFTS	HOST
✓	F		✓			✓	✓	T
✓	$	✓	✓			✓	✓	T
✓	F	✓	✓			✓	✓	I
	$	✓		✓	✓		✓	I
✓	$	✓					✓	I
✓	$	✓					✓	I
	F	✓	✓			✓		I
✓	F	✓		✓	✓		✓	I
	F	✓	✓					I
✓	$	✓	✓	✓	✓		✓	T
	F	✓			✓		✓	I
	F					✓	✓	I

T - TRIBAL EVENT I - INDIAN SPONSOR C - NON INDIAN SPONSOR

MONTH/DAY/ WEEKEND	EVENT	PHONE/FAX	LOCATION	DATE FIRST STARTED	POW WOW	RODEO & FAIR
MAY						
4TH WEEKEND	*CHEROKEE MEMORIAL DAY POW WOW CHEROKEE NATION PO BOX 460 CHEROKEE, NC 28719	800-438-1601 704-497-9195	CEREMONIAL GROUNDS CHEROKEE, NORTH CAROLINA	1985	✓	
*MEMORIAL DAY	*DELAWARE ANNUAL POW WOW DELAWARE TRIBE 108 S SENECA BARTLESVILLE, OK 74003	918-336-4925 918-531-2526	FRED FALL-LEAF FARM COPAN, OKLAHOMA	1964	✓	
24-26 '96 23-25 '97 22-24 '98 21-23 '99	INDIAN PLAZA INTER-TRIBAL POW WOW INDIAN PLAZA RT 2 CHARLEMONT, MA 01339	603-882-6007 413-339-4096	INDIAN PLAZA RT 2 CHARLEMONT, MASSACHUSETTS		✓	
	*OMAHA MEMORIAL DAY CELEBRATION OMAHA TRIBAL COUNCIL PO BOX 368 MACY, NE 68039	402-837-5391	POW WOW GROUNDS MACY, NEBRASKA		✓	✓
5TH WEEKEND LAST WEEKEND	CHOCTAW ANNUAL RODEO PO DRAWER 1210 DURANT, OK 74710	405-924-8280	JONES ACADEMY HARTSHORNE, OKLAHOMA			✓
— '96 30- 1 '97 29-31 '98 28-30 '99	WEASELTAIL POW WOW PO BOX 151 TOPPENISH, WA 98948	509-865-5121	WHITE SWAN PAVILION WHITE SWAN, WASHINGTON		✓	
JUNE	***YOUR EVENT CAN BE LISTED ! FAX US AT (520) 622-4900***					
1ST WEEKEND	ALABAMA-COUSHATTA P/W ALABAMA COUSHATTA TRIBAL NATION RT 3 BOX 659 LIVINGSTON, TX 77351	409-563-4391 409-563-4397	TRIBAL GROUNDS LIVINGSTON, TEXAS		✓	
31-2 '96 6,7,8 '97 5,6,7 '98 4,5,6 '99	KOOTENAI ANNUAL POW WOW TRIBAL OFFICE PO BOX 1269 BONNERS FERRY, ID 83805	208-843-2267 208-267-3519	POW WOW GROUNDS BONNERS FERRY, IDAHO		✓	
	OTSININGO INDIAN CRAFT FAIR & POW WOW PO BOX 288, HILTON RD APALACHIN, NY 13732	607-625-2221	RT 434, WATERMAN CONSERVATION CENTER APALACHIN, NY	1980	✓	
	UTE MOUNTAIN BEAR DANCE UTE MTN UTE NATION PO BOX 52 TOWAOC, CO 81344	970-565-3751 970-565-7412	TRIBAL FAIRGROUNDS TOWAOC, COLORADO			
2ND WEEKEND	OSAGE DANCE, ANNUAL OSAGE NATION ADMINISTRATION BLDG PAWHUSKA, OK 74056	918-885-2853	OSAGE INDIAN VILLAGE HOMINY, OKLAHOMA		✓	
	RED EARTH POW WOW NATIVE AMERICAN CULTURAL FESTIVAL 2100 NE 52ND ST OKLAHOMA CITY, OK 73111	405-427-5228 800-652-6552	DOWNTOWN OKLAHOMA CITY, OKLAHOMA		✓	

CALL BEFORE YOU GO !

POW WOW CALENDAR 1996-1999

CAMPING	COST	SOCIAL	CEREMONY	MARKET	EDUCATIONAL	CELEBRATION	ARTS & CRAFTS	HOST
✓	$	✓					✓	T
	F	✓					✓	T
✓	$						✓	I
✓	F	✓			✓	✓	✓	T
	$							I
	F	✓				✓	✓	I
✓	F	✓					✓	T
✓	F	✓				✓	✓	T
✓	$	✓		✓	✓		✓	C
✓	F	✓	✓			✓	✓	T
	F	✓						T
	$			✓		✓	✓	I

T - TRIBAL EVENT   I - INDIAN SPONSOR   C - NON INDIAN SPONSOR

MONTH/DAY/ WEEKEND	EVENT	PHONE/FAX	LOCATION	DATE FIRST STARTED	POW WOW	RODEO & FAIR
JUNE	***YOUR EVENT CAN BE LISTED ! FAX US AT (520) 622-4900***					
2ND WEEKEND	SAC & FOX ALL INDIAN PRO RODEO SAC & FOX INDIAN NATION RT 2 BOX 246 STROUD, OK 74079	405-273-0579 405-275-4270	5 1/2 MILES SOUTH ON HWY 377 STROUD, OKLAHOMA			✓
7,8,9 '96 13-15 '97 12-14 '98 11-13 '99	WHITE EARTH ANNUAL TRADITIONAL POW WOW WHITE EARTH NATION PO BOX 418 WHITE EARTH, MN 56591	218-983-3285 218-983-3641	POW WOW GROUNDS WHITE EARTH, MINNESOTA	1867	✓	
3RD WEEKEND	CHIEF JOSEPH MEMORIAL POW WOW NEZ PERCE TRIBAL OFFICE PO BOX 305 LAPWAI, ID 83540	208-843-7141 208-843-2253 208-843-7354	POW WOW GROUNDS LAPWAI, IDAHO		✓	
14-16 '96 20-22 '97 19-21 '98 18-20 '99	CREEK NATION FESTIVAL CREEK NATION OF OK FESTIVAL COMMITTEE PO BOX 580 OKMULGEE, OK 74447	405-756-8700 405-756-2911	POW WOW GROUNDS OKMULGEE, OKLAHOMA		✓	
	LUMMI STOMMISH WATER FESTIVAL LUMMI NATION 2616 KWINA RD BELLINGHAM, WA 98226	360-647-6218 360-734-8180 360-384-5521	NEAR GOOSEBERRY POINT FERNDALE, WASHINGTON	1987	✓	
	MOWA BAND OF CHOCTAWS ANNUAL POW WOW POW WOW CHAIRPERSON RT 1 BOX 330A MT VERNON, AL 36560	205-829-5500 205-829-5008	MT VERNON, ALABAMA		✓	
4TH WEEKEND	AMERICAN INDIAN WORLD PEACE DAY PO BOX 39 CROW AGENCY, MT 59022	406-638-2621 406-638-2382	LITTLE BIG HORN BATTLEFIELD CROW AGENCY, MONTANA			
21-23 '96 27-29 '97 26-28 '98 25-27 '99	COQUILLE RESTORATION POW WOW COQUILLE INDIAN NATION 250 HULL COOS BAY, OR 97420	503-267-4587 503-269-2573	OLD TOWN BRANDON, OREGON		✓	
	MIAMI TRADITIONAL P/W MIAMI VALLEY COUNCIL NATIVE AMERICANS PO BOX 637 DAYTON, OH 45401	513-275-8599	XENIA, OHIO	1988	✓	
	PI-UME-SHA POW WOW & TREATY DAYS WARM SPRINGS NATION PO BOX C WARM SPRINGS, OR 97761	503-553-1161 503-553-1294	CEREMONIAL GROUNDS WARM SPRINGS, OREGON		✓	✓
JULY	***"1200 INDIAN EVENTS"***		***POW WOW ON THE RED ROAD***			
1ST - 10TH	DRUM & FEATHER CLUB'S ANNUAL FOURTH OF JULY POW WOW PO BOX 150 NESPELEM, WA 99155	509-634-4711 509-634-4116	COLVILLE INDIAN AGENCY NESPELEM, WASHINGTON		✓	✓

CALL BEFORE YOU GO !

POW WOW CALENDAR 1996-1999

CAMPING	COST	SOCIAL	CEREMONY	MARKET	EDUCA-TIONAL	CELE-BRATION	ARTS & CRAFTS	HOST
	$							I
✓	F					✓	✓	T
✓	F	✓				✓	✓	T
	F	✓				✓		T
✓	F	✓				✓	✓	T
✓	F					✓	✓	T
	$				✓	✓	✓	I
	F	✓				✓		T
	$	✓				✓	✓	I
✓	F	✓	✓			✓	✓	T
✓	F	✓				✓	✓	I

T - TRIBAL EVENT **I - INDIAN SPONSOR** **C - NON INDIAN SPONSOR**

MONTH/DAY/ WEEKEND	EVENT	PHONE/FAX	LOCATION	DATE FIRST STARTED	POW WOW	RODEO & FAIR
JULY	*YOUR EVENT CAN BE LISTED ! FAX US AT (520) 622-4900*					
1ST WEEKEND	ARLEE POW WOW & CELEBRATION PO BOX 278 PABLO, MT 59855	406-745-3525 406-676-2770	FLATHEAD RESERVATION ARLEE, MONTANA		✓	
5,6,7 '96 4,5,6 '97 3,4,5 '98 2,3,4 '99	MASHPEE ANNUAL P/W PEOPLE OF THE FIRST LIGHT MASHPEE WAMPANOAG PO BOX 1048 MASHPEE, MA 02649	508-477-0208 800-352-0711	HERITAGE PARK NORTH RT 130 MASHPEE, MASSACHUSETTS	1988	✓	
	MESCALERO APACHE GAHAN CEREMONIAL MESCALERO APACHE NTN PO BOX 176 MESCALERO, NM 87340	505-671-4495	POW WOW GROUNDS MESCALERO, NEW MEXICO			
2ND WEEKEND	AMERICAN INDIAN INTER-TRIBAL CULTURAL ORG. TWINBROOK STATION PO BOX 775 ROCKVILLE, MD 20848	301-869-9381	RT 219 GARRETT COUNTY FAIRGROUNDS MCHENRY, MARYLAND	1982	✓	
12-14 '96 11-13 '97 10-12 '98 9-11 '99	BARRYVILLE POW WOW INDIAN LEAGUE OF THE AMERICAS PO BOX 613 PORT JERVIS, NY 12771	718-836-6255 914-858-8309	INDIAN LAND BARRYVILLE, NEW YORK	1984	✓	
	SOUTHERN UTE SUN DANCE SOUTHERN UTE NATION PO BOX 737 IGNACIO, CO 81137	970-563-4525 970-563-4033	POW WOW GROUNDS IGNACIO, COLORADO			
	TAOS PUEBLO POW WOW POW WOW COMMITTEE PO BOX 2441 TAOS, NM 87571	505-758-8731 505-758-1159	POW WOW GROUNDS TAOS, NEW MEXICO	1984	✓	
3RD WEEKEND	CHEYENNE HOMECOMING POW WOW PO BOX 38 CONCHO, OK 73022	405-262-0345	POW WOW GROUNDS CLINTON, OKLAHOMA		✓	
19-21 '96 18-20 '97 17-19 '98 16-18 '99	CHOCTAW INDIAN FAIR MISSISSIPPI BAND OF CHOCTAW INDIANS PO BOX 6010 PHILADELPHIA, MS 39350	601-656-5251	POW WOW GROUNDS PHILADELPHIA, MISSISSIPPI	1985	✓	
	COMANCHE HOMECOMING POW WOW HC 32 BOX 1720 LAWTON, OK 73502	405-492-4988	SULTAN PARK WALTERS, OKLAHOMA		✓	
	WALLOWA BAND NEZ PERCE DESCENDANTS FRIENDSHIP FEAST & POW WOW PO BOX 366 WALLOWA, OR 97885	503-886-2422	WALLOWA, OREGON		✓	
	"1200 INDIAN EVENTS" *POW WOW ON THE RED ROAD*					

CALL BEFORE YOU GO !

POW WOW CALENDAR 1996-1999

CAMPING	COST	SOCIAL	CEREMONY	MARKET	EDUCA-TIONAL	CELE-BRATION	ARTS & CRAFTS	HOST
✓	F	✓				✓	✓	T
✓	$	✓				✓	✓	I
✓	$		✓			✓	✓	T
✓	$	✓			✓		✓	I
✓	$	✓			✓		✓	I
✓	F	✓	✓			✓	✓	I
✓	$	✓				✓	✓	I
✓	F	✓				✓	✓	T
✓	$	✓			✓	✓	✓	T
✓	F	✓				✓	✓	T
✓	F	✓				✓	✓	T

T - TRIBAL EVENT I - INDIAN SPONSOR C - NON INDIAN SPONSOR

MONTH/DAY/ WEEKEND	EVENT	PHONE/FAX	LOCATION	DATE FIRST STARTED	POW WOW	RODEO & FAIR
JULY						
4TH WEEKEND	HASSANAMISCO INDIAN FAIR & POW WOW HASSANAMISCO NIPMUC 20 SINGLETARY AVE SUTTON, MA 01527	508-393-2080 508-839-7394	80 BRIGHAM HILL RD GRAFTON, MASSACHUSETTS	1988	✓	
26-28 '96 25-27 '97 24-26 '98 23-25 '99	THUNDERBIRD POW WOW A/I COMMUNITY CENTER 404 LAFAYETTE, 2ND FLOOR NEW YORK, NY 10003	718-347-3276 212-598-0100	QUEENS COUNTY FARM MUSEUM FLORAL PARK, NEW YORK		✓	
	WHITE MOUNTAIN NATIVE AMERICAN ART FESTIVAL LAKESIDE-PINETOP C OF C 592 W WHITEMOUNTAIN LAKESIDE, AZ 85929	520-367-4290	VARIES PINETOP, ARIZONA	1987	✓	✓
	WINNEBAGO ANNUAL POW WOW WINNEBAGO NATION PO BOX 687 WINNEBAGO, NE 68071	402-878-2272 402-878-2772	VETERANS PARK 1/5 MI. E HWY 75 WINNEBAGO, NEBRASKA	1866	✓	✓
5TH WEEKEND	AMERICAN INDIAN FED OF RHODE ISLAND ANNUAL POW WOW 21 RICHARD SMITHFIELD, RI 02917	401-231-0058 508-372-6754	STEPPING STONE RANCH, ESCOHEAG HILL RD, WEST GREENWICH, RI	1931	✓	
LAST WEEKEND	KAW TRIBAL POW WOW KAW TRIBE OF OKLAHOMA PO BOX 50 KAW CITY, OK 74641	405-269-2332 918-287-2359	WASHAUNGA BAY ON KAW LAKE KAW CITY, OKLAHOMA		✓	
AUGUST	*YOUR EVENT CAN BE LISTED ! FAX US AT (520) 622-4900*					
1ST WEEKEND	I.I.C.O.T. POW WOW OF CHAMPIONS INTERTRIBAL INDIAN CLUB 6941 E 7TH TULSA, OK 74112	918-836-1523 918-838-8276	TULSA STATE FAIRGROUNDS EXPO BLDG TULSA, OKLAHOMA	1977	✓	
2,3,4 '96 1,2,3 '97 31-2 '98 30-1 '99	OGLALA SIOUX NATION FAIR & POW WOW PO BOX H468 PINE RIDGE, SD 57770	605-867-5821	1/4 MILE WEST OF AGENCY PINE RIDGE, SOUTH DAKOTA	1985	✓	✓
	PLEASANT POINT INDIAN CELEBRATION PASSAMAQUODDY NATION PO BOX 343 PERRY, ME 04667	207-853-4641 207-853-2551	CEREMONIAL GROUNDS PERRY, MAINE	1965	✓	✓
	SOUTHERN CALIFORNIA INDIAN CENTERS POW WOW PO BOX 2550 GARDEN GROVE, CA 92642	714-520-0225 714-636-4226	ORANGE COUNTY FAIRGROUNDS COSTA MESA, CALIFORNIA	1968	✓	
	"1200 INDIAN EVENTS" *POW WOW ON THE RED ROAD*					

CALL BEFORE YOU GO !

POW WOW CALENDAR 1996-1999

CAMPING	COST	SOCIAL	CEREMONY	MARKET	EDUCA-TIONAL	CELE-BRATION	ARTS & CRAFTS	HOST
✓	$	✓				✓	✓	T
✓	$						✓	I
✓	F			✓	✓	✓	✓	C
✓	F			✓	✓	✓	✓	T
✓	F	✓				✓	✓	I
✓	$	✓						T
	$						✓	I
✓	F	✓	✓				✓	T
✓	F	✓		✓	✓	✓	✓	T
	$					✓	✓	I

T - TRIBAL EVENT **I - INDIAN SPONSOR** **C - NON INDIAN SPONSOR**

MONTH/DAY/ WEEKEND	EVENT	PHONE/FAX	LOCATION	DATE FIRST STARTED	POW WOW	RODEO & FAIR
AUGUST	***YOUR EVENT CAN BE LISTED ! FAX US AT (520) 622-4900***					
2ND WEEKEND	CROW INDIAN FAIR CROW NATION PO BOX 159 CROW AGENCY, MT 59022	403-684-5407 403-638-2601	CEREMONIAL GROUNDS CROW AGENCY, MONTANA	1918	✓	✓
9,10,11 '96 8,9,10 '97 7,8,9 '98 6,7,8 '99	OMAK STAMPEDE COLVILLE NATION PO BOX 150 NESPELEM, WA 99155	800-933-6625 509-634-4711	OMAK FESTIVAL GROUNDS OMAK, WASHINGTON		✓	✓
	PAUMANAUKE POW WOW B.A.C.C.A. 71 SAWYER AVE WEST BABYLON, NY 11704	212-757-0207 516-661-7559	TANNER PARK COPIAGUE LONG ISLAND, NEW YORK	1988	✓	
	SHOSHONI BANNOCK FESTIVAL & RODEO PO BOX 306 FORT HALL, ID 83203	208-785-2965 209-238-3700	POW WOW GROUNDS FORT HALL, IDAHO	1900	✓	✓
3RD WEEKEND	CHIEF SEATTLE DAYS CELEBRATION COMMITTEE SUQUAMISH NATION PO BOX 498 SUQUAMISH, WA 98392	206-598-3311	DOWNTOWN SUQUAMISH, WASHINGTON	1911		
16-18 '96 15-17 '97 14-16 '98 13-15 '99	GOOD MEDICINE POW WOW RT 5 BOX 261A ALBEMARLE, NC 28001	704-485-4255 704-753-1446	FRANK LISKE PARK, HWY 49 HARRISBURG, NO. CAROLINA		✓	
	MAKAH INDIAN DAYS PO BOX 115 NEAH BAY, WA 98357	206-645-2201	OCEAN FRONT NEAH BAY, WASHINGTON	1924		
	QUINNEHTUKQUT RENDEZVOUS & NATIVE AMERICAN FESTIVAL 19 BLINN ST EAST HARTFORD, CT 06108	203-282-1404	HADDAM MEADOWS STATE PARK, RT 154 HADDAM, CONNECTICUT	1984	✓	
	SANTA FE INDIAN MARKET S.W.A.I.A. 509 CAMINO DE LOS MARQUEZ # 1 SANTA FE, NM 87501	505-983-5220 505-983-7647	SANTA FE PLAZA & VARGAS MALL SANTA FE, NEW MEXICO	1924		
4TH WEEKEND	BALTIMORE AMERICAN INDIAN CENTER ANNUAL POW WOW 113 S BROADWAY BALTIMORE, MD 21231	410-675-3535	FESTIVAL HALL BALTIMORE, MARYLAND	1974	✓	
23-25 '96 22-24 '97 21-23 '98 20-22 '99	OIL DISCOVERY CELEBRATION & POW WOW POW WOW COMMITTEE PO BOX 1027 POPLAR, MT 59255	406-448-2546 406-768-5155	POW WOW GROUNDS POPLAR, MONTANA		✓	✓
	SPOKANE FALLS NW INDIAN ENCAMPMENT & POW WOW E 905 3RD AVE SPOKANE, WA 99202	509-535-0886	RIVERFRONT PARK SPOKANE, WASHINGTON	1989	✓	

CALL BEFORE YOU GO !

POW WOW CALENDAR 1996-1999

CAMPING	COST	SOCIAL	CEREMONY	MARKET	EDUCA-TIONAL	CELE-BRATION	ARTS & CRAFTS	HOST
✓	$	✓	✓			✓	✓	T
✓	$	✓				✓	✓	T
✓	$	✓		✓	✓		✓	C
✓	F	✓		✓		✓	✓	T
✓	F	✓				✓	✓	T
	F	✓					✓	I
✓	F	✓			✓	✓	✓	T
✓	$	✓		✓	✓	✓	✓	C
	F	✓		✓	✓		✓	C
	$	✓					✓	I
✓	F	✓				✓	✓	T
	F	✓				✓	✓	I

T - TRIBAL EVENT   I - INDIAN SPONSOR   C - NON INDIAN SPONSOR

MONTH/DAY/ WEEKEND	EVENT	PHONE/FAX	LOCATION	DATE FIRST STARTED	POW WOW	RODEO & FAIR
AUGUST	***"1200 INDIAN EVENTS"***		***POW WOW ON THE RED ROAD***			
5TH WEEKEND	COEUR D'ALENE POW WOW GENERAL DELIVERY PLUMMER, ID 83851	208-274-3101	COEUR D'ALENE RESERVATION PLUMMER, IDAHO		✓	
30-1 '96 29-31 '97 28-30 '98 27-29 '99	UNITED HOUMA INDIAN FESTIVAL OFFICE OF TOURISM START RT BOX 95A GOLDEN MEADOW, LA 70357	504-475-6640	TERREBONNE PARISH ARENA HOUMA, LOUISIANA	1991		
SEPTEMBER						
1ST WEEKEND	*CHEROKEE NATIONAL HOLIDAY & POW WOW CHEROKEE NATION PO BOX 948 TAHLEQUAH, OK 74415	918-456-0671 918-458-4295	CHEROKEE CULTURAL GROUNDS TAHLEQUAH, OK	1952	✓	✓
*LABOR DAY	*IROQUOIS INDIAN FESTIVAL IROQUOIS INDIAN MUSEUM PO BOX 7 HOWES CAVE, NY 12092	518-296-8949 518-296-8955	MUSEUM GROUNDS HOWES CAVE, NEW YORK	1982	✓	
6,7,8 '96 5,6,7 '97 4,5,6 '98 3,4,5 '99	*SPOKANE TRIBAL FAIR & PW WOW SPOKANE NATION PO BOX 100 WELPINIT, WA 99040	509-258-4581	POW WOW GROUNDS WELPINIT, WASHINGTON	1917	✓	✓
	*WHITE MOUNTAIN APACHE TRIBAL FAIR & RODEO PO BOX 1709 WHITERIVER, AZ 85941	520-338-4621 520-338-4346	POW WOW/ RODEO FAIRGROUNDS WHITERIVER, ARIZONA	1925	✓	✓
2ND WEEKEND	CHRISJOHNS IROQUOIS ART FESTIVAL RD 2 BOX 203 RED HOOK, NY 12571	914-758-6526 518-622-3324	RT 9 DUTCHESS COUNTY FAIRGROUNDS RHINEBECK, NEW YORK	1986	✓	
13-15 '96 12-14 '97 11-13 '98 10-12 '99	DALLAS FT WORTH INTER-TRIBAL ASSN NATL CHAMPIONSHIP POW WOW 2602 MAYFIELD RD GRAND PRAIRIE, TX 75052	214-647-2331 214-647-8585	TRADERS VILLAGE GRAND PRAIRIE, TEXAS	1962	✓	
	NAVAJO NATION FAIR PO DRAWER U WINDOW ROCK, AZ 86515	520-871-6702 520-871-6436 520-871-7381	POW WOW GROUNDS, FAIR ARENA WINDOW ROCK, ARIZONA	1946	✓	✓
	UNITED TRIBES INDIAN ART EXPOSITION & CHAMPIONSHIP POW WOW 3315 UNIVERSITY DR BISMARCK, ND 58504	701-255-3285 701-255-1844	UNITED TRIBES TECH COLLEGE BISMARCK, NORTH DAKOTA		✓	
3RD WEEKEND	CALIFORNIA AMERICAN INDIAN DAYS INDIAN HUMAN RES CTR 4040 30TH # A SAN DIEGO, CA 92104	619-694-3996 619-281-5964 619-281-1466	BALBOA PARK SAN DIEGO, CALIFORNIA	1983	✓	
20-22 '96 19-21 '97 18-20 '98 17-19 '99	CHICKASAW FESTIVAL CHICKASAW NATION FESTIVAL COMMITTEE PO BOX 1548 ADA, OK 74820	405-371-2175 405-436-2603	CITYWIDE TISHOMINGO, OKLAHOMA		✓	
	LUMBEE OLD STYLE DANCE PO BOX 68 PEMBROKE, NC 28372	919-521-0354 919-521-8625	NORTH CAROLINA CULTURE CTR PEMBROKE, NC	1989	✓	

CALL BEFORE YOU GO !

POW WOW CALENDAR 1996-1999

CAMPING	COST	SOCIAL	CEREMONY	MARKET	EDUCA-TIONAL	CELE-BRATION	ARTS & CRAFTS	HOST
✓	F	✓				✓	✓	T
		✓				✓	✓	T
	$	✓			✓	✓	✓	T
✓	$	✓					✓	I
✓	F					✓	✓	T
✓	$	✓	✓			✓	✓	T
✓	$	✓				✓	✓	I
✓	$	✓					✓	I
✓	$	✓	✓				✓	T
✓	$			✓			✓	I
	F	✓					✓	I
	F	✓					✓	T
✓	$	✓					✓	I

T - TRIBAL EVENT **I - INDIAN SPONSOR** **C - NON INDIAN SPONSOR**

MONTH/DAY/ WEEKEND	EVENT	PHONE/FAX	LOCATION	DATE FIRST STARTED	POW WOW	RODEO & FAIR
SEPTEMBER	*YOUR EVENT CAN BE LISTED ! FAX US AT (520) 622-4900*					
4TH WEEKEND	CHICKAHOMINY FESTIVAL 6801 S LOTT CARY RD PROVIDENCE FORGE, VA 23140	804-829-2261 804-829-2186	TRIBAL CENTER RT 609 & 602 PROVIDENCE FORGE, VIRGINIA		✓	
27-29 '96 26-28 '97 25-27 '98 24-26 '99	NARRAGANSETT INDIAN TRIBE GREAT SWAMP FIGHT CEREMONY PO BOX 268 CHARLESTON, RI 02813	617-961-1346 410-364-1100	ROUTE 2 SOUTH SO. KINGSTON, RHODE ISLAND	1675	✓	
29TH-30TH	ANNUAL FEAST DAY OF SAN GERONIMO TAOS PUEBLO TOURISM PO BOX 1846 TAOS, NM 87571	505-758-9593 505-758-8626	TAOS PUEBLO PLAZA TAOS, NEW MEXICO			
OCTOBER						
1ST WEEKEND	CHEROKEE FALL FESTIVAL CHEROKEE NATION PO BOX 460 CHEROKEE, NC 28719	704-497-9195 800-438-1601	CEREMONIAL GROUNDS CHEROKEE, NO. CAROLINA	1985		
4,5,6 '96 3,4,5 '97 2,3,4 '98 1,2,3 '99	SHIPROCK NAVAJO FAIR PO BOX 1893 SHIPROCK, NM 87420	505-368-5108 505-884-7715	FAIRGROUNDS SHIPROCK, NEW MEXICO	1923	✓	✓
2ND WEEKEND	21ST CENTURY NATIVE AMERICAN MESA POW WOW MESA SOUTHWEST MUSEUM 53 N MACDONALD MESA, AZ 85201	602-644-2169 602-644-2230	MESA SOUTHWEST MUSEUM MESA, ARIZONA	1984	✓	
11-13 '96 10-12 '97 9-11 '98 8-10 '99	AIS HOMECOMING DANCE AMERICAN INDIANIST SOCIETY 15 MATTSON WORCESTER, MA 01606	508-852-6271	CAMP MARSHALL ROUTE 31 SPENCER, MAINE	1968	✓	
	NATIVE AMERICAN POW WOW PE DEE INDIANS PO BOX 6068 CLIO, SC 29525	803-523-5259 803-523-6790	PE DEE TRADE SCHOOL MCCOIL, SO. CAROLINA		✓	
3RD WEEKEND	ALABAMA STATE WIDE P/W AL INDIAN AFFIARS COMMISSION 669 S LAWRENCE MONTGOMERY, AL 36130	334-242-2831	GARRETT COLISEUM MONTGOMERY, ALABAMA	1992	✓	
18-20 '96 17-19 '97 16-18 '98 15-17 '99	FIRE HAWK'S ANNUAL POW WOW 160 HORSE HILL RD ASHFORD, CT 06278	203-429-2668	WOLF DEN PARK JCT 44 & 101 POMFRET CTR, CONNECTICUT	1983	✓	
	"1200 INDIAN EVENTS" *POW WOW ON THE RED ROAD*					
4TH WEEKEND	APACHE JII DAY (SATURDAY ONLY) GLOBE MIAMI C OF C PO BOX 239 GLOBE, AZ 85502	800-804-5623 520-425-4495	DOWNTOWN GLOBE GLOBE, ARIZONA	1983		
25-27 '96 24-26 '97 23-25 '98 22-24 '99	INDIAN NATIONAL FINALS RODEO 1000 S MAIN SAPULPA, OK 74066	918-224-6511 415-583-6101	RUSHMORE PLAZA CIVIC CENTER RAPID CITY, SOUTH DAKOTA	1975	✓	✓

CALL BEFORE YOU GO !

POW WOW CALENDAR 1996-1999

CAMPING	COST	SOCIAL	CEREMONY	MARKET	EDUCA-TIONAL	CELE-BRATION	ARTS & CRAFTS	HOST
		✓					✓	T
✓	$	✓				✓	✓	T
✓	F		✓			✓	✓	T
	$	✓	✓	✓	✓	✓	✓	T
	$		✓				✓	I
	F	✓					✓	I
✓	$	✓	✓			✓	✓	C
✓	F	✓						T
	$	✓			✓		✓	I
✓	F	✓					✓	I
	F	✓			✓		✓	C
	$			✓			✓	I

T - TRIBAL EVENT I - INDIAN SPONSOR C - NON INDIAN SPONSOR

MONTH/DAY/ WEEKEND	EVENT	PHONE/FAX	LOCATION	DATE FIRST STARTED	POW WOW	RODEO & FAIR
NOVEMBER						
1ST WEEKEND	NATIONAL MISS INDIAN USA PAGEANT AMER. INDIAN HERITAGE 6051 ARLINGTON BLVD FALLS CHURCH, VA 22044	202-463-4267 703-532-1921	VARIES EACH YEAR WASHINGTON, DC			
1,2,3 '96 30,1,2 '97 6,7,8 '98 4,5,6 '99	OGLEWANAGI POW WOW 866 WILBETH RD AKRON, OH 44306	216-225-3416 216-628-5796	CHAPPARELL BINGO, 866 WILBETH AKRON, OHIO	1958	✓	
2ND WEEKEND	AMERICAN INDIAN FILM FESTIVAL 333 VALENCIA # 322 SAN FRANCISCO, CA 94103	415-554-0525	PALACE OF FINE ARTS SAN FRANCISCO, CALIFORNIA			
*VETERANS DAY	*SAN CARLOS APACHE VETERANS SAN CARLOS APACHE NTN PO BOX O SAN CARLOS, AZ 85550	520-475-2402 520-475-2361	SAN CARLOS APACHE RESERVATION SAN CARLOS, ARIZONA	1966	✓	✓
8,9,10 '96 7,8,9 '97 13-15 '98 12-14 '99	***YOUR EVENT CAN BE LISTED ! FAX US AT (520) 622-4900***					
	"1200 INDIAN EVENTS" ***POW WOW ON THE RED ROAD***					
3RD WEEKEND	NORTHERN PLAINS TRIBAL ART SHOW & SALE AMERICAN INDIAN SVCS PO BOX 1720 SIOUX FALLS, SD 57101	605-336-4007	CITY WIDE SIOUX FALLS, SOUTH DAKOTA	1992		
15-17 '96 14-16 '97 20-22 '98 19-21 '99						
4TH WEEKEND	*NATIVE AMERICAN MONTH SOCIAL POW WOW NA TRADE & INFO CTR PO BOX 27626 TUCSON, AZ 85726	520-622-4900 520-295-1350 520-292-0779	AMIGOS COMPLEX TUCSON, ARIZONA	1990	✓	
*THANKS-GIVING	*TEXAS RED NATIONS POW WOW PO BOX 758 CEDAR HILL, TX 75106	405-436-2063 817-924-1488	LOOS STADIUM FIELD HOUSE DALLAS, TEXAS	1990	✓	
22-24 '96 28-30 '97 27-29 '98 26-28 '99	*THANKSGIVING ANNUAL POW WOW UINTAH & OURAY NATIONS PO BOX 190 FORT DUCHESNE, UT 84026	801-722-5141	TRIBAL COMMUNITY BUILDING FORT DUCHESNE, UTAH	1985	✓	

CALL BEFORE YOU GO !

POW WOW CALENDAR 1996-1999

CAMPING	COST	SOCIAL	CEREMONY	MARKET	EDUCA-TIONAL	CELE-BRATION	ARTS & CRAFTS	HOST
	$					✓		I
	F	✓					✓	C
	$				✓			I
✓	$	✓				✓	✓	T
				✓			✓	I
	$	✓			✓		✓	I
	$	✓					✓	I
	F	✓				✓	✓	T

T - TRIBAL EVENT I - INDIAN SPONSOR C - NON INDIAN SPONSOR

MONTH/DAY/ WEEKEND	EVENT	PHONE/FAX	LOCATION	DATE FIRST STARTED	POW WOW	RODEO & FAIR
DECEMBER						
VARIES	SHALAKO CEREMONIAL BLESSING OF NEW HOMES ZUNI PUEBLO NATION PO BOX 338 ZUNI, NM 87327	505-782-4481 505-782-5800	PUEBLO PLAZA ZUNI, NEW MEXICO	∞		
1ST WEEKEND	CHRISTMAS ANNUAL ARTS & CRAFTS NAVAJO FAIR OFFICE PO BOX 308 WINDOW ROCK, AZ 86515	520-871-7303	LIBRARY WINDOW ROCK, ARIZONA	1977		
6,7,8 '96 5,6,7 '97 4,5,6 '98 3,4,5 '99	JEMEZ PUEBLO WINTER ARTS & CRAFT SHOW OFFICE OF TOURISM PO BOX 100 JEMEZ PUEBLO, NM 87024	505-834-7235 505-834-7331	JEMEZ PUEBLO CIVIC CENTER JEMEZ PUEBLO, NEW MEXICO			
2ND WEEKEND	ANNUAL WINTER POW WOW D Q UNIVERSITY PO BOX 409 DAVIS, CA 95617	916-758-0470 916-758-2518	CAMPUS GROUNDS DAVIS, CALIFORNIA	1969	✓	
13-15 '96 12-14 '97 11-13 '98 10-12 '99						
26TH - JAN 1ST	MICCOSUKEE ART FESTIVAL PO BOX 440021 MIAMI, FL 33144	305-223-8380	25 MILES WEST OF MIAMI MIAMI, FLORIDA			✓

CALL BEFORE YOU GO !

POW WOW CALENDAR 1996-1999

CAMPING	COST	SOCIAL	CEREMONY	MARKET	EDUCA-TIONAL	CELE-BRATION	ARTS & CRAFTS	HOST
	F		✓			✓		T
	F			✓			✓	I
	F						✓	I
	F	✓					✓	I
	$	✓		✓		✓	✓	T

NOTE:

DUE TO OUR SPACE LIMITATIONS WE HAVE LISTED ONLY THREE OR FOUR EVENTS FOR EACH WEEKEND, EQUALLY DISTRIBUTED ACROSS THE US, MOST EVENTS ARE OF AT LEAST TWENTY-FIVE YEARS CONTINUOUS DURATION, ie. SAME MONTH, SAME WEEKEND.

A MASTER LIST OF OVER 1200 EVENTS IS AVAILABLE TO THE SERIOUS POW WOWER.

WRITE FOR:

POW WOW ON THE RED ROAD

NATIVE AMERICAN CO-OP
PO BOX 27626
TUCSON, AZ 85726-7626 USA

T - TRIBAL EVENT   I - INDIAN SPONSOR   C - NON INDIAN SPONSOR

INDIAN NATIONAL FINALS RODEO ASSOCIATION

OKLAHOMA

Clem McSpadden, General Mgr.
PO Box 317
Chelsea, OK 74016
918-789-3237

Bob Arrington, Secretary
100 S Main
Sapulpa, OK 74006
918-789-2408

NATIVE AMERICAN RODEO ASSOCIATIONS BY REGION

REGION I

I.R.C.A
INDIAN RODEO COWBOYS
ASSOC/ALBERTA CORP
Box 214
Standoff, AB TOL 1YO
CANADA
403-328-5451
403-739-2149

REGION II

W.S.I.R.A
WESTERN STATES INDIAN
RODEO ASSOCIATION
2024 NE Brown Road
Washougal, WA 98671
206-835-3032

REGION III

U.I.R.A.
UNITED INDIAN RODEO
ASSOC/MONTANA CORP
PO Box 1143 Rocky Boy Rte
Box Elder, MT 59521
406-395-4133
406-395-4982
406-395-4412 FAX

REGION IV

R.M.I.R.A.
ROCKY MOUNTAIN INDIAN
RODEO ASSOCIATION/
WYOMING CORP
Route 3, Box 290-B
Blackfoot, ID 83221
208-785-6256
208-238-3702 FAX

REGION V

A.I.R.C.A.
ALL INDIAN RODEO
COWBOYS ASSOCIATION/
ARIZONA CORP
PO Box 1546
St. Michaels, AZ 86511
520-289-4152 MESSAGE
520-613-0310 MOBIL

REGION VI

N.N.R.C.A
NAVAJO NATON RODEO
COWBOYS ASSOCIATION/
NEW MEXICO CORP
PO Box 1202
Gallup, NM 87305
505-778-5396
505-722-6413 WK
520-871-7016 AZ

REGION VII

G.P.I.R.A.
GREAT PLAINS INDIAN
RODEO ASSOCATION/
SOUTH DAKOTA CORP
PO Box 726
Lame Deer, MT 59643
406-477-6562
406-477-6219 FAX

REGION VIII

A.I.R.A.O.
ALL INDIAN RODEO ASSOC
OF OKLAHOMA/
OKLAHOMA CORP
Rt 3, Box 630
Okmulgee, OK 74447
918-758-4303
918-445-1173 FAX

REGION IX

W.I.R.E.A.
WESTERN INDIAN RODEO
EXPOSITION &
ASSOCATION/ B. C. CORP
RR #7 Westside Road
Site 8A Comp 28
Vernon, BC V1T 723
CANADA
604-542-3520

REGION X

N.A.N.C.A
NATIVE AMERICAN
NATIVE COWBOYS
ASSOCIATION
PO Box 442
Hobbema, AB TOC 1NO
CANADA
403-585-3030
403-585-4227 FAX

REGION XI

P.I.R.A.
PRAIRIE INDIAN RODEO ASSOCIATION
PO BOX 442
Broadview, SK SOG OKO
CANADA
306-696-3540
306-696-3201

REGION XII

S.W.I.R.A.
SOUTHWEST INDIAN RODEO ASSOCIATION
Box 701
Globe, AZ 85502
520-425-9131

REGION XIII

E.I.R.A.
EASTERN INDIAN RODEO ASSOCATION
Rt 6, Box 750
Okeechobee, FL 34974
813-763-4483
813-763-5077

UNITED STATES

AMERICAN INDIAN SANCTIONED RODEO SCHEDULES

REGION I (IRCA)

Standoff, Alberta, Canada
403-328-5451
403-739-2149 FAX

Schedule Not Provided

REGION II (WSIRA)

Washougal, Washington
206-835-3032

Schedule Not Provided

REGION III (UIRA)

Box Elder, Montana
406-395-4133
406-395-4412 FAX

Schedule Not Provided

REGION IV (RMIRA)

Blackfoot, Idaho
208-785-6256
208-238-3702

Schedule Not Provided

REGION V (AIRCA)

Window Rock, Arizona
520-289-4152

1st Weekend	February	Sells, Arizona
1st Weekend	April	Sanders, Arizona
4th Weekend	April	Albuquerque, New Mexico
2nd Weekend	May	Shonto, Arizona
4th Weekend	May	Coalmine, Arizona
1st Weekend	June	Ganado, Arizona
2nd Weekend	June	Lower Greasewood, Arizona
3rd Weekend	June	Rock Point, Arizona
4th Weekend	June	Dilcon, Arizona
5th Weekend	June	Kayenta, Arizona
1st Weekend	July	Window Rock, Arizona

2nd Weekend	July	Sawmill, Arizona
3rd Weekend	July	Houck, Arizona
4th Weekend	July	Crownpoint, Arizona
5th Weekend	July	Chinle, Arizona
1st Weekend	August	Holbrook, Arizona
2nd Weekend	August	Gallup, New Mexico
3rd Weekend	August	Dilcon, Arizona
4th Weekend	August	Kayenta, Arizona
1st Weekend	September	Durango, Colorado
2nd Weekend	September	Window Rock, Arizona
3rd Weekend	September	Dilcon, Arizona
3rd Weekend	September	Bluff, Utah
4th Weekend	September	Pinehill, New Mexico
5th Weekend	September	Holbrook, Arizona (FINALS)
1st Weekend	December	Parker, Arizona
3rd Weekend	December	Phoenix, Arizona
1st Weekend	January	Phoenix, Arizona

REGION VI (NNRCA)

Gallup, New Mexico
505-778-5396
505-871-7016 FAX

Schedule Not Provided

REGION VII (GPIRA)

Lame Deer, Montana
406-477-6562
406-477-6212 FAX

4th Weekend	May	Lame Deer, Montana
4th Weekend	May	Lame Deer, Montana
3rd Weekend	June	Twin Buttes, North Dakota
Tentative	July	Fort Yates, North Dakota
Tentative	August	Oglala, South Dakota
Tentative	August	Rosebud, South Dakota
Tentative	September	Lame Deer, Montana
	September	Mitchell, South Dakota (FINALS)

REGION VIII (AIRAO)

Okumulgee, Oklahoma
918-758-4303
918-445-1173 FAX

Schedule Not Provided

REGION IX (WIREA)

Vernon, British Columbia, Canada
604-542-3520

Schedule Not Provided

REGION X (NANCA)

Hobbema, Alberta, Canada
403-585-3030
403-585-4227 FAX

Schedule Not Provided

REGION XI (PIRA)

Broadview, Saskatchewan, Canada
306-696-3540
306-696-3201 FAX

Schedule Not Provided

REGION XII (SWIRA)

San Carlos, Arizona
520-475-2550

2nd Weekend	November	San Carlos, Arizona
3rd Weekend	December	Phoenix, Arizona
2nd Weekend	April	Bylas, Arizona
3rd Weekend	April	Whiteriver, Arizona
2nd Weekend	May	Whiteriver, Arizona
2nd Weekend	June	Cedar Creek, Arizona
4th Weekend	June	Cibecue, Arizona
1st Weekend	July	Whiteriver, Arizona
4th Weekend	July	Cibecue, Arizona
1st Weekend	August	Bylas, Arizona
1st Weekend	September	Whiteriver, Arizona
3rd Weekend	September	To Be Announced (FINALS)

REGION XIII (EIRA)

Okeechobee, Florida
813-763-4483
813-763-5077 FAX

4th Weekend	March	Big Cypress Reservation
1st Weekend	May	Immokalee Reservation
4th Weekend	June	Hollywood Reservation
1st Weekend	July	Brighton Reservation
4th Weekend	July	Big Cypress Reservation
3rd Weekend	August	Atmore, Alabama
2nd Weekend	September	Location Unknown (FINALS)

*Rodeos are sometimes rescheduled but usually follow in sequence year after year. Call the respective Region Rodeo Association.

NAVAJO RUG WEAVERS SHOWS AND EXHIBITS

CROWNPOINT RUG AUCTION

The Crownpoint Rug auction has given buyers the unique opportunity to purchase Navajo rugs directly from the weavers themselves, at prices well below retail. The Crownpoint Rug Weavers Association has been auctioning rugs from all over the reservation since 1968. The auction has grown steadily in popularity, and brings buyers from all over the United States and the world.

The Crownpoint Auction is held every month, in the gymnasium of the Crownpoint Elementary School. There is no admission fee. Rug viewing begins at 3 p.m., and runs until 6:00. This gives prospective buyers ample time to examine each rug as the weavers bring them in.

Auctioning begins at 7 p.m., and usually ends around midnight. Purchases can be picked up any time after the sale until closing time. Cash and personal checks are accepted, no credit cards please.

The Crownpoint Elementary School provides a food and beverage concession, beginning at 5:00 p.m. Native American artisans also offer a large selection of jewelry, pottery, and crafts in the halls outside the gymnasium.

For more information about the Crownpoint Auction, and a list of Auction Dates, send a self-addressed, stamped envelope to:

Crownpoint Rug Weavers Association
Post Office Box 1630
Crownpoint, New Mexico 87313
505-786-5302

DIRECTIONS:

Take Interstate 40 to exit 53, at Thoreau. Turn directly onto Route 371 North. Stay on 371 North for about 25 miles, then take a left turn at the sign for Crownpoint. Turn right at the second four-way stop. The Crownpoint Elementary School is on the right hand side of the road, and the auction is held in the school gymnasium.

Hotel accommodations are available just off of I-40, in Gallup (50 miles west of Thoreau) and Grants (30 miles each of Thoreau).

You may also contact Christina Ellsworth at 786-7386 for information.

1996 DATES 3rd Friday of each month.

January 19, 1996
February 23, 1996
March 22, 1996
April 19, 1996
May 24, 1996
June 21, 1996
July 19, 1996
August 23, 1996
September 20, 1996
October 18, 1996
November 15, 1996
December 13, 1996

UNITED STATES

BUYERS GUIDE TO INDIAN STORES & GALLERIES

Buying from a reliable dealer is important. They will be honest in their opinions and represent exactly what they have. Beyond that, there are some other barometers that you can use to evaluate various items of Native art. Within the next few pages different excerpts will assist you in your selection.

Refund Policy: Ask about the dealers refund policy. Well made Indian art always holds it's value; Quite often it appreciates with time. Any dealer should be glad to give you a full refund if the customer is not fully satisfied with their purchase.

Personal Taste: "Beauty is in the eye of the beholder," and Native art is no exception! A piece of Indian art, whether baskets, beadwork, turquoise, or wood carvings should first of all please the owner. Like all fine art, you will own the piece for many years and enjoy it on many occasions. You should feel proud when displaying or wearing it. If the piece appeals to you, you can be sure it will appeal to others.

Spirit: Many times an Indian artist will not sign a piece of art because of deep traditional feelings. Traditional artists believe a part of their spirit is in each piece they create. If your spirit and the artist's spirit are in harmony the item will come into your possession. A pushy salesperson is not needed.

A signature is not a guarantee of fine quality art all the time. But some of the well known artists are starting to sign their work. It is nice to know who made your purchase for future references.

NORTH AMERICAN NATIVE AMERICAN INDIAN INFORMATION AND TRADE CENTER.

BUYER'S GUIDE

NAVAJO RUGS: THE PRODUCTS OF A DISAPPEARING ART

BUYING A NAVAJO RUG: A POTENTIAL INVESTMENT OPPORTUNITY

Buying a Navajo rug is a potential investment opportunity. The rugs almost never wear out and do not depreciate in value even after years of use.

Quality pieces of weaving from Navajo looms demand top prices and are finding their way into homes and offices of prominent people throughout the world. Fine weaving is being purchased as a long term investment and as a hedge against inflation. No other art object available in today's market can really offer the advantages of Navajo weaving. Usefulness, beauty, charm and price appreciation are among the attributes.

The number of weavers have declined steadily since the days of World War II. Family disruption, off-reservation job opportunities, educational advances and a changing way of life have all contributed to the decline in the number of weavers.

Weaving a Navajo rug is tedious work. It is demanding of time and patience. The weavers must first card the wool from the native sheep, then spin and dye it. Finally a loom is used to weave her own rug.

A survey of weavers by trading posts on or near Navajo reservations reveals that over 70 percent of active weavers are 35 years of age or older. Fewer than 10 percent are under 20. The 35-year statistic may not be alarming, but the fact is that most weavers do not weave after the age of 50. The demanding ritual of sitting before a loom for months constantly working with the hands at shoulder level, takes a physical toll.

NAVAJO RUGS: THE PRODUCTS OF A DISAPPEARING ART

If you have abandoned the rare-objects in despair of ever finding any bargains, consider buying a contemporary Navajo rug. High quality specimens are now appreciating at 20 percent a year. Few Navajo women are taking up the craft. The rewards are small for the Navajo weaver, who toils with her arms raised over her head. So the rugs will be getting scarce.

You can buy Navajo rugs from Museum shops and reputable Indian-crafts shops in most major cities, but you'll get more choice from top dealers in Navajo rug areas of Arizona and New Mexico.

The rugs are attractive and useful. Antique rugs are strictly for hanging on walls, but a new one can be trod for generations without showing much wear. Maintenance is an occasional dry cleaning and mothproofing.

Look for a pleasing design and good craftsmanship. The weave should be tight and even. View the rug flat on the floor to make sure it isn't crooked.

Collectors favor Two Gray Hills rug-subtle black brown and gray designs produced in one area of the Navajo reservation. Also popular Yei sandpaintings-rugs that copy designs medicine men make on the ground with colored sand. Pictorial rugs show everything from goats to motorcycles.

Contemporary Navajo rugs of good quality starts at around $600, but you'll pay many times that for the work of a name weaver. Among the best are Daisy Toglechee, Rose Mike, and Julia Jumbo, who make Two Gray Hills rugs; Mary Long and Lola Yazzie, who make Yei; Ruth Yabney (from the Teec Nos Pos area) and Bessie Taylor, who weave pictorials.

BUSINESS WEEK 9-5-77

*editors note: some of these weavers have passed on or are too old to weave since this article was written in 1977. Ruth Yabney died in 1994.

CLASSIC NAVAJO JEWELRY

A QUEST FOR BEAUTY

The jewelry designs that have become the trademark of the Navajo silversmiths of the world over are truly beautiful but borrowed.

They are the amalgam of many cultures.

From the Plains Indians came the fascination with silver. From the Pueblo Indians, the Spaniards, and the Mexicans came the designs and know-how. From the Anglos came the market. From the Navajo soul came the ability to blend them all in a beautiful experience.

The Navajos, who migrated to the Southwest 200 years ago carrying very little cultural baggage, proved to be highly adaptive and inventive people. They were quick to synthesize and weave the divergent customs, practices, and techniques of these divergent cultures into their own history. At the same time, they maintained the Navajo sense of harmony and flow.

In Quest of Beauty

Navajo jewelry emphasizes movement. It is an exploration of form and an artist's desire to express beauty.

The Navajo experiences beauty through expression, not through perception of what is deemed to be beautiful. It is experienced, not possessed. To be maintained, it needs to be renewed in all aspects of Navajo living - in art, song, dress, and daily living.

From the Plains Indians

Their introduction to the seductive silver material is believed to have come from their interaction with the Plains Indians. Gifts of silver trinkets were abundantly bestowed on the native Plains Indian tribes by the French, British, and Colonial military forces vying for territorial control of the new frontier.

Historians place the beginning of silver crafting among the Navajos at roughly 1850 as documented by the reports of Henry Dodge, an Anglo government agent at Fort Defiance. Hispanic blacksmiths, rather than silversmiths, are credited with teaching Navajos how to work metal. Scholars offer as evidence the designs found on Navajo Stamps used on leathers as well as the use of the cold chisel. Herrero Delgadito (Little Lean Iron Worker) who became head chief of the Navajo around Fort Defiance is believed to have been the first Navajo silversmith.

The early phase Navajo jewelry reflects the design preferences of the Plains Indians whose silver pieces were less massive than what has become known as Navajo style.

The Plains Indians made much of their jewelry from German silver alloys pounded into thin plates and then decorated. Early Navajo work incorporates the flat surfaced and the bangle style.

The designs of early pieces were also restricted by the crudeness of the wood and stone tools used. Early bangle bracelets were simply twisted metals of copper, brass, and even iron. Some were decorated with simple patterns with a cold chisel before the use of solder.

As the techniques were refined and the silver supply became more abundant, silver work moved into the middle phase and more massive and ornamented pieces were created for which the Navajo culture is now noted.

By 1875, the Navajos had acquired the technique of forge soldering that allowed them to join one piece of silver to another. About the same time, the Navajos also began to produce their own ingots which could be hammered into bar bracelets that expanded the surface and, therefore, the opportunity for ornamentation. The middle phase is simply a continuum of the advancing technological skill of the Indian artists. It is marked by greater elaboration of design. Some say the Victorian taste of the early 20th century Anglo market influenced the Navajo's tendency toward ornamentation.

The later phase of the last few decades is marked by clean and streamlined designs.

Familiar Designs

The concha belt is a prime example of the Navajo's deftness in synthesizing elements of alien cultures into a harmonious, truly Navajo expression. Round disks were used as hair ornaments by Eastern tribes; Plains Indians attached German silver disks to belts. To the simple designs, the Navajo added the Spanish element with richer relief and more exploratory ornamentation. Concha belts were worn to impress fellow tribesmen. The display of wealth was indicative of social position which was not hereditary, but rather based upon the abilities and responsibility of the individual. Wealth was believed to be a result of these qualities.

The crescent-shaped *naja* is one of the most familiar forms in Navajo jewelry. It clearly comes from outside the Navajo culture. It is thought to have originated in the Old World as a Spanish horse gear - a third eye placed on the animals forehead to ward off evil. It is often used as a focus piece in a squash blossom necklace, also of Spanish origin. The "squash blossoms" are actually pomegranate blossoms that were worn as trouser decorations by Spanish Colonial gentleman.

Curiously, Navajo jewelry artists of the early 20th century were experimenting with form at the same time young European sculptors, such as Brancusi and Lipschitz, were challenging the dictums of representational art, scholars have noted. From the beginning, the Navajo artist never embraced the practice of replicating nature.

Beauty Is an Experience in Active Pursuit of "Hozho"

An enhancement of "hozho", a concept of melding beauty, harmony, and well-being, is the mandate of the Navajo people. It is a state of nature to be sought, experienced, regenerated, and projected into the universe.

Jewelry art has been an exploration of beauty and form thus a fulfillment of "hozho".

Art Life Arizona, Volume 5 No. 2 1991

TURQUOISE, CORAL, JET AND SHELL

An untreated top grade Turquoise stone is rarer than one might think. If you are interested in a piece of jewelry with turquoise, you should examine the stone carefully. More than seventy percent of the turquoise colored stones on the market today are, in one way or another, treated, color colored or stabilized. This is not because of the dishonesty or frailties inherent in turquoise traders. It is simply because less than ten percent of the mined turquoise is fit to work and market in its natural form.

The supply of top grade turquoise will never meet the demand.

Turquoise has been mined in Iran for eight centuries and on the Sinai Peninsula since ancient times. Most of the turquoise used in Native American jewelry comes from the southwest, i.e. New Mexico, Arizona, Nevada, Colorado, and California. It ranges in color from light blue to gray-green; the robin's-egg blue varieties being most used in jewelry by southwest Indian silversmiths.

It is a semi-precious stone that is bought and sold by the carat; color, hardness, and matrix markings determine the value of each stone. American turquoise is marketed in one hundred fifty-two recognized shades of blue and green.

Methods of treating turquoise are quite numerous. They include; boiling in paraffin, soaking in paraffin oil, oil dyes, organic dyes, sodium silicate, treating with plastics and epoxy resin and lazer fracturing. Even Synthetic turquoise has hit the market at about the same price as good natural material. The buyer is faced with the problem of whether or not he is getting what he pays for. Actually, this is not as serious as it may seem if the buyer makes his purchases from reliable dealers. On today's market there are no "bargains". The demand for untreated turquoise is too great for anyone to have to sell at low prices.

In pieces with many small stones, often, treated turquoise is used, as treating gives the turquoise a hardness that is needed for cutting and working needlepoint and cluster settings.

With all of the above information even the experts can not often identify turquoise once it has left the mine. Turquoise is a product of nature.

Coral, the red stone often found in Indian jewelry comes from the sea in the Mediterranean. It is generally thought that the Spaniards introduced it to the southwest tribes. Today it often costs more than turquoise depending on it's qualities.

Jet, the black stone sometimes found in Indian jewelry is native to the Pueblos in the southwest and is generally collected in New Mexico.

Today various sea shells from all over the world are appearing in Indian Jewelry. These include mother of pearl, mussel, clam, spiny oyster and others.

Turquoise and other materials are very sensitive and one should be careful that they don't come in contact with oils, grease, hand lotions, perfumes, perspiration, soaps or any other foreign substances. A turquoise piece of jewelry is your guarantee of one form of fine Native art but must be protected against your own neglect.

BUYERS GUIDE

STABILIZED? SYNTHETIC? NATURAL? ENHANCED?

Is turquoise terminology confusing to you? Here are some definitions.

We are often asked where stone and shell materials come from. This list was compiled to help answer your questions.

BLUE VERDE - Turquoise from Old Vega Mine near the California-Nevada Border.

CHINESE TURQUOISE - From several locations in China, including Tibet.

ENHANCED TURQUOISE - Most of the enhanced turquoise is mined in Mexico and treated in Arizona.

LONE MOUNTAIN - Turquoise from Tonopah, Nevada.

MORENCI TURQUOISE - In Morenci, Arizona this good blue turquoise is found in an immense open-pit copper mine.

PERSIAN - Found in Iran, this turquoise has long been the standard of quality. It has been in short supply for several years.

SLEEPING BEAUTY - This turquoise is sky blue in its top grades. Like Morenci turquoise, it is found in an open-pit copper mine. The mine is near Globe, Arizona.

STABILIZED TURQUOISE - Chalk turquoise (pale and soft) is mined in Mexico and Arizona. It is commonly stabilized to produce clear blue material. Once treated, it is ideal for carving and heishi. Stabilized Sleeping Beauty turquoise is dark blue. Stabilized Mexican is light blue. Stabilized Chinese and other matrix turquoises are sometimes referred to as CHINA MOUNTAIN, although there is not an actual mine or location by that name.

LAPIS LAZULI - Afghanistan.

SUGILITE - South Africa.

SPINY OYSTER SHELL - Western Mexico, in the Sea of Cortez.

excerpt: INDIAN JEWELER'S SUPPLY CO CATALOGUE, 1992

NATURAL - Turquoise which has not been altered chemically or otherwise. Excludes any backing materials.
VALUE RATING: 20

NATURAL - Same as above, but having a tumble polished finish with inked matrix.
VALUE RATING: 12

ENHANCED - Hard turquoise with poor color which is treated electrochemically. No resins or dyes are used. Oxalic acid will react with enhanced turquoise, turning white. No reaction occurs with natural or stabilized turquoise.
VALUE RATING: 12

STABILIZED - 90% of mined turquoise is pale blue chalk. Resins are added to harden the turquoise and darken it. Stabilized turquoise is not brittle like natural or enhanced. We include fracture-sealed turquoise with this category, since the process is nearly identical.
VALUE RATING: 8

STABILIZED & COLOR-ENHANCED
VALUE RATING: 5

RECONSTITUTED - Chalk turquoise is crushed into a powder. Resins and dyes are added and the mixture is compressed into a solid form. "Block" material is frequently completely imitation rather than reconstituted.
VALUE RATING: 3

IMITATION - Any compound or mineral which is manufactured or treated so as to resemble turquoise in appearance.
VALUE RATING: 2

SYNTHETIC - A much abused term - Synthetics are artificially made substances which have all the physical properties and the chemical composition of natural substances. Synthetic turquoise is very rare. It is difficult to assign a value rating.
Value rating 20 is highest.
Value rating 2 is lowest.

excerpt: Indian Jeweler's Supply Co Catalogue, 1992

METALS INFORMATION

STERLING SILVER - 92.5% Silver, 7.5% Copper. Liquid at 1640°F, 893°C. Solid at 1435°F, 416°C. Specific gravity - 10.36. 1 cubic inch weighs 5.457 oz. Troy. Forms available: Sheet, wires, strip/bezel, tubing, discs/oval, grain, and several different solders. Sold by the troy ounce.

RED BRASS # 230 - 85% Copper, 15% Zinc. Melting point 1877°F. Forms available: Sheet, wires, tubing, bezel, discs/oval, solders.

NICKEL SILVER # 752 - 65% Cu, 18% Nickel, 17% Zinc. Melting point 1960°F. Forms available: Sheet, wires, tubing, bezel, discs/oval, solders. Note: There is no silver content.

14 K YELLOW GOLD - 58.33% Gold, 8.3% Silver, 29.2% Copper, 4.17% Zinc. Liquid at 1625°F, 885°C. Solid at 1525°F, 829°C. Specific gravity - 13.07. 1 cubic inch weighs 6.886 oz. Troy. Forms available: Sheet, wires, tubing, strip/bezel, grain, solders. Other golds available: 14K white grain, 18K yellow and white grain, and several different solders.

Editor's Note: This information is provided for the benefit of Mr. Andy Rooney, who asked these questions at one of our shows in New York City.

excerpt: Indian Jeweler's Supply Co Catalogue, 1992

QUICK NOTES !

**Information for this page is only available in the Library Edition.

QUICK NOTES !

**Information for this page is only available in the Library Edition.

Fred Synder, Director, Consultant

N.A.²I.I.T.C.

North American Native American Indian Information & Trade Center

QUICK NOTES !

**Information for this page is only available in the Library Edition.

Fred Synder, Director, Consultant

N.A.²I.I.T.C.

North American Native American
Indian Information & Trade Center

INDIAN OWNED STORES, GIFT SHOPS, & GALLERIES

ARIZONA

CAROLE J GARCIA
RESERVATION CREATIONS
San Xavier Plaza
PO Box 27626
Tucson, AZ 85726
520-295-1350
520-622-4900

NAVAJO ARTS & CRAFTS
ENTERPRISE
PO Box 160
Window Rock, AZ 86515
520-871-4095

CALIFORNIA

AMERICAN INDIAN
CONTEMPORARY ARTS
685 Market St # 250
San Francisco, CA 94105
415-495-7600

WILSON'S DEN
2225 S Sutter
Stockton, CA 95206

COLORADO

CHARLES EAGLE PLUME
STORE INC
Hwy 7
Allenspark, CO 80510
303-586-4710

MONTANA

DOUG ALLARD'S TRADING
POST
PO Box 460
St Ignatius, MT 59865
406-745-2951

NEW MEXICO

WANDA ARAGON
PO Box 302
Acoma, NM 87034

AGUILAR INDIAN ARTS
Rt 5 Box 318C
Santa Fe, NM 87501

AGUINO'S INDIAN ARTS
& CRAFTS
PO Box 52
San Juan Pueblo, NM 87566
505-667-8175

THE BALLOON
BUTTERFLY SHOP
PO Box 1298
Espanola, NM 87532
505-753-5657

CHARLES & ELSIE BENALLY
PO Box 1767
Shiprock, NM 87420

BLUE LAKE DRUM SHOP
PO Box 1846
Taos, NM 87571

BUFFALO DANCER
PO Box C
El Prado, NM 87529
505-758-8718

CORN STUDIO
PO Box 1420
Espanola, NM 87532
505-753-4588

CRUCITA'S INDIAN SHOP
PO Box 1536
Taos, NM 87571
505-758-3576

DURAN'S POTTERY
PO Box 339
Tesuque, NM 87574
505-983-7078

HIDDEN VALLEY SHOP
Picturis Pueblo Enterprise
PO Box 487
Penasco, NM 87553
505-587-2957

INDIAN CRAFTS & GIFT SHOP
PO Box 2004
Taos, NM 87571
505-758-8202

MARGART LUJAN TRUJILLO STUDIO
PO Box 324
El Prado, NM 87529
505-758-1699

MARTINEZ GIFT SHOP
PO Box 2208
Taos, NM 87571

MERROCK GALLERIA
PO Box 1619
Espanola, NM 87532
505-753-5602

MORNING TALK INDIAN SHOP
PO Box 2328
Taos, NM 87571
505-758-1429

NATIVE AMERICAN CREATIONS GUILD
PO Box 602
Taos, NM 87571
505-758-8935

NATIVE ARTS & CRAFTS
PO Box 2741
Taos, NM 87571
505-758-9519

O'KE OWEENGE
PO Box 1095
San Juan Pueblo, NM 87566
505-852-2372

POPOVI DA STUDIO OF INDIAN ARTS
R F D 5 Box 309
Santa Fe, NM 87501
505-455-3332

PUEBLO OF ZUNI
ARTS & CRAFTS
PO Box 425
Zuni, NM 87327
505-782-5531
505-782-2136 FAX

TONY REYNA INDIAN
SHOP # 1
PO Box 1892
Taos, NM 87571
505-758-3835

TONI ROLLER POTTER &
GREEN LEAVES STUDIO
PO Box 171
Santa Clara Pueblo, NM 87532
505-753-3003

SINGING WATER
POTTERY & TOURS
Rt 1 Box 472C
Espanola, NM 87532
505-753-9663

TAOS PUEBLO
INDIAN SHOP
PO Box 2802
Taos, NM 87571

TERESA TAPIA POTTER
Rt 11 Box 1
Santa Fe, NM 87501
505-983-7075

TIWA INDIAN ARTS
& CRAFTS
PO Box 471
Taos, NM 87571

WAHLEAH'S GIFT SHOP
PO Box 253
Taos, NM 87571
505-758-7250

NEVADA

TRAIL RIDGE GALLERY
PO Box 132
Virginia City, NV 89440
702-847-9001

Editor's Note: Due to the complexity and vagueness of the Indian Arts and Crafts Act of 1990 and the lack of decision from the Attorney General's office to the request of the Indian Arts and Crafts Board to clarify the Act, this section is incomplete. Even the Source Directory issued by I A C B is outdated and has not been published since 1987, with an update in July 1990. You can write to be added to their mailing list for the new edition -- its free:

Indian Arts and Crafts Board
Room 4004 - M I B
US Department of the Interior
Washington, DC 20240
202-208-3773

A mailing list of over 4,000 Indian Artists is also available by contacting:

N.A.[2]I.I.T.C. - North American, Native American Indian
Information and Trade Center
PO Box 1000
San Carlos, AZ 85550
520-622-4900

Note: To be listed forward your information to:

N.A.[2]I.I.T.C.
Attn: Indian Owned Stores
PO Box 27626
Tucson, AZ 85726
520-292-0779 FAX

NON-INDIAN OWNED STORES FEATURING EXCELLENT EXAMPLES OF TRADITIONAL NATIVE ART

ARIZONA

BARTON WRIGHT
4143 W Gelding Dr
Phoenix, AZ 85023

R B BURNHAM & CO
Hwy 666 Box 337
Sanders, AZ 86512
520-688-2777

BURNHAMS INDIAN BOOKS & TAPES
PO Box 398
Snowflake, AZ 85937
520-546-4985

DESERT SON INC
4759 E Sunrise Dr
Tucson, AZ 85718
520-299-0818

FOREVER RESORTS
PO Box 29041
Phoenix, AZ 85038
602-968-3999

THE GALLOPING GOOSE
162 S Montezuma
Prescott, AZ 86303
520-778-7600

GARLAND'S NAVAJO RUGS
PO Box 851
Sedona, AZ 86336
520-282-4070

HEARD MUSEUM STORE
22 E Monte Vista
Phoenix, AZ 85004
602-252-8344

JERRY JACKA
PO Box 9043
Phoenix, AZ 85068
602-944-2793

MANY NATIONS
13251 E Benson Hwy
Vail, AZ 85641
520-762-5266

MELJOY INDIAN TRADERS
165 Amarilla Dr
Globe, AZ 85501
520-425-0216

SUNDANCE INDIAN CRAFTS
217 W Mahoney
Winslow, AZ 86047

TRIBAL TREASURES
1601 Navajo Blvd
Holbrook, AZ 86025
520-524-2847

CALIFORNIA

AMERICAN INDIAN ARTIFACTS
PO Box 60
Salinas, CA 93902

CA-COON MAN OF MONTEREY
1815 Redondo Way
Salinas, CA 93906

GENE AUTRY WESTERN HERITAGE MUSEUM STORE
4700 Zoo Dr
Los Angeles, CA 90027
213-667-2000

JACKRABBIT TRADERS
PO Box 326
Sierra Madre, CA 91024

LADY OF THE EARTH
4141 Stevenson # 366
Fremont, CA 94536

RICHARDSON'S AMERICAN INDIAN ART
3876 E Fedora Ave
Fresno, CA 93726
209-222-3300

THE LAUGHING CROW
11314 Collins
N Hollywood, CA 91601
818-506-1821
818-506-1661 FAX

TROCHE'S INDIAN JEWELRY
34725 Clover
Union City, CA 94587
415-471-0664

GILBERT URQUIZU
5408 Camino Real
Riverside, CA 92509
714-685-7847

WINDFLOWER INDIAN ARTS
3271 N Raymond
Altadena, CA 91001
818-791-4561

YAAK RIVER BOOKS
PO Box 2716
Monterey, CA 93940
408-659-2661

COLORADO

AMERICAN RENAISSANCE
PO Box 1570
Pagosa Springs, CO 81147

CHARLES EAGLE PLUME STORE INC
Hwy 7
Allenspark, CO 80510
303-586-4710

FILTER PRESS
PO Box 5
Palmer Lake, CO 80133
719-481-2523

JOJABO'S INDIAN ARTS
300 S Clinton # 6C
Denver, CO 80231
303-344-2827

SKY UTE INDIAN GALLERY
PO Box 550
Ignacio, CO 81137
303-563-4531

SQUASH BLOSSOM INC
450 S Galena
Aspen, CO 81611
303-925-3214

TOH-ATIN GALLERY
145 W 9th
Durango, CO 81301
303-247-8277

WESTERN TRADING POST
32 Broadway
Denver, CO 80209
303-572-7979

WINTERCOUNT
303 W Main
New Castle, CO 81647
303-984-3685

GEORGIA

TEKAKWITHA
PO Box 338
Helen, GA 30545
404-878-2938

MASSACHUSETTS

PEACEWORK GALLERY & CRAFTS
263 Main
Northampton, MA 01060
413-586-7033

NEVADA

LARRY COOLEY
PO Box E
Sparks, NV 89432
702-358-0685

NATIVE AMERICAN ART
PO Box E
Sparks, NV 89432
702-358-0685

RAINBOW MESA
3006 La Mesa Dr
Henderson, NV 89126
702-451-3332

NEW MEXICO

ARROYO TRADING CO
2111 W Apache
Farmington, NM 87401
800-225-8340

BING CROSBY'S INDIAN ARTS
2510 W Washington NE
Albuquerque, NM 87110
505-888-4800

COYOTE MOON
PO Box 591
Taos, NM 87571
505-758-4437

CRYSTAL TRADERS
PO Box 5125
Farmington, NM 87499

FOUTZ TRADING CO
PO Box 1894
Shiprock, NM 87420
505-368-5790
505-368-4441 FAX

HOGBACK TRADING CO
3221 Hwy 64
Waterflow, NM 87421
505-598-5154

LUHAN'S TRADING POST
PO Box 372
El Prado, NM 87529
505-758-0075

PACKARD'S INDIAN
TRADING CO INC
61 Old Santa Fe Trail
Santa Fe, NM 87501
505-983-9241

RUSSELL FOUTZ INDIAN
ROOM
301 W Main
Farmington, NM 87401
505-325-9413

SOUTHWEST CONNECTION
4909 Poquita Cir
Farmington, NM 87401
505-326-2097

SOUTHWEST TREASURES
601 E 3rd
Portales, NM 88130
505-359-0446

TAOS INDIAN DRUMS
PO Box 1916
Taos, NM 87571
505-758-3796

TOBE TURPEN'S INDIAN
TRADING CO
1710 S 2nd
Gallup, NM 87301
505-722-3806

YELLOWHORSE
4314 Silver SE
Albuquerque, NM 87108
505-266-0600

NEW YORK

PAINTED PONY
TRADING CO LTD
14 E Broadway
Port Jefferson, NY 11777
516-473-5155

TEXAS

YSLETA DEL SUR PUEBLO
CULTURAL CENTER
122 S Old Pueblo
El Paso, TX 79907
915-859-3916
915-859-2889 FAX

UTAH

SUNRISE TRADING
PO Box 160
Montezuma Creek, UT 84534

WYOMING

GRAND TETON
NATIONAL PARK
SIGNAL MOUNTAIN LODGE
PO Box 50
Moran, WY 83013
307-543-2831

NATIVE AMERICAN TRADING POSTS FOR BUYING RAW CRAFT MATERIALS

CANADA

IROQRAFTS LTD
RR 4
Ohsweken, Ontario
Canada N0A 1M0
416-765-5633
416-765-4206 FAX

...largest Iroquois arts and crafts supplies in Canada...
...Since 1959...

→catalogue $ 3.00

IROQUOIS PUBLISHING & CRAFT SUPPLIES
RR 2
Ohsweken, Ontario
Canada N0A 1M0

...craft supplies, books, major interest on Iroquois Tribes...

→catalogue $ 1.00 and S.A.S.E.

ARIZONA

BOVIS BEAD CO
4500 E Speedway Blvd # 67
PO Box 13345
Tucson, AZ 85732
520-318-9512

...beads, beads, and more beads...

→catalogue $ 10.00

CANYON RECORDS
4143 N 16th St
Phoenix, AZ 85016
602-266-4823

...major producer of Native American music...full craft supply for Indian craftwork...

→catalogue free with S.A.S.E.

CASES UNLIMITED
8460 S Nogales Hwy
Tucson, AZ 85706
520-573-1218

...jewelry cases, display items, etc...

→catalogue free

JAY'S OF TUCSON INDIAN ARTS, INC
6637 S 12th Ave
Tucson, AZ 85706
520-294-3397
800-736-3381

...full selection of beads, findings, heshie for the do it yourselfer...

→catalogue free

MANY NATIONS
PO Box 460
Vail, AZ 85641
520-762-5266

...authentic American Indian items...
Wintercount notecards...

→catalogue

NATIONAL NATIVE AMERICAN COOPERATIVE
PO Box 1000
San Carlos, AZ 85550
520-622-4900
520-292-0779

...hard to find Indian craft supplies for tribes since 1969...tapes, books, herbal medicines and authentic crafts of 360 Indian Nations...

→catalogue - price sheet

NATIVE SEEDS / S.E.A.R.C.H.
2509 N Campbell Ave # 325
Tucson, AZ 85719
520-327-9123
520-327-5821

...traditional food seeds, crafts, music...

→catalogue $ 1.00

TREASURE CHEST BOOKS
1802 W Grant Rd # 101
PO Box 5250
Tucson, AZ 85703
520-623-9558
800-627-0048

...publishers and distributors of the best books from the Southwest...

→catalogue free

WINTERSUN TRADING CO
107 N San Francisco # 1
Flagstaff, AZ 86001
520-774-2884

...traditional herbs and American Indian arts...

→catalogue in progress

CALIFORNIA

PACIFIC WESTERN TRADERS
305 Wool St
Folsom, CA 95630
916-985-3851

...since 1971 California's American Indian trading post and resource center...supplies, books, herbs, crafts...

RISING ARROW
Box 70754
265-M Sobrante Way
Sunnyvale, CA 94086
408-732-2001

...chez beads, feathers, books...authentic Indian craft supplies...

→catalogue $ 1.00

SHENANDOAH FILM PRODUCTIONS
538 G St
Arcata, CA 95521
707-822-1030
616-536-0015

...health related films and videos on Native Americans...

→catalogue free with S.A.S.E.

CHUCK SNELL
PO Box 769
Trinidad, CA 95570
707-677-0460

...every kind of sea shell from all over the world...

→catalogue - free list

STAMPIN DESIGNER
1809 Westcliff Dr # 249
Newport Beach, CA 92660
818-796-0868

...largest selection of rubber stamps on American Indians and Southwest...

→catalogue free

WAKEDA TRADING POST
PO Box 19146
Sacramento, CA 95819
916-485-9838

...mail order only...beads, bells, feathers, hides, tapes...

→catalogue $ 1.00

COLORADO

AZUSA PUBLISHING INC
CHUCK LEWIS
PO Box 2526
Englewood, CO 80150
303-783-0073
303-783-0073 FAX

...American Indian postcards, posters, prints...historic photographic images...

STEVE EAGLES NATIVE AMERICAN REGALIA
PO Box 88142
Colorado Springs, CO 80909
719-495-0798
719-495-0897 FAX

...speciality in traditional reglia and materials to make your own regalia...

→catalogue $ 3.00

ORR'S TRADING CO
2654 S Broadway
Denver, CO 80210
303-722-6466

...beads, buckskin, feathers and a whole lot more...

→catalogue - price list

POW WOW NOTIONS
2648 W Colorado Ave
Colorado Springs, CO 80904
719-633-0960

...complete selection beads, beading supplies, fringe, shells, feathers, bells...

WESTERN TRADING POST
PO Box 9070
Denver, CO 80209
303-777-7750

...since 1952 quality craft supplies, books and more...

→catalogue $ 3.00

WINTERCOUNT
PO Box 889
New Castle, CO 81647
303-984-3685
303-984-3266 FAX

...American Indian art, prose, poetry...tee shirts, note cards, wall tiles, posters...

→catalogue $ 2.00

KENTUCKY

YA-TE-HEY GALLERY AND BOOKS
1841 Brownsboro Rd
Louisville, KY 40206
502-893-0250

...books, books, books, on American Indians...

→catalogue S.A.S.E. for price list.

LOUISIANA

WRITTEN HERITAGE BOOKS
8009 Wales St
New Orleans, LA 70126
504-246-3742

...books, videos, tapes, CD, ROM on American Indians...

→catalogue - price list

MASSACHUSETTS

AMERICAN BROADCLOTH
PO Box 5784
Marlboro, MA 01752
617-965-6938

...major source for tradecloth and four way blankets...

→catalogue $ 3.00 samples

WANDERING BULL INC
247 S Main St
PO Box 1075
Attleboro, MA 02703
508-226-6074
508-226-4878 FAX

...American Indian crafts, supplies, gifts...

→catalogue $ 2.00

MICHIGAN

NOC BAY TRADING COMPANY
PO Box 295
1133 Washington Ave
Escanaba, MI 49829
800-684-8000

...one of the best sources in Michigan for your indian craft supplies...

→catalogue $ 3.00

VEON CREATIONS
3565 State Hwy V
De Soto, MO 63020
314-586-5377

...books, publications on Indian beading...excellent resource... ...since 1964...

→catalogue free with S.A.S.E.

MONTANA

BUFFALO CHIPS
327 S 24th St W
Billings, MT 59102
406-656-8954

...great selection of Indian craft supplies, music, blankets...

→catalogue $ 2.00

FOUR WINDS INDIAN TRADING POST
PO Box 580
St Ignatius, MT 59865
406-745-4336

...American Indian artifacts, craft supplies, tradecloth...

→catalogue $ 3.00

PORCUPINES UNLIMITED
PO Box 20622
Billings, MT 59104
406-259-7552

...porcupine quills, guard hair, teeth, claws, hides, skulls...

→catalogue

NEVADA

LARRY G COOLEY
PO Box E
Sparks, NV 89431
702-358-0685

...turquoise in all forms..natural and stabalized...

→no catalogue

NEW JERSEY

LAKOTA BOOKS
PO Box 140
Kendall Park, NJ 08824
908-297-2253
908-940-9429 FAX

...largest selection of books, tapes, language...strickly on the Lakota tribes...

→catalogue

SUNRISE TRADING POST
35 Park Ave
Dumont, NJ 07628
201-384-4794
201-387-8186 FAX

...largest selection of Indian craft supplies in the east...speciality hand painted feathers...

→catalogue $3.50

NEW MEXICO

ALL ONE TRIBE DRUMS
PO Drawer N
Taos, NM 87571
505-751-0019
505-751-0509 FAX
800-442-DRUM

...unique drums for the serious drummer...unique handle and Indian painted designs...

→catalogue with S.A.S.E.

AMERICAN HERITAGE INDIAN ARTS
9709-A Trumbull SE
Albuquerque, NM 87123
505-271-1981
800-395-3962

...warbonnets, warbonnets, warbonnets...

→catalogue free with S.A.S.E.

INDIAN JEWELRY
SUPPLY CO
601 E Coal Ave
Box 1774
Gallup, NM 87301
505-722-4451
505-722-4172 FAX
800-545-6540 Ordering

Office also:
2105 San Mateo Blvd NE
Albuquerque, NM 87110
505-265-3701
505-266-5548

...full selection for the jeweler...silver, gold, tools, jewelry findings, stones, lapidary equipment...

→catalogue $ 6.00 per set of 3:
Findings and Metals
Stones, Lapidary
Metalsmithing tools and supplies

SUN WEST INC
324 Lomas NW
PO Box 25227
Albuquerque, NM 87125
505-243-3781
505-843-6183
800-771-3781

...silver, and gold...buttons, button covers, charms, chains, beads...

→catalogue - free

TAOS DRUMS
PO Box 1916
Taos, NM 87571
505-758-9844 FAX
800-424-DRUM

...since 1951 caretakers of the drum...

→catalogue free call 800 #

NEW YORK

GRAY OWL INDIAN CRAFT
SALES CORP
PO Box 468
132-05 Merrick Blvd
Jamaica, NY 11434
718-341-4000
718-527-6000 FAX

...over 4,000 items of craft supplies...

→catalogue $ 3.00

GREENFIELD REVIEW
LITERARY CENTER
PO Box 308
Greenfield Center, NY 12833
518-584-1728

...best selection of books by Native American authors...

→catalogue free with S.A.S.E.

MYSTIC FIRE VIDEO
PO Box 422
New York, NY 10012
212-941-0999
212-941-1443
800-292-9001

......Native America on mystic fire video...

→catalogue free call 800 #

NATIVE NATURALS
101 H Ellis St
Staten Island, NY 10307
718-227-0177
718-227-0079 FAX

...antlers, bones, claws, teeth, hides, skulls and much more...

NORTH CAROLINA

CHEROKEE PUBLICATIONS
PO Box 430
Cherokee, NC 28719
704-488-8856
704-488-6934 FAX

...books, maps and a whole lot more all on the Cherokee tribe...

→catalogue free with S.A.S.E.

OHIO

WOODEN NICKLE
TRADING CONCERN
1324 Woodrow St NW
North Canton, OH 44720
216-966-1408

...cedar feather boxes, walnut display boxes...craft supplies...

OKLAHOMA

FULL CIRCLE
COMMUNICATIONS
1131 S College Ave
Tulsa, OK 74104
800-940-8849

...videos on Indian culture...

→catalogue free with S.A.S.E.

OREGON

JIM & MIKE BOND
INDIAN TRADERS
35113 Brewster Rd
Lebanon, OR 97355
503-258-3645
503-258-5167 FAX

...one of the oldest, best selection, highest quality sources of raw craft materials, regalia, music...for all types of indian crafts...

→catalogue, price sheet

SOUTH DAKOTA

NATIVE AMERICAN
HERBAL TEA INC
PO Box 1266
Aberdeen, SD 57402
605-226-2006

...six specially blended traditional teas...

→catalogue - brochure with S.A.S.E.

SIOUX TRADING POST INC
415 6th St
Rapid City, SD 57701
800-456-3394

...world's largest selection of Italian beads...books, tapes, craft supplies...

→catalogue $ 2.00

TEXAS

CRAZY CROW
TRADING POST
PO Box 314
Denison, TX 75021
903-463-1366

...excellent selection of craft supplies and ribbon shirits...

→catalogue $ 3.00

WOODEN PENNY
TRADING POST
105 Bois D'Arc
Lake Jackson, TX 77566
409-297-8953
409-265-6813 FAX

...American Indian craft and ceremonial supplies...

→catalogue $ 2.00

UTAH

EAGLE FEATHER
TRADING POST
168 W 12th St
Ogden, UT 84404

...Indian arts and crafts, craft supplies, books...

→catalogue $ 3.00

WASHINGTON

MAC RAE'S INDIAN BOOK
DISTRIBUTOR
KEN MACRAE
1605 Cole St
Enumclaw WA 98022
206-825-3737

...largest selection of books on Indians...

→catalogue - price list

RINGS AND THINGS
214 N Wall Ave # 990
PO Box 450
Spokane, WA 99210
509-624-8565
509-838-2602 FAX
800-366-2156

...one of the largest selections of craft findings in the pacific northwest...

→catalogue - free with S.A.S.E.

SHIPWRECK BEADS
2727 Westmoor Ct SW
Olympia, WA 98502
306-754-BEAD (2323)

...one of the largest selections of beads from all over the world...

→catalogue $ 4.00

editors note:

This list is one of the most useful when starting your own Indian Trading Post, art & craft shop or gift shop. Often we get request where to buy beads, books, tapes, paper products, sidelines, herbs, teas and videos. Majority of those listed sell both wholesale and retail. Some are direct manufacturers, printers and sole sources. Always request information on your letterhead, copy of your business license, and a 9" x 12" self addressed envelope helps ensure a quick response. You should also realize many of these businesses will be at a major Indian festival/craft show on the weekends and may be on the road for a week or two occasionally. All beads and most supplies are available depending on overseas manufacturers, Nature's Growing Season, availability of supply, and many outside factors of which Indian traders, trading posts and direct sources have very limited control. It is very important when starting a craft project to order **more** than enough items for your project to complete it.

QUICK NOTES !

**Information for this page is only available in the Library Edition.

Fred Synder, Director, Consultant

N.A.²I.I.T.C

North American Native American
Indian Information & Trade Center

QUICK NOTES !

**Information for this page is only available in the Library Edition.

Fred Synder, Director, Consultant

N.A.²I.I.T.C.

North American Native American
Indian Information & Trade Center

DEALERS IN ANTIQUE INDIAN ART

ARIZONA

MICHAEL BRADFORD
PO Box 174
Cottonwood, AZ 86326
520-646-5596

...historic kachina, basketry, textiles of the Southwest...

GORDON FRITZ
PO Box 64445
Tucson, AZ 85728
520-888-8889

...American Indian art...

GALLERY 10 INC
Lee Cohen
7045 3rd Ave
Scottsdale, AZ 85251
602-994-0405

...textiles, pottery, paintings, basketry...

GARLAND'S
PO Box 851
Sedona, AZ 86336
520-282-4070

...Hopi carvings and Navajo rugs...

MICHAEL HIGGINS
4351 E Grant Rd
Tucson, AZ 85712
520-327-3115

...American Indian art...

JOHN HILL
6990 E Main 2nd Fl
Scottsdale, AZ 85251
602-946-2910

...Southwestern kachinas and jewelry...

NORTH AMERICAN INDIAN
INFO & TRADE CENTER
FRED SYNDER
PO BOX 27676
Tucson, AZ 85726
520-622-4900
520-292-0779 FAX

...the Indian connection for appraisal, buying and selling North American Indian art...

PRIMITIVE ARTS
PAUL SHEPARD
3026 E Broadway Blvd
Tucson, AZ 85716
520-326-4852

...North American Indian art...

CALIFORNIA

AMERIND ART INC
ANTHONY BERLANT
1304 12th
Santa Monica, CA 90401
213-395-5678

...textiles, pottery, jewelry of the Southwest...

ANACAPA & ORTEGA
MICHAEL HASKELL
Santa Barbara, CA 93101
805-962-9653

...North American Indian art...

BILL CASKEY & LIZ LEES
PO Box 1637
Topanga, CA 90290
213-455-2886

...North American Indian art...

JIM CONLEY
748 ½ La Cienega
Los Angeles, CA 90096
310-289-1601

...North American Indian art...

FAIRMONT TRADING CO
JIM & LAURIS PHILLIPS
PO Box 689
S Pasadena, CA 91030
818-796-3609

...jewelry, basketry, pottery and textiles...

SANDRA HORN
736 Alta Vista
Mill Valley, CA 94941
415-388-2245

...North American Indian art...

INDIAN TERRITORY
LEONARD WOOD
305 N Coast Highway
Laguna Beach, CA 92651
714-497-5747

...museum quality basketry, textiles, potter, jewelry, Plains Indian art...

JAMES JETER
PO Box 682
Summerland, CA 93067
805-969-6746

...North American Indian art...

KIM MARTINDALE
38 W Main
Ventura, CA 93001
818-889-5187

...North American Indian art...

RAMONA MORRIS
PO Box 620278
Woodside, CA 94062
415-851-8670

...American Indian art...

NATIVE AMERICAN
ART GALLERY
PHILIP GARAWAY
215 Windward Ave
Venice, CA 90291
213-392-8465

...Navajo, Hopi, textiles, kachinas, pottery, jewelry, California and Southwest baskets...

PRIMITIVE ARTS
LAURENT BERMUDEZ
1859 Solano Ave # B
Berkeley, CA 94707
510-527-1042

...American Indian art...

SHERWOOD'S SPIRIT
OF AMERICA
MICHAEL KOKIN
325 N Beverly Dr
Beverly Hills, CA 90210
213-274-6700

...rare examples of Plains, Northwest Coast, Southwest, Woodlands, California Indian cultures...

GARY SPRATT
PO Box 162
Rutherford, CA 94573
707-963-4022

...North American Indian art...

COLORADO

AMERICAN RENAISSANCE
MARK WINTER
PO Box 1570
Pagosa Springs, CO 81147
303-264-5533

...textiles of the American southwest...

BENZAV TRADING CO
STEVE & DAVID PICKELNER
PO Box 911
Fort Collins, CO 80522
303-482-6397

...North American Indian art...

JAMES COLLINS
PO Box 9174
Aspen, CO 81612
303-923-3190

...fine and rare textiles, jewelry, pottery of Navajo and Pueblo people...

ELK CREEK TRADING CO
JERRY BECKER
200 Aspen Ln
Pine, CO 80470
303-838-6245

...antique textiles of the Navajo, Pueblo, Saltillo, Rio Grande...

FINE AMERICAN ART LTD
DAVID COOK
1637 Wazee
Denver, CO 80210
303-623-8181

...fine textiles, jewelry, pottery, Plains Indian art...

JOANNE LYON GALLERY
525 E Cooper Ave
Aspen, CO 81611
303-925-9044

...American Indian ethnographic art...

GEORGE SHAW GALLERY
525 E Cooper Ave
Aspen, CO 81611
303-925-2873

...North American Indian art...

NEAL R SMITH FINE ART
2353 E 3rd Ave
Denver, CO 80206
303-399-3119

...North American Indian art...

MARTHA STRUEVER
1777 Larimer # 2108
Denver, CO 80202
303-298-1707

...Native American art...

CONNECTICUT

GUTHMAN AMERICANA
WILLIAM GUTHMAN
PO Box 392
Westport, CT 06881
203-259-9763

...French and Indian War period art...

FLORIDA

HOGAN GALLERY INC
BRUCE GREEN
PO Box 7901
Naples, FL 33941
813-455-1752

...North American Indian art...

IDAHO

AMERICAN WEST GALLERY
ALAN EDISON
PO Box 3130
Ketchum, ID 83340
208-726-1714

...North American Indian art...

PAWEL RACZKA
PO Box 647
Sun Valley, ID 83353
208-788-0102

...North American Indian art...

LOUISIANA

MERRILL B DOMAS GALLERY
824 Chartres
New Orleans, LA 70116
504-586-0479

...Southwest and California basketry, Southeastern art and artifacts...

MASSACHUSETTS

ROBERT BAUVER
R F D 1
Orange, MA 01364
508-544-0231

...19th century Navajo and Pueblo jewelry...

MARY DAHL
189 N Washington
Norton, MA 02766
508-285-4598

...North American Indian dolls a specialty...

HURST GALLERY
NORMAN HURST
53 Mount Auburn
Cambridge, MA 02138
617-491-6888

...American Indian art...

COLLEEN JAMES
120 Richards Ave
Paxton, MA 01612
508-347-2744

...art, basketry, textiles of North American tribes...

NASHOBA TRADING CO
ALAN SILBERBERG
PO Box 1190
Littleton, MA 01460
508-486-8250

...North American Indian art...

VISIONS LTD
MARK RUDDICK
1046 Great Pond Rd
N Andover, MA 01845

...pottery, baskets, weavings of the western tirbes...

MICHIGAN

RICHARD POHRT, JR
340 Brookside Dr
Ann Arbor, MI 48105
313-769-3942

...woodlands Indian art...

NEW JERSEY

JAMES HART, JR
6554 Irving Ave
Pennsauken, NJ 08109
609-663-1466

...North American Indian art...

NEW MEXICO

ARROWSMITH'S
REX ARROWSMITH
PO Box 175
Lincoln, NM 88338

...North American Indian art...

ART QUEST
LARRY FRANK
PO Box 292
Arroyo Hondo, NM 87513
505-776-2281

...New Mexico Indian art...

JOSHUA BAER INC
116 ½ E Palace Ave
Santa Fe, NM 87501
505-988-8944

...fine Southwest textiles...

TAYLOR DALE
53 Old Sante Fe Trl
Sante Fe, NM 87501
505-988-1487

...North American Indian art...

DEWEY GALLERIES LTD
RAY DEWEY
74 E San Francisco
Santa Fe, NM 87501
505-982-8632

...North American Indian art...

ECONOMOS WORKS OF ART
JAMES ECONOMOS
225 Canyon Rd
Santa Fe, NM 87501
505-982-6347

...American Indian art...

H J EVETTS &
R VANDENBERG
PO Box 2783
Corrales, NM 87048
505-897-4029

...historic Navajo and Pueblo jewelry, 19th century Plains Indian art...

ROBERT GALLEGOS
PO Box 247
Albuquerque, NM 87103
505-255-6740

...North American Indian art...

GALLERY 10 INC
PHILIP COHEN
225 Canyon Rd
Santa Fe, NM 87501
505-983-9707

...fine examples textiles, pottery, paintings, basketry...

KANIA/FERRIN GALLERY
JOHN KANIA
662 Canyon Rd
Santa Fe, NM 87501
505-982-8767

...historic kachinas, pottery, textiles and jewelry...

ALAN KESSLER GALLERY
836 Canyon Rd
Santa Fe, NM 87501
505-986-0123

...historic kachinas and 19th century Plains Indian art...

LANFORD-GILMORE
B LANFORD & R GILMORE
7512 Lantern NE
Albuquerque, NM 87109
505-888-3093

...North American Indian art...

MORNING STAR GALLERY
M GRIMMER & J DAVIS
513 Canyon Rd
Santa Fe, NM 87501
505-982-8187

...fine and rare art of the North American Indian...

JAMES REID LTD
114 E Palace Ave
Santa Fe, NM 87501
505-988-1147

...North American Indian art...

CHRISTOPHER SELSER
PO Box 9328
Santa Fe, NM 87501
505-984-1481

...antique Southwestern and Plains art...

SPANISH & INDIAN
TRADING CO
ERICH ERDOES
924 Paseo De Peralta # 1
Santa Fe, NM 87501
505-983-6106

...textiles, basketry, pottery, Plains Indian art speciality...

BOB WARD
PO Box 179
Santa Fe, NM 87501
505-983-2656

...North American Indian art...

NEW YORK

ALEXANDER GALLERY
ALEXANDER ACEVEDO
980 Madison Ave
New York, NY 10021
212-472-1636

...18th and 19th century woodlands and plains art...

JOSEPH G GERENA FINE ART
12 E 86th St # 627
New York, NY 10028
212-650-0117

...American Indian art...

GRAVEN IMAGES LTD
SCOTT RODOLITZ
475 Broome # 6B
New York, NY 10013
212-226-2550

...American Indian art...

JEFFREY MEYERS
12 E 86th St
New York, NY 10028
212-472-0115

...North American Indian and Eskimo art...

JOHN MOLLOY
212 E 70th # 2C
New York, NY 10021
212-249-1562

...North American Indian art...

TROTTA-BONO
TED TROTTA
PO Box 34
Shrub Oak, NY 10588
914-528-6604

...North American Indian art of the frontier, wood, bone, antler, implements...

PENNSYLVANIA

AMERICAN INDIAN ARTS
MARCY BURNS
PO Box 181
Glenside, PA 19038
215-576-1559

...19th century baskets, textiles, pottery a speciality...

CROWN & EAGLE ANTIQUES
Rt 202,
3 miles south New Hope
New Hope, PA 18938
215-794-7334

...museum quality 19th century crafts...

TEXAS

JAN DUGGAN
5423 Braxtonshire
Houston, TX 77069
713-440-9120

...California and Southwest basketry, beadwork, textiles...

WATERBIRD TRADERS
MICHAEL MCKISSICK
3420 Greenville Ave
Dallas, TX 75206
214-821-4606

...19th century Plains Indian art, beadwork, textiles, pottery, jewelry of the Southwest...

WASHINGTON

CURIOSERI
BRUCE BOYD
316 Occidental Ave S # 100
Seattle, WA 98104
206-223-0717

...American Indian art...

Note: Most dealers have been members of the antique Tribal Art Dealers Association Inc for three or more years.

Antique Tribal Arts Dealers Association
PO Box 23194
Santa Fe, NM 87502

INDIAN ART AUCTIONEERS

CALIFORNIA

Don Bennett Whitehawk, Inc
PO Box 283
Agoura, CA 91376
818-991-5596

Butterfield & Butterfield
220 San Bruno Ave at 15th St
San Francisco, CA 94103
415-861-7500

R G Munn Auctions
8625 Tumbleweed Terrace
Santee, CA 92071
619-596-7630

ILLINOIS

Dunning's Auctions
PO Box 866 (60121)
755 Church Road
Elgin, IL 60123
708-741-3483
708-741-3589 FAX

MASSACHUSETTS

Willis Henry Auctions
22 Main Street
Marshfield, MA 02050
617-834-7774

Robert W Skinner, Inc.
Bolton Gallery
Route 117
Bolton, MA 01740
508-779-6241

MONTANA

Allard Auctions
Col Doug Allard
PO Box 460
St. Ignatius, MT 59865
406-745-2951
800-821-3318
406-745-2961 FAX

Four Winds Indian Trading Post
Preston E Miller/Carolyn Corey
PO Box 580
3 Miles North on Highway 93
St. Ignatius, MT 59865
406-745-4336

NEW MEXICO

W E Channing Auctions
53 Old Santa Fe Trail
Santa Fe, NM 87501
415-988-1078

Crownpoint Rug Weavers
Auctions / Ena Chavez
PO Box 1630
Crownpoint, NM 87313
505-786-5302

Red Shell Auctions
John Hornbek
PO Box 764 (87305)
601 South 2nd
Gallup, NM 87301
505-722-6963

NEW YORK

Christie's Publications
21-24 44th Avenue
Long Island City,. NY 11101
718-784-1480

OHIO

Garth's Auctions
2690 Stratford Road
PO Box 369
Delaware, OH 43015
614-362-4771

Back issues of catalogs are not always available from the auction houses. For back issues of specific catalogs we suggest you contact:

Catalogs Unlimited
PO Box 327
High Falls, NY 12440
914-687-0484

Sotheby's Catalog Subscriptions
PO Box 5111
Norwalk, CT 06856-5111

PERSONAL QUICK NOTES

ANSWERS TO FREQUENTLY ASKED QUESTIONS

Who is an Indian?

No single federal or tribal criterion establishes a person's identity as an Indian. Government agencies use differing criteria to determine who is an Indian eligible to participate in their programs. Tribes also have varying eligibility criteria for membership. To determine what the criteria might be for agencies or tribes, you must contact them directly.

For its purposes, the Bureau of Census counts anyone an Indian who declares himself or herself to be such.

To be eligible for Bureau of Indian Affairs services, an Indian must (1) be a member of a tribe recognized by the federal government and (2) must, for some purposes, be of one-fourth or more Indian ancestry. By legislative and administrative decision, the Aleuts, Eskimos and Indians of Alaska are eligible for BIA services. Most of the BIA's services and programs, however, are limited to Indians living on or near federal reservations.

What is an Indian Tribe?

Originally, an Indian tribe was a body of people bound together by blood ties who were socially, politically, and religiously organized, who lived together in a defined territory and who spoke a common language or dialect.

The establishment of the reservation system created some new tribal groupings when two or three tribes were placed on one reservation, or when members of one tribe were spread over two or three reservations.

How does an Indian become a member of a tribe?

A tribe sets up its own membership criteria, although the U.S. Congress can also establish tribal membership criteria. Becoming a member of a particular tribe requires meeting its membership rules, including adoption. Except for adoption, the amount of blood quantum needed varies, with some tribes requiring only a trace of Indian blood (of the tribe) while others require as much as one-half.

What is a reservation?

In the U.S. there are only two kinds of reserved lands that are well known - military and Indian. An Indian reservation is land a tribe reserved for itself when it relinquished its other land areas to the U.S. through treaties. More recently, Congressional acts, executive orders and administrative acts have created reservations. Some reservations, today, have non-Indian residents and land owners.

Are Indians required to stay on reservations?
No. Indians are free to move about like all other Americans.

Did all Indians speak one Indian language?
No. At the end of the 15th century, more than 300 languages were spoken by the native population of what is now the United States. Some were linked by "linguistic stocks" which meant that widely scattered tribal groups had some similarities in their languages. Today, some 250 tribal languages are still spoken, some by only a few individuals and others by many. Most Indians now use English as their main language for communicating with non-tribal members. For many, it is a second language.

Do Indians serve in the Armed Forces?
Indians have the same obligations for military service as other U.S. citizens. They have fought in all American wars since the Revolution. In the Civil War, they served on both sides. Eli S. Parker, Seneca from New York, was at Appamattox as aide to Gen. Ulyssess S. Grant when Lee surrendered, and the unit of Confederate Brigadier General Stand Watie, Cherokee, was the last to surrender. It was not until World War I that Indians' demonstrated patriotism (6,000 of more than 8,000 who served were volunteers) moved congress to pass the Indian Citizenship Act of 1924. In World War II, 25,000 Indian men and women, mainly enlisted Army personnel, fought on all fronts in Europe and Asia, winning (according to an incomplete count) 71 Air Medals, 51 Silver Stars, 47 Bronze Stars, 34 Distinguished Flying Crosses, and two Congressional Medals of Honor. The most famous Indian exploit of World War II was the use by Navajo Marines of their language as a battlefield code, the only such code which the enemy could not break. In the Korean conflict, there was one Indian Congressional medal of Honor winner. In the Vietnam War, 41,500 Indians served in the military forces. In 1990, prior to Operation Desert Storm, some 24,000 Indian men and women were in the military. Approximately 3,000 served in the Persian Gulf with three among those killed in action. One out of every four Indian males is a military veteran and 45 to 47 percent of tribal leaders today are military veterans.

Are Indians wards of the government?

No. The federal government is a trustee of Indian property, it is not a guardian of individual Indians. The Secretary of the Interior is authorized by law, in many instances, to protect the interests of minors and incompetents, but this protection does not confer a guardian-ward relationship.

Do Indians get payments from the government?

No individual is automatically paid for being an Indian. The federal government may pay a tribe or an individual in compensation for damages for losses resulting from treaty violations, for encroachments on Indian lands, or for other past or present wrongs. A tribe or an individual may also receive a government check for payment of income from their lands and resources, but his is only because their resources are held in trust by the Secretary of the Interior and payment for their use has been collected from users by the federal government in their behalf. Fees from oil or grazing leases are an example.

Are Indians U.S. Citizens?

Yes. Before the U.S. Congress extended American citizenship in 1924 to all Indians born in the territorial limits of the United States, citizenship has been conferred upon approximately two-thirds of the Indian population through treaty agreements, statutes, naturalization proceedings, and by "service in the Armed Forces with an honorable discharge" in World War I. Indians are also members of their respective tribes.

Can Indians Vote?

Indians have the same right to vote as other U.S. Citizens. In 1948, the Arizona supreme court declared unconstitutional disenfranchising interpretations of the state constitution and Indians were permitted to vote as in most other states. A 1953 Utah state law stated that persons living on Indian reservation were not residents of the state and could not vote. That law was subsequently repealed. In 1954, Indians in Maine who were not then federally recognized were given the right to vote, and in 1962, New Mexico extended the right to vote to Indians.

Indians also vote in state and local elections and in the elections of the tribes of which they are members. Each tribe, however, determines which of its members is eligible to vote in its elections and qualifications to do so are not related to the individual Indian's right to vote in national, state, or local (non-Indian) elections.

Do Indians have the right to hold federal, state and local government offices?

Indians have the same right as other citizens to hold public office, and Indian men and women have held elective and appointive offices at all levels of government. Charles Curtis, a Kaw Indian from Kansas, served as Vice President of the United States under President Herbert Hoover.

Indians have been elected to the U.S. Congress from time to time for more than 80 years. Ben Reifel, a Sioux Indian from South Dakota, served five terms in the U.S. House of Representatives. Ben Nighthorse Campbell, a member of the Northern Cheyenne Tribe of Montana, was elected to the U.S. House of Representatives in 1986 from the Third District of Colorado, and is currently serving in his third term. He is the only American Indian currently serving in Congress. Indians also served and now hold office in a number of state legislatures. Others currently hold or have held elected or appointed positions in state judiciary systems and in county and city governments including local school boards.

Do Indians have the right to own land?

Yes. As U.S. citizens, Indians can buy and hold title to land purchased with their own funds. Nearly all lands of Indian tribes, however, are held in trust for them by the United States and there is no general law that permits a tribe to sell its land. Individual Indians also own trust land which they can sell, but only upon the approval of the Secretary of the Interior or his representative. If an Indian wants to extinguish the trust title of his land and hold title like any other citizen (with all the attendant responsibilities such as paying taxes), he can do so if the Secretary of the Interior or his authorized representative, determines that he is able to manage his own affairs. This is a protection for the individual.

Do Indians pay taxes?

Yes. They pay the same taxes as other citizens with the following exceptions applying to those Indians living on federal reservations: (1) federal income taxes are not levied on income from trust lands held for them by the United States; (2) state income taxes are not paid on income earned on a federal reservation; (3) state sales tax are not paid on transactions made on a federal reservation, and (4) local property taxes are not paid on reservation or trust land.

Do laws that apply to non-Indians also apply to Indians?

Yes. As U.S. citizens, Indians are generally subject to federal, state, and local laws. On federal reservations, however, only federal and tribal laws apply to members of the tribe unless the Congress provides otherwise. In federal law, the Assimilative Crimes Act makes any violation of state criminal law a federal offense on reservations.

Most tribes now maintain tribal court systems and facilities to detain tribal members convicted of certain offenses within the boundaries of the the reservation. A recent U.S. Supreme Court decision restricted the legal jurisdiction of federal tribes on their reservations to members only, meaning that an Indian tribe could not try in its tribal court a member of another tribe even though that person might be a resident on the reservation and have violated its law. There currently are bills in the Congress that would restore tribes' rights to prosecute any Indian violating laws on an Indian reservation.

Does the United States still make treaties with Indians?

Congress ended treaty-making with Indian tribes in 1871. Since then, relations with Indian groups are by congressional acts, executive orders, and executive agreements. The treaties that were made often contain obsolete commitments which have either been fulfilled or superseded by congressional legislation., The provision of educational, health, welfare, and other services by the government to tribes often has extended beyond treaty requirements. A number of large Indian groups have no treaties, yet share in the many services for Indians provided by the federal government.

The specifics of particular treaties signed by government negotiators with Indians are contained in one volume (Vol.II) of the publication, "Indian Affairs, Laws, and Treaties", compiled, annotated and edited by Charles Kappler. Published by the Government Printing Office in 1904, it is now out of print, but can be found in most large law libraries. More recently, the treaty volume has been published privately under the title, "Indian Treaties, 1778-1883". Originals of all the treaties are maintained by the National Archives and Records Service of the General Services Administration. A duplicate of a treaty is available upon request for a fee. The agency will also answer questions about specific Indian treaties. Write to: Diplomatic Branch, National Archives and Records Service, Washington, D.C. 20408.

How do Indian tribes govern themselves?

Most tribal governments are organized democratically, that is, with an elected leadership. The governing body is generally referred to as a "council" and is comprised of persons elected by vote of the eligible adult tribal members. The presiding official is the "chairman", although some tribes use other titles such as "principal chief", "president" or "governor".

An elected tribal council, recognized as such by the Secretary of the Interior, has authority to speak and act for the tribe and to represent it in negotiations with federal, state, and local governments.

Tribal governments generally define conditions of membership, regulate domestic relations of members, prescribe rules of inheritance for reservation property not in trust status, levy taxes, regulate property under tribal jurisdiction, control conduct of members by tribal ordinances, and administer justice.

Many tribes are organized under the Indian Reorganization Act (IRA) of 1934, including a number of Alaskan Native villages, which adopted formal governing documents (Constitutions) under the provisions of a 1936 amendment to the IRA. The passage in 1971 of the Alaska Native Claims Settlement Act, however, provided for the creation of village and regional corporations under state law to manage the money and lands granted by the Act. The Oklahoma Indian Welfare Act of 1936 provided for the organization of Indian tribes within the State of Oklahoma. Some tribes do not operate under any of these acts, but are nevertheless organized under documents approved by the Secretary of the Interior. Some tribes continue their traditional forms of government.

Prior to reorganization, the tribes maintained their own, often highly developed, systems of self-government.

Do Indians have special rights different from other citizens?

Any special rights that Indian tribes or members of those tribes have are generally based on treaties or other agreements between the United States and tribes. The heavy price Indians paid to retain certain "sovereign" rights was to relinquish much of their land to the United States. The inherent rights they did not relinquish are protected by U.S. law. Among those may be hunting and fishing rights and access to religious sites.

How do I trace my Indian ancestry and become a member of a tribe?

The first step in tracing Indian ancestry is basic genealogical research if you do not already have specific family information and documents that identify tribal ties. Some information to obtain is; names of ancestors; dates of birth, marriages and death; places where they lived; their brothers and sisters, if any, and most importantly, tribal affiliations. Among family documents to check are bibles, wills, and other such papers. The next step is to determine whether any of your ancestors are on an official tribal roll or census. For this there are several sources. Contact the National Archives and Records Administration, Natural Resources Branch, Civil

Archives Division, 8th and Pennsylvania Ave. N.W., Washington, D.C. 20408. Also, you may contact the tribal enrollment officer of the tribe of which you think your ancestors may have been members. Another source is the Bureau of Indian Affairs, Branch of Tribal Enrollment, 1849 C St. N.W., Washington, D.C. 20240. The key in determining your Indian ancestry is identification of a specific tribal affiliation.

Becoming a member of a tribe is determined by the enrollment criteria of the tribe from which your Indian blood may be derived, and this varies with each tribe. Generally, if your linkage to an identified tribal member is far removed, you would not qualify for membership, but it is the tribe, not the BIA, which makes the determination.

What does tribal sovereignty mean to Indians?

When Indian tribes first encountered Europeans, they were dealt with from strength of numbers and were treated as sovereigns with whom treaties were made. When tribes gave up lands to the U.S., they retained certain sovereignty over the lands they kept. While such sovereignty is limited today, it is nevertheless jealously guarded by the tribes against encroachments by other sovereign entities such as states. Tribes enjoy a direct government-to-government relationship with the U.S. government wherein no decisions about their lands and people are made without their consent.

What does the term "federally-recognized" mean?

Indian tribes that have a legal relationship to the U.S. government through treaties, Acts of Congress, executive orders, or other administrative actions are "recognized" by the federal government as official entities and receive services from the state. Others have neither federal or state recognition and may not seek such recognition. Any tribe or group is eligible to seek federal recognition by a process administered by a program of the Bureau of Indian Affairs or through direct petition to the U.S. Congress. Only the congress has the power to terminate a tribe from federal recognition. In that case, a tribe no longer has its lands held in trust by the U.S. nor does it receive services from the BIA.

Do all Indians live on reservations?

No. Indians can and do live anywhere in the United States that they wish. Many leave their home reservations for educational and employment purposes. Over half of the total U.S. Indian and Alaska Native population now lives away from reservations. Most return home often to participate in family and tribal life and sometimes to retire.

Why are Indians sometimes referred to as Native Americans?

The term, "Native American", came into usage in the 1960s' to denote the groups served by the Bureau of Indian Affairs: American Indians and Alaska Natives (Indians, Eskimos and Aleuts of Alaska). Later the term also included Native Hawaiians and Pacific Islanders in some federal programs. It, therefore, came into disfavor among some Indian groups.

The Eskimos and Aleuts in Alaska are two culturally distinct groups and are sensitive about being included under the "Indian" designation. They prefer, "Alaska Native".

Does the BIA provide scholarships for all Indians?

The Bureau provides some higher education scholarship assistance for eligible members of federally-recognized tribes. For information, contact the Indian Education Program, Bureau of Indian Affairs, 1849 C St. N.W., Washington, D.C. 20240.

American Indians Today third edition, United States Department of the Interior-Bureau of Indian Affairs, MS 2620-MIB, Washington, D.C. 20240-0001.

BASICS FOR INDIAN GENEALOGY

I. Determine what tribe

- A. If not known, consult John Swanton's book, The Indian Tribes of North America and check particular state for list of tribes.
- B. Once researcher chooses a tribe, determine whether the tribe is a "federally" recognized tribe. Indian Reservations: A State and Federal Handbook by the Confederation of American Indians will acknowledge the federal status of various tribes.
- C. If the tribe is federally recognized, where are the records?
    1. For records relating to Native Americans in the National Archives or one of its Regional Archives use Guide to Records in the National Archives of the United States Relating to American Indians.
        - a. For more detailed information about records in the National Archives, Washington, DC, use the Preliminary Inventory 163, Records of the Bureau of Indian Affairs, compiled by Ed Hill. See Select List of National Archives Publications (General Leaflet No. 3) for ordering PI 163.
        - b. Have the records been microfilmed by the National Archives as a microfilm publication? Consult American Indians: Select Catalog of National Archives Microfilm Publication.
            - (1) You may want to explain "M" and "T" numbers at this point.
            - (2) Microfilm may be purchased from the National Archives for $23 per roll. Also, check with the American Genealogical Lending Library, PO Box 244, Bountiful, UT 84010 to see if it has the film available for interlibrary loan.

(3) For additional information about Indian records in Regional Archives, obtain the address and telephone number from the brochure. The Regional Archives System of the National Archives , and contact the archivists for internal finding aids to their records.

2. Does the National Anthropological Archives, Smithsonian Institution, 10th Street and Constitutional Avenue NW, Washington, DC 20560 have any anthropological or sociological records about the tribe?
3. Has the tribe created a tribal archives? If so, where is it located and what does it have?
4. Other institutions having records about Native Americans may include special collections in colleges and universities, state archives, and historical societies.

II. Read about Native Americans and their relationship with non-Indians and the Federal Government.

III. **WARNING ! !** If the ancestor **did not** remain with the rest of the tribe during the various "Trails of Tears" as tribes were moved west, researcher must use other records as the tribal affiliation has been severed.

A. See Kent's article on "Wantabees and Outalucks" about problems in researching for Indian ancestors.

B. The Indian ancestor may be found on the federal population census schedules or among local government records about land, probate, marriage, divorce, birth, and death.

IV. Types of Indian records useful for genealogical research.

A. Tribal Census

1. Usually a base roll for membership

a. Five Civilized Tribes (Cherokee, Choctaw, Chickasaw, Creek, and Seminole) - "Final Rolls"

- b. Several other tribes use the 1936 census roll
2. Rolls for 1885-1940 on microfilm M595
3. See Wichita tribal census for 1936
4. Enrollment applications for Five Civilized Tribes contain more information than usual tribal census

B. Land allotment records
1. General Allotment Act of 1887 ("Dawes Act")
   - a. Read The Dawes Act and the Allotment of Indian Lands by D.S. Otis
   - b. Broke reservations into individual allotments
   - c. See Wichita tribe schedules of allotment
   - d. Did not apply to Five Civilized Tribes (Cherokee, Choctaw, Chickasaw, Creek, and Seminole)
2. Curtis Act of 1898 provided for enrollment of Five Civilized Tribes and allotments of land
   - a. See enrollment and allotment list
   - b. Items from land allotment file for member of Five Civilized Tribes

C. Annuity payrolls
1. Payment to tribal members for treaty obligations, loss of lands in the East, or lease or sale of lands
2. Osage annuity payroll of 1882
3. Notice the "large" dollar amount-no one will become wealthy by being a tribal member

D. Probate files
1. If an Indian was "restricted", or determined to be "incompetent" to manage his/her financial affairs, the Bureau of Indian Affairs and the Secretary of Interior were there to "protect" the Indian's land and money.
2. When a restricted Indian died, the Bureau of Indian Affairs became involved in his/her estate.
3. Probate files on restricted Indians can give additional information about family members.

V. Researching Indian Records

A. There are many other types of records that researchers can use to find information about ancestors, but the four types mentioned above are the most common and are generally easier to use.

B. This is not easy research-it requires patience, diligence, and some knowledge about Native Americans (more than is shown on TV).

Regional Archives System of the National Archives

National Archives-Alaska Region
654 West Third Avenue
Anchorage, AK 99501
907-271-2441; FTS 868-2441
Alaska

National Archives
Pacific Sierra Region
1000 Commodore Drive
San Bruno, CA 94066
415-876-9009; FTS 470-9009
Northern California, Hawaii, Nevada (except Clark County), American Samoa, the Trust Territory of the Pacific Islands

National Archives
Pacific Southwest Region
24000 Avila Road
P. O. Box 6719
Laguna Niguel, CA 92607-6719
714-643-4241; FTS 796-4241
Southern California, Arizona, and Clark County , Nevada

National Archives
Rocky Mountain Region
Bldg 48 - Denver Federal Center
Denver, CO 80225-0307
303-236-0817; FTS 776-0817
Colorado, Montana, North Dakota, South Dakota, Utah, Wyoming

National Archives
Southwest Region
1557 St. Joseph Avenue
East Point, GA 30344
404-763-7477; FTS 246-7477
Alabama, Georgia, Florida, Kentucky, Mississippi, North Carolina, South Carolina, Tennessee

National Archives
Great Lakes Region
7358 South Pulaski Road
Chicago, IL 60629
312-581-7816; FTS 353-0162
Illinois, Indiana, Michigan, Minnesota, Ohio, Wisconsin

National Archives
New England Region
380 Trapelo Road
Waltham, MA 02154
617-647-8100; FTS 839-1700
Connecticut, Maine, Massachusetts, New Hampshire, Rhode Island, Vermont

National Archives
Central Plains Region
2312 East Bannister Road
Kansas City, MO 64131
816-926-6272; FTS 926-6272
Iowa, Kansas, Missouri, Nebraska

National Archives
Northeast Region
Building 22
Military Ocean Terminal
Bayonne, NJ 07002-5388
201-823-7252
New Jersey, New York, Puerto Rico, the Virgin Islands

National Archives
Mid Atlantic Region
9th & Market Streets, Rm 1350
Philadelphia, PA 19107
215-597-3000; FTS 597-3000
Delaware, Pennsylvania, Maryland, Virginia, West Virginia

National Archives
Southwest Region
501 West Felix Street
P. O. Box 6216
Ft. Worth, TX 76115
817-334-5525; FTS 334-5525
Arkansas, Louisiana, New Mexico, Oklahoma, Texas

National Archives
Pacific Northwest Region
6125 Sand Point Way NE
Seattle, WA 98115
206-526-6507; FTS 392-6507
Idaho, Oregon, Washington

QUICK NOTES !

**Information for this page is only available in the Library Edition.

QUICK NOTES !

**Information for this page is only available in the Library Edition.

Fred Synder, Director, Consultant

N.A.²I.I.T.C.

North American Native American
Indian Information & Trade Center

QUICK NOTES !

**Information for this page is only available in the Library Edition.

Fred Synder, Director, Consultant

N.A.²I.I.T.C.

North American Native American Indian Information & Trade Center

QUICK NOTES !

**Information for this page is only available in the Library Edition.